3000 800045 00193
St. Louis Community College

⟨ **W9-DEA-619**

F.V.

St. Louis Community College

Forest Park
Florissant Valley
Meramec

Instructional Resources
St. Louis, Missouri

ALSO BY ALAN WALKER

A Study in Musical Analysis

An Anatomy of Musical Criticism

Franz Liszt: Volume One, The Virtuoso Years, 1811–1847

Franz Liszt: Volume Two, The Weimar Years, 1848–1861

EDITOR OF

Frédéric Chopin:
Profiles of the Man and the Musician

Franz Liszt:
The Man and His Music

Robert Schumann:
The Man and His Music

Living with Liszt.
The Diary of Carl Lachmund:
An American Pupil of Liszt, 1882–84

IN THE GREAT COMPOSER SERIES

Franz Liszt

Robert Schumann

Liszt, Carolyne, and the Vatican:
The Story of a Thwarted Marriage
(with Gabriele Erasmi)

Franz Liszt

THE FINAL YEARS

1861–1886

Alan Walker

Franz Liszt

VOLUME THREE

The Final Years

1861 · 1886

Alfred A. Knopf

NEW YORK · 1996

THIS IS A BORZOI BOOK
PUBLISHED BY ALFRED A. KNOPF, INC.

Copyright © 1996 by Alan Walker

All rights reserved under International and Pan-American Copyright Conventions.
Published in the United States by Alfred A. Knopf, Inc., New York.
Distributed by Random House, Inc., New York.

Musical examples drawn by William Renwick.

LIBRARY OF CONGRESS CATALOGING-IN-PUBLICATION DATA
(Revised for vol. 3)
Walker, Alan, [date]
Franz Liszt.
Vol. 2-3 : 1st ed.
Includes bibliographical references and index.
Contents: v. 1. The virtuoso years, 1811–1847—
v. 2. The Weimar years, 1848–1861—
v. 3. The final years, 1861–1886.
1. Liszt, Franz, 1811–1886.   2. Composers—Biography.
I. Title.
ML410.L7W27   1983   780'.92   82-47821
ISBN 0-394-52540-X (v. 1)

Manufactured in the United States of America
First Edition

FRONTISPIECE
Franz Liszt, an oil portrait by Mihály Munkácsy (1886).

*To Lisztians across the world,
wherever they may be, these volumes
are affectionately dedicated.*

Contents

Illustrations   xv

Acknowledgements   xvii

PROLOGUE

Franz Liszt: King Lear of Music   3

BOOK ONE: FROM WEIMAR TO ROME, 1861–1865

A Thwarted Marriage, 1861   21

Liszt says farewell to Weimar and sets out for Rome ⁓ he arrives in the Eternal City on October 20, where he is reunited with Princess Carolyne after a separation of eighteen months ⁓ their wedding is planned for October 22, his fiftieth birthday, but it is abruptly cancelled on the eve of the ceremony by order of the president of the Holy Congregation, Cardinal Caterini ⁓ aftershocks and recriminations ⁓ Carolyne blames "scheming Russian intrigues" ⁓ the role of Gustav Hohenlohe in the thwarted marriage considered ⁓ Carolyne takes up permanent residence in Rome, and lives at Via del Babuino 89 ⁓ Liszt moves to Via Felice 113, uncertain what to do and where to go.

The Eternal City   35

Liszt explores Rome's architecture: the Colosseum, the Sistine Chapel, the Forum, and the Baths of Diocletian ⁓ he laments the lack of public concerts and describes Rome as a "musical wilderness" ⁓ he acquires two new pupils: Giovanni Sgambati and Walter Bache ⁓ he strikes up friendships with important clerics, including Monsignor Francesco Nardi ⁓ his compositions include the two concert studies *Waldesrauschen* and *Gnomenreigen* and the "Weinen, Klagen" Variations.

The Death of Blandine, 1862   47

Blandine gives birth to Daniel ⁓ post-natal complications ⁓ the treatments of Dr. Charles Isnard ⁓ the death of Blandine, September 11, 1862 ⁓ Ollivier visits Liszt in Rome ⁓ Ollivier returns to La Moutte and falls ill ⁓ after seven years he takes a second wife, Marie-Thérèse Gravier.

The Madonna del Rosario, 1863–1865   54

Liszt withdraws to the Madonna del Rosario ⁓ a description of the monastery ⁓ he is visited by Pius IX and a clerical entourage on July 11, 1863 ⁓ Pius sings Bellini and Liszt accompanies ⁓ Liszt composes his two Franciscan Legends in the monastery ⁓ among his callers are Walter Bache, Eduard Reményi, and the diplomat Kurd von Schlözer ⁓ Liszt completes his Beethoven symphony transcriptions ⁓ at the pope's request Liszt plays in Rome at a charity concert for Peter's Pence ⁓ the pope invites him to his summer retreat at Castel Gandolfo ⁓ he attends the Tonkünstler-Versammlung festival at Karlsruhe ⁓ he visits Cosima and Hans von Bülow at Starnberg Lake ⁓ the growing turmoil between Cosima, Hans, and Wagner ⁓ Cosima confides to Liszt that her marriage to Hans is about to collapse ⁓ Liszt takes Cosima with him on his travels through Germany to keep her away from Wagner ⁓ Liszt's first return to Weimar since leaving the city ⁓ he meets Carl Alexander, who vainly tries to persuade him to return to the city ⁓ Liszt and Cosima travel to Paris and thence to Saint-Tropez, where they visit Blandine's grave ⁓ Liszt celebrates his fifty-third birthday at the Madonna del Rosario.

Book Two: The Abbé Liszt, 1865–1869

Liszt Enters the Lower Orders, 1865   85

Liszt receives the tonsure on April 25 ⁓ he is admitted to holy orders on July 30 ⁓ the reactions of his contemporaries ⁓ he moves into Hohenlohe's private quarters in the Vatican ⁓ he plays for Pius IX on the twentieth anniversary of the pontiff's coronation ⁓ accompanied by Cosima and Hans von Bülow, he visits Hungary and conducts his *St. Elisabeth,* wearing a cassock for the first time in public ⁓ the trio travels to Gran, where Liszt plays for Cardinal Scitovszky ⁓ from there they go to Szekszárd where Liszt stays as a guest of Baron Augusz ⁓ after a short trip to Venice Liszt returns to the Vatican ⁓ resumes work on his oratorio *Christus.*

Paris and the "Gran" Mass, 1866   95

Death of Liszt's mother ⁓ Emile Ollivier delivers the funeral oration ⁓ Sgambati conducts the first performance of the *Dante* Symphony in Rome ⁓ Liszt travels to Paris, where he settles his mother's estate ⁓ he meets many French musicians, including Saint-Saëns and Auber, and is "taken up" by Princess Pauline Metternich ⁓ the failure of the "Gran" Mass at its Paris première at the church of Saint-Eustache ⁓ Walter Bache's description of the débâcle ⁓ the hostility of the press ⁓ Liszt attempts to justify his setting of the mass to d'Ortigue, Berlioz, Damcke, and Kreutzer ⁓ he hears César Franck play the organ ⁓ Napoleon III invites Liszt to the Tuileries ⁓ from Paris to Amsterdam, where he is reunited with Cosima and Hans von Bülow ⁓ a "Liszt Festival" is mounted in his honour by the Dutch conductor Herman van Bree ⁓ Bülow gives the world première of the Spanish Rhapsody ⁓ back in Paris Liszt is received at the Tuileries by Empress Eugénie ⁓ he meets Marie d'Agoult on three occasions ⁓ she chooses this moment to re-publish her old novel *Nélida* ⁓ "Madame d'Agoult gives me no quarter," he writes ⁓ Liszt returns to Rome.

The Cosima-Bülow-Wagner Crisis I: The Triangle Forms, 1865–1867   106

The Bülows with Wagner in Munich ⁓ Cosima recalls giving birth to her daughter Blandine in Berlin unaided ⁓ Wagner's sumptuous life-style in Munich ⁓ the affair between Cosima and Wagner develops ⁓ the difficult question of Bülow's complicity ⁓ Wagner's relationship with King Ludwig II ⁓ his plans for a music school and a new opera house ⁓ Bülow makes enemies ⁓ the world première of *Tristan* and its attendant woes ⁓ Cosima gives birth to Wagner's daughter Isolde ⁓ the death of Ludwig Schnorr ⁓ Wagner requests more money from the Bavarian treasury ⁓ bags of coin in a taxicab ⌐ Wagner is banished from Munich ⌐ he moves to Switzerland ⌐ the death of Wagner's wife, Minna ⌐ he leases Triebschen, by Lake Lucerne ⌐ the Bülows join him there ⌐ of scandal and outrage ⌐ the strange case of Malvina Schnorr ⌐ Cosima gives birth to another Wagner daughter, Eva ⌐ Liszt visits the Bülows at Munich in a desperate bid to save their marriage ⌐ he confronts Wagner at Triebschen ⌐ his arrangement of the "Liebestod" from *Tristan*.

The Cosima-Bülow-Wagner Crisis II: The Triangle Breaks, 1868–1870   130

Bülow gives the world première of *Meistersinger* at Munich ⌐ his conflicts with Wagner ⌐ Cosima's continued infidelity ⌐ she deserts Bülow and lives openly with Wagner in Switzerland ⌐ their life at Triebschen ⌐ Liszt condemns Cosima ⌐ Bülow seeks a Protestant divorce ⌐ Bülow's letter to Claire de Charnacé ⌐ Cosima marries Wagner in Lucerne ⌐ Bülow resigns from Munich and embarks on a long concert tour of America ⌐ he suffers a nervous breakdown and becomes suicidal ⌐ Bülow's subsequent conduct towards Cosima and their daughters ⌐ he remarries.

Of Kings and Castles, 1867   147

The Compromise of 1867: the Dual Monarchy ⌐ Franz Joseph is crowned King of Hungary ⌐ Liszt's Hungarian Coronation Mass is performed at the ceremony ⌐ he is acclaimed by the public after the coronation ⌐ he re-visits Weimar ⌐ a performance of his *St. Elisabeth* in the restored Wartburg Castle ⌐ the Paris Exhibition of 1867 ⌐ inventions galore ⌐ an attempt on Tsar Alexander's life ⌐ the execution of Maximilian I of Mexico ⌐ Chickering wins first prize at the Paris Exhibition for his new grand piano, and he is awarded the Legion of Honour ⌐ the prize-winning piano is later shipped to Liszt in Rome ⌐ Liszt moves into the Santa Francesca Romana ⌐ among his distinguished visitors are George Grove, the American painter George Healy, Edvard Grieg, and Longfellow ⌐ Liszt sight-reads Grieg's newly composed Piano Concerto.

Of Cossacks and Countesses   171

Olga Zielinska's family background in Poland ⌐ her first meeting with Liszt in Rome, 1869 ⌐ her pathological character examined ⌐ of drugs and daggers ⌐ she assumes the title of "countess" ⌐ she accompanies Liszt to Budapest, and endures a public humiliation while playing Chopin ⌐ her family fortune collapses, she seeks redress at the gaming tables ⌐ her threats of suicide ⌐ Liszt's calming letter to Olga, 1871 ⌐ she leaves for America in a vain attempt to start a musical career there, and takes Liszt's Technical Studies with her ⌐ she returns to Budapest, having threatened to kill Liszt ⌐ her simulated suicide in his apartment ⌐ she leaves for Paris under threat of police expulsion and plots revenge ⌐ her novels *Souvenirs d'une cosaque* and *Souvenirs d'une pianiste* examined, their veracity questioned ⌐ she creates a spectacle on the boulevards of Paris ⌐ Liszt defends himself against Olga's books: his letter to his friends ⌐ Princess Carolyne's reaction to "la cosaque" ⌐ Olga in later life.

Book Three:
A Threefold Life Begins: Weimar, Budapest, and Rome, 1869–1876

The Hofgärtnerei: The Return of a Legend   193

Liszt takes up residence in Weimar ⌐ his "threefold life" begins ⌐ a description of the Hofgärtnerei ⌐ reunited with his old colleagues Lassen, the Schorns, the Mildes, and Pauline Viardot-Garcia ⌐ Liszt's friendship with Baroness Olga von Meyendorff ⌐ the "Starlings" and their musicales ⌐ Liszt starts his piano masterclasses ⌐ the Beethoven festivals of 1870 ⌐ he is shunned by the Vienna organisers ⌐ he mounts a Beethoven celebration in Weimar with Tausig as one of the soloists ⌐ Olga

Janina visits Weimar — the Franco-Prussian War is declared — Liszt goes to Hungary and is prevented by the military situation in Europe from returning to Rome.

The Franco-Prussian War of 1870   212

Napoleon III, Emperor of the French — his nemesis Prince Otto von Bismarck — pride and prejudice, contest and confrontation — the Franco-Prussian War of 1870 — Emile Ollivier's role: into war "with a light heart" — the armies of France and Prussia compared — the French are defeated at Sedan — a description of the battle — Napoleon surrenders to Bismarck — the Siege of Paris — the city is shelled and starved into submission — the armistice and war reparations — release of Napoleon, who settles in England — Liszt's reaction to the European catastrophe — Liszt as political spy — Wagner's jubilation at the outcome of the war: he composes a *Kaisermarsch* — Liszt in Hungary — he participates in the Beethoven festival in Budapest, December 1870 — Liszt is appointed Royal Hungarian Counsellor — there is talk of founding a Royal Academy of Music with Liszt as the first president.

The Lion of Weimar: Liszt and His Pupils   228

A description of the Weimar masterclasses — technique versus inspiration: "Wash your dirty linen at home!" — comparisons with Breithaupt, Kullak, and Deppe — Liszt on technique: "Technique should flow from spirit, not from mechanics" — an ear-witness account of Liszt's playing — Liszt's general principles of teaching — Liszt's classes described by Amy Fay, August Göllerich, and Carl Lachmund, respectively — Liszt as a sight-reader — the camaraderie between Liszt and his students — the Jena "Sausage Festival" of 1882 — Liszt and his American students celebrate the Fourth of July — his attitude to money — charges of sycophantism — Liszt is indisposed (July 1881) and Bülow decides to "clean out the Augean stables" — Liszt uses visual imagery and humour in his teaching — the Weimar town council passes a bye-law restricting the sound of piano practice on pain of a fine.

Excelsior! 1873–1875   255

Liszt completes *Christus* — Wagner and Liszt patch up their quarrel — the first complete performance of *Christus,* in Weimar, is attended by Wagner and Cosima — an account of the oratorio — the reaction of Cosima — Liszt's Weimar masterclasses are enriched by many new students — Liszt plays the *Hammerklavier* — he conducts the Ninth Symphony — the Hungarians celebrate Liszt's fiftieth jubilee — Hanslick on Liszt: "What a remarkable man!" — Liszt gives a series of charity concerts in Budapest — Ramann begins work on her "official" biography of Liszt — her troubled relationship with Princess Carolyne — Ramann's biography considered — its reception in England — Richard and Cosima Wagner join Liszt in Budapest to give fund-raising concerts for the Bayreuth enterprise — Liszt cuts his finger before playing the *Emperor* Concerto — the first performance of *The Bells of Strasbourg* — this cantata considered — he visits King Willem III of Holland — memorial concert for Mme Mouchanoff — Charles Stanford hears Liszt play in Leipzig — Liszt celebrates his sixty-fourth birthday with Princess Carolyne in Rome.

The Royal Academy of Music, 1875   288

Liszt is named president of the Hungarian Academy of Music — the role of Apponyi — a committee goes to work — a building is purchased at Fischplatz 4 — Liszt appoints the faculty and sets the curriculum — the academy opens its doors — of students and standards — the faculty workload — a description of Liszt's apartment — Liszt and his academy students: some eye-witness accounts — Liszt's ambivalent attitude towards the academy considered — the subsequent history of the institution.

The Last Years of Marie d'Agoult   301

Marie d'Agoult begins her *Mémoires* ⁓ her sanitized account of her years with Liszt ⁓ her mental illnesses considered ⁓ her treatments at the clinic of Dr. Emile Blanche ⁓ foretastes of death ⁓ a suicide attempt ⁓ she convalesces at the home of Louis de Ronchaud ⁓ some observations of Claire
de Charnacé on her mother: "she wanted to arrange the past" ⁓ the question of Liszt's attitude towards Marie's suicidal nature ⁓ Marie makes Ronchaud her literary executor ⁓ her career as a writer
considered ⁓ her relationship with her son-in-law Emile Ollivier ⁓ she moves away from Paris during the Franco-Prussian War ⁓ she visits Cosima and Wagner at Triebschen ⁓ reminiscences ⁓ the
deaths of her brother, Maurice, and her husband, Charles d'Agoult ⁓ the death and funeral of Marie
d'Agoult.

"External Weaknesses—Interior Causes"   319

Carolyne's lifelong ties to Liszt ⁓ her home in Rome ⁓ of foibles and fancies ⁓ her connections
with Roman society ⁓ she is acquainted with Pius IX ⁓ Carolyne as a writer ⁓ her *magnum opus*
considered ⁓ she is placed on the Index ⁓ the politics of Rome ⁓ Pius IX is besieged by problems
⁓ the assassination of Pellegrino Rossi ⁓ the rise of Victor Emmanuel and the battles of Magenta
and Solferino ⁓ Pius becomes a prisoner within the walls of the Vatican ⁓ official separation of
church and state ⁓ the death of Rosmini and the role of the Jesuits ⁓ Cardinal Hohenlohe and his
place in the politics of Rome ⁓ he becomes the target of assassins ⁓ his brother Chlodwig represses
the Jesuits in Germany ⁓ the death of Hohenlohe ⁓ Princess Carolyne's turbulent relations with
Church leaders ⁓ Liszt finds himself in opposition to her on doctrinal matters ⁓ of quarrels and rec-
onciliations ⁓ the accusations of Carolyne ⁓ her underlying grievance: his long absences from Rome
and from her.

BOOK FOUR: DE PROFUNDIS, 1876–1886

Liszt and Bayreuth   341

The rapprochement between Liszt and Wagner ⁓ they exchange letters, the first in nearly five years
⁓ the Wagners visit Liszt in Weimar, and he visits them in Bayreuth ⁓ Carolyne balks at Liszt's closer
relations with "pagan Bayreuth" ⁓ becomes a source of friction between them ⁓ some parallels between Cosima and Carolyne ⁓ Cosima turns Protestant after her marriage to Wagner ⁓ a rift develops between Carolyne and her daughter, Marie ⁓ Liszt takes the daughter's part, thus deepening
his own troubles with Carolyne ⁓ Liszt starts attending the Bayreuth Festivals; he witnesses all three
cycles of *The Ring* in 1876 ⁓ the background to this epoch-making production ⁓ the soil-turning
ceremony of the Festspielhaus ⁓ the wider reception of *The Ring* ⁓ Kaiser Wilhelm attends the third
cycle ⁓ Liszt and Wagner at Wahnfried ⁓ he plays at the soirées there, including the slow movement
of the *Hammerklavier* Sonata ⁓ Wagner pays a public tribute to Liszt: "For everything that I have at-
tained I have one person to thank . . ." ⁓ Liszt's benefit concerts for the Bayreuth project ⁓ the festival deficit ⁓ Wagner conducts at the Royal Albert Hall in London to pay his debts.

Wanderer Eternal, 1876–1881   357

Liszt the itinerant ⁓ Kellermann on Liszt's composing methods ⁓ Liszt's "threefold life" continues
⁓ the Danube floods of 1876 ⁓ Liszt gives a charity concert in the Vigadó ⁓ conducts the first performance of his choral prayer *To St. Francis of Paola* ⁓ his increasingly popular masterclasses in Weimar
⁓ trips to Düsseldorf, Loo Castle, Sondershausen, and Bayreuth ⁓ from Bayreuth to Hanover, where
he finds Bülow in a suicidal depression ⁓ Liszt's torn emotions ⁓ he plays his *St. Francis of Paola walking on the waters* for Lina Ramann in Nuremburg ⁓ returns to Budapest for the winter of 1876–77 ⁓

his busy life as president of the Royal Academy of Music ⌐ he sustains an accident to his right arm, then cuts his left index finger while being shaved ⌐ a Beethoven jubilee in Vienna, 1877, where the young Busoni hears Liszt play the "Emperor" Concerto ⌐ from Vienna to Bayreuth, where Wagner gives Liszt a signed copy of his autobiography, *Mein Leben* ⌐ at the Tonkünstler Festival in Hanover ⌐ the conductor Bott falls from the podium and Liszt takes over.

The public versus the private Liszt ⌐ he suffers from melancholia and contemplates suicide ⌐ with the cypresses and fountains of the Villa d'Este ⌐ he composes the third volume of his *Années de pèlerinage* ⌐ his cordial relations with the Jewish community of Budapest ⌐ he plays the *Moonlight* Sonata to friends in his home at Fischplatz ⌐ he plays the *Kreutzer* Sonata with Ole Bull ⌐ an anti-Liszt faction emerges in Budapest ⌐ Liszt retaliates by temporarily withdrawing from the city's concert life ⌐ with Cousin Eduard in Vienna ⌐ back to Bayreuth and thence to his masterclasses in Weimar ⌐ he now travels an average of four thousand miles a year in pursuit of his "threefold life" ⌐ driven by the needs of others rather than his own ⌐ the Franciscan element in his nature ⌐ at the Paris Exhibition of 1878 ⌐ the Tonkünstler Festival at Erfurt ⌐ Moriz Rosenthal and Adèle aus der Ohe become his pupils ⌐ Rosenthal recalls his lessons with the master at the Villa d'Este ⌐ Liszt composes his path-breaking *Via Crucis* ⌐ Cardinal Hohenlohe settles into the Santa Maria Maggiore ⌐ the further quarrels of Liszt and Carolyne ⌐ the river Tisza overflows its banks, disaster at Szeged ⌐ Liszt gives another charity concert for the victims ⌐ Hanslick on Liszt: "What magic still surrounds the elderly man!" ⌐ Liszt conducts his "Gran" Mass ⌐ the death of Cousin Eduard ⌐ Liszt is made an honorary canon of Albano ⌐ famine stalks the regions of Tivoli and the Sabine hills ⌐ Hohenlohe puts on a charity concert at which Liszt plays a fantasia on his *Ave Maris Stella* ⌐ the English cleric Reginald Haweis visits Liszt at Tivoli and hears him play his *Angelus!* and two Chopin nocturnes ⌐ Liszt meets the American sculptor Moses Ezekiel who produces a widely admired bust of him ⌐ Liszt moves into his apartments in the new Academy of Music, Budapest ⌐ Bülow plays Liszt's music in Budapest and Liszt writes a letter to the press in praise of his former pupil ⌐ Liszt and Géza Zichy raise money for the Hummel monument in Pressburg ⌐ Liszt visits his birthplace in Raiding (April 1881) ⌐ his travels become more extensive: to his "threefold life" he adds Berlin, Baden-Baden, and Brussels, where the King of the Belgians invests him with the Order of Leopold ⌐ by June, 1881, Liszt is showing signs of physical fatigue and the first symptoms of dropsy announce themselves.

Unstern!   403

Liszt falls down the stairs of the Hofgärtnerei, July 1881 ⌐ he is confined to his room for several weeks ⌐ the diagnosis of Dr. Brehme ⌐ the burdens of old age ⌐ Carolyne publishes her revised edition of *Des Bohémiens* ⌐ the Jewish press reacts ⌐ Liszt is branded a racist and pilloried as "the new Messiah" ⌐ the "blood trial" of Tiszaeszlár, and its connection to the reception of *Des Bohémiens* ⌐ Liszt replies to his Jewish critics in the *Gazette de Hongrie* ⌐ Ramann's dilemma: to translate or not to translate Carolyne's revisions ⌐ Liszt's problems with the Budapest opera-house: the *Königslied* affair ⌐ Liszt's *cri de coeur:* "Everyone is against me" ⌐ he takes to drinking absinthe ⌐ of dropsy and cataracts ⌐ the death of Liszt's manservant Achille Colonello ⌐ Lina Schmalhausen is charged with shoplifting ⌐ Scharwenka's lampoon ⌐ the subsequent fate of Schmalhausen ⌐ Liszt enters his twilight years.

Nuages gris   416

The world première of *Parsifal* ⌐ Wagner arranges a *Liebesmahl* for his friends and colleagues ⌐ he plays another public tribute to Liszt ⌐ Liszt composes his transcription of the "March of the Holy Grail" from *Parsifal* ⌐ Wagner conducts for the last time ⌐ Liszt is angered by a request for money to commemorate "Sedan Day" ⌐ an outing with his pupils to Arnstadt ⌐ the delights of *Pfeffermünzschen* en route ⌐ Eugène d'Albert makes his début ⌐ Liszt receives a grand piano from Mason & Risch ⌐ he reciprocates by sending them his portrait in oils by Paul von Joukowsky ⌐ Liszt spends the winter of 1882–83 in Venice with the Wagners ⌐ Siegfried Wagner's memories of his grandfather

— Liszt rails against the music of the local Catholic church: "an obscenity" — he composes his two "Funeral Gondolas" — Wagner celebrates Cosima's birthday with a concert at the Venice Conservatory: his youthful Symphony in C major is performed — Liszt departs Venice and takes his last leave of Wagner — the death of Wagner — Cosima accompanies Wagner's body on the long journey back to Bayreuth — she retreats into total seclusion and refuses to see her father — Liszt composes his *R.W.—Venezia* — he conducts the Good Friday Music from *Parsifal* — composes his *Am Grabe Richard Wagners* — the fate of some of Liszt's later manuscripts — Lina Schmalhausen offers to sell them to the British Museum — Liszt is asked by Cosima to return all the letters he received from Wagner across the years — he refuses to comply — Liszt is stalked by depression and superstition.

The Music of Liszt's Old Age   437

Liszt as "the father of modern music" — his late music as autobiography: its connections to his disturbed pathology — it falls into three categories: retrospection, despair, and death — some technical characteristics discussed — Friedheim on Liszt's "theory of the harmony of the future" — the modernity of *Nuages gris* and *Unstern!* — a first performance of the Bagatelle Without Tonality — Mansfeldt's letter — some unusual chord constructions — the reception of his late pieces — "I can wait."

Harmonies du soir, 1881–1885   457

Liszt moves into the Alibert Hotel, in the heart of Rome — visits to the Villa Medici — the annual festivals of the Allgemeiner Deutscher Musikverein at Leipzig (1883) and Weimar (1884) — Liszt makes his last appearance as a conductor — Rubinstein and Pachmann play Liszt's music in Budapest — he attends the Bayreuth Festival of 1884, but Cosima refuses to see him: her "spectral silence" — Liszt's health deteriorates, his eyesight fades — composes his Nineteenth Hungarian Rhapsody — meets Anton Bruckner in Vienna — a last farewell to Robert Franz — the Weimar masterclass of 1885, a letter from Hugo Mansfeldt — the Americans in Weimar once more celebrate the Fourth of July — from Weimar back to Rome — works on *St. Stanislas* — an encounter with Claude Debussy — on New Year's Day, 1886, he declares: "This will be an unlucky year for me."

Liszt's Last Visit to England, April 1886   477

Liszt is invited to England — his letter to Walter Bache — he is accompanied across the English Channel by Alexander Mackenzie and Alfred Littleton — a diversion at Penge — a warm reception in London, his first visit to the city since 1841 — his English itinerary traced in detail — a performance of *St. Elisabeth* in St. James's Hall — a visit to the Royal Academy of Music, where a Liszt Scholarship is established — he is invited to Windsor Castle, where he plays for Queen Victoria — an account of Liszt's visit in Victoria's diary — Bache puts on a reception at the Grosvenor Gallery — Liszt is reunited with Joachim — some all-Liszt concerts — he meets the Prince and Princess of Wales — an encounter with Henry Irving — in the "Beefsteak Room" for supper — he attends the London recitals of his two pupils Lamond and Stavenhagen — his bust is sculpted by Edgar Boehm — farewell to England — from London to Dover and back to France.

Approaching the End   498

Liszt makes brief detours to Antwerp and Brussels — he arrives back in Paris, where he stays as a guest of the Munkácsys — *St. Elisabeth* is performed in the Trocadéro — his pupils greet him at the Weimar railway station, his first return for more than six months — Liszt's physical condition causes concern — he consults Alfred Graefe at Halle and a cataract operation is scheduled for September — an all-Liszt concert at Sondershausen — *Christus* is performed at Weimar's Stadtkirche and Liszt offers advice during the rehearsal — Cosima visits Weimar unexpectedly and begs her father to attend the Bayreuth Festival later in the year — he serves as a witness at the wedding of his granddaughter

Daniela — stays at Castle Colpach for a holiday with the Munkácsys — he gives his last public recital in the Luxembourg Casino, July 19, 1886 — from Luxembourg he sets out for Bayreuth — he arrives in Bayreuth with a racking cough and a temperature — he becomes progressively ill.

The Death of Liszt · 508

The last ten days — the diary of Lina Schmalhausen — Liszt's symptoms — a description by Adelheid von Schorn — he attends a performance of *Tristan* on July 25 — he is treated by Dr. Landgraf, who diagnoses pneumonia — he becomes delirious — Cosima consults Dr. Fleischer from Erlangen University — she bans Liszt's pupils from his sickroom — he is humiliated by his granddaughters and is likened to King Lear — Liszt suffers a heart-attack: "Luft! Luft!" — he falls into a coma — the death of Liszt — Lina Schmalhausen tends the corpse — a death-mask is taken by the sculptor Weissbrod — an unsuccessful attempt to embalm Liszt's body — his funeral and burial in Bayreuth — orations at the graveside — the reactions of Princess Carolyne — Schmalhausen returns to view again Liszt's last resting-place.

Aftermath · 523

The struggle over Liszt's remains — Hungary and Germany argue over possession — the debate in the Hungarian parliament — a review of Liszt's own contradictory choices of a last resting-place — Liszt remains buried in Bayreuth — his will is contested — the background to the legal dispute — Carolyne's power of attorney — a permanent Liszt Museum is opened in Weimar, May 22, 1887 — the Liszt Foundation commences publication of the Collected Edition, 1907–36 — a Liszt Memorial Room is opened in Budapest, 1925 — La Mara begins the publication of Liszt's *Collected Letters* — the reaction of Princess Carolyne to Liszt's death — her last days and her death in Rome.

*Appendix I: Princess Carolyne's Death Notice, from the Register
of Santa Maria del Popolo, Rome* · 541

*Appendix II: Liszt Enters the Minor Orders of the Priesthood:
Entries from the* Liber Ordinationum *for 1863–1872,
Vicariato di Roma* · 545

Appendix III: Liszt's Titles and Honours · 549

Appendix IV: Catalogue of Princess Carolyne's Writings · 553

Sources Consulted in the Preparation of Volume III · 555

Index · 565

Illustrations

FRONTISPIECE   *Franz Liszt, an oil portrait by Mihály Munkácsy (1886).*

PAGE 78   *Franz Liszt, a rare photograph from circa 1864.*

PAGE 160   *The monastery of Santa Francesca Romana, a photograph by Pompeo Molins, circa 1870.*

PAGE 167   *Liszt at the door of the monastery of Santa Francesca Romana, an oil portrait by George Healy, 1869.*

PAGE 270   *A proclamation of Liszt's Jubilee, November 1873: "Our Compatriot Franz Liszt."*

PAGE 291   *The Royal Academy of Music: a proclamation dated September 5, 1875, signed by Ágoston Trefort, Minister of Education.*

PAGE 325   *Title page of Princess Carolyne's twenty-four-volume magnum opus* Causes intérieures, *1872–1887.*

PAGE 345   *Franz Liszt, a photograph taken in Hungary, 1876.*

PAGE 386   *A Liszt benefit concert in aid of the flood victims of Szeged and the Hungarian Plains, given in Budapest, March 26, 1879.*

PAGE 390   *A concert of Liszt's sacred choral music in Weimar, conducted by the composer, July 10, 1879.*

PAGE 397   *Franz Liszt, a photograph taken in Baden-Baden, May 1880.*

PAGE 479   *Liszt in Paris, a handbill for a performance of the "Gran" Mass, March 25, 1886.*

PAGE 491   *Liszt with his pupil Bernhard Stavenhagen in London, April 1886.*

PAGE 495   *Liszt in London, a photograph from April 1886.*

PAGE 516   *A facsimile page from the unpublished diary of Lina Schmalhausen, entry for July 31, 1886: "At 11:30 the Master received 2 morphine injections in the region of the heart."*

Acknowledgements

The writing of the third volume of my life of Liszt, like that of the earlier ones, involved me in much travel. I was sometimes reminded of Liszt's own evocative phrase "une vie trifurquée"—a life split in three—which he used to describe the endless circle of his existence during the last seventeen years of his life, divided as it was among the three cities of Rome, Weimar, and Budapest. This ceaseless movement also seemed to draw me into its orbit; hardly a year passed when I did not visit one or another of these cities—and sometimes all three of them in succession—in a constant search for Lisztiana. For it cannot be stressed too often that books on Liszt are hardly worth reading today, still less writing, unless they contain something new, unless they change the biographical landscape. Moreover, there were new destinations to add to the ones that had meanwhile become routine, including visits to such places as the monastery of the Madonna del Rosario in Rome, the Villa d'Este, the old city of Albano, and the grand duke of Weimar's summer castles at Belvedere, Ettersburg, and Wilhelmsthal—locations of great interest to anyone studying the last twenty-five years of Liszt's life. I may well be the first modern Liszt biographer to have visited Wilhelmsthal, which is difficult to find on present-day maps. But Liszt frequently stayed there as a guest of the grand duke, and it seemed to me to be important to locate it, if only to remain true to the idea of what I have elsewhere called "the geography of biography."

Somewhat similar motives drove me to seek out the Madonna del Rosario, on Rome's Monte Mario, where Liszt spent a two-year retreat during the years 1863–65. In his time the monastery was almost derelict, but any passing pilgrim could be assured of a bed for the night. Today the monastery is as difficult to breach as a fortress. It is run by an order of Dominican nuns who, much to the general despair, have taken vows of both silence and seclusion. This makes it particularly difficult for scholarship to proceed, for anyone who wishes to visit the Madonna del Rosario will find that there is absolutely no one with whom he can communicate. A closed order that actually refuses to allow itself to be penetrated by the Holy See has little difficulty in remaining impervious to the pleas of itinerant Liszt scholars, however elegant the language. More than one visitor has made the trek from the centre of Rome only to be confronted by locked doors, and has had to content himself with a glance at the marble plaque set into the front wall commemorating Liszt's sojourn there, before catching the next means of transport back to the city. When I first visited the monastery, in February 1984, the caretaker who lived in the adjoining premises possessed permanently damaged vocal cords and could not speak above a whisper. I have often wondered whether the fact that he could not speak was regarded as a prerequisite for his job by those who *would* not speak. Persistence brings its own rewards, however. The following year I breached the monastery's defences, thanks in large measure to help received from officials at the Academia Britannica and the British Embassy, and I spent several hours exploring this venerable building (during which time the nuns remained cloistered), admiring the view of St. Peter's distant dome just as Liszt himself had done from the window of his cell, a hundred and twenty years earlier. Such background is irreplaceable. It forever changes the way one hears works like the two Franciscan Legends, both of which were composed in the Madonna del Rosario, to say nothing of the oratorio *Christus,* which was completed in that self-same cell. The experience taught me afresh the old lesson of all biographical work: Unless and until you have seen for yourself where things happen, how and why they happen will remain obscure.

When I commenced work on my life of Liszt I could not have known that it would consume twenty-five years of my existence, but such has proved to be the case. Nor was the passage of the present volume made swifter by my work on two other books, both of which grew out of this biography and have meanwhile been published ahead of it. The first was *Liszt, Carolyne, and the Vatican: The Story of a Thwarted Marriage,* which I issued jointly with my colleague Dr. Gabriele Erasmi in 1990.[1] This book made available for the first time a very large number of hitherto unknown documents from the Vatican's Secret Archive which throw new light on the bitter, thirteen-year struggle between Princess Carolyne von Sayn-Wittgenstein and the Catholic Church, during which time she fought to secure an annulment of her first marriage in order to clear the way for her second—to Liszt. She won that fight in the Vatican itself, and contrary to all expectations her annulment was granted by Pope Pius IX, on January 8, 1861. The dramatic story of the dissolution of Carolyne's marriage brought the narrative of Volume Two to an end. Who and what thwarted her wedding to Liszt? That is where the narrative of Volume Three begins.

The other book to engross me was my annotated *Living with Liszt. The Diary of Carl Lachmund: An American Pupil of Liszt, 1882–84,* which appeared in the early part of 1995.[2] This volume provides an unprecedented glimpse of Liszt as a teacher, and I have cited it a number of times in the present work, particularly in the chapter "The Lion of Weimar: Liszt and His Pupils." Indeed, it

1. See WELC, cited on page 563.
2. See LL, cited on page 559.

changed the way I viewed this topic, and led me to modify a narrative that I had already written some years earlier.

Since my Liszt biography first got under way, the earlier volumes have been revised and re-published—the first in 1987 (again in 1990) and the second in 1993. That may seem a somewhat unusual thing to happen to a life-in-progress. Anyone who has worked in the field of Liszt scholarship, however, even on its periphery, will readily understand that a great deal of new and sometimes vital information flows into the topic daily, and it has to be assessed. The state of Liszt biography is probably more volatile than that of any other composer of comparable stature. In all the circumstances it seemed infinitely better for the earlier volumes to be revised even as the later ones were still coming out. The alternative might have delayed by a generation the issuing of a second edition, and with it many new facts.

I am fortunate in being able to include in my account of Liszt's final years a number of documents that have never before seen the light of day. From the start, I took it to be my chief task to present a more truthful picture of Liszt, one that was not warped by all the old unthinking generalizations that still pass for the story of his life. Thus, it seemed necessary to deal in somewhat greater depth than usual with such matters as the strange case of Olga Janina (the self-styled "Cossack countess") and to re-examine the precise nature of her relationship with Liszt—surely a classic example of musical biography run amok. And it will come as a surprise to many readers to learn of the circumstances surrounding the death of Blandine Liszt, to say nothing of the harrowing details of Liszt's own death, which several generations of biographers have managed to smooth over in order to create a happy ending. As well, I have made use of many of the unpublished letters of Princess Carolyne, especially where they throw light on situations that might otherwise remain obscure—such as the death of her husband, Prince Nicholas, her quarrels with her daughter, Princess Marie von Hohenlohe, and the accident Liszt suffered in July 1881, which changed the course of his life and may have shortened it. There is also a very great deal about Richard Wagner in this book, especially about his role in the break-up of Cosima's marriage to Hans von Bülow. While that story has been told many times before, of course, it has never been told from Liszt's perspective, a point of view that is possibly the most compelling of all.

It has almost become routine in these volumes for me to extend my thanks to the staffs of the Goethe- und Schiller-Archiv in Weimar, to the Library of Congress in Washington, D. C., to the British Library in London, to the National Széchényi Library in Budapest, and to the Vatican Library in Rome. The fact is that I owe them a debt that I cannot repay. These institutions became like second homes to me, for they not only gave me prompt access to a vast range of rare scholarly material, but did so with a friendliness and courtesy that remain all too rare in the field of musicology. There are also a number of individuals whose names should be entered in the roll-of-honour, including Gabriele Erasmi, Gerhart Teuscher, and László Jámbor—a formidable group of colleagues who, with the shining example of my irrepressible copy-editor, Patrick Dillon, before them, were ever ready to rescue me from confusion and error.

To Mária Eckhardt, the director of the Liszt Memorial Museum and Research Centre in Hungary, I owe special acknowledgements. She read through the entire manuscript and offered me some valuable suggestions. Few scholars can match Mária Eckhardt's command of the minutiae of Liszt's daily life, and I am glad that my text passed through the refining fire of her critical scrutiny before it was published. I am also grateful to Klára Hamburger, the secretary-general of the Budapest Liszt Society, who was unfailingly helpful to me on my various trips to the city of the Magyars and generously made available to me the fruits of her own research on a number of esoteric issues. Above all, I have to recognise the continued assistance of Pauline Pocknell, who has supported my work in a myriad of ways, but especially through translations, transcriptions, and archival work. She treated my book with the same respect as if it were her own. Without even realising it she also provided me with a bonus, for she fulfilled one of Liszt's own best maxims: "Create memories!" The pages that follow do indeed enshrine a wealth of memories—of difficulties confronted, of obstacles overcome, of problems solved, and of enigmas that remain.

My editor, Susan Ralston, proved to me time and again that there is no better home for a book of these dimensions than the house of Alfred A. Knopf, Inc. This institution surely sets the standards by which other publishers are judged. I remain grateful to the happy accident that led me to the venerable firm, and thence to Susan Ralston's office. She took my work into her protection many years ago and monitored its progress with care. No author could have received better treatment, and I am happy to celebrate that fact here.

Rome–London, 1995   ALAN WALKER

Prologue

Franz Liszt:
King Lear of Music

He who has a why to live can bear almost any how.
NIETZSCHE[1]

I

The threads that run through the last twenty-five years of Liszt's life are not easy to disentangle. This is the period that saw his departure from Weimar; his thwarted marriage to Princess von Sayn-Wittgenstein; his historic quarrel with Richard Wagner; the death of his elder daughter, Blandine; his growing estrangement from his younger daughter, Cosima; and his entry into the lower orders of the priesthood. Above all, it was a time of artistic frustration, arising from the widespread rejection of his music. He became an inveterate traveller, and from 1869 he spent three or four months out of every year in Weimar, Budapest, and Rome, in an endless circle. He himself called it his "vie tri-furquée"—a life split in three. Because of the many setbacks he endured, both public and private, Liszt's embattled character succumbed to a series of depressions, culminating in 1877 in a desire, several times repeated, to commit suicide—an act of despair from which only his devout Catholicism saved him. Liszt's correspondence with Olga von Meyendorff, which remained unknown until modern times, tells it all.

> . . . I am extremely tired of living; but as I believe that God's Fifth Commandment "thou shalt not kill" also applies to suicide, I go on existing. . . .[2]

---

1. NWB, vol. 2, p. 944.
2. WLLM, p. 299.

3

> . . . Last Friday I entered my seventieth year. It might be time to
> end things well . . . all the more since I have never wished to live
> long. In my early youth I often went to sleep hoping not to awaken
> here below.[3]

The darker side of Liszt's personality has long been suspected, but it has never
been more clearly revealed than in these letters. There is further correspondence in the Weimar archives, much of it unpublished, which helps us to understand the marked personality change of his old age—a change that stood in
such stark contrast to the buoyant, life-enhancing character that was Liszt during his halcyon days as a keyboard virtuoso in the 1840s.

II

Liszt, in fact, was to bear the tribulations of his old age with commendable fortitude. Among the many afflictions he had to endure as he entered his twilight
years were failing eyesight, ague, and dropsy. He also suffered from pyorrhoea
and lost most of his teeth; this meant that he was unable to eat anything which
required vigorous chewing, and his diet consisted mainly of soft foods. Liszt's
famous "warts," which were a chief characteristic of the face of his old age,
were really sycomas of an adipose tumorous growth; some, in the words of his
pupil Carl Lachmund, were "so narrow at the root that it seemed as if a snap
of the finger would have dislodged them." There is a possibility that they may
have appeared on the torso as well. Lachmund once helped Liszt adjust the
back of his collar, which had become unbuttoned, and he observed that just
below the collar-button was hidden a particularly large excrescence, flat and
long, "almost the size of a narrow fingernail."[4]

For the last six or seven years of his life, when he was easily overcome by fatigue, Liszt required help to get through the average day—a pupil to assist him
with his correspondence, someone to prepare his meals, and a friendly arm to
help him cross the road or to negotiate difficult steps. Since he liked to get up
before dawn to attend mass, he was usually tired by midday and insisted on taking a siesta. He hardly ever varied this routine in the 1880s. It was a major setback for him when he fell down the stairs of the Hofgärtnerei, on July 2, 1881,
an accident which shook him so badly that he was obliged to take to his bed for
several weeks, and for a long time afterwards he could walk only with difficulty.

Yet he kept going, filling his sixteen-hour days with a tremendous amount
of activity—teaching, playing, composing. "One is never ill," he used to say. "If

---

3. WLLM, p. 384.
4. LL, p. 52.

one does not enjoy good health, one should go out and acquire some." He would rarely tolerate any discussion of his health, in fact; and whenever anyone was indiscreet enough to broach this topic he quickly steered him to another subject. Humour was his constant defence against the frailties of old age. His letters are filled with jokes, puns, and barbed witticisms directed against himself, which disclosed the remarkable objectivity with which he watched the decaying of the mortal coil. It is hardly surprising that he became increasingly dependent on alcohol, the friend of his youth and close companion of his manhood. At the time of the Weimar masterclasses, in the 1880s, he was often observed to disappear from the music-room of the Hofgärtnerei into the adjoining bedroom for a quick glass of his favorite cognac, and return to the class a few moments later wiping the liquid from his lips. This apparently affected neither his piano-playing nor his conversation, and may in fact have stimulated both. Whether he was an alcoholic in the medical sense of that term we cannot be sure. But his consumption of wine and liquor in the course of a single day was considerable. For the last few years of his life Liszt regularly consumed one bottle of cognac daily and on occasion two bottles of wine as well. And in the early 1880s, he developed a strong liking for absinthe—a powerful distillation of grape-alcohol and wormwood.[5]

Achille Colonello, from whom this information ultimately derives, was one of a series of trusted manservants who entered Liszt's service during the last fifteen years of his life and accumulated much inside information about the master through their intimate daily contact with him. Their duties included setting out Liszt's clothes, shaving him, preparing his meals, announcing his visitors, undertaking special errands, and accompanying him on his foreign travels. Liszt had four such servants at various times during his final years. Miska Sipka was a Hungarian who remained with Liszt until 1875. He was a rather colourful personality who was renowned all over Weimar for insisting on speaking Hungarian to Liszt's visitors, with the result that anyone intent on meeting Liszt was obliged first to greet Miska in the Magyar tongue. Kornél Ábrányi called him "the stern Charon," and added that "many a German's mouth squeaks as they give [Hungarian] a try." Miska also had one other claim to fame: in the course of six years in Liszt's service he taught much of the local population to swear in Hungarian. So successful were these oaths that they began to travel across Thuringia; Ábrányi actually heard them come from the mouth of a German worker in a village many miles from Weimar, who was innocent of all knowledge of their origin.[6] Liszt was attached to Miska and visited him several times in the hospital of San Giacomo al Corso in Rome, where he died in 1875. Miska was succeeded by Spiridon Knežević, a Montenegrin who spoke Ger-

5. CLC, series 2, folder 5, pp. 166–67.
6. AAT, p. 78.

man, Italian, and Hungarian quite fluently. Spiridon was something of a man-
about-town in Weimar, where his position as Liszt's faithful servant gave him
a certain status among Liszt's friends and pupils there. He was always well attired, could conduct an intelligent conversation on a great variety of topics, and
was even treated with deference by the grand duke of Weimar. Spiridon often
complained when Liszt decided to travel second-class and subject him to the
indignities of carrying the luggage and sitting in cramped seats. As a member
of the Orthodox Russian Church, he had little sympathy with the hardships of
Franciscan poverty that Liszt liked to practise in old age. As Liszt grew older,
in fact, these hardships were pursued with ever more rigour. Whenever his
good friend Dr. Carl Gille came to stay with him in the Hofgärtnerei, Liszt
made a practice of giving up his bedroom and sleeping on a hard couch in an
adjoining room. If it became necessary to stay in a hotel, he would ask for "two
modest rooms for myself, and a third more comfortable for Signor Spiridon"—
an unusual reversal of their social stations.[7] In fact, Liszt became quite dependent on this manservant, and preferred to postpone his journeys whenever "the
inviolable Spiridon" was indisposed, rather than set out without him. Spiridon
left Liszt's service in August 1881 in order to get married. It was his second attempt at matrimony, and his new bride had no dowry. Liszt explained to Spiridon that he could not be responsible for a second household and he would
have "to seek his fortunes elsewhere than in my service."[8] That is how Achille
Colonello came to be engaged by Liszt. Alas, he died after a mere three years
in service, in 1884, and Liszt was forced to cast about for someone else. By this
time, Liszt himself was in failing health and needed a lot of attention, but he
found an excellent servant in another Hungarian, Mihály Krainer, who helped
to nurse Liszt during his last illness and tended him at his death. These servants
probably knew Liszt more intimately than many of his closest friends. Alas for
the biographer, not one of them is known to have kept a diary.

III

But many others did. Whenever Liszt announced his return to Weimar, the small
town filled up with pupils, friends, and disciples to await his arrival. Many of these
worthies got out their notebooks, sharpened their pencils, and lay siege to the
Hofgärtnerei in order to record their impressions of "der liebe Meister." Amy

---

7. PBUS, p. 219.
8. LLB, vol. 7, pp. 324–25. Incidentally, Liszt usually called Spiridon "Spiridion" after the character in
George Sand's novel of that name. A great deal of information about this servant may be found in
"Lisztiana, with three unpublished letters" by Miloš Velimirović, *Musical Quarterly,* October 1961, pp.
474–80.

Fay, August Göllerich, Carl Lachmund, Alexander Gottschalg, Emil von Sauer, Frederic Lamond, and Arthur Friedheim were but a small fraction of the people in Liszt's circle who left a memoir of the times. Useful as these records are to the biographer, they are by no means the most important. Adelheid von Schorn spent many years in the preparation of her book *Zwei Menschenalter* (1901), which chronicles the lives of Liszt and Princess Carolyne in impressive detail, particularly with regards to the Weimar connection. And her massive two-volume *Das nachklassische Weimar* (1911–12) puts other historians to shame. Were Liszt and his entourage to be banished from its pages, the book would be emasculated.

When Louis Held, the new "court photographer," arrived in Weimar in 1882 and opened his photography studio in Schillerstrasse, not far from the Hofgärtnerei, he gave the scribblers and chroniclers new standards of biographical exactitude to consider. With him the well-known phrase "A picture is worth ten thousand words" took on its literal meaning. Held found an unimaginably rich source of subjects in Weimar, a city which was peopled with individuals standing on the verge of history, and he forever changed the field of Liszt iconography. Held's portraits of Liszt and his circle are unsurpassed in both content and form. In May 1884 he thought nothing of setting up his camera in front of more than a hundred members of the Allgemeiner Deutscher Tonkünstlerverein and capturing that large throng for posterity. The puzzle is how he got everybody into the lens.[9] And there were intimate photographs as well, arranged on the spur of the moment, such as the long series of portraits he took of Liszt with individual students such as Bernhard Stavenhagen, Alexander Siloti, and the violinist Arma Senkrah. In 1886, Louis Held opened a studio at no. 1 Marienstrasse, on the same street as Liszt's dwelling, and from this coign of vantage it became even easier for him to capture Liszt on camera. From time to time Held set up his equipment in the Hofgärtnerei itself, with telling results. The last series of Weimar portraits is filled with the loving detail that was typical of Held's work—the facial lines, the skin-tone, the lustrous hair, and the points of light in the eyes which bring character to life. Nor does he spare the famous warts. He once asked Liszt whether he should remove them from a photographic negative. Liszt instructed him to leave them in. He might have been thinking of Cromwell, who used to say to his portrait painter: "Paint me as I am. Do not leave out a single wart, or you will not receive a penny." From that

---

9. See BFL, p. 298. An even greater challenge to his ability to handle "crowd scenes" came in 1902 when he captured the unveiling ceremony of the Liszt statue in Weimar's Goethe Park, and the Liszt centennial celebrations at the same site in 1911.

  Louis Held (1851–1927) had served his apprenticeship in Potsdam, had opened a professional studio in Berlin, in 1879, but had seen possibilities of greater expansion in Weimar through an attachment to the royal court. His outdoor scenes—the parks, the vegetable and flower markets, the regimental parades, and even the trams which were already trundling through the streets by the turn of the century—capture far better than do words the diversity of daily life in this city.

moment Liszt was Held's favourite subject. Held may even have changed the
way in which Liszt's biography came to be written; for during these later years
he left much pictorial evidence of the "saintly" Liszt, an image that aroused ven-
eration in his disciples and derision in his enemies. Without such pictures, en-
hanced as they were by the clerical collar, the abbé's soutane, the long grey hair,
and the face—above all, the face—with its piercing gaze and craggy profile, our
literary descriptions might be different, for they would rest on hearsay. But Held
brings Liszt into our living rooms. The famous photograph taken of Liszt on
October 22, 1884, his seventy-third birthday, surrounded by eleven of his pupils
sitting on the steps outside Armbrust's restaurant[10] in Weimar, speaks volumes.
This is more than a mere gathering of some students and their local music
teacher: a master is holding court with his disciples. (Some critics, with malice
aforethought, have seen in this picture a hint of the Last Supper, even though
one disciple is missing.) To many of these acolytes Liszt was a guru-figure, and
they came from all over the world to bask in his presence.

Yet there was more to the "saintly" Liszt than mere externals. Those char-
acter-traits that had been present in him from childhood received in old age a
new impetus, and they were allowed free play. He became careless of criticism,
tolerant of rivals, forgiving of enemies, and generous to the needy. He had always lent his name and his fame to charitable causes, often in a fanfare of publicity, but in his old age he began to do much good by stealth. Janka Wohl, a
Hungarian student, never forgot how she came upon him unexpectedly in his
Budapest apartment one afternoon, putting a pile of banknotes into envelopes.
It transpired that for years he had made a habit of answering personally the
scores of begging letters with which he was beleaguered.[11] Carl Lachmund
once observed something similar. During the years 1882–84, when he was a
pupil of Liszt, he and his wife, Caroline, got to know Liszt socially and were
sometimes invited to join him for dinner at the Hofgärtnerei. On one occasion, after the meal was finished, the guests went into an adjoining room for
coffee. There they found a young Polish girl, who had recently travelled to
Germany especially to study with Liszt, waiting for the master. He nodded to
her, as if expecting her, went to a desk drawer, and handed her an envelope. She
took it and, without any acknowledgement whatever, departed. Lachmund
later discovered that this was a routine visit, that the mother was suffering from
tuberculosis, that there was a younger sister in the family, and that they had difficulty in living from one day to the next. Liszt had meanwhile been support-

---

10. BFL, p. 303. The photograph was not taken outside the Hofgärtnerei, as is commonly supposed.
Armbrust's used to be located in the Schützengasse, less than half a mile away. Liszt had been in the
habit of gathering there with his friends since the 1850s (see, for example, the entry in HML, vol. 6,
p. 254). Evidently it was Siloti who suggested this birthday picture, and who paid for it as well.
11. WFLR, p. 219.

ing them.[12] The genteel poverty into which Liszt fell during the 1870s and '80s today arouses our bewilderment. Since 1847 he had not earned a penny from piano playing, and as he always refused to accept a fee from his pupils he now had virtually no income. During his Weimar period his salary (or "cigar money," as he jokingly dubbed it) had amounted to no more than a few hundred dollars a year. Meanwhile, he had been financially responsible for his three children and had supported his ageing mother in Paris, all of which had helped to deplete his resources. As he gave money away quite freely, his capital also dwindled. His main source of income during his twilight years was from his published compositions, but this gradually dried up as they became less popular and sold fewer copies. It was a paradoxical position to be in. Here was the world's greatest pianist; all he had to do was to announce a public concert and the money would come pouring in. But he always steadfastly refused to return to the concert platform for personal profit. An amusing sidelight to all this came in 1874 when the secretary of a musical festival about to be held in Liverpool wrote to Liszt to find out what was his fee. Liszt treated this functionary gently but firmly.

> [Villa d'Este,
> June 21, 1874]

> Dear Sir,
>   Your friendly communication rests upon a harmless mistake. You appear not to know that for twenty-six years I have entirely ceased to be considered as a pianist; consequently, I have not given concerts for a long time, and have only occasionally played the piano in public for some very special reason in Rome, in Hungary (my native country), and in Vienna—nowhere else—to aid some charity or to further some artistic cause. And on these rare and very exceptional occasions no one has ever thought of offering me any remuneration in money. Excuse me, therefore, dear sir, if I do not accept your invitation to the Liverpool Musical Festival, because there is no way I can consider wearying the public with my *erstwhile* piano playing.
>
>   Respectfully yours,
>   F. LISZT[13]

A much more lucrative situation presented itself in the summer of 1885, when Liszt received a visit from an American concert agent, who offered him two

---

12. LL, p. 227. We now know that this young Polish girl was Anna Konopacka, a one-time pupil of Liszt. She and her sick mother are portrayed in Ernst von Wolzogen's novel *Der Kraft-Mayr* (1897).
13. LLB, vol. 2, p. 203.

million marks if he would visit the United States the following season. The
agent assured him that since he would share the platform with other artists he
would be expected to play only one item in each concert. Liszt was highly
amused at this bizarre offer, for he replied: "What, at the age of seventy-four, am
I expected to do with two million marks? Am I supposed to play 'Erlkönig' three
hundred times in America?"[14] By the year 1875 Liszt observed that he was receiving nearly fifty letters a week from various countries, "not counting ship-
ments of manuscripts, pamphlets, books, dedications, and all kinds of music."[15]
That is a remarkable number on which it does not do to dwell. It amounted to
two hundred a month, nearly two thousand five hundred a year. Liszt was besieged by his mail, and complained constantly that it got in the way of his creative work. He knew full well that the time taken to deal with this mountain of
paper might have been better spent in writing new compositions or polishing
old ones. Yet deal with it he did. "Some ask for concerts, for advice, for recom-
mendations; others for money, for jobs, for decorations, etc. etc."[16] He called it
"playing providence." The rest of the world might call it folly; the underprivi-
leged, after all, are always with us. Such was Liszt's essential goodness, however,
that he utterly failed to comprehend that to answer a human need is like cutting off a Gorgon's head: for every one severed, six others spring up in its place.
Indeed, he would probably have found the analogy offensive, since the only lesson one can logically draw from it is to turn one's back on humanity altogether,
in which case one might as well withdraw from life itself.

Liszt had no intention of withdrawing from life, his dark depressions
notwithstanding. Yet there remains the interesting question of his two-year retreat in the monastery of the Madonna del Rosario, on the Monte Mario outside Rome. That it was a withdrawal cannot be denied, yet there is some
evidence to suggest that when Liszt sought sanctuary within those cloisters, in
the early summer of 1863, he wanted no more than a temporary haven from
which to escape the vicissitudes of the outside world, recover his sense of direction, and emerge psychologically refreshed. What actually happened does
not appear to have been planned, yet could have been forseen. Liszt underwent
a spiritual regeneration in the Madonna del Rosario, and emerged as "Abbé
Liszt." The monastic life gave him a chance for uninterrupted periods of quiet
contemplation and drove him back to the innermost recesses of his personality. It was there that he re-discovered in himself the old childhood longing for
the priesthood, but this time there was nothing and no one to deter him. His
own justification for donning the cassock is worth pondering: "When the
monk is already formed within, why not appropriate the outer garment of

14. SE, p. 99.
15. WLLM, pp. 123 and 213.
16. WLLM, p. 213.

one?"[17] Just how much of the monk there was in Liszt is still a matter of speculation among scholars, and the topic will be addressed elsewhere in this narrative. But even if his sojourn in the Madonna del Rosario had not led him to
take holy orders, it would still have provided him with the tranquillity for
work. During his stay there he completed not only his vast oratorio *Christus*
but also the two Franciscan Legends and several of his piano transcriptions of
the Beethoven symphonies. The view of Rome from the Madonna del
Rosario was, and is, spectacular. The whole city rolls away from the Monte
Mario like a map. From the window of his cell, Liszt would have gazed out at
many a famous landmark, including the dome of Saint Peter's. And in his day,
the monastery would have been quite isolated, accessible only by way of a secondary road. It was an ideal retreat for composition.

By 1865 Liszt had already taken four of the seven orders of priesthood and
had become an abbé in the Roman Catholic Church—an act that was not
merely intended to bring repose into his troubled life but which, in his own
words, "corresponds with the antecedents of my youth":[18] we recall that Liszt
had wanted to enter a Paris seminary in his sixteenth year. The archival material that forms the background to this absorbing aspect of Liszt's life is contained in Rome, some of it in the Vatican Library, and it has never been
consulted until now. The personal papers of Cardinals Hohenlohe and Antonelli throw much light on Liszt's complex relationship with the Church.

IV

One fact to emerge with wonderful clarity during the last twenty-five years of
Liszt's life was his gift as a teacher. The long series of masterclasses Liszt held
in Weimar during the years 1869–1886 created an epoch. Young people gathered around him by the multitude and were happy to trail after him on his
peregrinations through Europe. He has been described as "the Pied Piper of
Weimar," and the image is compelling. Many of these young musicians left a
wealth of personal testimony, so it is not difficult for the biographer to revive
the excitement of those times and to capture for posterity Liszt's views on
piano playing and musical interpretation, from which, incidentally, there are
still new things to learn.

It is well known that Liszt never charged a penny for his lessons—one of the
factors that contributed to the "genteel poverty" of which we spoke. Since Art,
for him, was God-given, it was unthinkable to turn it into a business, and he had
little patience with those who did. Shortly after Theodor Kullak died, and

---

17. LLB, vol. 2, p. 81.
18. Ibid.

the details of his will had become widely known, the conversation in Liszt's class turned on the large fortune that he had accumulated as a teacher. "Yes," said Liszt, "but no endowment for needy musicians. It is a shame, a burning shame."[19] Liszt's view of such matters was a very simple one: give back what you take out. Music had been very generous to Kullak, but he had not been particularly generous in return. As Liszt told Lina Ramann: "As an artist, you don't rake in a million marks without performing some sacrifice on the altar of Art."[20] Coming from anyone else, such comments would have been little better than an impertinence; after all, a man may do what he likes with the money he has acquired through honest labour. But coming from Liszt, the criticism was unanswerable. Quite apart from the gift of his teaching, he had given away a fortune to charity through his playing. His example in such matters was unassailable.

Those who were privileged to attend Liszt's classes in the seventies and eighties were fortunate in another respect. Long after he had retired from the concert platform, he continued to play for his pupils. Liszt liked to teach by example, and he often sat down at the piano in order to illustrate how a particular passage should go. Such experiences were priceless. The most sophisticated audiences in the world were denied the possibility of hearing Liszt in the concert hall; yet his pupils heard him several times a week, for no charge at all. Young as they were, many of them realised that they were witnessing history and had the good sense to record their impressions.

Bettina Walker attended Liszt's classes in the summer of 1883, and left a vivid description of his playing.

> He gave one the impression of possessing an almost terrible mastery over every imaginable variety of passage—especially in leaping intervals so wide apart, that to play them with ease is as nearly as possible like being in two different places at the same time. I have listened to him twice in the "Patineurs" [from Le Prophète], and a cold shiver has passed through me, not so much at what he actually bestowed on us, as what he suggested as having still in reserve. To his interpretations of Chopin—three of whose Ballades, many of the Preludes, several Etudes, three Polonaises, and one Concerto, I heard him play in Weimar—I have listened with delight mingled with awe.

---

19. LL, p. 226. Kullak's Neue Akademie der Tonkunst had become the biggest private institution of its kind in Germany, with about one hundred teachers and eleven hundred students. Kullak had amassed a personal fortune of several million thalers in the course of his productive career. Liszt felt so strongly about the "Kullak affair" that on September 5, 1885, he wrote a letter to Otto Lessmann, the editor of the *Allgemeine Musikalische Zeitung,* in which he suggested that Kullak's sons ought to consider setting up such an endowment for needy musicians in the name of their father (see RL, p. 297–98).

20. RL, p. 298.

His sight-reading of difficult manuscript compositions, which were brought to him on different occasions, was simply marvellous.[21]

Similar accounts abound in the literature. One of the more thoughtful comes from Arthur Friedheim, who had many opportunities to hear Liszt during the last six years of his life, and addresses a somewhat wider question.

If Liszt were with us today, more than one hundred years after he reached the peak of his powers, would he be likely to duplicate the sensation he created then and would our critics and audiences react as they did in the ripest period of Romanticism? I say "Yes," for Liszt's genius, insight, versatility and personal magnetism would be as potent now as they were then, and would enable him to adapt himself to every modern requirement. . . . I would go even further and hazard the logical opinion that Liszt would have developed in our time as he did in his own, and perhaps even shown us things altogether new in ideas and execution.[22]

This was the legendary Liszt. But there was an all-too-human side as well. Carl Lachmund paints an unforgettable picture of Liszt shuffling about the Hofgärtnerei in a pair of old slippers which had no supporting heels. In order to prevent them from falling off, he was obliged to slide around in them, a mode of locomotion which was virtually noise-free. During a performance by a student Liszt would often glide silently in and out of the group of listeners, who were unsure where he might turn up next. He found these magic slippers more comfortable to wear than anything else, and he even received the Grand Duke of Weimar in them. Princess von Sayn-Wittgenstein was referring to this decrepit footwear when she remarked that they made Liszt look like "an old organist." And she added: "You could float from Civita-Veccia to Naples in them."[23] It was not merely for domestic comfort that Liszt wore those slippers, however. His feet were by now so bloated with dropsy that no other footwear was practical.

V

Among the lasting achievements of Liszt's old age was the foundation of the Royal Academy of Music in Budapest, which was opened in November 1875 with Liszt as its first president. This institution, today called the Liszt Academy

---

21. WMME, pp. 126–27.
22. FLL, p. 161.
23. CLBA, p. 10.

of Music, is one of the great music schools, and it remains a source of justifiable pride to Hungary. Over the years Liszt made many sacrifices to help launch this ambitious enterprise. He participated in the drawing up of its curriculum, in the appointment of its faculty, and in the teaching of its more gifted piano students. While the history of the institution has already been ably dealt with by Hungarian scholars, we have nonetheless devoted a chapter of the present book to the academy's fledgling years because its story is a part of Liszt's biography, and is inseparable from it. In fact, the composer's Hungarian connections are traced in much greater detail than has hitherto been possible in a life of Liszt. Even a decade ago, he was widely regarded as a cosmopolitan figure whose links to his native country remained weak. Today that notion has to be radically revised, thanks in large measure to Dezső Legány's magnum opus, *Liszt and His Country.* His two-volume work was brought to completion while the present biography was still in progress, and I have taken advantage of it a number of times in the pages that follow.

Liszt's long-standing quarrel with Richard Wagner, which began in the mid 1860s, was finally patched up in 1872, after which he became a frequent guest at Wahnfried in Bayreuth, where Wagner now lived. The Hungarian composer's support for Wagner's artistic cause was dealt with in Volume Two and need not be stressed here. The practical point to be borne in mind is that over the years a sizable legacy accumulated as a result of his many visits—letters, manuscripts, newspaper articles—which are today preserved in both the Richard Wagner Archive and the Stadt Archiv in Bayreuth. Add to this the fact that Liszt is buried in Bayreuth, and it becomes clear that this city (like Weimar, Rome, and Budapest) is important to any biographer who wishes to base his narrative on the results of field work rather than hearsay.

VI

Musical criticism has not been kind to Liszt in the century since his death. Even during his lifetime the critics rose up in a fury of invective and, with devastating force, condemned his music as worthless and trivial. Eduard Hanslick led the attack. "After Liszt," he once wrote, "Mozart is like a soft spring breeze penetrating a room reeking with fumes." The English critics, not to be outdone, followed suit. "Liszt's themes," observed Frederick Corder, "stick out like almonds in a Dundee cake; they fail to cohere."[24] Sir Henry Hadow told his readers that he "would not give up [Haydn's] *Creation* for all the works of the Hungarian master put together."[25] But perhaps the most sanctimonious ut-

---

24. CFL, p. 133.
25. HSMM, p. 201.

terance in the history of criticism came from Sir George Macfarren, the principal of the Royal Academy of Music, who piously declared that Liszt "was working a great evil upon music." Anxious, no doubt, to protect his students against Liszt's pernicious influence, he tried to dissuade them from listening to his music lest it corrupt them. This was an extreme measure, but, as he put it, "were you to preach temperance at a gin-shop door, and let your congregation taste the poison sold therein, that they might know its vileness, they would come out drunkards."[26] Such comments have nothing to do with musical reality, nor even with musical criticism (the two things are not always the same), yet they exist in abundance. It would be easy to show that if all the invective ever levelled against Liszt were to be gathered between hard covers, the resulting tome would far surpass in bulk the size of a full-scale biography.

Liszt was well aware of the negative criticism that he and his music aroused, and he purported to ignore it. Yet in the end it affected him profoundly and did him psychological harm. The bitterness of heart is there for all to see. There are wrenching letters from his old age in which we catch a glimpse of the turmoil which raged within him whenever he tried to reflect on his work and understand the strange fate that had befallen it. We know of occasions in which he not only discouraged performances of his music but actually banned them. To Jessie Laussot he once wrote:

> Knowing by experience with how little favour my works meet, I have been obliged to force a sort of systematic heedlessness on myself with regard to them, and a resigned passiveness. Thus, during my years of foreign activity in Germany, I constantly observed the rule of never asking anyone whatsoever to have any of my works performed; more than that, I plainly dissuaded many persons from doing so who showed some intention of this kind—and I shall do the same elsewhere.[27]

And to the conductor Johann von Herbeck:

> To say "no" to my friends always comes hard to me. But how to act differently in face of negative criticism? . . . Nowadays people hear and judge only by reading the newspapers. . . . I want to profit from this fact, insofar as the leading and favourite journals of Vienna, Pest, Leipzig, Berlin, Paris, London, etc., which abhor my humble

---

26. BGM, p. 296.
27. LLB, vol. 2, p. 78.

compositions and declare them worthless, shall be relieved of all
further outward trouble concerning them. . . . What is the good of
performances to people who only want to read newspapers?[28]

In 1877 Liszt's pupil Berthold Kellermann arranged a performance of *Christus*
in Berlin at great personal expense. When Liszt heard of it, he refused to sanction the performance and asked Kellermann to cancel it. Kellermann was hurt
by this decision and travelled to Weimar to talk to Liszt about it. It was only
then that he learned of Liszt's true motive in banning the performance. "It
mattered less to him, he told me, that he would once again be torn to pieces
by all the newspapers, than that I would suffer from it. I would be the first target of the poisoned arrows of his adversaries, and he knew the latter well
enough to know that to ruin me they would stop at nothing."[29] This attempt
to impose a ban on performances of his own music was unprecedented. One
has to move into the twentieth century to find similar attitudes—from
Kaikhosru Sorabji among others. Liszt would surely have admired Arnold
Schoenberg's adroit solution to the problem of getting a fair hearing for new
compositions: the formation of the Society for Private Musical Performances
in Vienna, in 1918, from which gatherings the music critics were excluded.
The issue pursued Liszt into old age. During a masterclass held in June 1885,
August Stradal was playing Liszt's "Weinen, Klagen" Variations. Liszt turned to
the class and remarked: "If you want a bad criticism, you must play this. It will
then be said: 'the young artist is not lacking in talent—it remains only to regret that he made such a poor choice of piece.' "[30]

What kind of music, and what kind of man, could provoke such hostility as
this? Liszt's music, like his life, is filled with contrast and unfolds across a variety of genres. It moves from the sacred to the secular, from the stage to the
study, from "programme" to "absolute" music, from God to the devil. And
these categories are themselves made more complicated by the variety of styles
which cut across them. Some of Liszt's works are full-blooded, outgoing, flamboyant. Others are withdrawn, economical, ascetic. All this is difficult for criticism, which traditionally abhors "lack of consistency." Yet there is no reason
why contrasting styles should not jostle for expression within the same mind;
indeed, it should be a matter for rejoicing, since it happens but rarely in the history of art. It remains a fact, however, that when one person expresses qualities
which are the opposite of his qualities he arouses the world's suspicion as to the
integrity of any of them. Likewise, if a composer appears to turn his back on
himself with each succeeding work, he ought not to be surprised if the world

---

28. LLB, vol. 2, p. 220.
29. KE, pp. 62 and 200.
30. GLK, p. 68.

follows suit and turns its back on them as well. Many musicians, in fact, have shrunk away from Liszt, bewildered and even offended by the stylistic parade that constitutes his oeuvre. This reaction is narrow, but it is difficult to demonstrate that it is narrow. Busoni's example is worth recalling. Tireless in his devotion to Liszt, and with few peers as an interpreter of his music, Busoni started out by actively disliking his idol. The change came when he was in his late twenties, and it had all the force of a religious conversion. Bartók underwent a similar metamorphosis, and at a similar time of his life. When were these two great composers wrong about Liszt—before or after they had changed their minds about him? Equally significant was the case of Richard Strauss, who from his earliest days had been a chief beneficiary of Liszt's creative legacy. Strauss had been Eduard Lassen's assistant conductor at Weimar, and his tone-poems *Don Juan* and *Macbeth* had received their first performances there—by some of the same players who had known and worked with Liszt. The "Liszt question" was one that came to absorb Strauss. In 1948, when the eighty-four-year-old composer was at Montreux, the conversation turned to Liszt and he became so emotional that those around him thought he might become ill. The thing that agitated him was that Liszt was "tragically misunderstood in Germany."[31]

Nowadays, thanks partly to Busoni's and Bartók's pioneering efforts, we are beginning to see Liszt in a new and unexpected light. Historically, he has come to assume enormous significance for our time. One of the most remarkable discoveries our generation has made about Liszt is the music of his old age. Its idiom is advanced and uncompromising. It prompted Bartók to exclaim that Liszt was the true father of modern music. Time is already beginning to bear out this interesting judgement.

For the rest, the rough-and-tumble of critical debate about Liszt is likely to continue, although it is today better informed. Let us never forget, however, that a composer's worth is not settled by debate, however distinguished the debators. If history should ever pronounce a final verdict on Liszt, it will not be because the views of one group of musicians have prevailed over those of another. It will be because the music itself, properly performed and appreciated, has prevailed over both.

---

31. BFL, p. 196.

BOOK ONE

From Weimar to Rome
1861 · 1865

A Thwarted Marriage, 1861

*My long exile is about to end. In five days' time I
shall find in you a home, a hearth, an altar!*
FRANZ LISZT TO CAROLYNE VON SAYN–
WITTGENSTEIN, OCTOBER 14, 1861[1]

I

On Saturday, August 17, 1861, Liszt checked out of the Erbprinz Hotel and set
out on foot for the Weimar railway station. Along the way he made a detour in
order to catch a last, nostalgic glimpse of the Altenburg from the outside. Even
though he was late, he could not resist taking a leisurely stroll around the garden. The windows of Princess Carolyne's bedroom and those of the Blue
Room were now boarded over, the main doors sealed.[2] The place resembled a
deserted shrine which continued to echo with the remembrance of times past.
Only the plumed peacocks were still in residence, whose mournful cries had so
attracted the attention of the princess that she herself used to feed them. A few
days earlier Liszt had even given three or four thaler to a local resident to make
sure that these exotic creatures did not suffer during his absence.[3] Still lost in his
thoughts, Liszt wended his way towards the railway station and boarded the 1:30
p.m. train for Wilhelmsthal. Weimar slipped into the background and the train
began to thread its way through the Thuringian hills. At that moment Liszt had
no idea if he would ever see the city of Goethe and Schiller again.

Why was Liszt visiting Wilhelmsthal? It was one of the summer homes of
Weimar's royal family; Liszt wanted to take his leave of Grand Duke Carl
Alexander in person. The grand duke was affable, as always, but it soon became

---

1. LLB, vol. 5, p. 238.
2. LLB, vol. 5, p. 218.
3. Ibid.

clear that he had no idea why Liszt was there. When he learned that his erst-while Kapellmeister might leave Weimar for good, he refused to hear of it. During Liszt's four-day stay at the castle, he dined with the grand duke and his wife, Princess Sophie, and he had several heart-to-heart chats with them, but neither of them could penetrate his reserve. In reply to all their questions he told them that he simply desired to leave Germany for a time "and look for a hut where I can work in peace . . . perhaps in the South of France, the Hyeres islands, Athens or Spain."[4] He did not breathe a word about his forthcoming marriage to Princess Carolyne, for reasons that will shortly be made clear. It was in these circumstances, and in this summer retreat, that Carl Alexander made Liszt a Chamberlain of the Weimar Court. This was not only a great honour for the composer but also a shrewd move on the part of the grand duke. With such a powerful and dignified title, Liszt was now a virtual ambassador for Weimar. However far he wandered, he remained attached to the city as if by a golden thread.[5]

By August 22 Liszt had arrived in Löwenberg, where he remained as a guest of Prince Constantin von Hohenzollern-Hechingen for nearly a month. This was the first real holiday that Liszt had enjoyed for many years (merely to mention the word "holiday" in connection with Liszt's driven personality strikes a chimerical note), and he found the experience refreshing. He spent his time mainly in "reading, writing, and playing the piano," and he dined every evening with the music-loving prince.[6] Occasionally he made forays into the surrounding villages of Rankau, Dalkau, and Bunzlau, so that he could sink himself in the peace and quiet of the countryside. On September 10 he received an unexpected visit from the pianist Adolf Henselt, who had contracted malaria in St. Petersburg and was now convalescing on his estates at nearby Gersdorff.[7] Two days later they were joined at Wilhelmsthal by Cosima, who was on a brief trip from Berlin; after the trio had spent some convivial hours together, Cosima and her father accompanied Henselt back to Gersdorff. It was the last recorded meeting between the two great pianists. Shortly afterwards Henselt returned to St. Petersburg, where he held the elevated position of inspector-general of piano classes to His Imperial Majesty Tsar Alexander II of

---

4. LLB, vol. 5, p. 221.
5. See the letter that Liszt wrote to Hans von Bülow on August 24, about a week after his encounter with the grand duke. "My gracious master absolutely refuses to accept the idea that I am leaving Weimar for a long time, and in order to emphasise the fact that he is determined that I should continue to play a role in his household, he appointed me Chamberlain." (LBLB, pp. 310–11) When Liszt wrote to his mother to inform her of the honour, he took special delight in reminding her of a colourful prophecy foretold at his birth and repeated to him throughout his infancy: "You see, dearest mother, that the prophecy of the midwife in Raiding ('Franzi will come back in a glass coach') is pretty well fulfilled." (LLBM, p. 136) In this connection see also Volume One, p. 55.
6. LLB, vol. 5, p. 221.
7. LLB, vol. 5, pp. 225–26.

Russia. Cosima's presence at Löwenberg prompted Liszt to give thought to the next stage of his leisurely itinerary, and he decided to join her and Bülow in Berlin. As he told Princess Carolyne: "Although Prince Hohenzollern is extremely gracious and amiable towards me, I do not think it proper to prolong my stay here for more than four or five days. I have already enjoyed his hospitality for three weeks, and it is not one of my habits to weary even my best friends by my presence."[8]

Liszt got to Berlin on September 19 and put up at the Hotel de Pologne, about a hundred yards from the Bülows' apartment on Schöneberger Strasse. This was a convenient arrangement, since it enabled him to take his meals with Hans and Cosima while at the same time giving him the opportunity to socialize with some of his old friends. He saw Meyerbeer, the painter Cornelius, and Carl Weitzmann, and he also spent an evening in the company of Anton Rubinstein. It was the first time that Liszt and "Van II" had met since the latter's ignominious flight from Weimar, and the music of Berlioz, in 1855.[9] The occasion was friendly enough, although Liszt's attitude towards Rubinstein's own music remained unchanged. "As usual, he spends his time composing a mass of works. To my regret, the last two he played to me are not an advance on the earlier ones."[10]

Liszt caught the night train from Berlin on October 6 and arrived in Frankfurt at half past nine the following morning. His itinerary now began to unfold with great rapidity. The following day he was in Basel, and the day after that in Lyons. By October 12 he had arrived in Marseilles, where he put up at the Hôtel des Empereurs. Although the Olliviers were daily expecting him at nearby Saint-Tropez, he made no attempt to contact them. He lingered in Marseilles for five days and then booked a berth on the steamship *Quirinal* (the same boat that had transported the princess to Italy seventeen months earlier) and set out for Italy on October 17. As it sailed past Saint-Tropez, on a calm Mediterranean sea, Blandine thought that she could see it in the distance from the windows of La Moutte, and wished her father Godspeed.[11] Three days later Liszt was in Rome. He arrived in the Eternal City on Sunday, October 20, and was reunited with Carolyne in her apartment at Piazza di Spagna 93 that same day.[12]

---

8. LLB, vol. 5, p. 224.
9. See Volume Two, pp. 257–58.
10. LLB, vol. 5, p. 229.
11. OCLF, p. 295.
12. Liszt himself confirmed the date of his arrival in Rome in his *Memento Journalier,* VLKN, p. 86. The princess had been occupying a three-room apartment on the Piazza di Spagna, one of the most fashionable quarters in Rome, since June the previous year (LLB, vol. 5, p. 14).

II

More than two months had elapsed since Liszt left Weimar, and his journey to
Rome had unfolded so erratically that it calls for an explanation. Even a cur-
sory glance at the map shows that he was at times literally moving around in
circles, pausing here, hurrying forward there, choosing the name of his next
destination as if it were no more than a card in a game of chance. Most bewil-
dering of all, he put out misleading statements to his friends about his plans for
the winter—first Athens, then Saint-Tropez, possibly Vienna, but *never* Rome.
Even his nearest and dearest were not made privy to his movements; they knew
only that the way was now clear for his marriage to Carolyne, but they had no
idea when or where it would take place. Blandine fully expected him to stay
as her house guest at Saint-Tropez, but he never turned up. As for Cosima, it
was the indecisive month that he spent with her and Hans in Berlin that convinced her that her father looked forward to his marriage "as to a burial service." The detached observer is bound to ask: Why did not Liszt simply catch
the next train to Rome, which would have got him there the following day
and ended all speculation? In order to answer this question we have to read the
letters that he was exchanging with Carolyne, which point to an astonishing
conclusion: Carolyne herself kept Liszt on the move, kept even *him* in the dark
as to his ultimate destination, and then, when it was revealed, swore him to secrecy. Speculation, in short, was exactly what she wanted to create.[13] As late as
August 28 he told her: "If you definitely fix on Rome as the terminus of my
journey, please tell me whether it will be via Vienna, Ancona, or Marseilles,"[14]
a proof that he left Weimar with no clear idea of what was happening or what
was expected of him. A month later he was still unsure, and wrote from Berlin:
"It is up to you to set the date of my voyage."[15] It was not until October 4 that
he learned from Carolyne that she had fixed the date of the wedding for October 22, his fiftieth birthday, and that it would definitely take place in Rome,
in the church of San Carlo al Corso. He hastened to assure her: "To [Count
Mulinen] I shall speak only of Saint-Tropez and Athens."[16] Despite his best efforts, however, the newspapers somehow got wind of Carolyne's last-minute

---

13. This had happened once before in their long and tortured relationship. It will be recalled that when
Carolyne had first planned her escape from the Wittgensteins and had fled across the Russian border
in the early spring of 1848, she had designed a choreography of similar complexity. She had zig-zagged
her way towards Liszt, before finally meeting him at Kryzanowicz Castle, just as he now zig-zagged
his way towards her—and for the same reasons: to throw off their pursuers. The one journey could
almost be described as a dress-rehearsal for the other.
14. LLB, vol. 5, p. 220.
15. Ibid.
16. LLB, vol. 5, p. 235.

instructions to him and broke the story of his journey to Rome. When Carolyne chastised him, Liszt hotly defended himself and told her that the papers must have "plucked this piece of news entirely out of the air, because I have never spoken of this journey as probable. I have firmly promoted plans for Saint-Tropez and Athens."[17]

What motivated Carolyne to behave in so secretive a manner? And why did Liszt allow himself to be pushed hither and thither without complaint? In order to answer these questions we must not forget the long ordeal that Carolyne had endured in Rome as she pursued her annulment through the corridors of the Vatican.[18] Even though she had secured a resounding victory, and her annulment had been upheld by Pius IX himself, she had made some powerful enemies along the way, and the struggle had left a permanent imprint on her character. She was in a state of near-paranoia with regard to the hostility of the Wittgenstein and Hohenlohe families, and she still feared that they were malevolent enough to harm her cause. Liszt was caught in the middle. He knew that he had become for Carolyne a pawn on a chessboard of European dimensions, and he willingly allowed himself to be moved from one location to another as the game she played with the Roman clerics became ever more intricate. Did Carolyne also fear that she and Liszt were being watched by tsarist agents? Since Carolyne's arrival in Rome the Russian legation had never ceased to conspire against her. She was an exile, who had been stripped of her citizenship by Tsar Alexander II, and that made her an object of their special contempt. Now she had become the centre of a struggle between Rome and St. Petersburg, and that made her dangerous. The Russian legation wanted at all costs to frighten Carolyne away from her marriage to Liszt. In Volume Two of this biography we already made it plain that this legation was a tool of the Wittgenstein and Hohenlohe families, who feared that they might lose millions of roubles if the marriage went ahead.[19]

Carolyne never underestimated the malevolence of which her Russian foes were capable. Neither she nor Liszt would soon forget the attempt on the part of the tsar's police to kidnap Princess Marie from Weimar, in the early days of her struggles with the Wittgenstein family. What better way to bewilder her adversaries than by staying put in Rome while sending Liszt off on a series of peregrinations that no one else, including Liszt himself, would be able to interpret? The evidence for such a conclusion lies everywhere to hand. Less than

---

17. LLB, vol. 5, p. 233.

18. This long struggle is described in detail in the chapter "Of Marriage and Divorce" in Volume Two of the present work.

19. Volume Two, pp. 521–22. Carolyne's unpublished letters to Liszt confirm that the Russians constantly meddled in her affairs. She reported that they had attempted to turn Monsignor Quaglia, the secretary of the College of Cardinals, against her, and also Monsignor Berardi, an associate of Cardinal Antonelli (WA, Kasten 36, August 30, 1860).

two weeks after he had closed down the Altenburg, and had begun to drift from one location to another, Liszt told Carolyne: "Only tell me where I must go, and where I shall have to set out—and I shall arrive."[20] By the time he eventually reached Marseilles, on October 12, he still had no idea of the date of his arrival in Rome. Carolyne even tried to choose a Marseilles hotel for him in which he might remain incognito, and she instructed him to embark on the *Quirinal* on October 17. The date was selected with special care. It was the last possible ship which would enable Liszt to arrive in the Eternal City on October 20, which was a Sunday, a day on which all those high-ranking clerics with an interest in her case would be engaged in their more spiritual pursuits.

III

Seventeen months had elapsed since Liszt and Carolyne had last seen one another. This was a very long separation, and it is difficult to imagine the emotions that stirred in both of them. But there can be no question that Liszt's resolve to go through with the marriage ceremony was as strong as ever, whatever the sceptics have said about it.[21] On October 20, within hours of his arrival in Rome, he and Carolyne went to the Vatican and were ushered into the presence of Monsignor Bernardino Maggi, who was obviously expecting them. After warning them of the gravity of the oaths they were about to make, and of the penalties generally meted out to those who committed perjury, Monsignor Maggi took their sworn statements. What followed in those chambers deserves to be stated with force. With the Holy Gospel in his hand, Liszt swore (a) that he was single, (b) that he had not taken vows to become a priest, (c) that he was not promised in marriage to another, and (d) that he had come

---

20. LLB, vol. 5, p. 220.

21. A good deal of literature has been devoted to the question of whether Liszt really wanted to marry Carolyne, or whether he would have preferred instead to abandon her at the altar. It would be a pity to waste another word on the sceptics, who included some of Liszt's closest friends. When Carolyne left Weimar, in May 1860, everyone assumed that she would return in a matter of weeks. But as the months rolled by, and it became clear that she was not going to come back, the small town started to buzz with speculation. Peter Cornelius was convinced that Liszt and Carolyne had gone their separate ways. "Take note of my words," he wrote to a friend, "this is a separation. God grant that I may be mistaken!" (CLW, vol. I, p. 474). Carl Tausig, who was often given to blunt speech on such matters, dismissed Liszt's trip to Rome as a *blague*. Perhaps the most damaging comment of all comes from Adelheid von Schorn, who, years later, solemnly recorded her opinion that during their seventeen-month separation Liszt had become indifferent to Carolyne and no longer wanted a legal union with her. She admits that Liszt's sense of chivalry towards the princess was as strong as ever, and that this alone would have been enough for him to lead her to the altar. But the princess, she went on, with her "fine womanly feeling," sensed that it would have been a duty, and refused to accept this sacrifice from him. And so, Schorn concludes, the matter was never referred to again. (SZM, p. 107)

    The documents, as we shall see, tell a somewhat different story.

to Rome for the purpose of contracting marriage. He then affixed his signature to the document, which had been prepared in advance; and after similar
oaths were sworn by Carolyne, she affixed hers.[22]

Only one obstacle now stood in the way of Carolyne's nuptials with Liszt:
the marriage banns had not yet been read. This is borne out by a telltale document drawn up within hours of Liszt's arrival in Rome in which it was requested that the customary reading of the banns be waived. The grounds were
ominous: the couple wished "to join in holy matrimony in haste and secrecy
on account of just and legitimate reasons presented verbally. . . ."[23] What lay
behind the request? Carolyne feared yet another plot to disrupt her wedding
to Liszt, and she reasoned that a series of public announcements could only invite disaster. Her anxieties were well-founded, as we shall shortly discover.[24]

The scene now shifted to the church of San Carlo al Corso, about three
miles away, where the officiating priest, Father Francesco Morelli, was awaiting confirmation that the wedding would indeed proceed on October 22 as
planned. Morelli was the father superior of San Carlo, and as such was not
only Carolyne's parish priest but the cleric who would have conducted the
wedding service. Indeed, no other cleric had the authority to officiate at the
ceremony without Morelli's approval, and there is no evidence that this was
either sought or given. Morelli had known Carolyne ever since she became
one of his parishioners, in June 1860, in which capacity he would have taken
her confession. He would also have had a number of discussions with her
about the forthcoming marriage arrangements; but he had yet to meet Liszt.
Liszt and Carolyne must now have made their way to San Carlo to meet
Morelli, in order to hold the customary pre-nuptial rehearsals. We know that

---

22. The statement, which bears the signature of Monsignor Bernardino Maggi, is reproduced in Volume Two (Appendix II, doc. 7, p. 579), and its importance lies in the fact that it is the only legal document we have in which Liszt declares before a witness his intention to marry Carolyne.

23. AVR. Reproduced in Volume Two, Appendix II, doc. 6. We know that this undated request to
waive the marriage banns must have been made *after* Liszt got to Rome, because the document mentions the fact that he was already in the city.

24. The question has often been asked: Why did Carolyne arrange to marry at San Carlo al Corso,
one of the biggest churches in Rome, where it would have been virtually impossible to keep the ceremony secret? The answer is that San Carlo lay within the boundaries of her parish; the Piazza di
Spagna was less than half a mile distant. She also had a sentimental attachment to this particular church:
San Carlo was her patron saint. But why arrange the wedding in Rome at all, where so many of her
clerical enemies were at hand? Rome was also where many of her clerical friends were, and she probably thought that the pros and the cons of this particular problem balanced themselves out.

Into the same category of mystery and menace with which Carolyne now viewed everything to
do with her forthcoming marriage, we must place the curious business of her choice of confessor for
Liszt. Before receiving the sacrament of marriage, both Liszt and Carolyne (like any other couple
about to enter holy matrimony) would have to confess and seek absolution for their sins. Long before
he got to Rome this matter had begun to exercise Carolyne's mind. The ears that received Liszt's confession, it seems, might well pick up information that could later be used against her. Liszt's attitude

at six o'clock on the evening of October 21, the pair attended communion at San Carlo.[25] The altar at which they were to be married the following morning was already decorated with candles and flowers.

What happened next has become part of the mythology of Liszt biography, and it comes to us from Princess Carolyne herself. At eleven o'clock in the evening a message was delivered to her in her apartment from Father Morelli telling her that he had just learned that Pope Pius IX had withdrawn his sanction for the wedding to take place. Her case would have to be re-examined. Years later, Carolyne told Lina Ramann that the Vatican's last-minute intervention was the result of "scheming Russian intrigues."[26] What did she mean?

On October 20, even as Liszt and Carolyne were in the Vatican swearing out their statements before Monsignor Maggi, a Russian cousin of Carolyne was seeking an urgent audience of Cardinal Caterini, the prefect of the Holy Congregation of Cardinals which had reviewed Carolyne's case. The name of this cousin was Calm-Podowski, and he was accompanied by two of Carolyne's female relatives.[27] This powerful deputation carried with them a message which confirmed the one brought earlier by Denise Poniatowska, the cousin who had unsuccessfully conspired against Carolyne in the late summer of 1860.[28] The Wittgenstein-Iwanowska marriage was not forced, as Carolyne insisted that it was, but was entered into freely. Calm-Podowski had actually been present at the first introductions between Carolyne and Nicholas in 1836, so he claimed, and he had observed their courtship and nuptials unfold without constraint.[29] The annulment granted for *vis et metus* should therefore be quashed. It remains to observe that the testimony of such witnesses could never have reached the ears of Cardinal Caterini at this late stage without the backing of a powerful cleric. The finger of guilt points directly towards Gustav Hohenlohe. In the Secret Archive of the Vatican there exists a letter that proves

---

appears to have been that it was not important to him who his confessor was, but that if it was important to her she should go ahead and choose someone for him. Carolyne then suggested to Liszt that the best cleric to receive his confession would be Father Ferrari (LLB, vol. 5, p. 224), whom she knew to be friendly to her cause. Liszt then reminded her that if she did indeed approach Father Ferrari she would have to tell him that he did not know enough Italian to make his confession in that language. This exchange took place more than a month before Liszt got to Rome, and it is an indication that Carolyne knew her case to be so notorious among the clergy that she no longer trusted even the sanctity of the confessional.

25. RL, p. 89.
26. Ibid. Their conversation took place in June 1876, shortly after Ramann had begun work on her Liszt biography. Ramann was in Rome, acquiring first-hand material for the book, and Carolyne had taken her to San Carlo so that she could see the church for herself.
27. RLKM, vol. 3, pp. 10 and 434. The two female relatives are identified only as "Princess O" and "Countess B." We surmise that the former must have been Princess Orloffsky, the married name of the second of Dyonis Iwanowsky's daughters.
28. See Volume Two, p. 527.
29. RLKM, vol. 3, pp. 10–11; LSJ, p. 42.

Hohenlohe's complicity beyond doubt. It is addressed to Cardinal Caterini and dated Friday, October 18—that is, two days before Liszt's arrival in Rome and four days before his projected marriage.

> To the Most Eminent Lord Cardinal [Prospero] Caterini
> [Prefect of the Holy Congregation of the Council]
> etc. etc.

Most Eminent Prince:

My conscience and my sense of duty compel me to ask Your Most Reverend Eminence to deign yourself to grant an audience to the bearers of this letter, the most Reverend Father Semenenko from St. Claudius in Poland and His Lordship Count Potoczki [*sic*][30] who are both known in Poland as well as in Rome for their piety and integrity.

They are to speak about a very troublesome marriage case concerning a Princess Wittgenstein-Iwanowska and they wish to forestall a great scandal. While I am sure that you will consent to do this favour, I have the great honour of signing myself, as I bend with the greatest respect to kiss your Most Reverend Eminence's holy purple,

> Your humblest, most devoted and obedient servant
> GUSTAV VON HOHENLOHE
> Archbishop of Edessa[31]

---

30. Hohenlohe has mis-spelled the name Podowski, a relative of Carolyne's on her mother's side.

31. ASVR (2). If further evidence is sought of Gustav Hohenlohe's complicity in this matter, it will be found in the Secret Archive of the Holy Congregation of the Council for 1859–1861 (shelf mark Z60). There are a number of letters from Hohenlohe, including the one cited above, which show that he intervened in this case almost from the start. The Italian daily press was well aware of his activities. It appears that someone highly placed within Vatican circles, with unfriendly intentions towards Hohenlohe, "leaked" the essential details of Carolyne's case to the editor of *La Nazione,* a political daily, which published the following on December 4, 1861.

> . . . Liszt, already celebrated for his pianistic talents, is acquiring a different kind of notoriety as a consequence of the problems he has encountered in trying to celebrate his nuptials with Princess Wittgenstein. This lady's husband is still alive, and yet, so many years after that wedding was celebrated, the Roman Court declared that marriage null and void. In the wake of appeals made with the typical persistence and cleverness that characterize a woman in love, and thanks to *the notorious penchant of the Curia for bowing low* before titles and gold, Rome allowed the Princess to marry a second time. Just as the preparations for the wedding had been completed and the bride and groom had come to Rome, they received a formal prohibition to get married. Prince von Hohenlohe, a relative of the Princess, managed to obtain the veto. This proves that the Prince must be richer than Liszt and Frau Wittgenstein!

Whatever the mantle of secrecy with which the Hohenlohes so skilfully managed to wrap this case in later years, it was widely understood at the time that they, and they alone, were responsible for pre-

The timing of this letter was perfect, and it was aimed with deadly accuracy towards the one man in Rome with the power to stop Carolyne's wedding in its tracks: Cardinal Caterini, who had headed the Holy Congregation's two inquiries into this matter on September 22 and December 22, 1860, and had the ear of Pius IX. Hohenlohe's warning phrase "to forestall a great scandal" must have struck a chill in Caterini's heart, since he was the only member of the Holy Congregation to have voted against Carolyne's annulment.[32] But who was Father Semenenko? This Polish priest had for some years been attached to an order of Polish seminarians at the church of San Claudio, in Rome, and his role appears to have been to confirm the identity of Carolyne's Ukrainian relatives in the presence of Caterini.[33] But why were her kith and kin so eager to testify against her? It will be recalled that when her father, Peter Iwanowsky, died in 1844, her three cousins (daughters of his brother, Dyonis Iwanowsky) came forward with a false will which named them, not Carolyne, as the legal beneficiaries of his vast properties in Ukraine. The princess was able to prove that this will was a forgery, since its water-mark postdated her father's death.[34] This painful episode created a permanent divide between the two halves of the family. Gustav Hohenlohe would have had no difficulty at all in recruiting Carolyne's relatives to his cause.[35]

---

venting Carolyne's marriage to Liszt. When the documents pertaining to the case were eventually gathered together and placed in the Vatican's Secret Archive, the Hohenlohes doubtless breathed a collective sigh of relief, for this was the best way to cover their tracks. The article from *La Nazione*, incidentally, is the last item in the Vatican file, which was closed in December 1861. Ironically, it reveals the fact that Gustav von Hohenlohe's charges of bribery against Carolyne had backfired, for he himself here stands accused of having bought the Vatican's veto.

32. Not long after Volume Two of this biography appeared, one hundred and thirty-three documents pertaining to Carolyne's annulment case, which are presently in the Secret Archive of the Vatican Library, were published by me and Professor Gabriele Erasmi with the permission of the Vatican authorities. Among the many new facts to come to light was the exact membership of the Holy Congregation that reviewed her case. Eight cardinals took part in the deliberations, and the vote was not unanimous. Cardinals Cagiano, d'Andrea, Milesi, Marini, Silvestri, and Bofondi voted in favour, although the latter expressed some reservations. The prefect of the Congregation, Cardinal Caterini, voted against the resolution. See WELCV, p. 189.

33. In the archival documents for the church of San Claudio de' Polacchi, now stored in the Vicariato di Roma, Father Pjotr Semenenko is described as "forty-seven years old" and a "consultant for the Index." In this latter capacity he would have been well-known to the Vatican hierarchy.

34. LSJ, pp. 15–16. This information was given to La Mara by Carolyne's daughter, Princess Marie.

35. Princess Marie Hohenlohe was convinced that her mother was mistaken about the hostility of her Ukrainian relatives. She genuinely believed that the only thing that motivated Carolyne's kith and kin to act against her was concern for her immortal soul. If, as they thought, Carolyne's annulment had been secured through perjury, then she would suffer eternal damnation if she went ahead and married Liszt. Princess Marie was spared many details of her mother's case, however, and since she was under the sway of the Hohenlohe family, she knew only what they wanted her to know.

I V

The crisis of October 21 appears to have had a devastating effect on the princess. After thirteen years of litigation her nerves were shattered; for the first time her will failed. The intervention of Calm-Podowski and his entourage could not have been strong enough to do more than postpone the marriage by a week or two (the problem of perjury had already been examined by the cardinals), and there is no evidence in the Vatican file to suggest that the document of annulment was ever upturned. Carolyne was free to rebut these latest charges, like all the others she had rebutted in the past; but she did not bother to do so. The marriage between Liszt and Carolyne did not take place because Carolyne herself lost heart. Lurking behind everything else was the legal effect that a marriage to Liszt might have on her daughter. The first inkling that Carolyne had that Marie could be stigmatized as a bastard, and that she herself could be branded as a bigamist, had come in one of her unpublished letters to Liszt, dated August 30, 1860.[36] Such difficulties had been foreseen by the Hohenlohes as well, for one month before Marie's wedding she had petitioned Pius IX to declare her the legitimate offspring of a legitimate marriage. While this petition is in the Vatican files,[37] the response is not, and Carolyne had become frantic about the matter. Furthermore, she well knew that annulment cases are never closed. Anyone can re-open them if the evidence is strong enough, no matter how many years may have elapsed, and call for a review of earlier proceedings. The Iwanowskys were against her, the Wittgensteins were against her, the Hohenlohes were against her—and now even her daughter was against her, a particularly hard blow for Carolyne to bear.[38] Marie had recently given birth to her first child, Franz Joseph, and Carolyne had been neither allowed to see her grandchild nor invited to the baptism. The nightmare scenario in which Carolyne's grandchildren might become the "illegitimate" half of

---

36. WA, Kasten 36.

37. ASV, CC, doc. 11.

38. One of the most difficult situations that Carolyne had been called upon to face while obtaining her annulment was the deteriorating relationship with her daughter. After Marie's wedding, in October 1859, there was an ever-widening rift between the pair. Carolyne blamed Konstantin Hohenlohe for poisoning the atmosphere and convinced herself that he was intercepting her mail to her daughter. It seemed never to have occurred to Carolyne that Marie had much to lose in the fanatical battle that her mother was waging against the Church. In desperation, Marie had turned to Liszt, and in the summer of 1860, when the annulment case was still in turmoil, she had written to her "dear, great and impartial judge" for help. Carolyne, she told Liszt, expected her daughter to obey her without hesitation, "even if she ordered me to throw my fortune into the Danube. . . . I suffer cruelly, for the rapid torrent of circumstances makes me more and more incapable of being good for anything. It is as much as I can do to maintain my peace of mind, confidence, and serenity. . . . Burn this letter, dear Great One, and do not reply to it. The negotiations are secret." (WA, unpublished letter of July 16, 1860)

her family line and be deprived of their legacy loomed large with everyone. Worse still, if Carolyne and Liszt married, and she bore him a child, any future challenge by the Hohenlohes to the validity of Carolyne's second wedding ceremony would almost certainly be defended by their offspring. Would Carolyne's remarriage expose everybody to endless litigation in the years ahead? Even though Carolyne protested that it would not, she could not be sure. Nobody could. Time changes many things.

These were the burdens that became too much for the princess to bear. Thereafter she had many opportunities to marry Liszt, but after October 21 the matter was allowed to subside. The essential correctness of this view is borne out by the fact that when Prince Nicholas died, in March 1864, the last remaining obstacle to Carolyne's union with Liszt was removed, and yet their marriage plans were never revived. Carolyne herself has told us that she refused to marry Liszt "as soon as that refusal became possible for me."[39] Liszt himself corroborates the idea that it was a mutual decision. In 1864 he made his first return to Weimar since exchanging the city for Rome, and while he was there he was re-united with Grand Duke Carl Alexander. During the course of their conversation, the grand duke inquired about Carolyne and the prospects of the much-postponed marriage. Liszt's little-known response is worth quoting: "[The grand duke] was unable to imagine that one might have pursued a goal for fifteen years only to withdraw from it at the moment when nothing more opposed its realization."[40]

---

39. EKFL, p. 68.
40. LLB, vol. 6, p. 55. A few months later, there was a postscript to the conversation. Carl Alexander told Liszt that now Prince Nicholas was dead, there was "no longer any human reason, nor earthly power which could oppose your union. If it is not accomplished, the reason lies in you, or in her." (LLCA, p. 127) To which Liszt responded with Pascal's famous sentiment: "The heart has its reasons of which reason knows nothing." (LLCA, p. 128)

When news of the death of Nicholas was brought to Carolyne in Rome by his relatives, it provoked an extraordinary reaction in her. In a letter to Liszt she described her late husband as "a madman who has committed infamous deeds of which I am, at the present moment, the victim, without a fortune, without a country." But what of the burning question that must have been igniting their thoughts at that moment? Now that she had been so abruptly elevated to widowhood, and she and Liszt were free to marry, what did she tell him? "The happiness of Liszt, and the accomplishment of my fate, is quite independent of what has happened to Nicholas." That is a cold statement. To objectify the emotional turmoil of the last seventeen years, by putting Liszt into the third person to his face, so to speak, tells us that she still viewed him as part of her "problem" with the Church. Carolyne was not the first litigant to endure a sustained legal action only to find that she was psychologically incapable of dropping the case long after it was settled. But she found some softer sentences for Liszt's consumption as well. "My first words, two and a half years ago [that is, after the Vatican had granted her an annulment], were: 'It's a question of leading the life one can lead.' . . . At our age, it is not a question of an action of the moment, but of giving up one's life one fine autumn evening, without too many conflicts of the heart, of position, of habit. Nothing will separate us. Nothing can separate us." And Carolyne summarized her attitude with the words: "I hope you will approve of this point of view as a *formality*. It is logical." (Hitherto unpublished; WA, Kasten 41, u. 1) Liszt evidently agreed

". . . only to withdraw from it." It is an unexpected coda to this strange and complex business, but it comes from Liszt and Carolyne themselves. We must surely leave the last word with them.

V

Carolyne remained at the Piazza di Spagna for a few months, and then moved into apartments at Via del Babuino 89, a short distance away, but still in the parish of Santa Maria del Popolo, where she remained until her death, more than twenty-five years later. There was no question of resuming her former *menage à deux* with Liszt, and a moment's reflection will tell us why. That kind of life had been difficult enough in Weimar; in Rome it would have been impossible. She now lived under the very nose of the Vatican, she was known to the church's leading clerics, and for the past seventeen months she had rested her case on the sanctity of the marriage bond. Under such circumstances, to resume her old liaison with Liszt would have been to flaunt defiance, not in the face of the world (which she had never minded) but in the face of the Church which had now ruled against her, and that she could never have brought herself to do.

As for Liszt, he appears to have taken the wedding fiasco calmly. We say "appears" because there is not a single letter, document, or diary entry that would allow us to divine his true feelings.[41] Perhaps he thought that he and Carolyne merely faced a temporary setback, indistinguishable from dozens of others they had experienced across the years. But with the passing weeks, and with Carolyne's fundamental change of heart, it must have quickly dawned on Liszt that this particular setback would be permanent.

What to do, and where to go? Even Liszt's most conscientious biographers do not seem to have realized that he was in Rome by default. It had never been his idea to be married there, and he had never planned to live there. He stayed on because the alternatives were too painful to contemplate. To return to Weimar, Berlin, Paris, or Vienna would have been to expose himself to ques-

---

with Carolyne's assessment of their position. Whatever his earlier feelings on the matter may have been, his life, like Carolyne's, had taken on a new direction, and he was no longer about to give it up "one fine autumn evening."

41. His *Memento-Journalier* entry for October 22 (VLKN, no. 2, p. 86) consists mainly of a series of aphorisms of the kind that he had always liked to collect in order to mull them over at leisure:

"I am Roman citizen!"

"All misfortune is conquered through suffering."

"Unless an order comes expressly from the Pope, I plan to go on doing what I am doing." (Montalembert)

There is not the slightest hint in all this of a spiritual crisis.

tions about the thwarted marriage-service that he was not prepared to answer. And so he lingered. He took apartments at Via Felice (which is today the Via Sistina) 113, not far from the Via del Babuino, which enabled him to walk over to see Carolyne every day and offer her some comfort during this period of crisis. He also engaged a manservant, Fortunato Salvagni, to look after his everyday concerns, and he installed a small upright Boisselot piano so that he could continue to compose.[42] But what the immediate future held, he had no idea.

---

42. LLB, vol. 8, p. 153.

The Eternal City

*Oh Rome! My country; city of the soul; the Niobe
of Nations.*

FRANZ LISZT[1]

I

Liszt spent the first few weeks of his stay in Rome acclimatizing himself to his
new environment. His apartment was situated in the heart of old Rome, and the
cobbled streets that led away from the Via Felice pointed in all directions towards
antiquity. At one end of the Via Felice lay one of the most beautiful of Bernini's
fountains; at the other, the Spanish Steps. The street running parallel to Liszt's was
the Via della Purificazione, where Daniel had been born twenty-two years earlier. The entire district vibrated with memories of his earlier stay there. He loved
the city's ancient monuments and he spent much time exploring such shrines as
St. Peter's, the Pantheon, and the Forum. He was particularly impressed with the
Colosseum, and jokingly told Franz Brendel that he thought it would make a
good concert hall.[2] Every morning he was awakened by what he described as a
concert of bells from the surrounding churches, which, he humourously maintained, was superior to anything one might hear in the Paris Conservatoire.[3] On
Sundays he regularly visited the Sistine Chapel "to bathe and steep my mind in

---

1. VLKN, p. 32. Written in English by Liszt. The words come from Lord Byron's *Childe Harold,* canto
4, stanzas 78–79.
2. LLB, vol. 2, p. 18. "I sometimes imagine the [Sondershausen] orchestra set up there, with the con-
founded instruments of percussion in an arcade—our well-wishers Rietz, Taubert, and other braggarts
of criticism close by (or in the Aquarium!)—the Directors of the Deutscher Musik-Verein resting on
the "Pulvinare," and the members relaxing all around on soft cushions; and sitting resplendent in the
reserved seats of Subsellia the Senators and Envoys of old."
3. OCLF, p. 298.

the dark waves of the *Jordan* of Palestrina,"[4] an indication of his increasing inter-est in the church music of the sixteenth century. The beauty and majesty of the Eternal City was beginning to exert its spell, and by the end of the year he was ensnared. On Christmas Day, 1861, he wrote to Blandine:

> My life here is more peaceful and harmonious and better organized than in Germany. I hope that this will be to the advantage of my work and will succeed in reaching a good end. I'm living in a very pretty apartment, very near the Pincio, on the first floor, 113 Via Fe-lice, where Leopold Robert lived for seven or eight years. The stu-dios of Tenerani and Overbeck, the Quirinal, Santa Maria degli Angeli, and Santa Maria Maggiore are in my immediate neigh-bourhood, and I really am planning to return there often in order to take possession [of them], since beautiful things belong in fact to those who know how to feel them and be absorbed by them.[5]

About the thwarted marriage service he kept quiet, except to tell her that "since my arrival in Rome, I have learned this proverb: 'Stando, stando, si rompono le pietre' [Constant dripping wears away the stones]"—an indication that he thought that the Vatican might still be worn down, given time. Mean-while, he had to set about finding a niche for himself in the Eternal City.

II

In the 1860s the musical life of Rome was practically non-existent. There were no professional symphony orchestras, no concert halls, no conservatories, and as yet no real public for the music that Vienna, Berlin, and Leipzig now took for granted. Nadine Helbig, who moved to Rome in 1865, was not wrong to describe the city as "a musical wilderness."[6] Whenever musicians put on con-certs, they did so in conditions which can only be described as makeshift. The Ramacciotti chamber concerts, for instance, were given in a dark, narrow room in the Via della Frezza, which was totally unsuitable for music-making. In 1866 the Dante Sala was opened for public concerts (it was part of the Palazzo Poli, whose east wall supports the background of the Fontana di Trevi), but it left much to be desired as far as its acoustics were concerned.[7] When Pius IX

---

4. Ibid.
5. OCLF, pp. 297–98.
6. HLR, p. 71.
7. The Dante Sala was opened on February 26, 1866, with a performance of Liszt's *Dante* Symphony conducted by Giovanni Sgambati. The hall no longer exists today.

arranged his great concert for "Peter's Pence" in March 1864, the only auditorium spacious enough to contain the large throng of people was the L-
shaped New Building of the Praetorian Camp.[8] Half the listeners could not see
the performers they heard because the platform lay around the corner, at the
other end of the ninety-degree angle. It was small wonder, then, that Duke
Michelangelo Caetani expressed bewilderment that Liszt would want to stay
in Rome at all, and he added: "Here a reputation has no tomorrow. Everything
falls asleep."[9]

The instrumental music of Mozart and Beethoven was still unknown. When
Giovanni Sgambati conducted the *Eroica* Symphony in December 1866, "the
audience did not seem fully to understand it."[10] It is an indication of the poor
taste which prevailed in Rome at this time that one of the biggest draws in the
1860s was an Irish violinist who billed himself as "Paganini redivivo" and gave
a recital in a small downtown theatre every night. He appeared out of a cloud
of steam, played the solo caprices of Paganini while bathed in garish spotlights,
and then, enveloped once more in steam, sank beneath the stage.[11]

It is tempting to explain all this by the fact that Rome's population stood at
a mere 215,000 souls, hardly larger than that of a modern provincial town, until
we recall that Vienna, Berlin, and Paris had first come to musical prominence
with populations still smaller. Unlike them, however, Rome was not an au-
tonomous secular city standing at the head of a sovereign nation. It was still in
the embrace of the Vatican, and its position as the national capital of a unified
Italy lay in the future. What that meant for music can easily be imagined: the
historical importance of sacred over secular music had created such an imbal-
ance that the latter was everywhere in a state of arrested development.

The best music-making went on inside the homes of the aristocrats and the
higher clergy. Monsignor Francesco Nardi's soirées were known across the city,
and Liszt became such a regular contributor to them that he eventually moved
a Bechstein grand into this cleric's music-room.[12] The powerful Caetani family also put on concerts in their sumptuous palace; the head of the clan, Duke
Michelangelo Caetani, became a personal friend of Liszt and opened many
doors for him. Some outstanding musical events also took place in the home
of Baron Felix von Meyendorff, the Russian ambassador to Rome, whose
young wife, Olga, would later become one of Liszt's closest friends and confi-

8. For an account of Liszt's participation in this particular concert, see *Dwight's Musical Journal,* Saturday, May 28, 1864.

9. HLC, p. 256.

10. SRB, p. 293.

11. HLR (English translation only), pp. 214–15.

12. Francesco Nardi had been a professor of philosophy and canon law at the University of Padua before settling in Rome. Liszt was befriended by this cleric towards the end of 1861, and soon came to
admire the breadth of Nardi's intellectual and artistic interests.

dants. Another benefactor was Count Harry von Arnim, the Prussian ambassador, whose musical evenings were a highlight of the social season. Once it was learned that Liszt had taken up permanent residence in the city, he became a much-sought-after guest at their gatherings. It was about this time, too, that he got to know a gifted twenty-one-year-old musician named Giovanni Sgambati, who lived on the Piazza di Spagna, not far from the apartment of Princess Carolyne, and who became his pupil. Liszt wrote to Franz Brendel: "I have fished out here a very talented young pianist, Sgambati by name, who makes a first-rate partner in duets, and who, for example, plays the *Dante* Symphony boldly and correctly."[13] Sgambati became Liszt's best-known Italian pupil, and went on to develop a twin career as pianist and conductor. He was eventually appointed professor of the piano class in the recently opened Santa Cecilia Academy of Music, and later still he became its director.[14] Another pupil that Liszt acquired about the same time was the English pianist Walter Bache. Bache, who had just completed his piano studies in Leipzig, had travelled to Italy with no particular purpose in mind other than to soak up as much of the culture of that country as he could before returning to Britain. He found himself in Florence, made the acquaintance of Jessie Laussot, and was advised by her to go to Rome and seek out Liszt.[15] Bache arrived in the city in early June 1862, and lost no time in contacting his future mentor. When he first saw Liszt, he was so nervous that he became tongue-tied. Liszt misinterpreted the long silence and thought that Bache had come to borrow money. (Later, when Bache told his sister Constance about this scene, she observed: "What an insight it gives into Liszt's life that this should be his first thought when a young stranger came to him.")[16] Bache was dreadfully hurt by the misunderstanding, but once Liszt realized his mistake he could not do enough to help the young man. On June 6 Bache wrote to his father: "Liszt has been very kind indeed to me." And again: "My visit to Rome has been satisfactory in every respect. . . . Liszt has told me to come to him and he will give me an occasional lesson:

---

13. LLB, vol. 2, p. 17.

14. There is a useful memoir of Sgambati in WMME, pp. 51–98.

15. Since her love-affair with Richard Wagner in the early 1850s, the wealthy Jessie Laussot had settled in Florence, where she had founded a choral society named after Cherubini, and was seeking to spread the message of German music through Italian artistic circles. Born Jessie Taylor, this English-woman had studied music in Dresden, and while still in her early twenties had entered into an unhappy marriage to Eugène Laussot, a wine merchant. It was Jessie, together with Frau Franziska Ritter, who, in 1850, had offered to put up three thousand francs a year in order to save Wagner from destitution. Eugène, by contrast, offered to put a bullet through his head when he discovered that his young wife was planning to elope with Wagner. The story is told in NLRW, vol. 2, pp. 133–61. It was through her connections with Wagner that Jessie had first met Liszt and was able to point Walter Bache in the latter's direction.

16. BBM, p. 154. The name of Constance Bache is almost as well known to Liszt scholars as that of her brother, since she eventually translated the first two volumes of Liszt's letters into English.

this is the greatest possible advantage I could have."[17] Bache, whose father was a Unitarian minister in Birmingham, managed to secure a job as an organist in the English Church in Rome, which was located not far from where Liszt lived, and that is how he supported himself for three years while having lessons from Liszt. His letters of the period are filled with references to the times they spent together, and he heard Liszt play a lot of his own music—pieces from the "Swiss" book of the *Années de pèlerinage,* the Prelude and Fugue on the name B-A-C-H, and above all the Sonata in B minor.[18] Liszt helped the young man prepare for a number of public concerts in Rome, and persuaded him to take on some difficult repertory which at first he felt unable to play—including Liszt's transcriptions of Gounod's *Faust* Waltz and Meyerbeer's "Patineurs" Waltz from *Le Prophète.* But he mastered them with Liszt's help and a lot of hard work. On one occasion, when Liszt turned up at Bache's apartment to give him a lesson, he found him with a sore thumb, unable to play. So Liszt himself sat at the piano and delivered a performance of his Fantasie and Fugue from *Le Prophète.*[19] When he returned to England in the spring of 1865, Bache made it his life's mission to promote Liszt's cause in that country, and for more than twenty years put on concerts of Liszt's music, often at his own expense. We shall hear more of Bache's attachment to Liszt at a later point in the narrative.

But this was not the end of Liszt's musical activities. In an attempt to rouse Rome from its slumbers, he mounted six historical vocal concerts during the winter of 1862–63, which featured the music of Bach, Handel, and others. Rarely had such music been heard in the Eternal City. Bernhard Scholz[20] happened to be in Rome at this time, and wrote:

> . . . I saw Liszt in the street the other day in the company of a priest. His manner was humble, and he was continually smiling politely and obsequiously . . . Six concerts of classical vocal music were given here this winter under his auspices, at which Palestrina, Bach, Handel, Curschmann, Mendelssohn, Mozart—and Liszt were sung. He moves much in clerical circles. . . .[21]

---

17. BBM, pp. 155–56.

18. Since documented performances by Liszt of the B-minor Sonata are rare, it might be worth recording that this one took place in Rome in March 1865.

19. BBM, p. 180. This is an interesting observation since the "Ad nos" Fantasie and Fugue is for organ and was never officially arranged for piano solo by Liszt. But it is evident from Bache's comment that Liszt had such a version in his fingers.

20. It will be recalled that Bernhard Scholz was a friend and colleague of both Joachim and Brahms and had been one of the co-signatories of the famous "Manifesto" against Liszt and the so-called New German School. See Volume Two of the present work, p. 349.

21. JMBJ, vol. 2, p. 302.

". . . He moves much in clerical circles." Liszt had always followed the Vatican calendar with interest, but now that he was in Rome he could observe it unfolding at first hand, and he mingled with clerics across the spectrum of the Church. On June 8, 1862, the Feast of the Pentecost, Pius IX summoned to Rome the whole of the Catholic Episcopate in order to witness the canonization of the twenty-six Japanese martyrs. Among the thousands of clerics who converged on the city for the ceremony was Father Augustin, otherwise known in the Liszt literature as Hermann ("Puzzi") Cohen, who was now a Barefoot Carmelite monk. Liszt also witnessed the ceremony and ran into Father Augustin by chance.[22] The two men had not seen one another for more than twenty-five years, and the reunion was charged with memories for both of them. A few days after their encounter, Liszt visited Father Augustin at the convent of the Vittoria, where he received Holy Communion from his former pupil. Afterwards he joined Puzzi and the other monks for a small repast, at the conclusion of which the two pianists took turns to play on an old, out-of-tune piano.[23]

Liszt began to cut a familiar figure as he criss-crossed his way through the winding complex of streets that constituted Old Rome. Tall and thin, his long hair streaming in the wind, he was often observed alighting from the hackney carriages which he used to transport himself to various locations in the city. A few months after his arrival in Rome he encountered the great historian Gregorovius, to whom we are indebted for some of the best eye-witness descriptions of Liszt to come down to us from these years. "Have made Liszt's acquaintance; a striking, uncanny figure—tall, thin, and with long grey hair. Frau von S. maintains that he is burnt out and that only the outer walls remain, from which a little ghost-like flame hisses forth."[24] It is a telling image which captures something of the psychological strain under which he was labouring at this time.

---

22. In a letter dated June 12, 1862, Liszt told Franz Brendel about the ceremony, and of the "overpowering moment in which the Pope intoned the Te Deum." (LLB, vol. 2, p. 10)

23. SLFH, pp. 183–84. Not long after their meeting, "Puzzi" wrote to his sister from Rome: "I have found Liszt here. I often see him: he comes to see me. This morning I went to him with Msgr. de la Bouillerie, Louis Veuillot, and Marie Bernard. He played several pieces to us, very amiably." (Ibid.) Presumably this gathering of Puzzi and his colleagues took place in Liszt's apartment on Via Felice. Shortly afterwards, Father Augustin was received in audience by Pius IX, who sent him to London to found a convent there. In the true tradition of the Barefoot Carmelites, he set out from the Eternal City with no money in his purse and had to borrow from friends in Paris in order to cover the costs of the journey.

  Some details of Liszt's earlier relationship with Puzzi Cohen will be found in Volume One, especially pp. 213–16.

24. GRT, p. 201. Ferdinand Gregorovius, who wrote this comment in his diary on April 13, 1862, was born in East Prussia, the youngest of eight brothers and sisters. He came of a clerical family and was

III

Work, as always, was his consolation. While he was living in the Via Felice he brought to completion a number of important compositions, including the two concert studies *Waldesrauschen* and *Gnomenreigen,* which he had promised to write for the Lebert and Stark *Klavierschule* while he was still in Germany. It is nonetheless strange to think that these brilliant showpieces were born in the Eternal City. On deeper reflection, however, they are best understood as autobiographical utterances; they are really nostalgic annotations to the spectacular keyboard pieces of the Weimar period, and even of the *Glanzzeit,* now lost almost beyond recall. To modify that telling image of Gregorovius, a ghost-like flame hisses forth now and again, and stirs old memories of the Transcendental studies. But there is something new as well. The first of these studies, *Waldesrauschen,* points the way towards the shimmering textures of Ravel's "Ondine."

Equally audacious is its form. *Waldesrauschen* consists in its entirety of a set of metamorphoses on the above phrases. Many years after he had written this

trained as a theologian at Königsberg University. His eventual dislike of theology, however, caused him to abandon this discipline in favour of philosophy—the philosophy of Kant and Hegel in particular. For some years he earned his living as a teacher while slowly building up a reputation as a writer. His first novel was the romance *Werdomar and Wladislav,* which he published at the age of twenty-four. Gregorovius settled in Rome in 1852, and it was here that he embarked upon his magnum opus, *The History of Rome in the Middle Ages.*

study, Liszt was charmed to know that Queen Elizabeth of Rumania had been so moved when she heard it that she had been inspired to write a poem about it.[25] The other study, *Gnomenreigen,* is absorbed with the problem of alternating hands. And it is a piece (most unusual in Liszt) that improves with speed, an observation that can easily be tested. Its gossamer lightness summons up memories of the young Mendelssohn and the Scherzo from *A Midsummer Night's Dream.*

Liszt composed both pieces on the small Boisselot upright piano that he had earlier installed in his apartment at the Via Felice. The spectacle of him playing such music on this relatively fragile instrument defies the imagination, until we remember that neither study calls for force, but for extreme dexterity. They prove conclusively that even though he never practised, the magician of Weimar had not lost his cunning.

     Two other "autobiographical" compositions for solo piano must be mentioned here. The first is the strangely neglected *Evocation à la Chapelle Sixtine,* which emerged directly from a visit to the Sistine Chapel in the second half of 1862. After his arrival in Rome, Liszt had often sought out the spot where, in 1770, the fourteen-year-old Mozart had astonished the musical world by copying down from memory Allegri's *Miserere,* an unpublished composition whose performance was confined to the Sistine Choir during Holy Week and whose circulation was restricted on pain of excommunication. On one such occasion, Liszt observed, "it seemed to me as if I saw him [Mozart], and as if he looked

---

25. LLB, vol. 8, p. 410. The poem was published in *Über Land und Meer,* 1892, no. 8, under the queen's literary pseudonym, Carmen Sylva.

back at me with gentle encouragement. Allegri was standing by his side, basking in the fame which his *Miserere* now enjoyed."[26] Overcome with emotion, Liszt was inspired to capture this scene in music.

> I have not only brought them closer together, but, as it were, bound them together. Man's wretchedness and anguish moan plaintively in the *Miserere*; God's infinite mercy and the fullfilment of prayer answer it and sing in [Mozart's] *Ave Verum Corpus*. This concerns the sublimest of mysteries, the one which reveals to us Love triumphant over Evil and Death.[27]

Liszt places the *Miserere* in a low register of the keyboard, from where it gradually swirls out of the depths.

After clothing this simple theme in anguished, chromatic harmonies, Liszt works up a storm and offers his listeners a terrifying glimpse of Apocalypse Now. Both flesh and spirit are taxed to the verge of exhaustion. The music then collapses and gives way to the *Ave Verum Corpus*, first in the serene key of B major, and then in Liszt's "divine" key of F-sharp major.[28]

---

26. LBLCA, p. 116. This letter was scrutinized in some detail in Volume One, pp. 84–85. The apparition of Beethoven emerged from the shadows, or so it seemed to Liszt, and stood over those of Allegri and Mozart.

27. Ibid. The *Evocation* exists in two other versions—for organ and for full orchestra. This last version received its world première in Budapest, in 1993.

28. Mozart's original is actually in D major, which makes Liszt's transposition of this passage all the more evocative. For further examples of Liszt's use of F-sharp major to represent divinity, see Volume Two, p. 154.

Love and Death struggle for supremacy, with the work ending to the distant strains of the *Ave Verum Corpus*.

When Liszt was an old man, his pupils sometimes brought the *Evocation* to his masterclasses, and it became clear from his comments that he felt protective towards it. He once told Göllerich that such music should only be played in private . . . "it is not for the great public." Even allowing for Liszt's self-irony (a marked characteristic of his old age), he was saying something important, and we can only hope that the twenty-six-year-old Göllerich grasped it. There are some works, Liszt seemed to imply, which sound better in private than in public; bring them into the full glare of the concert hall and they literally change their personalities.[29] With the rise of a new and more sympathetic generation of pianists (about whom Liszt could only dream, since they hardly existed in his own day), the distinction between "public" and "private" performances has lost some of its meaning. The very greatest performances are all private ones, and the great public itself is merely there to eavesdrop. Under these ideal conditions the *Evocation* emerges as a sovereign achievement, and it will last as long as interest in Liszt's life and works endures.

Closely connected to this piece of musical autobiography is another, the transcription of a linked pair of movements from Mozart's *Requiem*, the "Confutatis maledictis" and the "Lacrymosa." We surmise that it was the death of Liszt's daughter Blandine in the summer of 1862 (a tragedy that is dealt with in the following chapter) that acted as a catalyst here. Although the date of composition remains circumstantial, these transcriptions sprang from his first, unsettled years in Rome. They bear a strong spiritual resemblance to the *Evocation,* and were in fact published in the same year, 1865. Liszt had been familiar with Mozart's *Requiem* for most of his adult life. We recall that he had even conducted the entire Dies Irae at the Vienna Mozart Centenary Festival of 1856, so he brought an insider's knowledge to his task. The thunder of the "Confutatis" almost engulfs the piano in its sea of sound.

---

29. GLK, p. 69.

Whether or not Liszt knew Carl Czerny's piano reduction of the "Lacrymosa" we cannot be certain. It is a serviceable arrangement, but it cannot compare with the grandeur of Liszt's. His brilliant command of the topography of the keyboard is everywhere in evidence, and comes out in such seemingly simple passages as the following,

which have to be played to be appreciated. And at those points where the tears and lamentations of souls rise to the heavens, Liszt's keyboard is large enough to encompass the sound of a full choir.

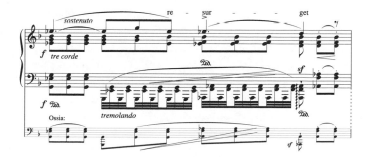

These Mozart transcriptions have yet to find their way into the standard repertory. Even among Liszt players they remain one of the composer's best-kept secrets. Nonetheless, they are stellar examples of their kind, inseparable from his Roman years.

I V

Not long after Liszt had arrived in the Eternal City, he had apotheosized it in his *Memento Journalier* with an immortal phrase: "Oh Rome! My country; city of the soul; the Niobe of Nations."[30] The words, of course, are Lord Byron's, but they expressed Liszt's deep feelings about a place he had come to love. Rome offered Liszt the prospect of personal happiness, a new life, and a harmonious existence such as he had not known for many years. He could look back on his first few months there and know that his time had been well spent. He had overcome a serious personal crisis, had made a host of new friends, had acquired new pupils, had composed some important works, and had gained a modest place for himself in the upper reaches of Roman society. Whatever the future held in store for him, the Eternal City would always remain an integral part of it.

---

30. VLKN, p. 32.

The Death of Blandine, 1862

Angiolin dal biondo crin . . .[1]

I

When Liszt and Blandine waved farewell to one another at Weimar's railway station in August 1861, they had no idea that it would be for ever. Her unexpected death at the early age of twenty-six was a major blow for Liszt, and it has never been reported in the depth that it deserves. The cause is usually given as "childbirth." There was a little more to it than that, however, as we shall presently discover.

Blandine and Émile Ollivier had already celebrated their fourth wedding anniversary, but their union had not yet been blessed with children. This seems to have been a deliberate choice on the part of the young couple, who wanted to establish a proper home at La Moutte before bringing up a family there. It was a special delight to Blandine, therefore, to be able to inform her father of her long-delayed pregnancy in a letter dated January 23, 1862.

> I pray in hopes of a great joy, but I am not rejoicing all the same, and I confess that if I bore a man of mediocre heart, of whom there are so many, I would be very little flattered. Besides, I fully share in this matter the opinion of Michelangelo. They announced to him, with great pomp and stupidity, the birth of one of his nephews. "It

---

1. "Little angel with the blond hair" (Bocello). Blandine was three years old when Liszt wrote this song for her, in 1839. (RL, p. 389)

47

is not when a man is born that one should rejoice," he replied, "but
after he has lived—if he has lived well."[2]

She told Liszt that her father-in-law, Démosthène Ollivier, was "crazy with
joy" about the news, and that Anna Liszt was already knitting small socks for
the new arrival. It was the sort of letter that any daughter might write to her
father in such circumstances, full of excitement and affection. About the middle of May, 1862, Ollivier decided to send Blandine to the home of Dr. Charles
Isnard, his brother-in-law, there to await the confinement and delivery. Ollivier
himself called this separation "cruel," but he felt that there would be advantages in it for Blandine and her unborn infant. Isnard, who was a specialist in
obstetrics, was married to Ollivier's younger sister Josephine. They lived in
Gemenos, not far from Saint-Tropez, had two small children of their own, and
held Blandine in great affection. The idea was for Blandine to enjoy the warm
Mediterranean sunshine, build up her strength, and receive the best possible
pre-natal care. No one had any inkling that such a sensible plan would lead to
such tragic consequences. On July 3 Blandine went into labour and after
"scarcely two hours of pain," in Isnard's words, was safely delivered of a son.[3]
It was one of the easiest births that Isnard had ever attended, he said, and there
were no immediate post-natal complications. When Blandine was told that she
had given birth to a boy, she asked: "Is he pretty?" Then she quickly corrected
herself and added: "In any case, it does not matter to me; I am sure that he will
be intelligent."[4] The child was given the names of Daniel-Emile, in memory
of Blandine's dead brother and the child's father.

                                    II

Within a few days of the birth Blandine was on her feet and able to care for
Daniel herself. In fact, she may have over-exerted herself, for on July 27 she
wrote to Liszt: "I am writing to you from my bed where I have again been
forced to take refuge since yesterday."[5] She then went on to give Liszt a detailed description of his grandson's physiognomy, and added: "Fortunately, he

---

2. OCLF, p. 301.
3. Our information about Blandine's confinement, labour, and death comes from the detailed series
of unpublished letters written by Dr. Isnard to Ollivier between August 3 and September 29. They
are preserved in the Bibliothèque nationale under the shelf-mark NAF 25193, ff. 7–14. When Madame
Liszt heard about the easy birth she exclaimed: "Cicero's mother also gave birth without pain." To
which Ollivier added the poignant observation: "I hardly dare believe that this is an omen. . . ." (Unpublished letter of Ollivier to Zélie de Sourdeval, dated July 12, 1862; from the Ollivier Archives, La
Moutte)
4. TOS-W, p. 42.
5. OCLF, p. 324.

is a good child: he cries only enough not to cause worry about his health. He is not big . . . but he is vigorous, and his little hand squeezes my wrist hard. I am feeding him, my milk seems to suit him, because he sleeps well and leaves me in peace for five hours a night."[6] The next few days passed without incident, and Blandine spent a lot of time lounging on the terrace, reading Victor Hugo's *Les Misérables.*

In early August, Isnard noticed that Blandine was having difficulty in feeding her infant at the left breast. There was an ominous swelling which made it awkward for the boy to suckle. In order to make the milk flow more freely, Isnard brought in two or three local infants, aged two months or so, who were able to suckle more vigorously. He also used what he called "a special little machine" and, as a last resort, a woman whose specialty was withdrawing milk. The end results of all these efforts was that the swelling increased and submerged the nipple. Henceforth, Daniel had to be nursed at the right breast alone. Despite, or because of, the attentions of Isnard, Blandine's condition worsened, and about August 9, Ollivier (who had been receiving regular bulletins in Paris) decided to come to Gemenos himself. The report that awaited him was not good. By now, even Isnard was alarmed. The left breast was inflamed, and there was a suppuration which required constant attention. In order to dull the pain, Isnard prescribed a mixture of arsenic and laudanum, to be taken in water four or five times a day. A round-the-clock vigil was arranged at Blandine's bedside to cater to her needs. "Never was a queen surrounded by so much care, devotion, and love," she said. "Not a single paid hand."[7] The turning-point came on August 16, when Isnard was confronted with an abscess and an imminent collapse of the breast. Having seen many similar cases, he knew that he could delay no longer, and he decided to make an incision.

> That cut of the scalpel, that impassibility disconcerted me! Under the surgeon's knife I have seen the old sailor, . . . the war veteran, the man of bronze. Not a contraction, not a gasp, not a movement of the eyebrow! I have never seen such stoicism! The immobility of a king! Was it the effect of that energetic will? Was it insensitivity to pain? Evidently this constitution did not react like others! It was my first and terrible warning![8]

From Isnard's description we conclude that this operation was carried out without an effective anaesthetic and without the benefit of proper antiseptic

---

6. Ibid.
7. BN NAF 25193, f. 14.
8. Ibid.

safeguards. Blandine's condition deteriorated rapidly after that ordeal; and, possibly as a result of Isnard's scalpel or even his "little machine," she now had to battle with septicaemia. She was unable to eat or sleep, suffered from out-breaks of fever, and experienced frightening episodes of breathlessness. Towards the end of August she begged Ollivier to take her home to Saint-Tropez. Somehow he managed to get her to La Moutte, where she took to her bed, never to leave it. Isnard continued to travel from Gemenos in order to administer laudanum and other palliatives, but it was to no avail. On September 8, Blandine was in such a critical condition that Ollivier alerted Liszt to the impending catastrophe.[9] Mercifully, this arrived without much further delay. She passed away during the early hours of September 11. A few days later she was buried in the small cemetery at Saint-Tropez, overlooking the Mediterranean Sea.[10]

III

Emile was devastated; he told Liszt that his happiness had been destroyed for ever.[11] He became obsessed with finding out the causes of Blandine's death. In his distraught frame of mind, he seems to have blamed himself for placing her in Isnard's care. He insisted that Isnard inform him in writing of all her post-natal symptoms, and of the various medical precautions taken to treat them. This was a painful situation for both men, but Isnard did not shirk the task. His unpublished reply to Ollivier runs to eight closely written pages, giving many medical details which have hitherto remained unknown.[12] Was the early treat-ment of withdrawing milk from the breast a correct one? Were the doses of ar-senic and laudanum too large? Was the pain of the incision too traumatic? Was it possible that she was in a coma at the end, and buried alive by mistake? To all such questions Isnard gave Ollivier soothing replies. The last question, in fact, was a symptom of the young husband's distraught emotions and of his in-ability to accept the reality of Blandine's death.

---

9. OJ, vol. 2, p. 55.
10. Some unnecessary confusion surrounds the actual date of death. The notion that she may have died two days earlier rests on a letter that Ollivier wrote to Liszt on September 9, in which he de-clared: "Blandine died this morning." (OJ, vol. 2, p. 56) We now know that the date of that letter is wrong. In the holograph of his *Journal,* Ollivier gave the true date of Blandine's death as September 11 "at six o'clock in the morning." For this information I am indebted to Anne Troisier de Diaz, the present custodian of the Ollivier *Journal,* which is kept in the Ollivier archives at La Moutte. Blan-dine's death-certificate also gives September 11 (Town Hall of Saint-Tropez, certificate no. 62, 1862). The mayor of Saint-Tropez, one Désiré Cauvin, who signed the death-certificate, based his informa-tion on a report of the local sacristan, François Martel, who was present at the burial.
11. OJ, vol. 2, p. 56.
12. BN NAF 25193, f. 14.

At the end of September, Ollivier, still in a state of shock, travelled to Rome in order to give Liszt a first-hand account of Blandine's last days. Liszt put him up in his apartments at Via Felice 113, where the two men shared their grief.[13] The experience drew them closer together and helps to explain the special intimacy they enjoyed in later years. Liszt did all he could to console his son-in-law and lift him out of his depression; he took him to soirées and restaurants, played the piano to him, and showed him the sights of the Eternal City.[14] The day after his arrival was September 27, which happened to be Cosima's name-day; so Liszt and Ollivier marked the occasion by visiting the ancient temple of Romulus and Remus, which had meanwhile been converted into a church dedicated to saints Cosmas and Damien.[15] They also went over to see Princess Carolyne, and Emile was touched by the warmth of her reception. Not long after he got back to Saint-Tropez he told her: "There has not been a day since I left Rome that I have not planned to write to you, not a day that I have not thought with affection and gratitude of your maternal welcome . . . of the long conversations in which I poured out my sorrow and assuaged it by telling you about it."[16] Both Liszt and Carolyne sensed that Ollivier was psychologically ravaged, and that his period of mourning would last for several years.

IV

Liszt brought forth his Variations on "Weinen, Klagen, Sorgen, Zagen" during this very period of turmoil with Ollivier and the shared anguish over the loss of his daughter. The emergence of such a piece in the second half of 1862 was not accidental. It is best understood as a symptom of the grieving process, and like so much else in Liszt's output this music is really autobiographical. Liszt found in the first movement of Bach's cantata "Weeping, Wailing, Mourning, Trembling" a wonderful vehicle for his grief. He composed his own variations on its ground bass. Bach's version of the theme (which he also used in the Crucifixus of the B-minor Mass) runs like this:

---

13. In a letter Liszt wrote to his mother on September 27, he informed her that Ollivier had been staying with him since the previous day. (VFL, p. 113) As in the case of Daniel Liszt's death, three years earlier, Liszt's first thought was to console his own mother. "My first and constant thought in this tragedy which strikes us is you, dearest mother. You who had such a share in that gentle and dear existence . . . by the care, the tenderness, and the love that you poured out every day, every hour, in her childhood. . . . I weep and upset myself about it more than I can tell you!" (VFL, p. 112)

14. OJ, vol. 2, pp. 56–57.

15. VFL, p. 113. Cosmas was the patron saint of Cosima. See Volume One, p. 248.

16. TOS-W, p. 41.

Liszt, however, begins his own variations with an arresting statement of the theme in the "wrong" key of D-flat major, which gradually collapses into the home tonic of F minor—Liszt's key of mourning *par excellence*.[17]

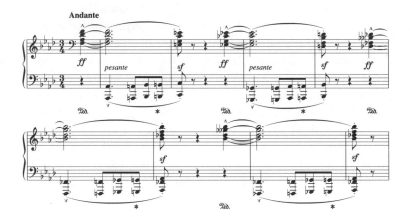

Once again his Boisselot upright in the Via Felice was the unlikely recipient of some forward-looking textures. The variations grow towards a cataclysm and the keyboard starts to weep and wail beneath the player's hands.

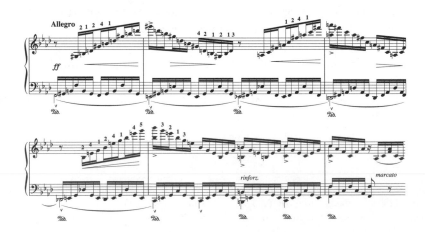

Liszt ends his variations with a statement of the old Lutheran chorale "Was Gott tut, das ist wohlgetan" ("What God does, that is well done"), an unmis-

---

17. Both *Funérailles* and *Héroïde funèbre* are in this key.

takable reference to the personal loss that he himself had suffered, and his acceptance of it.

V

When Ollivier got back to La Moutte, he fell ill. At first he wanted to sell up,
since every room, every brick, and every stick of furniture reminded him of
Blandine's presence. Later he changed his mind and resolved to "conserve and
embellish this piece of land she loved."[18] In fact, he added to it by buying, bit
by bit, the lots from thirteen different proprietors, which enabled him to push
his property all the way to the shoreline. He planted palm trees, eucalyptus trees,
and vineyards, and cut paths to the seafront. Hard physical labour, in the end,
proved to be Ollivier's salvation, and restored him to sanity and a normal life.[19]

---

18. TOS-W, p. 42.

19. In 1869 Ollivier took as his second wife a nineteen-year-old girl named Marie-Thérèse Gravier.
Despite the twenty-five-year difference in their ages, she proved to be the perfect helpmate in his political career. Nor did she represent an obstacle in the way of his friendship with Liszt and Carolyne,
who got to know her well and happily accepted her into the family circle.

   And what of the infant Daniel? When Ollivier got back to Saint-Tropez from Rome, he found
his son badly undernourished and almost "dying of hunger." A wet-nurse was brought in from Piedmont and within a brief time the child was "as though resurrected." (TOS-W, p. 42) It is clear that in
his bereavement Ollivier had difficulty in adjusting to what were now the burdens rather than the joys
of fatherhood. He confessed to Carolyne: "Up to now the sight of [Daniel] upsets me and increases
my sorrow." Daniel spent his early years at La Moutte, in the care of his doting grandfather Démosthène, and Ollivier saw the child mainly during the summer holidays. There were in any case
strong practical reasons for this arrangement. Ollivier's career was in Paris. His apartment was very
small, and one of its rooms contained the ailing Anna Liszt, for whom Ollivier continued to care.
Daniel eventually became a lawyer, like his father and grandfather before him. We recall that he eventually inherited Marie d'Agoult's papers and later published her *Mémoires* and her *Correspondance* with
Liszt. (See Volume One, pp. 7–8.)

The Madonna del Rosario
1863-1865

My stay in Rome is not an accidental one.
FRANZ LISZT[1]

I

The premature death of Blandine, following so hard on that of Daniel, weighed heavily on Liszt's mind, and he spent his fifty-first birthday in a state of depression. Walter Bache, who was about to begin taking lessons from him, caught a brief glimpse of him that very day and reported, "He is still very sad indeed."[2] Three weeks later, Liszt referred to a "great affliction which recently occurred in my life" but about which he felt unable to unburden himself.[3] Liszt, in fact, was now entering the blackest and most troubled phase of his life. He suffered a marked personality change. His sense of boundless optimism temporarily deserted him. He became introspective. His hair turned gray, and on his face appeared the numerous warts with which anybody who has seen photographs of him in later life is familiar. In order to bring some repose into his troubled life, he knew that he must get away from the hustle and bustle of Rome, and he appealed to an old acquaintance, Father Agostino Theiner, to help him find somewhere else to live.[4] Theiner at once suggested that they should journey up the slopes of the Monte Mario together and visit the Madonna del Rosario, where he himself kept humble accommodations. From the moment that Liszt caught sight of the old monastery he knew that he had found a perfect retreat.

---

1. LLB, vol. 2, p. 54.
2. BBM, p. 158.
3. CLBA, p. 91.
4. Father Theiner was prefect of the Secret Archive of the Vatican Library. He had been introduced to Liszt by Carolyne, who had known him since 1859.

In those days the Madonna del Rosario lay about an hour's journey from Rome. It occupied a commanding position on Monte Mario, near the Via Trionfale, along which the Roman legions had returned in victory, and it enjoyed some spectacular views of the surrounding countryside. Founded in 1628, the monastery was not completed until about a hundred years later, when it was given to the Domenican monks by Clement XI. By 1863 the old building had become dilapidated, and only three members of the original order actually lived there—a priest, a monk, and a lay brother. These clerics lived a life of extreme simplicity, eking out a bare living from a small fruit-and-vegetable garden and a few chickens which they kept in a wire enclosure inside the grounds. Attached to the monastery was a small church, the Santa Maria, where daily mass was celebrated and sometimes attended by passing pilgrims. In order to reach the monastery at all, visitors had to climb a formidable series of steps up to the front door, which was always closed. They had to pull on a bell rope and wait until the leisurely reverberations had echoed through the deserted corridors and attracted attention.

This peaceful haven was to remain Liszt's home for the next five years. He moved into the Madonna del Rosario on June 20, 1863,[5] and with but two exceptions he remained there until 1868.[6] He was given a small cell on the ground floor at the front of the monastery, with whitewashed walls, whose floor space was a mere fifteen feet by twelve feet. His only furniture was a wooden bed, a work-table, a bookcase, and a small upright piano with a missing D. The windows offered a panoramic view of Rome, however; from one side he could see the dome of St. Peter's shining in the distance, from the other the Albano Hills stretching along the horizon beyond the older part of the city. In these inspirational surroundings Liszt found the freedom to work without interruption and a great deal of time in which to meditate. He even joined the monks in their ministrations, and he sometimes officiated during mass on the small harmonium (the church was so poor it did not possess a pipe organ). This monastic life-style seemed to harmonize with his deepest needs; he himself expressed it best of all when he wrote: "My life is simplifying itself, and the Catholic piety of my childhood has become a regular and also a regulating feeling."[7]

Three weeks after Liszt moved into the Madonna del Rosario, there occurred an event that put this isolated monastery on the map and set the whole of Rome talking. On July 11, 1863, Liszt was visited in his cell by Pope Pius IX, in company with Monsignors Hohenlohe and Frédéric de Mérode. Liszt himself left a description of the occasion.[8] After chatting for a brief period to his

---

5. LLB, vol. 2, p. 41.
6. From April 1865 until June 1866 he occupied quarters in the Vatican. And from November 1866 he also lived in the Santa Francesca Romana.
7. LLB, vol. 3, p. 161.
8. LLB, vol. 2, p. 46. See also the *Allgemeine Zeitung* (no. 203), July 22, 1863, p. 3363.

"dear Palestrina," the music-loving pontiff asked Liszt to play something for him. Liszt sat down at his "pianino" and delivered the first of his Franciscan Legends, *St. Francis of Assisi preaching to the birds.*[9] Then followed a performance of the aria "Casta diva" from Bellini's *Norma.* The pope was so moved by this melody that he sprang to his feet, went to the keyboard, and in his fine baritone voice sang the aria from memory, with Liszt accompanying. Afterwards he admonished Liszt, "in the most gracious manner possible," to strive after heavenly things in earthly ones, and to use his temporal harmonies as a means of preparing himself for the timeless ones.[10] Before leaving he presented Liszt with a ring. A few days later, Liszt was received in audience at the Vatican, and the pope gave him a beautiful cameo depicting the Madonna.

Liszt's circle in Rome speculated a great deal about the significance of these meetings. Was Liszt about to embrace holy orders? Was he being given serious consideration for the job of director of the Sistine Choir? Liszt certainly discussed the reform of church music with Pius IX, but there is no evidence that the pontiff was about to dismiss Salvatore Meluzzi from his post at St. Peter's. Nor is there any reason to suppose that Liszt coveted such a position. Years later, he said that he "neither expected nor wished for an appointment or title of any kind at Rome." And he added that he was "under no illusions as to the difficulty and vexations of such a task."[11] In fact, Liszt's music was considered by many of Rome's leading clerics to be far too advanced for the taste of the church. As for taking holy orders, this step was still a distant one.

I I

Among the works which Liszt brought to completion at the Madonna del Rosario were the two Franciscan Legends. It is said that the first of them, *St. Francis of Assisi preaching to the birds,* was inspired by the thousands of sparrows that sometimes rose in clouds above the Monte Mario. Liszt had in mind the charming story of Francis of Assisi, who beheld the multitude of birds which filled the wayside and was moved to preach to them. "And forthwith those which were in the trees came around him, and not one moved during the whole sermon; nor would they fly away until the Saint had given them his

---

9. The identity of the pieces Liszt played to Pius IX has been much disputed. See RL, p. 88.

10. LLB, vol. 2, p. 46. Was this the only visit of Pius IX to the Madonna del Rosario? Although the standard biographies of Liszt never mention it, there may have been a second one a few months later, according to reports in the Pest newspapers. On November 8, 1863, the *Pesti Napló* (citing the *Frankfurter Europa)* wrote that the pontiff had visited Liszt at the monastery "for a second time" and that Liszt had beguiled the pope for more than an hour with his playing. Similar reports appeared in the Spanish press. See LLR, p. 91, n. 14.

11. LLB, vol. 7, p. 73.

blessing."[12] It is an evocative story, and Liszt has matched it with equally evocative music in which we hear the chirping and twittering of birds. Here is one of many of Liszt's "ornithological effects":

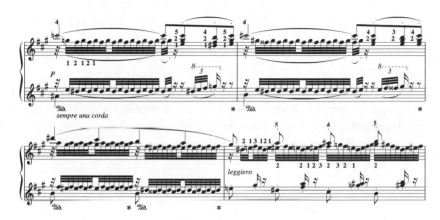

At the first entry of St. Francis (duly marked in the score) Liszt has the monk address the flock in recitative and subdue their joyous song to his words. The sermon itself rises heavenwards in a series of solemn chords whose expanding harmonies suggest that God himself is looking down on the scene with approval.

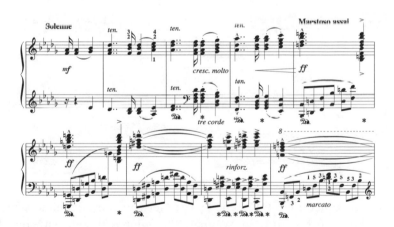

In his preface, Liszt apologizes to St. Francis ("the glorious poor servant of Christ") for his lack of ingenuity in capturing this remarkable scene. In fact, he reveals such skill in conjuring up bird sounds from the keyboard that the work must be regarded as the historical link between Couperin's "Le Coucou" and Messiaen's *Catalogue d'oiseaux*.

---

12. The story is related in Chapter 16 of the *Fioretti di San Francesco*.

The other Legend is called *St. Francis of Paola walking on the waters.* It is based on the well-known story of St. Francis of Paola being turned away by the boat-man at the ferry-crossing of the Straits of Messina because he could not afford the fare. "If he is a saint," remarked the boatman, "let him walk." Whereupon St. Francis, having blessed his cloak in the name of God, placed it on the wa-ters, lifted up one part of it like a sail, and floated safely across the straits to the other side. When the boatman saw what had happened, he fell on his knees, implored pardon for his refusal, and begged the saint to return to the boat. "But God, for the glory of His holy name . . . caused him to refuse this offer and to arrive in port before the boat."[13] We hear the menacing sound of the waves and the tremendous swell of the waters, and through it all there sounds the "St. Francis" theme floating serenely across the seascape.

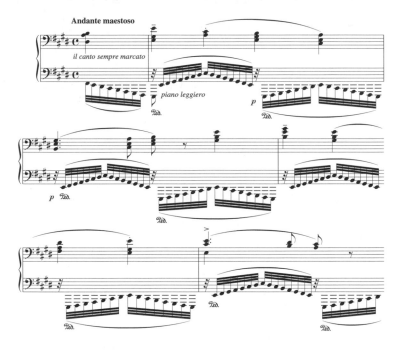

Liszt possessed a picture of this scene by the German painter Steinle, which in later years hung in his study in Weimar. The saint is shown with his cloak spread out under his feet; one hand is raised as though to command the ele-ments, in the other he holds a live coal, a symbol of inward fire; his gaze re-mains fixed on heaven, from where the divine word "Charitas" shines forth. The coda of the Legend, in fact, contains a reminiscence of a short choral work for male chorus and organ, *An den heiligen Franziskus von Paula,* composed

13. The story may be found in Chapter 35 of Miscimarra's *Life of St. Francis of Paola.*

three years earlier but not yet published.[14] The words associated with this passage are: "O let us preserve Love whole."

The moral of the Legend, wrote Liszt, was to show that the laws of faith govern the laws of nature.[15] St. Francis of Paola, incidentally, was Liszt's patron saint, which may have been one reason why he retained a particular affection for this piece until the end of his days.

III

He was by no means cloistered on the Monte Mario. Twice a week he would leave his retreat, walk down the Via Trionfale, cross the River Tiber, and give a piano class in the home of his pupil Giovanni Sgambati. A small contingent of Italian and foreign students gathered around him on those occasions, which

---

14. In his will (1860) Liszt mentions this piece as being one of the compositions he would like to see published (LLB, vol. 5, p. 61). However, it did not appear in print until 1875.
15. Preface to the work, CE, II, vol. 9. In a particularly vicious review of these pieces, published a year after Liszt had taken holy orders, Eduard Hanslick told his readers: "The worldly Liszt performed miraculously, but the Abbé Liszt performs miracles." Then, after regaling his audience with the stories that Liszt had attached to his two Legends, Hanslick continued in his most sarcastic vein: "If, after all this, you examine the two pieces of music themselves, you find two ordinary brilliant concert studies, one of which spins out for a musical motive the twitter of birds, and the other imitates the roar of the sea. The pieces are grateful to a virtuoso, and not without some piquant spice of dissonance; of course, the birds preaching provide for the *bravura* of the right hand, and the walking on the waves for that of the left hand. These compositions might just as well have been called 'Les Amours des Oiseaux' and 'Souvenirs des Bains d'Ostende,' and ten years ago they probably would have received these titles. Perhaps Liszt will bring the rest of the saints before us, one by one, in the same pleasant manner. We must confess, this rigging out of the saintly halo for the concert hall, these hammering and trilling miracles make an unspeakably childish impression on us." (HGC, Vol. 2, pp. 409–10) Hanslick's arguments about the interchangeability of Liszt's titles could have been applied with equal justice to Berlioz, Mendelssohn, Schumann, Brahms, and others, some of whom had composed music with literary connections a good deal more vague than those of Liszt. But Hanslick was driven by bias, and we have reproduced his own words as the best evidence of that fact.

Hanslick had now reached his definitive position as the critic of Vienna's *Neue Freie Presse,* in which capacity he was widely feared. His theoretical picture of music was by now very well known, for it was all contained in his little book *Vom Musikalisch-Schönen,* which had already gone through

included Walter Bache, Ettore Pinelli, Carlo Lippi, and Gilda Perini. On Thursdays he would usually attend a soirée in the home of Monsignor Nardi, where he would mix and mingle with aristocrats, embassy officials, and the higher clergy. Liszt's best piano, a particularly fine Bechstein grand, was kept at Nardi's house, and Liszt would often thrill the assembly by playing on this instrument. He never taught or socialized in the Madonna del Rosario; that was reserved for work and for meditation. Liszt's friends and pupils would sometimes reciprocate his visits to them, however, brave the long climb up the Monte Mario, pull on the bell-rope, and ask to see Commendatore Liszt. He was unfailingly hospitable on such occasions, and would drop whatever he was doing in order to devote himself to his guests. Walter Bache well recalled making such a visit in October 1863, and wrote to his father:

October 19, 1863

. . . Liszt has removed to Monte Mario, about two and a half miles from my part of town: on a high hill, and adjoining or forming part of a beautiful country church. . . . He was *very, very* kind— more than I can tell you. He has removed to this place on purpose to get away from people and live quietly. It is a magnificent country, with a splendid view of Rome, and no houses for miles. But this will make no difference to my visiting him, he said. He is writing a great deal: but he put it aside and took me for a beautiful walk, and played me several things (amongst others a Prelude and Fugue of his own for organ—on the name B.A.C.H . . .) and ordered dinner on purpose for me; and so I stopped all day, and have just had a most magnificent walk home—but descriptions of scenery are always stupid and fall so far short of reality—I wish you could have seen it. He accompanied me part of the way home, and promised to come to see me tomorrow evening.[16]

---

several editions. Music, for Hanslick, was a self-contained communication—somewhat like a mathematical formula—and the best of it was untouched by time and place. This was the central idea that had always separated Hanslick from Liszt and his contemporaries, and which had driven the "War of the Romantics" for more than a decade. The years had not mellowed Hanslick's thinking, and he continued to pursue the idea of music's abstractness with tenacity. Like a religious zealot, his goal was to switch off the light and make his readers see by the flame of one candle—his own. We now know something of which Hanslick's contemporaries were unaware. The candle did not belong to him, however much he pretended otherwise. It was stolen from an obscure Bohemian music critic named Bernhard Gutt, who died in 1849, five years before his ideas were plagiarized by the up-and-coming Hanslick in the first edition of *Vom Musikalisch-Schönen*. (See the penetrating exposé of Hanslick in PHB, pp. 107–15.) Hanslick's high place in the history of music criticism has become untenable and needs to be urgently reassessed. He had one idea for which he became famous, and he did not even discover it for himself.
16. BBM, p. 169.

Another frequent visitor to the Monte Mario was Kurd von Schlözer, a Prussian diplomat based in Rome, who was also a keen amateur pianist. No account of Liszt's early years in the Madonna del Rosario is complete without reference to Schlözer's *Römische Briefe*, which contain some of the best descriptions of Liszt in his monastic setting to come down to us. Schlözer tells of one occasion, towards the end of May 1864, when Liszt was visited in his cell by his old compatriot Ede Reményi, who turned up in the company of the British vice-consul to Naples, Mr. Douglas, together with the latter's wife and daughter. It was not long before Reményi took out his violin and, to everyone's delight, played his own arrangement of Liszt's "Die drei Zigeuner" (Lenau), with Liszt himself playing the accompaniment on the pianino (minus the D). The performance became so animated that Reményi was virtually dancing about while playing, after the fashion of the Magyar peasants. The session came to an end with a truly British scene. Schlözer tells us that Douglas went up to Liszt and asked him: "May I request a favour of you?"—"With pleasure."—"May I play a chord on your piano?"—"As many as you like." With that, Douglas walked proudly towards Liszt's pianino and played a solitary chord. Then he took out his diary and solemnly wrote down that at 4:00 p.m. on Monday afternoon, May 30, 1864, at the monastery of Monte Mario, he had played a chord on the piano which belonged to Franz Liszt.[17]

Schlözer goes on to tell us that Liszt was in a first-rate mood that day, and he disclosed the reason: Liszt had just received from Wagner a transcript of the famous letter from King Ludwig II of Bavaria in which the young monarch had asked the impecunious musician to come to Munich, where he would be guaranteed a life free from material care. From his earliest youth, the king told him, he had been the greatest admirer of Wagner and his music, and he now wanted to repay him for all the joy his compositions had brought him. Wagner's fortunes were at their lowest ebb when the king's letter arrived, and he was about to flee his creditors. The scope of the king's benefaction was unprecedented in the history of music, as we now know, and it was to change Wagner's life. Wagner himself regarded Ludwig's offer as heaven-sent. So too did Liszt, who could not get over this unexpected change in Wagner's fortunes and kept showing his copy of the letter to all his influential friends in Rome.[18]

---

17. SRB, p. 74.
18. On June 17, 1864, Liszt sent a transcript of the letter to Agnes Street-Klindworth (WA, Kasten 75, no. 12). The text runs as follows.

> Most honoured sir:
>   I have charged Councillor Pfistermeister with the matter of talking over with you a suitable dwelling place for you. Rest assured that I shall do everything within my power to compensate you for your past sufferings. I shall banish from your mind forever the petty cares of everyday life. I shall give you the peace you have longed for, so that you may freely

IV

While Liszt was at the Madonna del Rosario, he brought to completion his remarkable series of piano transcriptions of the Beethoven symphonies. The task
had occupied him, on and off, for many years.[19] Nobody understood the art of
transcription better than Liszt, yet even he regarded these symphonies as a difficult prospect for one pair of hands. In his preface to the collection he declared
his aims:

> I confess that I should have to regard it as a rather useless employ-
> ment of my time, if I had added but one more version of the Sym-
> phonies in the usual manner; but I consider my time well employed
> if I have succeeded in transferring to the piano not only the grand
> outlines of Beethoven's compositions but also those numerous fine
> details, and smaller traits that so powerfully contribute to the com-
> pletion of the ensemble.
>
>   Rome, 1865[20]

---

deploy the commanding wings of your genius on the pure altar of blissful art!
    Unbeknownst to you, you were the sole source of my joy from my early youth, my
friend who could speak to my heart like no one else, my best teacher and mentor.
    I want to repay everything to you to the best of my ability! Oh, how I have looked
forward to the time when I would be able to do this! I scarcely dared hope to be so
soon in a position to prove my love for you.

                                    With my most cordial greetings.
                                    Your friend,
                                    LUDWIG OF BAVARIA

                                    May 5, 1864

    It was eventually published in KLRWB, vol. I, p. II.
19. The impulse to complete the entire set came from Breitkopf and Härtel. They were aware that
years earlier, during his heyday as a concert pianist, Liszt had already transcribed the Fifth, Sixth, and
Seventh symphonies, together with the Funeral March from the *Eroica*; after he got to Rome they
urged him to tackle the others. Liszt agreed, on condition that he be allowed to revise his earlier efforts and issue all nine symphonies together. To help get him started, Breitkopf sent him the orchestral scores in their "critically revised" editions. (See his letters to Breitkopf dated March 26, August
28, and November 16, 1863, in LLB, vol. 2.) The correspondence shows that Liszt embarked on the
task shortly after Easter, 1863, and completed it some time before July 1865. Perhaps the most piquant
part of the business was that the bulk of the creative work was done in Liszt's small cell on his anti-
quated "pianino," with the missing D, and the first ears to hear the strains of these arrangements were
those of the Domenican brothers.
20. CE, II, vols. F.B. nos. 2 and 3. Although this preface is dated "Rome, 1865," it is an exact reprint
of the one that Liszt published for the first edition of the Fifth Symphony in 1840 (see Volume Two,

Liszt was not content, then, merely to reduce Beethoven's symphonies to two staves, after the manner of the "hack" arranger. The thing that gripped his imagination was the challenge these symphonies represented in defying ten fingers to reproduce them *without harming Beethoven's thought*. It was a challenge that no other arrangement had so far successfully met. The results, as we know today, are spectacular; these transcriptions have remained a model of their kind. Sir Donald Tovey said of them that they "prove conclusively . . . that Liszt was by far the most wonderful interpreter of orchestral scores on the pianoforte that the world is ever likely to see."[21]

Liszt's transcriptions differ from the routine arrangements of the Beethoven symphonies in two important respects, both of which represent the twin ideals towards which he constantly strives. First, they remain unsurpassed in the amount of fine orchestral detail incorporated into their texture. Second, the seemingly impossible technical problems posed by such an accomplishment are solved in the most pianistic way.

A simple illustration occurs at the beginning of the Fifth Symphony. A respectable, and respected, arrangement by Otto Singer runs:

Compare that with Liszt's solution. There is not a note to choose between the two arrangements (except for Liszt's octaves in bar 4, which are in Beethoven's score anyway). But how much simpler is Liszt's to play!

---

pp. 377, of the present work, where a part of the preface is reproduced in facsimile). Liszt uttered similar thoughts to Breitkopf and Härtel when he accepted from them the commission to complete these transcriptions in their entirety. "A pianoforte arrangement of these creations must, indeed, expect to remain a very poor and far-off *approximation*. How to instill into the transitory hammers of the piano breath and soul, resonance and power, fullness and inspiration, colour and accent? However, I will at least endeavour to overcome the worst difficulties and to furnish the pianoforte-playing world with as faithful as possible an illustration of Beethoven's genius." (LLB, vol. 2, p. 35)

21. *Essays in Musical Analysis,* vol. 1, p. 193. Among the piano arrangements which had preceded Liszt's were Kalkbrenner's (1840), Hummel's (before 1837), and above all Czerny's (1827–29).

The fingering, a crucial aspect of each solution, is reproduced exactly as the arrangers left it.

Equally revealing is the slow movement of the Fifth. All other arrangements give the famous cello tune to the right hand, and its pizzicato accompaniment to the left—all except Liszt's.

At first sight this seems perverse. Why cross the hands to do something which can be done perfectly well without? Nevertheless, it is Liszt's arrangement which shows the deepest insight. What could be more natural to a pianist than to make his left hand "play the cello"? By disposing of the melody in this way, its phrasing and articulation, and its relationship to the accompaniment, are naturally assured.

As for the "fine orchestral detail," Liszt will sometimes go to enormous trouble to incorporate Beethoven's original phrasing, even where it may not always coincide with the pianist's best interests. Consider Kalkbrenner's phrasing of this figure from the first movement of the *Eroica*.

It is marvellous to play, but it is not what Beethoven wrote. What is the point of "playability," Liszt might well have asked, if what we play cheats us of the very thing we are trying to reproduce? Liszt does not compromise on such matters. He leaves Beethoven's phrasing unharmed.

This is difficult. Even professional pianists do not always rise to this kind of challenge.

Naturally there are times when Liszt is unable to transfer to the piano even the simplest of Beethoven's motifs, because they fight the keyboard. We know that the opening of the finale to the Eighth Symphony gave him some trouble, and that he consulted Ferdinand David about it.[22] How does one transcribe the following measures? They spring from the innermost nature of the violins, and sound crude when reproduced on the piano.

At such moments, Liszt chooses the nearest pianistic equivalent, and his selection here cannot be bettered. The music moves so rapidly that the ear takes the will for the deed:

One is reminded of a remark that Cosima once quoted from Liszt: "In matters of translation there are some exactitudes which are the equivalent of infidelities."[23]

The Ninth Symphony poses problems which even Liszt was unable satisfactorily to resolve. The choral finale proved quite intractable, and we find him writing in 1864 to Breitkopf and Härtel (who had expected to publish all nine symphonies complete) asking to be excused from the task of transcribing it.

---

22. LLB, vol. 2, p. 48.
23. CWHSC, p. 114.

> After various endeavours one way and another, I became inevitably
> and distinctly convinced of the impossibility of making any pi-
> anoforte arrangement of the fourth movement *for two hands,* that
> could in any way be even approximately effective or satisfactory. I
> trust you will not bear me any ill-will for failing in this, and that you
> will consider my work with the Beethoven Symphonies as con-
> cluded with the third movement of the Ninth, for it was not part
> of my task to provide a simple *pianoforte score* of this overwhelming
> fourth movement for the use of chorus directors. Arrangements of
> this kind have already been made, and I maintain that I am *not* able
> to furnish a better or a more satisfactory one for helpless pianofortes
> and pianists, and I believe that there is no one nowadays who could
> manage it.[24]

Breitkopf and Härtel refused to be brushed aside, however. They wrote back to
Liszt insisting that he address himself more vigorously to the problem. In a letter dated October 1, 1864, Liszt agreed to make a further attempt.

> In compliance with the wish you so kindly express, I will again
> make an attempt to "adapt" the fourth movement of the Ninth
> Symphony to the piano, and soon after my return to Rome will set
> to work upon the required *tentative* [attempt]. Let us hope that the
> variation of the proverb "Tant va la cruche à l'eau qu'à la
> fin . . . *elle s'emplit*"[25] may prove true.[26]

The finished result is a model of how to proceed in such circumstances. Liszt
openly acknowledges his difficulty by printing the choral parts on separate
staves above the transcribed orchestral score. While the music is at times strictly
unplayable, it has the great advantage of not impairing Beethoven's thought—
as it surely would have done if Liszt had attempted to squeeze everything into
two hands.

---

24. LLB, vol. 2, p. 76.
25. "So often goes the pitcher to water that at last it is filled."
26. LLB, vol. 2, p. 77.

Kalkbrenner, like Liszt, falls back on the expedient of printing the choral parts on separate staves. But in every other respect his version falls lamentably short of the high standard adopted by Liszt. The opening of the finale, in Kalkbrenner's arrangement, gives no idea of the grandeur of Beethoven's original.

Beethoven's "dominant thirteenth" chord is apparently so offensive to Kalkbrenner that he emasculates it. Liszt, as we would expect, transcribes the grinding, glorious dissonance in full.

Note Liszt's pedal marking.

These transcriptions show Liszt in an unfamiliar light. They dispel the popular view of him as a showman, taking other composers' works and turning them into a fireworks display for his own glorification. The act of self-denial Liszt here discloses, suppressing his own creative impulses in the interests of Beethoven's music, has few parallels.

V

During his sojourn at the Madonna del Rosario, Liszt rarely played in public. But there were exceptions. On March 21, 1864, he descended from his hilltop retreat to take part in a charity concert for Peter's Pence. It was Passion Week, and Rome was filled to overflowing with higher clergy and pilgrims from all over the world. Pius IX himself had requested Liszt's presence at the "Sacred Academy," as it was called. Since Rome had no decent concert hall, the event took place in the unfinished New Building of the Praetorian Camp, near the Baths of Diocletian. Soldiers were on duty at the entrance, directing the guests to their seats, while a military band played popular operatic airs in the background. The bare brick arches of the interior were festooned for the occasion with flags, wreaths of flowers, and crosses. A large plaster-cast of the figure of Christ occupied one wall, and a Virgin Mary another. A hastily constructed "stage" supported a grand piano, around which were seated a number of cardinals and other high-ranking dignitaries wearing their mitres and their crimson and purple robes. As the hall filled up, people rushed to the front seats, the better to see the keyboard. A silence then fell across the gathering while the members of the Sistine Choir assembled beneath the figure of the Virgin and sang a motet of Palestrina. The Order of Service called for four sermons in four languages, which were delivered from a pulpit next to the keyboard; interspersed among them were four performances by Liszt. Because of the special nature of the occasion, he chose to play music with a religious flavour: the *Ave Maria* from his *Harmonies poétiques et réligieuses,* and his two transcriptions of numbers from Rossini's *Stabat Mater*—the aria "Cujus animam" and the chorus, "La Charité." The congregation applauded loudly after each of the sermons, but it was Liszt's playing which roused them to a pitch of enthusiasm rarely observed at such festivals. Sitting in the audience was a reporter from the American journal *Christian Inquirer,* who wrote:

> When I took music lessons in a little street at the west end of Boston, a picture of Liszt hung over the teacher's piano. It was the common picture. Liszt surrounded with distinguished musicians, enrapt in the melody which he plays, his head thrown back, hair flowing, and hands arched. He still resembles that picture. His long, gray, unparted hair, brushed straight back, swings about his smooth shaven face as he bends to the piano before him, like a heavy silk

fringe. His face is sharp and steadfast, lights up "e'en at the sounds
he himself has made," but not too full of amiable beauty. And his
playing! Add an exquisite touch, refinement of modulation, rapidity of execution, to the playing of the best pianists America ever
heard, and you begin to appreciate Liszt. Such diminuendos, such
melody! May I criticize? He lifts his hands unnecessarily high in the
air. He bows too often in a catch-courtesy way on taking his rest
and when he is rising. He has too much the air of a man playing before "the highest nobility" and depending upon their smile. These
are but parts of him, and do not affect the whole.[27]

At the end of the service Monsignor Nardi rose to give thanks on behalf of the
poor, and the benediction was pronounced. There was prolonged applause
when it was learned that the final sum raised was more than 4,000 scudi.[28]

This was a time of deepening connections between Liszt and the Church hierarchy. In mid-July 1864, Pius IX invited Liszt to join him at his summer
palace at Castel Gandolfo, where the pianist gave some command performances for the pontiff and his retinue.[29] Afterwards he travelled on to Albano
in the company of Gustav Hohenlohe, where he caught his first glimpse of the
old city whose canon he was later to become.[30] Although Liszt's circle was
dominated by clerics, they represented a wide cross-section of intellectual interests, and even included scientists. Not far from the Madonna del Rosario
was the famous observatory of the Jesuit College, whose chief astronomer was
Father Angelo Secchi. Liszt got to know Secchi, and in the summer of 1864 he

---

27. Reprinted in *Dwight's Musical Journal*, Saturday, May 28, 1864. For another press report see also
L'Osservatore Romano, March 23, 1864, in which we read: "The power of the music which was exercised upon all the pure hearts moved, enthused, and caused the audience to become ecstatic in the
harmonies that Professor Liszt extracted with the magisterial touch of his fingers from the piano."
Gregorovius reported that there was "tremendous applause in the Praetorian Camp. Liszt shows himself fanatically Catholic." (GRT, p. 263)

28. The following month the pontiff bestowed on Liszt the "Order of Pius IX, Third Class," in recognition of his services at this Peter's Pence concert. The diploma is dated April 15, 1864. (WA, Kasten
127, u. 2)

29. One of them occurred on July 30 and was reported in *Le Monde*, August 10, 1864:

> On Saturday, July 30, Pius IX, having granted an audience to Commander Liszt, wanted
> to hear him play some piano pieces. An instrument having been placed in the throne
> room, scarcely had the great artist begun preluding on one of his compositions, than the
> audience was plunged into silence and listened with rapture. After every piece the pope
> gave the signal for the applause; then he warmly complimented the Commander, who
> recommends himself as much by his Christian beliefs as by the marvels of his musical
> genius.

30. LLB, vol. 6, p. 26.

and a group of friends went over to the observatory to inspect the Jesuits' magnificent telescope.[31] Secchi pointed the instrument first towards Jupiter and then towards Saturn and its moons, while Liszt and his companions marvelled at the heavenly panorama before them.

VI

Liszt had now been in Italy for nearly three years, yet he had hardly ventured beyond a twenty-mile radius of Rome. This was a new situation for him, which he thoroughly relished. He had so far refused all invitations to travel abroad, but in the summer of 1864 it became clear that he would have difficulty in ignoring the growing clamour for his presence at the forthcoming meeting of the Tonkünstler-Versammlung, in Karlsruhe, of which organization he was the president. His letters to Brendel and Bülow indicate that he was at first hesitant to consider the journey, but by July 1 he had definitely made up his mind to attend.

On Thursday, August 11, Liszt boarded the steamship *Montebello*, in the company of his manservant Fortunato Salvagni, for the short sea voyage to Marseilles. Although the day was bright and sunny, the crossing was a rough one. The vessel was pitched and tossed about in heavy seas, and Liszt was seasick.[32] When it reached the entrance to the port, it had to remain outside the harbour, bobbing up and down for six hours, unable to dock. Only when he was safely in Marseilles did Liszt make a good-humoured reference to St. Francis and remark that "Brother Wind blew up a bit too much in praising the good God."[33] From Marseilles Liszt caught the early morning "stopping train" for Strasbourg, which stopped rather more than he had bargained for—four hours in Dijon, three hours in Belfort, and three hours in Mulhouse. While the other passengers fumed, Liszt passed the time by reading a cheap edition of *Manon Lescaut* which he picked up for fifty centimes at a little bookshop at Belfort Station. He got to Karlsruhe on Tuesday, August 16, only to find the festival arrangements in disarray. Brendel met him at the railway station and on their way to the hotel unfolded a litany of woes. Bülow, who should have directed the festival, had succumbed to "nervous fever" and was unable to appear. Hans von Bronsart and Ingeborg Starck, who had been engaged as soloists, both sent their regrets. Richard Pohl had decided not to commit himself at all at Karlsruhe, since he was heavily involved in the editing of the *Baden Gazette*. "This is how he understands his function of General Secretary of the

---

31. The visit took place on July 1, in the company of Bishop Haynald, Kurd von Schlözer, and Dr. F. Castano (SRB, pp. 105–06).
32. LLB, vol. 6, p. 28. Liszt was never a very good sailor. See Volume One, p. 109.
33. Ibid.

Musikverein!" grumbled Liszt.[34] Brendel himself remained loyal, however, and he had done wonders in holding the organization together. To replace the ailing Bülow, Max Seifriz was hurriedly brought in as festival director, while Alide Topp (a Bülow pupil) stood in for Ingeborg Starck. Liszt was delighted with her talent. "[She] is quite simply a marvel. Yesterday she played for me by heart my Sonata and the Mephisto Waltz in a way which enchanted me."[35] Ede Reményi, who had earlier been commended to Brendel by Liszt, turned up as planned, and his playing of the Hungarian Concerto by Joachim was one of the highlights of the occasion. As usual, Liszt's hotel room became a camp, with scores of visitors dropping in at all hours—Pauline Viardot-Garcia, Henry Chorley, Ivan Turgenev, Eduard Lassen, Alexander Serov, Carl Gille, Edmund Singer, Eduard Devrient, Bishop Haynald, and Agnès Street-Klindworth.[36] In the midst of these comings and goings Cosima arrived unexpectedly from Starnberg Lake, in Bavaria, with news of Hans. She had been under the vague impression that her father had stopped off at Saint-Tropez and Paris, where she had telegraphed him about Hans's illness. She knew that the main reason Liszt was in Germany was to see Bülow direct the Tonkünstler Festival. When she heard from a third party that her father was already in Karlsruhe, she travelled there post-haste. She had not seen him since the summer of 1861, and they had both changed. Did Liszt already sense the psychological strain to which her marriage to Hans had subjected her? If so, he had so far kept silent about it. But the sensational news that Cosima was about to impart to him concerning her private life would shake him to the core, and we shall shortly have to consider it in detail.

Although Liszt was not a "platform personality" at Karlsruhe, he was well represented as a composer. The opening concert featured his Thirteenth Psalm ("How long, O Lord?"), with Herr Brandes, a tenor in the Court Opera, as soloist. Three days later, his Sonata in B minor and "Mephisto" Waltz were played by Alide Topp. Then came a group of his songs in the chamber series—"Es muss ein Wunderbares sein," "In Liebeslust," and "Mignons Lied." At the final orchestral concert his symphonic poem *Festklänge* was performed, together with the orchestral version of the "Mephisto" Waltz. Liszt himself rehearsed the orchestra on the morning of the concert and magnetized the players with his conducting.[37] In fact, he emerged from the Karlsruhe festival

---

34. LLB, vol. 6, p. 34.
35. LLB, vol. 6, p. 35.
36. Agnès had travelled from Regensburg, where she had been looking after some business interests of her father's. On the question of her earlier liaison with Liszt, see Volume Two, pp. 209–24.
37. The festival ran from Sunday, August 21 to Friday, August 26. Most of the concerts took place in the Court Opera House—the large ones in the main auditorium, and the small ones in the theatre foyer. A series of detailed reports appeared in the *Neue Zeitschrift für Musik* for the issues of September 2, 9, 16, 23, and 30 and October 14, 1864.

to general critical acclaim. "It is almost the first time that such an accident has happened to me!" he remarked ironically.[38] Despite his reluctance to play the piano, he is known to have made at least one private appearance before friends—at a reception for Pauline Viardot-Garcia, at which he played his *St. Francis of Assisi preaching to the birds* and his first "Mephisto" Waltz.

After the festival Liszt travelled back with Cosima to Starnberg Lake in order to assess the seriousness of Bülow's illness for himself. He found that his irascible son-in-law had checked into the Bayerischer Hof Hotel in Munich, where he was in the grip of a black depression, confined to his bed, and showing some alarming side-symptoms. For about a week there had been a "floating paralysis" in both legs, which now had moved up into the left arm and was causing him pain. He had been treated by one Dr. Wolfsteiner, the royal physician, who diagnosed his condition, somewhat unhelpfully, as "nervous." Bülow, the worst of patients, suffered most from his enforced inactivity. As Liszt observed: "To endure things patiently is to some natures an absolute impossibility."[39] Although Bülow was incapable of crossing the room, much less of venturing out of doors, he was already insisting on returning to Berlin, whose air, he stubbornly maintained, was better for him than that of any of the spas of Bavaria.

Why were the Bülows in Bavaria at all? They were there at the express invitation of King Ludwig II, who, on Wagner's advice, was about to appoint Bülow his court pianist at an annual salary of 2,000 florins. Ever since the dramatic turnaround in Wagner's fortunes earlier in the year, he had been angling to have the couple brought to Munich. He considered Hans to be absolutely indispensable to his cause, for there were already plans to mount a number of Wagner operas in the court theatre, and Bülow's intimate knowledge of the scores would be of vital assistance when they went into rehearsal. Thus it had come about that the Bülows came to Bavaria as Wagner's guests so that negotiations might proceed more quickly. It was a difficult decision for Hans, who was well established in Berlin. Moreover, the King of Prussia was already putting out discreet feelers to see how much it would cost to keep him there.[40] As for Bülow, it was the state of anguished indecision into which all this had plunged him that had brought on his latest "migraine mood." What nobody knew at the time was that Wagner and Cosima were in love. They had first declared their feelings for one another the previous year,[41] and Wagner was de-

---

38. LLB, vol. 6, p. 37.

39. LLB, vol. 2, p. 75.

40. LLB, vol. 6, p. 40. An appointment was made for Bülow to meet Count Redern, the king's envoy in Munich, but at the last moment Bülow cancelled it. Wagner had already shown him King Ludwig's letter in which the monarch had said: "Tell my dear Bülow how much I have grown to love him in so short a time" (LLB, vol. 6, p. 40). No Prussian king would have addressed him so warmly. The invitation to Munich was irresistible.

41. WML, p. 876. See also p. 73, n. 43.

termined to have her by his side. This act of duplicity, when it became generally known, strained his relations with the king, with Bülow, and of course with Liszt himself, and it was to create a scandal within the Bavarian court.

In order to understand the growing turmoil within the Liszt-Bülow-Wagner circle, the events leading up to the arrival of the Bülows at Starnberg Lake have to be placed in sharper perspective. Ever since Wagner's political exile had ended, in the summer of 1861, his career had lacked direction. Although he was now free to enter Germany, he had no regular means of support, and his debts had steadily mounted. At the same time, his relationship with his wife, Minna, had declined to the point where it had become both abusive and violent and could not go on, and in November 1862 they had finally agreed to separate. From this point Wagner regarded himself as abandoned and homeless. The year 1863 was one of the worst in his life. He was obliged to take on a number of freelance conducting engagements (in such far-flung cities as Prague, St. Petersburg, Moscow, and Breslau) to help stave off his creditors. All creative work was temporarily abandoned, which depressed him still further. What he needed was a hearth and a home to protect him from what he perceived to be the rigors of an increasingly hostile world. He sought consolation in the arms of a number of women,[42] and especially those of a Viennese lady named Mathilde Maier, whom he begged to become his housekeeper. Mathilde, who was twenty years his junior, refused. He then held out the prospect of marriage to her, once he was legally freed of the ties that still bound him to Minna.

This was the state of affairs with Wagner when he was re-united with the Bülows in Berlin in November 1863, in a deeply troubled frame of mind. He had long admired Cosima and suspected that she was unhappily married. He began to pay court to her, without any clear notion of where it might lead. She for her part was vulnerable, and during this visit their feelings came boiling to the surface. There was an emotional scene in which the pair had declared their love for one another.[43] This secret lay locked in their hearts for eight months. Meanwhile, Wagner's financial situation grew rapidly worse. He had been forced to flee his Viennese creditors and seek refuge in Switzerland. From this

---

42. Among those towards whom Wagner was amorously inclined at this time were Stephanie Mauro (referred to as "Puppe" in his letters), Friederike Mayer, Henriette von Bissing, and of course, a love of longer standing, Mathilde Wesendonck.

43. According to the account Wagner later gave to the world in *Mein Leben,* their declaration of love took place on the afternoon of November 28, 1863. The pair had gone for a drive while Bülow was professionally occupied. "We gazed speechless into each other's eyes; an intense longing for avowal of the truth mastered us, and led to a confession—which needed no words—of the boundless unhappiness which oppressed us. With tears and sobs we sealed our confession to belong to each other alone. . . ." (ML, p. 876) The last sentence was deleted from earlier editions of *Mein Leben.*

temporary sanctuary he wrote to Cornelius in April 1864 that it would need a miracle to save him, "otherwise I am done for!" As we know, that miracle occurred the following month when he was contacted by Ludwig II of Bavaria, brought to Munich, and relieved of all his financial cares. Shortly afterwards, Wagner had moved into the Villa Pellet, a sumptuous home on the edge of Starnberg Lake, which King Ludwig had placed at his disposal; but he quickly realized that so large an establishment would require a female hand to help him run it. Once again he wrote to Mathilde Maier and proposed a *ménage à deux*, a letter he soon had cause to regret having sent. For Bülow now responded to Wagner's invitation to come to Bavaria by sending Cosima ahead of him to help Wagner with his domestic arrangements. She arrived at Starnberg Lake with their two small daughters, Daniela and Blandine, on June 29, 1864; Bülow himself did not get there until July 7. During that period Wagner and Cosima became lovers; their first child, Isolde, was born on April 10, 1865. Mathilde Maier must have been very confused to receive a further letter from Wagner, written on the day of Cosima's arrival, which told her: "Of any change in our mutual status there can for the present be *no* question."[44] Did Bülow know in 1864 just how matters really stood between Wagner and Cosima? The question has often been asked, but it cannot be answered with certainty; we believe that he suspected enough to make him physically and mentally ill. Once he threw a violent tantrum when he discovered that Cosima was in Wagner's bedroom, the door locked. That was during the first week of August. Bülow left Starnberg in a fury and checked into the Bayerischer Hof Hotel in Munich, while Cosima journeyed to Karlsruhe to meet her father and "explain" Hans's absence from the Tonkünstler Festival. And that was not all she explained. From an entry in Wagner's "Brown Book" we gather that Cosima told Liszt that her marriage to Hans was threatened and that she was in the middle of an affair with Wagner.[45] It was this news, more than anything else, that prompted Liszt to travel back to Starnberg with her to try to help Hans and his daughter patch things up.

Liszt had not expected to see Wagner at Starnberg, and would have preferred to avoid him. It was August 25 when he and Cosima got there, King Ludwig's nineteenth birthday. Wagner had gone to pay homage to the young monarch, who was with his family at Hohenschwangau.[46] Late that evening, however, Wagner unexpectedly returned to the Villa Pellet. There was a reunion between the two musicians, tempered on both sides by the magnitude of the problems which now faced them. The next day, Liszt and Wagner trav-

44. RWBB, p. 35.
45. RWBB, p. 65.
46. Wagner had taken with him the score of his newly composed *Huldigungsmarsch* as a birthday gift. The piece was first performed in Munich on October 5.

elled to Munich, where they spent many hours in conversation. We know that Liszt seized the occasion to admonish Wagner in the severest way for his treatment of Hans and Cosima. He warned Wagner that no good would come of it, and he threatened to hold his friend in contempt if he persisted.[47] If Liszt thought that a reproof was all that was needed, he was gravely mistaken. In any case, there were more pleasant matters to discuss. For the first time, Liszt learned of the full extent of King Ludwig's benefaction, and of the untold power and wealth that Wagner was now able to muster in the service of his artistic ambitions. He showed Liszt a number of Ludwig's letters to him, which left no doubt in Liszt's mind as to the sincerity of the king's intentions. "Solomon was wrong," exclaimed Liszt. "There *is* something new under the sun!"[48] He could not help noticing how success had softened some of the asperities in Wagner's character.[49] Wagner played to Liszt parts of his new opera-in-progress, *Die Meistersinger*, which Liszt, even on such a fleeting encounter, unhesitatingly described as "a masterpiece of humour, wit, and lively grace."[50] Liszt then reciprocated by playing to Wagner his Beatitudes, about which Wagner "seemed more than pleased."[51] This cosy scene was deceptive, however, and Liszt misled himself very badly when he observed that nothing had basically changed between them.[52] Everything had changed, in fact. Hans was in turmoil, Cosima was pregnant with Wagner's child, and Wagner himself was supremely indifferent to Liszt's warning advice. Liszt was too shrewd a man of the world not to know that some further action was required on his side, and he did his best to break up the relationship between Cosima and Wagner. During the weeks that followed, as we shall see, Cosima spent much time in her fa-

47. This knowledge comes to us from Wagner's "Brown Book," which was only published in 1975. Wagner implies that Liszt warned him he would be courting disaster if he persisted in trying to win Cosima's affections. "In the end your father's right—he told me a year ago of course 'it would turn out like this—he would treat me with contempt!' " (RWBB, p. 64). Although this entry dates from September 1865, the context makes it abundantly plain that the conversation between Liszt and Wagner could only have taken place during their talks in Munich.

48. LLB, vol. 6, p. 36.

49. LLB, vol. 6, p. 40. There is one other matter that requires attention while we are dealing with the "benign" Wagner whom Liszt observed during their conversations in Munich. We may scan the programmes of the recent Tonkünstler-Versammlung in Karlsruhe in vain for any mention of a single work of Wagner. Far from being due to some unaccountable neglect on the part of the organizers, it was the deliberate choice of Wagner himself, and it could only be interpreted as a snub. Now that he enjoyed royal patronage, it seems that Wagner felt that he no longer needed the support of the Tonkünstler-Versammlung, many of whose members had done so much to sustain him during his long exile, and he simply decided to cut them adrift. The timing makes no other conclusion possible. Within two or three weeks of Wagner's historic encounter with King Ludwig, he had started to develop an attitude of sublime indifference towards those friends and colleagues whose loyal support he could now so easily have repaid. As early as June 1864, and with less than two months to go before the start of the festival, it had become transparently obvious to poor Brendel that Wagner no longer wished to be associated with the Versammlung. In the flurry of correspondence exchanged between Liszt and Brendel immediately prior to the festival, the latter had already expressed his anxieties, to which Liszt replied from Rome: "If [Wagner] definitely refuses to attend the Tonkünstler-

ther's company—travelling with him to such places as Weimar, Berlin, Paris, and Saint-Tropez—part of a deliberate ploy to keep her away from Wagner, and one which Liszt would repeat the following year.[53] Her physical condition must have been a daily reminder of the terrible dilemma she now faced as a result of her unfaithfulness to Bülow. To tell her father or not to tell him? In the event she kept silent, and Liszt never knew for sure that his granddaughter Isolde was Wagner's child, although he later came to believe that she was.[54]

These, then, were the circumstances surrounding the Bülows' visit to Bavaria. By early September, Bülow had the fixed notion that only the "Roman baths" in Berlin would enable him to complete his cure. On Saturday evening, September 3, Cosima somehow got him to the Munich railway station. There he cursed the world in general and his doctor in particular while waiting for the train. Wagner saw them off. The fate of all three of them was now sealed. Bülow was bound to Wagner, Wagner was bound to Cosima, and Cosima—she was for the moment bound to both of them, and when the choice had to be made, she was torn asunder.

VII

Liszt's trip to Germany came to an emotional climax with his brief return to Weimar and the Altenburg early in September. He arrived at Weimar's railway

---

Versammlung all we can do is to obtain his consent to give the extracts . . . from his *Meistersinger* and other of his works (together with the scores and voice parts). In my opinion these pieces are indispensable for the principal day of the Karlsruhe programme. It would be best if Bülow alone brought the matter to the desired issue. It seems to me impossible that Wagner could give him and all of us the pain of an absolute refusal!" (LLB, vol. 2, p. 71) But give such pain Wagner did. By now he appeared to be so drunk with elation at having netted a reigning monarch for his cause that he was anaesthetized to the finer feelings of those around him.

50. LLB, vol. 6, p. 41.

51. Ibid.

52. Ibid.

53. See pp. 91–92.

54. Bülow officially carried the honour of paternity until the Bayreuth Landesgericht ruled on the succession case in June 1914. Isolde herself asked the court to rule that she was Wagner's child, since the Wagner family was at that moment in the middle of a dispute concerning the disposition of his artistic legacy. This was a particularly painful trial, in which a great deal of family linen was washed in public. (Among other things, Isolde was driven by the desire not to have her son, born in 1901, excluded from the Bayreuth succession—a situation precipitated by the marriage of her sister, Eva, to the conspiring Houston Stewart Chamberlain.) In her deposition Cosima testified that between June and October 1864 she had sexual relations only with Wagner. But her testimony was weakened when Wagner's housekeeper at the Villa Pellet, the then-ancient Anna Mrazéck, testified that Cosima shared Hans's bedroom. To the court it seemed most likely that Cosima slept with both men at this time, and it was unable to rule in Isolde's favour. One "outsider" who knew how matters stood, however, was Claire de Charnacé, Cosima's half-sister. In her unpublished diary Claire noted that while "Cosima never confessed anything to me, looking at the dates I know that a monstrous

station about midnight on the evening of September 3. Since the only carriage waiting in the street outside was almost full, Liszt insisted that his servant Fortunato occupy the last remaining seat while he himself trudged two miles through the dark, deserted streets on foot. "What ghosts did I not meet!" he exclaimed, and was reminded of Schubert's "Der Doppelgänger."[55] When he got to the Altenburg, the maid, Augusta, let him in.[56] As he walked through the rooms he was overcome by memories; at 3:00 a.m. he was still in the Blue Room, the place of so many of his earlier creative endeavours. In the morning he asked Augusta for the key to Carolyne's room. Everything had remained unchanged, except that her bed had been dismantled in order to get rid of the mice which had taken up residence inside the mattress.[57] In its place hung Scheffer's *The Three Magi* and a portrait of Princess Marie. "This room has become my chapel," Liszt wrote to Carolyne, "and no one goes in there during my stay!"[58]

Liszt had returned to the Altenburg not out of sentimental reasons, but because there was a distinct possibility that the court might rent one of the upper floors to a new tenant, and certain rooms had to be emptied. The place housed a small fortune in terms of its furnishings and paintings, and the manuscripts that Liszt had temporarily stored there were priceless. Fortunato spent much of the time helping Augusta to pack and bring things down to the lower floors; particular objects were set aside for Liszt to transport back to Carolyne.[59] Most important of all, perhaps, Liszt was in Weimar because he wanted to see Carl Alexander, but he only now learned that the grand duke had been detained on business in Ostend. Meanwhile, Liszt tried to remain incognito. He had no intention of shackling himself with the chains of his former life. The only people he saw during the first two days were Eduard Grosse, Count Beust (to whom Carolyne was directly responsible for the running of the Altenburg), and Father Anton Hohmann, the parish priest. With the best will in the world it was impossible to keep his visit secret, and word spread that he was back. He showed himself at the Court Theatre, where his old rival Dingelstedt kindly placed the

---

seduction took place. . . . Since Bülow was unable to leave [Berlin] immediately, Cosima went on ahead of him and went to talk to Wagner in a hotel. Nine months later to the day, Isolde was born! During that time Cosima calmly organized in Munich a life as a threesome. Bülow never recognized Isolde as his child. . . ." This last point was true only later, when Wagner's features had impressed themselves on the young girl's face. (VA, F859, carton 11) Isolde was known by the surname Bülow until the time of her marriage, and Hans left her a legacy in his will.

55. LLB, vol. 6, p. 43.

56. Augusta Pickel had accompanied Carolyne to Rome in May 1860. When it became evident that the princess's stay in the Eternal City was to be a long one, Augusta returned to Weimar on June 2, 1862, in order to get married. Subsequently she lived in the Altenburg as a caretaker. (See RL, pp. 241–42, and RLKM, vol. 3, p. 439, n. 2.)

57. LLB, vol. 6, p. 42.

58. Ibid.

59. LLB, vol. 6, p. 58.

Franz Liszt, a rare photograph from circa 1864.

intendant's box at his disposal. The play was Schiller's *Wallenstein's Camp,* a production that had been put on at the express command of the grand duke: the
Prussian army manoeuvres were in full swing, and the audience consisted
mainly of soldiers from the Weimar regiment. Dingelstedt was very friendly
towards Liszt, and he convened a special gathering of the Neu–Weimar–Verein
for a supper party in Liszt's honour.[60] Liszt could not help observing that Dingelstedt was now in his (Liszt's) former position of having to squabble endlessly
over the day-to-day running of the theatre; he was currently embroiled in a violent argument with Carl Gutzkow, the chairman of the Schiller *Stiftung,* and
the two men had almost come to blows. "I was thinking to myself yesterday,"
mused Liszt, "that there are towns which perform the opposite function to that
of orthopedic institutions. They make bent that which is straight!"[61] One unfortunate consequence of his higher profile in the town was that he attracted
the attention of a group of local merchants who issued a summons against him
for unpaid debts. Liszt dismissed them as "arrogant," but the matter was serious
enough for him to consult a lawyer, Dr. Keil;[62] although the case was never
brought to court, it served to remind him of what a provincial city Weimar was.
It was a diversion for him to have Cosima visit him once more from Berlin.
They usually dined alone in the Altenburg every evening, although close friends
and colleagues sometimes dropped by to see them—Friedrich Preller, Hoffman
von Fallersleben, Carl Gille, and Franz Carl Götze, to the last of whom he entrusted the full score of his oratorio *St. Elisabeth* for copying. One of his happi-
est encounters was with Alexander Gottschalg, with whom he had a long
working session on the organ of the Herder Church, after which he drove his
"legendary cantor" all the way back to Tiefurt in a carriage.[63]

The grand duke's continued absence from Weimar extended Liszt's own stay
in Germany and gave Cosima the opportunity to take her father back to Berlin
for a brief visit. In the Bülow household the big talking-point was Ludwig II's
recent offer to bring Hans to Munich. It was while Liszt was their house-guest,
in fact, that Hans "wrote an extremely brilliant letter," as Liszt put it,[64] in
which he accepted the title of *Vorspieler seiner Majestät.* Liszt could never stay

---

60. LLB, vol. 6, p. 47.
61. Ibid.
62. LLB, vol. 6, p. 54.
63. LLB, vol. 6, p. 49. According to a report in the *Neue Zeitschrift,* this session took place on September 10 and its purpose was to familiarize Gottschalg with some of Liszt's newer organ compositions. Liszt himself also played the instrument—presumably to demonstrate some of the registrations.
64. LLB, vol. 6, p. 52. The King's formal offer was contained in a letter from State Minister Franz von
Pfistermeister, dated September 12, 1864, and reproduced in BB, vol. 4, pp. 598–99. Bülow made fun
of the title *Vorspieler des Königs* and disparaged himself as "ein zur Disposition gestellter Pianist"—a
beck-and-call pianist.

with the Bülows and not be reminded of Daniel's death there five years earlier. Together he and Cosima travelled out to the Catholic cemetery and knelt
by Daniel's tomb.[65] It was the last time that Liszt was known to have visited the
grave.

On September 28 Liszt journeyed to Wilhelmsthal, where he had his long-
awaited interview with Carl Alexander. The substance of their conversation
has never been recorded, but we know from circumstantial evidence that they
discussed Liszt's cancelled wedding and his plans for the future. The grand duke
listened patiently as Liszt recounted the events that had transpired immediately
after his arrival in Rome, in October 1861. He then reminded Liszt that he had
written several times to Antonelli, and Liszt thanked him for this token of
friendship. During the course of their chat Liszt pointed out to Carl Alexander something about which, so he said, he had so far spoken to no one, and the
burden of which was this: he and the princess had released one another from
whatever obligations they might once have felt to get married.[66] The grand
duke seemed somewhat taken aback, and went on to talk about a rank and a
residence for Liszt should he ever decide to return to Weimar. At this point,
Liszt remarked that everything he desired by way of rank was in his inkwell,
and his inkwell could not be better placed than in the Madonna del Rosario.[67]
Five more years would elapse before Liszt felt that the time was ripe for him
to reside once more in Weimar, and even then it would only be on an occasional basis. The German atmosphere oppressed him, he said, and for the time
being he knew that he could live nowhere else but in Italy.

VIII

One more journey faced Liszt before he could return to his beloved Monte
Mario. He had promised his mother that he would come to Paris, and he was
now eagerly awaited at 29, rue Saint Guillaume, where a room had been set
aside for him. On October 3 he set out from Wilhelmsthal and travelled to
Eisenach,[68] where he was joined by Cosima and Eduard Lassen, the latter of
whom had travelled from Weimar especially to say goodbye to him. The three
of them spent the day touring the Wartburg: it was Cosima's first visit to this

---

65. Ibid.
66. LLB, vol. 6, p. 55.
67. Ibid.
68. LLB, vol. 6, p. 59. It is an indication of the friendly relations that obtained between Liszt and Carl
Alexander that the grand duke accompanied his erstwhile Kapellmeister on the train for several miles
and then got out at a small way-station—the Hohe Sonne—to join his followers on a hunt. Cosima's
decision to meet Liszt at Eisenach and accompany him to Paris was prompted in part by the fact that
she was now alone in Berlin, Hans having left for Munich, and his new job, the previous day.

historic site. From Eisenach, Liszt and Cosima journeyed overnight to Paris, arriving at 5:00 a.m. That same day they lunched with Anna at her bedside; it was the first such family reunion in years. Liszt found his mother "in perfect health, and [she] holds firm ideas on many matters which she spices up with charming good humour, not lacking in a certain sweet malice."[69] Liszt was being somewhat euphemistic. His mother was bed-ridden, and however alert she was mentally, her physical prognosis was bleak. He talked about her future with Monsignor Bucquet, the family's confessor. It seems that there may have been a plan to move Anna to a place where she might receive constant care (since Blandine's death, Anna was often left alone when Ollivier was out of town), and Monsignor Bucquet was considered to be the best person to pursue this delicate matter, which everyone knew the old lady was sure to resist.[70] In the event the idea went nowhere, and Anna died in Ollivier's home eighteen months later. The present occasion was the last on which Liszt saw his mother alive.

Liszt and Cosima departed the City of Light on October 12. They travelled via Toulon and Saint-Tropez and got to La Moutte on October 15, where Ollivier was expecting them.[71] The three of them went to the graveside of Blandine, and for the second time in less than a month Liszt found himself kneeling by the tomb of one of his dead children. The experience penetrated his soul and made him ponder afresh the meaning of his own life. A few hours later, he was on his way to Marseilles, where he took ship for Italy, while Cosima went back to Germany.

Liszt spent October 22, his fifty-third birthday, in his cell at the Madonna del Rosario, where he was visited by a number of his friends and some Franciscan and Dominican monks.[72] As he gazed around the room at his work-desk, his pianino, his wooden bed, and then beyond to the glorious vista of the Roman Campagna, he knew that he had no need of anything beyond these simple confines. He had come back home.

---

69. LLB, vol. 6, p. 59.

70. LLB, vol. 6, pp. 62–63. In this connection see also the letter that Ollivier wrote to Princess Carolyne on July 10, 1863, in which he tells her: "I really regret having abandoned [Mme Liszt], but my brother will replace me at her side, and after my brother my maid, who is extremely intelligent, will watch over her. Some of my friends have also promised me to visit her regularly." (TOS-W, p. 49)

71. OJ, vol. 2, p. 159.

72. SLG, pp. 16–17. Even Princess Carolyne trekked up the Monte Mario from her rooms in Via Babuino to deliver her birthday greetings in person. On October 23 Liszt wrote to her: "This room is still perfumed by your presence yesterday." (LLB, vol. 6, p. 63)

BOOK TWO

The Abbé Liszt
1865 · 1869

Liszt Enters the Lower Orders, 1865

When the monk is already formed within, why not appropriate the outer garment of one?

FRANZ LISZT[1]

I

It was in the peaceful surroundings of the Madonna del Rosario that Liszt prepared himself for one of the gravest decisions of his life, that of entering the lower orders of the priesthood. To the outside world this decision has always represented a paradox. Here was a supreme man of the world who had rubbed shoulders with kings and princes; for much of his life he had commanded power and luxury; he had only to open a piano and audiences swooned; he had enjoyed the favours of beautiful women, and his illicit union with Marie d'Agoult had produced three children. How could such a man take holy orders? Predictably, Liszt was accused of lack of sincerity. His detractors, doubtless recalling his clanking medals, the Sword of Honour, and the Lola Montez episode, took it to be a superb *coup de théâtre* by a master showman. The charge will hardly bear scrutiny, however. Liszt had pondered his decision for a long time. As he himself put it, it harmonized with all the antecedents of his youth. Indeed, in his will he had confessed that he had always felt the Church to be his true vocation "from the age of seventeen when, with tears and supplications, I begged to be permitted to enter the seminary in Paris, and I hoped that it would be given to me to live the life of the saints and perhaps die the death of the martyrs."[2] To re-phrase our earlier question: How could such a man *not* take holy orders?

---

1. LLB, vol. 2, p. 81.
2. LLB, vol. 5, p. 52.

Before donning the cassock Liszt made a "farewell" appearance in the Palazzo Barberini, on April 20. Gregorovius, who was there, wrote in his journal:

> [Liszt] played [Weber's] *Invitation to the Dance* and [Schubert's] "Erl-könig"—a curious farewell to the world. No one suspected that he had the abbé's stockings already in his pocket. . . . He now wears the abbé's frock, lives in the Vatican, and, as Schlözer told me yesterday, looks well and contented. This is the end of a gifted virtuoso, a truly sovereign personality. Am glad that I heard him play again; he and the instrument seem to be one, as it were, a piano-centaur.[3]

The next day Liszt left the Madonna del Rosario and went to stay for a short time in the Lazarite monastery in Rome, in order to prepare himself spiritually for his entry into the lower clergy.

II

Liszt entered the ecclesiastical state on April 25, 1865, when he received the tonsure in the private chapel of Monsignor Gustav Hohenlohe. Only three people knew in advance of his decision: Pope Pius IX, Princess Carolyne, and Gustav Hohenlohe himself, who performed the ceremony. A motley assortment of individuals had been brought along to witness the rite. They included Liszt's confessor, Father Ferrari; his valet, Fortunato Salvagni; two priests from Hohenlohe's entourage, Monsignor Corazzo and Don Marcello; and Hohenlohe's houseman Antonio.[4] That evening Liszt was granted a brief audience by the pope. At the end "the Holy Father gave me his blessing *in extenso,*" wrote Liszt.[5] Two days later, he broke the news to his mother, who wept when she read it.

---

3. GRT, pp. 298–99. Gregorovius wrote this journal entry on April 30, nine days after Liszt's concert. It is evident that he had no idea at the time of the concert that Liszt had arranged to enter the clergy four days later. His description of this concert as a "farewell" was something that only dawned on him later, and it proved to be wrong. Nonetheless, it was widely felt at the time that Liszt had turned his back on the world. There is a very long description of this concert in *Dwight's Journal of Music* (June 10, 1865, p. 44), which bears the title "The Last of Liszt," and which begins with the announcement that "the greatest artistic celebrity of modern times has at last taken his farewell of the world which, after all, has not treated him so badly. . . . Franz Liszt, though living still, is dead to us." All this is yet one more confirmation of the fact that the world at large consistently misrepresented Liszt's actions. Far from withdrawing from the world, and especially the musical world, Liszt, by his subsequent behaviour, proved that he always remained an important part of it.

4. LLB, vol. 6, p. 70.

5. LLB, vol. 6, p. 74. This was probably the starting-point for a story, first put out by William Wallace with absolutely no authority, that the pope had heard Liszt's confession, and that it had gone on for five hours. Eventually, so the tale continued, the Holy Father cried out, "Basta, caro Liszt! Go and tell the rest of your sins to the piano!" (WLWP, p. 104) Such fiction was readily accepted as fact by a world

"My dear child," Anna replied, "people often talk of things at such great length that they finally happen, and so it is with your present change of status. There have been frequent reports in the newpapers here that you had chosen clerical status, but I have vigorously contradicted them whenever they were mentioned. And so your letter of April 27,[6] which I received yesterday, upset me deeply, and I burst into tears. Forgive me, but I really was not prepared for such news from you."[7]

After reflecting on his decision ("the night brings counsel"), Anna bowed to what she called the will of God. And she told him: "If the blessing of a feeble old mother can achieve aught with the Almighty, then I bless you a thousand times."

Shortly afterwards Liszt gave a fuller account of the event to Prince Constantin von Hohenzollern-Hechingen, which is one of the most detailed to come down to us.

> Convinced as I was that this act would strengthen me in the right road, I accomplished it without effort, in all simplicity and uprightness of intention. Moreover, it agrees with all the antecedents of my youth, as well as with the development that my work of musical composition has taken during these last four years—a work which I propose to pursue with fresh vigour, as I consider it the least defective form of my nature.
>
> To speak familiarly, if "the cloak does not make the monk," it also does not prevent him from being one; and, in certain cases, when the monk is already formed within, why not appropriate the outer garment of one?
>
> But I am forgetting that I do not in the least intend to become a monk, in the severe sense of the word. For this I have no vocation, and it is enough for me to belong to the hierarchy of the church to such a degree as the minor orders allow me to do. It is therefore not the frock but the cassock that I have donned. And on this subject

which hungered for gossip about the great pianist. The reality was far less interesting. Nineteenth-century popes never heard confession, and Liszt himself tells us that the interview lasted "about ten minutes." (LLB, vol. 6, p. 74)

6. VFL, pp. 137–39. In this letter, dated April 27, 1865, Liszt told his mother that he had been admitted to the minor orders. It has often been pointed out that this was not so, that Liszt had merely received the tonsure. In fact, he was not admitted to the minor orders until July 30, more than three months later. How to account for the anomaly? We surmise that Liszt had already taken the decision to proceed, and that he was presenting his mother with a *fait accompli* in order to forestall some later resistance to the idea on her part. It has to be recalled that twice in his life he had tried to enter a seminary, only to be deflected from this path. (See Volume One, pp. 117, 132.)

7. LLB, vol. 6, p. 78.

> Your Highness will pardon me the small vanity of mentioning to
> you that they pay me the compliment of saying that I wear my cas-
> sock as though I had worn it all my life.[8]

Even those close to Liszt were bewildered by his decision. Emile Ollivier called
it "a spiritual suicide,"[9] while Wagner wondered what sins could possibly be so
great that only Liszt's entry into holy orders would wash them away.[10] As for
the outside world, the unexpected transitions in Liszt's life had always been a
source of gossip. August Ambros, one of the most distinguished musicologists of
the time, who had met Liszt on a number of occasions, took it upon himself to
point out that "the whole cultural world" was stunned by Liszt's seemingly
abrupt decision. The world was used to the sudden transitions in Liszt's music,
Ambros observed. But when the papers announced this latest *volte face,* everybody was caught by surprise. The man who had provoked so much "Lisztola-
trie" during his life had now bowed his head to the tonsure![11] Actually, the
tonsure placed Liszt under no obligation to proceed any further in his spiritual
odyssey. Nonetheless, on July 30 he entered the four minor orders of the priesthood—doorkeeper, lector, exorcist, and acolyte. Once again, Gustav Hohenlohe
officiated at the ceremony, this time in his private chapel at Tivoli.[12] The limited extent to which Liszt had committed himself to the Church should be
clearly understood. Although he was now able to use the title "Abbé," he could
not celebrate mass, nor could he hear confession. He undertook no vows of
celibacy, was free to marry, and was able at any time to retract. And he always
made it clear that he had no desire to become a monk "in the severe sense of
the word."[13] Nevertheless, there is evidence that he was at first actively interested in pursuing the subdiaconate—the next order in the sequence of steps towards the priesthood—and for a few months he entered a fairly intensive study
of theology towards that end. He eventually abandoned the idea, for it would
have imposed obligations on him that he was not prepared to fulfil, and, as he
himself pointed out, it would have robbed him of leisure for composition,
which daily became more precious to him.

---

8. LLB, vol. 2, p. 81.
9. OJ, vol. 2, pp. 188–89.
10. RWBB, p. 65.
11. ABB, p. 53.
12. The Liszt literature generally makes no mention of the second ceremony, on July 30, but it was by
far the more important. Liszt spent the three months separating the two dates in studying for the four
minor orders. His examination on July 30 was conducted by Monsignor Audisio, who received special
permission to do it in one session instead of the customary two. A record of both ceremonies is preserved in the Vicariato di Roma, *Liber Ordinationum, 1863–1872,* pp. 114 and 131. See Appendix II, where
these documents are reproduced in full.
13. After the four minor orders come the three major ones: the subdiaconate, the diaconate, and the
priesthood. Incidentally, the major orders, unlike the minor ones, are regarded as part of the sacrament,
and they involve vows of celibacy. Seminarians entering the last two orders must be ordained by a bishop.

The fact that it was Gustav Hohenlohe who performed the ceremony served to strengthen the "conspiracy theory" to which his meddling in Liszt's marriage plans had earlier given rise.[14] What better way to keep Liszt and Carolyne apart, so the argument ran, than to have Liszt enter the priesthood? And who better to seduce Liszt into the arms of the Church than Hohenlohe, who by now had got to know the musician very well? In light of Hohenlohe's past behaviour, he and his family certainly had a vested interest in the outcome. (We know that he was against Carolyne's re-marriage, not only to Liszt but to anyone.) Yet in this instance, Hohenlohe appears to carry no blame. It was Liszt himself who desired to don the cassock, and he was under no outside pressure from anyone to do so. The conspiracy theory is further weakened when we consider the warm friendship that had developed between Liszt and Hohenlohe, based on mutual respect and admiration. To claim that Liszt had become Hohenlohe's victim is to fly in the face of the facts, to say nothing of Liszt's long attachment to the Church itself, an attachment which had begun in his childhood. The child had simply become father to the man.[15]

III

Altogether Liszt lived in Hohenlohe's private apartments in the Vatican for a period of fourteen months—from mid-April 1865 to June 1866. He did not suffer any of the privations usually associated with a seminary, as he himself was the first to admit. In fact, his quarters were sumptuously furnished. They were on the same floor as Raphael's *stanze,* whose famous walls were decorated with this artist's murals. Liszt had a wonderful view of St. Peter's Square; from his windows he often observed the religious processions file past on their way into St. Peter's. His daily routine was simple. He arose at dawn and sometimes assisted Hohenlohe as a sacristan in the celebration of early-morning mass. Then he would set aside an hour or two for the study of theology under a private tutor especially assigned to him for this purpose, Father Antonio Solfanelli from the faculty of St. Peter's Seminary. He also devoted a part of each day to the reading of Italian and Latin religious texts. Nor did he neglect his composing. This was the period in which he wrote his Missa Choralis, which he dedicated to Pope Pius IX. The Vatican was also the unusual setting in which he checked the proofs of his piano transcriptions of the Beethoven symphonies. A far more unlikely work was also completed within the Vatican walls: his piano "Illustrations" of Meyerbeer's *L'Africaine.*

---

14. See Volume Two, p. 516n.
15. Liszt himself confirmed this. Twelve years to the day on which he had taken holy orders he wrote: "The feelings which led me [into the ecclesiastical state] have never dried up. They date from my childhood years, and from my first communion in a little village church." (Letter dated April 25, 1877, LLB, vol. 7, p. 188)

Pius IX took a keen interest in Liszt's presence in the Vatican, and it was in-evitable that the music-loving pontiff would call on the services of the famous pianist. An occasion arose on June 21, the twentieth anniversary of the pope's coronation. Hohenlohe was asked if Liszt would consent to mark the event by giving a recital. Liszt readily agreed and had his piano transferred to the pope's private library. It was probably the first time that a piano recital had been given in these august surroundings, especially by an artist dressed in a clerical habit. After Liszt had regaled the pope and his entourage with his playing, Pius IX approached him and complimented him on his attractive appearance.[16]

Liszt became a familiar figure in Rome, walking through the cobbled streets of the old city with his long grey hair streaming in the wind and his abbé's soutane fluttering behind him. Gregorovius, who spotted him getting out of a hackney carriage, described him unforgettably as "Mephistopheles disguised as an abbé. Such is the end of Lovelace!"[17]

I V

Just a few days after he took holy orders, Liszt set out for Hungary in order to conduct the first performance of his oratorio *St. Elisabeth.* This was in fulfill-ment of a long-standing invitation to attend a festival celebrating the twenty-fifth anniversary, on August 15, of the founding of the Pest Conservatory of Music (which Liszt had helped to establish in 1840). He travelled from Italy by rail, and arrived in Buda's new South Railway Station on August 8. It was the first time that he had travelled to his native land by train.

During his stay in the Hungarian capital Liszt lived with Father Mihály Schwendtner. Schwendtner had been a chaplain in the Hungarian army during the War of Independence and had later been imprisoned by the Austrians. After his pardon he had become the officiating priest at the Pest Parish Church, over-looking the Danube River, where he was looked after by his niece, Fräulein Resi. He and Liszt became fast friends, and Liszt thereafter often stayed with the Schwendtners.[18] The location gave him the opportunity to renew his old ties with the Franciscans of Pest, some of whom he had known from his boyhood. Inspired perhaps by the feelings of collegiality that always overwhelmed him when he found himself among them, Liszt decided on August 10 to have him-self measured for a Franciscan habit. The Franciscan tailor who measured him, cut the cloth, and fitted the cassock at twenty-four hours' notice was Brother

---

16. Hitherto unpublished letter of Liszt to his mother, dated June 30, 1865. (BN NAF 25,179 24/1)
17. GRT, p. 300.
18. See Liszt's letter of thanks to the Schwendtners for their hospitality to him on this occasion. (LLB, vol. 2, pp. 85–86)

Hubert Hatos. It was in this garment that Liszt mounted the podium on August 15 to conduct the world première of *St. Elisabeth*.[19]

The performance, which was given in a Hungarian translation by Kornél Ábrányi, took place in the recently opened Redoutensaal. It was sold out days in advance. Five hundred players and singers were gathered on the stage, and there were more than two thousand people in the audience. The oratorio proved to be so successful that it was repeated on August 23. The Leipzig *Illustrierte Zeitung* reported "extraordinary scenes of jubilation as Liszt stepped up to the conductor's podium," and referred obliquely to his Franciscan habit as "the mantle of renunciation."[20] The same newspaper observed that the conductor was much more subdued than hitherto: "The composer, whom we have been accustomed to seeing storming irrepressibly ahead with his symphonic poems, keeps the musical reins much more firmly under control in this oratorio." Two days later there followed an all-Hungarian festival concert at which Liszt conducted the first part of his *Dante* Symphony, together with new works by Robert Volkmann, Mihály Mosonyi, and Ferenc Erkel. Sunday, August 20, was the feast day of St. Stephen, the patron saint of Hungary. Fifty choral societies from across the land converged on the capital for this celebration, and the resulting thousand-strong choir gathered in the woodlands outside the city to give voice to an outbreak of national rejoicing. The scenes of jubilation went on far into the night, illuminated by bonfires.

V

Throughout his six-week stay in Hungary Liszt was accompanied at all his major engagements by Cosima and Hans von Bülow. What were the Bülows doing in Hungary? They were there at Liszt's express invitation.[21] Liszt had not seen his daughter and son-in-law since the previous year, when he had first learned that Cosima and Wagner were lovers. Liszt had taken Cosima away with him at that time, in order to reason with her, but he had failed to change her mind. In April 1865 she had given birth to Wagner's child, Isolde. While we cannot know with certainty when Bülow and Liszt began to suspect the true paternity of this infant, we do know the bond between Cosima and Hans was now

---

19. This somewhat esoteric information may be gleaned from an unpublished letter of Father Vilmos Kurtz, dated "Pest, August 10, 1865," and addressed to the father provincial in Pressburg. The document has been located in the Franciscan Archives of that city (see GFLF, Appendix V). Immediately after the fitting, Liszt posed for photographs in the studio of Canzi and Heller (BFL, p. 230).
20. Issue of September 16, 1865.
21. Bülow wrote four articles about Liszt's visit which were published in the Hungarian newspaper *Pesti Napló* on August 22 and 23 (the *St. Elisabeth* première) and August 26 and 28 (the all-Hungarian concert, which included part of the *Dante* Symphony). These articles are reproduced in BB, vol. 3, pp. 72–98.

very weak, and their permanent estrangement was close at hand. In a desperate attempt to save their marriage, Liszt had invited them to Hungary, to get them away from what he now perceived to be Wagner's malignant influence.[22] Ever since the publication of Wagner's "Brown Book" in 1975, we have known that Wagner suffered accordingly, and he allowed himself to record in this personal diary (which was meant for Cosima's eyes only) some devastating remarks against his former friend.[23] Liszt never knew about them, of course, but he did not need to; he was as aware as anyone of the dark cloud that now hung over his relationship with Wagner. Throughout this stay in Hungary, Liszt and Wagner were engaged in an emotional tug-of-war, with Cosima as the prize. The famous photograph of Hans, Cosima, and Liszt (together with Leó Festetics), taken around the time of the première of *St. Elisabeth,* gives a small hint of the turmoil that swirled in the background. Although they are gathered in a circle, with Liszt at the piano, everybody avoids looking at anybody else. Cosima stares into the distance, Hans (facing her) glares over her head, Festetics has a downcast gaze, while Liszt glances over his shoulder at nothing in particular.[24]

Liszt was also in demand as a pianist. On August 27 he travelled to Gran in the company of Hans, Cosima, Schwendtner, and Reményi to play before Cardinal János Scitovszky and his retinue. Liszt had not been to this city since the performance of his "Gran" Mass in 1856, and this reunion with the primate of Hungary was very dear to him. Afterwards there was a banquet to celebrate the tenth anniversary of the opening of the basilica, at which Liszt and Cosima were the guests of honour, seated on either side of the cardinal. Two days later Liszt made another important appearance as a pianist in the Redoutensaal when he gave the first public performances of his two Franciscan Legends. Hans and Cosima were sitting in the audience. Although these pieces were not yet published, Cosima already knew that they were dedicated to her; she was unlikely ever to hear such stellar performances again.

At the beginning of September Liszt travelled down to Szekszárd in the company of Hans, Cosima, and Reményi, to stay as the guests of his old friend Baron Antal Augusz. On September 3 Liszt was serenaded by an immense crowd of nearly eight thousand people gathered outside the house in Liszt's honour. By way of thanks, he had a piano wheeled to an open window, and he and Reményi regaled the crowd with a spirited performance of his Twelfth Hungarian Rhapsody. Afterwards, Liszt and Bülow played a four-handed arrangement of the *Rákóczy* March. It was a remarkable ending to a memorable journey, and it reminded Liszt once more of the powerful links that bound him to his native land.

---

22. The full story of this tangled matter is told in the two chapters dealing with the Cosima-Bülow-Wagner crisis, entitled "The Triangle Forms" and "The Triangle Breaks," pp. 106–29 and 130–46.
23. RWBB, pp. 62–65.
24. BFL, p. 233. Festetics is often wrongly identified as the violinist Wilhelm Ernst, who did not visit Budapest in 1865.

And there were family links too. It so happened that in this very district of Hungary two of Liszt's cousins were practising priests. One of them, Father Alois Hennig, was now a teacher at the Jesuit seminary at Kalocsa. Another, Father Anton Vetzkó, was a parish priest in the nearby village of Bedegh. Liszt attended early-morning mass at his church, and Vetzko heard his confession.[25]

After promising to return again soon, Liszt left Hungary on September 12. It had been his plan to take the Bülows with him to Venice, where he hoped that they might enjoy a second honeymoon, but they turned down his invitation and boarded the train for Munich. He might have consoled himself with the thought that he had at least kept Cosima and Wagner apart for five weeks.[26]

And so Liszt travelled alone to the city of canals, bridges, and romantic lagoons. He spent three days exploring the "symphonic architecture" of Venice, as he described it, including St. Mark's Cathedral and the Palace of the Doges. He finally arrived back at his old quarters in the Vatican on September 18. Almost at once, he was plunged into a round of social calls. Princess Carolyne had to be brought up to date with his Hungarian successes (he went over to her apartments, and the following day she visited him in the Vatican), and the pair talked at length about the dismal marriage of Hans and Cosima. Hohenlohe also arranged for him to dine with Cardinal Manning, Archbishop of Westminster, who was visiting Rome at that time. But Liszt's greatest pleasure was to be received in audience by Pius IX within a few hours of his return from Hungary. When the time came to take their leave of one another, Pius turned to Liszt and said, "Il mio Liszt," which touched the composer deeply.[27] (Liszt tells us that before the audience, he had spent the entire day indoors working on his *Papst-Hymnus*—Hymn to the Pope—which he later incorporated in his oratorio *Christus*.) Liszt also resumed his theological studies with Solfanelli, with whom he began to make "a little bit of progress" in Latin and Italian. One of the first letters he wrote was to Father Schwendtner, thanking him for his recent hospitality and asking that a mass be said for him on his birthday in the Franciscan Church at Pest.[28]

October 22 itself he spent quietly at his former residence, the Madonna del Rosario.[29] "My health is good," he told Brendel, "and I can unconcernedly allow people the pleasure of referring to me as 'physically broken down' and a 'decayed wreck' (as I have been described in the *Augsburger Allgemeine*

---

25. LLB, vol. 6, p. 90. Liszt had last met Father Hennig in Gran, in 1856, and had attended a low mass in his church. See Volume Two, p. 405.
26. By this time Wagner, in a paroxysm of rage, was accusing Cosima of having abandoned Isolde, who, as Wagner well knew, was being very well cared for in Munich, together with Cosima's other daughters, Blandine and Daniela. It was all part of the tug-of-war, and intended to bring Cosima back to Munich as quickly as possible.
27. LLB, vol. 6, p. 91.
28. LLB, vol. 2, p. 85.
29. LLB, vol. 2, p. 89.

Zeitung)."[30] His dearest wish was to resume work on *Christus,* which was now half finished and would require from him another six to eight months' work. In the event, the composition moved slowly. He told Carolyne that he was having trouble with the Storm, which did not blow as he wanted it; he joked that he was "becalmed" in the peaceful weather that preceded it. Hohenlohe did not help matters by introducing his famous guest to the ceaseless round of visitors (clerical, political, and ambassadorial) that descended on him at all hours of the day and night in the Vatican, and whom he used to organize into *conversazioni* in his apartments.

Liszt's correspondence of the period makes it clear that he was also under pressure to arrange further performances of *St. Elisabeth.* Carl Gille wanted it for Jena, and Herbeck wanted it for Vienna. Kahnt came forward with a request to be allowed to publish the mammoth score. To all of these requests Liszt replied in the negative. He told Eduard Liszt: "You know how much against my wish it is to bring this work into *circulation.* However flattering it may be to me (perhorrescised composer!) to receive inquiries from various places about it, it seems to me advisable to avoid being precipitous, and not to expose my friends so soon again to the sort of unpleasantness that my earlier works brought upon them."[31]

He was clearly nervous about the prospect of this three-hour composition being mounted in Vienna without adequate rehearsals, and he harboured vivid memories of the failure of his *Prometheus* Choruses there in 1860. Nonetheless, he was grateful for the unusual attention lavished on *St. Elisabeth* (much of which may have had to do with the articles Hans von Bülow wrote for *Pesti Napló,* and which Brendel had just re-printed in the *Neue Zeitschrift).* And there was one request that he had no desire to refuse. Ludwig II of Bavaria (to whom the oratorio is dedicated) wanted it for Munich, and commanded that a performance be mounted there. (It took place on February 24, 1866, with Bülow conducting; Liszt was not present.) These were matters which diverted his time, and it was November before he could open the score of *Christus,* pick up his pen, and resume uninterrupted work on his choral masterpiece.

---

30. LLB, vol. 2, p. 87.
31. LLB, vol. 2, p. 89.

Paris and the "Gran" Mass, 1866

*The mistake I made was not to have forbidden a per-
formance given under such deplorable conditions.*

FRANZ LISZT[1]

I

At the beginning of February 1866 Liszt received the disquieting news from Emile Ollivier that his mother was ill, and he made preparations to visit her in Paris. In mid-January Ollivier had still been able to report that Anna, whom he looked after devotedly, was in "perfect health"; but she then contracted pneumonia and failed to rally. Ollivier called in Monsignor Bucquet and requested that he give Anna the last rites, because he knew that this is what her son would have wanted.[2] It was not a moment too soon; shortly afterwards, during the evening of February 6, Anna expired in the arms of Adolphe, Ollivier's brother. As Liszt was about to leave Rome, he received a telegram from Ollivier informing him of Anna's death and the date of the funeral service: February 8, less than thirty-six hours later. Since he could not get to Paris in time for the interment, Liszt reluctantly decided to abandon the attempt. He had in any case been invited to the French capital for performances of his "Gran" Mass the following month, and he knew that his presence in Paris, which Ollivier required in order to go through the formalities of tidying up Anna's estate, could wait until then.[3]

---

1. LLB, vol. 2, p. 373.
2. TOS-W, p. 75.
3. Cosima, who was in Munich, did not attend the funeral either. Three days later, on February 11, she wrote to her half-sister, Claire de Charnacé: "All my childhood belonged to my grandmother, to whom I could not say a last farewell. . . . A very entangled situation at the moment prevents me from leaving." (Hitherto unpublished. VMA, Carton 30) The "entangled situation" was a veiled

Anna's funeral cortège set out from 29, rue Saint-Guillaume at 10:30 a.m. on Thursday, February 8. A small group of mourners led by Emile and Adolphe Ollivier followed the hearse to the church of St. Thomas Aquinas, where a short mass was held. Also in attendance were Madame Céleste Spontini (one of the Erard daughters), Ferdinand Denis, and M. Schaefer. After the service, Anna's body was buried in the Montparnasse cemetery. Ollivier himself delivered the graveside oration.

> I would not have fulfilled my entire duty if, in the name of him who is not present, if, in my own name, I did not say farewell to the woman before us. She deserves that we do not take our leave of her without expressing a feeling of deep sorrow. She had all the gifts which inspire affection: a lively and serious intelligence, a lovable character, always even tempered and always kindly; a goodness whose depths one could never plumb; and overlaying it all, a serenity which even her simplicity did not prevent from being impressive, and which she owed to the nobility of her thoughts, to the elevation of her feelings, and to that admirable purity which, during the whole of a long life, was never even sullied for a moment by a fleeting temptation.
>
> She had one great joy. The fruit of her womb was blessed, and that dream with which every mother caresses the head of her child—of making a strong, valiant, famous, and good man—she saw that dream realized to the full.
>
> But her heart was not swollen by this, and she was not ungrateful to Providence. Having had such a joy she did not seek others; until her last day, she was solely a mother for her son, and then for her grandchildren.
>
> Now she is departing from us. She will leave on earth people who will piously and faithfully preserve her memory. Elsewhere she will meet again those others for whom she wept as long as she lived, and whom she did not think she should have survived. She will talk to them about those who remain behind. Farewell![4]

reference to the complications in her love-affair with Wagner, who had been forced to leave Munich five or six weeks earlier and was temporarily homeless. At the moment of her grandmother's death, Cosima was pre-occupied with the task of helping him find a house. By April, Wagner was settled in Triebschen.

    See also the interesting sketch of Anna Liszt's last days by Alexandre de Bertha (BFLE, pp. 1160–63). According to Bertha, who saw her just a few hours before she expired, Anna had had her bedroom stripped of most of its furniture so that she could walk round and round on crutches and get her daily exercise.

4. Published in *La Presse,* issue of Saturday, February 10, 1866.

The following day, February 9, Liszt wrote to Ollivier from Rome:

> Blandine is with Grandma—and I shall not be long. For the rest of my life I shall owe to you the most effective consolation of my sorrow: the sanctifying union of my mother's soul with mine through the grace of the sacraments she received when dying!
>
> Never will I be able to thank you enough for this saintly act. . . .[5]

One of Liszt's last public appearances in Rome, just before he set out for Paris, was on Monday, February 26, when his *Dante* Symphony was conducted by Sgambati to mark the opening of the Dante Gallery. Although the hall was full, the work was not particularly well received. The Romans found the music "formless." Liszt himself, however, was accorded a warm enough reception. According to Gregorovius, he was almost felled by one of the floral bouquets with which the "ladies of Paradise" showered him at the conclusion of the work.[6]

I I

Liszt got to Paris on Sunday, March 4, and took up accommodation in his mother's old rooms at 29, rue Saint-Guillaume. He was to remain in the City of Light for more than ten weeks, departing on May 22. It was his longest stay there since the days of his youth. His visit was the result of an invitation from the mayor, M. Dufour, who had earlier suggested a charity performance of the "Gran" Mass in the church of Saint-Eustache for needy children of the Second Arrondissement.[7] One of the first things Liszt did was to visit his mother's grave, where he gave full expression to his grief. Later he and Ollivier had the melancholy task of sorting through Anna's personal effects. "We have just opened my mother's desk and cupboards," he wrote to Carolyne. "She left very few things of worth—a bracelet, two watches, a few rings, a shawl, some false teeth—that's about all!"[8] Ollivier and Liszt spent much time exchanging family news and clarifying some legal issues that had arisen as a result of Anna's death. Ollivier wrote in his journal: "[Liszt] is basically sad and unhappy, and his soul is certainly not joyful; but he is very good and affectionate towards me, and I feel a genuine pleasure in seeing him."[9]

---

5. BN NAF 25180, f. 46.
6. GRT, pp. 321–22.
7. Liszt had written to his mother on January 14 telling her of the "friendly letter" he had received from M. Dufour, and how this visit to Paris would bring him the joy of seeing her again. (LLBM, p. 151)
8. LLB, vol. 6, pp. 111–12.
9. OJ, vol. 2, p. 238.

During the ten days prior to the performance of the "Gran" Mass, Liszt bus-
ied himself with numerous social calls. On March 8 he was a guest in the salon
of Princess Pauline Metternich, where about fifteen people were present, including Saint-Saëns. The two composers played the Sanctus and the Credo
from the "Gran" Mass, for four hands. Saint-Saëns tells us that he was sight-
reading from the full orchestral score and was extremely nervous. But the performance went so well that Liszt offered his young colleague a compliment
never to be forgotten. "It is possible to be as much of a musician as Saint-Saëns;
it is impossible to be more of one!"[10] It was a special treat when Liszt sat down
and played some solo pieces—the Two Franciscan Legends and the *Soirées de
Vienne.* Saint-Saëns later wrote of that evening:

> I already thought of him as a genius, and had formed in advance an
> almost impossible conception of his piano playing. . . . As I write I
> see again that long pale face casting seductive glances at his audi-
> ence while from beneath his fingers, almost unconsciously, and with
> an astonishing range of nuances, there murmured, surged, boomed,
> and stormed the waves of the *Legend of St. Francis of Paule walking on
> the waters.* Never again shall we see or hear anything to compare
> with it.[11]

A few days later Liszt was back again in Princess Metternich's salon. On this
occasion he made the acquaintance of the pianist Leopold de Meyer, who was
already launched on his concert career. According to *La Presse* (March 16,
1866), "the famous pianists surpassed themselves, each in his own style, and
produced the strongest effect. Both played on a magnificent piano (which was
greatly admired) from the firm of Henri Herz."

Hardly a day passed without the newspapers carrying some mention of
Liszt. Princess Julie Metternich called him the most sought-after man in
Paris,[12] and there was truth in the observation. The American singer Lillie
Moulton left a memoir of Liszt's visit which confirms it. "The famous pianist
Liszt, the new Abbé, is pervading Paris just now, and is, I think, very pleased to
be a priestly lion, taking his success as a matter of course. There are a succession of dinners in his honour, where he does ample justice to the food, and is
in no way bashful about his appetite. He does a great deal of beaming; he has
(as someone said) 'so much countenance.' " Moulton then goes on to tell us
about a remarkable feat of sight-reading she witnessed one evening. Just before
dinner, Liszt spotted a manuscript which Auber had brought with him. After

---

10. MGGE, p. 106.
11. HSC, pp. 48–49.
12. LLB, vol. 6, p. 101.

picking it up and glancing briefly at it, he put it down again with the words "C'est très jolie!" The company then went in to dinner, and after Liszt had dined and smoked his usual cigar, he went over to the piano and played the "jolie" little thing of Auber's from memory. "Was not that wonderful that he could remember it all the time during dinner? He seemed only to have glanced at it, and yet he could play it off like that from memory."[13]

It was not only high society that was mesmerised by Liszt. The Parisian public, which had always associated his name with notoriety and scandal, was likewise agog to see the "Abbé Liszt" in his clerical collar and black soutane. Perhaps the most notable example of his public impact occurred when Liszt attended a concert at the Conservatoire and sat in a box made available by Auber, who was at that time the director. The programme included Wagner's *Tannhäuser* Overture, which was received with less enthusiasm than Liszt thought it deserved. So he stood up in his box and clapped so loudly that the audience turned towards the source of the disturbance, and, recognizing the Abbé Liszt, one of the first champions of this piece, began to clap with him. Soon the whole hall was clapping loudly and shouting "Bis! Bis!" until the orchestra repeated the overture. At the end, the audience turned towards Liszt and cried out "Vive Liszt!" Auber said that such a thing was unknown in the annals of these concerts.[14] Behind these public demonstrations of enthusiasm, however, there was a good deal of scepticism. Many Parisians remained unconvinced by the "Abbé," and they put his clerical garb into the same category as his sword-of-honour and his clanking medals: they were stage-props designed to attract attention. As for the newspapers, they were determined not to be taken in by Liszt's strange metamorphosis, and when the "Gran" Mass was performed at the Church of Saint-Eustache, on March 15, they were waiting for him.

III

To call that performance a failure hardly does justice to what actually occurred: it was a disaster from which Liszt's reputation in Paris recovered with difficulty. From a purely musical standpoint the state of the choir left much to be desired. Since the authorities at Saint-Eustache did not permit women in the choir, the upper choral parts of the 170-strong ensemble had to be sung by boys, and the vocal texture lacked clarity. Moreover, the eighty-piece orchestra was made up of players from different groups, unused to working with the music director of Saint-Eustache, M. Hurand. But it was the extra-musical circumstances sur-

---

13. H-LL, p. 162.
14. H-LL, pp. 163–65.

rounding the event that placed a curse over it. Liszt had agreed in advance that the proceeds would be donated to the schools of the Second District. While this had the advantage of attracting a large crowd of four thousand people, it was a crowd of the wrong sort. Many of them behaved as if they were at the theatre, chatting through the music and moving about from one social group to another.[15] Since the mass was placed in the setting of a full church service, there was a sermon preached by Cardinal Henri de Bonnechose on the topical subject of charity. That was the cue for the patrons to come round the church, unceremoniously rattling their collection boxes as a background accompaniment to Liszt's score. But there was worse. Liszt had reckoned without the official presence of the military, a detachment of which had marched into the church, knapsacks on back, rifles in hand, and had then proceeded to turn a part of the church into a parade ground. Even as the choir began the Kyrie, a roll on the military drums rudely interrupted them. And the tenor had hardly begun the Credo when an officer barked the command "Shoulder arms!" Walter Bache, who had travelled to Paris especially for the performance, was dumbfounded.

> Just fancy, there was a detachment of soldiers in the church, and occasionally during the music the officer gave the word of command at the top of his voice! During the Sanctus the drummer performed an obbligato! Can you believe me? Before the Mass we had several polkas played by the military band, and the Mendelssohn Wedding March badly played on the organ! (One of the papers said that Liszt did it.) Directly after the last notes of the Agnus Dei, orchestra and chorus began some other piece belonging to the service in a Donizetti style, all the people believing that it was by Liszt! During the music, lady patronesses came round rattling money boxes, and upsetting chairs with their crinolines! The audience was just like the one at the Palazzo Barberini.[16]

The only consolation for Liszt was that the performance raised more than forty thousand francs. But there was no doubt that art had been sacrificed on the altar of charity.

The men of the press now fell upon Liszt and turned the event into a carnival. Most of the articles either attacked the music or lampooned the composer. A favourite ploy was to liken Liszt to Wagner and attack him accordingly. Even before the performance, Albert Wolff had commented sarcastically

---

15. According to *La Presse* (March 17, 1866) the audience also contained distinguished representatives from the fields of jurisprudence, the military, science, literature and the arts, and finance. Liszt himself walked into the church as part of the clerical processional, headed by Cardinal de Bonnechose.
16. BBM, pp. 192–93.

in *L'Univers Illustre* (March 14), "After being the patron, defender, champion, and performer of the great blusterer Wagner, it is time to think about being reconciled with God." Guy de Charnacé, the son-in-law of Marie d'Agoult, also entered the fray and wrote a scathing review of the mass for *La Liberté*. The fact that Charnacé lacked credibility as a music critic did not prevent him from going to work with a will. "It is a pendant to the most solemn page of Wagner," he remarked of the Credo. "For the uninitiated it is a chaos of horror."[17] One of the worst reviews was written by Léon Escudier in *L'Art Musical* (March 22). "People have spoken of a disappointment. The word is inaccurate. Disappointment implies unfulfilled hopes. What grounds were there for hoping that Liszt's mass would be a masterpiece? . . . The mass is simply a succession of chopped-up, broken, fragmentary, and disjointed periods, a conglomeration of shrill sonorities, achieved by means of a dogged and monotonous use of crescendo. . . . As each number came to an end, hope was transferred to its successor." Perhaps the review that hurt Liszt the most, however, was the one in the *Journal des Débats* (March 23). Berlioz should have written it, but he backed away from the task and at the last minute he handed it to one of Liszt's old friends, Joseph d'Ortigue.[18] After attending both rehearsal and performance, d'Ortigue confessed to his readers his "deficient perceptiveness," declared his "incompetence," and asked to be excused from judging the work. "God knows that I suffered, and suffer still, at not being able to admire the work of this great artist, a pianist of genius whose talents have transported me many times, and whose person will always remain dear to me."

In order to compensate Liszt for the débâcle, an additional performance of the Credo was hurriedly arranged at the Cirque Napoléon, on Good Friday, March 30, conducted by Jules Pasdeloup. Liszt himself, still smarting from the reviews, did not even bother to go. But Emile Ollivier was there and later told Liszt that the performance was "slack and confused, the soloists had colds, the choir was insecure."[19] The best thing that the anonymous reviewer of *La Revue et Gazette Musicale* could find to say about this second performance was that

---

17. Charnacé's piece was commissioned by Emile de Girardin, Marie d'Agoult's old friend. Liszt believed that "Nélida" herself had dictated the article to Charnacé. (LLB, vol. 6, p. 102)

18. Berlioz had seen the score of the "Gran" Mass during his last visit to Weimar, in 1855, when Liszt had put on a festival of Berlioz's music there. At that time he had been impressed with this composition. But now he feared that he might not like the music when he heard it performed, and he did not want to be placed in a position where he would be forced to say so publicly. While acknowledging Berlioz's entirely commendable desire not to want to compromise his critical impartiality, we note in passing the complete lack of interest in doing for Liszt in Paris what Liszt had done for him so often in Germany: namely, to promote Liszt's cause with as much energy as Liszt had promoted his. It would have been a simple enough matter for Berlioz to have written an article of a general nature, one that did not even mention the "Gran" Mass by name, but which, by its tenor, would have told the reader that Liszt's visit to Paris was an artistic event of some magnitude. But that, apparently, was more than Berlioz could now bring himself to do.

19. LLB, vol. 6, p. 108.

"the chief effect of this piece, listened to with heroic endurance, was to ensure enormous success for the Agnus Dei of Mozart which immediately followed."

How can we explain the failure in Paris of a work that had enjoyed such a great success in Prague, in Vienna, and above all in Pest? The inferior performance certainly had a lot to do with it, but there was something else as well. While the Parisians continued to idolize Liszt as a performer, they steadfastly refused to regard him seriously as a composer. *L'Art Musical* summed up the general mood on April 4 when it wrote that after the hostile demonstrations Liszt had suffered at the hands of the press, "the musician could still raise himself again in the public eye and make amends for his shameful defeat as a composer. Taking off his cassock, he only had to go onto the stage, sit down at the piano, and let his marvellous fingers run over the ivory keys."

That Liszt was humiliated by the failure of his mass cannot be doubted. But whatever the reaction of the public and the press, he was determined not to be misunderstood by his friends. On April 21 he met with d'Ortigue, Berlioz, and Berthold Damcke in the home of Léon Kreutzer, and, with the aid of the piano–duet version of the work, he explained "in less than an hour" how he proceeded in his compositions. "I went out of my way to vindicate myself against the unjust charge of overturning the prevailing notions of harmony, rhythm, and melody. Far from overturning them, I believe that I have developed and enriched them." Damcke, a teacher of harmony who until then had been opposed to Liszt's music, was forced to admit that there was not a single bar of the mass which infringed upon the rules of harmony and that "he could teach at any conservatoire in accordance with the examples found in [Liszt's] work." Berlioz appears to have remained silent, but Liszt concluded that "I imagine this hour of friendly conversation has not lessened the good opinion he may have of my bit of musical *savoir-faire.*"[20]

This was uphill work. By any realistic standards Liszt was not required to justify himself before the bar of professional opinion. (After all, one cannot imagine Berlioz having to justify himself before Liszt.) That he felt compelled to do so is an indication of how deep were the wounds left by the débâcle. Fortunately, most of Liszt's other musical colleagues mustered around him, and such figures as Auber, Saint-Saëns, Rossini, Gounod, and Jules Massenet (whom he had first met in Rome two years previously) were generally supportive of his work. He also met César Franck at this time, whose early chamber compositions he had championed fifteen years earlier in Weimar.[21] On April 3, Liszt visited the Church of Sainte-Clothilde in order to hear Franck play some of

---

20. LLB, vol. 6, p. 113.

21. Especially the three piano trios, op. 1. In gratitude for this early encouragement, Franck had dedicated his Piano Trio in B minor, op. 2, to Liszt.

his own compositions on the massive organ built by Cavaillé-Coll.[22] According to Franck's pupil Vincent d'Indy, Liszt sat in the organ-loft, lost in amazement, and "evoked the name of J. S. Bach as an inevitable comparison."[23] Ten days later Franck put on a special organ recital in Liszt's honour. According to *Le Ménestrel,* sitting with Liszt in the audience were Charles-Marie Widor, M. Chauvet (organist at Saint-Merry), d'Ortigue, and Princess Pauline Metternich. Afterwards Liszt complimented Franck warmly on the style of his works and their masterly performance.[24]

On Saturday, April 21, Napoleon III invited Liszt to visit him at the Tuileries. Five years had elapsed since the two men had last seen one another. The audience lasted for half an hour—a rare privilege, since Napoleon was often plagued with illness. (He had started to suffer excruciating agonies from gallstones and was often confined to his bed.) "The emperor received me with Napoleonic grace," Liszt wrote laconically.

Three days later, on April 24, Liszt journeyed to Amsterdam, where he was met by Hans and Cosima. Although there was a great deal of family news to exchange, the main purpose of the reunion was a professional one. Liszt and Bülow were in Amsterdam at the invitation of the Dutch conductor Herman van Bree, who was directing a small Liszt festival in the composer's honour. On April 25 his Psalm 13 was performed in the Zaal van het Park, under van Bree's direction, and in the same concert Bülow played Liszt's arrangement of Schubert's *Wanderer* Fantasy and his *St. Francis of Paola walking on the waters.* During the prolonged applause Liszt mounted the platform and was presented with an inscribed silver laurel-wreath. (Ever mindful of anniversaries, Liszt could not help noting that this concert marked the first year of his residence in the Vatican.)[25] A second concert followed on April 27 in which Bülow was the soloist in Beethoven's G-major Piano Concerto. In the same concert he gave the world première of Liszt's Spanish Rhapsody (composed in 1863). This visit to Amsterdam was crowned with a performance of the "Gran" Mass on April 29, conducted by van Bree, in the church of Moses and Aaron. From Amsterdam Liszt proceeded to The Hague in response to an invitation from Queen Sophie of Holland (the sister-in-law of Grand Duke Carl Alexander), who "overwhelmed him with hospitality." From there he returned to Paris via Brussels on May 1.

---

22. Aristide Cavaillé-Coll has been described as the true creator of the French Romantic organ. Apart from the instrument at Saint-Clothilde, he also built the organs of La Madeleine, Notre Dame, the Trocadero (all in Paris), and that of Sheffield Town Hall, in England.
23. ICF, p. 18.
24. *La Revue et Gazette Musicale,* issue of April 22, 1866.
25. LLB, vol. 6, p. 116.

He had now been in Paris for nearly eight weeks, and the social whirl in which he was ensnared showed no signs of abating. He took part in a matinée at the home of Rossini, where he and the pianist Francis Planté played *Les Préludes* and *Tasso* on two pianos, performances which "succeeded beyond my expectations."[26] Then followed a soirée at the home of Gustave Doré, the famous illustrator, which included a performance of the *Dante* Symphony on two pianos with Saint-Saëns. Liszt also had a three-hour tête-à-tête at Charles Gounod's, where he heard parts of the latter's new opera, *Roméo et Juliette.* On May 10 he was unexpectedly summoned back to the Tuileries by Empress Eugénie. "Her Majesty did not ask me to play, but since the conversation took a musical turn I proposed that I should make my Saint walk on the waters before her, and we went into the salon. The Empress had received me alone at first; but she summoned her two ladies-in-waiting and her chamberlain to the salon—so that they would not be disappointed!"[27]

IV

Liszt saw Marie d'Agoult no fewer than three times during this long visit to Paris. The meetings were inspired by Ollivier and his friends, who thought that a reunion would be beneficial. They could not have been more wrong. The first two meetings took place before the disastrous performance of the "Gran" Mass at Saint-Eustache. Louis de Ronchaud, who was present at one of them, reported that Marie asked Liszt why he had taken holy orders. "So that I never marry!" was Liszt's supposed reply. The anecdote is suspect, since everybody knew that the minor orders did not impose vows of celibacy. Perhaps Liszt uttered the remark, as Haraszti suggests, in order to get rid of the eternal reproaches about himself and Carolyne.

The last encounter, which occurred a few days after the performance of the mass, was filled with tension. Liszt knew that Marie still directed intrigues against him; she had chosen the occasion of his visit to Paris to re-publish her novel *Nélida,* which had been out of print for more than twenty years. (Everyone recognized that Guermann had long since painted his "bare walls," and that Marie's action was based on spite. "It is time to finish with [Guermann] once and for all," wrote Liszt to Carolyne. "Mme d'Agoult gives me no quarter.") He had good cause to be annoyed. During this meeting Marie informed him that she was thinking of publishing her *Confessions.* Liszt retorted that he did not think it possible for her to write her *Confessions,* that a better title for

---

26. LLB, vol. 6, p. 119.
27. LLB, vol. 3, p. 121.

them might be "Poses and Lies." And he went on: "For the first time I put bluntly to her the question of the True and the False. These are big words but it was necessary to pronounce them in order to fulfil my duty."[28] Marie's reply has not come down to us. This was the last time that the lovers of Geneva ever saw one another. The acrimony and bitterness that now characterized their relations accompanied them to the grave.

On May 22 Liszt returned to Rome. Before leaving Ollivier's house he took a last nostalgic look round his mother's sitting-room, played a few chords on Blandine's open piano, as if to say farewell, and then went out. Ollivier accompanied him to the railway station. "On the train he could not hold back his tears," wrote Ollivier. "I, too, was deeply moved."[29]

---

28. LLB, vol. 6, pp. 110–11. On the question of the re-publication of *Nélida,* Marie herself once made the astonishing assertion that the motive for publishing this character-assassination was not to harm Liszt but to idealize him. In October 1850 she had struck up a correspondence with Dr. Ange Guépin, a well-known oculist who had been treating her weak eyes, and from whom she later received a lot of first-hand information for her magnum opus *The History of the Revolution of 1848.* Dr. Guépin took an interest in his distinguished patient and drew her out on a number of topics which are of more than passing interest to her biographers. He pumped her about *Nélida* and obtained from her the response:

> When I published *Nélida* I neither *wanted* nor *thought* to harm Liszt. I knew that he was fond of every kind of publicity; this novel only spoke of his peccadillos, and not of his true faults. I thought I was almost idealising him; however, I was wrong, but unthinkingly wrong. This book was not composed in a premeditated way; it came out of me like an eruption, like measles. Liszt did not consider himself wounded by it at the time; but perhaps he has felt retrospective anger. (Letter dated October 28, 1850, VLR, p. 18)

It will come as a surprise to students of *Nélida* to learn from the author herself that she did not mean to harm Liszt, that she wrote her autobiographical novel, as it were, "without thinking"! Did Marie expect Dr. Guépin to believe her? When she wrote these words, only four years had elapsed since the publication of her *roman à clef,* and Liszt had indeed felt "retrospective anger" towards her, a fact that Marie d'Agoult knew full well, although he made no public protest. But let us suppose for a moment that she was speaking the truth when she told Guépin that the novel was a spontaneous outbreak, like the measles. If that was the case, why did she feel the need to re-publish this work, twenty years after its first appearance, and at the very moment of Liszt's re-appearance in Paris? One cannot have measles twice. It is sometimes argued that the reason was that she needed the money. That makes a good deal of sense if we recall her declining fortunes in the fifties and sixties, and also allows us to see the matter for what it really was: an exercise in the gathering of lucre at someone else's expense.
29. OJ, vol. 2, pp. 246–47.

The Cosima-Bülow-Wagner Crisis I: The Triangle Forms, 1865-1867

I went through the death of his son with him, as well of those of his daughter Blandine and of his mother—but nothing that can be compared with this despair.

PRINCESS CAROLYNE ON LISZT,
TO LINA RAMANN[1]

I

The daily misery that had become a part of Cosima's lot as the wife of Hans von Bülow does not excuse her duplicitous relationship with Wagner, but it goes far to explain it. By the time of her first emotional encounter with Wagner in Berlin, on November 28, 1863, she and Bülow had grown apart to such an extent that they were almost strangers to one another. It is difficult to imagine the depths of human despair to which the ill-starred couple had sunk, but there had already been one indicator. On March 20, 1863, Cosima had given birth unaided to their second child, Blandine Elisabeth, while her mother-in-law, the irascible Franziska von Bülow, and Hans himself were in another part of the house, unaware that Cosima was in the final stages of labour. Cosima herself tells us that she paced up and down the room all by herself, wriggling like a worm and whimpering. One cry of pain she could not suppress, and it aroused the household. They got her to bed just as the baby was born. By the time the midwife was summoned it was all over. Cosima was on bad terms with her mother-in-law and suffered greatly from her hard, cruel nature. As for Hans, she later wrote: "I hardly dared tell him that I was pregnant, so unfriendly was his reaction, as if his comfort were being disturbed." This incident, which almost passes belief, came to light only with the publication of Cosima's *Diaries* in 1976.[2] She herself never spoke of it to anyone, least of all to Liszt, and did not

1. RL, p. 76.
2. WT, pp. 75–76.

even confide it to her diary until six years later, on the anniversary of her suffering. She regarded the episode as a final turning-point in her marriage, for she wrote: "I cannot think without shuddering of that night in Berlin, which serves to make utterly clear to me the subsequent course of my destiny."[3]

When Bülow accepted the position of court pianist in Munich in October 1864, he could have had no notion of the crucifixion that awaited him there. Wagner had brought him in, it will be recalled, as a result of the "miracle" of his meeting with King Ludwig II of Bavaria, and he had done so for two reasons. First, there was no one else in Munich whom he could trust with the preparation of his music dramas—above all the "unperformable" *Tristan*—which were scheduled for production in the Royal Opera House at the king's command. Second, Cosima was now Wagner's mistress and had become indispensable to his emotional well-being; if the only way to have her by his side was to have her husband there as well, then so be it. Bülow's only official duty at first was to act as *Vorspieler des Königs,* although there was talk of him directing a Royal Music School in Munich—a scheme which Wagner was currently pressing on the king. Bülow, in short, was free to devote most of his time to Wagner, and he flung himself into this work with all his usual fanaticism: a conference at nine, an orchestral rehearsal at ten, three hours' teaching in the afternoons, and in the evening a piano rehearsal for the principals in *Tristan* which might last until nine. These twelve-hour days left him exhausted, with little enthusiasm for anything else.

II

Wagner now lived rent-free in a magnificent private residence, the Hotel Jôchum on the Briennerstrasse, which Ludwig eventually purchased for him in the hope of keeping him bound to Munich in perpetuity. The Bülows, by contrast, occupied a smaller dwelling on nearby Luitpoldstrasse. Cosima di-

---

3. WT, p. 76. In the general rush to condemn Cosima's long deception of Hans von Bülow, the suicidal state into which he often threw her is usually overlooked. In an unpublished letter she wrote to her sister Blandine on May 28, 1862, she offers a glimpse of her heart of darkness. Blandine was in Saint-Tropez, awaiting the birth of her first child, Daniel, and Cosima wrote to her from Berlin: "At least you have rest and a blue sky; when I was pregnant I would, I think, have given up my place in heaven not to see anyone and to be able to walk by a river or the sea, or look at the sky and trees. I had to give birth in a town, and what a town! The hubbub around me never let up, and it was amidst noise, dust, and stones, without anyone *belonging to me,* that I delivered a child." This was the birth of her first child, Daniela; the circumstances surrounding the birth of her second, in 1863, were worse, as we have already indicated. Later in this same letter to Blandine, Cosima writes: "I am going through a difficult phase. Hans has been overcome again by attacks of hypochondria which hurt and frighten me so much. I call to my aid all the bohemianism nature gave me, in vain, and I barely manage with great difficulty to keep calm and cheerful on the surface." (BN, Archive Daniel Ollivier, Vol. V, 25179, NAF 25179)

vided her time between the two establishments, often on a daily basis. At Luit-poldstrasse she was Frau von Bülow, wife of Hans and mother of his two children. At Briennerstrasse she shed this mundane role and became an altogether different creature. She acted as Wagner's secretary, adviser, and confidante; she dealt with his correspondence, issued orders to the domestics, supervised his meals, protected him from the swarm of petty officials connected with the theatre, and generally assumed all his burdens. And she also continued her most important role: that of being his mistress. She was already pregnant with their first child.

Although the theatre was soon abuzz with gossip about the adulterous relationship between Cosima and Wagner, that part of it which reached Bülow's ears, according to him, appears to have been unworthy of serious attention. It is difficult to know with certainty when he discovered the truth. The literature itself is hardly helpful, since it contains elisions and suppressions which are designed to mislead even the most intrepid scholar. If Bülow's own account is to be believed,[4] he had at first no knowledge of the love-affair which by the time he arrived in Munich in November 1864 was not only in full swing but was obvious to everybody else. Did Bülow really expect the world to believe him? As early as the previous summer, when he and Cosima had visited Wagner at Starnberg, Bülow had known of his wife's infatuation with "the Master." And even assuming that he was at first unaware of her infidelity, everything changed once the couple had settled in Munich. It is stretching credulity to the breaking point to assume that for a period of four years, up to the moment when Cosima left him in November 1868, Bülow remained innocent of all knowledge of the true state of affairs. We are, in fact, left with an extraordinary conclusion: that the love-affair between Wagner and Cosima was tacitly acknowledged by Bülow, and he chose to look away.

Three possible reasons suggest themselves as the cause of such remarkable behaviour. First, he still loved Cosima after his fashion, and he did not want to lose her, a fact that came out in his subsequent correspondence. Second, his near-idolatry of Richard Wagner made it impossible for him to deal with the matter in any rational way. Third, he wanted to spare Liszt, who was now a Roman Catholic cleric, the pain that a Protestant divorce would create. In the event, none of these things, either separately or in combination, was sufficiently strong to keep the faltering marriage together. What Bülow endured in the meantime in an effort to lead the semblance of a "normal" existence in Munich can hardly be imagined. By his own account he was in daily contact with a crowd of musicians, professors, and pupils who laughed behind his back, and he was not spared the most merciless exposure by the local press.

---

4. Set forth in detail in a letter to Claire de Charnacé, dated September 15, 1869, and reproduced on pp. 138–42.

Wagner's dwelling on Briennerstrasse quickly became the talk of the capital. He had embarked on an orgy of extravagance that stunned his visitors. In answer to a summons from Wagner, Bertha Goldwag, his Viennese milliner, had arrived in Munich with a team of decorators and had set about creating a fantasy-world, decorating the house with silks, satins, and laces to the level of comfort usually associated with an Oriental potentate. One of the main rooms became known as the "Satin Room." It was sixteen feet long by fourteen-and-a-half feet wide, with a ceiling eleven-and-a-half feet high. A fine yellow satin covered the walls; folded pink satin covered the recesses at each end of the room; the ceiling was bordered with pearl-grey ruches and artificial roses. The floor was covered by an expensive Smyrna carpet. In the middle was a soft couch on which Wagner would recline. Bertha's work cost Wagner ten thousand gulden.[5] But it did not end there. Expensive perfumes were imported from Paris, and Wagner's wardrobe became worthy of the king who paid for it; we read of velvet jackets, silk shirts and dressing-gowns, monogrammed slippers. The ordinary citizens of Munich who walked past the baroque façade of the Hotel Jôchum were mesmerized by a pair of peacocks that roamed the grounds, showing off their opulent plumage (Wagner named them Wotan and Frigge, the old Nordic spelling of Fricka). Ludwig's subjects were reminded of his grandfather, Ludwig I, who, not so many years earlier, had indulged in a similar folly when he had brought Lola Montez to his court and set her up in her own equally luxurious palace. Lola had eventually had her doors and windows smashed in and had been chased out of Munich by an angry mob. Would history repeat itself? No one could be sure, but in the meantime history could be helped. The satirical magazine *Punsch* pinned on Wagner the insulting epithet "Lolotte of the Briennerstrasse." The good citizens of Munich now awaited further developments.

With crass indifference to the public-relations disaster that he was creating for himself, Wagner obligingly provided his enemies with further ammunition. In early February 1865 he sent Friedrich Pecht's portrait of him to the king with a request for payment, an action which irritated Ludwig, who had every reason to suppose that he would receive the likeness of his hero as a gift. To this gaffe Wagner quickly added another. In an unguarded moment he referred to his royal benefactor as "mein Junge" ("my boy") in the presence of the cabinet secretary, an insult which reached the king's ears and deeply offended him. On February 6, 1865, Wagner was refused an audience. "Do you wish me to

---

5. Bertha Goldwag later wrote of this adventure: "I travelled incognita on Wagner's instructions. At Salzburg, during the customs declaration, I made out that the silk shirts, the dressing-gowns, the counterpanes and so forth were actually intended for a countess in Berlin." (KBWP, p. 29) When Bertha finally presented Wagner with her bill, he found himself unable to meet it in full, so the profligate paid her 500 francs on account and the rest in installments. In Wagner's world, no one required money so urgently that they could not be kept waiting for it—except he himself.

leave, or do you wish me to stay?" he asked Ludwig. "Stay," came the reply. Ludwig, after fuming for several days, had decided to blame his ministers for coming between himself and Wagner, people "who can have no conception of our love," and he continued in the language of the New Testament: "Forgive them, for they know not what they do."[6] So Wagner stayed.

The hostility of both press and court to Wagner at this time was vitriolic and unremitting. He was perceived by those closest to the king as having a malevolent, hypnotic influence over the young monarch. Worse, he dabbled in politics and appeared to be in league with Bismarck and betraying Bavaria to Prussia. But the most serious charge of all was that he was draining the royal coffers. This was not an exaggeration. Ever since King Ludwig had placed his protective mantle around Wagner's shoulders in 1864, a stream of gold had been diverted from the treasury and into Wagner's pockets. It had settled his debts, bought him private properties, attired him with an expensive wardrobe, and at colossal cost was now producing his music dramas: *Tannhäuser, Lohengrin, Der fliegende Holländer,* and *Tristan* were all in rehearsal, awaiting the king's pleasure. Wagner's spendthrift ways had already attracted the attention of *Punsch*. In one lampoon he is depicted playing a keyboard instrument while moneybags, each marked "1000," dance to his endless melody. The caption tells us that though the Orpheus of old merely moved rocks, the new Orpheus casts a spell over metal itself.[7]

Another bone of contention was Wagner's plan to create a music school, which he insisted was necessary to train singers for the demanding roles he had created for them. Wagner's ideas were expressed in a fifty-page brochure entitled *Report to His Majesty King Ludwig II of Bavaria upon a German Music School to be Founded in Munich*. It seems that Bülow helped Wagner to prepare the document, and it was understood that when the time came Bülow would be appointed director.[8] Nowhere in the whole of Germany, according to Wagner, was there an institution capable of fulfilling this noble purpose. Munich had a perfectly good music conservatory, but Wagner brushed it aside as of no consequence, and a number of local teachers felt threatened.

But the projected music school paled when set beside Wagner's vision of an opera house. Munich's existing house, he asserted, was acceptable only as the site of those nightly entertainments of the frivolous sort that characterised opera

---

6. KLRWB, vol. I, p. 57.

7. KFW, p. 40.

8. Long before the brochure appeared, the population at large knew about its contents. Once again *Punsch* obliged its readership and pilloried Wagner in a merciless cartoon, which shows a Bavarian army officer taking a bag of money out of a chest marked "The Bavarian Royal Treasury," while Wagner, standing next to him, urges: "Do not take it *all* out, dear friend. Leave a few gulden to pay for my Conservatoire of the Future." (KFW, p. 34) It was the time of the military buildup for the forthcoming Prusso-Austrian War, and the implication was that the cause of Wagner was more important to Bavaria than the needs of the army.

seasons across Germany. For Wagnerian music drama a new theatre would have to be built which was worthy to receive such masterpieces. Wagner's brochure was published, with exquisite timing, in the early spring of 1865, just as *Tristan* was about to go into rehearsal. The very people whose support he now needed, particularly the ones in the opera administration, felt insulted, and decided to oppose him. Wagner pressed ahead anyway, bringing in the abrasive Friedrich Schmitt to teach singing and architect Gottfried Semper (a fellow revolutionary of '48) to design the new opera house. To do Wagner justice, his ideas were not to be explained entirely by his megalomania. Nowhere in Germany was there an opera house capable of mounting *The Ring,* for example, which the king was determined to have for Munich; and Wagner despaired of finding leading singers who would not collapse beneath the strain of their roles. As so often with him, however, it was not so much the bold ideas as the arrogant way in which they were pressed which the world found objectionable.

Hans von Bülow, master of polemics that he was, was not slow to enter the fray. He was living on his nerves throughout the entire month that *Tristan* was in rehearsal, driving himself and the players to the brink of exhaustion. (He actually fainted during one rehearsal.) On May 2, when the theatre machinist Penkmayr objected to his demand that thirty stalls be removed to make more room for the orchestra, Bülow barked: "What does it matter whether we have thirty *Schweinehunde* more or less in the place!" The remark, which was made in the half-darkened theatre and was meant only for the players, was leaked to the *Neueste Nachrichten* on May 7, which offered its columns to Bülow for a reply. Bülow published a lame apology on May 9, in which he said that the comment had been made on the spur of the moment; it was not intended to insult the "cultivated Munich public" as a whole, but merely that wicked part of it which wanted to stand in Wagner's way. The *Nachrichten* accepted Bülow's explanation, but other newspapers were less obliging. The *Volksblatt* called him a "typical specimen of truly Prussian self-esteem" and told him that if he had made his offending remark in the beer halls of Munich, the "Zervierteln" would be the least of his worries. It urged Bülow to follow the advice of the old Müncheners at such moments: "Go abroad." This was the cue for which the *Neuer Bayerischer Kurier* was waiting. Every day for a week it displayed the headline "Hans von Bülow Is Still Here!" in letters which increased in size with each issue.

III

It was the triumph of *Tristan* that did more than anything else to consolidate Wagner's position in Munich. The first rehearsals of his operatic masterpiece began at ten o'clock on the morning of April 10, 1865. By one of those bizarre coincidences which regularly attached themselves to Wagner's biography and gave it the appearance of a romantic novel, Cosima had given birth to his daughter Isolde only two hours earlier.[9] In the six years that had elapsed since Wagner completed *Tristan,* there must have been times when he thought that he would never hear the opera performed. Indeed, the rehearsals themselves were fraught with crises, any one of which could have brought the enterprise to a standstill. Memories of the Vienna production of 1863–64, which had been abandoned after seventy-seven rehearsals, were always uppermost in his mind. For the roles of Tristan and Isolde, Wagner had summoned from Dresden Ludwig Schnorr von Carolsfeld and his wife, Malvina, the only two singers in Germany whom he thought capable of doing justice to these roles at that time. Halfway through the rehearsals it became clear to Wagner that the cosy Residenz Theatre, which he had originally selected as the site of the production, was in fact far too small to contain the massive volume of sound produced by the orchestra, and so everything was transferred, lock, stock, and barrel, to the Royal Court and National Theatre, which held about two thousand people. By May 11—the day of the final dress-rehearsal—Bülow had had twenty-one full rehearsals and even he was satisfied. This particular performance took place before the king and six hundred specially invited guests. Just before ten o'clock in the morning Wagner came on stage and in a voice charged with emotion thanked Bülow for his unremitting labours, calling him "my second self." He went on to thank the players for their hard work and devotion, telling them that he had boundless faith in the opera, which he now left in their hands. A spontaneous outbreak of applause followed his words. He was succeeded by Bülow, who was equally agitated. Bülow told the singers and players that without their efforts he would have been unable to fulfil the trust that Wagner had placed in him. He then turned to the orchestra, lifted his baton, and the first notes of the *Tristan* Prelude filled the theatre. He conducted the entire opera from memory. By a quarter past three the performance was over. After each act the audience called for Wagner, but he failed to appear.[10]

The public première of *Tristan* had been planned for May 15, 1865. That date has been described as one of the most extraordinary in the Wagner calendar. Early in the day bailiffs broke into Wagner's home and began to remove his furniture in settlement of a five-year-old debt to Madame Julie Salis-Schwabe, which Wagner, either through forgetfulness or indifference, had failed to liquidate. Cosima was obliged to rush over to the royal treasury bearing a note in

9. In all the circumstances, it was inevitable that she would bear the name Isolde. Had this child been a boy, the Wagner genealogy would surely have been graced by a Tristan Wagner. The infant's full names, incidentally, were Isolde Ludowika Josepha. The "Ludowika" was in honour of King Ludwig.
10. This dress-rehearsal was considered by King Ludwig to be such an important date that he marked it by granting a pardon to all those who had been condemned for their part in the 1849 uprising.

which Wagner begged for the immediate release of 2,400 florins, which the officials there set against his salary.[11] No sooner was that little drama resolved than Ludwig Schnorr turned up on Wagner's doorstep with tears in his eyes to say that his wife had gone down with catarrh, aggravated by a "vapour bath" she had taken the previous day, and her voice was now so hoarse that she was incapable of going on stage that evening. Wagner was thrown into a fit of despair but had no alternative but to postpone the première while Malvina went off to Bad Reichenhall in search of a cure.

While this whirlwind was blowing around Wagner's head, he had had to cope with the news, brought to him on May 14, that his wife, Minna, lay dying in Dresden. Although this information was contradicted the following day by a somewhat more optimistic prognosis, we can only ponder the emotions that stirred in Wagner's heart. Even as the bailiffs were attempting to remove his furniture, he had to gather sufficient composure to write a letter to his old friend Anton Pusinelli, the Dresden publisher, who had kept him informed about Minna's condition. "The sudden change after the most terrible apprehension," Wagner told Pusinelli, "is only to be compared with my whole strange destiny." But worse was to follow, as we shall see.

When the announcement of *Tristan*'s postponement was made public on the afternoon of May 15, the town was swept with the wildest rumours: Malvina's voice had been destroyed by singing Wagner's music; the orchestra, worked to the point of exhaustion, had struck for more pay; Bülow had been threatened with assassination for his "Schweinehunde" remarks, and so on and so forth. Such gossip and innuendo were hardly new for Wagner, of course. A much more serious source of embarrassment for him was that Munich had meanwhile filled up with friends and supporters who had come from all over Europe to hear *Tristan*—and many of them could not afford to linger and were forced to return home. In an attempt to compensate his disappointed admirers, Wagner had tried to persuade Schnorr to return from Reichenhall and take

---

11. Wagner had borrowed this money in Paris. The loan was originally arranged for one year, and although Wagner had successfully negotiated an extension of a further year, the debt was now long overdue. Like many other people to whom Wagner owed money, Julie Schwabe had heard of the composer's new-found wealth and the lavish life-style he was currently enjoying, and she saw no good reason why she should wait any longer for her bill to be settled. Since she now lived in Rome, she had engaged the services of a local Munich lawyer, Dr. von Schauss, who had written "an extremely polite note" to Wagner as early as March 20 asking him to delay no longer, since any legal action he (Schauss) might have to take would only serve to generate adverse publicity during the forthcoming *Tristan* production. But Wagner had delayed, as he always did when the usual situation was reversed and people asked *him* for money, not thinking that Schauss would have the temerity to carry out the distraint order he had meanwhile placed on Wagner's possessions. A whole literature has sprung up around this case. There were many, starting with Wagner himself, who believed that his enemies had bought Frau Schwabe's bill and used it to embarrass him while the first performance of *Tristan* was taking place. But ever since the publication of Schauss's letter, we know that this could not have been so. (KLRWB, vol. 5, pp. 229–30)

part in performances of *Der fliegende Holländer* and *Tannhäuser* towards the end of the month; but the tenor was not to be drawn from his wife's side.

The much-heralded first public performance of *Tristan* finally took place on June 10—a delay which Bülow had turned to good advantage by fitting in three more rehearsals. Although the audience was thin, it included Joachim Raff, Karl Klindworth, Felix Draeseke, Richard Pohl, and Anton Bruckner, who had travelled especially from Linz for the occasion and who remained devoted to Wagner all his life. Wagner was upset by the absence of a number of his more important friends, who, he thought, should have made a sacrifice to be there. Carl Bechstein and Peter Cornelius were absent, and so was Liszt, who was at that moment in the Vatican preparing to enter holy orders. Despite all the difficulties, some of which had appeared insurmountable at the time, Wagner had the immense satisfaction of seeing *Tristan* go out into the world. The unproduceable had been produced, the unperformable performed. Everyone agreed that it was a personal triumph for Hans von Bülow. He had nailed his colours to Wagner's mast, and his handling of the complex score had been inspired. Even so, the gossip-mongers and muck-rakers did their best to sully his artistic victory by dwelling on the sordid details of his personal life. During the dress-rehearsals, for example, there had appeared a particularly pernicious drawing by M. Schultze, which claimed to have been "sketched from life," showing Cosima and Wagner walking arm-in-arm through the streets of Munich with Hans von Bülow following them at a respectful distance with a copy of the full score under his arm.[12] The implication was obvious: while Bülow was serving Wagner, Wagner was in turn serving Bülow's wife.

As if to punish Wagner for mounting *Tristan* at all, the gods now rose up in a fury and struck down Ludwig Schnorr. The sudden death of his Tristan so soon after the first performance of the work had a shattering effect on Wagner, who saw in it yet another example of the terrible curse under which the opera had always laboured. By the third performance, on June 19, Schnorr had already been complaining to Wagner that despite his protestations the theatre authorities had done nothing to shield him from the cold draughts that swept across the stage of the theatre and chilled him to the bone while he was in a fever-heat of perspiration from the effort of singing act three. Schnorr had always been susceptible to colds and chills, which usually led to more serious consequences with him. Although he took part in a performance of *Der fliegende Holländer* on July 15, it was evident to everyone that he was already ill. Even so, Wagner was totally unprepared for the news of his death, which occurred on

---

12. It is reproduced in PW, p. 70.

July 21, and there is little doubt that he felt himself to be partly responsible. The following day he and Bülow caught the train to Dresden to attend the funeral. Wagner had asked that the burial be delayed for half an hour so that he could gaze on Schnorr's face for the last time, but owing to the intense summer heat and the rapid decomposition of the body the funeral was in fact brought forward. By the time Wagner and Bülow arrived in Dresden it was all over. All they could do was to commiserate with the devastated Malvina, let her pour out the horrifying details of her husband's last moments,[13] and catch the next train back to Munich. They were in Dresden for less than two hours.

I V

Wagner lost little time in turning the success of *Tristan* to his personal advantage. In August 1865 he wrote the king a letter that has been described as "a masterful symphony of sophistry and arrogance."[14] Whatever earlier arrangements had been made between himself and the crown, Wagner declared, must now be amended to take into account his additional needs. Nothing short of a settlement of two hundred thousand gulden would suffice for this purpose, of which forty thousand should be paid out immediately in cash, the rest to form the capital for his trust fund, the interest from which would be paid to him for life. The sum represented two-thirds of the money set aside from the Civil List for the king himself. The government of Bavaria trembled, and the king, sensing political danger, backed away from the request. So drunk had Ludwig become on Wagner and his music, however, that by the autumn he had overcome the opposition of his officials to the extent that he granted a part of the request: Wagner would be paid his forty thousand gulden in cash. It is well known how the lower functionaries attempted to make this arrangement unworkable. If Wagner wanted coin of the realm, then coin of the realm he would get. When Cosima went round to the royal treasury to pick up a draft, the officials there attempted to embarrass her by releasing the money in sacks of coin. Nothing daunted, she loaded the bags into two hackney-cabs and brought the treasure back to Briennerstrasse.

The Bavarian court could not stagger under such burdens in perpetuity, and Ludwig's advisors resolved to bring Wagner down. Two of them in particular—Cabinet Secretary Franz von Pfistermeister and Minister-President Baron

---

13. This could not have been easy for her. The cause of Schnorr's death is still obscure. His fever was described as a *springende Gicht,* or "leaping gout . . . that travelled from his knee joint to his brain." In his delirium he roared like an animal and tore out his hair, which had to be sheared. During his final hours three people were required to restrain him. His doctor put it out that his distinguished patient had died of *Tristan.*

14. GRW, p. 253.

Ludwig von der Pfordten—stirred up a campaign of hatred against him. Wagner was referred to in the press as an "AntiChrist." From Munich the press war
spread outwards across Europe; the "Wagner question" aroused international
interest. Even the ageing Grillparzer, who had delivered the graveside oration
at Schubert's funeral, was moved to send a poem from Vienna to the citizens
of Munich in which he advised them to fling the *Salbader*[15] into a debtor's
prison.

Wagner was incapable of taking such matters calmly. With Cosima's help he
wrote a pseudonymous article for the *Neueste Nachrichten* in which he vigorously defended himself in the third person.[16] Certain conspirators, he charged,
among them Pfistermeister, planned to pour slander into the ears of the Bavarian people. Their only purpose was to frighten the king and prevent the latter
from supporting Richard Wagner and his music. The solution was simple,
Wagner went on: "the removal of two or three persons" from the ministry. This
was the sort of language that his enemies were waiting for, and Pfistermeister
and Pfordten (humorously referred to by Wagner as "Pfi" and "Pfo" in his private correspondence) now began to exert pressure on the young king to rid
Bavaria of its former "barricade man" who, true to form, was once more conspiring against the government. Their task was made all the easier by the fact
that Wagner had mentioned the king in free and familiar terms and had talked
in his article about their "unshakeable friendship." It was one thing to say such
things in private, quite another to do so in the popular press. Wagner's identity
as the author was quickly revealed, despite his denials, for Cosima herself had
delivered the article to the newspaper office. The crisis came on December 6,
when Ludwig, under pressure from his ministers, decreed that Wagner must be
banished from Bavaria—at least for a while. When news of his fate was brought
to Wagner, he was dining with Cosima at the Hotel Jôchum. "She nearly
fainted," he wrote later, "and I helped her to regain her composure with difficulty." Four days later he left Munich, accompanied by his faithful servant
Franz Mrazéck and his old dog, Pohl. Cosima and Peter Cornelius were at the
railway station to see him off. It was five o'clock in the morning. As Wagner
boarded the train, Cornelius wrote that he "looked ghostly, pale, with a confused expression and the long, loose hair quite grey. . . . Cosima was completely broken. As the train pulled away and disappeared behind the pillars, it
was like the melting of a vision."[17]

---

15. That is, someone known for his interminable twaddle. Grillparzer's poem is reproduced in MCW,
vol. 1, pp. 265–66.
16. *Neueste Nachrichten,* November 29, 1865.
17. CLW, vol. 2, p. 318.

V

For Cosima it was a nightmare come true. Wagner was banished. Bülow had left on a concert tour a week before the royal decree was issued and would not return until just before Christmas. She was alone in the city of her enemies, who now turned all their venom against her. It was here that Cosima showed her true mettle. She took it to be her primary duty to keep in contact with the king, without whose continued support there could be no hope of Wagner's return. First she secured a guarantee that Wagner's salary would be continued, and then she established a correspondence with the king in which she kept him regularly informed about the fate of his "friend." This was a shrewd decision on her part, for she rightly guessed that by feeding the king a little news she would tempt his appetite for more.

Wagner spent his temporary banishment in Switzerland. He stayed for a few days in Vevey and then found a house in Geneva, Les Artichauts, with a magnificent view of Mont Blanc. By any standards it was a comfortable dwelling, but even this refuge failed to raise his sagging spirits, for he found it difficult to compose. It was winter, and he claimed that the doors and windows let in too many draughts. He left for a short trip to the south of France. While he was in Marseilles, towards the end of January 1866, news was brought to him of the death of Minna—a major turning-point in his life.[18] In March 1866 Cosima visited him in Switzerland, in the company of her eldest daughter, Daniela. While they were on an excursion to Lake Lucerne they spotted a house called Triebschen, which stood on a piece of land jutting out from the lake, surrounded by poplar trees. Across the water there were sensational views of the mountains of Pilatus and Righi. Wagner immediately became enamoured of

---

18. She died during the early hours of January 25. Minna had evidently got up from her sickbed in the middle of the night with a feeling of suffocation, and after opening a window had been felled by a stroke. She was laid to rest on January 28, after a funeral attended by musicians and singers from the Dresden Kapelle and a number of relatives. Wagner did not attend, but asked his friend Pusinelli to supervise the burial arrangements. He has been harshly criticised for this seeming display of indifference, for with the benefit of hindsight it is today clear that he would have had time to reach Dresden from Marseilles. Ernest Newman has dealt with this matter; he makes it clear that the telegramme which communicated the mournful tidings of Minna's death was delayed, and mentioned neither the day of her demise nor the time of the funeral. (NLRW, vol. 3, pp. 503–04)

It is a telling commentary on Wagner's confused frame of mind at this time that when he got back to Switzerland he discovered that his dog, Pohl, had died during his absence. Upon learning that the animal had been dropped without ceremony into a hastily dug grave, he exhumed the dead pet and placed it in a specially built coffin. Although the body had started to decompose, and Wagner was almost fainting with emotion, he somehow placed a collar about the animal's neck and re-buried it in the middle of a grove of trees, with a Jura stone to mark the site. Robert Gutman has put forward the interesting speculation that this extraordinary ritual was a cleansing process intended to expatiate the guilt Wagner felt at not walking with his wife's coffin to her grave. (GRW, pp. 262–63)

the place and inquired about renting it. To help him with this expensive proposition he asked King Ludwig to send him the rest of his year's salary; in a fit of
generosity the king made a gift to him of the 5,000 francs required for the first
year's rent. It was at Triebschen that Wagner found the peace of mind he
needed to compose, and it was there that he created much of *Die Meistersinger.*

After acquiring Triebschen, Wagner was more determined than ever to have
Cosima permanently by his side. To this end, he invited the entire Bülow
household to spend the summer of 1866 with him in order to give the liaison
some semblance of respectability. Cosima got there on May 12; Bülow did not
arrive until the middle of June. It was a repeat of the Starnberg episode two
years earlier, with exactly the same consequences. By the time Bülow got there
Cosima was pregnant with Wagner's second daughter, Eva. From this point in
the story Bülow's conduct becomes questionable, for he appears to have been
a party to the intrigue. Wagner was not satisfied merely to have the husband's
acquiescence, however; he wanted that of the whole world as well. He knew
that some means had to be found to quell the rising tide of gossip in Munich
if the trio was ever to return to that city. Hitherto King Ludwig had remained
commendably quiet about the whole business; but what if he could be
prompted to take sides in this matter, and to do so publicly?

Within days of having banished Wagner from Munich, in fact, the king had
started to pine for his return. The exile that the composer was now enduring
was in many ways as great an ordeal for Ludwig as it was for Wagner. Ludwig
began to nourish a secret desire to visit his hero in Switzerland, but he knew
that his ministers would never allow it. Once Wagner was installed at Triebschen, however, the temptation proved irresistible. Ludwig surreptitiously
slipped away from Munich in order to be with Wagner on May 22, the composer's fifty-third birthday. The king arrived in disguise, accompanied only by
a solitary aide, and asked to be announced as "Walther von Stolzing." Although the romantic escapade only lasted for two days, it was the worst time
for the monarch to be away from the capital, since Austria and Prussia were
girding for war, and Bavaria would have to take sides. The visit was "leaked"
and the cabinet of Bavaria trembled at the thought that Ludwig had absented
himself from the country at a time of national crisis, and for so trivial a purpose. On May 31 the *Volksbote* unleashed a vitriolic attack against Cosima,
whom it blamed, not without reason, for the king's continued attachment to
Wagner.

> Not a year has passed since the well-known "Madame Hans de
> Bülow" got away in the two famous cabs with forty thousand
> gulden from the Treasury for her "friend" (or what?). But what are
> forty thousand gulden? "Madame Hans" ought to be looking
> round again for more cabs; for the day before yesterday an action

was entered against Richard Wagner in connection with bills for no less than twenty-six thousand gulden—a fact absolutely vouched for to the *Volksbote*. Meanwhile, the same "Madame Hans," who has been known to the public since last December by the descriptive title of "the carrier pigeon," is with her friend (or what?) in Lucerne, where she was during the visit of an exalted person.

Bülow, who was still in Munich, was outraged by this public attack against his wife's morals, and he challenged the editor of the *Volksbote*, Dr. Zander, to a duel. The challenge was ignored, so Bülow published a reply in the *Neueste Nachrichten* on June 3. He was clearly rattled, and his response suffered accordingly. Peter Cornelius thought that it should never have been sent; he later said he would have counselled silence had Bülow thought to consult him first. On June 6 Bülow set out for Switzerland with one question on his mind: how to muzzle the Bavarian press. When he reached Zürich, en route for Triebschen, he found Cosima waiting for him with the answer.

The plot that Wagner, Cosima, and Bülow concocted to restore their "good name" was nothing less than to draw the monarchy itself into their grand deception, and it was breathtaking in its audacity. Wagner despatched an appeal to the palace, begging Ludwig to intercede in their behalf. He told the king that Cosima was being dragged through the public mire simply because of her "devotion to her father's friend, her husband's mentor." King Ludwig, he went on, should write a letter that recognized all the positive things that Bülow had done for Munich, urge him not to resign his post, and, while he was about it, compliment the character of Cosima, "his noble wife." To this Cosima added an appeal of her own. She told Ludwig that she was falling on her knees before him "in humility and distress" and implored him to send the letter that Wagner had requested in support of her husband. Not only would such a document vindicate her husband's honour, she insisted, but it would allow her to transmit to her three children "their father's honorable name unstained." (This was a particularly bold piece of pretence when we recall that one of those children was Wagner's, and that he had just impregnated her with another.)[19] Wagner then enclosed a draft of the letter with a request that the king copy it and affix the royal seal. Ludwig, in short, was to be manipulated by the three conspirators and, like some dutiful puppet, was expected to dance to the tune they had composed for him. To make sure that his royal patron took him seriously, Wagner hinted that he had resolved never to see the king again if such a document was not forthcoming. In his blind devotion to Wagner, the king had little alternative but to heed this emotional blackmail and comply. The letter was

---

19. Cosima's letter to the king is given in detail by Ernest Newman in NLRW, vol. 3, pp. 548–49. Newman calls it "the basest act of Cosima's whole life."

written, signed, and delivered to Bülow, who promptly published it in the *Neueste Nachrichten* on June 19 and in the Augsburg *Abendzeitung* on June 20. The trio had now perjured themselves.

The *Volksbote* refused to budge, declaring that it would not retract a single word it had printed about the Bülows. If the charges were false, it went on, then the Bavarian courts had remedies for such things. And it suggested that Bülow's reluctance to bring a legal action was a clear indication of guilt. In any case, it added loftily, considering the dangerous conditions which the Fatherland now faced, the *Volksbote* had better things to do than to concern itself with the private lives of foreign musicians. It is a fact that on the very day that Bülow sent the king's letter to the newspapers, Bavaria took sides with Austria and declared war on Prussia, an event which diverted attention away from the Bülow-Wagner scandal. What the triangle hoped to achieve by their mendacious behaviour has taxed some of the best minds in Wagner scholarship. True, they may have gained for themselves a brief respite from the wagging tongues; but in the long run they could not win. Once the king discovered the truth, as he was bound to do, they were in a worse position than before, for they all stood revealed as conspirators unworthy of his royal protection.

And the truth came from an unexpected quarter. Ever since the tragic death of Ludwig Schnorr, his widow, Malvina, had firmly believed that she was in contact with his spirit. She was encouraged in this notion by one of her pupils, Isidore von Reutter, who claimed to have some gifts as a medium. In séances Malvina and Isidore had established a three-way communication with her dead husband. Under Isidore's influence Malvina wrote long letters to her deceased Ludwig and received his replies by way of her dreams. Isidore was a charlatan, of course, who was subjecting poor Malvina to the most shameful manipulation in her hour of grief. Isidore, in fact, shaped Malvina's ideas on many matters concerning Wagner and the king. It was she who had first supported Malvina in the latter's extraordinary idea that it was her destiny to marry Wagner, a notion that she insisted had received the dead Schnorr's blessing. Wagner extricated himself from this potentially embarrassing situation with his usual adroitness, only to have Malvina press him with even more intimate disclosures that she claimed to have received from beyond the grave.

Having established that Bülow had left Triebschen for Basel, Malvina turned up there, in the company of Isidore, in November 1866. She had not expected to find Cosima in residence, and the discovery rattled her. Cosima held her and Isidore at bay in the living room while Wagner worked upstairs, but she eventually agreed to send up to him an extraordinary document from the medium which purported to contain revelations dictated by Schnorr's spirit, the boldest of which was that she, Isidore, was to marry King Ludwig and that Wagner, because of his immense influence over the king, was to help her fulfil this mission. Wagner, thoroughly alarmed, went downstairs to the three women and saw at once that Malvina was on the verge of a mental breakdown.[20] He treated his Isolde with kindness and gentleness and somehow got her and Isidore back to their hotel in Lucerne. As they parted, Wagner said that Malvina gave him "an indescribably insane amorous look"—which convinced him that the poor woman had fallen hopelessly in love with him.

The next day, Cosima delivered to Malvina a letter from Wagner in which he told her that he would have no further dealings with her until she had got rid of Isidore; whereupon Malvina broke into a torrent of abuse against Cosima and threatened "to smash her."[21] From this moment she regarded Cosima as Wagner's "evil spirit." Wagner suspected—not without reason, as it turned out—that she was quite capable of doing him and Cosima immeasurable harm. He despatched a letter to the king, alerting him to the possibility of a communication from Malvina, and enclosed a copy of the revelation in which Isidore's destiny as the king's consort was set forth. There now ensued a three-way correspondence among Malvina, Wagner, and the king, the result of which was a personal catastrophe for Wagner. For in her letters, sent via the king's adjutant Captain von Sauer, Malvina disclosed more and more of the personal nature of the relationship between Wagner and Cosima. On December 20 Ludwig sent on to Cosima a letter from Malvina whose contents he described as "shocking." He told Cosima that he regarded it as his duty to let her read what Malvina had been saying about her and Wagner. A thoroughly agitated Wagner, in turn, wrote back to the king advising him to banish Malvina from Bavaria, on pain of losing the Bavarian pension that she had been granted as a result of the death of Schnorr. The climax came on January 12, 1867, when Malvina, convinced that Wagner and Cosima would do everything they could to discredit her, wrote the king a highly detailed letter in which she informed him that he had been duped. She advised him to make some private inquiries about the Bülow-Cosima-Wagner triangle, and not take their protestations of innocence at face value. "Your royal ermine is to cover their shame; but consider well, my king, that the royal ermine itself will be soiled." For the first time the king came to the realization that the letter he had written at Wagner's behest, which Bülow had published in the Munich press, had been obtained by

---

20. The full story of Malvina's visit to Triebschen was told by Wagner to August Röckel in a letter dated November 23, 1866, KLRWB, vol. 5, pp. 46ff.
21. Ibid. When Malvina arrived at Triebschen she saw at once that Cosima was ensconced there and in charge of Wagner's affairs. She also noticed that Cosima was in an advanced state of pregnancy, an observation that further inflamed her passions. On this matter she required no help from seers and soothsayers to conclude that a deception was being practised on the king. During the *Tristan* days, when she and Ludwig Schnorr were working under Wagner's direction, she had almost deified him. Like everybody else, she had lived through the ceaseless barrage of gossip pumped out by the Bavarian press, and she marvelled that Wagner had not been broken by his enemies. She never had much sympathy for Cosima, who from Malvina's narrow perspective had brought much grief into the composer's life. But after the confrontation in her Lucerne hotel, Malvina held Cosima beneath contempt.

fraud. The conspiracy that Wagner, Bülow, and Cosima had so carefully created collapsed. Henceforth, the king's dealings with all three of them, but especially with Wagner, were marked by a distant coolness verging on estrangement.

VI

Bülow and Cosima remained at Triebschen for more than two months during that summer of 1866, keeping up the pretence of a happily married couple living as guests under Wagner's roof. The king's letter of support had calmed the troubled waters, and the trio had as yet no inkling that Malvina was about to agitate them again. It was in the relative solitude of Triebschen that Bülow took stock of his position. He still had a lease on his apartment in the Luitpoldstrasse; his contract at the Royal Opera House did not expire until 1868. But the atmosphere there was poisoned, and Bülow actually feared that he and Cosima might be threatened with physical violence if they returned to Munich too soon. Nor had he any desire to go back to Berlin, for the court there still harboured a small resentment against him for leaving the Prussian capital and going to Munich in the first place. He was powerfully attracted to Italy (and he even began to study Italian in preparation for a journey there), but it was unrealistic for him to move on to his preferred destinations of Milan or Florence just then. The prospect of earning his living as a "nomad-pianist," as he put it, was also one he actively considered at this time, but it filled him with apprehension.

In any case, he had badly neglected his piano-playing of late. While he was at Triebschen he could not get near the instrument, since Wagner monopolized it from eight in the morning until five in the afternoon, working on the score of *Die Meistersinger*. The creation of this work was one that Bülow witnessed at first hand, and it cast a spell over him. Although he had good cause to be embittered with the world in general and with Wagner in particular, he nonetheless waxed ecstatic over *Die Meistersinger*, and told Raff: "It seems to me that this work represents the culmination of his genius; it is incredibly vigorous, plastic, richer than *Tristan* in musical detail: I count on it having an immense effect in the national sense."[22] Bülow could not wait to get his hands on the finished score and conduct the first performance—an ambition that was to be fulfilled two years later.

The autumn of 1866 arrived, and Bülow was still undecided about what to do and where to go. Tired, depressed, and thoroughly at odds with himself, he decided to live for a while in Basel, where, he told Raff, he hoped to find "obscurity." There he set up as a piano teacher and concert performer with no

---

22. Letter dated August 12, 1866. BB, vol. 4, p. 136.

other plan in his tortured mind than to wait until things had cooled down in Munich. Basel was in any case close enough to Lucerne for the Bülows to remain in constant touch with Wagner, and they did so. Cosima, as was now her established custom, willingly flitted back and forth between the two men, wife to one and mistress to the other. It was at Triebschen, in fact, that she gave birth to Wagner's second daughter, Eva, on February 17, 1867. Bülow got there just in time to see her deliver the child.[23] He stayed on for a week, to keep up appearances; then, his duty done, he returned to Basel and resumed his bachelor's existence. It is evident that he was willing to endure almost any indignity imposed upon him by this *ménage à trois* rather than face up to the one question that really mattered: would he, or would he not, divorce Cosima and have done with the whole sorry business?

Bülow's indecision, which lasted for another two years or more, has not helped him in the eyes of posterity. Was there some personal advantage to him in his present relationship with Cosima and Wagner that he did not want to lose? The idea is not implausible when we consider what happened next. Wagner wanted Bülow back in Munich, and so did the king. Neither of them had bargained for this show of independence on Bülow's part. How could Bülow be coaxed to pick up the baton again? Wagner now drew up the terms under which Bülow might be persuaded to return to Munich. First, he was to be appointed director of the projected music school, with a full salary and with the authority to run it according to the principles that Wagner himself had set forth in his brochure of 1865; second, he was to be authorised to put *Meistersinger* into production and bring in the best singers for that purpose, from abroad if necessary; third, he was to be given plenipotentiary powers over all matters which concerned the operatic side of the theatre's administration, and given the title of Royal Kapellmeister; fourth and last, he was to receive a Bavarian decoration. By the early part of 1867 the king had agreed to all these terms, even to the decoration,[24] and the Bülows returned to Munich in April of that year. This was Wagner's "gift" to Bülow, and it raises a difficult question. Did Hans accept it in exchange for his acquiescing in Wagner's continued relationship with Cosima? Subsequent events have always caused some mild bewilderment among scholars of the topic. Hans rented a large apartment on the Arcostrasse for himself and his family, which was far more spacious than his needs warranted. Two rooms were set aside for Wagner's use whenever he was in town, furnished from the Briennerstrasse house. To the outsider the conclusion was irresistible: the *ménage à trois* was back in town under condi-

---

23. The day before the birth, February 16, Bülow wrote to Carl Bechstein: "Tomorrow morning (it is now 11:00 p.m.) I go to Lucerne to see my wife. I am rather anxious about her: she is on the eve of her confinement and is in bed with a temperature." (BNB, p. 217)

24. Bülow was invested with the Order of the Cross of St. Michael, first class, in October 1867.

tions which seemed to favour Bülow. Rightly or wrongly, a deal appeared to have been struck.

It is a fact that from the moment Bülow returned to Munich his career took wing. His newly acquired authority as Royal Kapellmeister helped, of course, since he no longer had to work against an unfriendly administration. "Pfi" and "Pfo" had gone into retirement, and with them many of his and Wagner's earlier troubles.[25] Most of all, however, there seemed to be a groundswell of public sympathy for much of his work in the opera house, which may have had its origins in the shabby treatment meted out to him as a "wronged" husband. Whatever the cause, the work that Bülow now did represents a landmark in his career and justified his return to Munich, however painful it may have been for him on a personal level. As he himself put it: "I conduct everything now—*Trovatore, William Tell, Hans Heiling,* music to *Egmont*—and we have nothing but model performances and the house is sold out."[26] He also put into regular production *Tannhäuser* and *Lohengrin* and, as light relief, *The Merry Wives of Windsor.* Wagner became distinctly worried by what he perceived to be this sustained show of independence on Bülow's part, for such a wide-ranging repertory inevitably deflected attention away from himself and his works.

VII

Matters took a new and dramatic turn when Liszt arrived in Munich on September 20, 1867, and stayed in the city for more than a month. Although he put up at the Hotel Marienbad, he spent a great deal of time with Hans and Cosima at their home on Arcostrasse, and had ample opportunity to survey the wreckage that was now the Bülows' marriage.[27] He found Hans in poor health, suffering from a mild fever and an infected throat, which not even a recent cure at St. Moritz had helped. The doctor had forbidden Bülow to talk, but the irascible patient, even while his affliction was at its height, showed his contempt for such advice by directing a six-hour rehearsal of *Lohengrin,* followed by a complete performance. It is unthinkable that Liszt would not have raised with the Bülows the question of their *ménage à trois,* since that was his chief reason for being in Munich. Even so, the documents are sparse and this episode can only be reconstructed with difficulty. Wagner knew that Liszt was in the city,

25. Bülow wrote to Bechstein on May 9, 1867: "All the *cochonneries* have ceased, now that the Pf's (not the 'pianofortes') have been banished." (BNB, p. 220)

26. BNB, p. 221.

27. Cosima herself only got back to Munich on September 14. She had lived with Wagner at Triebschen since August 11, while Bülow was in St. Moritz. Evidently her return to Munich at this time with her three older daughters (Eva was left behind with Wagner) was meant to maintain the fiction of her marriage to Bülow while her father was in the vicinity.

but he deliberately stayed clear because he feared a confrontation. Liszt nevertheless decided to arrange one for him. If Wagner would not come to Munich, then Liszt would have to go to Triebschen.

Liszt was too well versed in the ways of the world not to know what the press would do with this information, so he obscured his tracks. On October 3 he kept an engagement in Stuttgart, which was far enough away to throw even the most zealous of journalistic bloodhounds off the scent. There he was joined by Richard Pohl; by October 6 the pair had moved on to Basel. It was not until two days later that Liszt surprised Pohl with the abrupt announcement that he intended to return to call on Wagner at Triebschen. For the first time Pohl realized that he and Basel were part of an elaborate subterfuge, that it had been Liszt's intention all along to visit Wagner.[28]

Liszt arrived at Triebschen on Wednesday, October 9, at three o'clock in the afternoon. He and Wagner had not seen one another since the summer of 1864, and neither of them could have relished the circumstances under which they were now obliged to confront one another. For six hours they were closeted together, but nothing is known of their conversation. All that Wagner would say later about the visit was that it was "dreaded but pleasant."[29] Liszt put it more vividly when he said that it was like visiting Napoleon on St. Helena. That there was plain speaking on both sides is obvious. Liszt never visited Triebschen again, and in fact he broke off relations with Wagner for five years; the two composers were not re-united until the summer of 1872. Having said all that was to be said on the subject of Hans and Cosima, they turned their attention to *Die Meistersinger*. Liszt sight-read substantial sections of the work from the full orchestral score, while Wagner sang the vocal parts. They were joined that evening by Pohl, who, while patiently awaiting Liszt's return to their hotel in Lucerne, had been summoned to Triebschen and transported there in Wagner's carriage. Nineteen years later Pohl said that he never heard a more remarkable rendering of *Die Meistersinger* than the one he witnessed that night. As for Liszt, he immediately recognized the enormous power of the work and declared it to be a masterpiece. Of Wagner himself Liszt said very little, except to observe that he had changed a good deal outwardly. His face was pinched and lined, yet "his genius has not weakened at all. The *Meistersinger* astonished me by its incomparable vigour, boldness, abundance, verve, and *maestria*."[30]

---

28. Pohl's account of Liszt's visit to Triebschen will be found in RWJK (1886), pp. 78–84.
29. RWBB, p. 124.
30. LLB, vol. 6, p. 159.

VIII

Knowing what we do of Liszt's generosity of spirit, we should find it no surprise to learn that it was during the very worst days of the Cosima-Bülow crisis that he composed his magnificent piano paraphrase of Isolde's "Liebestod" from *Tristan*. It nonetheless still gives us pause for thought that he should come forth with such an arrangement at such a time. It dates from 1867, the very year of his visit to Triebschen. Wagner was now the source of much pain in Liszt's life, and by any standards of human decency Liszt had good reason to shun his tormentor. But that did not mean he had to shun the music. Many times in the past Liszt had shown that he served Art, however base the individual artist in whom that Art resided. Was this his way of telling Wagner that whatever his opinion of him as a human being, they would always remain united in music? We can only speculate. It is enough to know that the paraphrase of the "Liebestod" is one of the pinnacles of this branch of Liszt's art, and that it has been justly praised as a model of its kind. With the obvious exceptions of Wagner and Bülow, no musician in the world was more intimately acquainted with Wagner's complex score than Liszt. (We recall that he had conducted the second public performance of the *Tristan* Prelude from manuscript in the summer of 1859, and Wagner had sent him each of the three acts as they came off the printing press.)

The formidable task which faced Liszt when he attempted to transfer such a rich texture to the piano was twofold. First, he had to find a way in which ten fingers might do justice to the contrapuntal fabric which comprises so much of this music. Second, he had to find a means of matching some of the biggest climaxes in Romantic orchestral music on a keyboard of a mere eighty-eight notes. After all, the orchestra is a sustaining instrument of tremendous power, while the sounds of the piano start to decay from the moment they are born. Through the judicious use of three devices—arpeggios, tremolandos, and repeated chords—Liszt feeds a continuous stream of sound into the instrument, and then scatters diamond dust across the length and breadth of the keyboard by releasing all the upper partials through the sustaining pedal. The result is a texture which glows with peculiar incandescence. In fact, the "Liebestod" is much more than a literal transfer (such a thing would fail lamentably as a concert paraphrase). Liszt lays bare the paradox that lies at the heart of all such work: the more faithful you are to the letter, the less faithful you become to the spirit.[31]

---

31. If a note-for-note rendering of the text is all that we require, then we might as well play Bülow's piano reduction of *Tristan* and have done with it.

After a brief introduction, the "Liebestod" begins with that most difficult of keyboard textures: a tremolando, shimmering in the heavy lower register, which Liszt marks *ppp*. It is almost a violation of the instrument's true character, as many an inferior pianist has discovered to his cost. Yet Wagner leaves Liszt with little choice in the matter, for it is on a string tremolando that he himself floats Isolde's line.

Liszt often said that he liked such tremolandos to be played rapidly, "with as many notes as possible." If, through technical limitations, the player plays them too slowly, the magic is lost, and with it the piece.

As the music takes wing, Liszt manages to incorporate all the essential detail within two hands, the occasional spread chord even suggesting the presence of the orchestra's harp. His pedal markings deserve special attention. Both pedals are used constantly; in fact, the first half of the "Liebestod" (with two brief exceptions) is played with the soft pedal throughout, and lest the player forget this unusual injunction Liszt is constantly at his ear, reminding him "sempre una corda."

Liszt appears to have taken some trouble with the great climax. At any rate, it exists in three versions in the Collected Edition, and the player may choose among them.[32] Timbre, melodic clarity, and physical comfort will help to determine the final selection. The version printed below in bold type is the most frequently heard, and it is the one through whose texture the greatest volume of sound is most likely to escape.

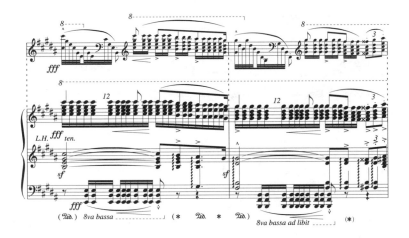

We cannot be certain exactly where the "Liebestod" paraphrase was composed. Liszt's home in 1867 was at the Santa Francesca Romana, in which case the first strains of this composition would have emerged from his prize-winning Chickering grand piano in Rome. Published in 1868, the paraphrase was slowly taken up by his piano pupils, who brought it to his masterclasses.[33] As he sat in his studio—in Weimar, Budapest, or Rome—listening to his pupils' innocent fingers play the piece with varying degrees of failure, he must have asked himself what they could possibly have known of its inner significance. For the piece is musical biography made manifest. What emotions must have swept his soul at such times, emotions which would perforce have had to remain suppressed! Joy and sorrow, elation and despair, resignation from the things of this world—all are mixed and mingled in the crucible of the "Liebestod." It may be Wagner's music, but it is of Liszt that we think when we hear the paraphrase itself. At its centre it contains a bitterness of heart—for those with ears to hear.

---

32. They are given by Liszt's pupil August Stradal in CE, (FB) vol. I, pp. vi and 118.

33. It was, for example, played to him by the twenty-one-year-old Adèle aus der Ohe on August 17, 1885, and by Etelka Willheim on March 2, 1886. See GLK, pp. 95 and 133.

While Liszt was in Munich he attended performances of both *Tannhäuser* and *Lohengrin*. Observing the way in which Bülow had matured as a conductor since he had last heard him, he wrote to his cousin Eduard: "If Bülow remains active here for a few years, Munich will become the musical capital of Germany."[34] That is a fairly clear indication that Bülow was no longer in a hurry to wash his hands of Munich, whatever his critics were saying; otherwise Liszt would have been the first to learn of it. In order to please Hans and Cosima, Liszt agreed to stay on and celebrate his fifty-sixth birthday with them and his grandchildren. It was an emotional occasion. Peter Cornelius had sent over a poem he had written, which was recited to perfection by seven-year-old Daniela. Both Cosima and Liszt found the scene so touching that they wept like children.[35] The tragedy that was casting its darkening shadow across the Bülow household affected everything, and not even Liszt's birthday celebration could dispel the gloom.

---

34. LLB, vol. 2, pp. 107–08.
35. LLB, vol. 2, p. 108. The poem, entitled "Zu Liszts Geburtstag, 22 Oktober 1867" will be found in CLW, vol. 4, p. 285.

The Cosima-Bülow-Wagner Crisis II:
The Triangle Breaks,
1868-1870

I only had the choice between two situations: that of being viewed with the most insulting pity as an individual unaware of what everyone knew, or that of being accused of infamy, as someone who had accepted the most shameful bargain as the favourite of the favourite of a king.

HANS VON BÜLOW[1]

I

In March 1868 Bülow's chief purpose in returning to Munich began to assert itself. That was when the rehearsals for the world première of *Die Meistersinger* began, a performance which took place on June 21, 1868, before King Ludwig and fifteen hundred guests from across Europe. Wagner was seated in the royal box, next to the king, and was called upon to take bows during the intervals. He refused to appear after the first act, but the king prevailed upon him to show himself after the second and third acts, and he acknowledged the applause showered upon him. It was undoubtedly the highest point of his Munich period—higher by far than that reached by the *Tristan* performances three years earlier—and the reason is not difficult to fathom. *Meistersinger* is set in the heart of Old Germany, in the sixteenth century. Its appearance coincided with a rising tide of German nationalism and the urge to unify the various German states into a single Reich. At last the great public had found something in Wagner with which they could easily identify, for the opera is drawn from local history. Wagner claimed from the start that his intention in composing it was nothing less than the regeneration of German art. Everything in *Meistersinger* was familiar to that first audience: the city in which the opera was set (Nuremberg), the central drama towards which it moved (the singing contests held under the aegis of the medieval guilds), and the destiny of the German nation.

---

1. VML, Charnacé Archives, Ms. F 859(3).

Hans Sachs's jingoistic address at the end of the final act urges the audience to "honour your German Masters would you forefend disasters!"

This was probably Bülow's greatest period as a conductor. He had reached commanding heights; no one else on the scene could presently be compared with him. From Munich he could have gone on to almost any conducting position in Europe. But his world was about to shatter into a thousand pieces, and when it did so he seemed unable to put all the fragments back together again. While *Meistersinger* was in rehearsal his fretted nerves often got the better of him. Once, when he was going through the score of the opera with a few musicians in his house, a photo of Wagner and little Eva fell out of the composer's manuscript score, and Bülow had to leave the room, overcome by a flood of emotion. Wagner's "Brown Book" also records a number of conflicts with Bülow. In May, during a piano rehearsal, Wagner experienced a "heavy, oppressive feeling from Hans's deep hostility and estrangement." And in June we read the terse entry: "Orchestral rehearsals: serious trouble with Hans."[2]

Now that he was Munich's Royal Kapellmeister, it was natural that Bülow should be sought out by other composers anxious to have their operas conducted by him. One such was Wendelin Weissheimer, who turned up in Munich bearing the score of his opera *Theodor Körner*. Wagner had already refused to hear the work, on the grounds that he was too deeply immersed in *Meistersinger*, but Bülow agreed to go through it with the composer on the piano. As they were playing and singing from the score one morning in the house on Arcostrasse, the maidservant came in with a request from Wagner that Bülow stop playing the piano, as he was trying to sleep. "It was eleven o'clock in the morning!" exclaimed Weissheimer. Bülow slammed the piano lid shut and jumped up with the words: "It is a high honour for me to live with the great Master—but it is often more than one can endure!"[3] There must have been many such scenes which have not entered the literature. Throughout the *Meisteringer* period, in fact, Bülow's nerves were frayed to the breaking-point. Nor was the appearance of Franziska von Bülow, who arrived in the early summer to look after Hans, calculated to make life simpler for the inhabitants of Arcostrasse. The love she bore her son existed in inverse ratio to the hatred she bore her daughter-in-law, and Cosima detested her.

II

In the summer of 1868 Cosima left Munich for a few weeks, ostensibly to visit her half-sister, Claire de Charnacé, in Versailles. In reality, she went once

---

2. RWBB, p. 167.
3. WEW, pp. 392–93.

more to Switzerland to be with Wagner. Cosima, well practised in the art of living a double life, wrote to Bülow the most reassuring letters about the children and about Claire, which, according to his later testimony, led him genuinely to believe that whatever it was his wife was doing, she could not possibly be doing it in Wagner's company. (The reader who has followed the tangled story of the Bülows' marriage so far can only stand back in bewilderment that Bülow would expect anyone to accept his version of events without serious question. By now Cosima had shown her true colours to such a degree that whenever she was not in Bülow's company he had every reason in the world to suppose that she was in Wagner's.) The blow, when it came, appears nonetheless to have struck him with devastating force. He received from Cosima a request for funds to enable her to accompany Claire on a trip to Italy, only to read in the newspapers a short time later that Cosima and Wagner had been spotted together there. From this moment Bülow's life in Munich began to collapse. As he himself finally acknowledged, he was perceived as "the favourite of the favourite of a king" who had entered that most shameful of bargains: a place in the sun in exchange for sexual favours granted by his wife to his benefactor. He handed in his resignation to the king; it was at first refused, so he handed it in again. All he could do when pressed by friends and colleagues was to maintain the fiction that his wife was indeed in Versailles with Claire de Charnacé and pray for the nightmare to disappear.

Even if the relationship between Cosima and Hans had been a normal one prior to her first encounter with Wagner, the birth of a child to Cosima outside wedlock would have been sufficient to eat away at the very foundations of her marriage. Five years is an extremely long time to sustain such a deception. And in this case there was not one child but three: Isolde was born in April 1865; Eva arrived in February 1867; and then came Siegfried in June 1869. In fact, it must have been the knowledge that she was again pregnant by Wagner that, in October 1868, prompted her to tell her husband that the time had come to live openly with the man she loved. Although Bülow was a Protestant, his marriage to Cosima had been celebrated within the Roman Catholic Church and was therefore a sacrament and indissoluble. The only ray of hope in an otherwise hopeless situation was for Bülow to petition the Prussian courts for a civil divorce. At first he had steadfastly refused to do this, but rather chose to go on bearing what he called "the structure of my cuckoldry" with Prussian fortitude. Only when the utter impossibility of continuing the relationship had been borne in on Cosima did she take the one option now left to *her*, albeit one frowned upon by church and state. She gathered up Isolde and the infant Eva and fled to Wagner. The two older girls were

left behind at boarding school in Munich, with their nurse, Hermine, to supervise them.[4]

III

One of the most revealing sources concerning the difficult question of
Cosima's transfer from Munich to Triebschen is the sequence of unpublished
letters that she wrote to her half-sister, Claire de Charnacé, whom she calls
"my only friend." They provide the biographer with a generous supply of detail that might otherwise remain unknown. We gather that Cosima at first had
no one to help with the supervision of her children, and even lacked proper
domestic help. But that did not matter, she wrote, since "I fear servants as
much as masters"; she resolved to wash, comb, and feed her young charges
herself.[5] Triebschen was cold, and she had to light the fires. "I am a victim of
the fireplaces," she told Claire. "Either I'm cold or burning hot." She asked
Claire to pick up two fire-screens on one of her shopping trips to Paris. "It
goes without saying that if you do not have time to do these errands, you will
let me roast."[6] At this time Cosima was three months pregnant and far from
well. She also lived in constant fear that Daniela and Blandine would be taken
from her. "I have no news of the children, and I am frightened that some order
has come down from *on high* to bring me to heel in that way."[7] It was this fear
of losing her children that prompted Cosima to begin keeping a diary on January 1, 1869. The very first paragraph makes it clear that the initial purpose of
the diary was to give an account of her life to her young family. She tells her
children:

> You shall know every hour of my life, so that one day you will come
> to see me as I am; for if I die young, others will be able to tell you
> very little about me, and if I live long, I shall probably only wish to
> remain silent. In this way you will help me do my duty. What I

---

4. Cosima arrived at Triebschen on November 17, 1868. "I made the journey alone with these little
ones," she wrote to Claire the following day, "which, in the transfer from the train to the boat, and
vice versa, was no easy task." (VMA, F 859, carton 30, unpublished letter from Cosima) Franziska von
Bülow once again travelled down from Berlin to Munich to look after Hans in his hour of need.
(Ibid.) It also fell to Franziska to close down the house on Arcostrasse a few months later and transport the furniture back to Berlin. Since Hans soon proved to be incapable of looking after the two
older girls, they were sent to join the rest of the family in the spring of 1869. He told them they should
be very happy that they were at Triebschen. "Thank good Uncle Richard often for permitting you
to live there with Mama."
5. VMA, F 859, carton 30, unpublished letter dated November 18, 1868.
6. Ibid.
7. VMA, F 859, carton 30, unpublished letter dated January 16, 1869.

mean by that you will find out later. Your mother intends to tell you everything about her present life, and she believes she can do so.[8]

Later, after Daniela and Blandine came to live in Triebschen, she had the help of the nurse, Hermine, who actually stayed on with the family for a number of years. But one of her biggest worries during these first few months was the illness first of Eva and then of Isolde, who came down with a serious case of croup in early May, not long before the birth of Siegfried. Cosima was isolated with Isolde for several days to protect the rest of the family from infection.[9] She emerged in time to arrange the celebrations surrounding Wagner's fifty-sixth birthday, on May 22. She got up in the middle of the night to set up Wagner's bust and surround it with flowers. Hans Richter, who had travelled especially from Munich, arose before breakfast and awakened the household by blowing Siegfried's forest call on the French horn. Aroused by this theme, Wagner came down to breakfast and found his room had been transformed into a flower garden, while Cosima's four daughters were dressed as Rienzi's Heralds of Peace. At 10:30 a.m. the Morin-Chevillard String Quartet arrived from Paris, following a secret invitation from Cosima, and played three of the late Beethoven quartets for Wagner. Cosima herself was in an emotional frame of mind and watched the day pass by "like a dream."[10]

The birth of Siegfried on Sunday, June 6, is described in compelling detail in the diary. A lunch had been arranged for Friedrich Nietzsche, who happened to be visiting Wagner at that time, the first occasion on which the philosopher had stayed the night at Triebschen. Although Cosima's labour pains had started, she did not wish to disturb these arrangements, so she sent for a local midwife and retired to her room alone. Later she was joined by Wagner, who witnessed a part of her labour; then, assisted only by the midwife, she gave birth to their son amidst piercing cries of pain while Wagner paced anxiously back and forth in the next room. At one point he heard a servant go in and exclaim "Oh God in heaven!" Thinking that a calamity had occurred, he rushed in to hear the words "A *son* has arrived!"[11]

IV

The letter that Cosima wrote to Liszt telling him of her decision to leave Bülow has not survived, but we have a copy of Liszt's reply. His anger, frustra-

---

8. WT, vol. 1, p. 21.
9. VMA, F 859, carton 30. Unpublished letter dated May 27, 1869.
10. WT, vol. 1, p. 97.
11. WT, vol. 1, p. 104.

tion, and genuine grief over the plight in which Bülow found himself are evident throughout.

> Where are you going? What are you telling me? What! Every-
> thing is dead for you except a single person to whom you think you
> are necessary, because he says he cannot do without you? Alas! I can
> foresee that this *necessity* will soon be an encumbrance, and by pos-
> sessing you in his fashion, you will necessarily become inconve-
> nient, annoying, contrary to him. Although you might well only
> want to live for him, that would not be enough at all, and would
> hardly be feasible because fatal poisons would begin to seep from
> the rock on which you aim to rest yourself.
>
> God save me from judging you wrongly. I know that "nothing
> infamous, nothing low, nothing futile is subjugating you" but you
> have become giddy and are dissipating the vital and holy forces of
> your soul by sealing an evil deed with approval. This perversion, this
> adulteration of God's gifts breaks my heart!
>
> You speak of living alone and raising your children. How will
> you manage that? W.'s notoriety and his extremely dependent po-
> sition from a material point of view will work against your best
> plans. After such a scandal, I doubt whether convention will allow
> you to live in Switzerland or Germany. Probably you will be forced
> to seek some refuge as far away as America. The hand of your royal
> friend and benefactor might slacken its grip, if not withdraw, as a
> consequence; embarrassment and shameful financial difficulties
> would dog your footsteps. Even if you were to bear them bravely,
> would the *other one* put up with them because of this?
>
> And what about your children? What are you teaching them?
> Does not the model contain the precepts? Will they understand
> that one should call Evil Good, call night day, call bitter things
> sweet?
>
> Yes, my daughter, what you are planning to do is bad in God's
> eyes and man's. Indeed, my convictions and experience protest
> about it to you, and I beg you by your maternal feelings to re-
> nounce this fatal plan, drive away the subtleties of sophisms, stop
> sacrificing [yourself] to the implacable idol. Instead of abjuring
> your God, fall on your knees before him; he is truth and mercy in
> one; invoke him with all your soul and the healing light of repen-
> tance will enter your conscience.
>
> It is Hans to whom you are *necessary;* it is him you must not fail.
> You married him of your own free will, with love—and his behav-
> iour towards you has always been so noble that on your side it calls

for another "gegenseitige Übereinstimmung" than the one pleaded before the courts. What madness to ask him now to subscribe legally to your dishonour!

You are also *necessary* to your four children, and deserve their respect, [which] must be for you the first priority. Now the more than precarious future the yoke of your passion would bestow on them exposes you to their most cruel reproaches, which your conscience will ratify. I will not speak to you about public opinion, [about] which nonetheless one should not exaggerate one's contempt to the point of absolving everything it condemns, and Jean-Jacques [Rousseau] himself warns of the danger of this contempt when it "pushes us to the other extreme, and even makes us brave the sacred laws of decency and honesty."

By falsely crushing the sublime, one does not change the immutable nature of duty. You must not leave the noblest of husbands; you must not mislead your children; you must not bear witness against me and plunge madly into an abyss of moral and material misery; and finally you must not deny your God.

Passion consumes itself when it is not enlivened by the sense of superior duties. It withers away or becomes poisoned in wealth, dies in poverty, and passes with frightful rapidity; but remorse remains.

Not only do I rightly condemn what you are proposing, but I am telling you this while begging you to take hold of yourself and not allow yourself to be removed from my blessing.

May God grant my prayers, and may the memory of your father make you become again the child of God our Father and our All in Eternity.

F. Liszt

November 2, 1868, Rome[12]

Now that the scandal was in the open, Bülow was free to do "the honorable thing" by commencing divorce proceedings. Even so, he waited a year before launching the action, since he wanted to give Cosima time to "find herself," as she put it.[13] Bülow also found that as a divorce by mutual consent was impossible under Prussian law, there were only two alternatives open to him. The first was to bring a charge of adultery against Cosima, but for that he would have had to name Wagner as co-respondent, subpoena friend and foe

---

12. Hitherto unpublished. VMA, Ms. F 859, 1/3. In the same archive there is a letter from Cosima to Claire de Charnacé in which she tells Claire that Bülow received a letter from Liszt by the same mail, exhorting him not to give Cosima a divorce.
13. VMA, Ms. F 859, carton 30, unpublished letter dated November 18, 1869.

alike for their sworn testimony in open court, and possibly face the prospect of having at least one and possibly two of the children who presently bore his name officially stigmatized as bastards. From that prospect Bülow shrank. The only other option was a charge of desertion, which he eventually pursued. Another reason for the delay was that he hesitated to expose Liszt to the humiliating consequences of a Protestant divorce. Since Cosima was a Catholic whose marriage had been sanctified within the Catholic Church, no divorce procured by Bülow would ever give her the freedom to re-marry within that church—nor, according to Catholic doctrine, within any other. By having her union to Wagner blessed according to Protestant rites, she became in the eyes of Catholics a public concubine. The ultimate rejection of her Catholic faith caused Liszt more distress than any other aspect of the tragedy. He could forgive Cosima much, but not what he called the denial of her God. The result was that he did indeed withdraw his blessing from his only surviving child, and a number of years elapsed before it was restored.[14]

We shall probably never understand the full extent of Bülow's misery. His personal life became a wasteland, ravaged by depression and a series of nervous illnesses. In only one or two letters does he lay bare his tortured soul. The first surviving letter to Cosima, for instance, written eight months after their separation, gives us a glimpse of what he was enduring.

> Munich
> June 17, 1869

> . . . Since you left me, I have lost my sole support in life and in my struggle. It was your mind, your heart, your patience, indulgence, sympathy, encouragement, and advice—last and most especially, your presence, your face, your speech—which, taken all together, constituted that support. The loss of this supreme good, whose full value I recognize only after its loss, has brought about moral and artistic collapse—I am bankrupt.[15]

The last three words are so eloquent that they require no embellishment. Yet Bülow himself later embellished them in what is perhaps the most revealing account he ever gave to the world about the whole sorry business. In a letter to Claire de Charnacé dated September 15, 1869—not long after Bülow had

---

14. Not long after her marriage to Wagner, Cosima converted to Protestantism. When she raised with Bülow the delicate matter of the conversion of his children as well, he told her of his hatred of the Protestant church, which he described as "the Germanic religion *par excellence*." But he added that he ought not to encourage his children to hate it too, and agreed that his daughters "should follow the mother's religion." (BNB, p. 486)

15. BNB, p. 477. This letter delicately forbears to mention that less than two weeks earlier Cosima had given birth to Siegfried Wagner, a fact which Bülow had already gleaned from the newspapers.

commenced divorce proceedings—he attempted to justify the action he was taking. No other document reveals his purgatory so clearly, and no other puts his version of the case so well.[16]

Madame:

There are few people in the world for whom I have as much respect as you, so it is natural, with any kind of self-pride excepted, to be very anxious not to be badly esteemed by people one venerates. It is this feeling which impels me to importune you with these lines, in which, to keep it short, I shall have to avoid paraphrases at the risk of using terms which are not sufficiently veiled, and for which, madame, I ask your pardon in advance.

You have been kind enough until now, madame, to give flattering praise to the spirit of equity and disinterested conciliation that I have shown in a situation which it is really difficult [for me] to bear. I have reason to fear that you are disposed to withdraw your very precious approbation in view of the last action I have had to take and which could well seem to you to be a serious inconsistency. It is almost as painful for me to justify myself about it as it is to abandon the explanation to the passing of time.

Believe me, madame, I did everything humanly possible to avert a public scandal. I imposed a life of incessant torture on myself for more than three years. You can have no idea of the devouring agitation to which I was prey without respite. As a last resort, I even sacrificed my artistic and material position. The only thing left was the sacrifice of my life, which, I admit, would have been the simplest way to arrange things, to cut the inextricable knot. I backed away from this sacrifice—can it be considered a crime on my part?—perhaps I would not have backed away if I had encountered on the side of the maestro [Wagner], who is as sublime in his works as he is incomparably abject in his actions, the slightest sign of an

16. We use the phrase "his version of the case" advisedly, for it occasionally parts company with the facts as we know them. For example, Bülow had been aware of his wife's infidelity for five years, not three; he talks about Cosima's lying "from morning till night" about her affair with Wagner, yet overlooks to mention that he also was a party to the deception practised on King Ludwig to preserve his wife's good name; and, finally, he suggests that Wagner was cruel to have forced Cosima to give birth to Siegfried at Triebschen, which, according to Bülow, had created much more gossip than if she had escaped into the anonymity of Paris or Versailles. The truth as far as this last assertion is concerned was exactly the opposite—namely, that both Cosima and Wagner had planned all along for the birth to take place in their home, precisely *because* it was free of strangers. There are other inconsistencies in Bülow's letter which it would serve no practical purpose to pursue. The basic fact is that he had been placed under terrible pressure and he can be forgiven if his record of events contains elisions and circumlocutions. Few other people could have retained such public composure in such a hopeless situation.

impulse of loyalty, the most ephemeral indication of a feeling of up-
rightness. Alas, I must not proceed with accusations, so as not to tarnish the only thing left to me, the conscience of having been less
guilty towards others than they have been towards me. But this ac-
cusation that I have just made, and which twenty years' acquain-
tanceship have put me in an ample position to prove, is not
necessary to exonerate another person, who formerly, as much by
the superiority of her intelligence as by her loyalty, frankness, and
the nobility of her character, resembled you as if she were a sister.
Well, this character has been perverted, tarnished, corrupted by the
pernicious influence of the third party [Wagner]. I do not despair
that this eclipse will only be temporary. When, madame, your step-
sister is free (we will perhaps have to wait as long as *one year* from
now for the result of the separation trial), when she has legitimised
before "public opinion" her liaison with her lover, she will become
herself again—she will no longer have to lie from morning till
night. Allow me, madame, to give a fairly striking example in support of my statement. A year ago I was, as I am now, in Wiesbaden
at the home of my friend Monsieur Raff. Cosima, since June, had
been in Switzerland with the children. We were corresponding very
often. One day she informed me that she wanted to take a trip to
Italy, Genoa, etc., and that you, madame, had promised to accompany her there, that you were going to arrive in Lucerne within
twenty-four hours—at the same time she asked me to send her a
sum of money she had entrusted to me for this purpose.

I was delighted with this plan, and I encouraged her in it the best
I could, foreseeing the most fortunate influence on her moral well-
being from your company, madame. Soon she told me that she had
left and three times a week I received the most interesting and kind-
est of letters, and the recital of her travelling impressions enchanted
me. Only, not a word about you, madame. I paid little attention to
that—the "we" used in her accounts deceived me, that is to say, it
reassured me. I attributed to a very forgivable distraction on her part
the fact that the news and greetings I addressed to you, madame, remained without the slightest acknowledgement.

How could I suppose that she was up and down the roads alone?
The correspondence still continued. Then one fine day I learned in
Munich *through one of the most widely circulated newspapers of Vienna*
that Monsieur Wagner and Madame de Bülow had visited such-
and-such a place in Italy.

I had the delightful job of maintaining before society that I was
aware of this, and had consented to this pseudo-marital excursion!

I acquitted myself in the role admirably; but what was hard, especially, was to have to improvise. Cosima, if she had not been subju-
gated to the influence of the most cowardly of all the great men,
would not have been capable of such jesuitical behaviour. The first
step must have cost her something. She could have refrained from
taking the others.

What pains, what precautions (at every instant in a life busy beyond my strength) did I not take to maintain the fiction of the stay
in Versailles. The people in my house almost laughed in my face.
Finally the situation became more and more intolerable—it
gnawed at my heart and my mind. I will spare you the frightful
episodes that the *imprudences* of *the other party* brought about (and
which the most active efforts on my part could no longer suppress). Therefore, I handed in my resignation, but it was not accepted by the king. I handed it in again. I wrote to Cosima that I
was leaving her my name, that she was free as far as the rest was
concerned. This letter, which in her reply C. described as overwhelming for her in its generosity, they are now using as a weapon
against me with M. l'Abbé Liszt, to whom they have sent it
through the intermediary of Madame de Mouchanoff to justify the
behaviour in Lucerne, etc. However indescribable this procedure
might be, I find it beneath my dignity to reply in defence. I have
promised myself not to see, not to write, to my former father-in-
law before the divorce is pronounced definitively and I shall not
deviate from this line of conduct.

Now why my inconsistency about the separation, in connection
with which I had first excluded the judiciary method? In November, when I asked her an almost indelicate question about the motives for her sudden departure (I had begged her in vain to wait for
Liszt's arrival in January), C[osima] thought fit to answer me with
a false oath.[17] It is that about which I was informed a few months
ago by the *newspapers,* who announced without the least delicacy
the happiness of the maestro to whom his mistress (the very word)
had just finally given a son, baptised with the name "Siegfried"—a
happy presage of the early completion of his opera.

The structure of my cuckoldry was thus crowned in the most
splendid way. I could not flee from Munich, but the hell I endured
during the last stages of my work there is unimaginable. Always in
contact with a crowd of musicians, teachers, pupils—in short, with

---

17. Bülow can only mean that he had asked Cosima, in however circuitous a fashion, if she was pregnant by Wagner, and that she had denied it.

the publicity which scarcely spared me—after the last conducting engagement, that of *Tristan,* the most widely read newspaper mentioned the devotion I had put into studying the work of my wife's friend. I only had the choice between two situations: that of being viewed with the most insulting pity as an individual unaware of what everyone knew, or that of being accused of infamy, as someone who had accepted the most shameful bargain as the favorite of the favorite of a king. At the same time, the newspapers were announcing the imminence of my divorce before I had even taken the first step. There was no other escape except suicide—or to follow this last advice. There is no sacrifice that I did not make in order to try to obtain the least scandalous divorce, the most amiable one. But I cannot change Prussian legislation. By mutual consent, "impossible." Only the plea of "desertion" remains.

I think that C. is not responsible for the shame that she has heaped on me, and which she will no longer be able to wash off me. I know that once more she has yielded to the domination of the scoundrel who prevented her from *giving birth* in Paris (or Versailles). She could not foresee that her confinement would provide the topic for the conversations of all the foreigners in the different inns in Lucerne and would be welcome game for the journalists—scavengers who simply wanted to be re-imbursed for their pleasure trip.

The maestro's article against the Jews (the autocratic lords of the whole German press) did a great deal to stimulate the ardour of these gentlemen in burying three more or less famous people in the public mire.

I think that I have been much too loquacious in my explanations. May they be of use, madame, in saving me from an unfair judgement on your part, which would give me the only sorrow which is still possible for me. They say that time heals many injuries, but this power has its limits. I am too covered with shame to be capable of expecting any benefit from that. I am exiled from my homeland as a musician, exiled from all civilised countries. I will try to eke out my poor future in the obscure position of a chaser after vouchers for lessons as a music-teacher.[18] The only satisfaction that sustains me is that of having found here below the complete compensation of what I have been able to salvage from it. I am not ex-

---

18. In Bülow's day, established music teachers who did not have the time to teach all their students often made extra money by issuing vouchers which were put on the market and bought by those who needed the work.

pecting a reply, madame, and I will not write to you any more, but encouraged by your offer of goodwill and friendship, I am asking you for the favour of not judging with unfair severity

Your very respectful servant
Hans von Bülow[19]

Although Bülow had to move mountains in order to procure his divorce, Cosima's ordeal was in some ways greater. Lucerne was blessed with a particularly obtuse Catholic priest who took it to be his duty to make life as difficult as possible for Cosima by pointing out the devastating consequences to her soul if she proceeded with her folly. This worthy was particularly upset by the fact that the infant Siegfried was already nearly a year old and had still not been baptised. He told Cosima that his parish was scandalised at such contempt for divine law. He attempted to get the local police chief to harass her into arranging a Catholic baptism, but the latter quite properly decided that neglect of baptism was not a criminal offence. Unfortunately, it became necessary for Cosima to visit the priest for a "clerical interrogation" before he would sign the necessary legal documents required in the case. In a letter to Claire de Charnacé, Cosima reported the farcical confrontation thus:

> COSIMA: It is not to amuse myself that I do not have this child baptised; I am waiting to be re-married to make of him both a Christian and a citizen at one and the same time—that is to say, to give him the name of his father. Besides, since the child is in good health, thank God, there is no hurry, and he will have the religion of his father, that is to say Protestantism.
> PRIEST: You know that the Gospels (!!) and the Catholic dogma forbid re-marriage during the lifetime of the first husband.
> COSIMA: Yes, monsieur.
> PRIEST: And that the Catholic Church excludes those of its members who disobey this law?
> COSIMA: Yes, monsieur.

The priest, who must have been stunned at such swift acquiescence, which undermined all his efforts to draw Cosima into a theological debate, quickly moved on to a critique of the events of May 22 at Triebschen, when the dawn had been shattered by a military band serenading Wagner on his fifty-seventh birthday. To all this Cosima made no reply but simply said: "May I have my let-

---

19. VMA, Charnacé Archives, Ms. F 859(3).

ter, please?" and left. As her report to Claire makes clear, there was little point in arguing with a man whose moral code was such that he had had a doll removed from a local hairdresser's window because it was displaying its *chignon* opposite a picture of the pope.[20]

Bülow was finally granted a divorce on July 18, 1870. Although he was the injured party, he paid all the legal costs himself.[21] Wagner and Cosima were married in the Protestant church of Lucerne at eight o'clock on the morning of August 25—King Ludwig's birthday. The witnesses were Hans Richter and the writer Malwida von Meysenbug. Later in the day a telegramme of congratulations arrived from Marie von Mouchanoff, also signed by Tausig and Lenbach. Liszt only heard about the wedding a week later through the newspapers.[22]

V

Now that the burden of life with Hans von Bülow had been lifted from Cosima's shoulders, it was replaced by an infinitely greater one—guilt at having left him. This cross Cosima bore to the end of her days. At the very moment of her wedding, the pain that mingled with the pleasure was well expressed in her diary: "My prayers were concentrated on two points: R's well-being—that I might always promote it; Hans's happiness—that it might be granted to him, separated from me, to lead a cheerful life."[23] Neither prayer was to be completely granted. It is a myth that Richard and Cosima Wagner went on to live a life of unalloyed bliss: there is abundant evidence that their marriage experienced its fair share of tension during the thirteen years still remaining to Wagner.

---

20. VMA, F 859, carton 30. Hitherto unpublished letter from Cosima to Claire, dated May 28, 1870. The matter of the children's conversion to Protestantism was long delayed; Cosima did not sign the papers until October 2, 1872. (WT, vol. I, p. 579) In an earlier letter to Claire, Cosima revealed great animosity towards the Catholic Church when she wrote: "Meanwhile the Pope has people hanged and put on the rack. How that holds one and attracts one to the fold!" (Ibid. Hitherto unpublished letter dated December 1868)

21. An entry in Cosima's diary runs: ". . . In answer to my inquiry about my liabilities, [the lawyer Simson] says that Herr von B[ülow] has decided to bear all the costs of the suit. This distresses me, but there is nothing I can do about it." WT, vol. I, p. 281.

22. LLB, vol. 6, p. 265. Nor was the situation without its comical side. According to Ernest Newman, shortly after the wedding Wagner received a letter from the president of "the Society of the Friends of Divorce" in Paris (who had picked up news of Wagner's marriage to Cosima from the French newspapers) informing him that he had been made an honorary member of the society. (NLRW, vol. 4, p. 274, n. 9) Wagner's response has not been recorded, but he must have been perplexed: he was never divorced.

23. WT, vol. I, p. 263.

From the depths of his despair Bülow emerged with painful slowness. He moved at first to Florence, where he remained for two years. There he buried himself in work and returned with renewed zeal to the piano. By 1872 he was ready to resume his career as a travelling virtuoso, and he won memorable triumphs in England, Russia, and America, particularly as an interpreter of Beethoven. Some idea of his punishing itinerary may be gained from the fact that during his American tour (1875–76) he gave no fewer than 139 concerts. He continued to suffer from his old depressions, however, and his letters from abroad give evidence of his manic-depressive state. After his return from America, his loyal friend Hans von Bronsart procured for him the post of music director at the court of Hanover, an appointment that nearly ended in catastrophe. Carl Bechstein tells us that having been alerted by one of Bülow's letters to the suicidal condition of his old friend, he travelled to Hanover and walked into Bülow's garden just in time to prevent him from shooting himself.[24] In 1880 Bülow achieved his definitive position when he became conductor of the Meiningen Court Orchestra, which he raised to international prominence. It was at Meiningen, too, that he met his second wife, the German actress Marie Schanzer, whom he married in 1882 and who brought a degree of stability into his troubled life.[25] For the rest of his days, he continued to conduct the music of Wagner, a fact which never ceases to arouse astonishment when the pain that Wagner had inflicted upon him is considered.[26] But Bülow had long since recognized that Wagner the man (whom he had described to Claire de Charnacé as "the most cowardly of all the great men") was a completely different being from Wagner the composer, and he behaved accordingly.

---

24. The immediate cause of the crisis was a serious quarrel with Bronsart which anyone else would have forgotten about within three or four days but which in the case of Bülow, with his knife-edge temperament, had gnawed at his soul. (BNB, p. xxii)

25. Marie Schanzer is one of the unsung heroines. She must have been haunted by many of the ghosts of Bülow's past, yet during his life she protected his interests and devoted herself to his cause. And after his death she built a fine monument to his memory by publishing seven volumes of his correspondence and a volume of his collected writings. See her memoir of her husband, published in 1925 (BBLW).

Incidentally, Bülow served at Meiningen for five years, and then stepped down in favour of the twenty-one-year-old Richard Strauss. The special interest that Bülow took in Strauss's career represents a touching postscript to some of the difficulties that Bülow had had twenty years earlier with Richard's father, Franz Strauss, the principal horn player of the Munich Court Orchestra (see Volume Two, p. 297, n. 39). Strauss's first appearance as a conductor, in fact, was entirely Bülow's doing. He invited the young musician to direct the Meiningen Orchestra in a performance of his (Strauss's) Suite for Winds, op. 4, on November 18, 1884, in Munich.

26. More than that, Bülow also gave many piano recitals in behalf of the Bayreuth Festival Fund, which Wagner set up for the eventual establishment of a suitable opera house in that city. One of the more sickening aspects of Bülow's correspondence with Wagner is the deferential tone of many of the letters. With his life in a shambles, and at his wits' end to know what to do with himself, Bülow still refers to Wagner as "my dear Master" and writes of the "piety" which he feels towards Wagner's music. Bülow's utter subjugation before the man who had brought him to the brink of personal disaster is worthy of a psychopathological study.

While the wretched business of his separation and divorce was under way, Bülow deliberately held aloof from Liszt, who was wracked by the sufferings of his son-in-law but was powerless to help him. Liszt not only understood Wagner's malevolent influence over Cosima, but had on occasion done his best to weaken it, sometimes with telling results. In this respect, as in so many others, the literature is hardly helpful. It has been frequently argued that since Liszt was now a cleric with powerful connections in the Roman Catholic Church, the last thing he needed was another family scandal; that his own past indiscretions hardly qualified him to preach to Cosima about hers; and that the practical reality of his life in Rome, many hundreds of miles from this do-mestic drama, effectively removed him from the scene of the action, and so on and so forth. Yet Liszt had constantly come between Cosima and Wagner, as a glance at his itinerary in the 1860s will show. He had spent much of the au-tumn of 1864 in Cosima's company, when she had first told him of her affair with Wagner. Moreover, when Liszt invited Cosima and Hans to accompany him to Hungary in the summer of 1865, his chief purpose had been to remove Cosima from Wagner's sphere of influence, and her absence from his life tore Wagner apart. And when the scandal of the *ménage à trois* could no longer be contained, Liszt had visited Wagner at Triebschen, in October 1867, a journey that had no other purpose than to persuade Wagner to break off relations with his daughter.

Bülow could hardly expect his father-in-law to sanction the Protestant di-vorce he had given Cosima, and so he resolved not to have any contact with Liszt until the matter was settled. The result was that he did not see Liszt for nearly three years. There was a reunion on October 22, 1871, in Rome, on the occasion of Liszt's sixtieth birthday, and Bülow described the "sweet and pow-erful emotion which filled my heart."[27] As for Liszt, he never ceased to love Bülow like a son, and he continued to search out professional opportunities for him. In 1874 he would even offer Bülow a professorship at the newly formed Royal Academy of Music in Budapest, but Bülow turned him down.[28]

Bülow continued to hold himself responsible for the financial support of his daughters; this fact alone meant that he remained in fairly regular touch with Cosima. His subsequent letters to her reveal his constant interest in the welfare of his children and his readiness to help with money. Not long after the sepa-ration, he told Cosima: "The allowance from your father, as well as that made

27. BNB, p. 484.
28. See p. 290.

you by your mother, belongs to the children."[29] One of the principal motives for his tour of America, in fact, was to make enough money to support his young family. Long before he arrived in the New World he told Cosima that "I shall remain in America as long as it is necessary to attain the minimum of the sum destined for my daughters during my lifetime: a hundred thousand francs, of which there exists at the moment only one fifth. . . ."[30] Within three years he was able to tell Cosima that as a result of his German tours a sum of forty thousand francs had already been amassed for Daniela and that a similar amount would shortly be available for Isolde.[31] As for Blandine, "[she] may expect the ten thousand thalers which my mother has often said she wishes to leave me."[32] Nevertheless, it would be misleading to suppose that Bülow played an important part in the upbringing of his children. This he was happy to leave entirely in the hands of their mother. And with such blanket phrases as "I repeat, madame, that I agree with all you say about the children," he withdrew from many of the major decisions affecting their lives.

---

29. BNB, p. 481.
30. BNB, p. 485.
31. The fact that he was ready to support Isolde is a clear indication that he had no inkling at that time that she was not his own flesh and blood. Even as late as 1875, when he wrote to Cosima about the terms of his will, we find Bülow referring to "our three daughters in common." He made no such provision for Eva, whom he knew to be Wagner's child.
32. BNB, p. 494.

Of Kings and Castles, 1867

*It was not the king, but it was a king, to whom were
addressed the sympathies of a grateful nation. . . .*[1]

I

On June 8, 1867, Emperor Franz Joseph of Austria was crowned King of Hungary. This was a political event of the first magnitude, which was welcomed on all sides. Ever since the Austrians had crushed the Hungarian uprising in 1849, Hungary had been little better than a vassal state. Its finances, its political institutions, and its foreign policy were all governed from Vienna. The leaders of the uprising were either dead or in exile. Hungary had never formally acknowledged Austrian hegemony, however, and Austria gradually discovered that the burdens of being an occupying power far outweighed the advantages. During the eighteen years of Austrian domination, debate and discussion had gradually emerged as the only means of ending a fruitless confrontation. The historical truth was that the destinies of both nations had always been intertwined, and some means had now to be found to reflect that reality. The so-called Compromise of 1867 was the result. Briefly stated, the crown of Hungary would be placed on the head of Emperor Franz Joseph, with all the pomp and circumstance accorded the old Hungarian kings. If the same head wore both crowns, so it was argued, many of the major problems of government could be resolved. The complex ritual of the Dual Monarchy embodied a fundamental point: the Hungarians were expected to promise allegiance not to the emperor of Austria but to the crown of Hungary. The measure of independence that this secured for Hungary was great, as subsequent developments

---

1. WFLR, p. 21.

showed. It was a noble effort which deserved to succeed. The Austro-Hungarian Empire, which was born of the Compromise, would last for fifty years, until it collapsed in the ruins of World War I.

A musical controversy had already begun to swirl around the ceremonials. Months earlier the primate of Hungary, Archbishop János Simor, had invited Liszt to compose a coronation mass for the occasion. To this idea the Austrians had made vigorous objection on the grounds that tradition dictated that the Imperial Chapel in Vienna should provide the music for such solemn occasions. The Hungarian press whipped up a storm of protest, and the Austrians were obliged to yield to Magyar national feeling.[2] Still, the debate went on for a long time, and it was only on April 30 that Liszt received a formal commission to provide such a work—less than six weeks before the coronation. By then the work was already finished, however, since Liszt had correctly sensed the outcome of the discussion.[3]

The coronation took place inside the ancient Matthias Church at Buda Castle, a national shrine which contained the remains of several Hungarian kings. The Compromise was well named, and it began for Franz Joseph on the very day of the coronation. As he and Empress Elisabeth entered the church and walked down the aisle towards their thrones, they had to pass beneath the royal banners of ten of the provinces of Hungary, each borne aloft by a Hungarian magnate, while the ceremony was led by Archbishop Simor. As the primate placed the crown of Hungary on the emperor's head, Franz Joseph may have realised for the first time the full gravity of the burden he was about to assume. The crown weighed four pounds, and he had to wear it for ten hours. Since he had fasted for several hours before arriving at the church, in accordance with the requirements of the ceremony, the physical ordeal should not be underestimated. Even at the subsequent banquet the crown was still in place when the emperor got up to make a toast. He raised his glass and proclaimed the words "Éljen a haza!" ("Long live the country!") Was Franz Joseph recollecting the last words uttered by Prime Minister Lajos Batthyány before he was executed by the Austrians in 1849? This was a day filled with symbols and tokens. After the long ceremony was over, the finance minister distributed "coronation money" at random. Mounted on a charger, he rode through the crowds scattering a hundred golden ducats and three thousand silver medals that had been struck for the occasion. Even the soldiers broke ranks and joined the crowds in a friendly scramble for this benefaction.[4]

---

2. SRB, p. 321.
3. See the letter that Liszt wrote to Baron Augusz on April 14, 1867: "Today I finished my Coronation Mass." Although he does not say so, he composed it in the brief span of three weeks.
4. For an eye-witness account of the coronation, see B-KMCE, pp. 44–52.

Since Liszt received no formal invitation to the ceremony, still less a request to conduct his own music, he was obliged to ensconce himself in the choir loft, from which coign of vantage he not only had a good view of the coronation but could also appreciate the performance of his music. The players, imported from Vienna, looked magnificent in their red tail-jackets and their white trousers. They had been well rehearsed by Gottfried von Preyer, the Kapellmeister of St. Stephen's Cathedral in Vienna. Liszt was so pleased with the result that he wrote to Princess Carolyne the same day: "The musical success of my mass is complete. Everyone was surprised by its brevity, its simplicity, and—if I dare say it—by its character."[5]

That last word, "character," is important. In his Hungarian Coronation Mass, Liszt expressed two contrasting qualities: the religious and the nationalistic. Was this a symbolic way of enshrining the idea of compromise in music, an idea which lay at the heart of the coronation? In any event, the combination strikes the ear as fresh and original. The *verbunkos* style is much in evidence, and so is the "Hungarian" scale with its mournful augmented fourths and seconds. Nonetheless, this is not a complicated work. As Liszt told Mihály Mosonyi, "The mass is built up in such a way that it can well be sung at sight. . . ."[6] For the coronation Liszt provided only six movements, which resulted in a work of half an hour's duration. After the first performance he added the Offertory, and two years after that the Gradual. The Gloria underlines the element of Hungarian nationalism by presenting a fragment of the *Rákóczy* March, albeit transfigured by the ecclesiastical context in which it is heard. This is a subtle piece of symbolism that the weight of Franz Joseph's crown during the long coronation ceremony may not have allowed him to appreciate. By the time the music has reached the "Qui tollis" section of the Gloria, however, the "Hungarian" scale would have penetrated even the Habsburg ears.

The violin solo in the Benedictus may have been inspired by the one Beethoven composed for the Benedictus of his Missa Solemnis. It was originally composed for Ede Reményi, but the exigencies of the premiere perfor-

5. LLB, vol. 6, p. 130.
6. CLBA, p. 123.

mance made it difficult for Reményi to participate, and the solo was played by
Joseph Hellmesberger instead.[7]

The brevity, colour, and simplicity of the Hungarian Coronation Mass always
gave pleasure. That pleasure ultimately extended to the emperor himself, who,
across the years, enjoyed a number of friendly encounters with Liszt and eventually, in 1874, made him a Commander of the Order of Franz Joseph.

After the coronation ceremony there occurred one of those scenes which
could have been drawn straight from a novel. As Liszt left the Matthias Church,
he decided to walk back to his lodgings. His route took him down the hill
leading away from the castle to the Danube, across the Chain Bridge, and
thence to his apartments at the Pest Parish Church, which had been set aside
for him as usual by his friend Father Mihály Schwendtner. Tens of thousands
of people were lining the route in a fever of suspense, waiting for the blast of
cannons from the Gellert Hills that would signal the start of the royal procession. Janka Wohl picks up the story:

> . . . The tall figure of a priest, in a long black cassock studded with
> decorations, was seen to descend the broad white road leading to
> the Danube, which had been kept clear for the royal procession. As
> he walked bareheaded, his snow-white hair floated on the breeze,
> and his features seemed cast in brass. At his appearance a murmur
> arose, which swelled and deepened as he advanced and was recog-
> nized by the people. The name of Liszt flew down the serried ranks
> from mouth to mouth, swift as a flash of lightning. Soon a hundred
> thousand men and women were frantically applauding him, wild

---

7. During his exile for his part in the Hungarian uprising, Reményi had whiled away his time as "Violinist to Queen Victoria," in which capacity he had led the orchestra at Windsor Castle. In 1860 he
was granted an amnesty, after which he started out on a series of tours which consolidated his international reputation.

with excitement of this whirlwind of voices. The crowd on the
other side of the river naturally thought it must be the king, who
was being hailed with the spontaneous acclamations of a reconciled
people. It was not *the* king, but it was *a* king, to whom were addressed the sympathies of a grateful nation proud of the possession
of such a son. . . .[8]

Although it had been two years since Liszt had visited his native country,
and he was fêted everywhere he went, he was unable to linger. About the middle of June he was obliged to hurry back to Rome in order to help supervise
the rehearsals of his "Christmas Oratorio" from *Christus,* which was to be conducted by Giovanni Sgambati in the Dante Sala on July 6. This was a trial performance of the still-unfinished work, and it aroused interest in Rome. The
newspapers tell us tantalisingly little about the event. According to the journal
Eptacorde (July 9) the Dante Sala was "full," while *L'Osservatore Romano* (July
18) contented itself with telling its readers that the long work contained "profound beauties." For Liszt, however, the experience of hearing a part of his
magnum opus in Rome was useful, for it helped him in the ongoing struggle
to express what was to become in its definitive form a three-and-a-half-hour
work.

II

From Italy, Liszt now travelled to Germany in order to be present at the
celebrations surrounding the eight-hundredth anniversary of the Wartburg.
Thanks to Grand Duke Carl Alexander, this ancient castle had been restored
to something like its former glory. A number of festivities had been planned to
mark its restoration; perhaps the most important of these was a performance of
Liszt's oratorio *St. Elisabeth,* which was arranged for August 28, the anniversary of the birthday of Grand Duke Carl August.

Liszt's journey to Weimar was almost a replica of the one he had undertaken
three years earlier. He travelled to Marseilles by boat and then boarded the express train for Lyons, which this time took him through Strasbourg and Mainz.
When he finally arrived in Weimar on July 29, he found Augusta the maid
waiting for him at the railway station, in response to a telegramme he had sent
her. They proceeded to the Altenburg, where Augusta had prepared the Blue
Room for Liszt's use, and where he was based throughout his visit. It was only
his second return to the Altenburg since he had closed down the house in

---

8. WFLR, pp. 20–21. See also Kornél Ábrányi's accounts of Liszt's visit in ALUK and AMS, pp.
338–43.

1861, and the visit was charged with emotion. The Altenburg was always filled with ghosts for him, and he told Carolyne: "Thirteen years of joys and sorrows, of *Wahrheit und Dichtung* enclose me, and sing, weep, exclaim, moan and shine around me in this place! Every object—what am I saying?—every atom of air and light contains a part of your soul!"[9]

A part of the venerable house was now occupied by "grace and favour" tenants of the royal family, but Liszt and Carolyne still had the use of several rooms, in which they had been allowed to store some of their furniture. It was now that Count Friedrich Beust, the marshal of the Weimar Court, explained to Liszt that the Altenburg would shortly be required as a home for Colonel Karl von Bessel, the commander of Weimar's 94th Infantry regiment, and that he ought to begin the sad task of putting his and the princess's personal effects into permanent storage. At the same time, Beust told Liszt that the grand duke had left instructions that the Blue Room, together with its small adjoining rooms and separate staircase, was to be set aside for Liszt's use in perpetuity.[10] Liszt suspected that this offer may have been made because the court was embarrassed at having to ask him to vacate the other rooms, so he declined. He told Carolyne: "I no longer want to return to this house."[11] One part of his and Carolyne's remaining effects went to auction that same year, and the other part went into storage in the nearby home of Frau Rosina Walther. Until Carolyne's death, in 1887, she paid Frau Walther rent for the use of this space.[12]

For several weeks before Liszt arrived in Weimar, the choirs of Eisenach and Weimar (eighty singers in all) had been rehearsing *St. Elisabeth* under the watchful eyes of Carl Müller-Hartung. At the same time, the orchestras of Weimar, Jena, and Eisenach had been rehearsed by Carl Stör—about 150 players in all. The strings were strengthened by some of the best orchestral leaders in Germany, including Ferdinand David (Leipzig), Edmund Singer (Stuttgart), Leopold Damrosch (Breslau), and Ede Reményi. The role of Elisabeth was sung by Sophie Dietz (a soprano from the Munich Court Opera), while that of Landgrave Ludwig was sung by Liszt's old friend and colleague Feodor von

9. LLB, vol. 6, p. 133. Liszt wrote this emotional letter on July 29, 1867. It was almost certainly a reply to the one that Carolyne had written to him from Rome on July 25, in which she had told him:

> God alone knows what it has cost me not to return anymore to Woronince, not to return anymore to Weimar! But the same feeling sustained me in both crises—the feeling that we are not placed here below to be attached to the place, but to the idea, to the work! . . . Therefore, I sacrificed Woronince for Weimar, and Weimar for Rome—for you are and will be greater in Rome than you were capable of being in Weimar. . . . Meanwhile, greet our treasured past—every pine-tree in the little wood, every ripple of the Ilm, every pebble of the paths in the park! (LAG, pp. 428–30)

10. LLB, vol. 6, p. 137.
11. LLB, vol. 6, p. 144.
12. For further details of Liszt's final removal from the Altenburg, see Volume Two, p. 552.

Milde.[13] It was Liszt's primary task to fuse these disparate forces into one en-semble. At first things did not go well. Many of the players were unused to Liszt's free gestures, which, as always with him, indicated the shape of the phrase rather than the metronomic beat of the pulse. The rank-and-file play-ers relied upon their section-leaders to beat time for them from within the body of the orchestra. Adelheid von Schorn put it well when she said that while the Weimarers understood him, strange orchestras were at first confused. Liszt, she said, "was no time-beater, but a *spiritual leader,* who did not simply conduct with his baton but conveyed his wishes with every feature of his face, nay, with every movement of his fingers."[14] There was only one rehearsal, but miraculously everything came together for the performance, and the vast en-semble began to make music. It was the old story, and one which we have en-countered many times in the course of Liszt's conducting career.

It is not easy for the modern reader to recapture the significance that the Wartburg had for nineteenth-century Germans. Although it lay within the do-mains of Thuringia, the stories and legends associated with it were woven deeply into the fabric of the German nation. Every schoolchild knew that this was where Martin Luther had sought refuge after his defiance of Emperor Charles V at the Diet of Worms in 1521, and where he had begun his transla-tion of the Bible. Likewise, the medieval song-contests were firmly embedded in the historical imagination. The Wartburg was also the place where St. Elis-abeth of Hungary had been taken as a child and had later experienced the "Miracle of the Roses." Liszt's oratorio *Die Legende von der heiligen Elisabeth,* then, could not have had a more appropriate setting for its performance, nor the Wartburg a more appropriate work to mark its emergence as a pre-eminent symbol of German unity. By the summer of 1867, Moritz von Schwind's fres-cos had begun to attract attention. He had completed work not only on the Elisabeth Gallery (which depicts the life of the saint from childhood to death in a series of thirteen scenes) but also on the great fresco in the Singers' Hall

---

13. Sophie Dietz was not Liszt's first choice for the role of Elisabeth, although she sang well. He would have preferred either Rosa von Milde or Emilie Genast, with both of whom he had worked many times. But the first was ill, while the second was now married and living in Basel.

14. SZM, p. 122. Adelheid von Schorn's comment might be dismissed as fanciful rhetoric were it not for a marginal note that Liszt himself placed in the full score of *St. Elisabeth*. At the point where the "Miracle of the Roses" occurs, Liszt writes:

> At this point, and at the entry of the choir "A wonder hath the Lord performed," the orchestra should sound as if transfigured. The conductor is requested hardly to beat the time ⌣⌣⌣⌣⌣ and that said, it should be added that the composer considers the usual sort of time-beating as a senseless, brutal habit which he would like to prohibit in the case of all his works. Music is a series of tones that long for and embrace each other, and they must not be fettered through the action of brutally beating the time!

We have provided similar examples of Liszt's "phrase-beating," rather than time-beating, in the chap-ter "Liszt as Conductor" in Volume Two of the present work.

itself. In this last picture, called *Der Sängerkrieg auf der Wartburg,* Schwind followed a time-honoured Thuringian tradition when he depicted a number of prominent individuals among the large gathering—including Liszt and Carl Alexander.[15] Martin Luther's rooms were also on view, together with the large stain on the wall where he was supposed to have thrown his inkwell at the devil. In other rooms were exhibited suits of armour and medieval weapons.

III

Important though the Wartburg celebrations were in Germany, to say nothing of the establishment of the Dual Monarchy in Austro-Hungary, they were not the events that captured the imagination of the world during that memorable summer. That signal honour was reserved for the Paris Exhibition (known to historians as the Great Exhibition in order to distinguish it from all the lesser ones), which was designed to convince the world that France, under the Second Empire, had reached the apex of cultural and scientific development.

Within months of ascending the throne in 1852, Napoleon III had begun an ambitious plan to transform Paris into the most modern city in Europe. Until the middle of the century, much of the capital had consisted of medieval slums infested with vermin—a crazy warren of narrow, zigzag alleyways and dark pathways which has been well described as "a sea of squalor" lapping across the Ile de la Cité, Montmartre, the rue Saint-Denis, and washing almost to the doors of Notre Dame and the Louvre. Within fifteen years, much of medieval Paris had been torn down to make way for the lofty mansions that lined the broad new boulevards leading towards the heart of the city. Napoleon entrusted the awesome task of rebuilding his capital to Georges-Eugène Haussmann, and eventually made him a baron in recognition of his services.

Street lighting was introduced, and at night it turned Paris into a wonderland—a "City of Light," as it became known. New aqueducts provided the older districts of Paris with fresh running water for the first time in their history (water had hitherto been brought in by porters bearing barrels on their backs). The sewers of Paris had been little better than open cesspools whose foul-smelling effluents were drawn off and taken away by night in cart-drawn barrels, then dumped in the forest areas beyond the city limits. As recently as 1848, more than twenty thousand Parisians had died in an outbreak of cholera directly attributable to the use of fetid water. Haussmann swept these obscenities away, and in the place of medieval sewer pits and neglected cemeteries he created more than five thousand acres of parks and gardens, many of them with

---

15. See *Die Fresken Moritz von Schwinds auf der Wartburg* by Helga Hoffmann, p. 47. Liszt is depicted as one of the contestants. He stands to the immediate right of the central dais and carries a lute.

drinking fountains. He allowed Paris to breathe. The boulevards transformed the family life of the people; Parisians became a society of strollers, especially on warm summer evenings, when they would meet one another in the cafés and outdoor restaurants that proliferated almost overnight. The great railway stations—the Gare du Nord and the Gare Lyon—which were also built at this time eventually offered Paris its superior links with the rest of the country. Napoleon decided not to charge the Parisians a penny in taxes for these miracles, but raised the money instead by issuing city bonds. (An issue of 60 million francs was sold out on the very first day.) It is a measure of his success that fifteen years after his reign began, Paris was able to mount the Great Exhibition and play host to the world.

The Great Exhibition opened on April 1 and lasted until November. Invitations went out to eighty sovereigns and potentates, and Paris filled up with the high and mighty from across the world—Tsar Alexander II of Russia, Emperor Franz Joseph of Austria, the sultan of Turkey, the khedive of Egypt, the viceroy of India, the Prince of Wales, and their various retinues. The king of Prussia turned up in the company of Bismarck. Only Queen Victoria and the pope declined to attend (the former was still in mourning for Prince Albert, while the latter was preoccupied with stopping Garibaldi's march on Rome). Tens of thousands of tourists converged on Paris, and the cross-Channel ferries did a brisk trade, bringing in visitors from as far away as Canada and America.

The director of the exhibition was Frédéric Le Play, a mining engineer, who conceived things on a massive scale. The enterprise occupied twenty-three hectares of land on the Champs de Mars, the parade ground of the military academy. There were fifteen different entrances to this park, whose walkways were lined with magnificent groves and banks of flowers. At its centre stood the Palais de l'Industrie, a huge building of 140,000 square metres, built of glass and iron. A series of concentric walks revealed to the promenader a panorama of national booths in which the countries of the world vied with one another to display their wares—fifty-two thousand exhibitors all told. The scientific marvels included such diverse inventions as a specially balanced truck for "Conveying Lengthy Goods on Railways with Sharp Curves," a model of a Siamese elephant, a "Speculum for Obtaining a View of the Larynx," and, most audacious of all, a machine which swallowed rabbit-skins and turned out felt hats. The pride of the British section was a mechanical swan which floated on water. When it was wound up, it curved its neck in pride, plunged its head beneath the water, and emerged with a fish in its beak, which it would then swallow before returning to rest, its head nestling behind its wings. But even this crowd-pleaser was outclassed by one in the French department. A local jeweller had designed a series of electrical cravat pins—a drummer with his drum, a death's head with a loose jaw, a dog—which were connected to a wire and a small battery carried in the pocket. When a concealed button was pressed, the drummer drummed, the jaw of the death's head chattered, and the dog growled and snapped.[16] Modern armaments were also represented; at the German booth, people marvelled at the Krupps' "Needle Gun," a cannon capable of firing from German territory and hitting targets in Paris. Bismarck viewed the gun and was impressed; a Franco-Prussian war was already a possibility in his mind. Three years later, in fact, he was to encircle Paris with such guns in a ring of iron.

On the cultural side things were equally dazzling. Baron Haussmann put on a ball at the Hôtel de Ville for eight thousand guests. Not to be outdone, the Metternichs roofed over the garden of the Austrian embassy and put on one of their own. It was at the Metternichs' ball that Johann Strauss II and his orchestra created a sensation by playing for the first time in Paris the *Blue Danube* waltz. The Parisians were literally transfixed by it: no one danced, they were rooted to the spot while they listened.[17] Thereafter, Strauss and his orchestra appeared every night at the Austrian booth. Offenbach, too, had a runaway success on his hands: *La Grande-Duchesse de Gérolstein* played to packed audiences in the Théâtre des Variétés. The title role was sung by the beautiful Hortense Schneider, who became the toast of Paris. Her song "Voici le sabre de mon père" stopped the show, and even raised the question whether the year 1867 would be remembered for the Great Exhibition or for *La Grande-Duchesse*. Certainly there was some confusion about that in the common mind. When Schneider drove around the exhibition on a sight-seeing tour, she was told by a low-level functionary that certain parts were open only to royalty. "I am the duchesse de Gérolstein," she retorted, and was admitted.

The presence of so many dignitaries in the city raised fears for their personal safety. Mingling with the crowds were many malcontents. On June 6 came the great review at Longchamps, in the Bois de Boulogne, where sixty thousand French troops paraded before Napoleon III, Tsar Alexander II, and King Wilhelm of Prussia. Afterwards, thousands of people lined the streets to see the potentates pass by in their carriages. Without warning, a Polish revolutionary sprang out of this sea of humanity, took aim with his revolver, and fired at the

---

16. From *The Times*, April 11, 1867, which gave very generous coverage to the exhibition throughout the summer of that year. Its praise was not untinged by criticism, however. In particular *The Times* was offended by the admission charges to many of the exhibits, and it retailed a joke that was started by the Parisians themselves: namely, that the only place in the exhibition that one was not relieved of money was the exit. Another bone of contention was what *The Times* (April 16) called "the great lavatory question." Apparently the French had placed the lavatories at strategic points among the restaurants which formed the outer perimeter of the exhibition, and people had to push their way through crowds of wine drinkers and beer tipplers to reach their place of refuge. The door was of glass, and it was set in a glass wall. "One can scarcely imagine an English lady going into such a place," the newspaper commented loftily.

17. The piece was performed by Strauss for the first time without the inane words which had led to its failure in Vienna.

tsar. The bullet was taken by the horse of one of the outriders, who had seen the would-be assassin elbow his way to the front and had spurred his steed forward to block the attack.[18]

Less than two weeks later the crowned heads of Europe received an even sharper reminder of their mortality. On June 19 the thirty-five-year-old emperor Maximilian I of Mexico was executed by the Mexican republican army. Maximilian, the younger brother of Emperor Franz Joseph, had been placed on the throne largely by force of French arms in 1864. News of the death of his protégé was not brought to Napoleon until July 1, during the climax of the exhibition's prize-giving ceremonies. The "Sphinx" carried on with his public duties at the Palais de l'Industrie, showing no trace of the emotional turmoil seething within him, and hoping against hope that the report was false.[19]

I V

In America, the Paris Exhibition had at first seemed far distant. The New World was singularly unimpressed by the extravaganzas of Vanity Fair, especially in a European production. And even when one of the exhibition's most prominent actors was almost shipped back to St. Petersburg in a coffin, and the brother of another was stood against a wall and shot, just south of the United States' own border, it caused scarcely a headline. Tsars, after all, are immediately replaced by others of their kind, whose chief role in life is to wait in the wings for that hallowed moment, however it occurs. As for puppet emperors, they were only as strong as the strings to which they were attached, and Maximilian's had been cut. In July 1867, however, the attention of the American public was rivetted by a little contretemps which broke out in the press and kept the general population amused for several weeks. It was to have interesting consequences for Liszt himself.

---

18. This attempt on the tsar's life might have been foreseen. From the moment he set foot in Paris, the crowds had greeted him with the cry "Vive la Pologne!" The assassin was a young mechanic named Beregowski, from Volhynia. He had travelled from Poland to Paris, via Belgium, for the express purpose of murdering the tsar, and had no accomplices. His double-barrelled pistol was overloaded; it exploded in his hand, shattering his left thumb. The ball pierced the nostril of the outrider's horse, passed through the animal, and wounded a lady who was travelling in the tsar's coach. The London *Times* called the attempted assassination a "detestable outrage" (June 8, 1867), thereby depriving its Polish readers of any suitable words to describe the Russian hangings of the leaders of the Polish insurrection in 1864. The outrider who had come between the bullet and the tsar, one M. Rainbeaux, was given the Legion of Honour by Napoleon the next day. The horse died.

19. Rome was even slower to receive the news. On July 8 Gregorovius noted in his journal: "Three days ago we received the news of Maximilian's execution. He has suffered the fate of the tamer of wild animals, who is at last torn to pieces by the savage beasts." (GRT, p. 363) And on July 17 he wrote: "The emperor . . . has been shot, in obedience to the same law by which he caused Arteaga and Salazar, the republican generals, to be executed." (GRT, p. 364) Liszt was already back in the Eternal

The American firm of Chickering and Sons had decided to enter one of its new grand pianos in the Paris Exhibition, where it virtually swept the boards. When the gold medals were announced, the instrument shared top honours with the entry of the much more famous Steinway and Sons. To the consternation of Steinways, however, Frank Chickering was admitted to the Legion of Honour. On July 1 the ribbon was pinned on him by Napoleon III during a glittering ceremony before twenty thousand people in the Palais de l'Industrie.

Was this a sign that the Chickering was actually a better instrument? Frank Chickering thought so; immediately after the investiture he cabled his firm in Boston:

> Paris,
> July 1, 1867
>
> In addition to our Gold Medal, I have today received a decoration of the Legion of Honor, which puts us at the head of all Piano Exhibitors.
>
> C. F. CHICKERING[20]

Here was an issue that America could understand; two of their own manufacturers had entered an international exhibition, had beaten out the foreign competition, and were now not only in a neck-and-neck race to the finish, but had started to argue as to what that finish represented. Which firm had the higher award? Had the Legion of Honour been bought? Since such distinctions were rare in the United States, the press was filled with commentary. The tongue-wagging became so unpleasant that Chickering was moved to issue a rebuttal.

> Paris,
> November 19, 1867
>
> . . . Knowing full well the source from which these statements emanate,[21] and as the facts with official proofs had already been published, I had up to this time considered it unnecessary to make any denial of these reports; but, as I find that such statements are still being extensively copied and reproduced, I feel it a duty to myself

---

City when word of the calamity began to spread. He commemorated the death of Maximilian in two works: a "March Funèbre," which later turned up in the third volume of his *Années de pèlerinage*, and a Requiem for male voices (R. 488), which Princess Carolyne described as "one of his greatest works." (SZM, p. 142). The Requiem for Organ, which is based on the one for male voices, was played at Carolyne's own funeral, in 1887.

20. Reprinted in *Dwight's Journal of Music*, Saturday, July 6, 1867.
21. Chickering was pointing the finger at his arch-rival, Steinway and Sons.

and to the interests of the firm of which I am a member, to make a *positive denial* of all such statements, which are evidently written and published for the sole purpose of giving to this award a false and deteriorated value in the opinion of the American public. . . .

. . . I never in any way, either directly or indirectly, asked for, nor did I ever use any influence, personal or otherwise, to obtain this high distinction.

My official notification of the award is dated June 30, 1867, and was received by me on the 1st of July. . . .

C. F. CHICKERING[22]

To this letter Chickering attached statements from three members of the jury, notably François-Joseph Fétis, Ambroise Thomas, and François Gevaert, which declared that his clarification was accurate.

As the controversy showed no sign of dying down, he decided to turn it to his advantage with a telling stroke of publicity. Instead of sending his prize-winning piano back to Boston, he sent it to Liszt, who was at that time living in semi-seclusion in the Santa Francesca Romana in Rome. What better fate could there be for the best piano in the world than to be given to the best pianist in the world? The reasoning was impeccable; and it worked. From the moment the instrument arrived in Rome it attracted many visitors, who regarded it as yet another monument to admire on one's peregrinations across the Eternal City—the Forum, the Colosseum, the Baths of Diocletian, and Liszt's Chickering grand.

V

Liszt had moved into the Santa Francesca Romana on November 22, 1866, St. Cecilia's Day, and it remained his principal Roman residence until 1871.[23] His sumptuously furnished rooms, which commanded magnificent views over the Forum, had formerly belonged to Cardinal Piccolomini. Many visitors, some of them famous, descended on Liszt while he was there, and were not slow to record their impressions. Adolf and Fanny Stahr said that Liszt "had a beautiful apartment with a view that was scarcely equalled in the world: on the right

---

22. *Dwight's Journal of Music,* December 21, 1867, vol. 27, no. 20, pp. 159–60. Chickering's letter is a long one, and we have quoted only short extracts from it.

23. On June 22, 1866, Gustav Hohenlohe had been made a cardinal and took up his new position as bishop of Santa Maria Maggiore. This had made it necessary for Hohenlohe to relinquish his Vatican apartments and for Liszt to seek another Roman address. Liszt lived in the Santa Francesca Romana until 1871, when the monastery was secularized. He then moved into an apartment in the Vicolo de' Greci, situated opposite the Santa Cecilia Academy, which remained his Roman base for the next several years.

The monastery of Santa Francesca Romana, a photograph by Pompeo Molins, circa 1870.

lay the Forum with its monuments, on the left the Colosseum, and straight ahead was the marble arch of triumph, of Titus."[24]

In December, Frank and Mrs. Chickering travelled with the prize-winning piano to Rome. By the end of the month it was installed in Liszt's music-room after a brief ceremony. Word soon spread through Rome that the piano had arrived, and people vied with one another not only to see it but to hear Liszt play it. In early January 1868, Kurd von Schlözer heard him play his arrangement of the *Tannhäuser* Overture on the new Chickering. "During the performance he stopped several times with the despairing cry: 'Sapristi, I am too old!' which I do not believe for a moment." Schlözer pronounced the instrument to be the most sonorous that he had ever heard.[25] For two years the piano was the talk of Rome. Almost a year after its arrival Liszt told Grand Duke Carl Alexander: "A superb American piano which was brought here for Christmas by the maker himself was the pretext for a growing flood of visits."[26]

Among the "flood of visits" several call for special mention. Karl Birkenbühl described the Santa Francesca Romana as "a melancholy, plain little monastery" which, because of its position on the old Via Sacra and its proximity to the Forum, was nonetheless an incomparable home. As he arrived at the doorsteps and pulled the green cord, it crossed his mind that this was Liszt's Sans-Souci—the equivalent of Frederick II's luxurious retreat at Potsdam. The visitor was let in by two manservants, a fact which surprised him, because he had expected to see signs of Franciscan poverty. He was also surprised by the elegance of Liszt's drawing-room.

> The door was opened, and the well-known artistic figure advanced in a friendly manner towards me. That the skilful fingers of the great pianist pressed the hand of me, a simple writer, is a fact which, for the completeness of my narrative, must not remain unmentioned. The first and most immediate impression produced upon me by Liszt's appearance was that of surprising youthfulness. Even the unmistakably grizzling, though still thick, long flowing hair, which the scissors of the Tonsure have not dared to touch, detract but little from the heart-entrancing charm of his unusual individuality. Of fretfulness, satiety, monkish abnegation, and so on, there is not a trace to be detected in the features of Liszt's interesting and characteristic head. And just as little as we find Liszt in a monk's cell do we find him in a monk's cowl. The black soutane sits scarcely less

24. The visit, which took place in January 1867, was recorded in their *Ein Winter in Rom* (Berlin, 1869, p. 132).
25. SRB, pp. 354–55.
26. LLB, vol. 8, p. 202.

elegantly on him than, in its time, the dress coat. Those who look upon Liszt as a riddle will most decidedly not find the solution of it in his outward appearance.

They talked about Hungary—and in particular about the forthcoming Coronation Mass and *St. Elisabeth,* works with which Liszt just then was deeply preoccupied. Liszt remarked that the coronation ceremony would be short, and so the mass had to be short too. And as he drank a glass of fiery Tokaj wine he promised his guest that he would try to put some "essence of Tokaj" into the music.

> . . . The cigar, which did not look, between the lips of the great musician, as if it had been treated with particular gentleness or care, had gone out. Liszt got up to reach the matches. While he was again lighting the narcotic weed, he directed my attention to the pretty statuette of St. Elisabeth which had attracted my gaze as I entered the room.

A long conversation then ensued about Liszt's role in the Church, and finally Liszt led his visitor through two smaller rooms to a wooden outhouse with a small window, through which were to be seen the Colosseum, in all its gigantic proportions, and the triumphal arch of Constantine close by, overtowered by Mount Coelius, now silent. "A splendid balcony might be erected here," observed Liszt, "but—*the poor Franciscan Monk has no money for such a purpose.*"[27]

Liszt also held masterclasses every Wednesday afternoon in the inspirational surroundings of the Santa Francesca Romana. The Roman students who grouped themselves around him at this time included Giovanni Sgambati, Ettore Pinelli, Carlo Lippi, Gilda Perini, and Nadine Helbig, who left some detailed reminiscences of those times. Born Princess Nadine Shahavskaya, this eighteen-year-old Russian aristocrat had arrived in Rome in 1865 after a period of study in Germany with Clara Schumann. The following year she had married the German archaeologist Wolfgang Helbig, and in November 1866 she had become Liszt's pupil—the very month of his removal to the Santa Francesca Romana.[28] Helbig well remembered a lesson, on Schumann's

---

27. From Karl Birkenbühl's *Federzeichungen aus Rom,* reprinted in *Dwight's Journal* on August 31, 1867; vol. 27, no. 12. It appeared under the title "A Visit to Franz Liszt at Rome."

28. Helbig and her husband lived in a large modern house built for them on the Tarpeian Rock by the German Archaeological Institute, and here she gave many musical parties. An extremely large lady (Gregorovius described her as "a woman of remarkably colossal figure"), after her marriage she became stout. When she sat down at the keyboard she sometimes pulled the grand piano towards her, rather than adjust her chair to the instrument—a sensible arrangement made possible by the balance of forces. (CMW, p. 75)

F-sharp minor Sonata. It was very different from the instruction she had received from Clara Schumann on the same piece. "I was impressed by his strange and pregnant remarks," Helbig wrote. "Of the heavy bass he said: 'Think how strong the arches must be that are to support this magnificent melody.' "[29] It was exactly the sort of imagery for which she had been searching. Whenever Liszt sat down at the Chickering to illustrate his interpretations, she was overwhelmed by his playing. "Under his divine fingers [the instrument] sounded heavenly," she observed, "but none of us cared to play on it." Evidently the action of the Chickering had become irregular, and because of the damp conditions of the monastery some of the black keys used to get stuck. These things never bothered Liszt, but they bothered his students.[30]

In April 1868 George Grove (the future editor of *Grove's Dictionary of Music*) was in Rome. Deciding on impulse to visit Liszt at the Santa Francesca Romana, he wrote a note "fragrant with incense, asking him to deign to receive his slave." For more than two hours Grove chatted with Liszt, mingled with other guests, and heard Liszt play a few pieces, including two of his Schubert arrangements from the *Soirées de Vienne.* "He was not tall," Grove recalled, "but in that limited space was concentrated the pluck of thirty battalions. He was in an Abbé's dress, long black coat and knee breeches, with buckles in his shoes; which became him well. His hair is grey, his face very refined and *luminous,* and his hands the perfection of delicacy."[31]

V I

Whatever advantages the Santa Francesca Romana might have had as a place of residence, and however sumptuous its furnishings, it lacked the solitude of the Madonna del Rosario. While the latter place, high above Rome on the Monte Mario, had been a retreat, the former had almost become a public thoroughfare. Liszt, who was by now one of the city's tourist attractions, must have felt at times like a statue planted opposite the Forum for people to gaze at on their way to the Colosseum. But temporary relief was at hand. One of his close friends in Rome was Father Antonio Solfanelli, his erstwhile tutor in theology. When Solfanelli, who was recovering from a serious illness, asked Liszt to accompany him on his convalescence, the composer required no further prompting. In early July 1868, the pair set out for Grotta Mare, on the Adriatic coast. They followed the ancient route of the pilgrims, which took them through Spoleto, Cascia (where they paid their respects before the preserved remains of

---

29. HLR, pp. 74–75.
30. HLR, p. 76.
31. GLL, p. 164.

St. Rita), Assisi, Fabriano, and Loreto. In Grotta Mare, they stayed in the house of Count Fenili, Solfanelli's uncle. Liszt's apartment was close to the edge of the sea and was surrounded by lemon and orange groves. He regularly went sea-bathing (an unusual experience for him), soaking in the fresh air and warm sunshine. He also studied the breviary daily, with Solfanelli as his instructor. And in Grotta Mare, too, Liszt began work on his set of Technical Studies for the piano. This could have been no accident. The psychological compensation is there for all to see. In these exercises Liszt reverses his role as a student and asserts himself as a master. Each day Solfanelli pressed the basic Latin texts on his pupil, and each day Liszt went away and pressed in turn the basic keyboard configurations on his imaginary acolytes. They are, in short, the musical equivalent of a breviary of piano playing, an "order of service" for all novices who aspire to keyboard excellence.[32] The piano aficionado should know that many of these exercises were invented in the absence of a keyboard. As Liszt drily observed in a letter to Carl Gille: "To be sure, they kindly offered to order an instrument and have it placed in my sitting-room, but I raised the most decided protest."[33] It was an idyllic existence, one of the first real holidays he had had in years. He described his time at Grotta Mare as "two months of tranquillity and simple contentment. . . . Such an occupation is enough to live and die well."[34] He got back to the Santa Francesca Romana on September 1, refreshed in mind and body.

VII

Liszt's brief sojourn at Grotta Mare reminded him of how unsatisfactory the Santa Francesca Romana had become for his peace of mind, and of the absolute necessity not to get caught up in the whirlwind of activity brought on by the company of other people. But what to do and where to go?

It was at this juncture that he received an invitation to visit Cardinal Hohenlohe at the Villa d'Este, the latter's new residence at Tivoli, about twenty kilometers from Rome. Princess Carolyne described the villa as "a fairyland, a dream, a most beautiful vision of Italy."[35] Its gardens were spectacular, with their huge cypress trees and hundreds of splashing fountains, and the villa itself commanded superb views of the surrounding countryside. Liszt arrived there

---

32. Liszt finished his Technical Studies two years later, but he did not live to see them published. They were eventually brought out in 1887 by Alexander Winterberger in a set of twelve volumes (WTS). For an account of their chequered history during his lifetime, see pp. 177–78.
33. SLG, p. 33.
34. LLB, vol. 6, p. 186.
35. SZM, p. 142.

on November 17 and stayed for a month. He knew that he had found an artistic paradise which was likely to satisfy all his creative needs.

The Villa d'Este takes its name from Cardinal Ippolite d'Este, the sixteenth-century governor of Tivoli, who had been responsible for developing the Benedictine monastery that was the original site of the villa and for turning it into an architectural wonder worthy of the seat of his government. It was a stroke of genius that led d'Este to bring in the architect Pirro Ligorio and charge him with the task of creating the gardens and fountains. Ligorio diverted the river Aniene for his purpose (a major feat of hydraulic engineering), and through a series of aqueducts and graded waterfalls created whatever force was required to "drive" the fountains into infinity. By the seventeenth century the villa was already regarded as one of the marvels of Italy. It was eventually acquired from the d'Este family by the Habsburgs, who allowed it to fall into disrepair. By the mid-nineteenth century, the villa and its gardens stood in urgent need of restoration. When the duke of Modena invited Cardinal Hohenlohe to become his tenant (the villa never belonged to Hohenlohe), the cardinal embarked on the project which absorbed so much of his time and money, but which eventually rescued for posterity some of the major fountains, which had become clogged and broken. By the time Liszt arrived, the spectacular water-displays were once more functioning as they had in Ligorio's time.[36] Liszt would certainly have sat inside Ligorio's masterpiece, the Fontana dell' Ovato (the so-called Queen of Fountains), and contemplated from inside the marble chamber the wall of water rushing over him. He always found in the Villa d'Este a wonderful source of inspiration. Some of the best piano music of his old age was composed there.

Cardinal Hohenlohe, who occupied the ground floor of the villa, had set aside a small wing, approached by means of a small spiral staircase, for Liszt's exclusive use. There was just enough room for an upright piano. This study had but a single window, from which Liszt could see the countryside for miles around and even glimpse the dome of St. Peter's. The cardinal himself had chosen the wallpaper: large roses on a light blue background, symbolic of the Miracle of the Roses in the story of St. Elisabeth. The place was sparsely furnished, and in the winter it was ice-cold. Yet it was here that Liszt got up every morning at three o'clock and walked by the light of a little tin lantern to the nearby church to celebrate early mass. In those days, Tivoli was not yet connected to Rome by the railway, and the only way to reach the place was by horse and cart along a road that was full of pot-holes—a bone-breaking journey that could take three or four hours. It was a trip that his pupils were glad to endure if they wanted to continue their lessons. One of Liszt's first visitors

---

36. Liszt had visited Hadrian's Villa, just a few miles away, in 1839. The reason he did not mention seeing the Villa d'Este at that time is fairly obvious: it was run-down, and there was little or nothing to see.

was Nadine Helbig, who reported that his hands were red and his fingers covered with chilblains, presumably from the cold. That did not prevent him from playing for her his *Bénédiction de Dieu dans la solitude* with "quite extraordinary rapture."[37]

At the Villa d'Este, Liszt brought to completion his editions of Weber's and Schubert's piano sonatas, begun in Rome a short time earlier. We do not readily think of him as a scholar and editor; yet these editions reveal him to have been both judicious and restrained in his presentation of the text, and quite free from Romantic excess. His introduction to the Schubert sonatas sets forth a set of editorial principles still acceptable today, the main one being the clearest visual separation of Schubert's text from his own (few) interpretative suggestions. "Our pianists scarcely realize what a glorious treasure they have in Schubert's piano compositions," he told his editor, Professor Sigmund Lebert.[38] Evidently this music transported him back in memory to his adolescence, for in an emotional outburst he exclaimed: "O never-resting, ever-welling genius, full of tenderness! O my cherished hero of the heaven of youth!"[39]

By mid-December Liszt was back in Rome. Although he was to have a number of different addresses there in the years to come, the Villa d'Este remained his Italian residence of choice.

VIII

One of Liszt's frequent visitors in Rome was the American painter George Healy, who towards the end of 1868 executed a fine oil-painting of him playing the Chickering.[40] This portrait captured the imagination of a far more prominent member of the American colony, the poet Henry Wadsworth Longfellow, who prevailed upon Healy to arrange an introduction. On New Year's Eve, 1868, Healy tells us, he and Longfellow drove up to the old monastery and rang at Liszt's private entrance. It was already dusk as they stood in the vestibule, and there were no servants in sight.

> But the Abbé himself came down to greet us, a Roman candlestick
> held aloft to light the way. His characteristic head, with its long,
> iron-grey hair, sharply etched features, and penetrating black eyes,
> and his tall, slim figure shrouded in priestly vestments produced so

---

37. HLR, pp. 175–76.
38. Lebert was one of the co-founders of the Stuttgart Conservatory and was now engaged as a general editor for the firm of Cotta, in Stuttgart.
39. LLB, vol. 2, p. 133.
40. It hangs in the Newberry Library, Chicago. See BFL, p. 245.

Liszt at the door of the monastery of Santa Francesca Romana,
an oil portrait by George Healy, 1869.

impressive a picture that Longfellow let out an involuntary whisper:
"Mr. Healy, you must paint that for me!"[41]

Healy reports that Liszt was amiability itself. He brought his visitors indoors,
showed them round his luxurious dwelling, and then played for them on his
Chickering. Taking advantage of his host's pleasant disposition, Healy told him
of the striking impression his appearance in the darkened vestibule had made
on him and Longfellow. He asked Liszt to sit for him so that he could capture
the scene before leaving. Liszt willingly consented, and the finished result is
one of the best likenesses of him in later life.[42] On January 4, 1869, Liszt was a
dinner-guest of the Healy family. The day after that he invited the Healys and
the Longfellows for a social gathering at the Santa Francesca Romana. Again
he played on his Chickering grand. "I never imagined such wonderful playing
before," wrote Alice Longfellow, the poet's daughter. "His hands were all over
the piano; I don't believe he left a note untouched."[43]

An important musical consequence sprang from these encounters between
Liszt and Longfellow. A few days after their last meeting in the Santa Francesca
Romana, Liszt took Longfellow and his family to visit Princess Carolyne, who
got on so well with the poet's sister, Mrs. Anne Pierce, that the two ladies
struck up a brief correspondence. This was the origin of Carolyne's suggestion
that Liszt should consider setting some of Longfellow's verse. At Liszt's request,
she provided him with a German translation of the famous poem *The Golden
Legend,* the second part of the poet's *Christus* trilogy. Liszt was fascinated by the
idea, but he took his time. It was not until 1874, while he was staying at the
Villa d'Este, that he finally completed his twenty-minute cantata *The Bells of
Strasbourg Cathedral,* for orchestra, chorus, and baritone soloist.[44]

IX

Of all the visitors who descended on Liszt at the Santa Francesca Romana, the
one best known to musical history is the young Edvard Grieg, who was in
Rome enjoying the benefits of a government stipend which Liszt himself had
helped to secure.[45] Having heard that Grieg had arrived in the Eternal City,

---

41. G.P.A. Healy, *Reminiscences of a Portrait Painter* (Chicago, 1894), pp. 219–21.
42. Today it hangs in Craigie House, the former residence of the Longfellow family in Cambridge,
Massachusetts.
43. WLL, p. 10.
44. See pp. 280–83 for details of the first performance.
45. Until now, Liszt and Grieg had not met. The Norwegian composer had earlier asked Liszt for a
recommendation in helping him to get a travel grant from the Ministry of Education in Norway.
Liszt's brief letter, which is dated December 29, 1868, says some flattering things about Grieg and his
Sonata in F major for violin and piano (1865), which the young composer had sent him.

Liszt expressed the wish to meet him. In February 1870 Grieg turned up at the old monastery to thank Liszt in person. Under his arm he carried a copy of his newly composed Sonata for Violin and Piano in G major (1867), which Liszt had never seen. Liszt insisted that Grieg sit down at the piano and play it. Grieg tells us that his courage "dropped below zero"[46] because he was unprepared to play the sonata from the open score, but somehow he stumbled through the first movement, with Liszt sitting next to him and occasionally picking out the violin part at the top of the keyboard. Liszt was entranced by the originality of the piece, and especially by the first entry of the violin. "That is bold! Listen to that again, I like that. Once again, please!" Liszt himself then took over the performance, and Grieg had a chance to witness his legendary powers of sight-reading for himself.

> Now you must bear in mind, in the first place, that he had never seen nor heard the sonata, and in the second place that it was a sonata with a violin part, now above, now below, independent of the piano part. And what does Liszt do? He plays the whole thing, root and branch, violin and piano, nay, more, for he played fuller, more broadly. The violin got its due right in the middle of the piano part. He was literally over the whole piano at once, without missing a note, and how he did play! With grandeur, beauty, genius, unique comprehension. I think I laughed—laughed like an idiot.[47]

Grieg's second meeting with Liszt occurred a few weeks later, in early April. This was a yet more memorable encounter because Grieg brought with him the manuscript of his unpublished Piano Concerto in A minor, which he had just retrieved from his Leipzig publishers. A number of other musicians were present, including Sgambati and the Danish composer August Winding. Liszt asked Grieg to play the concerto, but the young man declined, for he had not yet been able to practise it. Liszt then took the manuscript to the piano and read the concerto at sight, making commentaries to the audience as he went along. When he began, he took the first movement too quickly. But after Grieg had corrected him, Liszt went on in fine style and played the difficult Cadenza best of all. Again, it was the Chickering grand that helped to enshrine this moment in musical history. "In conclusion," wrote Grieg, "he handed me the manuscript and said in a peculiarly cordial tone: 'Keep right on; I tell you that

---

46. Grieg left a very full account of both these visits to Liszt in two letters to his parents, written in Norwegian, and dated February 17, 1870, and April 9, 1870, respectively. They are reproduced in M-JEG, pp. 137–42.
47. M-JEG, p. 140.

you have the ability to succeed. Do not let yourself be deterred.' "[48] Grieg treasured the remembrance of that hour and often recalled it in times of adversity.

In 1871, with the collapse of the papal army and the triumphal entry of King Victor Emmanuel's troops into Rome, the Santa Francesca Romana was secularized, and Princess Carolyne arranged for the instrument to be transferred to the home of Baron Augusz in Szekszárd. There it remained until Liszt's death, when it was transferred to the Liszt Academy of Music, in Budapest.[49]

---

48. M-JEG, p. 142. Twenty-two years later, when Grieg published selections from these letters to his parents in the Oslo periodical *Samtiden,* he allowed himself the luxury of adding various sentences that will not be found in the original text. One such passage has become famous. It concerns the moment when the Finale's second subject is recapitulated on the full orchestra, and the G-sharp becomes a G-natural. "When he got to the above-mentioned G," Grieg later wrote, "he gestured imperiously with his arms and cried: 'G, G, not G-sharp! Splendid! That is real Swedish Banko!' to which he added very softly as in a parenthesis: 'Smetana sent me a sample the other day.' " Grieg was justly proud of his Liszt connection. Did this prompt him to elaborate on it? See RFLEG, p. 36.

49. Today the old academy (on Sugár Street) is the Liszt Memorial Museum, and the piano is on permanent display there.

Of Cossacks and Countesses

*My father feared that women would trouble my ex-
istence and dominate me.*[1]

FRANZ LISZT

I

In the early summer of 1869, a new pupil joined Liszt's circle in Rome. This
was Olga Janina, the self-styled "Cossack countess," who was to taint Liszt's
life with scandal. Much has been written about this strange individual, who oc-
cupies a position in the Liszt literature out of all proportion to her modest
place in his life. If we propose to examine the case afresh, it is for a very good
reason: the veil of mendacity that she wrapped around herself, and which did
duty for her biography until modern times, can now be pulled aside. It has long
been known that her real name was not Janina, that she was not a Cossack, and
that she was not a countess. This was the image she projected of herself, especially in her four autobiographical novels, written after her connection with
Liszt was ended. The very fact that such fundamental things as her name and
her family background were falsified should have alerted us to the possibility
that other things about her might have been falsified as well. And they were.
We have new material to offer the reader, and it reveals a somewhat different
character than the one she liked to portray.[2]

Olga's family name was Zielinski, and she was born around 1845, in Lemberg. Her parents were Ludwik Zielinski and Lopuszanska Sabina, and Olga
had an older brother named Wladislaw. The family was reasonably wealthy,

---

1. LLB, vol. 7, p. 82.
2. One of the most reliable accounts of Olga's early life may be found in LLC, vol. 1, especially pp.
64–66, 98–100, and 239.

since her father had taken out a patent on the manufacture of an improved boot polish from which he had made money. Olga therefore enjoyed the leisure to pursue a musical career. Her first piano teacher was her mother; when it became evident that Olga was not lacking in talent, the young girl took lessons from Antoni Wrana, a former student at the Prague Conservatory, and Vilem Blodék, who had been a pupil of Dreyschock. In 1863, when she was in her eighteenth year, Olga married her first husband, Karol Janina Piasecki. The match was unhappy and she left him shortly afterwards, adopting his second name as her professional one because she thought it might project a better image. There was one child of the marriage, a daughter named Hélène. Freed from her marital yoke, Olga entertained serious ambitions of becoming a concert pianist. To this end she travelled to Paris in April 1865, in the company of her mother, and remained there for at least a year, taking lessons from Henri Herz. It is an indication of her talent that she started to give public concerts at this time.[3] After a mere eighteen months in the French capital, however, she returned to Poland and continued her studies with Karol Mikuli, a pupil of Chopin.

In April 1869, during some further travels through Central Europe, she heard Liszt play in Vienna. Here was music-making of an order she had hitherto only dreamed about. She wrote to him in Rome, received a positive reply, and the following month travelled to Italy to become his pupil. Liszt was surprised to see a young woman; he had expected a man, since she had signed her letter "O. Janina." At first Olga lived on the Via del Babuino, not far from Princess Carolyne, who was therefore able to observe her at first hand; later on she moved to the Piazza Trajane. Liszt was still living in the Santa Francesca Romana at that time, and that is where she first joined his large circle of students and colleagues.

II

From the start Olga stood out from the others because of her dress and her bizarre behaviour. She wore a jacket and trousers, smoked cigars, and cut her hair short like a man. Contemporary photographs show that she was not endowed with good looks; indeed, she was downright plain, her face hard and masculine. She had the habit of biting her fingernails right down to the quick and making them bleed; so assiduous was she in this ungainly occupation that "when she played she stained the keyboard with the blood of her gnawed fin-

---

3. One of them was given on April 23, 1866, in the Salle Herz. According to the *Revue et Gazette Musicale,* which described her as "a young and charming Polish pianist," she made a great sensation with a new operatic paraphrase of her teacher's, based on Meyerbeer's *L'Africaine.* (Issue of April 29, 1866)

gers."[4] She liked to draw attention to herself through her "advanced" ideas on such matters as free love, atheism, and female emancipation. Among her other charming accoutrements was her Circassian belt and dagger which, according to her, bore a poisoned tip; she also carried a revolver, much to the consternation of the other students, who regarded her as unstable.

When Olga arrived in Rome in the summer of 1869, she had already inhaled the vapours of Liszt's music and had become intoxicated by it. Music was not all she inhaled, apparently. She was addicted to opium, laudanum, and a variety of other pharmaceutical products; in fact, Olga never seemed to have any difficulty in acquiring drugs, and whenever she travelled she always appeared to have with her a deadly supply of pills, powders, and potions—and evidently their antidotes. And to judge from what Liszt later said on the topic, he knew that she was suicidal. This had a profound effect on the way he handled their subsequent relationship.

That Olga had formed an obsession for Liszt from the moment of her arrival in Rome, and that she had already put this obsession on public display, was apparent to all. Gregorovius met her in October 1869 and observed that "she has left her children in her headstrong passion for Liszt," and went on to describe her as "a little, witty, foolish person, mad about Liszt."[5] From 1871 Olga affected the title "countess," and even added it to her passport, a right which was hers neither by birth nor by marriage. In common with several other pupils, she accompanied Liszt on some of his journeys beyond Italy. For example, she was a part of the entourage that he took with him to Weimar for the Beethoven festival in the spring of 1870, and she also went with him to Pest later that year. It was in Weimar that her passionate and unstable nature got the better of her. She claims she was seduced by Colonel von Bessel, the Prussian army commander who lived in the Altenburg. In order to escape his attentions, she then eloped to Helgoland with Imre Sertrich, the under-secretary of the

---

4. DAF, p. 333. Nadine Helbig made a similar observation. She remarked that Olga's nails were cut down to the quick and were often bloody, "like the talons of some bird of prey." (LBFL, p. 217) Another eye-witness account of Olga in those early days in Rome comes to us from the sculptor Josef von Kopf:

> Madame Janina described herself as a "countess"; but all Polish ladies abroad were supposed to be countesses! Small, lively of speech, quick of movement, passionate, excitable, and short-tempered—she was a great pianist. With her wide mouth, upturned nose, hair cropped short like a man, she made an unbeautiful impression. But that quickly disappeared when she spoke or sat at the piano, and played her sonatas like a virtuoso. She often came to my studio; I also sculpted her in relief. She had a man's suit made for her, of the kind I was accustomed to wear in my workshop. Decked out like this, she would walk around the streets in the evening and through the night, a dagger in her dress. She amused herself, as she said, "royally." (KLB, pp. 370–71) A photograph of Olga wearing her man's apparel will be found in BVL, p. 199.

5. GRT, p. 458.

Russian legation in Weimar.[6] We surmise that it was also in 1870 that Olga's father died, because her income suddenly dried up and brought financial crisis into her life. From Helgoland she sent Liszt a letter of apology, and he took her back into his class. She rejoined him that autumn in Szekszárd, where he was staying in the home of Baron Augusz. Olga occupied rooms across the street, in the Hotel Szabó. On October 18 she actually put on a reception in honour of Liszt. On October 22, his birthday, she took part in a concert, together with Ede Reményi, to raise money for the French wounded in the Franco-Prussian War.

There is no doubt that Liszt valued Olga's talent, and he engaged her as a copyist. Perhaps he did this to help her manage her dwindling resources; in any case, he told Princess Carolyne that Olga's calligraphy was beautiful enough to display in an exhibition.[7] But he also praised her playing and encouraged her to study some of his own large-scale compositions, including the A-major Piano Concerto, which she played in public. She spent the winter of 1870–71 with Liszt in Pest, where he arranged for her to be featured in a number of concerts, though not always with the success that she craved. Janka Wohl was a witness to a distressing scene in which Olga suffered a memory lapse and was humiliated.

> Liszt was then living at the house of his friend, the curé Schwendtner. . . . He had at his disposal a fine suite of rooms, among which was a large hall well suited for concerts. . . . Every Sunday afternoon a select company used to meet there. The entire aristocracy flocked to his room, in the hope of not only hearing his best pupils and the artists who, with the object of visiting the master, happened to be passing through Budapest, but Liszt himself, who, like a popular prince, poured out with a lavish hand his unique talent. . . .
>
> At one of these *matinées* the Countess played Chopin's Grand Ballade in G minor, and she played it with such *bravura* and fire that the master publicly congratulated her.
>
> She had promised to play at a charity concert which was to take place shortly, and we all advised her to play this Ballade which she played so admirably. But we none of us knew that we were giving her the worst kind of advice.

---

6. These peccadillos are described by Olga herself in JSP, chapter 42, pp. 182–83, and chapter 48, pp. 202–03. In keeping with her usual practice, Olga identifies the amorous colonel simply as a Prussian captain "with the name of B. . . ." She goes on to describe him as "unintelligent, vulgar, and beastly . . . with an enormous nose that had turned blue through frequent libations." The undersecretary to the Russian legation is identified only by his diplomatic rank. The holder of that position in real life was Sertrich, and any reader of Olga's book would have been able to identify him.

7. LLB, vol. 6, p. 234.

On the evening of the concert a brilliant audience assembled. The Countess arrived, on the arm of Liszt, wearing a violet velvet dress buttoned up to her throat. He got her a seat in the little drawing-room with open colonnades facing the audience, which was reserved for the artists.

When her turn came she was very graciously received, and she commenced her Ballade, of course playing by heart. All went well until the sixth page, when she hesitates and gets confused. In desperation she begins again, encouraged by indulgent applause. But, at the very same passage, her overwrought nerves betray her again. Pale as a sheet she rises. Then the master, thoroughly irritated, stamps his foot, and calls out from where he is sitting: "Stop where you are!" She sits down again, and, in the midst of a sickening silence, she begins the wretched piece for the third time. Again her obstinate memory deserts her. She makes a desperate effort to remember the final passages, and at last finishes the fatal piece with a clatter of awful discords.

I was never present at a more painful scene. Going out, the master upbraided her more than angrily, as she clung to his arm. He had been severely tried, and he at last lost all patience with the freaks of his pupil. And, this breakdown confirming as it did, his oft-expressed opinion that she was not of the stuff that artists are made of, he no longer spared her.[8]

Talented though she was, Liszt had better students than Olga in his circle, and the question must be asked why he promoted "La Cosaque" so actively during the winter of 1870 71. We surmise that since her income had dwindled, her artistic future was now at stake, to say nothing of her much-cherished independence. It is not difficult to imagine what such a dramatic shift in her fortunes would have had on her hysterical nature. We believe that she now subjected Liszt to emotional blackmail, and Liszt began to experience the full force of her inflammatory character. According to a letter that Liszt wrote to Carolyne from Weimar on May 10, Olga had already made several unsuccessful attempts at suicide, and he went on to describe her character:

You know that Mme Janina has been in Rome for more than a fortnight, at the home of her friend Szemere.[9] Your reflexions on her are very just. For years, she has been feeding her spirit exclusively on the most perverse theories and sophisms. The blasphemies, imprecations,

---

8. WFLR, pp. 37–38.
9. This was Miriam Szemere, the daughter of Count Bertalan von Szemere, the exiled former minister of the interior in the short-lived Batthyány revolutionary government of 1848.

the extravagances of Proudhon and of the new Atheist school, and of the Asamists and Anarchists, are her familiar litanies. George Sand seems faint and timid to her! . . . The loss of her fortune, and several attempts at suicide, do not augur well for her future. But please, for Christian charity's sake, keep all that I have said to you to yourself.[10]

Suicide attempts would have been viewed by a man of Liszt's religious views with deep apprehension, and we believe that Olga used that fact to blackmail her way onto the concert platform. Even if she was not yet ready for a public career (as Janka Wohl's description of her playing seems to confirm), public indignities of the kind that occurred during her performance of the Chopin ballade were infinitely preferable to Liszt than Olga's demise.[11] And so he acceded to her ambition to perform out of a simple desire to bring back some meaning into her life.

III

In May 1871, Olga and her brother visited Baden-Baden in an attempt to make good their depleted resources at the gambling tables, to no effect. She also tried unsuccessfully to launch a concert career by giving recitals in Warsaw and Russia. The only letter from Liszt to Olga that has survived was written at this time. Dated May 17, 1871, it was addressed to her in Warsaw. What prompted him to write such a tender letter to his wayward pupil? Rather than jump to wrong conclusions, we would do better to consider the date. May 16 was Olga's birthday (Liszt never could resist an anniversary, although he mis-remembered this one by one day).[12] Moreover, Liszt knew that she had reached a turning-point in her life.

> Madame Olga Janina, née Countess Zielinska
> Hotel d'Europe, Warsaw
>
> Weimar, May 17, 1871
>
> On this May 17, did you feel the loving embrace of my soul? It is sad unto death, and my peace only arises from my extreme bitterness. (*Ecce in pace amaritudo mea amarissima.*)[13]

---

10. LLB, vol. 6, pp. 299–300.
11. It is not entirely irrelevant to dwell on the case of the poor young pianist from Hanover who, according to August Stradal, followed Liszt to Budapest in the hopeful expectation of studying with him. After the man played *St. Francis of Paola walking on the waters* abominably, Liszt expressed an unfavorable opinion of his talent, and told him not to come back. The young man was devastated and shortly afterwards shot himself. Everyone tried to hide this news from Liszt; if he had learned of it, "he would certainly have given way to despair." (SE, p. 137)
12. ZRPC, p. 8.
13. "Behold, for peace I had great bitterness." (Isaiah 38:17)

Why do you chatter about the "alms of anger and hatred"? Here at my side are the two red notebooks with the golden star that you brought to the Villa d'Este for me. They say something different. Do not deny them, and follow *this* star which shines for you in my heart.

You are right not to "*exploit*," but rather to foster your very rare and admirable musical talent. However, in order not to weaken its development, you must correct your fantastic and capricious moods, intolerable in good company, and not least contrary to my wishes for dignity in your character.

Your salamander-like nature, and your obsession for work, assign you a noble rank in art. Is it possible that you might renounce it, despite the protest of your conscience, and that the shameful pleasures of the charivari of "*degradations*" with their pharmaceutical attractions, revolvers, and other nauseating stupidities will engulf you?

Let me say No and No again, and embrace you and kiss your hand.

F.L.

I await your news from Russia.[14]

How should we interpret the words Liszt attributes to Olga, "the alms of anger and hatred"? Had she asked Liszt for money and received a refusal? Words would have been no substitute for cash to a woman in Olga's position, especially if she needed it for "pharmaceutical attractions."

Liszt now made his first serious attempt to rid himself of her. With his encouragement she set out in July for New York in search of work. Although she remained in America for more than three months, the New World was even less ready than the Old to provide her with opportunities for a career. It was the middle of the summer, the concert season was at an end, and she could procure no engagements. According to Olga, she wrote Liszt a number of letters concerning her plight, but his reply was "pitiless" (no such reply has come down to us). She met a number of people who were acquainted with Liszt, including Leopold Damrosch and the music publisher Julius Schuberth, who alerted Liszt to the fact that Olga appeared to be deranged and had issued a death threat against him.[15]

Why had Olga sought out Schuberth? The story is of interest to all piano aficionados. At Liszt's request Olga had taken with her to New York the three-volume manuscript of the Technical Studies that he had begun in Grotta Mare

---

14. BDLL, p. 22.

15. About the middle of November 1871, Liszt received two letters from Schuberth in New York, and one from Hébert in Paris, warning him to be on his guard "against the vengeance of a hysterical madwoman." (LLB, vol. 6, p. 330)

three years earlier, of which Olga had evidently begun to make a fair copy during her tenure in Rome. Earlier that year Liszt had concluded an agreement with Schuberth, according to which the latter was to hand over a thousand dollars on receipt of the precious package.[16] Olga not only pocketed the thousand dollars but failed to deliver the third volume of studies, which she may have sold when her career in the New World failed to materialize. At the end of her tether, Olga cabled Liszt that she was returning to Europe to kill him and left New York on October 15 on the French steamship *Saint Laurent*. She got to Hungary during the third week of November. On the twenty-fifth she burst into Liszt's apartment in Budapest, brandishing a revolver and several phials of poison—"ornaments that she had already shown me twice, last winter," according to Liszt.[17] She may have been under the influence of drugs. For several hours Liszt attempted to calm her down. Ödön Mihalovich entered the room, followed shortly afterwards by Antal Augusz. (They were not there by chance. Liszt had taken the precaution of forwarding to Mihalovich all of Olga's letters, so Mihalovich was by now very well-informed about her hysterical nature.) Olga repeated before everyone that she had no other object in life than to kill Liszt and then commit suicide. Liszt assured his two colleagues that he could handle the hysterical woman without assistance, and they left. Suddenly Olga swallowed a dose of "poison" and went into convulsions. In the early hours of the morning Liszt somehow got her back to the Hotel Europa, on the corner of Nádor Street, where she was staying. A doctor was summoned, and the poison was found to be harmless. Olga's little "scene" had all the makings of a low-class farce, but however much Liszt would have liked to keep it quiet, it was not possible for him to do so. Since he knew that within a very short time word would reach Princess Carolyne, he sent her a preliminary account of the confrontation. His letter is dated November 29, 1871.

> Last Saturday a terrible disturbance occurred here. I was unable to resolve it until the evening of the day before yesterday. Mme Countess Janina—this title now appears on her Austrian passport—has spent three days here. Spare me the catalogue of her acts of vi-

---

16. This information comes to us from an unpublished letter of Liszt's, dated June 10, 1871, to an unknown correspondent. The holograph is preserved in the Heinemann Collection of the Library of Congress under the call number 168-B.

The memoirs of Alexander Gottschalg confirm many of the details of the strange case of Olga and the Technical Studies, including the story of her absconding with Liszt's fee and the third volume. (GLW, pp. 117–18) When Liszt discovered what had happened, he found the prospect of making another copy so irksome that publication of the project was delayed. The first two parts appeared in 1887, shortly after his death, in an edition by Alexander Winterberger. But what of the missing third part? It eventually came into the possession of another of Liszt's students, the German pianist Karl Goepfart, and was published for the first time in 1983.

17. LLB, vol. 6, p. 330.

olence and anger, and do me the favour of not speaking about her to anyone. My guardian angel protected me in the moment of danger. After another attempt to poison herself in my room, Madame Janina left for Paris, where she will probably remain. But once again, I urge you not to talk about it—not even to me—for I wish to forget this episode as soon as possible which, thanks to my guardian angel, did not end in catastrophe or in a public scandal.[18]

The public scandal may have been avoided for the present—it came later—but Carolyne was not satisfied with Liszt's explanation and pressed him for further details. He did not provide them until February 3, 1872, more than two months later. Only then did Carolyne learn for the first time of the death threat from New York, the warnings from Schuberth and Hébert, and the dramatic confrontation with the revolver in his apartment. Liszt even reported some of the dialogue between himself and Olga. As Janina advanced on him with her pistol, Liszt told her: "What you are about to do is wicked, madame, and I beg you to desist, but I shall not try to prevent you." Carolyne, and anyone else who has thought about the matter, must have wondered why Liszt and his friends did not summon the police there and then and prosecute Olga for her criminal behaviour. Liszt himself provides the answer.

> I protested firmly against the intervention of the police, for Mme Janina was quite capable of firing her revolver before they had time to handcuff her. Enough, and more than enough on this subject. The next day she left for Paris. . . . I ask you, once again, not to mention this to anyone. Do not write to Augusz—your silence will do me honour.[19]

Immediately after her simulated suicide, La Janina was given an ultimatum by Augusz and Mihalovich: Either leave Budapest voluntarily or be deported by the police. She left, with venom in her heart, and took up residence in Paris, where she plotted her revenge.

IV

In 1872 Olga gave a number of public recitals in Paris which featured the music of Liszt and Chopin.[20] On March 31 and April 22, 1873, she actually lectured

---

18. LLB, vol. 6, pp. 316–17.
19. LLB, vol. 6, p. 330.
20. See the article about one of Olga's appearances in *La Revue Musicale,* December 8, 1872; also *L'Art Musical,* December 12, 1872.

on Liszt at the Salle des Conférences.[21] This, together with some teaching, bought her the necessary time to enable her to work on her four autobiographical novels, the first of which was published in 1874 under the title *Souvenirs d'une cosaque*. She used the pseudonym "Robert Franz," the name of the well-known song composer and one of Liszt's most loyal friends and associates. This fictional account of her imaginary life with Liszt had no other purpose than to humiliate him in the eyes of his friends and colleagues. In pursuit of this aim she sent copies to the pope, Grand Duke Carl Alexander, and other prominent individuals who knew Liszt. The novel eventually went through thirteen editions and was followed by an anonymous sequel, *Souvenirs d'un pianiste*, which pretended to be Liszt's reply. In 1875 two further novels appeared from her pen, for which she used the pseudonym Sylvia Zorelli: *Les Amours d'une cosaque par un ami de l'Abbé "X"* and *Le Roman du pianiste et de la cosaque*. We shall briefly consider the contents of the books in a moment.

V

These are the probable facts as they are known to us. We now come to the fiction. It is a sad commentary on the way in which biographies of Liszt are generally written that Olga's novels have been regarded as a more truthful account of her relationship with him than the scholarly documents which pertain to the case—to say nothing of the views of those who knew her well. Ernest Newman went so far as to say that Olga's first book was "one of the most valuable documents we possess for the reconstruction of the real Liszt," and "we are bound to accept it as a perfectly truthful record."[22] Even Sacheverell Sitwell, one of Liszt's more sympathetic biographers, says that "the story is complicated because both actors in the drama give their own accounts of it"[23]—as if the one "account" balanced the other—without even bothering to find out which one coincided with reality.[24]

---

21. Reported in *Avenir National,* April 5, 1873. The text of the lectures may be found in Jules Janin's *Journal des Débats* for April 7, 1873, and Henri Roche's *La Presse Musicale* for April 26, 1873.

22. NML, pp. 250–51.

23. SFL, p. 289.

24. One can only be grateful to Hortense Voigt for not leaving any memoirs that might constitute "the other side" of *her* case. This name is unlikely to stir many memories, even among Liszt aficionados. Yet for years Fräulein Voigt went around calling herself Liszt's fiancée, and became such a nuisance to him that the police were called in. The facts of the matter may be summarized briefly. Voigt pursued Liszt to Hungary in February 1874, proclaiming her love for him. She lay siege to the house of Imre Széchenyi in Horpács for four days, hoping to catch a glimpse of her idol. Széchenyi was forced to get a restraining order from the authorities, barring her from the neighbourhood. She then went to Budapest, where she approached both a Catholic priest and a Protestant pastor to discuss her wedding with Liszt, unfortunately delayed "by intrigues of the blackest hue." (WLLM, p. 123) In a letter to Baron Augusz, Liszt spoke of "the intrusions of the fiancée, who qualifies for the madhouse."

In the first of her novels, *Souvenirs d'une cosaque,* she tells her readers that she was raised on the steppes of Ukraine in one or another of the family's castles, and often went out hunting for wolves with her bare hands. Already we have entered her world of fantasy: the Zielinski family owned no castles, Olga was brought up hundreds of miles from the steppes, and anyone who hunted wolves with their bare hands would hardly have survived the experience. According to the novel, her mother died when Olga was only eighteen months old, and she was free to roam as she wished. This is strange, since her mother accompanied her to Paris years later when she took up a musical career. She tells us that she was only fifteen when she married Karol Piasecki (she was nearly eighteen) and that on the morning after the wedding night she horse-whipped him for his cruelty and left him. Fantasy is now piled onto fiction until her narrative groans beneath the weight of its own mendacity. We are asked to believe that when she subsequently began her musical studies in Kiev, people fled from her in all directions because of the tiger that she kept on a chain. One day, in an unguarded moment, the beast bit the principal of the Kiev Conservatory, and the unfortunate fellow succumbed to gangrene.[25] For-

---

Augusz alerted the Budapest police, who picked up Fräulein Voigt for questioning. The commissioner of police, Elek Thaisz, sent an account to Augusz on February 18:

> My most esteemed friend:
>
> Miss Hortense Voigt was here at 12 noon. I gently reminded her of the inappropri-ateness of her behaviour toward Liszt, to which her tears started showering like rain and she was able to excuse herself only by saying, "Das wird sich Liszt selbst verantworten müssen" ["Liszt will have to hold himself responsible for it"]. After repeated attempts to convince her that nobody should be expected to tolerate intrusions similar to those of hers, and that everybody is entitled to police protection in such cases, I cautioned her very seriously that she should leave Liszt alone in the future or I should be compelled to use the most severe police measures against her.

> Your sincere and devoted friend,
> Elek Thaisz

> Budapest, February 18, 1874. (VLES, pp. 81–82)

The warning does not appear to have had much effect on Hortense. Three years later we find her writing to Liszt and signing herself "Thy loving bride"—a spectacular advance on her earlier modest claim to be merely his fiancée. Dr. Eduard von Liszt had something to say about Hortense Voigt in his book *Franz Liszt: Abstammung, Familie, Begebenheiten* (1937; p. 78). The letter he quotes from her there has her addressing Liszt as "Mein heissgeliebter Bräutigam, mein Süsser, herziger Franz!" ("My ardently loved bridegroom, my darling, lovely Franz!").

The only reason to recall the hysterical ravings of Hortense Voigt at this stage in the Janina saga is to point out that Liszt attracted such emotional cripples all his life, and Olga Janina was but one of them. If she had not written her novels, and had simply faded into the sunset like Hortense and a dozen others of her ilk, it is unlikely that biographers would find it necessary to devote more than a couple of lines to her tortured soul.

25. ZRPC, p. 44. This particular elaboration comes from the last novel, *Le Roman du pianiste et de la cosaque* (1875), written under the pseudonym "Sylvia Zorelli." What is of psychological interest here is that we have a fictitious "Sylvia Zorelli" writing a first-hand account of her friend, the equally fic-

tunately he lingered just long enough to introduce her to the music of L[iszt]. Is it necessary to take this account of her early life any further to sense that we are in the presence of a practised liar? One of the few truthful accounts in her entire description of her early years is the birth of her daughter, Hélène (conceived, so she would have us believe, during the cruelty of the solitary honeymoon night), a product of the union that would in any case have been impossible for her to hide.

It is when we come to her account of her first meetings with Liszt, however, that her gifts as a writer of fiction are revealed in all their dazzling splendour. Nowhere is Liszt openly identified, of course. He is thinly disguised as the "Abbé 'X.'" She describes one of their first encounters at the Santa Francesca Romana, in 1869, shortly after Liszt had accepted her as a pupil. As he entered the room there was a general rush of admirers towards him, wanting to kiss his hand. Olga tells us that she did not join in, finding the atmosphere of idolatry and hero-worship suffocating. Liszt received her coldly, a reaction which stood in such sharp contrast to the warmth of his earlier greetings that she attributed it to the fact that he was irritated that she had not joined the others in prostrating herself before him and paying homage. He then had her play a few things but was so critical of her playing that she felt humiliated. After the lesson was over, she entered the Colosseum and smoked a cigar to soothe her fretted nerves. The plot now thickens. A short time later there was a knock on Olga's door. It was Liszt, come to apologise for his brusque behaviour towards her. She would have us believe that he suggested that she would achieve nothing by coming for lessons with all the others, and that they should meet at either his place or hers for private instruction. Unable to resist the impulse, Olga seized his hand and kissed it with ardour, an action she instantly regretted, so she says, because it made her no better than the crowd of sycophants whose behaviour had aroused her revulsion on that earlier occasion. Olga's tale now moves quickly towards its first climax. The lessons began, and an unspoken love sprang up between the pair. One evening in July he told her that he had to leave for Germany on a short trip. The news acted like a catalyst on their relationship. As she was about to leave his apartment, Liszt took her in his arms and she in turn clasped him to her savagely, her blood on fire. They remained in a locked embrace until she heard him say: "Do not speak to me of love. I must not love." Stunned, she rushed out of the building, her heart on fire and her thoughts in a whirl.

---

titious "cosaque," as if to provide the world with some badly needed verification of the first novel. By now Olga has such a multiplicity of personalities at her disposal that she almost eludes detection. Zielinska hides behind Janina, who in turn hides behind "la cosaque," who finally hides behind Zorelli. This infinite regression was continued at the time of her second marriage, when she hid behind the title Marquise de Cézano, sometimes adding the suffix "née Princess Orbeliani." See pp. 189–90.

During Liszt's absence abroad Olga had much time to think. "I must not love": his last words haunted her. If it was the Church that was constraining him, then she would wrest him from the Church. "He would be mine, or I would kill him," she resolved. Liszt returned to Rome, and the lessons resumed. At their first reunion "he drew me into his arms, resting my head on his shoulder. I do not know how long we remained like that. It may have been centuries. . . . So he loved me!" " 'Call me Ferencz, *tutoie-moi,*' " she has him say, "and he covered me with passionate kisses."[26]

The novelist in Olga was now in full flood, and her story moved quickly towards its dénouement. In the winter of 1869 Liszt moved to Tivoli and took up residence at the Villa d'Este. Olga visited him twice a week for her lessons, and she claims that they frequently dined alone on the terrace. On one occasion, as she entered his room he drew her to him with the words "I can resist you no longer!" and they became lovers in the physical sense. As he lay there sleeping, Olga wondered what his first words would be when he awoke. Would they be words of love or words of remorse? If the latter, she resolved to kill him with the poisoned dagger which had fallen at the foot of the bed after she had disrobed. She drew the blade from the sheath and held her breath. Liszt awoke. His first words were of love. He was saved.[27]

VI

The first novel was evidently so successful that it was quickly followed by another, which purported to be a "reply" to the first; that is to say, it pretended to come from Liszt. Bearing the title *Souvenirs d'un pianiste: Réponse aux Souvenirs d'une cosaque,* but published anonymously, it established from the beginning the appropriate tone of titillation for what was to follow. After declaring in the preface that "he who writes these lines acts out of neither Vengeance nor Justice," Olga writes:

> Taking up the pen for the last time, he has set himself a more elevated task.
> A Christian, a priest, he lapsed one day, one hour.[28] For such a terrible crime he thought that there was only one expiation and

---

26. JSC, p. 139.
27. JSC, pp. 175–76.
28. Liszt was never a priest, of course, nor had he taken vows of chastity. But Olga was not about to let the facts stand in the way of a good story.

only one consolation: a public confession. On his knees before God and man, he retraces step by step the story of this great fall.

G . . . September 1874.[29]

Olga was now as notorious in Paris as she had been in Budapest. And she was just as unstable. Thinking that her new-found fame would not harm her flagging concert career, she took to sending publicity material about her forthcoming appearances to the local newspapers. On one occasion this had an unexpected result, and she was pilloried in the press.

Quite a violent scene took place this evening at the Café de la Paix. By giving a brief account of what led up to it, we come just as quickly to the climax of the story. Mme Olga Janina, Liszt's student, the author of a book which recently appeared in Paris, and which is called *Souvenirs d'une cosaque,* is known less than she would doubtless like to be. Mme Olga Janina is getting ready to give a concert in the Taitbout room next Saturday and to this end she sent to many Parisian newspapers short publicity announcements which several inserted without malice. A few others treated her quite badly about this matter, among them this evening's *Le Pays.*

Mme Olga de Janina set great store, so she says, by *Le Pays'* publicity. Thus during the day she sent to M. Paul de Cassagnac someone who professed to be one of her friends, a priest, so it seems, who received from the chief editor of *Le Pays* this very simple reply:

"I cannot insert your little publicity article, for I have just seen among our proofs an article from a collaborator which damages it somewhat."

It appears that M. de Cassagnac added that he was surprised to see a priest request publicity coverage for the concert of Mme Olga de Janina, whose behaviour in society had been quite rowdy. The friend left and recounted the event to Mme Olga de Janina.

The latter, boiling with rage, dressed as a man, and carrying a thin cane, went off to the Café de la Paix to find the editor of *Le Pays.* She found M. Paul de Cassagnac, and after she had berated him, she struck him twice, on the shoulder and the face. M. de Cassagnac received it with the disdainful smile which such a vulgar lack of man-

---

29. JSP, p. 6.

ners merited, and in the middle of the uproar, Mme Olga de Janina was taken back home, where she could be looked after, if the need arose. This evening, the whole boulevard was talking about this latest escapade of the sprightly Cossack.

One could think this method of drawing publicity in the heart of Paris a little cavalier, and we wonder now if the police will allow the concert announced for next Saturday to take place. If it does, what might happen there?[30]

Who was the "priest"? The image we are left with is that of Olga's publicity agent dressed in clerical garb, hawking his client's brochures around the boulevards. Did she hope that the uninformed public might even mistake him for Liszt? The speculation is not so far-fetched when we recall that on the garish cover of *Souvenirs d'un pianiste* was a caricature of Liszt playing the piano to two scantily clad cherubs, one scattering flower-petals before him and the other proffering him a goblet of wine.[31]

VII

Among the many people who clamoured for Liszt's reaction to Olga's *Souvenirs*, none was more persistent than that other Olga, Baroness von Meyendorff, who knew La Janina, had met her on a number of occasions, and loathed her—a feeling that was reciprocated. Her letters to Liszt on the topic have not survived, but to judge from Liszt's reply, she advised him that after reading the book she was now going to disinfect her library. On July 27, 1874, Liszt wrote to her:

> Do not fear that I shall ask for the Cosaque book: the summary you have been good enough to make for me is amply sufficient, and I shall certainly do nothing to prevent you from "disinfecting" your library of that "fabulous flower from Brazil," which blooms only every hundred years. Besides people have written to me about it from Paris and from Rome. Should you happen to be curious about the nature of my reply I shall try to remember it and write it down once again for you.[32]

---

30. From a Paris newspaper, 1874, undated. (WA, Kasten 288, u. 1)

31. The cover of this rare book is reproduced in BVL, p. 199.

32. July 27, 1874. WLLM, p. 151. The colourful phrase " 'fabulous flower of Brazil,' which blooms only every hundred years" actually comes from La Janina herself, and is her description of the passion aroused in her by Liszt. (JSC, p. 121) Baroness Meyendorff had evidently included it in the summary of the book which she made for Liszt.

With this letter he included two others, his "official" and only responses to the many people who had written to him about Janina's book and had asked him what he intended to do about it. "Here," he told Meyendorff, "is the extract from my two letters about *la Cosaque*."

> Before reading the *Novel of a Cosaque*:
>
> I have not yet read the *Souvenirs* in question; but from what I have heard about them the writer delights in making me look both ridiculous and odious. She and her friends are free to behave according to their good or evil pleasure; I can only oppose certain scandals with a decent silence, which does not sink into the mire and leaves to others the responsibility for their debasement. That *la Cosaque* should excel in decrying me and flaying me with the learned *Nélida* is none of my business; each of them has in the past written me numerous impassioned letters on the nobility of my character and the uprightness of my feelings. In this I shall not contradict them, and will continue to prize sincerely their remarkable and brilliant talents as artists, writers, and inventors, while regretting that they should turn them so energetically against my poor self. The last volume will serve as a final warning, I hope, against my mistake in tolerating the artificial excitement of artists in the art of contraband and the blaze of intrusive passion. . . .
>
> After reading it:
>
> *La Cosaque,* an interloper like *Nélida,* but an incendiary, prowled for whole nights around my lodgings in Rome. My great wrong lies in my having let myself finally be taken in by her make-believe eccentric heroism, by her babble which is not devoid of wit nor of a disconcerting kind of eloquence; she has, moreover, astonishing energy in her work and a very rare talent as a pianist. Assuredly, I should have sent her packing immediately after her first avowal of love and not have yielded to the silly temptation of imagining that I could be of use to her in any way. Little snakes of this kind can only be tamed by riding in coaches with powdered footmen and by flaunting their shame in lodgings adorned with fantastic furniture and tropical plants. Their ideal of happiness is to preen themselves in boxes at the theatre and at orgies in the private rooms of restaurants . . . *Vade retro me, Satana: quoniam non sapis quae Dei sunt* ["Get thee behind me, Satan: for thou savourest not the things that be of God"]—On such occasions one must resolutely and right away follow the edifying example of St. Thomas Aquinas who, in the castle of St. John, put a woman to flight "with an incandescent ember." Unfortunately, my modest Thomist knowledge was not up to the

occasion. However, if it were a matter of explaining my conduct before a Court of Honour, even one composed of people prejudiced against me, I would not find it in the least embarrassing to clear myself by correcting, in accordance with the truth, facts and dates repeatedly attested to by the adversary party itself.

I add that the real Robert Franz has written to me in the most decorous manner, asking me to authorize him to protest in the press against the abusive use of his name by the pseudo Franz. I replied that the respectable public would certainly never confuse the author of the lovely *Lieder* and *Gesange* with the croakings of *la Cosaque,* and that, for my part, I was so enthralled by the former that the Cossack dissonances hardly reached my ears and disturbed them not at all.[33]

Liszt evidently made several copies of these letters for private distribution.[34] He was wise not to send one to the press. That would have revealed that he had been stung by Olga's book—despite his protestations to the contrary. He preferred to greet her slanders with a wall of silence. While that stratagem may have been good enough for the public, what of his close friends? His approach to the difficult problem of what to tell them about La Janina is not without interest. Liszt's response falls into two parts. In the first, he gives his general reactions to news of the book before having read it. In the second, he reveals his feelings *after* having read it. We have only Liszt's word for it that this is how the texts actually came to be written, and he may well have constructed them like that after reading the book in order to make himself appear more detached. Certainly, the language of the second letter is unusually strong for him. He admits that he should have sent her packing, and likens her to a "little snake." By placing her in a context of "powdered footmen" and in the company of women who flaunt their shame "in lodgings adorned with fantastic furniture," he is really calling her a prostitute.

Since Liszt was not about to make a public protest, Olga did that for him. In the middle of September he received an anonymous package containing a copy of *Souvenirs d'un pianiste*—his purported "reply" to Olga's first novel. He told Baron Augusz that he did not know who sent it to him and that he was completely ignorant of the author's name.[35]

Others besides Liszt were maligned in La Janina's books. The most obvious case, of course, was Robert Franz. He was now very frail, almost totally deaf, and lived in near-isolation in Halle. Franz, as we have seen, was only dissuaded from

33. WLLM, p. 178.
34. For example, another copy went to Baron Augusz on September 29, 1874 (CLBA, pp. 17–19). Liszt's basic draft was published by Robert Bory in BDL, pp. 20–22.
35. CLBA, pp. 18–19.

making a public protest by Liszt himself.[36] Another recipient of Janina's venom was the beautiful Polish-born Marie von Kalergis (now Countess von Mouchanoff), whom Janina had often seen in Weimar walking through the Goethe Park on the arm of Liszt, a spectacle that was more than Janina could abide. Inflamed by jealousy, she described Mouchanoff as "the belle of the Berlin balconies"—thoroughly false—false graces, false ideas, false hair, and false posterior. "There was nothing genuine about her but an issue in her leg, and her breath."[37] This last comment was especially cruel; for some years Marie von Mouchanoff had been a cripple, and she could now walk only with a crutch. She suffered from cancer of the leg, a painful disability which she bore with dignity, and which killed her within weeks of the appearance of Janina's book. Olga has the pair weaving their way across the park, with Mouchanoff leaning on Liszt's arm, "cooing her whole repertory of recitatives, nocturnes, and cantilenas" into his ear. Another glancing blow was struck against Julius Schuberth, who Janina says refused to help her after she had declined to sleep with him.

VIII

Perhaps the person who was caused most distress by the book, however, was Princess Carolyne, who was not even pilloried in it. When she read it in the

---

36. Franz's unpublished letter to Liszt on the topic of "la cosaque" is dated July 23, 1874. (WA, Kasten 15, u. 9) He had received word of Olga's book from a friend who had read a review of it in the Viennese press and had sent him a copy of the newspaper in question. Franz told Liszt: "That notwithstanding, I consider it my duty, *vis à vis* a person to whom I have been indebted in so many ways [i.e., Liszt himself], not to leave the slightest appearance of a suspicion that I am disturbed."

Why did Olga choose the pseudonym Robert Franz? As far as we know, the question has never been asked, but the answer lies readily to hand. She was aware of the ties of loyalty that bound Franz to Liszt, ties that had recently taken on a strikingly visible form. On March 2, 1873, Liszt had taken part in a benefit concert for Franz in the main ballroom of the Hungária Hotel, Budapest. He had played Beethoven's A-flat major Sonata, op. 26, one of his *Soirées de Vienne* (no. 4), and his own transcriptions of two songs by Schumann and Franz himself. Unable to make a proper living, Franz now stood on the verge of destitution. It was his friend the singer Baron Senfft v. Pilsach, who had alerted the profession at large to Franz's plight, and eventually succeeded in raising more than 30,000 thalers which were put into a trust fund for Franz and ensured that he lived in comfort for his remaining days. To this context we can add something else. Liszt's book on Franz had been published in April 1872 (by F. Leuckart of Leipzig). It comprised a revised version of a flattering text that had appeared in the *Neue Zeitschrift* as early as the 1850s. Franz's gratitude towards Liszt was both touching and genuine. In March, just before the book appeared, he had written to Liszt to tell him that when he looked back on his past life, he found Liszt running through it "like a golden thread," and that at critical moments Liszt had always stood protectively beside him. "Accept a thousand thanks for so much love and goodness." (LBZL, vol. 3, p. 113) Olga's choice of pseudonym now becomes clear. The connection between Liszt and Franz was topical, and anyone who read what Liszt had to say about his colleague would have been aware of the high esteem in which Liszt held him. No greater damage could have been done to Liszt than to use his friend's name as the author of this calumny. The choice of "Robert Franz" as Olga's pseudonym was well considered, and calculated to wound.

37. JSC, p. 207.

summer of 1874, she was aghast to think that the man for whom she had made so many sacrifices was now a laughing-stock. We know from her unpublished letters to Liszt that she expressed some blunt thoughts on the matter. He told her essentially the same thing that he had at first told Baroness von Meyendorff: namely, that while he was curious about the book, he had not yet read it. But Carolyne hit back: "You wish to read La Cosaque—here it is. I pray to God that reading this will give you as much pain as it gives me."[38] These were hard words, and they prompted him to recall his father's deathbed utterance, made forty-seven years earlier at Boulogne-sur-mer, in which Adam Liszt had warned his fifteen-year-old son that he feared that women would trouble his existence and come to dominate his life.[39] We may be sure that Carolyne accepted Adam's premonition—with the noble exception of herself. In fact she now proceeded to take the high moral ground.

> Of all the women who reached the apotheosis of passion—who is still yours? Nélida and the Cossack ended with venomous pamphlets. . . . It is the good Christian woman, who has never accepted the theories of Leone Leoni nor any flaming apotheosis of passion, who loves you after all.[40]

Whatever satisfaction the publication of Janina's books may have brought their author, the reviews must have enraged her. She was badly gored by Jules Barbey d'Aurevilly in *Le Constitutionnel*. "The only originality in this book lies in the word 'cosaque,' " he wrote. "Cosaques do not write every day in Paris. Its sole success has been the scandal."[41] Barbey d'Aurevilly also slyly revealed that he knew the identity of the author. Olga replied in the preface of the thirteenth edition of her book, published in 1878.

After the publication of her novels, very little more was heard about Olga Janina. In later life she married Paul Guy Cézano, a Russian subject of private means, and lived with him at Lancy-St. Georges, a small community south of Geneva.[42] There she set up as a piano teacher under the name of Olga de Cézano, occasionally affecting the title of "marquise," with "née Princess Or-

---

38. Hitherto unpublished. WA, Kasten 205, u.1 (Abschrift). Undated.
39. LLB, vol. 7, p. 82. See also Volume One of the present work, p. 127, n. 8.
40. Hitherto unpublished. WA, Kasten 205, u. 1 (Abschrift).
41. See Jules Barbey d'Aurevilly, *Les Bas-Bleus,* vol. 5, of the Oeuvres et les Hommes, chapter XVIII, Paris, 1878.
42. This information comes from the Geneva census register of August 15, 1884, no. 104, held in the Archives d'Etat, Geneva. It shows that Olga had entered Switzerland on a temporary permit in the spring of 1883. Her household was situated at no. 16, rue de la Grenade, and consisted of husband Paul (b. 1843), a cook, and a dog.

beliani" sometimes added for good measure. According to Bülow, she was still living there as late as 1886. He heard her play some Beethoven sonatas and was impressed with her interpretations.[43] The last official mention of her was in 1887, when Ludwig Nohl listed her in his *Dictionary* as still teaching in Geneva.

Of all the crises that Liszt was called upon to endure in his long and chequered life, it is arguable that none caused him more anguish than his relationship with Olga Janina. He could easily have rid himself of her, yet he chose not to do so and he did himself incalculable harm in consequence. That fact may speak against him. But we do well to recall that there are some personalities whose weakness becomes their strength, and others whose strength becomes their weakness. Bring them together and you have a recipe for a human tragedy. Olga was one of those professional victims who have mastered the art of making strong men quail by first arousing their chivalry and then holding them responsible not only for all the subsequent misfortunes that fall on their miserable lives but for their very survival. This last responsibility was almost more than Liszt could bear, until Olga herself brought about her own downfall and it was no longer necessary for him to carry the burden.

Towards the end of his life, Liszt remarked in a conversation with Lina Ramann: "The mistake I made was to have trusted her."[44] And just before his death, he told Sophie Menter that La Janina was not bad, merely exalted.

---

43. RL–B, p. 29.
44. RL, p. 212.

BOOK THREE

A Threefold Life Begins: Weimar, Budapest, and Rome 1869 · 1876

The Hofgärtnerei:
The Return of a Legend

Create memories!
FRANZ LISZT[1]

I

Ever since Liszt left Weimar in 1861, Grand Duke Carl Alexander had been tactfully trying to persuade him to return. He had never ceased to take an interest in Liszt's career, as their correspondence testifies, and he had followed events in Rome with close concern. Eight years had now elapsed since Liszt had lived and worked in the city of Goethe and Schiller. Although he had drunk his cup of bitterness in that city, he was still tied to it through the bonds of affection that attached him to the royal family, and to the many individuals who still lived there and had remained loyal to him. We recall that one of Carl Alexander's last acts before Liszt's departure, in August 1861, had been to make Liszt a Chamberlain to the Royal Court, an honour which, while it carried no duties, gave him a high status within the establishment there. As to the general Weimar community, the old antagonisms had died down. There was a slow but certain realisation that Liszt had brought honour and prestige to the city, and that unless some initiative was taken he would be lost to Weimar forever. But what sort of an association would be best? There could be no question of Liszt resuming his former duties at the opera house. For one thing, he had no desire to return to such a mundane profession; for another, the post was now well filled by Eduard Lassen. In any case, the grand duke understood Liszt through and through. He believed that it would be enough to announce Liszt's return to Weimar to ensure a revival of the artistic activity of the 1850s, when it

---

1. LL, p. 331.

seemed that the whole of the cultural world had descended on the small town simply to bask in Liszt's presence. Could it happen again? It was well-remembered that such giants as Bülow and Tausig had received their training from Liszt in Weimar. But since those far-off days, a new and formidable generation of pianists had appeared. Many of them had never heard Liszt play a note, let alone received a lesson from him. But they revered his name which was now a part of the mythology of the piano. As soon as it was realised that Liszt was about to return to Weimar, young pianists the world over started to pack their bags in the hopeful expectation of studying with him.

By August 1868 the preliminary arrangements were in place, and the grand duke wrote to Liszt:

> Beust has informed you that a house has been prepared for you in Weimar, according to your wishes, which assures you of both comfort and independence, in a retired position and with proximity to society, if that is what you would like, in an enclosed part of the Weimar park. Come here, then, among your many friends and be near the one who has the right to count on it even without writing these lines. Come, I say, and put into deeds Goethe's saying:
>
> > Warum willst du weiter schweifen?
> > Sieh, das Gute liegt so nah,
> > Lerne nur das Glück ergreifen,
> > Denn das Glück ist immer da![2]
>
> Goodbye then, and God willing we will see you soon—such is the call of
>
> > Your old friend,
> > C.A.[3]

The grand duke's offer came at a good time for Liszt. Since his arrival in Rome he had lived at no fewer than four addresses, and his tenure at the Santa Francesca Romana would end in a few months' time. Moreover, since the Altenburg had been closed to him for more than a year, he no longer had a permanent residence in Weimar either. It was this anomaly that Carl Alexander now corrected. Liszt's return marked the beginning of his so-called *vie tri-*

---

2. From Goethe's poem "Erinnerung," the first line of which the grand duke has slightly misquoted.

> Would you roam forever onward?
> See the good that lies so near.
> Only learn to grasp that fortune,
> Fortune that is always there.

3. LBLCA, p. 140.

furquée, or life split in three, in which he divided each year more or less equally among Weimar, Budapest, and Rome. The phrase is a good one; it came from Liszt himself.

The dwelling which Carl Alexander had set aside for Liszt's personal use was the Hofgärtnerei—the court gardener's house—which lay at the end of Marienstrasse, near Belvedere Allee. Built in 1798, the Hofgärtnerei was a small, two-story villa which backed onto the Goethe Park and was therefore well secluded. Earlier it had housed the studio of the painter Friedrich Preller. The grand duchess herself supervised the decorations and furnishings, everything being arranged with Liszt's physical comfort in mind.[4] A large music-room dominated the first floor, with tall windows overlooking the gardens. This room was to become the scene of the most famous piano classes in history: for seventeen years Liszt was to teach there, and a brilliant stream of pupils passed through his hands. Leading off from one end of this room was a bed-room, and from the other a dining-room.[5]

In the Hofgärtnerei Liszt lived a life of simple routine. Always an early riser, he sometimes got up before dawn, and after attending morning mass and taking a light breakfast he was already at his desk composing by seven o'clock. Around midday he was ready to receive visitors, and three afternoons a week he would teach. In the evening he liked to socialize. By eleven o'clock he was usually in bed. His housekeeper, Pauline Apel, had earlier been one of Princess Carolyne's domestic servants in the Altenburg. She was an ideal choice for the position, and ran the Hofgärtnerei with quiet efficiency—never obtrusive, always supportive. For seventeen years it was usually Pauline who opened the door to visitors—musicians, painters, actors, aristocrats, politicians, pupils, and friends—took their hats and coats, showed them into the reception-room, and served coffee, cognac, and cakes that she herself had baked. As the galaxy of guests crossed back and forth across the threshold, Frau Apel became an ear- and eye-witness to history and soon came to be regarded as an authority-figure on all matters concerning Liszt and his Weimar circle. And when, after Liszt's

---

4. At first he found it somewhat too comfortable for his modest needs, and talked of a "Wagnerian" luxury that was out of place among the plain townspeople of Weimar. (LLB, vol. 6, p. 196)
5. When Carl Alexander offered Liszt the use of the Hofgärtnerei, he may not have known what a symbolic gesture he was making to the world of piano playing. On the opposite side of the street, no. 8 Marienstrasse, Hummel's widow, Elisabeth, and his granddaughters Johanna and Augusta lived in the same family house in which Hummel himself had lived and worked some forty years earlier. The three ladies passed the Hofgärtnerei every day on their walks to and from the Goethe Park, and we know that they viewed the various goings-on there with suspicion. Liszt, according to them, had "destroyed the true art of piano-playing" as embodied in the classical ideals of a wonderful husband and grandfather. The polarity established between Liszt and Hummel on the professional level spilled over into the private one as well. We do not know of a single occasion when the Hummels were invited to socialize at the Hofgärtnerei, or when Liszt was invited to join the Hummels. It was as if an invisible wall ran down the middle of Marienstrasse, forever separating the two "rival" buildings, which still face one another today.

death, the house became a museum, Pauline stayed on as a custodian and visitors' guide.

II

Liszt arrived at the Weimar railway station at midnight on January 12, 1869, after travelling via Florence and Munich. The next day the small town was filled with excitement at the prospect of having him back in its midst. One of the first people he met was Eduard Lassen, who was in the middle of concert rehearsals. Together they went to see August Kömpel, the new orchestral leader, and Liszt was persuaded to take part in some spontaneous chamber music. "He played divinely, as always," wrote Lassen.[6] That evening Liszt went to the theatre to hear a performance of Weber's *Oberon* under Lassen's direction. He spent the next few days receiving callers, accepting invitations, meeting old friends, and getting used to his new home. Among the residents who saw much of him at this time were Henriette and Adelheid von Schorn, Emilie Merian-Genast, Feodor and Rosa von Milde, and his old friend Hofrath Carl Gille, who lived in nearby Jena.

Distinguished visitors to Weimar also started to look him up, including Ede Reményi and Anton Rubinstein. Reményi, who got to Weimar not long after Liszt had settled in, was one of the first guests to be entertained at the Hofgärtnerei. On one occasion he and Liszt improvised on Gypsy melodies, and Adelheid von Schorn could not help observing that when Reményi played the whole man danced. "The two Hungarians not only *played* music, they *were themselves* the music—in every nerve—down to their fingertips."[7] Afterwards Reményi fell at Liszt's feet and clasped his knees. Schorn could not tell whether he was laughing or crying from sheer joy. Rubinstein came to Weimar at the beginning of February in order to give a solo recital. He visited Liszt several times in the latter's new home, and the two pianists played four-handed Schubert marches to a delighted gathering.

Liszt himself made an appearance as a pianist at the Weimar Court on January 20, when he played before the royal family. The concert was to have been given by Reményi and the tenor Wachtel, who withdrew at the last moment, so Liszt stepped in. "He played like an angel and looked like a saint," wrote Henriette von Schorn.[8] Carl Alexander was delighted that Liszt was once more a part of Weimar's glory. In fact, the informality that had always marked the relationship between the two men intensified after Liszt's return to Weimar. In

---

6. SNW, vol. 2, p. 187.
7. SZM, p. 155.
8. SZM, p. 152.

the years to come, Carl Alexander would often visit Liszt at the Hofgärtnerei, and even attend a matinée or a masterclass there—something he could never have done in the old days, when Princess Carolyne lived with Liszt and was *persona non grata* at court. He sometimes grew impatient, however, at the way in which Liszt was diverted by his many female admirers. The grand duke often had to make a special appointment before he could be sure of catching his old friend at home—a role reversal that he did not relish.

> The devil with women, especially when they are beautiful and lov-able in your eyes! They tear you away from my company. I am nei-ther one nor the other, but indeed a friend who is fruitless in his efforts to see you, since you are always being carried off! I am call-ing now on your friendship to stay at home for once and wait for me today, Monday, between noon and one o'clock. Meanwhile, compose for me an elegy on patience. C.A.[9]

Adelheid von Schorn was not only a frequent visitor to the Hofgärtnerei but also its faithful chronicler.[10] She has been called Carolyne's "spy" because of the vast correspondence the pair exchanged on Liszt's comings and goings during the seventies and eighties. Carolyne was desperate for news of Liszt at this juncture in his life, for she had not expected him to return to Weimar—the graveyard of so many of her own dead hopes and desires. At first Adelheid's mother, Henriette, was her chief informant. She had been Carolyne's closest friend in Weimar during the fifties, and it was natural that Carolyne should turn to her for news, information, and gossip about Liszt. After Henriette's death (later in this same year of 1869) the burden of the correspondence was taken over entirely by Adelheid. The biographer can only remain grateful that such devoted sleuthing took place at all. Without it, our knowledge of Liszt and his Weimar circle would be the poorer.[11]

The celebrated mezzo-soprano Pauline Viardot-Garcia turned up in Weimar in February 1869 in the company of her husband, their two children,

---

9. LBLCA, p. 147.
10. See her two books SZM and SNW (the latter in two volumes).
11. Within days of Liszt's arrival at Weimar, in fact, Carolyne had asked Henriette von Schorn for a full report of his new home. Carolyne must have walked down Marienstrasse, and past the Hofgärt-nerei, many times during the ten years that she herself had spent in the city, and she now wanted to know more about it. On receiving Carolyne's request, Henriette, who was ill, had despatched Adel-heid to the Hofgärtnerei. Adelheid proved on this and subsequent occasions to have inherited her his-torian-father's sharp eye for detail. Liszt must have been quite dazzled by the depth of Carolyne's knowledge of his abode, by the sort of problems he faced settling in, and above all by her certain knowledge of how best to solve them—an intelligence-gathering operation directed from Rome! As early as January 22, 1869, Carolyne told Liszt that she had learned that the grand duke had "felt *very*

and Ivan Turgenev—her *cavaliere servente*—and stayed for several weeks. Although she had formally retired from the stage, she still made occasional "command" appearances, and one such had been issued by Carl Alexander, a great admirer of her talents. She was in Weimar to supervise the rehearsals of her opera *Le Dernier Sorcier* (libretto by Turgenev), which was performed in Weimar on April 8, 1869, the birthday of Grand Duchess Sophie, in an orchestration by Lassen. The friendship between Liszt and Pauline went back for many years. It is not always recalled that as a child she had been a piano pupil of his in Paris in the late 1820s, and that at the height of her meteoric career as a singer (which came close to rivalling that of her better-known sister, Maria Malibran), she had sung under Liszt's baton at the Weimar Court concerts.[12] It was inevitable that Pauline, too, would wend her way to the Hofgärtnerei and that her reunion with Liszt would include some memorable music-making. During February and March the little town was treated to some world-class song recitals—sung in French, Spanish, and German—including the Lieder of Lassen.[13] The Viardots were so enchanted with Weimar that they spent the following winter in the town as well.

One of the most striking friendships of Liszt's later years was formed at this time, and we must say a few words about it here because of its special importance to the composer's private life. Baroness Olga von Meyendorff was the wife of Felix von Meyendorff, who had been appointed Russian ambassador to the court of Weimar in 1867. That was the year in which Liszt had become re-acquainted with the young couple, at the performance of his *St. Elisabeth* in the Wartburg, and he had predicted a brilliant career for the thirty-three-year-old diplomat. Not long afterwards, Meyendorff was transferred to Karlsruhe, where he died in January 1871, leaving behind his thirty-two-year-old widow and four small sons. Unable to bear the loneliness of her new situation, in a city that held little attraction for her, Olga moved back to Weimar with her family, primarily to be near Liszt, with whom she had meanwhile struck up a correspondence.

---

cold at your home. . . . If he, accustomed to that climate, felt cold, what will it be like for you, who at *your age* have already spent several winters in succession in Italy, and who is sensitive to cold?" She went on to warn him of the dangers of rheumatism, and told him to move his bed away from the outside wall where it was presently located to an inner wall, where he would be warmer. The Hofgärtnerei, she told him, "is a house of cardboard, exposed to every wind, and not at all sheltered. It is a summer residence, not a winter one." (WA, Kasten 42, u.3; hitherto unpublished) This was the first of many such missives which Liszt received from Carolyne. There is no evidence that he resented her attempts to interfere, and he even preserved her letters in which she hectored him. But from the moment he arrived in Weimar he was under no illusions; he knew that everything he said and did was being reported back to her.

12. Her last professional appearance in Weimar had been in Rossini's *Barber of Seville,* on December 22, 1859, directed by Lassen. In that same year Liszt had eulogized her in an article first published in the *Neue Zeitschrift.* See RGS, vol. 3, part 1, pp. 121–35.

13. SZM, p. 161; SNW, vol. 2, p. 181.

Olga and Liszt remained intimate friends for the rest of his life. She often accompanied him on his travels in order to provide him with the material comforts that his bachelor existence lacked. In Weimar, she provided him with a much softer environment than he might otherwise have enjoyed; in fact, Liszt did not hesitate to turn to Olga whenever he entertained, either taking his friends to her house or having her act as a hostess at his.

This new attachment aroused Carolyne's curiosity, and then her jealousy. She referred to Olga sardonically as Liszt's "Russian muse." The fact is, Baroness von Meyendorff was not popular among the members of Liszt's circle. She was perceived as being cold and remote, although stunningly elegant. She invariably dressed in black, as though in perpetual widowhood; and this, together with her jet-black hair, made her pale face look even more pallid. (Liszt's students nicknamed her "the black cat.") Amy Fay often used to glimpse Olga walking in the Goethe Park, trailing her "sable garments like the night" and surrounded by her four beautiful boys, "each handsomer than the other."[14] To Miss Fay the baroness looked like a woman with a history. Inevitably, the tongues started to wag, especially in Weimar, and they have been wagging in the literature ever since; but there is no evidence that the relationship between Liszt and Olga was more than platonic. The large correspondence that they exchanged across a period of fifteen years reveals an emotional bond of uncommon strength, but it does not reveal the love-affair that some commentators have tried hard to uncover.[15]

Liszt's circle in Weimar was further enlivened through his friendship with the explorer Gerhard Rohlfs, who settled in Weimar with his family in 1870 and became acquainted with Liszt the following year. Rohlfs was by then world-famous for his travels in Africa, and he became one of the brightest jewels in Carl Alexander's crown. Fifteen years earlier, he had joined the French Foreign Legion; he had learned Arabic and had then begun a series of dramatic explorations across North Africa. He was the first European explorer to traverse Africa from the Mediterranean to the Gulf of Guinea, starting out in Tripoli in 1865, crossing the Sahara desert, and arriving at the Atlantic Ocean, near Lagos, in 1866. Carl Alexander kept urging Rohlfs to introduce himself to Liszt. The two men finally met in 1871, and thereafter Rohlfs and his wife, Leontine, were frequent guests at the Hofgärtnerei. Rohlfs was an amateur pianist with a special admiration for Beethoven, but his playing had been brought to an untimely end as a result of injuries sustained during his first great trek through Morocco, in 1861–62. Liszt valued Rohlfs's intelligence and wide-ranging humanity, qualities which attracted attention in such a small town as Weimar. After Liszt's death, Rohlfs wrote an interesting mem-

---

14. FMG, pp. 259–60.
15. See WLLM.

oir about his friendship with the composer, which only came to light long
after his own demise.[16]

This is also the place to say something about a musician who had recently
moved to Weimar at Liszt's suggestion in order to assist Lassen with the orchestra, and became one of the composer's loyal supporters. The sterling work
of Carl Müller-Hartung in behalf of Weimar's musical life was such that after
Liszt he was the dominant force there for the rest of the century.[17] Although
Weimar boasted an orchestra and an opera house, it had no school of music—
unlike Leipzig, Berlin, and Cologne. The Leipzig Conservatory had been in
existence since 1843, and under the direction of Felix Mendelssohn it had
quickly won international renown. Its three main divisions—strings, piano, and
composition—were headed by Ferdinand David, Ignaz Moscheles, and Moritz
Hauptmann respectively, three of the most prominent teachers of the time.
Berlin had followed with a conservatory of its own in 1850, and Cologne in
1852; both institutions were modelled on that of Leipzig. The huge success of
these centres of musical learning was a cause for concern among progressive
musicians, because their curricula were based largely on the music of the past.
To make matters worse, a number of distinguished private conservatories had
meanwhile sprung up throughout Germany, which were allied with the national ones in spirit. Joseph Joachim had founded the Berlin Hochschule für
Musik in 1869; and in 1878 the Hoch Conservatory had started work in Frankfurt, with Clara Schumann as the head of the piano department. The well-
known friendship between Joachim and Schumann, and the near-idolatry in
which they both held the memory of Mendelssohn, forged strong links among
the three institutions they represented, and even helped to define them. By the
early 1870s a whole generation of young musicians had emerged from these
places who were conservative in their outlook and reserved in their tastes. They
acted as a barrier to the wider reception of the new music of Liszt, Wagner,
and, a little later on, Richard Strauss. It was in an attempt to meet this threat
that Carl Müller-Hartung pressed the case for an orchestral school in Weimar.
The institution opened its doors on June 24, 1872 (Carl Alexander's birthday),
with Müller-Hartung as its first director. Among its teachers were Alexander
Gottschalg, the Weimar court organist, and Feodor and Rosa von Milde—all
old friends of Liszt's. The violinist Carl Halir also joined its faculty.[18]

---

16. It was discovered among his papers, which he had bequeathed to his native Bremen, and published
for the first time in 1993 under the title *Erinnerungen an Franz Liszt* (REL).

17. Carl Müller-Hartung (1834–1908) was the son of the organist and choirmaster J. Christian Müller
and his wife, Wilhelmine, *née* Hartung. It was only after his professional career got under way, when
he was in his early twenties, that he combined the names of both his parents.

18. Halir's attachment to modern music was demonstrated in various ways, but the best known was
his world première of the revised Sibelius Violin Concerto, which took place in Berlin in 1905, with
Richard Strauss conducting.

From the start, the Orchesterschule was designed to be different from its rivals. The emphasis was on orchestral training, particularly in the modern repertoire. Soon the school had a well-disciplined student orchestra quite capable of playing the symphonic poems of Liszt and the orchestral music of Bülow, Raff, and Cornelius. They even managed orchestral excerpts from the Wagner operas—all the more commendable when we learn that the Orchesterschule admitted students at the age of fourteen. Such ensembles were notably lacking in Leipzig and Berlin. Müller-Hartung drew up a rigorous schedule of work for his young charges, which included not only the usual private lessons but large numbers of daily rehearsals as well. Moreover, each student had to study two orchestral instruments, not one as demanded by Leipzig and Berlin. Students were also expected to show some knowledge of keyboard harmony. Later on, Müller-Hartung added an opera division to the school and formed a chorus. The central mission of the school, then, was not to train virtuosi but to cultivate all-round performers with a catholic taste. Within the first five years no fewer than 112 students had graduated from its courses; and within the first twenty years more than a thousand. As the reputation of the school began to grow, young musicians were enrolled from all parts of Germany and from America as well. Hans von Bülow was so impressed with Müller-Hartung's work that he donated ten thousand marks for the establishment of a scholarship, while Liszt donated three pianos and a harmonium. After Liszt's death the Weimar Orchestral School was eventually re-named the Franz Liszt Hochschule für Musik, a title it still bears today.[19]

III

Of all the friends and admirers who grouped themselves around Liszt after his return to Weimar, none were more colourful than the Stahr sisters, and none more hospitable. At their Sunday afternoon at-homes, which were renowned in

---

19. Typical of the kind of dogsbody work that Müller-Hartung's student orchestra eagerly undertook in Weimar were the occasional concerts given in the Erholung, the old ballroom that stands on the east side of the city's Goethe-Platz. These informal occasions always aroused great local enthusiasm, and they were in marked contrast to the more formal concerts mounted in the theatre on the opposite side of the square by the court orchestra. Whenever Liszt's students played a concerto, he encouraged them to approach Müller-Hartung. On September 21, 1883, for example, an all-Liszt concert was given in honour of the composer, and we learn from the press that

> the assisting orchestra is composed of boys from fourteen to twenty years of age, and the precision and good taste shown in their playing is really astonishing. Their director Prof. Müller-Hartung, is to be heartily congratulated on the success of his boy orchestra [sic]. . . . Prof. Müller-Hartung's orchestral school and its energetic leader deserve a widespread fame; and I am glad to note among his students four young American gentlemen. (*Chicago Indicator,* December 15, 1883)

Weimar, Liszt was a regular visitor. Anna and Helene Stahr were known locally as "the starlings." They dressed exactly alike, "carefully and neatly attired in the style of schoolgirls at a Sunday-school picnic," as Carl Lachmund once put it. Their father was the historian Dr. Adolf Stahr, a professor at the university of Jena whose book *Weimar und Jena* had made him an authority on the two cities; their step-mother was the writer Fanny Lewald. They lived on Schwanenseestrasse in a pretty cottage set among trees, where they gave music lessons to a coterie of young pupils. They had known Liszt since the early 1850s, when he had met them in their father's home in Jena and had thereafter given them some informal piano instruction. While everybody regarded them as eccentric, they were highly cultivated and regularly held soirées of distinction in their home to which the whole of musical Weimar was invited. Lachmund used to say that on these occasions the "starlings" seemed to be here, there, and everywhere, giving the impression that they were in all the rooms at once. They served coffee in dainty little cups and offered their guests home-baked cookies. The rooms were so stuffed with memorabilia that it seemed impossible to accommodate any further objects. Liszt was very amusing about this, observing: "They are elastic rooms; for no matter how many guests I may bring, they expand to meet the emergency."[20] The walls of the various rooms and the hallway were covered with pictures of famous visitors of the past. One room, devoted entirely to Liszt, contained so many photographs and engravings that one could not see the wallpaper behind it. The "starlings" were absolutely devoted to Liszt and fussed over him as if he were a member of their own family.[21]

This was the background from which Liszt's masterclasses in Weimar emerged. The social and artistic life of the town was the catalyst—with its soirées, its "at-homes," and its special get-togethers. Every Sunday morning, from 11:00 a.m. to 1:00 p.m., Liszt held a matinée of his own at which artists considered it an honour to be invited to perform.[22] The grand duke rarely missed these matinées, for they were usually peopled by artists of distinction, and Liszt himself would sometimes play. As more and more young pianists formed a circle around him, he announced that he would receive them twice a week, from 4:00 to 6:00 p.m. The numbers grew, and these "at-homes" were

---

20. LL, p. 78.

21. Anna and Helene are buried together in the Weimar Stadtfriedhof. On their tombstone is inscribed in musical notation the first four measures of Liszt's song "Es muss ein Wunderbares sein." Beneath it is the phrase

> Unermüdlich in gemeinsam Streben
> Unzertrennbar in Freud u. Leid
>
> [Tireless in striving jointly
> Indestructible in Joy and Sorrow.]

22. SZM, pp. 148–49.

increased to three a week.[23] Although they soon came to be regarded as a training ground for pianists, especially by the pianists, Liszt's classes never entirely lost their old-world charm. They were essentially social hours, in which he was the host and they were the guests, with the ever-present Pauline serving iced tea and chocolate cake and whatever other delicacies she had in her kitchen that day. That said, Liszt's at-homes masked a deep seriousness of purpose, and they forever changed the history of piano playing.

Liszt left Weimar towards the end of March 1869 and made his leisurely way back to Rome via Vienna and Pest. Although his stay in the "Athens of the North" had lasted barely twelve weeks, it had changed the course of his life. This contact with his past had had a rejuvenating effect on him. Perhaps it was the striking contrast with Rome, and its lack of genuine musical life ("Here there is no tomorrow; everything falls asleep"), which he found so refreshing. As he contemplated the artistic activity with which he had been surrounded almost from the moment he had stepped off the train, he could well have echoed Goethe's sentiment expressed a century earlier: "Hier bin ich ein Mensch." He had renewed old friendships, formed new ones, and had found in Carl Alexander the same admirer and supporter as of yore. Above all, Liszt now had a comfortable home to which he could return whenever he wished. His "threefold life" had begun.

I V

The year 1869 also marked an important renewal in Liszt's relationship with Vienna. Thirty years earlier the city had witnessed some of his most spectacular triumphs as a concert pianist. There were still many people who could recall those golden times, although the artistic life of the city had changed almost beyond recognition. The Kaiserstadt was now a bastion of conservatism in which Liszt and his music were not always welcome. True, during the long years of his residency in Weimar Liszt had made sporadic trips to the city, both as a conductor and as a composer. But his removal to Rome had weakened his musical links with the Kaiserstadt, and his stock had dwindled. The presence of Eduard Hanslick in the city was a constant reminder that the War of the Romantics was still in progress, and Liszt could always expect a hostile reception from the press, even *in absentia*. Nonetheless, it is not entirely true to depict Vi-

---

23. Among the first students to arrive at the Hofgärtnerei in the early part of 1869 were Anna Mehlig, Georg Leitert, Irma Steinacker, and Rafael Joseffy—the son of a Budapest rabbi, who, in Liszt's words, promised "to become a second Tausig." (LLB, vol. 6, pp. 212–13)

enna as a closed city. Liszt had supporters there, whose work in his behalf deserves mention.

On April 4 and 11, 1869, Johann Herbeck conducted two successful performances of *St. Elisabeth* in Vienna's Redoutensaal. Although the oratorio had already been presented in Budapest, Munich, and the Wartburg, Liszt had so far denied Herbeck the opportunity to present the work in Vienna, because he feared a repetition of the débâcle that had surrounded his *Prometheus* Choruses when they had been given under Herbeck's direction in 1860.[24] Herbeck had remained one of Liszt's strongest supporters, however, and his career had lately taken on some powerful new directions. Not only was he now the director of the Gesellschaft der Musikfreunde, but since 1866 he had been the Kapellmeister to Emperor Franz Joseph as well. In his enthusiasm to mount *St. Elisabeth* Herbeck had found a keen ally in Joseph Hellmesberger, the director of the Vienna Conservatory. So when in 1868 Herbeck once more raised the question of doing the oratorio there, Liszt not only withdrew his earlier objections but agreed to attend the performances.[25]

There is no doubt that Herbeck threw the whole of his considerable resources into the preparation of the work. For more than two weeks he rehearsed a combined ensemble of some four hundred vocalists and instrumentalists, to ensure a performance of substance. To underline the importance of the occasion, he invited more than seven hundred members of the musical profession to witness the final dress-rehearsal. He had just taken his place at the conductor's desk when the doors of the hall opened and Liszt walked down the aisle. Hellmesberger was the first to recognise the tall, lean figure with the long grey hair and the abbé's cassock flowing behind him, and he whispered something in Herbeck's ear. Herbeck turned round, saw Liszt advancing on him, sprang down the steps leading from the platform to the auditorium, and exclaimed loudly, "Der Meister! Der Meister!" As he kissed Liszt's hands the audience and performers rose to their feet and greeted the composer with applause. Liszt then took his seat near the conductor's podium and stayed throughout the rehearsal, which lasted well over three hours. Despite the length of the session, no one left the hall, and afterwards a large crowd of wellwishers surrounded Liszt. The performance on April 4 was considered to be so satisfactory that it was repeated a week later, on April 11.

Liszt remained in Vienna for another week at the home of his cousin Eduard, who now lived in the Schottenhof with his second wife and children.[26]

---

24. On this difficult question see Liszt's letter to János Dunkl in PBUS, p. 122.
25. For the correspondence between Liszt and Herbeck on the Vienna première of *St. Elisabeth,* consult HJH (Appendix), pp. 23–26.
26. Eduard's first wife, Karolina Pickhart, had died of cholera in 1854. He had remained a widower for five years before taking as his second wife Henriette Wolf. There were three children from each marriage. See the "Liszt Family Tree I" in Volume One.

A tastefully furnished room had been set aside for Liszt's permanent use, where he could relax, play the piano, compose, and receive his friends. It became a "home away from home" where he stayed whenever he was in Vienna. With the passing years these quarters were filled with memorabilia—furniture, carpets, paintings, and pianos—and the "Blue Salon" (as it became known) remained something of a Liszt shrine for nearly a century, until everything was transferred to the Burgenländisches Museum in Eisenstadt, in 1970.

The English writer William Beatty-Kingston saw much of Liszt at this time and even heard him play at various private homes in Vienna. Many years later he was able to recall the memory of those occasions in detail.

> At that time all his capabilities of invention, memory, and technique, were still entirely at his disposal; and, as a pianist, he was not only unrivalled, but unapproachable. Practice and will had so thoroughly disciplined his fingers and accustomed them to fulfil infallibly the orders transmitted to them from his brain, that he was absolutely free from any preoccupation as to their ability to execute, and was at liberty to give full play to the creative and constructive faculties of his intellect without giving a thought to the mere mechanical contrivances attached to his wrists. His interpretations of Beethoven and Bach were sublime revelations; his improvisations bewildering realisations of the seemingly impossible.[27]

Now that Liszt had permanent quarters in Vienna his visits to that city became more frequent (from 1871 he managed to return practically every year). He travelled back to Italy via Regensburg and Pest, where he conducted two performances of his Hungarian Coronation Mass in the Redoute. This visit was notable for his first meeting with his pupil Sophie Menter, on whom he eventually bestowed the famous accolade "my only legitimate daughter as a pianist." Liszt finally got back to Rome on May 17 and installed himself in new quarters at 43, Vicolo de' Greci, dividing his time for the rest of the year between the city and the Villa d'Este.

v

As the year 1870 was ushered in, the thoughts of musicians everywhere began to turn towards Beethoven and the forthcoming centennial celebrations. During the past twenty-five years the German master had been eulogised as the greatest composer in history, and plans were now developed to enshrine him

---

27. B-KMCE, pp. 123–24.

among the immortals. Festivals were planned in Bonn, Berlin, Pest, and above all in Vienna, the city most closely associated with Beethoven's name and fame. Committees can be peculiarly obtuse, and so it was with the one struck in Vienna for the purpose of marking this historical event. While the chairman, one Dr. Franz Egger, and his colleagues doubtless acted in good faith, they had either forgotten or, worse, never known of the enmities that had been sown among the leading musicians of the 1850s and '60s and now bore poisoned fruit. With crass indifference to reality, Egger and his cohorts now began to issue invitations to Brahms, Joachim, Clara Schumann, Liszt, and Wagner to participate in the proceedings. They would have had better luck establishing a peace conference at the height of the Franco-Prussian War. And the notion is not far-fetched, since the War of the Romantics, unlike the forthcoming European conflict, was not to subside during the lifetime of the parties.

Joachim replied to Egger's invitation on May 21, 1870. To anyone familiar with the murky background of malice and intrigue that had characterised the War of the Romantics ten years earlier, Joachim's letter was not only predictable but could have been written for him by anyone with a ready pen and a knowledge of his unbending character.

> . . . The concerts have been entrusted to the conductorship of two foreign artists, the heads of the New German School, and although I admit that it would not have been possible to find more famous names [Liszt and Wagner], I cannot conscientiously conceal from myself the fact that they destroy my vision of Beethoven as a great, sublime yet simple spirit, whose unassuming majesty has gradually conquered the world.
>
> Since it would be impossible for me, under these circumstances, to participate heart and soul in the Festival, I feel sure that I shall be acting in accordance with the wishes of the Committee in absenting myself so that the harmony of the centenary may be undisturbed.[28]

But Joachim did more than "absent" himself. He made sure that both Clara Schumann and Brahms absented themselves as well. Three days after his letter to Egger, Joachim dashed off another in which he told Brahms that "Abbé Liszt is chosen by [the Beethoven committee] to conduct the *Missa Solemnis!* The worship of Rossini during Beethoven's lifetime . . . is nothing compared to this flippant comedy."[29]

This disparaging mention of Rossini is revealing. Tens of thousands of music lovers admired him. And yet, according to Joachim, they were worshipping at

---

28. JMBJ, vol. 3, pp. 41–42.
29. JBB, vol. 6, p. 62.

the wrong shrine. As for Liszt-worship, that had now become a "flippant comedy." It does not seem to have occurred to Joachim that a love of Beethoven does not exclude a love of Rossini—or any other composer for that matter. In fact, there is something deeper at work in Joachim's letter: his belief in German supremacy in music, which Beethoven had come to symbolize. Needless to add, Liszt did not share this belief and spent much of his time trying to demolish it.

Joachim also started a correspondence with Clara Schumann on the same topic. "I feel as you do," she confessed to him, "—the idea of a Beethoven Festival with Liszt and Wagner oppresses me, but how to get out of it? I, as a *woman,* cannot act as you did and say what I think, it would seem too arrogant if I, a woman, were to address men in this way, so I must invent a lie!"[30] Whereupon Joachim told her that "as far as art is concerned you are 'man enough.' I should simply tell Herbeck that I wished to have particulars of the entire programme before binding myself, and then either consent or refuse."[31]

V I

In the event, Clara and Joachim could have saved themselves much hand-wringing. For many months Liszt had been planning a Beethoven festival of his own in Weimar, and had no time to become involved in one in Vienna. He had set out from Rome on April 2, and by the sixth he was installed once more in the Hofgärtnerei. From the moment he got back to Weimar he had one over-riding aim: to implement a long-standing plan to transform the regular festival of the Tonkünstler-Versammlung (scheduled to take place between May 25 and 29) into a celebration of Beethoven. Rehearsals began, invitations went out, and by mid-May Weimar was already gearing up for the arrival of a flood of visitors, including Camille Saint-Saëns,[32] Joseph Hellmesberger, Károly Goldmark, Pauline Viardot-Garcia, Ferdinand David, Leopold Damrosch, Joachim Raff, Anton Rubinstein, Max Seifriz, Theodor Ratzenberger, Franz Servais, Ludwig Nohl, Lina Ramann, and Eduard Liszt. Undoubtedly, Liszt scored a coup when he engaged the services of his former pupil Carl Tausig, who was then at the height of his fame as a virtuoso. Although the two men rarely met, they were connected by golden threads of friendship that went back to Tausig's thirteenth year and his first lessons with Liszt.

---

30. JMBJ, vol. 3, p. 42.

31. Ibid.

32. At Liszt's prompting, Saint-Saëns had arrived in Weimar early in order to attend rehearsals of his cantata *Prometheus's Wedding Feast.* This immense score not only calls for a full orchestra but for "extra" instruments such as two harps, three saxophones, English horn, contrabassoon, contrabass trombone, three vocal soloists, and chorus. By the time the full ensemble was gathered together, the players would

[Weimar, beginning of May, 1870]

Dear Tausig:

    . . . I long to chat with you again here. Can you come from the 25th to the 29th of this month? Will you grant all of us, but especially me, the great pleasure of hearing you at one of the concerts of the Tonkünstler-Versammlung? I have taken it upon myself to urge you [to come], and your pupil M. Weber, who will hand you these lines, will tell you in greater detail how much I want you to celebrate with me the Beethoven festival in Weimar. If you will be content with a somewhat cramped lodging, I invite you to share mine. Try not to refuse me—and believe in all my constant affection.

F. LISZT[33]

At first Tausig was unwilling to oblige his old master, and Liszt was somewhat hurt by his firm refusal, "which prevents me from re-issuing the invitation." But he would not give up, and in a second letter he pointed out slyly that it would please him exceedingly if Tausig were to find himself unexpectedly moved to stop by for at least the last concert, Sunday the twenty-ninth, and play the *Emperor* Concerto for the greater glory of Beethoven.[34] Tausig finally yielded to Liszt's invitation and played the concerto, with Liszt conducting. It was the last known occasion on which the two men were together.[35] The full programme of the closing concert, which took place in the Hoftheater, was as follows:

---

have been hard pressed to find a place on the stage of the Weimar Court Theatre. The performance of *Prometheus* took place on May 27. Saint-Saëns had originally composed the cantata for the Paris Exhibition of 1867, but it had not been given at that time because of political in-fighting among the administrators; subsequently, only portions of the work had been performed in France. The Weimar performance, then, may well have been the first complete one. An exchange of letters on the topic will be found in LBZL, vol. 2, p. 340; and LLB, vol. 8, p. 164.

    Saint-Saëns himself tells us that it was during this visit to Weimar that Liszt encouraged him to begin work on his opera *Samson et Dalila,* and that without Liszt's encouragement the work might never have been finished. As is well known, it was given its first performance in the Weimar opera house, in Liszt's presence, in 1877.

33. LLB, vol. 8, pp. 216–17.

34. LLB, vol. 8, p. 219.

35. The following year Tausig succumbed to typhoid fever, aged twenty-nine. For an account of his death see Volume Two, p. 183 and n.

    Although Tausig died in nearby Leipzig, Liszt did not attend the funeral, and for a very good reason. According to a letter from Emilie Genast to Lassen, dated August 10, 1871:

> Liszt was deeply affected by the death of Tausig, and the first few days were made still more distressing because a great uncertainty hovered over whether the body would be brought to Berlin. Finally that was done, and consequently Liszt was spared the painful duty of attending the funeral.

His old friend Marie von Mouchanoff, who had nursed Tausig through his final illness and had watched the death-struggle, stopped off at Weimar for a couple of days to describe Tausig's last days

LASSEN   A Beethoven Overture (conducted by the composer)

LISZT   Beethoven Cantata, for chorus and orchestra (first
performance) (conducted by Müller-Hartung)[36]

BEETHOVEN   Concerto No. 5 in E-flat major (*Emperor*) (soloist:
Carl Tausig) (conductor: Liszt)

Interval

BEETHOVEN   Symphony No. 9 in D minor (*Choral*)
(conductor: Liszt)
(soloists: Frau Otto-Alvsleben,
Frau Krebs-Michalesi, Josef Schild,
Feodor von Milde)

La Mara, who was present throughout the festival, described Tausig's performance of the *Emperor* Concerto as "great and mighty." An extremely large body of musicians had been assembled for this concert, consisting of the combined orchestras of Weimar and Sondershausen. The rank-and-file was also strengthened by no fewer than six orchestral leaders—from Sondershausen (Ulrich), Breslau (Leopold Damrosch), Leipzig (Ferdinand David), Vienna (Joseph Hellmesberger), Meiningen (Fleischhauer), and Weimar (August Kömpel)—as well as by other prominent individuals from those same orchestras. Of Liszt's account of the Ninth Symphony, La Mara observed that "everyone was electrified. Liszt's interpretation of the gigantic work was for me a fresh revelation . . . a performance that I can compare with no other of the many I have heard."[37]

Liszt lingered in Weimar for several more weeks. Performances of his "Gran" Mass were arranged in his honour in Leipzig and Jena, and he was in attendance on both occasions. The trip to Leipzig was more than a passing af-

---

on earth. She and Liszt and Emilie Genast spent an entire evening reminiscing about the great pianist. The experience was a most painful one for Madame Mouchanoff, who was herself mortally ill and had just two more years to live, and this reunion with Liszt generated great emotion.

> In the evening [Emilie Genast continued], as I sat together with Liszt and Frau von Mouchanhoff, serious and silent, he suddenly opened the piano and played your Lied "Das Leben draussen" ["The life beyond"]. I would like you to have been able to participate in the experience which we received. I think it must make you happy that on that evening this was the only music he could bear. (SNW, vol 2, p. 295)

36. Raabe claims that Liszt conducted this performance (RLS, vol. 2, p. 334), but the local newspapers and the concert billing make it clear that Müller-Hartung directed the work. The first version of this Festival Cantata had been composed as early as 1845 for the unveiling of the Beethoven monument in Bonn and had remained unpublished (see Volume One, p. 423). Liszt had meanwhile thoroughly revised and re-orchestrated the piece, whose central section contained his orchestration of the slow movement of Beethoven's Piano Trio in B-flat major (the "Archduke"). The original poem, by Professor O. L. B. Wolff, was now replaced with a new text by Adolf Stern, with some additions by Ferdinand Gregorovius. Liszt dedicated this version to Grand Duchess Sophie of Weimar.
37. LDML, vol. 1, p. 116. There is in the Weimar Archive a rare copy of the Beethoven Festival booklet, from which many of the programme details have been culled. (WA, Kasten 242)

fair. The Carl Riedel Choral Society mounted the first three parts of the "Gran" Mass on Sunday, July 3. The performance took place in the Church of St. Nicholas, where Liszt shared the honours with J. S. Bach. Carl Riedel's choir was now one of the best in Germany, and Liszt knew that his work was in safe hands. He arrived by train at the head of a bevy of friends and supporters, including Adelheid von Schorn, her cousin Octavie von Stein, La Mara, and his new pupil Olga Janina, who had attached herself to him in Rome a few months earlier. On July 5 they all went over to the Johann Zschocher Institute (situated opposite the St. Thomas Church) for a concert of Liszt's music. Zschocher was taking his fledgling choristers through a performance of Liszt's "Ave Maria." "That is an old work," Liszt mused. "I once performed it in Leipzig." "I was lucky enough to hear it on that occasion," replied La Mara, "and it made a deep impression on me." "You could hardly say that today," Liszt remarked with a smile as the young amateurs did their best. Then came a performance of his song "Es war ein König in Thule," in which he accompanied the nervous young soloist and inspired her to soar far above her usual modest level of interpretation. La Mara observed that he needed a lot of patience that morning, because his *Consolations* came next and they were played "inconsolably." When the time came to leave, Liszt was asked to write something in the institute's guest-book. While his back was turned, the incorrigible Janina took it upon herself to record beneath his entry her displeasure that Liszt had had to endure such inferior performances of his music that day. Liszt publicly upbraided her for her bad manners and forced her to erase the offending sentence; she emerged from the institute weeping. Even while they were in the coach that took them on to the Riedels' house for lunch, Liszt continued to rail against Olga. "You do not know that beautiful saying of Goethe, you do not know what is fitting!" Olga tried to defend herself in French, only to be found guilty of the same offence. "We do not speak French here!" he interrupted. "It is not the fashion in Leipzig; here we converse in German." And when she continued to address him in French, he refused to acknowledge anything she said until she reverted to German.[38]

Liszt tarried in Weimar for several weeks more. But the chief thing that prevented his early departure from Germany was the forthcoming world premières of Wagner's *Das Rheingold* and *Die Walküre,* in Munich, which Hans von Bülow was planning to conduct in the Royal Opera House. Accordingly, Liszt set out for Munich during the second week of July and stayed in the city from July 13 to 26, during which period he saw both operas twice. In his spare moments he sat for the painter Franz Lenbach, who produced a well-known oil portrait of him.

---

38. LDML, vol. 1, pp. 118–21.

VII

While he was in Munich something happened to make Liszt bring forward his travel plans with great urgency. On July 19 France declared war on Germany. There had been many warning signals of the conflict to come. For the past several weeks regiments of soldiers had been mustered across Thuringia—in Weimar, Jena, Eisenach—and Liszt must have observed them being transported to the western front. Carl Alexander, who was the colonel-in-chief of the 94th Infantry Regiment of Sachsen-Weimar, left Weimar to join his men on August 4. Adelheid von Schorn tells us that a large "field altar" had been erected outside the Weimar barracks. During the last days of July the troops had assembled there to be blessed by the garrison priest, Reverend Christian Schweitzer.[39] The entire royal household had taken part in these ceremonials, including the grand duke, the grand duchess, and the two princesses. Hymns were sung to the accompaniment of a military band, the grand duke called out "Auf wiedersehen!," and the troops marched off to do battle for the fatherland.

Liszt was shaken by these developments, and he could not wait to put as much distance as possible between himself and Germany. Immediately after the last performance of *Die Walküre* he set out for Hungary. He arrived in Pest on July 30. After a brief stopover in the Hungarian capital, he continued his journey to the town of Szekszárd, where he stayed as a guest of Baron Augusz. Altogether he was to remain in "exile" in Hungary for eight months. Why so long a period? An early return to Rome was prevented by the military situation there. The French troops that had secured the Eternal City for the Vatican for the past ten years were now required for the battlefields of Western Europe, and Victor Emmanuel was poised to take Rome by force the moment they were withdrawn. Princess Carolyne herself advised Liszt not to attempt to return to Italy until the turmoil there had subsided.

---

39. SNW, vol. 2, p. 197.

The Franco-Prussian War of 1870

*The huge events that startle the world also bear on
my little existence.*

FRANZ LISZT[1]

I

No account of these turbulent times can avoid mention of the Franco-Prussian
War or of the two personalities who were at the centre of the conflict: Emperor Napoleon III and Prince Otto von Bismarck. When these two characters clashed, Europe trembled. Liszt was, we recall, personally acquainted with
Napoleon III, had been decorated by that monarch with the order of Commander of the Legion of Honour, and had played before him at various "command performances" at the Tuileries.[2] He had no time for Bismarck, nor did
he believe that any good would come of the Iron Chancellor's policy of weld-
ing the smaller German principalities to Prussia by force. Liszt followed the
events of the Franco-Prussian War with mounting despair, and the defeat of
France caused him genuine anguish.

Louis Napoleon III had been proclaimed Emperor of the French in 1852.
His rule, which lasted for eighteen years, was filled with both triumph and
tragedy. Among the triumphs were the re-building of Paris and the introduction of the franchise for large numbers of ordinary French citizens. Among the
tragedies were a series of foreign catastrophes, which ended in the downfall of
the Second Empire. In matters of foreign policy, in fact, Napoleon was surrounded by experts who frequently gave him conflicting advice. But none of
them caused him greater difficulty than his wife, Empress Eugénie, whose in-

---

1. HLSW, p. 144.
2. See Volume Two, p. 541.

fluence over him was so complete that she was formally barred from cabinet meetings. Eugénie was popular neither at court nor in the country at large. A commoner from Spain (she had been nicknamed "the Imperial Harlot" in France), she had wed Napoleon in 1853 over the objections of his family and his advisors, and in one move was raised from obscurity to empress. She had actively meddled in France's policies towards Rome, Poland, and above all Mexico—the fiasco that had ended in the execution of the emperor of Mexico, Archduke Maximilian of the house of Habsburg.

II

Napoleon's nemesis was Otto von Bismarck, whose lifelong ambition was the unification of the German states with Prussia at their head and Berlin as their capital. Some of the smaller principalities were not at all enthusiastic about being swallowed up by a large and militant Prussia, and they resisted. To break their will, Bismarck embarked on a long and arduous process of public and private diplomacy, involving treaties, agreements, secret understandings, and even bribery. And when this failed, he was willing to go to war. He had already shown his true feelings as early as 1862, when he had remarked to some political colleagues in Prussia: "The great questions of the day will not be decided by speeches and resolutions of majorities—that was the blunder of 1848–49—but by blood and iron."[3] And blood and iron it was to be. During the next decade Bismarck's policies led to three European wars—with Denmark (1864), Austria (1866), and France (1870). But in the end his great goal of German unification had been achieved.

Napoleon had watched with growing concern as Denmark had been forced to give up Schleswig, and then as Austria had been obliged to back down after the "Five Weeks' War." By 1870, France was the only power capable of containing Bismarck, who, moreover, lacked a provocation to create a further conflict. Therefore, one had to be found. It came in the form of the infamous "Ems Dispatch," which has been described as one of the most notorious editing jobs in history. Briefly, in the summer of 1870, while King Wilhelm of Prussia was enjoying the waters of Ems, he was approached by an agitated French ambassador, Count Vincente Benedetti, who wanted certain guarantees for France regarding the future of the Spanish throne. Wilhelm was irked by this confrontation, which breached protocol since it occurred in the public gardens, in full view of the general population, and had not been arranged ahead of time through diplomatic channels.

---

3. This famous phrase was first coined at a meeting of the budget committee of the Prussian Chamber of Deputies on September 30, 1862.

What was the background to this hasty encounter? The Spaniards had recently toppled the licentious and corrupt Queen Isabella and had a vacant throne. This vacancy Bismarck resolved to fill with his own candidate, Prince Leopold of Hohenzollern-Sigmaringen, thereby extending German influence over yet another corner of Europe. The French government had objected that Spain had a right to choose its own monarch, free from bullying by Germany. Foreign minister Antoine Agénor had made a bellicose speech in the French legislature, in which he described the Hohenzollern candidacy as "an insult to France." This phrase brightened Bismarck's day, for he saw in it something "insolent" and "possibly leading to war." The urgent crisis that poor Benedetti was trying to defuse when he rushed off to Ems in search of King Wilhelm was nothing less than a European conflict. But Wilhelm, exasperated at the insistence with which Benedetti pressed his arguments, terminated the conversation. Benedetti then requested a further meeting, which Wilhelm turned down while at the same time instructing his aide Heinrich Abeken to send a dispatch to Bismarck in Berlin describing the events of the day. Abeken correctly reported that Wilhelm had decided to keep Benedetti informed through an intermediary and would not himself participate in any further direct discussions. This dispatch Bismarck now proceeded to doctor. He changed the wording to read: "His Majesty has nothing further to communicate to the ambassador," and then released the text to the *Norddeutscher Allgemeine Zeitung,* with copies to all the German embassies around the world, in order to embarrass the French. "This will be like a red rag to the Gallic bull!" Bismarck exclaimed. Within hours it had been picked up by the French newspapers and was on sale on the streets of Paris. The next day there were mobs on the boulevards howling for a confrontation with Germany. As one modern commentator has put it, by this one action Bismarck snatched a war from the jaws of peace.[4]

Bismarck had made a point of studying Napoleon III, and he understood his adversary through and through. Napoleon was by nature introspective; he liked to mull over his more difficult problems in silence before coming to a decision. Because of his inscrutable exterior, he had earned for himself the nickname "the Sphinx." Bismarck was not impressed. To him the emperor was simply "a sphinx without a riddle." Moreover, Bismarck's spies must surely have informed him that Napoleon was beset by chronic personal indignities which were not widely known at that time. For most of his reign Napoleon suffered the unspeakable agonies of kidney stones. He was often incapacitated by the sharp pains which pierced his side, and this private affliction must have affected his public judgement. His mind was often fogged by the drugs he took to dull the wracking tortures of the body. On one occasion before entering a public gathering, he was known to have held his arm over a candle's flame in order

---

4. BNCE, p. 328.

to secure relief from the change of pain.[5] Just as the crisis of the Spanish succession was coming to a head, in fact, Napoleon was taken ill at Saint-Cloud. He was examined by a panel of five doctors who, however, failed to agree on a course of treatment. Incapacitated by drugs, and unwilling to oppose the implacable will of Empress Eugénie and her cohorts, who wanted war with Germany at whatever cost,[6] Napoleon was carried forward on a tide of national sentiment towards a catastrophe.

III

When France declared war on Germany, it fell to Prime Minister Emile Ollivier to announce that sombre fact in the legislature. He told the nation that he was taking on the challenge of war "with a light heart."[7] This phrase eventually came back to haunt him and blight his political career. In vain did Ollivier later protest that he meant that he took France into war "with a clear conscience"; posterity remembered only the "light heart." As France began to suffer her first military reverses, Eugénie saw in Ollivier a perfect scapegoat, and even while the war was in progress, she had him removed from office.

On July 28 the emperor boarded the train for Metz, in the company of his fourteen-year-old son, Prince Louis, to take command of the French army, which had been slow to mobilize and was ill-prepared for war.[8] As the train pulled away, Eugénie called out to her husband: "Do your duty!" She had persuaded Napoleon to place himself at the head of the army—a mistake of the first magnitude, as later events proved. It was not simply that he lacked the proper experience: the generals of his military high command could have compensated for that. But by placing himself at the head of his troops, he ensured that a surrender on the field of battle meant not only that the army would fall

---

5. MRSE, p. 518.

6. The views of Eugénie and her "war faction" were so well documented by her contemporaries that it was pointless of her to deny in later life that she had ever wanted war with Germany. "Everyone here, the Empress foremost, is so desirous of war that it seems impossible that we shall not have it," remarked the Comtesse de Garets, one of her maids of honour. (GSE, p. 187) And her enthusiasm for the impending conflict so impressed the Austrian ambassador, Prince Richard Metternich, that he reported her as saying that "military preparations were proceeding on a grand scale," and that "war with Prussia was inevitable." (WCN, pp. 326–27)

7. He made this famous speech to the French legislature on July 15, 1870. Ollivier, who had until recently been the leader of the liberal opposition party, had been asked by Napoleon III to form a government in January 1870. There is a strong possibility that it was Liszt himself who was responsible for persuading Ollivier to leave the opposition and join ranks with Napoleon. (HLEO, pp. 73–75, and VFL, pp. 25–26)

8. Prince Louis survived the Franco-Prussian War, only to die in the service of England nine years later. He and a party of British officers were ambushed while on patrol in Zululand, and he fell under a hail of Zulu spears.

but that France would fall with it, for the emperor *was* France. Had Napoleon been content to remain in Paris and entrust the army to one of his field marshals, or to behave like Crown King Wilhelm and stay well behind the lines of battle and watch his generals practise the art of war in their own way, a defeat might have left him immune from subsequent criticism. It would certainly have saved him from the ignominy of imprisonment. But none of this could have been foretold. In July 1870 the mood in France was jubilant and the prospect of defeat unthinkable.

Napoleon had been wrongly informed by his generals that he had four hundred thousand well-trained field troops at his immediate disposal; less than half that number were available at the beginning of the conflict, and many of them were not properly equipped. Thousands of soldiers were instructed to report to their units near the front lines, but had no idea where those units were or how to reach them. There was also an exodus of civilians moving in the opposite direction, and the French transport system broke down under the weight of people travelling to all points of the compass simultaneously. Those soldiers who made it to the front lines were not always given arms, nor were they told precisely what was expected of them. Evidently it was enough for them to know that they were there in defence of *la patrie*. The Prussian army under Helmut von Moltke, on the other hand, knew exactly what was required of it: to inflict such a heavy blow against Napoleon that he would henceforth be unable to prevent the further expansion of Germany.

IV

The first shots were fired on July 30, when Napoleon dispatched six divisions across the German border to take the town of Saarbrücken. Although they were heavily outnumbered, the Germans fought a pitched battle before retiring with the loss of four officers and seventy-nine men, as opposed to French losses of six officers and eighty men. Napoleon watched the battle from a vantage-point outside Saarbrücken, with Prince Louis at his side. Later he telegraphed Eugénie that Prince Louis had received his baptism of fire (he was well away from the battle lines) and had picked up a spent bullet as a souvenir. After the skirmish, Napoleon was in such pain from his kidney stones that he had to be lifted from his horse and could hardly walk to his carriage.

Forty-eight hours later there was an outbreak of rejoicing in Paris as rumours of a great victory reached the Bourse: "25,000 Prisoners Taken, Including the Crown Prince," read the headlines. Crowds rushed onto the streets, singing and dancing, and brought the traffic to a standstill. Within a few hours, however, Paris learned the truth. The French army had sustained many casualties at Froeschwiller in Lorraine, and Marshal Patrice MacMahon was retreating in disarray. And on the same day, the French had not only lost Saarbrücken to a Prussian advance, but had been pursued back across their own frontier; and when they had turned and fought, the Prussians had scattered them at Spicheren, forty miles to the west. The Prussians were now advancing deep into the heart of France, and Napoleon sensed a disaster in the making. When news of these twin defeats reached Empress Eugénie, she called the Chamber of Deputies into session and forced Ollivier out of office on a vote of no confidence. From that moment Ollivier was made the principal scapegoat of the war; he never recovered his position in political life. Eugénie appointed as his successor General Charles Cousin-Montauban, Comte de Palikao,[9] who immediately declared Paris to be in a state of siege, and began to raise a "citizen's army" to defend the capital.

V

The French army had now been broken in two. One force, under Marshal Achille-François Bazaine, was surrounded at Metz; the other, under Marshal MacMahon, was pinned down at Sedan. MacMahon had a depleted and demoralized army of 110,000 men; facing them were 250,000 Germans under General von Moltke, with five hundred artillery pieces.

The battle of Sedan began in darkness, at 4:00 a.m. on the morning of September 1, when Bavarian troops crossed the river Meuse and attacked the French positions. The fighting spread quickly along the entire front and the German artillery poured a stream of deadly fire into the French lines. General Barthélémi Lebrun, amazed at its accuracy, called it "an avalanche of iron." As the rising sun burned off the morning mist, the carnage was revealed in vivid detail to the observers on the German side of the river—King Wilhelm, Bismarck, various princes and dukes,[10] the foreign military attachés, and William Howard Russell, the war correspondent for the London *Times*. It is to Russell that we owe some of the most vivid reporting of the battle. As the struggle progressed, he observed that "the day had become so clear that through a good glass the movements of individual men were plainly discernible . . . bayonets glistened, and arms twinkled and flashed like a streamlet in moonlight."[11] To Wilhelm, who viewed the conflict from the safety of his vantage-point several

---

9. His colourful title dated from 1860 when he had led a punitive expedition against the Chinese.
10. Including Grand Duke Carl Alexander of Weimar (MF-P, p. 212). Among the foreign military observers was General Philip Henry Sheridan of the United States Army, who a few years earlier had come to prominence in the American Civil War. His presence as an observer in the German high command was not surprising. In 1867 Sheridan had been transferred to the Gulf of Mexico, where his presence along the Texan border had helped to overthrow the French puppet Emperor Maximilian.
11. HCS, p. 321.

miles away, the battle looked quite beautiful, as if it were being waged by toy soldiers marching to and fro, their ranks occasionally distorted by a shell-burst. At the height of a particularly heroic cavalry charge by the French dandy the Marquis de Galliffet, Wilhelm's enthusiasm could not be contained, and he burst out "Ah, the brave fellows!" To Russell, who later went down to the field of battle, things did not look beautiful at all. He reported that "no human eye ever rested on such revolting objects as were presented by the battle-fields around Sedan."[12] As he wandered across the terrain, he saw bodies that were nothing more than "masses of coloured rags glued together with blood and brains and pinned into strange shapes by fragments of bones." There were

> men's bodies without heads, legs without bodies, heaps of human entrails attached to blue and red cloth, and disembowelled corpses in uniform, bodies lying about in all attitudes, with skulls shattered, faces blown off, hips smashed, bones, flesh, and gay clothing all pounded together as if brayed in a mortar, extending for miles. . . .[13]

What fascinated Russell was the force of the German shell-blasts as they burst above the heads of the French soldiers. In one place he saw "eight French soldiers who must have been struck down by the bursting of a shell over a company, for they lay all round in a circle with their feet inwards, each shattered in the head or chest by a piece of shell and no other dead being within a hundred yards of them."[14]

Through this carnage Napoleon III rode back and forth all day, courting death, impervious to Prussian bullets. Though soldiers fell all around him, he himself was unscathed. Two officers accompanying him across the battlefield had been blown to bits by a single shell-burst, but the emperor escaped without a scratch. Strapped to his horse because of his condition, convulsed by pain, he doubtless prayed for a shell fragment to dispatch him to his death. But it did not come. In the last stages of the battle, and only after the French generals had refused to sign a letter asking the Prussians for terms, Bismarck ordered the Prussian artillery to concentrate all its fire-power on the town of Sedan itself. Demoralized and disorganized, Napoleon's army stared disaster in the face. To prevent further killing, Napoleon himself issued the order for the white flag to be hoisted. When the Prussians saw it fluttering in the breeze, they ceased fire and sent Colonel Paul Bronsart von Schellendorf[15] across the Meuse in order

---

12. *The Times,* Tuesday, September 6, 1870.
13. Ibid.
14. Ibid.
15. A younger brother of Liszt's pupil Hans Bronsart, who was himself temporarily enlisted as an officer in the conflict.

to negotiate terms. It was only then that the Prussians learned that Napoleon himself was on the field of battle. Bismarck and King Wilhelm could hardly comprehend their good fortune. Whatever happened now, the Second Empire was doomed. Napoleon had no choice but to sign the instrument of surrender, and he was then conducted from Sedan by a detachment of Prussian soldiers. As darkness fell, there arose from the campfires of the German army the strains of the old Lutheran chorale "Nun danket alle Gott." For the rest of the war, Napoleon and his entourage were held under house arrest at Wilhelmshöhe.[16]

When news of the defeat at Sedan reached Paris on September 4, huge mobs roamed the streets in a frenzy and converged on the legislature. They demanded, and got, the proclamation of a republic. The next day the crowds approached the Tuileries, and when they began to look dangerous, Empress Eugénie's advisors urged her to escape. Prince Richard Metternich, the Austrian ambassador, and the Cavaliere Constantino Nigra, Italy's foreign minister, were with her. The little party gathered in the anteroom leading to Eugénie's bedchamber. Unable to leave by the usual exits, they made their way through a secret passage from the palace museum into the old Louvre, and from there into the streets, where, in the unlikeliest episode of all, Eugénie hailed a passing cab.[17] It was at this point that all her instincts for self-preservation came to the fore. Instead of trying to flee the city, she sought temporary sanctuary in the home of her American dentist, Dr. Thomas Evans. The next day Evans drove her to Deauville in his carriage. From there she crossed over to England in a small yacht (named the *Gazelle*) during a storm in which the tiny craft

---

16. The message that Napoleon sent to King Wilhelm at the moment of surrender has gone down to posterity.

> Not having been able to die in the midst of my troops, nothing remains for me but to place my sword in the hands of Your Majesty.

> > Je suis de Votre Majesté,
> > le bon Frère.
> > Napoléon.

> Sedan, September 1, 1870

According to a report from military intelligence, posted in Berlin and published in *The Times* on September 7, 1870, fifty French generals were taken prisoner at Sedan, together with eighty thousand officers and men. Prussia began transporting this mass of humanity back to various parts of Germany and requested that the other German states help out by dividing the captured army at the rate of two prisoners for every one thousand citizens.

Many of the prisoners were transported back to Spandau prison in Berlin, where Liszt's former pupil "Puzzi" Cohen, now Father Augustine, tended the dead and the dying. He himself died at Spandau in January 1871 after contracting typhoid fever from the prisoners.

17. Eugénie had always poured scorn on the undignified way in which Louis-Philippe had made his escape from Paris, twenty-two years earlier. It was now her turn to flee France, and she chose exactly the same means of locomotion.

tossed and turned for twenty-four hours and almost foundered. The empress and her party finally made landfall at Ryde, on the Isle of Wight.

V I

The Germans now advanced on Paris, and by September 23 they had encircled the city. Already the citizens had prepared themselves for a siege. After the defeat at Sedan the work of provisioning the city had rapidly got under way. Enough flour and corn were stocked to last for eighty days. A quarter of a million sheep and forty thousand oxen were brought in from outlying areas and made to graze in the Bois de Boulogne. It was also reckoned that there was enough coal to last for seventy-eight days. No one believed that the siege would last long. Everyone was convinced that the Germans would attack. And if that happened, the government told itself, the Germans would suffer a crushing defeat. Nothing in military history suggested that a city the size of Paris could be taken by a frontal assault. There were now more than a million men under arms for the defence of the capital, under the overall command of General Louis Trochu. The 13th and 14th Army Corps were there, the Garde Mobile, the Garde Sédentaire of Paris, the Légion des Volontaires de France (consisting of Polish exiles), Les Amis de France (a mixture of Belgian, Italian, and British residents in Paris), and dozens of heterogeneous guerrilla formations created out of the many workers' groups and the professions. France had seen nothing like this since the days of Napoleon I, whose name was often invoked to stiffen the pride of the army. On September 14 General Trochu reviewed his monster force in the Champs-Elysées; the whole of Paris turned out to watch. Trochu later wrote that the parade stretched from the Place de la Bastille to the Arc de Triomphe—a distance of nearly four miles. "At every window of surrounding buildings, on the balconies and the terraces there were further ranks of moving heads, of flags, of patriotic emblems. Every voice was shouting, all arms were moving, it was a delirium!"[18]

Paris now awaited the German assault, but it did not come. Instead, Moltke decided to starve the city into submission. The siege of Paris would last for four months, creating much misery for the inhabitants. Meanwhile, the new, young minister for war, Léon Gambetta, escaped from the city by balloon in order to continue the struggle from Tours. His attempts to raise an army and send it north in order to relieve the siege of Paris were frustrated by Moltke. Gambetta also sent emissaries abroad to muster support from the foreign powers, but they turned him down. The Prussians tightened the noose around Paris and began to bombard the city on December 27. Three hundred to four hundred shells

---

18. Trochu, *Oeuvres posthumes*, vol. 1 (Tours, 1896), p. 218.

fell on the civil population every day. Altogether 97 citizens were killed and 278 were wounded. During the siege there was such serious starvation that people routinely ate cats and dogs. Even the animals in the zoo were killed for human consumption—elephants, rhinos, and ostriches among them. Verlaine reported that he ate giraffe. Victor Hugo consumed a veritable smorgasbord of wildlife, including rat pâté, bear steak, and leg of antelope.[19]

The French were obliged to sign an armistice with the Prussians on January 28, 1871, much to Gambetta's dismay and over his angry protests. The terms of the peace treaty were severe. France had to pay a war indemnity of five billion francs, in addition to the cost of maintaining a German army of occupation in eastern France, which would remain entrenched there until the indemnity was paid. Alsace and Lorraine were to be annexed to the new German empire. The final humiliation came when the German army was authorized to stage a victory march through the Arc de Triomphe.[20]

During this period the German high command established itself at Versailles, where King Wilhelm and his retinue also took up a temporary residence. It was at Versailles on January 18 that Wilhelm, flushed with his recent victories, proclaimed the creation of the first German Reich in the famous Hall of Mirrors. In a communication to Bismarck, written out on the back of an envelope, he scribbled the words "Chancellor of the German Empire," and established Bismarck's right to direct the empire he had created. It was from this time that Bismarck's famous appellation "the Iron Chancellor" dates.

When the terms of the armistice became known, civil war broke out in Paris, and by March 1871 the Paris Communards had seized power. They controlled Paris for two months, until Louis-Adolphe Thiers (who had meanwhile been elected to lead the republican government) resolved to oust them by force. The German army still ringed Paris but respected the armistice and did not interfere in the local fighting. In the course of the "Bloody Week" (May 21–28), the Communards fought the French army street by street. As they fell back, they took hostages whom they executed, among them the Archbishop of Paris, and they also set fire to public buildings, including the Tuileries and the Hotel de Ville.[21] Their final stand was at the Père-Lachaise Cemetery, where they were mown

---

19. See Hugo's *Choses vues,* vol. 2 (Paris, 1913; pp. 158–74), in which he records his unusual diet for the months of November and December. On December 30 he wrote: "I'm beginning to get stomach cramps. We are eating unknown things." (p. 167)

20. When Empress Eugénie was ninety-five years old, news of the defeat of Germany in the 1914–18 war was brought to her, together with the severe peace terms imposed at the insistence of France—which included the return of Alsace and Lorraine. She remarked: "Today I can understand why God has made me live so long. Our dead of 1870 . . . are at last requited for their sacrifice."

21. The home of Emile Ollivier, who had become highly unpopular as a result of his association with the war, was severely damaged by fire at this time. His own possessions went up in flames together with the legacy of Anna Liszt—including her correspondence with Adam and other precious documents associated with Liszt's childhood.

down in great numbers. Twenty thousand Communards were killed in the fighting; thousands of others were taken prisoner and deported to penal colonies.

The siege of Paris left no aspect of the city's artistic and intellectual life untouched. Vincent d'Indy, who was nineteen years old at the time, served in the National Guard and left a graphic account of those difficult days.[22] Jules Massenet also lived through the siege and later wrote about it in his *Recollections.* "As if the lesson of that bloody time would never fade away, and as if its memory would be perpetuated, bits of burnt paper were brought into our garden from time to time on the wings of the wind. I kept one piece. It bore traces of figures and probably came from the burning of the Ministry of Finance."[23] Auber, too, survived the siege. When he heard of the summary executions of Generals Thomas and Lecomte, the latter of whom was a personal friend (the Communards had stood them against a wall and shot them, failing to kill Lecomte with the first volley, so they held up his body and fired into it until he died), Auber said: "My heart bleeds when I gaze on all that is going on about me. Alas! I have lived too long."[24]

Napoleon III was finally released from captivity in March 1871, and travelled to England and his final place of exile, Camden Place in Chislehurst. There he was reunited with the empress and their son, and there he lived out his remaining years in constant agony from his kidney stones. He finally consented to undergo a series of operations for the removal of the stones by the British surgeon Sir Henry Thompson. After the first, exploratory operation, during which Napoleon was chloroformed, Sir Henry discovered a stone the size of a full-sized date blocking the royal bladder. It was decided to remove it by lithotrity, a procedure which involved crushing the stone and removing it in sections. Two operations were carried out, and more than half the stone was removed. But Napoleon expired before the final operation commenced— possibly from an overdose of anaesthetic. He died on January 9, 1873.[25]

VII

Liszt looked on helplessly as the catastrophe of the Franco-Prussian War unfolded. His career tied him both to Germany and to France, and he was torn.

---

22. Vincent d'Indy, *Histoire du 105e bataillon de la Garde Nationale de Paris, en l'année 1870–71, par un engagé volontaire dudit bataillon âgé de 19 ans* (Paris, 1872).

23. MMS, p. 83.

24. H-LL, p. 288.

25. When Liszt heard of the emperor's passing, he eulogized him in a letter to Princess Carolyne. "Napoleon III dead. Magnanimous heart, comprehensively universal intelligence, the wisdom of experience, a gentle and generous character—an unlucky destiny! He was a thwarted Caesar, but was animated by a breath of the divine Caesar, an ideal personification of the terrestrial Empire!" (LLB, vol. 7, p. 2)

But there was no question that his deepest loyalties lay with Napoleon III and France. He believed with all his heart in the democratic ideals of the Second Empire. In the autumn of 1868 he had written to Agnès Street-Klindworth: "I confess my *patriotic* passion for Paris, especially for the *imperial* Paris of the present."[26] One of the worst aspects of the war for Liszt was the pro-Bismarckian stand of Cosima. He gradually came to believe that Cosima had betrayed her French background. For this he blamed Richard Wagner, whose public gloatings over each Prussian victory had become nauseating.[27] And when Cosima and Wagner were married, in Lucerne, just five weeks after the outbreak of hostilities, Liszt knew that his daughter would become irredeemably German.[28] Liszt himself never wavered in his feelings of personal loyalty towards Napoleon III. He wrote to Carolyne on August 31, 1870, after the tide of the war had turned against France: "If the Empire were to collapse, I should personally feel extremely sad. I absolutely do not believe that the personal rule of Napoleon III has been corrupting and oppressive for France—but quite the contrary, it is demonstrably necessary, conciliatory, progressive, and genuinely intelligent and democratic in the best sense of the word."[29] When news of France's defeat reached him, Liszt was shattered. On September 4 he observed bitterly: "As Voltaire predicted, the century of the Prussians has at last arrived!"[30]

Liszt's interest in the outcome of the Franco-Prussian War, his friendship with Napoleon III, and the crucial role played in the events of 1870 by his son-in-law Emile Ollivier have led some scholars to speculate that the composer regularly spied for the French and sent secret despatches back to Paris. This theory—Liszt as secret agent—has come to enjoy a certain vogue in the liter-

---

26. LLB, vol. 3, p. 203.
27. Even allowing for the usual expression of patriotic sentiment in time of war, Wagner's jingoistic utterances place him beyond the pale. His infatuation with Bismarck, King Wilhelm, and German nationalism in general knew no bounds at this time, although this alone would not fault him since it was shared by millions of Germans at home. At the height of the war Wagner wrote his *Kaisermarsch*, whose choral finale extols the Kaiser to the heavens. And during the siege of Paris, while the Parisians were starving, he made them the butt of his wit in a tasteless farce entitled *Eine Kapitulation*. Perhaps his most blatant surge of nationalism, however, came in his poem "To the German Army before Paris," a copy of which he sent to Bismarck in the early part of 1871. Bismarck responded with a flattering reply from Versailles on February 21, telling him that with his works Wagner had won a victory of his own over the French. (BBW, 1901, p. 220) In the face of behaviour such as this, it is not surprising that many French musicians developed an all-consuming hatred of Wagner and his works which survived long after the war ended.
28. This is borne out by Cosima's diary entries of the period. Thus, on January 10, 1871, she wrote: "The news of the bombardment of Paris is good, and it seems the French themselves realize the hopelessness of their position." (WT, vol. 1, p. 320) And on January 14 comes the entry: ". . . Our splendid Germans continue to make good progress. Heaven's blessings on them!" (WT, vol. 1, p. 322) These observations, it should be remembered, were made at a time when the friends of her youth were daily being maimed and killed by Prussian shells. There is not a single expression of sadness at the carnage.
29. LLB, vol. 6, p. 263.
30. Ibid.

ature, thanks in part to Emile Haraszti's influential essay on the topic.[31] That Liszt often talked politics in his correspondence cannot be denied, and he doubtless had many personal conversations about the political structure of the Second Empire with Ollivier (who had been in opposition before he rallied to Napoleon's side, a move constantly urged on him by Liszt). He also received political despatches from Agnès Street-Klindworth, who *was* an agent,[32] which he regularly passed on to others. But this is a far cry from spying in the generally accepted sense of the term. Haraszti rested his case mainly on some remarks that Liszt is supposed to have made in later years to Kornél Ábrányi, the secretary of the Royal Academy.

> Certainly [Liszt told Ábrányi] the European situation would be quite different today if my son-in-law, Emile Ollivier, and if particularly Napoleon III had paid more heed to my items of information—always received from trustworthy sources—than to the reports of narrow-minded and painfully credulous diplomats devoid of conscience, like presumptuous Goliaths making fun of David's sling-shots. . . .[33]

Liszt then goes on to report the enormous influence that Wagner had over Ludwig II, and its effect on the latter's decision to break his word to Napoleon, enter the war, and commit Bavarian troops to the Prussian side, a military event that may well have tipped the scales in Bismarck's favour.

> Timely warning was given to my son-in-law, Emile Ollivier, to the French diplomats, to the Empress, who was rather inclined to enter the war, and to the Emperor, Napoleon III, who at first hesitated but was at length swept along with the tide . . . but all this good advice was a voice crying in the wilderness. The die was cast, and its fatal consequences have been written in some of the gloomiest pages of history.[34]

None of this turns Liszt into a spy, although it does confirm that he was a highly interesting *raconteur*. And where are the documents that Liszt is supposed to have sent to Napoleon III and to Emile Ollivier? Haraszti's case is not strengthened when he tells us that they must have been destroyed when the Tuileries was set on fire—a convenient conflagration. As the Hungarian Liszt

---

31. "Franz Liszt and Richard Wagner in the Franco-German War of 1870," *Musical Quarterly,* vol. 35, no. 3 (July 1949). Written in collaboration with Bertita Paillard.

32. See Volume Two, pp. 209–224.

33. *Musical Quarterly*, vol. 35, no. 3 (July 1949), p. 386.

34. Ibid., p. 387.

scholar Klára Hamburger drily remarked: "It was totally out of keeping with Liszt's character. Nor is it likely that [Liszt] would have sung so openly the praises of a man for whom he was secretly spying."[35]

VIII

Liszt was not idle during the four months that he spent in Szekszárd as a guest of Baron Augusz. He had already warned his host that he planned to turn his home into an athenaeum while he was there, one whose music would equal that of the leading capitals. And he tried to keep his word. Ede Reményi, Nándor Plotényi, Ödön Mihalovich, Franz Servais, Sophie Menter, and Olga Janina all turned up, as did the painter Wilhelm von Kaulbach, the sculptor Ernst Rietschel, and the world-famous chemist Baron Justus Liebig. It was the kind of circle that Liszt enjoyed, and the large, well-appointed home of the Augusz family was well suited for music-making.[36] Another distinguished guest who journeyed to Szekszárd was the Hungarian composer Mihály Mosonyi. He presented Liszt with one of his best compositions, the *Souvenirs of Happiness.* No one guessed the foreboding in the title. Mosonyi was already unwell at this time. As he set out on the return trip to Budapest, he was overtaken by a torrential downpour of rain and soaked to the skin. He never recovered, and the following month he died.[37]

About the middle of September, Augusz took Liszt and some of his entourage to Kalocsa, to visit Cardinal Lajos Haynald, the primate of Hungary. After lunch, they repaid Haynald by putting on a concert in the great hall of the archiepiscopal residence, during which Liszt played some of his *Mélodies hongroises,* and took part in a performance of Beethoven's *Kreutzer* Sonata with Reményi. In fact, Liszt played the piano a great deal while he was with the Augusz family. The most memorable occasion was on October 22, his fifty-ninth birthday, which he celebrated together with the entire village. As dusk fell on the eve of the birthday, every house on the main street illuminated its windows, and there were displays of fireworks around the Augusz residence. At six o'clock the main square started to fill with people and a torchlight procession moved towards Liszt's windows. A Gypsy band turned up and played a medley of Hungarian pieces, including the *Rákóczy* March, while Liszt looked on. A local teacher then emerged from the crowd and addressed a speech to Liszt

---

35. "Musicien humanitaire," *New Hungarian Quarterly,* Budapest vol. 27, no. 103 (Autumn 1986), p. 5.
36. One of these musical at-homes at Szekszárd has been depicted in a drawing by Kollarz. It shows Liszt at the piano, with Augusz, Reményi, Ábrányi, and Mosonyi looking on. (BFL, p. 248)
37. Liszt commemorated their long friendship with his *Mosonyi's Funeral Music,* which was published in November 1870. A second version appeared in 1885 as the last of the seven *Hungarian Historical Portraits.*

in which he begged the composer to remain in Hungary. The crowd took up the call, cheered wildly, and cried, "Long live Ferenc Liszt!" Augusz then replied for Liszt in Hungarian, at which there was an even greater outbreak of enthusiasm. This was the cue for Liszt to have a piano pushed near the open window, so that he and Antal Siposs could play *Mosonyi's Festival Music*. This was meant as a tribute to Mosonyi, who lay dying in Pest. The party then moved to the hotel on the opposite side of the street, and during the course of the evening Reményi gave a recital in aid of French soldiers wounded in battle. There followed a banquet for 130 people, put on by the Ladies' Civic Society of Szekszárd. The following day, Liszt rose early and went to morning mass, during which he and Reményi played the Benedictus from his Hungarian Coronation Mass. Augusz then hosted a birthday banquet for his distinguished visitor, at the end of which Liszt got up and made an unusual speech.

> St. Francis of Assisi had a pupil who would have liked to know what his master said during his prayers. So he listened to him, but on the first morning he heard only these words: "O my Lord!" On the following morning he heard the very same words. There is nothing I can say either, as this idea contains within itself all that is great, sublime, and noble. Therefore when I turn to my Lord I also remember my friends, for whose devotion and friendship I can only show myself worthy if I devote my activities hereafter to my country.[38]

This theme of devotion to country came to dominate Liszt's thoughts. He was overwhelmed by the outpouring of affection for him by his fellow Hungarians at this time, but as yet he had no clear idea of how he might reciprocate. "I am so terrified at the prospect of being thrown back into an active career!" he wrote.[39] His fears were well-founded; there was already talk in the Hungarian press of some kind of official position for him in the musical life of Hungary. Yet all he really wanted was to be left in peace to compose. As he told Princess Carolyne: "My whole career lies in my head and at the tip of my pen. If I succeed in writing a few good pages of music, then I do not ask for more."[40]

The year 1870 ended as it had begun, with celebrations in honour of Beethoven. In order to mark the composer's one hundredth birthday, which fell on December 16, Liszt was persuaded to direct an all-Beethoven concert—this time in the Pest Vigadó. Once again he chose as the centrepiece the Ninth Symphony; the other works in the programme were the Violin Concerto, with Reményi as soloist, and the second version of his own Beethoven Festival Can-

---

38. *Szépirodalmi Közlöny,* October 27, 1870.
39. HLSW, p. 145.
40. LLB, vol. 6, p. 274.

tata, this time in a Hungarian translation especially undertaken for this concert by Kornél Ábrányi. This was a glittering occasion, of a kind that had not been seen in Hungary since before the War of Independence. It was attended by many prominent individuals in politics and the arts. The journal *Zenészeti Lapok* summed up the national sentiment when it reported that "our festival borrowed the prestige and lustre of an artistic genius, Franz Liszt, through which the celebration not only achieved European significance but also aroused the envy of other nations."[41] Such public appearances, far from satisfying those Hungarians who wanted Liszt to take a leading role in their affairs, only created a national clamour for him to take on yet more. On December 22 Liszt's long sojourn in Hungary was crowned by a visit from the prime minister, Gyula Andrássy. It was the wish of the government, Andrássy told him, that he take over the leadership of the newly planned National Academy of Music; the legislature had already voted to set aside money for its creation.[42] Liszt was flattered by the invitation, not least because of the august office from which it came; but he realized that it was an attempt to bind him permanently to Hungary, and for that he was not yet ready. Five more years were to elapse before Liszt formally assented to take on this job, and there was to be much soul-searching along the way.

One honour that Liszt did accept from Andrássy, however, and which was extended to him as a direct result of this visit, was the title of Royal Hungarian Councillor. The position carried with it an annual stipend of four thousand forints and entitled Liszt to sit in the Hungarian legislature. While this was a privilege he never exercised, the fact that it was extended to him at all meant that he was now recognised not only in word but also in deed as one of the leaders of his nation.[43]

---

41. *Zenészeti Lapok,* 1870/71, pp. 134–35.

42. There was a report of the visit in the *Zenészeti Lapok,* January 1, 1871: "Last Sunday the prime minister, Count Gyula Andrássy, visited Franz Liszt and remained with him for more than half an hour. The outcome of this visit was that the matter of Liszt's abode in Budapest was settled."

43. Emperor Franz Joseph bestowed the title on June 13, 1871; the letter from Prime Minister Andrássy confirming Liszt in this important position is dated June 21, 1871. It is preserved among Liszt's papers in Weimar. (WA, Kasten 131, u. 2)

The Lion of Weimar:
Liszt and His Pupils

*I possess no talent for the pedantic discussion of the
rules of playing, of interpretation, and of expression.*
LISZT TO LINA RAMANN (1874)[1]

*Liszt has the gift of doubling the talents of others
while he is talking to them.*
GRAND DUCHESS SOPHIE OF WEIMAR TO MME
MOUCHANOFF–KALERGIS (1870)[2]

I

Liszt was the greatest piano teacher of his generation. From his mid–adolescence
in the 1820s, right up to the last month of his life, July 1886, teaching was central to his musical existence. More than four hundred students are said to have
passed through his hands, and a number of them became eminent.[3] Liszt virtually created the "masterclass," a concept that still flourishes today. He believed
that young masters would find one another artistically stimulating and that the
competitive climate would raise artistic standards. The first generation of his students had included Tausig, Klindworth, Bronsart, and Bülow. But the second
also featured some impressive names, including Moriz Rosenthal, Alexander
Siloti, Emil Sauer, Eugène d'Albert, and Arthur Friedheim, some of whom lived
well into the 1940s. Their gramophone records give us a fascinating glimpse into
a golden age of piano-playing, now vanished forever.

What was Liszt like as a teacher? There is a wealth of testimony on the subject, much of it from the pupils themselves. He was not interested in playing
the pedagogue. He had no "method," no "system," little technical advice to
offer his students. Not for him an analytical pursuit of the technical processes
of piano playing. The last thing that the supreme master of the keyboard was
concerned with was the physical problems associated with the instrument.

---

1. RL, p. 39.
2. LLB, vol. 6, p. 248.
3. A comprehensive list will be found on pp. 249–52 of this volume.

Since they had ceased to exist for him he no longer considered them. "Wash your dirty linen at home," he used to tell those of his pupils who still required technical help. By the same token, he was singularly unimpressed by students who flaunted their technique. "Do I care how fast you can play your octaves?" he once thundered at a pupil in the middle of the celebrated octave passage of the Chopin A-flat-major Polonaise. "What I wish to hear is the canter of the horses of the Polish cavalry before they gather force and destroy the enemy."[4] Interpretation, not mechanical attainment, was what interested him. Of course, by observing Liszt himself play—watching the lie of his hands on the keyboard, seeing how certain passages were fingered, studying his pedal effects—his pupils had access to the best possible model, and they learned far more than they might have done from a dry, academic description of these events.

The Weimar classes were usually held three afternoons a week, on Mondays, Wednesdays, and Fridays, between 3:30 and 6:00 p.m. As the students assembled in the music room of the Hofgärtnerei, they placed their music in a growing pile on the piano. An air of expectancy hovered over the room while they waited for Liszt to appear. Then the moment arrived for which everyone was waiting. A voice at the back whispers, "Der Meister kommt!" They all rise and stand in respectful silence as Liszt enters the room and makes his way to the piano. After greeting everyone, he turns to the heap of music, leafs through it until he finds something he wants to hear, holds up the copy, and asks: "Who plays this?" The luckless student then comes forward and the class begins.

Two pianos stand in the music room, a full-size Bechstein grand and a small upright.[5] The student goes to the Bechstein while Liszt seats himself at the upright. After a few general words of introduction from Liszt, the student plays, with Liszt and the others looking on, after which Liszt makes a few observations and perhaps even plays through the work himself. These are moments to treasure, and the atmosphere becomes electric when Liszt, displeased with the way a performance is going, pushes the student off the stool in an attempt to revive the flagging music. The whole keyboard thunders and lightens, and the trembling student gets a glimpse into a mighty conception of the work which, until then, lay locked up behind the notes of the music. Liszt was an inspirational force. Simply to be in the same room with him, as more than one student testified, turned one temporarily into a better pianist.

All this stood in marked contrast to Liszt's contemporaries, some of whom were obsessed with technique. Many pedagogues of the day—Rudolf Breit-

---

4. LM, p. 68.
5. The Bechstein was sent to him courtesy of Carl Bechstein, and put into storage whenever Liszt was not resident in Weimar. Bechstein replaced it with a new one whenever it needed repair. The well-known Ibach upright, at which Liszt posed for a number of photographs with his students, was not delivered to the Hofgärtnerei until April 1885. In the early years the upright piano was supplied by G. Höhle, a local Weimar manufacturer.

haupt, Theodor Kullak, and Ludwig Deppe among them—thought that pianists could be produced somewhat like soldiers, by regimental drill. After a
suitable lapse of time, so the theory ran, the "soldiers" would come marching
out of the studios and conservatories, poised to conquer the world. Kalkbrenner's hand-rail was supposed to make the wrists "conform" to the correct lat-
eral motions of playing. Kullak, who used to frown on all surplus movement,
insisted that his pupils play with a coin balanced on the back of the hand. (All
this did, as one pupil wrily observed, was to give people plenty of practice in
picking up fallen coins off the floor.) The most notorious of these mechanical
aids was Johann Logier's "Chiroplast," an amazing invention of rods and rings
through which the victim was obliged to insert his thumbs and fingers, all freedom restricted, like a manacled prisoner. Far worse than Kullak's coin, Kalkbrenner's hand-rail, and Logier's Chiroplast was the growing fashion of having
the webbing of the fingers cut to increase the stretch.[6] For Liszt this kind of
thing was a scourge; and since he knew that hundreds of aspiring pianists
looked up to him as a role-model, he condemned it. When one of his students,
Johanna Wenzel (who later became a teacher at the Brussels Conservatory and
the wife of another of his pupils, Juliusz Zarembski), asked his advice about
some such operation, he responded:

> My dear young lady:
>   In reply to your friendly lines I earnestly beg of you to think no
> more of having the barbarous operation. Better to play every octave
> and chord wrong throughout your life than to commit such a mad
> attack upon your hands.
>   With best thanks, I subscribe myself yours respectfully,
>   F. LISZT
>
>   Weimar, June 10, 1872[7]

Liszt regarded such ideas as both false and dangerous. They were based on
externals and overlooked a deeper truth. Pianists, like plants, were placed there
by nature. The gardener may cultivate the plant, but he does not create it. So
too the teacher of pianists; he can cultivate but he cannot create. Moreover, in-

---

6. By 1885 this operation had been "refined" to the point where the tendons themselves were cut. In
August of that year *The Musical Times* reported that a London surgeon, one Mr. Noble Smith, had successfully carried out a new operation for freeing the "subcutaneous division of the exterior tendon
slip of the ring finger," a description that it took over from the *British Medical Journal*. See "Mirror of
Music," vol. 1, pp. 334–35.
    Among the more exotic aids to technical perfection was something called the "Musical Glove,"
which was advertised in *The Musical Times* as early as 1878, together with the bogus claim that it
strengthened the hand muscles.
7. LLB, vol. 2, p. 174.

side every good pianist is a musician struggling to get out. Liszt took it to be his duty to set the musician free and lead him forth. Everything else would follow once the musician had been released, including his technical development. In a comment Liszt once made to his biographer Lina Ramann, he delivered an aphorism which still offers food for thought: "Technique should create itself from spirit, not from mechanics."[8]

I I

It is a tantalising paradox that from his earliest youth Liszt had punished his own hands and fingers in the unceasing quest for a transcendental technique. Even in his later years, when he claimed to be above it all, he still devoted much time and effort to the production of such things as his three volumes of Technical Studies (1869–71). Yet as far as his own pupils were concerned, he rarely lost an opportunity to avoid mentioning the topic of technique. Nonetheless, nothing is simpler for the biographer than to show that technical problems (and their solutions) were for Liszt himself a constant preoccupation. He was like an advanced chess-player who has spent so much time playing the game that the complex moves leading up to "check" and "checkmate" invade every aspect of his mental life. He reviewed them all the time.

Kurd von Schlözer once visited Liszt in the Santa Francesca Romana and found him amusing himself at a little dumb keyboard by practising a trill from a Beethoven sonata (op. 109) "which until that moment he had played his

---

8. "Aus dem Geist schaffe sich die Technik, nicht aus der Mechanik!" (RL-P, p. 6) Liszt frequently touched on this concept. He once explained to Carl Lachmund: "When I have the will to do, I can do. But when that will is lacking, I can not do more than the ordinary." Knowing Liszt's strong religious convictions Lachmund immediately saw a connection. "Yes," he observed, "it is the spirit that quickeneth." Years later, when Lachmund told Rafael Joseffy of Liszt's remarkable playing, notwithstanding that "three score years and ten" had bowed his shoulders, Joseffy remarked: "I have always held that great technique does not so much come from the fingers; it is the *intellectual spirit* that gives the power for the technique." (LL, p. 33) This remark could only have originated with Liszt himself, since it is so much in tune with his own views on the topic.

Giuseppe Ferrata, who studied with Liszt in Rome during the years 1884–85, reported an interesting conversation on the same subject.

> More than once I accompanied him to the church of San Carlo al Corso, Rome, to hear mass. We would often walk from the hotel in Via Aliberti to the church, a little distance off, arm in arm, and once he said to me: "Many students of the piano run up and down scales for hours every day, thinking that they will reach the heaven of technical attainment; but athletes develop their muscles and get resistance and control of them by exercises which are based on sudden contraction and expansion. These principles should apply also to students of piano who should formulate exercises for sudden expansion and contraction of the muscles of their arms and hands." (CLC, series 1, folder 36, unpublished letter to Lachmund, dated December 5, 1917)

whole life long with the second and third fingers." Now in later life, observed Schlözer, Liszt had suddenly taken it into his head to do it with the third and fourth fingers.[9] It was the same years earlier when William Mason had turned up at the Altenburg and played Liszt's arrangement of one of the Weber overtures. Liszt, struck by the strange fingering that Mason was using, stopped him and said: "What fingering is that you are using?" Mason hesitated, then replied: "Klindworth gave it to me." "Leave Klindworth's fingering to Klindworth," Liszt retorted. "*He* can do very well with it; *you* must use this"—whereupon Liszt jotted down a more straightforward solution.[10] By itself the story is trivial, but it indicates Liszt's belief that each hand is different, that the only "correct" solutions are the ones that each individual player finds the most comfortable—and discovers for himself through trial and error. And what is comfortable at one time of life may be uncomfortable at another. This was why Liszt refused to teach technique. The empirical process was sacrosanct. That process had worked for him, so let it work for others. To interfere in such a primary activity would be like getting in the way of nature. It is clear from a study of his methods that Liszt held his chief duty to be to place before his students a clear and correct "sonic image" of each piece to be studied. Only picture the image, he seemed to say, and the body will find its own way to project it.

Memorable were those days on which Liszt played to his students. None of them ever forgot the experience. But no one could ever be certain when these impromptu performances would take place. They usually arose out of some piece that had taken his fancy, had stirred some distant memory, or illustrated some point he was particularly anxious to make. He rarely played anything complete, but over the years he presented his students with hundreds of fragments, both great and small, of whatever repertory they happened to bring along. And he usually played everything from memory. When the spirit moved him, however, he delivered major performances of complete pieces that reverberated in the mind. One such occasion took place in the Hofgärtnerei on August 10, 1883, and was recorded by Carl Lachmund in his diary. It happened unexpectedly, while the students were preoccupied with other things. Suddenly Liszt approached the piano.

> The mood had seized him! There were half audible exclamations of joy and astonishment; some drew quickly nearer; and then there was perfect quiet.

Incidentally, Ferrata (1867–1928) was later sent to America by his uncle Cardinal Domenico Ferrata as a result of a scandalous love-affair with a Russian princess, Olga Cheramateff—a banishment that he appears to have turned to good advantage, since he eventually became head of the music department at Newcombe College in New Orleans, a post he held until his death. He was also the editor of *Modern Music and Musicians.*

9. SRB, p. 354.

10. *The Musical Standard,* August 26, 1916.

Sitting at ease, as if comfortable, and with his hands in anything but a conventional position, he began the beautiful A flat Etude, the first from Chopin's op. 25. Oh, how convincingly every melody note, as he intoned it, spoke to one's heart, and how beautifully the rippling accompaniment shaded its emotional meaning. This he followed with the second, in the relative key of F minor, the one with the tricky combination of two-quarter (six-eight) against three-quarter time.

. . . Both etudes he played with that same quiet ease and lucidness of phrasing that always impressed one in his playing, and there was an entire absence of any show of virtuosity or of dynamic extremes, so often heard in the playing of great piano virtuosos. His apparent disregard of metric time, without disturbing the symmetry of rhythmic balance, which lent the Lisztian charm to his phrasing, was to me most characteristic and wonderful.

He had finished. No one could find words. We knew not what to say or do. We could merely, as is the custom in foreign lands, kiss his hands, those hands that had done such wonders for nearly two-thirds of a century.[11]

Liszt was seventy-three years old when he delivered these performances, and he never practised; yet his playing had evidently lost nothing of its former plasticity.

Did Liszt have any general principles of interpretation? The answer to this question is not unlike that given by the Irish judge who once declared that as a general principle he had no general principles. Still, two of Liszt's more thought-provoking ideas can be mentioned here, since they are indicative of the way in which he taught and played. For example, Liszt spoke ironically of the "Pontius Pilate offence" in art. By this he meant that he had no time for those artists who ritually washed their hands in public of the music they played, who claimed classical "objectivity," who detached themselves from their performances. He argued that the "cult of personality" was less harmful to music than the "cult of anonymity."[12] He knew that Diderot's celebrated paradox about actors (that in their art they can only be true by being false) cannot possibly be applied to musicians, who can only be true *by being true*. As for virtuosity, Liszt did not despise it as such; it was the mindless display of virtuosity which aroused his ire. The mind had to drive the body, not body the mind. He

---

11. LL, pp. 244–45.

12. On this topic, see Liszt's letter to Wilhelm Joseph von Wasielewski, LLB, vol. 1, p. 258. Elsewhere Liszt once observed: "It is annoying that virtuosos, both instrumentalists and singers, behave towards the works they perform as if they were simple reciters. Virtuosity is not a passive slave. All the attractions of a work depend on it to some extent. It can resuscitate all [a work's] charms . . . or make it ugly, destroy it." Henri Gil-Marchex, *Revue musicale,* special Liszt numbers, May–June 1928, p. 88.

saw his first duty as a teacher to encourage his pupils to discover themselves, and then to declare himself unnecessary. It is almost as if he believed the cynical aphorism "There are no great teachers, there are only great pupils." How well he succeeded in releasing the individual within each of his students is borne out by the enormous diversity of playing he encouraged among them. Only the bad teacher is interested in producing copies of himself.

The other idea is equally stimulating. In 1875, after the Royal Academy of Music had opened in Budapest and he had been appointed its first president, he was able to influence its curriculum. He insisted that all piano students study composition and that all composition students study the piano. This injunction seems harsh today. What modern conservatory would tolerate it? Liszt, however, thought that the separation of performance from composition was detrimental to both, that Music was indivisible. Until his death, all his students at the Royal Academy had to graduate in improvisation. It is a fact that of Liszt's students who later dominated the field of performance (to the names of Bülow, Tausig, and Rosenthal can be added those of Sauer, Weingartner, and Friedheim), every one of them composed. The link is so consistent that we can postulate a causal connection between their interest in *creation* and their excellence in *re*-creation. Certainly it could be said of Liszt himself that he played with the insight of a composer and composed with the outlook of a performer.

III

When Liszt told his students to "create memories," he could have had no idea that so many of them would take him at his word. It is almost easier to identify those students who did *not* chronicle those times than those who did. One of the best eye-witness accounts of the Weimar masterclasses comes from Amy Fay, who travelled from the United States in 1869 to study in Germany and first encountered Liszt in 1873. Miss Fay's descriptions of her lessons with Liszt are so famous that they have become part of the folklore surrounding his classes, and it is almost impossible to think of them at all except through her eyes. Her observations are rivetting, and widely accessible. The modern Liszt biographer could easily be criticized for even mentioning Miss Fay, who in this particular area has rendered everybody else speechless. But not to quote her would be worse; quite simply, her prose is irreplaceable.

Amy Fay first caught sight of Liszt during a visit to the Weimar theatre on May 1, 1873. A few days later she was invited to a tea-party, where she met him again and was transfixed.

> . . . The door suddenly opened and Liszt appeared. We all rose to our feet and he shook hands with everybody without waiting to be

introduced. Liszt looks as if he had been through everything, and has a face *seamed* with experience. He is rather tall and narrow, and wears a long abbé's coat reaching down nearly to his feet. He made me think of an old time magician more than anything, and I felt that with a touch of his wand he could transform us all. . . .[13]

After making Liszt's acquaintance and becoming his pupil, she wrote:

> In Liszt I can at last say that my ideal in *something* has been realised. He goes far beyond all that I expected. Anything so perfectly beautiful as he looks when he sits at the piano I never saw, and yet he is almost an old man now. His personal magnetism is immense, and I can scarcely bear it when he plays. He can make me cry all he chooses. . . . Liszt knows very well the influence he has on people, for he always fixes his eye on some one of us when he plays, and I believe that he tries to wring our hearts.[14]

Miss Fay's book was first published in 1881, well within Liszt's lifetime. It acted like forked lightning on a whole generation of young pianists (especially in the New World), firing them with the ambition to go to Liszt and Weimar, regardless of the effort.

Another account of these classes, albeit of a very different nature, came from the diary of August Göllerich, who was a pupil of Liszt between 1884 and 1886. While Amy Fay sums up the colour, excitement, and sheer magic of the classes, Göllerich provides a careful record of the repertory played (and Liszt's reactions to it), together with the precise date, location, and identity of the performer. Of a performance of his Second "Mephisto" Waltz (played by Adèle aus der Ohe), Liszt remarked drily: "I consider it my duty to reject nothing."[15] After Moriz Rosenthal had delivered a performance of the Brahms "Paganini" variations, Liszt laughed and remarked: "It pleases me that through my own variations I have been of use to Brahms with his; it gives me great pleasure!"[16] In fact, Göllerich's diary often records autobiographical asides that are unobtainable elsewhere. István Thomán once turned up at the class and played Schumann's *Novellette* in D major. It jogged Liszt's memory, and he observed: "When in the 1840s I came to Germany for the first time from Paris, Schumann showed me the manuscript of this piece, on which was written: 'Wel-

---

13. FMG, p. 207.
14. FMG, p. 227.
15. GLK, p. 142.
16. GLK, p. 53. A comparison of the two sets of variations leaves little doubt that Brahms turned to Liszt for his model.

come to Germany, Franz Liszt.' "[17] Shortly afterwards Ilona Krivácsy played the *Ernani* Paraphrase to Liszt. After she had finished, his only comment was: "My coda amused Verdi."[18] Small scraps of information, admittedly, but they add something to the total picture.

Occasionally, when Liszt's remarks on the playing were damaging, Göllerich would cloak the identity of the player in anonymity. On July 6, 1885, Liszt became so angry at a performance of Chopin's B-minor Sonata that he released a torrent of criticism: "That was definitely not played, but skewered [*gestochen*]. If you have no ears to hear, why do you play the piano? With whom did you study that? With Marmontel it costs 20 marks an hour—here everything is free. There you learn nothing, whereas here you can at least learn something. You must go to some conservatory, but not come to me."[19] This anecdote contradicts the widely held view that Liszt was all sweetness and light when dealing with his students. His kindness and generosity, which were indeed legendary, did have their limits. He could work himself into a temper if a poor performance warranted it, and woe betide the unfortunate student at the receiving end of his tongue. Bettina Walker, who spent an entire summer with Liszt in Weimar, reports that on one occasion a young man attempted to play a Liszt polonaise. He had not progressed far into the piece when he came down with a jumble of wrong notes. Three times Liszt made him begin again, but each time it got worse. "Then, indeed, there was a scene which I cannot easily forget. Liszt's voice trembled with anger and scorn, as, flinging the music from the desk, and saying more than once in a voice which was calculated to terrify us all, 'Do you know to whom you have been playing? You have no business here. Go to the Conservatoire; that is the place for such as you.' "[20] The young man retired to the back of the room, oblivious to the fact that he had spoiled the afternoon for the next student, one of the Grosskurth sisters, who came to the piano with a Chopin nocturne. The young man's performance had stirred up Liszt's bile, and the master "absolutely clawed" the poor girl, to whom he was normally so kind. He thrust the music into her hands and dismissed her from the keyboard with the dreaded words "We do not wash dirty linen here." She retired to a far corner in order to hide her tears.[21]

A third source also stands out from the plethora of "reminiscences," "conversations," "notebooks," "sketchbooks," and therapeutic musings that emerged from Liszt's classes in the 1880s. When the American pianist Carl Lachmund arrived in Weimar in April 1882, he resolved from the start to keep a careful record

17. GLK, p. 120.
18. GLK, p. 127.
19. GLK, p. 80.
20. WMME, p. 120.
21. WMME, pp. 120–21.

of all his meetings with Liszt, and brought with him a set of blank, leather-bound diaries for that purpose. He lived in Weimar for three consecutive summers, and his account of the period 1882–84 is one of the best that we have.[22] On one occasion Lachmund was playing Schumann's Toccata in C major to Liszt. "Ah," remarked Liszt, "this is a difficult piece." He then turned to Katharina Ranouchewitsch, a pupil of Henselt who was attending the class that day, held up the music, and said: "That is something you should work at; it is solid and one must learn to bite it while still young—when one is old the bite has gone!"[23] Once, as the Dutch pianist Henryk van Zeyl was playing the Scherzo from Chopin's B-minor Sonata, Liszt approached the piano and gazed at the player as if to re-charge the dying performance. He snapped his fingers and rocked his hands back and forth. "The grey eyes sparkled," wrote Lachmund. "Not a word did he say; but van Zeyl understood perfectly." The performance came alive, and "the effect was magical."[24] We shall quote again from the Lachmund diaries, since they add bright detail to the picture.

IV

Liszt's ability to perform whatever was brought to him never ceased to arouse astonishment. Bach, Mozart, Beethoven, Mendelssohn, Schumann, Chopin, and Brahms were all represented in his classes, of course; but so were a host of lesser composers such as Henselt, Rubinstein, Raff, Moszkowski, and Scharwenka; whoever they were, Liszt seemed to know everything that they had ever written. The only two pieces that he discouraged his students from bringing were Chopin's Scherzo in B-flat minor (which he called the "Governess" Scherzo, because "every governess plays it," and towards which he seemed to have had a genuine antipathy) and his own Hungarian Rhapsody No. 2 in C-sharp minor, because it was so popular. Since he no longer practised regularly, he relied heavily on his memory and on his phenomenal powers of sight-reading. This ability continued well into old age, until failing eyesight prevented him from reading and writing altogether.

Kornél Ábrányi, who spent a few weeks in Weimar in the summer of 1873, attended Liszt's masterclasses and various social events at the Hofgärtnerei. He had heard Liszt play many times, but the thing that struck him with force was Liszt's sight-reading.

---

22. See LL. The diaries form part of the Lachmund Archive in the Special Collections Department of the New York Public Library. Together with other memorabilia of his encounters with Liszt, they became the basis of Lachmund's book *Living with Liszt,* which was only published in its original English text in 1995. A truncated German translation of this work, in which the text is badly mauled, appeared in 1970 under the title *Mein Leben mit Franz Liszt.*
23. LL, p. 157.
24. LL, p. 19.

Liszt's reading of music is spectacular. He plays everything at first sight as do others after having studied the score for half a year. Moreover, he would sight-read music that many first-class virtuosi could not even play. . . . The best-trained reader could not read letters, or words, with the same ease as he reads notes. He sees complete scores at once and expresses the same on the piano. He does not even pay attention to his hands. They move as if he had kept his eyes on them. What his eyes see, his hands strike in the same thought (a bat of the eye is too long a span). In the swiftness, his hands disappear (apart from him we had experienced this only with Tausig) and in these instances it seems as if the piano thundered by itself, as if a supernatural power moved it with an invisible force.[25]

Of course, Liszt was fallible, and he sometimes hit wrong notes; but his students found even that to be a constructive experience. Amy Fay relates that

an accident of this kind happened to him in one of the Sunday matinées, when the room was full of distinguished people and of his pupils. He was rolling up the piano in arpeggios in a very grand manner indeed, when he struck a semi-tone short of the high note upon which he had intended to end. I caught my breath and wondered whether he was going to leave us like that, in mid-air, as it were, and the harmony unresolved, or whether he would be reduced to the humiliation of correcting himself like ordinary mortals, and taking the right chord. A half smile came over his face, as much as to say—"Don't fancy that *this* little thing disturbs me,"— and he instantly went meandering down the piano in harmony with the false note he had struck, and then rolled deliberately up in a second grand sweep, *this* time striking true. I never saw a more delicious piece of cleverness. It was so quick-witted and so exactly characteristic of Liszt. Instead of giving you a chance to say, "He has made a mistake," he forced you to say, "He has shown how to get out of a mistake."[26]

Musicians who recalled the Liszt of yesteryear were generally agreed that he was now a different pianist—more subdued, less flamboyant, and lacking in the physical endurance required to do justice to the war-horses of his youth. Nevertheless, he did from time to time play them. Kurd von Schlözer recalled that Liszt once gave a small matinée concert in Rome, in 1868. He decided to play

---

25. AAT, p. 85.
26. FMG, p. 243.

his arrangement of Schubert's "Erlkönig," but had to go away and practise the octaves for half an hour beforehand so that he could pull them out of his sleeve when they were required.[27] That was in 1867. Six years later Anton Rubinstein told the American conductor Theodore Thomas to "make haste and go [to Europe] at once; [Liszt] is already beginning to break up, and his playing is not up to the standard of former years, although his personality is as attractive as ever."[28]

V

The camaraderie that Liszt had always enjoyed with his pupils, from the earliest days, was continued in Weimar. He could often be seen walking down the street with a group of pupils at his heels, talking as they went. There is a charming anecdote told by Anton Strelezki, who was a pupil of Liszt from 1869 onwards. He once collided with Liszt, who was coming out of a cigar-shop. "Lazybones!" exclaimed Liszt. "You ought to be at home practising." Strelezki explained that he had already done four hours' practice that morning, and was now on his way home to do more. "In that case," said Liszt, "if you have already done four hours' slavery, come home with me." Karl Heymann, the pianist, was with them, and as soon as they reached the Hofgärtnerei Liszt went straight to the piano and started playing. "Karl," he called out, "what is that? It's been running through my head all afternoon, and I can't for the life of me think what it is." Several times Liszt played the passage, and eventually Strelezki thought he recognized it and suggested that it came from Balakirev's *Islamey.* "Bravo! Bravo!" shouted Liszt. "Of course it does. I haven't heard it since Tausig studied it with me, and it has haunted me all afternoon."[29]

Such stories, which abound in the literature, indicate the degree of informality and friendliness that existed between Liszt and his pupils, quite unusual for those times. A Turkish student, Francesco Della Sudda Bey (who had studied with Leschetizky and Kullak before coming to Weimar), once gave a reception for Liszt in the Erbprinz Hotel.[30] In the centre of the table stood a magnificent flower-piece, shaped like a pyramid, three feet high. Resting on a base of laurel leaves in a profusion of blooms were the letters LISZT. Liszt's favourite dishes were served, including eggs *à la Russe,* rice and chopped ham (Italian style), dessert and champagne. The Bey made a modest speech in halting German, which was followed by a more fulsome one from Gottschalg, in which he attached various themes in Liszt's life to the colours of the floral

---

27. SRB, p. 425.
28. MMML, pp. 111–12.
29. SPRL, pp. 10–11.
30. On September 9, 1882. LL, pp. 154–55.

arrangement before them. The group then retired to the garden for coffee. Suddenly Liszt turned to Friedheim and van Zeyl and exclaimed: "Show off the ball duet of which I've heard so much!" The two young men exchanged grins and took up their posts. One went out into the street while the other remained in the garden. Each had a ball which he kept throwing right over the roof of the hotel as fast as possible. The point of the game was to keep the "ball duet" in the air, to the general stupefaction of the onlookers. And whoever was caught off-guard had to scramble for the incoming ball, to the amusement of all concerned.[31]

On June 26, 1882, Liszt and a group of his students set out for Jena to attend the annual concert of his choral music arranged in his honour by his friend Hofrath Carl Gille. By now the tradition was at least ten years old, and within Liszt's circle it was colloquially known as the "sausage concert." It derived its unusual name from the fact that after the concert Gille used to invite everyone back to his house and give a garden-party at which hot sausages and cool beer were served, amidst much merrymaking. At eleven o'clock in the morning everyone assembled on the platform of the Weimar railway station. The party included about thirty pupils and disciples, among them Martha Remmert, Eugène d'Albert, Alfred Reisenauer, Alexander Gottschalg, Vera Timanova, Carl Lachmund, and Olga von Meyendorff. As the little train pulled into the station, amidst screeching brakes and clouds of steam, many heads bobbed out of the windows in order to catch a glimpse of Liszt standing in the middle of this motley crowd. The journey from Weimar to Jena lasted less than an hour, and everyone went straight over to the church for the mid-day rehearsal. Afterwards, they followed Liszt to the Hotel Zum Bären, where two long tables had been set up for lunch. Liszt and his entourage made a striking impression as they zigzagged their way, crocodile-style, through the narrow streets of the old city. The "sausage concert" was well known to the inhabitants of Jena, who looked forward to the arrival of Liszt and his party of young bohemians each year in much the same way as other towns looked forward to an annual parade. During lunch, which featured the usual round of toasts and speeches, Gottschalg rose to his feet and read an original poem in which he had changed Goethe's dying words, "Mehr Licht," to "Mehr Liszt, mehr Liszt!" Gottschalg may not have been able to get away with such a vile pun in a different time and place, but this was the Jena "sausage-festival," and everybody entered into the spirit of the occasion by raising their glasses yet again to the venerable master.[32]

The concert took place at 5:00 p.m. It was noteworthy because it contained a performance of his cantata *The Bells of Strasbourg Cathedral* conducted by Liszt himself, an event which has somehow escaped the attention of his chroniclers.

31. LL, pp. 154–55.
32. LL, p. 91.

Liszt wore a long frock coat and he conducted without a baton. It has often been remarked that he did not beat time in the usual way, but indicated the phrasing and dynamics with slow, wave-like motions of the hands and arms. At times, when he was sure that his intentions were understood, he would cease conducting altogether. Even at the cataclysmic climax of *The Bells* he remained detached from the clamour and opened his arms wide, like the wings of an eagle, to engulf the sound. The audience received an object-lesson in Liszt's individual approach to conducting that day, made all the more telling by the flailing arms of the local conductor, who had worked himself into a perspiration in the preceding composition.[33]

As the audience streamed out of the church, they made their way in small groups to the home of Dr. Gille, who did his old friend proud. Broiled chicken and Rhine wine were served, and maids in white aprons wove in and out of the clusters of guests, serving sausages and rolls. At the close of the evening Gille made a short speech in honour of Liszt, but was moved to tears at the recollection of his wife and daughter, both of whom had died since the previous year's concert. The evening ended all too soon for the Lisztianer. But as darkness fell they wended their way back to the station, boarded the train, and got back to Weimar in the small hours of the morning.[34]

What other teacher could have led his students into such an enchanted world? The atmosphere at Weimar was truly magical for those young people who were fortunate enough to be included in Liszt's inner circle, and they carried away with them a rich store of memories which remained with them for life. They were far more than pupils; they were members of one family, held together by ties of mutual affection. Nonetheless, Liszt expected his students to know a good deal about music before he admitted them to the class. This point is very well expressed by Etelka Willheim, a Hungarian student who later married an American and settled in California: "His pupils were somewhat in the position of a student of philosophy sitting at the feet of a wise man. The student must needs know a good deal about philosophy to have gained the wise man's confidence to the extent that he was allowed his friendship. So it was with Liszt."[35]

In the 1880s Liszt even carried his sense of collegiality to the extent of celebrating American Independence Day, to please his growing band of American students. Morris Bagby recalls one such occasion (in 1885), when Liszt

---

33. Ibid.

34. Amy Fay recalled attending a similar event as early as July 1873. Then, too, Liszt put on a lunch at the local hotel. Among the vegetables were new potatoes, boiled with their skins on. Liszt threw one of these hot potatoes at Fay, and she caught it, part of the "endless fun" that went on that day. After the meal Liszt announced: "Now we'll go to Paradise." So the group rambled along the river bank until they arrived at "Paradise," so-called because of its special beauty. Later they all attended the concert, and then stopped off for tea at the house of Dr. Gille, where, Fay tells us, everyone lay on the grass and ate hot sausages. (FMG, pp. 244–47)

35. Hitherto unpublished. CLC, series 1, folder no. 169.

arranged to have a group of his students learn Anton Rubinstein's Variations on "Yankee Doodle." Since these variations can last for nearly forty minutes, and since they become progressively more difficult, the students had their work cut out. July 4 dawned and Liszt turned up wearing a button-hole of flowers in the American national colours. "We are all Americans today," he remarked in stirring tones. After Liszt's *Festklänge* and a specially commissioned paraphrase on "Yankee Doodle" by Arthur Friedheim (which incorporated the closing chorus from Beethoven's Ninth and the "bell" theme from Wagner's *Parsifal* in outrageous combinations) came Rubinstein's monster variations. But they proved to be so long that they were temporarily suspended—much to the general relief. Meanwhile, the July 4 concert was highlighted by a telegramme from Carl Gille in Jena, which read "Amerika und Meister hoch!" It was not until two days later that Moriz Rosenthal finally brought "Yankee Doodle" to its rousing conclusion, all the other pianists—Friedheim, Sauer, and Göllerich among them—having declined to have anything more to do with it. For the rest of the week, a flag of flowers in the American colours stood on the table. And even after they had turned brown and started to die, Pauline Apel had them ostentatiously placed on the entrance steps to the Hofgärtnerei, where they remained for the rest of the summer—a silent reminder to all those who entered the building of America's most important holiday.[36]

Did Liszt carry the notion of collegiality too far? The question has often been asked, and with reason. Whenever one walked into the music room of the Hofgärtnerei, one could be sure of seeing two things close to the piano: a decanter of Liszt's favourite cognac and a lighted candle on which the young men would keep alight their cigars. Smoking and drinking were a way of life with Liszt; in fact, they were ranked by him among the social graces, and all young men who were desirous of making their way in the world were supposed to master them as soon as possible. Liszt therefore considered it perfectly natural to offer alcohol and tobacco to his young charges. Sad to say, some of them became addicted, and one or two ended up as alcoholics. Alfred Reisenauer was among these unfortunates; he died in Latvia in 1907, after a heavy bout of drinking during a concert tour. He was only forty-four years old. Arthur Friedheim was arrested during his first visit to New York, in 1892, taken to the East Twenty-second Street precinct, and charged with causing an affray in the lobby of Amberg's Theatre while inebriated.[37]

---

36. BSLW, pp. 659–62.
37. It was claimed that Friedheim struck the doorkeeper, one August Bartenhauser, a violent blow; about half an hour later Bartenhauser became ill and had to be taken home. Later that night he died and the police revised the charge against Friedheim to one of murder. The pianist was held without bail, pending a coroner's report, and the case (which had by now attracted the attention of the press) was heard at Yorkville Court. The coroner revealed that the dead man had a history of heart disease and that Friedheim's blow was not the cause of death. While the presiding judge, Justice Taintnor, dis-

There was another area, too, in which Liszt's "beneficence" sometimes cast a shadow. Exceedingly generous with money, he was regarded by a number of his less reputable pupils as a "soft touch." He disliked to think that any of his students suffered material hardship, and he often went out of his way to help them—usually with loans or outright gifts of money. Inevitably he became the target of abuse and was besieged by people who saw in him a Midas-figure with unfathomable wealth at his disposal. It seems never to have occurred to these money-grubbers that had they studied with any other teacher they would have been obliged to pay for their lessons. But with Liszt, it almost seemed in some cases that they expected *him* to pay them for the privilege of teaching them! It quickly became necessary for him to defend himself against their rapacious demands, which accounts for his occasional habit of questioning prospective students about their finances—a habit that was sometimes misunderstood. Edwin Klahre, an American student (who later taught at the New England Conservatory), was sent to Liszt in Weimar in the spring of 1884 with a letter of introduction from Xaver Scharwenka, who warned the young man never to mention the word "money" in Liszt's presence. When Klahre got to Weimar there was a moment of tension. "After playing to him he asked me if I would like to study with him. I naturally said yes! Then he asked me the question: how about money? Imagine my surprise and consternation. Smiling his kindly smile he said: 'You don't have to pay *me*,' but he couldn't look after *my* finances."[38]

V I

Posterity has sometimes criticised Liszt for the air of sycophantism which seemed to hover over these classes, and for the fawning attitude, bordering on servility, of certain individual students (which usually stood in inverse ratio to their talent). A number of critics have chastised him for "holding court," for actively seeking to surround himself with young disciples whose homage was the price of admission to the class. It was the idolatry and hothouse atmosphere of the Hofgärtnerei which bothered the twenty-year-old Walter Damrosch when he visited Liszt in 1882. He later wrote a critical account of what he had

---

missed all charges against Friedheim, the case must have had serious consequences for the pianist's professional life, to say nothing of his state of mind. In his memoir *Life and Liszt* he makes no mention of the episode, but claims that his lack of success in America during the 1891–92 season was due to the unfortunate coincidence that Paderewski was giving highly successful concerts there at the same time. Friedheim returned to Europe, where he spent several years conducting and teaching before settling in New York permanently during World War I. His arrest and arraignment were reported in three separate editions of the *Evening World* on April 21, 1892.

38. Hitherto unpublished letter, dated November 14, 1922. CLC, series 1, folder no. 74.

witnessed.[39] His description of the class of '82 as a "pitiful crowd of sycophants and incompetents" drew a powerful response from Carl Lachmund, who pointed out that the "crowd of incompetents" included six young men who would one day be counted among the world's greatest pianists: Friedheim, Rosenthal, Siloti, Reisenauer, Sauer, and d'Albert.[40] It was a telling rebuttal. Still, Damrosch was by no means alone when he argued that these were exceptions and in general Liszt really deserved better students. Even Hans von Bülow used to draw attention to the paradox that in the best pianist's house one could hear the worst playing.

Bülow had formed that conviction from personal experience: he sometimes took over the classes when Liszt was indisposed. These were occasions that the students dreaded, since they knew that Bülow regarded many of them as "hangers-on" without any talent. In June 1880 Bülow used the opportunity to "clean out the Augean stable," as he put it. He assembled the class and addressed them in the following terms: "Ladies and gentlemen! Do not forget that the Master was born as long ago as 1811, or that he is the essence of goodness and gentleness; and do not misuse him in this revolting way. You ladies in particular: most of you, I assure you, are destined for the myrtle rather than the laurel."[41]

Everybody trembled, and most of them left. Dori Petersen then played Liszt's *Mazeppa*—atrociously. She was a rough-and-ready player, with an overbearing personality. Bülow rounded on her: "You have but *one* qualification for playing this piece—the nature of a horse."[42] Shortly afterwards Berthold Kellermann told Liszt what had happened. "Bülow was quite right," remarked Liszt. "But he was too hard. I suppose that you will see all those people tonight in the Sächsischer Hof? Just tell them to wait until Bülow has left, and then to come back here."[43] Bülow could never understand why Liszt failed to appreciate what he had done. As he put it to Adelheid von Schorn, he had merely provided the same service for Liszt as he did for his own dog in ridding him of his fleas.

Nevertheless, the fleas came back. There was another dramatic confronta-

39. In his autobiography *My Musical Life* (DMML, pp. 36–40). Parts of this book were serialised in New York's fashionable *Ladies' Home Journal* beginning in October 1922 (which is where Lachmund first read it), a year before the book itself was published.

40. With exquisite timing, Lachmund's letter was published in *The New York Times* (section 8, p. 4) on Liszt's birthday, October 22, 1922. It ended with the phrase: "In reverence to the great master and justice to the class, these facts are submitted." Walter Damrosch was moved to reply a week later, on October 29.

41. BBLW, p. 273.

42. Ibid. Marie von Bülow, from whom this anecdote comes, does not identify the pupil. Since the publication of the diary of Carl Lachmund in 1995, however, we know it to have been Dori Petersen. (LL, p. 20)

43. KE, p. 26.

tion between Bülow and the Weimar masterclass in the summer of 1881. Shortly after the lesson had begun, Liszt became unwell and the pupils urged him to withdraw.[44] This he refused to do. ("One is never ill," he used to say.) Just then, and quite by chance, the door opened and Bülow walked in. He was on a two-week visit to Weimar, and he and his daughter Daniela were staying as guests of Liszt. "His very appearance created a feeling of apprehension," recounted Emma Grosskurth. "It was as if a great hawk had swept down among us. Several tried to flutter to cover, to the further end of the salon, or behind the curtains that divided the rooms."[45] Bülow sized up the situation at once, and insisted that Liszt lie down in his bedroom while he, Bülow, continue with the lesson. And with that he led Liszt firmly into the adjoining chamber. Consternation followed. Lina Schmalhausen (whom Bülow rightly took to be an amateurish pianist) had been playing when the class was interrupted. Now she gathered up her music and tried to retreat. "No, it is you I wish to hear first," Bülow barked.[46] Total humiliation ensued; and when, through nervousness, she could not even play in time, Bülow exclaimed in withering tones: "I have heard it said that there are people who cannot count three; but you cannot count two!" (Afterwards, Lina wrote to Liszt that she had been ridiculed in front of the class and could not possibly return. Liszt went round to visit her next day, to console her and tell her that it would be perfectly all right for her to come back.) During the same session poor Dori Petersen was once more at the receiving end of Bülow's sharp tongue. He listened to her with growing impatience and then cut her dead. "I hope never to see you here again," he told her. "You should be swept out of here—not with the broom, but with the handle!"[47] By now, Bülow was under no illusions about the magnitude of the problem as he saw it. The following year he told Daniela: "*A propos* of vermin, let us not rejoice too much on your grandfather's account over the little revolution at the Hofgärtnerei. I believe that in matters of insecticide 'things are destroyed only to be replaced.' "[48]

Although Liszt could be sarcastic, unlike Bülow he was not deliberately cruel. Only with incompetents and poseurs was he harsh. A young man once presented himself to Liszt and produced a letter of introduction from the Queen of Holland. "Play to me first," said Liszt, "and then I'll read the letter." Alas, this poor unfortunate was singularly lacking in talent. Liszt became angry, and he turned on his visitor. "Instead of carrying around letters from queens,"

---

44. This was not long after Liszt's fall down the stairs of the Hofgärtnerei, and during his subsequent convalescence, discussed in detail on pp. 403–05.
45. LL, p. 20.
46. Ibid.
47. Ibid.
48. BNB, p. 594.

he remonstrated, "it would be better if you did some serious practising."[49] His ire was particularly aroused whenever he heard that some local incompetent was billing himself as "a pupil of Liszt." On one occasion he turned up on the doorstep of one such imposter, a lady pianist, whom he greeted with the remark: "I must apologise to you for this sudden intrusion. Perhaps you would be kind enough to play something for me, so that I may at least have heard you once."[50]

It was mainly in the defence of Beethoven and Bach that he would display the greatest aggression. A very good example of this occurred in June 1882, when some poor young man had the misfortune to bring Beethoven's *Waldstein* Sonata to the class; Liszt spotted it among the pile of music on the piano and asked to hear it. Although the student had previously studied the work with Kullak, in Berlin, it soon became clear that he did not really know it, and Liszt kept stopping him every few bars. One spot in particular did not suit Liszt, and he made the miscreant go over it again and again. Liszt finally flew into a rage. He snatched the music from the rack, flung it onto the piano, scattering the leaves as it hit, and his features became distorted with wrath as he spurted out in broken phrases: "Cannot even notice a *forte* where it is marked. . . . No—I do not take in washing here—do your washing at home." And most telling of all: "We have conservatories to do such work." The poor fellow just stood there liked a whipped dog, head hanging in shame, while the other students turned away in embarrassed silence.[51]

Such outbursts were rare. Liszt preferred to rely on his biting humour to convey displeasure. If trills and tremolandos sounded hesitant, he would declare: "Such economy of notes!" And when a performance was bungled, he would shake his head sadly and mutter: "Let it go—at discount!" To Julie Lourie, who was playing Chopin's A-flat-major Study, he remarked: "You play it as though you were knitting stockings."[52] Carl Lachmund recalls a young lady attempting to play *La campanella* who simply could not leap to the infamous high D-sharps without striking wrong notes. Liszt stopped her and made her try the offending measures again and again, but the harder she tried, the more nervous she became. Finally, Liszt took his seat at the piano and played

---

49. FLL, p. 47.
50. FLL, p. 49. Perhaps this was the same lady mentioned in the memoirs of Liszt's grandson Siegfried Wagner. He tells us that a young woman who was preparing to give a recital in Jena thought that she might attract a larger audience if she announced that she was a pupil of Liszt. Unluckily for her, Liszt himself unexpectedly arrived in the town on the very day of her concert, and she knew that she would be exposed. With a thumping heart the girl went to Liszt and confessed her deception. "Come, Fräulein, sit yourself at the keyboard and go through your programme for me," Liszt ordered her. She did as she was instructed, and for two hours he corrected the things that displeased him. He then turned to her with the remark: "So, child, now you can say that you are a pupil of Liszt." (WE, p. 22)
51. LL, p. 72.

the first page for her without missing a single note and without the slightest effort. "He did not keep his eyes on the keys," notes Lachmund, "but looked up at us as his hands flew from one key to another in leaps two octaves apart." And when in a careless moment he missed the top note, he immediately repeated the mistake, "making the same error on purpose, like a foxy grandpa."[53] On such occasions his face would assume a Mephistophelian air, as if to say: "I, too, can make mistakes if I try!" Liszt habitually referred to wrong notes as "uninvited guests," a phrase that caused hilarity, especially when in the course of a performance he would ask "the guests" to leave. One student who was notoriously careless of wrong notes had formed the habit of hesitating at skips in order to be sure of hitting the right key. Liszt remarked amusingly: "You should not always stop as if to look at the house-number."

Such comments were what Frederic Lamond and others had in mind when they said that Liszt taught by parable, and that he always liked to have some poetical image in mind when he played. That made him a refreshing change from those teachers who thought that the solution to every problem was a further dose of scales and arpeggios. Liszt understood the power of an idea, and he knew that the inspired human being has the capacity to turn ideas into reality. Once, when Arthur Friedheim was playing *Harmonies du soir* late one afternoon, Liszt stopped the performance, pointed towards the beautiful sunset that had mellowed the landscape outside, and said: "Play that. There are your evening harmonies."[54] But he also had the gift of reversing this process: that is, he drew images from the many bad performances he was obliged to endure. Della Sudda Bey once brought Chopin's Barcarolle to the class. At the recapitulation, where the left-hand motif returns in octaves, he was clumsy. Liszt stopped him and said: "That is like a Westphalian horse." The joke was not lost on the Germans there, who were all familiar with these plodding animals. He was particularly fond of culinary images and once told van Zeyl, who had just begun to play the *Waldstein* Sonata: "Do not chop beefsteak for us." To another pupil, whose tremolandos contained surplus movement, he remarked: "Do not make omelettes."[55] And to a French lady student who was trying to perform

---

52. LL, p. 101.

53. LL, p. 32.

54. FLL, p. 52.

55. Liszt was probably the first serious composer to introduce the tremolando into piano music on a regular basis. The device is so rare in the music of Chopin and Schumann that it may be said not to exist for them. Like his two great contemporaries, Liszt well knew that the tremolando is a dangerous effect which can sound tawdry in the wrong hands. Yet he requires the device whenever he wishes to transform the piano into a sustaining instrument, as opposed to the percussive instrument that it actually is. Works like *Les jeux d'eaux à la Villa d'Este* and his transcription of the "Liebestod" from Wagner's *Tristan* would not be possible without it. Liszt's own tremolandos involved a hardly visible, extremely rapid *trembling* of the hand, with the keys halfway depressed—as if the fingers themselves were thrumming against the strings.

his *Gnomenreigen,* and getting her fingers tangled, he made the witty remark "There you are mixing salad again." Liszt's verbal imagery might be considered idiosyncratic today, but anyone who is familiar with these piano textures will understand how apt his comments were.

With dullness he would have nothing to do. One thing he could not abide was playing that was flat, lifeless, and ultimately boring. The phrase "a temperance man" was often used by Liszt to describe performances that were sober— and dull. Such players and their playing, he seemed to be saying, stood in the same relation to great performance as did a cup of tea to a glass of whiskey. They lacked spirit! His young pupil d'Albert occasionally played in a wild and impetuous fashion. Liszt's recommendation was that he should join a temperance society— "but only an honorary member!"[56] To inspire became his chief function, and nothing was more remarkable than the way in which his students learned to draw strength from his playing. When Edwin Klahre turned up in Weimar for his first lesson (on May 2, 1884), he tells us, he played Liszt's Ballade in B minor. He had formed the habit of

> moving my body from side to side, my nose close to the keys. He stopped me, one hand under my chin, the other on top of my head, and said to sit still and hold my head erect.
>
> His first remark was at the opening period of the Ballade, [that] it should be broad and majestic and [that one] should sit accordingly. He put me aside and sat down and played from the beginning. It was a revelation to me. Every note of the melody of the right hand he played with a very marked and large tone, his hand at least a foot high, remarking that one should not play for the people that sit in the front row and usually have free tickets, but play for those in the gallery that pay ten pfennigs for a ticket. They should not only hear but see.[57]

Such alchemy did not always last, however. Even a magician like Liszt could not continue to pull white rabbits out of hats if the rabbits were not there in the first place.

---

56. LL, pp. 67–68.
57. Hitherto unpublished letter dated November 14, 1922. CLC, series 1, folder 74.

A Summary Catalogue of Liszt's Pupils and Disciples Grouped by Nationality (1829–1886)

Liszt is said to have taught more than four hundred pupils in the course of his long life, but the figure is impossible to prove. In order to command a proper view of the topic we must first cross a difficult stretch of territory with care. The plain fact is that not all the young people who experienced personal contact with Liszt enjoyed equal status; and some of them were not all that young. Many of the names on the list would be rejected by some as stretching the definition of the phrase "a pupil of Liszt" beyond reasonable limits. Liszt himself was partly to blame, because of the mixed nature of the groups of musicians with whom he liked to surround himself. Moreover, he constantly proclaimed that he was "no piano professor" and sent those who came to him for technical instruction back to the conservatories. The dilemma is one of exclusion rather than inclusion, and it disappears the moment we view Liszt not as a piano teacher but as a guru-figure encircled by disciples and admirers. And there were circles within circles. At the centre were those pianists like Bülow, Tausig, Rosenthal, d'Albert, Sophie Menter, and Arthur Friedheim, who studied with Liszt for years, played for him constantly, and later went on to enjoy international careers; their links with him are not in doubt. Then there were those in the middle circle, pianist-musicians of the calibre of Walter Bache (who was with Liszt every summer for seventeen years), Martin Krause, and Amy Fay, none of whom had any real success on the concert platform but who went on to enjoy distinguished careers as teachers. Finally, there were those in the outer circle who, while they may have been passive members of the class, nonetheless learned much by simply watching and listening. "Watching and listening": is that not how all the best education takes place? For that reason, it is impossible to deny a place in the pantheon to such musicians as Felix Weingartner, who was primarily a conductor, who never once played the piano for Liszt, yet who regularly attended the masterclasses and was proud to be known as a Liszt pupil; to Richard Pohl, who was a distinguished critic; to Alexander Gottschalg and Alexander Winterberger, who were organists; and to Morris Bagby, who later became a concert manager. The contact that all these people had with Liszt was deep and profound; it changed not only their musical outlook, but in some cases the course of their lives.

American

Bagby, Albert Morris
Bartlett, Miss
Benedict, Milo E.
Bird, Arthur
Bock, Anna
Boise, Otis
Dayas, William
   Humphrys
Fay, Amy
Fischer, Auguste

Gaebler, Sophie
   Charlotte
Gaul, Kathie
Geiser, Adele
Hanchette, Estelle
Hastings, Adèle
Hatsch, Harry
Hoeltge, May
Hubbard, Louis
Klahre, Edwin
Lachmund, Carl
   Valentine

Lambert, Alexander
Liebling, Georg
Liebling, Saul
Mansfeldt, Hugo
   Leonhardt
Mason, William
May, Ida
Orth, John
Petersilia, Carlyle
Pinner, Max
Piutti, William
Pratt, Silas Gamaliel

Riesberg, Frederick
Rivé–King, Julie
Sherwood, William Hall
Sternberg, Constantin
  von
Stevens, Neally
Tracey, James M.
Trimble, Mary

Austrian

Esinger, Hermine
Fiebinger, Anna
Fichtner, Pauline
Göllerich, August
Golz, Amalie
Liszt, Hedwig von
Liszt, Marie von
Raab, Antonia
Schönberger, Benno
Seidel–Furani, Maria
Weingartner, Felix

Belgian

de Greef, Arthur
Guricks, Camille
Servais, Franz

Bohemian

Grünberger, Ludwig
Stradal, August

British

Albert, Eugène d'
Bache, Walter
Glynne, Catherine
Goodwin, Amina
  Beatrice
Hatton, George
Lamond, Frederic
  Archibald
Strelezki, Anton
  (Theophilus Burnand)
Walker, Bettina
Waller, Henry

Canadian

Lauder, Waugh

Danish

Bendix, Otto
Bendix, Victor
  Emanuel
Langgaard, Siegfried
Olsen, Sophie

Dutch

Coonen, Louis
Falk-Mehlig, Anna
Kluit, Anna
Lönen, Louis
Sandt, Max van der
Zeyl, Henryk van

Finnish

Lindberg, Alexandra

French

Bennet-Ritter, Théodore
Falke, Henri
Jaëll-Trautmann, Marie
  von
Laprunarède, Adèle
  (Duchess de Fleury)
Montigny-Rémaury,
  Caroline de
Musset, Hermine de
Risler, Edouard
Saint-Cricq, Countess
  Caroline
Vial, Hortense
Viardot-Garcia, Pauline

German

Adler, Elsa
Ansorge, Konrad
Bach, Leonhard Emil
Baermann, Karl
Bendel, Franz
Benfey, Rudolf

Berger, Wilhelm
Blassmann, Adolf
Bloch, Ida
Blume-Ahrendts,
  Charlotte
Bödinghausen, Frl.
Brassin, Louis
Bregenzer, Antonie
Breidenstein, Marie
Brendel-Trautmann,
  Elisabeth
Bronsart, Hans von
  Schellendorf
Bülow, Hans von
Burmeister, Johanna
Burmeister, Richard
Cohen, Hermann
Diedrich,
Dingeldey, Ludwig
Draeseke, Felix
Eckhof, Paul
Ehlert, Louis
Eisenhauer, Theodor
Elisabeth, Princess of
  Saxen-Weimar-
  Eisenach
Fokke, Margarethe
Forchhammer,
  Theophil
Friedenthal, Flora von
Fritze, Wilhelm
Gärtner-Hirschfield
Geibel,
Gierl, Josef
Goepfart, Karl Eduard
Gottschalg, Alexander
  Wilhelm
Greipel-Golz, Amalie
Grosskurth, Emma
Grosskurth, Lina
Grützmacher,
  Friedrich
Hasert, Rudolf
Herzer, Gertrude
Hoffbauer, Karl
Hundt, Aline
Jadassohn, Salomon
Jagwitz, Charlotte
  von

Jahn, Hr.
Jeppe, Elisabeth
Jeschke, Klothilde
Jungmann, Louis
Kahrer, Laura
Klindworth, Karl
Klinkerfuss-Schulz,
   Johanna
Koch, Emma
Krause, Klara
Krause, Martin
Kroll, Franz
Lagemann, Fräulein
Leitert, Gustav
Lessman, Otto
Levysohn, Elsa
Levyson, Elsa
Lichterfeld, Ottilie
Lomba, Josef
Lüders, Hermine
Lutter, Heinrich
Mass, Louis
Menter, Sophie
Metzsdorff, Richard
Meyendorff, Klemens
   von
Meyer, Max
Mildner, Henriette
Müller, Franz
Ohe, Adèle aus der
Petersen, Dori
Pflughaupt, Robert
Pflughaupt, Sophie
Pohlig, Karl
Pruckner, Dionys
Rappoldi-Kahrer,
   Laura
Ratzenberger,
   Theodor
Reisenauer, Alfred
Remmert, Gertrud
Remmert, Martha
Rennebaum, Auguste
Reubke, Julius
Reuss, Eduard
Richter, Hermann
   Julius
Riese, Klara
Rilke, Anna

Rosenstock, Fräulein
Roth, Bertrand
Sauer, Emil von
Schilling, Ernst
Schmalhausen, Lina
Schnobel, Marie
Schwarz, Heinrich
Singer, Otto
Sonntag, Elsa
Sorman, Alfred
Sothmann, Fräulein
Spierling, Anna
Stade, Friedrich
Stahr, Anna
Stahr, Helene
Stasny, Carl Richard
Stasny, Ludwig
Stavenhagen, Bernhard
Street-Klindworth,
   Agnès
Urspruch, Anton
Valeska, Ivanka
Viole, Rudolf
Westphalen, Herr
Winterberger,
   Alexander
Zopf, Hermann

Hungarian

Ábrányi, Kornél
Aggházy, Károly
Almássy, Miklós
Altschul, Frigyes
   Rezső
Bahnert, József
Basch, Stefánia
Batka, János
Bauholzer, Júlia
Beliczay, Gyula
Bertha, Sándor
Boas-Antone,
   Bogáthy, Elza
Dunkl, János
Elbert, Imre
Endrey, Paulina
Ferenczy, Ferenc
Feigler, Janka
Filtsch, Károly

Forrai, Sándor
Forster, Stefánia
Frank, Hermina
Freund, Róbert
Fritz, Vilma
Gál, Anna
Gaál, Ferenc
Gobbi, Henrik
Gosztonyi, Béla
Grün, Ilona
Guttmann, Emma
Haitsch, Vilma
Háry, Piroska
Hegyi, Géza
Hodoly, Katalin von
Jerusalem, Júlia
Joseffy, Rafael
Juhász, Aladár
Knapp-Barnay, Ilona
Koderle, Róza
Kont, Ilona
Korbay, Ferenc
Kramer, Ernesztina
Krausz, Gusztáv
Krausz, Lujza
Krautwald-Annau,
   Jozefin
Krisztinkovics, Béla
Krivácsy, Ilona
Kuliffay, Izabella
Kun, Margit
Kupis, Melánia
Lépessy, Ilona
Máday, Ella
Major, Gyula
Márkus, Dezső
Mihalovich, Ödön
Müller, Eugénia
Müller, Katalin
Nágy, Ida
Neumann, Gizella
Nikó, Hortenzia
Nobl, Irén
Pászthory-Voigt, Gizella
   von
Rausch, Károly
Ravasz, Ilona
Rigó, Anna
Schuk, Anna

Schwarz, Irma
Singer, Szidónia
Siposs, Antal
Solomonson, Ella
Sonntág, Elza
Steinacker, Irma
Swoboda, Károly
Szendy, Árpád
Telbisz, Jenő
Thomán, István
Utassi, Etelka
Varga, Vilma
Vaszilievits, Olga
Végh, Baron János
Vörös-Várkonyi,
    Paulina
Weisz, József
Willheim, Etelka
Wohl, Janka
Zaphiry, Helén
Zichy, Count Géza
Zichy, Zsófia

Italian

Bazzini, Antonio
Boccaccini, Pietro
Buonamici, Giuseppe
Cognetti, Luisa
Coop, Ernesto
Falcioni, Don
    Zefiriono
Ferrata, Giuseppe
Forino, Ferdinando
Guili, Fräulein
Gulli, Luigi
Latelli
Lippi, Carlo
Mazza, Magdalena
Mettler, Emma
Perini, Gilda
Pinelli, Ettore
Sgambati, Giovanni

Monacan

Bärmann, Karl
Brodhag, Emil

Norwegian

Backer-Grondahl, Agathe

Polish

Janina, Olga (Olga
    Zielinska-Piasecka)
Konopacka, Anna
Kownacka, Kamilla
Majewska, Maria
Marek, Ludwik
Rosenthal, Moriz
Tarnowski, Wladislaw
Tausig, Carl
Zarembski, Juliusz

Portuguese

Vianna da Motta, José

Russian

Bensch, Albert
Damian, Rössel
Drewing, Viktoria
Friedheim, Arthur
Helbig, Nadine von (née
    Princess Shahavskaya)
Hippius, Fräulein
Kettwitz, Fräulein
Paramanoff, Mele
Ranouchewitsch,
    Katharina
Sabinin, Martha
    Stepanova von
Siloti, Alexander von
Timanova, Vera
    Victorovna

Spanish

Rendano, Alfredo
    (Alfonso)
Rosario de las Hierras

Swedish

Bersén, Robertine
Hyllested, August
Magnus-Heintze, Sara
Starck, Ingeborg
Thegerström, Hilda

Swiss

Boissier-Gasparin,
    Valérie
Calame, Amélie
Cannut, Count C.
Darier, Louise
Demelleyer, Marie
Gambini, Jenny
Kautz-Kreutzer,
    Clémence
Lourie, Julie
Milliquet, Ida
Raffard, Julie
Turettini-Necker,
    Albertine
Wallner, Joséphine
Wolff, Pierre Etienne

Turkish

Sudda Bey, Francesco
    Della

Nationality not known

Bauer, Jacques
Breitner, Ludovico
Brodhag, Emil
Hahn, Arthur

When in the company of his pupils, Liszt often jokingly referred to "first-class" pianists and "second-class" pianists. Such a distinction does not strike the modern reader with the biting humour that he originally intended. He was making ironical allusion to the mania of nineteenth-century royal households for creating orders with lists of first-class and second-class recipients, with medals to match. (Liszt himself had been awarded several such honours—the Order of the White Falcon, Second Class, being a good example.) Who decided on the difference, and what did it actually mean? The grouping of pianists after the aristocratic model was the whole basis of the joke. Liszt was genuinely amused by the practice, since he believed that beyond a certain level it was both difficult and pointless to grade performers. Providing each player had sufficient technique to express the artist within, that was enough. What he would have made of the modern obsession with piano competitions (one of the most important of which today bears his name), where the competitors emerge with first-, second-, and even third-class distinctions, beggars the imagination.

V I I

Since Liszt charged nothing for his lessons ("Génie oblige!"), and all were welcome to attend, Weimar was crowded with students during the months that he was in residence. So many pianists converged on the town, in fact, that the sound of practising filled the air and provoked complaints from the general citizenry. Eventually the town council was forced to pass a bye-law restricting practising to certain times of day, and then only with the windows shut.[58] Offenders were fined two marks on the spot and given an official receipt, according to Arthur Friedheim, who was himself found guilty on a number of occasions. Since it took the best part of a day for the fine-collector to traverse the city (a number of Liszt's students deliberately invited him indoors to imbibe a glass of cognac, which had the effect of slowing down his perambulations), the windows were usually opened again the moment he had turned the corner.[59] The thought that he had become a public nuisance in his old age, to

---

58. In the second half of June 1871, Marie von Mouchanoff wrote: "Weimar has returned to its usual calm [after a performance of *St. Elisabeth*]....In the silent streets, undisturbed by any vehicles, one can hear the sound of practising in all directions." (LMM-K, pp. 266–67)

59. FLL, p. 53. The same point was made by Carl Lachmund in an article he wrote for *Music and Drama* (July 8, 1882, p. 6), where he observes that the rules were even stricter on Sundays, because the miscreants were supposed to be in church:

> This classical town has some severe laws in regard to "making music" as the German calls it. It is not allowed to have the windows open while playing or practising, and a fine of 2 marks is promptly imposed on anyone who plays at all during church hours on Sunday morning. During this time all places of business should be closed. A transparent curtain hangs in the shop window and you can walk right in and purchase what you wish. So much for German mock piety.

say nothing of a means of raising revenue for the town council, probably gave Liszt deep satisfaction.

If Liszt was a solace to his students, they were certainly a solace to him. He called them his "children" and saw in them his posterity. At a time when the world had started to shun his music, he knew that he could safely entrust his legacy to the gifted young.

Excelsior! 1873-1875

. . . Still grasping in his hand of ice
That banner with the strange device.
Excelsior![1]

I

Among the many milestones that marked these years, none was more important for Liszt than the first complete performance of his oratorio *Christus*. No other composition cost him nearly so much labour or was composed over such a long period of time. He had first conceived the idea of a large-scale oratorio on the life of Christ as early as 1853. But one of the main problems for him was to find a suitable text for what was an admittedly complex story. At various times Liszt considered inviting the poet Georg Herwegh, Peter Cornelius, and Princess Carolyne to help him prepare the text, but in the end he took on the task himself by selecting passages from the Bible, the Catholic liturgy, and various medieval Latin hymns. The result was a choral masterpiece which, after decades of neglect, is now being hailed as the finest oratorio to come out of the nineteenth century.[2]

When Liszt declared that he had at last finished the mammoth score (at the Madonna del Rosario on October 2, 1866), it still had only twelve of its fourteen numbers.[3] The following year he added the section called "The Founda-

---

1. From the poem "Excelsior" by Henry Wadsworth Longfellow.
2. Elgar's *Dream of Gerontius,* its closest rival, appeared in the year 1900.
3. CLBA, p. 115. This is borne out by the British Library holograph of *Christus,* which contains only the original twelve numbers. (BM Add. 34182) Liszt inscribed on this manuscript the precise dates on which he finished three sections of the oratorio:

Stabat mater speciosa	October 20, 1865
"Das Wunder"	November 2, 1865
Stabat mater dolorosa	September 7, 1866

tion of the Church," and in 1868 he provided the Easter Hymn, "O filii et filiae." Sections of *Christus* had been performed before, of course. "The Beatitudes" had actually been heard at Weimar as early as 1859, as part of the nuptials
of Princess Marie von Sayn-Wittgenstein. And Sgambati had conducted the
whole of Part One, the "Christmas Oratorio," in the Sala Dante in Rome, on
July 6, 1867 (the "Stabat mater speciosa" had already been heard in Rome, on
January 4, 1866). But by far the most interesting of these "previews" had been
presented by Anton Rubinstein, who had conducted the "Christmas Oratorio" in Vienna in December 1871, in Liszt's presence, with Anton Bruckner
presiding at the organ. Nonetheless, these highly selective glimpses of the work
left its true dimensions to the imagination. Until the full score was published
(it was brought out by Julius Schuberth in 1872), and the music performed in
its entirety, it was hardly possible to grasp its significance. Liszt himself always
claimed that he was in no hurry to hear the oratorio that he dubbed his "musical will and testament"; he used to say that it was sufficient for him to have
composed it without having to promote it. Five years elapsed before the long-
awaited first complete performance took place in Weimar's Herder Church
under Liszt's baton on May 29, 1873. His soloists were Rosa von Milde (soprano), Fräulein Dotter (alto), Herr Borchers (tenor), and Feodor von Milde
(baritone), singers whom Liszt knew well and with whom he had worked before. The large chorus was drawn from groups in Weimar, Jena, and Erfurt, and
the orchestras of Weimar and Sondershausen were combined. The performance started at 6:00 p.m. and went on for three hours. Since the event had
been widely publicized, the historic church was filled to capacity with a large
and distinguished audience. Richard and Cosima Wagner were there (with
Bülow's eldest daughter, Daniela), together with Marie von Mouchanoff,
Countess Marie Schleinitz, Ödön Mihalovich, Eduard Lassen, Count Albert
Apponyi, Kornél Ábrányi, Carl Riedel, and Joachim Raff.

We do well to pause here and cast a second glance at this list of special guests.
The presence of the Wagners in the Herder Church was little short of sensational, given the upheavals that had marked their relations with Liszt. What were
the circumstances that had prompted them to journey from Bayreuth to
Weimar in order to hear this most Catholic of Liszt's compositions?

In May 1872 the two composers had patched up their historic quarrel. It was
Wagner who took the initiative. He wanted Liszt to be present at the laying of
the foundation-stone of the Festspielhaus in Bayreuth—a crowning achievement of his life's work. The ceremonials were planned to take place on May
22, his fifty-ninth birthday. Cosima appears at first to have been against the idea
of inviting her father, for she was convinced that he would not attend. But
Wagner's desire to see his old friend again proved irresistible. His letter of reconciliation is an important and moving document, and it led to consequences
which changed the course of musical history. On May 18, 1872, he wrote:

My Great and Dear Friend:

Cosima maintains that you would not come even if I were to invite you. We should have to endure that, as we have had to endure
so many things! But I cannot refrain from inviting you. And what
is it I cry to you when I say, "Come"! You came into my life as the
greatest man whom I could ever address as an intimate friend. You
gradually went apart from me, perhaps because I had become less
close to you than you were to me. In place of you there came to me
your deepest new-born being and fulfilled my longing to know you
were very close to me. So you live in full beauty before me and in
me, and we are one beyond the grave itself. You were the first to en-
noble me by his love; to a second, higher life am I now wedded in
her, and can accomplish what I should never have been able to accomplish alone. Thus you could become everything to me, while I
could remain so little to you. How immeasurably greater is my gain!
If I now say to you "Come," I thereby say to you "Come to yourself!" For it is yourself that you will find here. Blessings and love to
you, whatever you decide to do!

Your old friend,
RICHARD[4]

Wagner was right to appeal to the great-hearted Liszt. He knew that the last
thing required now was a rehearsal of all the murky details that had led to the
quarrel in the first place, above all the shame that Wagner had heaped on Hans
von Bülow, and the furnace of public abuse through which he had drawn
Cosima. In a masterpiece of circumlocution Wagner sweeps it all aside with the
phrase "you gradually went apart from me, perhaps because I had become less
close to you than you were to me." And whatever Liszt may have thought of
such metaphysical notions as "we are one beyond the grave itself," it was the
kind of language calculated to appeal to his sense of forgiveness. For the rest,
Liszt recognized that Wagner's letter was a symbol, that Wagner and Cosima
now needed him. In the event, he was unable to attend the ceremonials, but he
responded to the letter. It was the language behind the language that had to be
addressed.

May 20, 1872

Sublime Dear Friend:

Too deeply moved by your letter I cannot thank you in words.
But from the depths of my heart I hope that every shadow of a cir-

---

4. LLB, vol. 6, pp. 349–50.

cumstance that could hold me fettered may disappear, and that soon we may see each other again. Then shall you see in perfect clearness how inseparable is my soul from you both, and how intimately I live again in that "second and higher life" of yours in which you are able "to accomplish what you could never have accomplished alone." Herein I recognize Heaven's pardon! God's blessing on you both, and all my love.

F.L.[5]

These letters deserve scrutiny. For five years the two men had not seen each other, let alone corresponded. Yet the old fire of their friendship had proved impossible to quench, and it burned as brightly as ever at the moment of Wagner's greatest triumph. The weeks passed, and Liszt received a second letter from Wagner asking if he and Cosima would be welcome to visit Liszt in Weimar. Liszt replied in the affirmative, and on September 2, 1872, the Wagners travelled from Bayreuth to be reunited with him.[6] Their presence in Weimar for *Christus* in May 1873 was their second within a few months. To the outside world it was a family reunion. But to the Wagners, as we shall eventually discover, it was a calculated investment in their future. Subsequent developments in their complex relations with Liszt prove that this was so, and lead us to conclude that they were in Weimar as part of a sustained recruitment drive to attach Liszt to the Bayreuth cause. Wagner had not even wanted to come, but as he told Cosima on the occasion of their earlier visit: "One must play at diplomacy."[7] None of this was apparent to Liszt at the time. As he mounted the podium that evening, clad in his abbé's cassock, to conduct the massed orchestras and choirs in a performance of his magnum opus, his thoughts and feelings must have drawn sustenance from the simple fact that his closest relatives were in church to witness it.

The full score of *Christus* is headed with a Latin quotation from the Book of St. Paul to the Ephesians: "Veritatem autem facientes in caritate, crescamus in illo per omnia qui est caput: Christus" (Ephesians 4:15. "But speaking the truth in love, may we grow up into him in all things, which is the head, Christ"). The oratorio falls into three parts, and depicts the life of Christ, from the Annunciation to the Resurrection.

---

5. LLB, vol. 6, p. 350.
6. This reunion aroused great misgivings. Cosima's diaries tell of the indecisions and struggles they endured before resolving to go to Weimar. (WT, vol. 1, pp. 568–572) From this same source we learn that it was Marie von Mouchanoff who served as an intermediary and helped to bring the Wagners and Liszt together.
7. WT, vol. 1, p. 568.

PART ONE: *Christmas Oratorio*

1. Introduction ("Rorate coeli desuper et nubes pluant justum; aperiatur terra et germinet Salvatorem," Isaiah 45:8)

2. Pastorale and Annunciation of the Angels ("Angelus ad pastores ait," Luke 2:10–14)

3. "Stabat mater speciosa" (Hymn)

4. Shepherd's song at the Manger

5. The Three Holy Kings (March "Et ecce stella, quam viderant," Matthew 2:9)

PART TWO: *After Epiphany*

6. The Beatitudes ("Beati pauperes spiritu," Matthew 5:3–10)

7. The Lord's Prayer ("Pater noster")

8. The Foundation of the Church ("Tu es Petrus," Matthew 16:18; "Simon Joannis, diligis me?," John 21:16–17)

9. The Miracle ("Et ecce motus magnus factus est in maris," Matthew 8:26)

10. The Entry into Jerusalem ("Hosanna, benedictus qui venit in nomine Domini," Matthew 21:4–9)

PART THREE: *Passion and Resurrection*

11. "Tristis est anima mea" (Mark 14:34–36)

12. "Stabat mater dolorosa"

13. "O filii et filiae" (Easter Hymn)

14. "Resurrexit" ("Christus vincit")

A biography of Franz Liszt is no place in which to embark on a full-scale analysis of *Christus*. It would require another book to do justice to this long and intriguing work. Nonetheless, there are certain highlights that clamour for attention. The first thing that will strike the detached observer of *Christus* is that its sonic surface gradually moves from the very simple to the highly complex. Within the span of three hours, the work progresses through a century of harmonic development. This impression of "history in motion" was surely a deliberate stratagem on Liszt's part, meant to symbolize the increasingly rich and dramatic life of Christ. It begins with music of pastoral simplicity, depicting the Nativity and Christ's childhood; and it ends with the music of prophecy, symbolizing the Crucifixion and the Resurrection. And "prophecy" is not too strong a word to describe those passages towards the end of *Christus* that have no counterpart until modern times. We shall come to them presently. Yet another observation that we must not fail to register is that this oratorio contains hardly any use whatever of the metamorphosis of themes—a unifying technique that Liszt had invented and was almost *de rigueur* for him in his large-scale compositions. To give unity to his life of Christ, he relies instead on motivic cross-references, thematic reminiscence, and recapitulation. He also generates melodic material from plainsong in the belief that Catholic audiences at least might find it familiar. Finally, there is the superior orchestration. It is in most respects flawless, and Liszt's handling of this rich tapestry of sound, which involves large-scale instrumental forces (including an enlarged percussion section, a harp, and an organ), as well as a large mixed choir and six soloists, is beyond reproach.

The orchestral introduction to Part One ("Christmas Oratorio") begins with music which is generated from the plainchant "Rorate coeli desuper" ("Drop down ye heavens from above, and let the skies pour down righteousness").

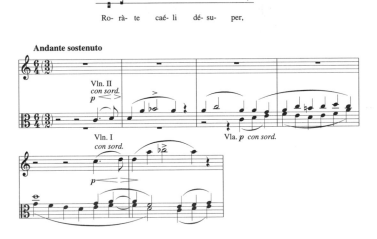

Liszt weaves the threads of this theme into a hushed, contrapuntal tapestry on muted strings, later enriched by woodwinds, an unmistakable depiction of the ethereal glow of the heavens on the night of Christ's birth in Bethlehem. Then follows the music of the Nativity, as the Angel, addressing the shepherds tending their flocks by night, gives them "tidings of great joy." The melody is a variant of the plainchant "Angelus ad pastores ait" ("And the Angel said unto the shepherds"), here cast in 12/8 time and presented on the cor anglais, the pastoral instrument par excellence.

Liszt had very little to guide him when it came to the rhythmicization of plain-song. While he had made a special study of Gregorian chant during his years in Rome, his knowledge could hardly be described as scholarly. Even today, this particular field remains fraught with difficulty—as the controversy surrounding the unmetrical speech-rhythms of the Solesmes school will testify. Liszt's metrical version of "Angelus ad pastores ait," sung at the first entry of the Angel, is a perfectly acceptable solution—the important point being not so much whether it is right or wrong, but what becomes of it as the movement unfolds.

Part One of the oratorio concludes with the brilliant "March of the Three Holy Kings," in which the Three Wise Men follow the Star of Bethlehem and lay their gifts before the infant Jesus. Liszt places within the score two biblical quotations, as if to underline the fact that he is writing programme music whose meaning he wishes to make clear: "And lo, the star, which they saw in the East, went before them," and "When they had opened their treasures, they presented to him gifts; gold and frankincense and myrrh."

This purely instrumental movement is sometimes performed as a separate or-chestral piece, in which capacity it can make a powerful effect.

The most gripping moments in Part Two ("After the Epiphany") are found within the movement Liszt called "The Miracle," a setting of the familiar

Gospel story of Christ calming the tempest. ("And behold, there arose a great tempest in the sea, insomuch that the ship was covered with the waves"— Matthew 8:24.) Of the various miracles of Christ enshrined within the Bible, this is the one that offered Liszt the greatest musical opportunities. He builds up a tremendous orchestral storm, one of the finest he ever composed, at the climax of which the disciples cry out: "Lord save us, we perish!"

These storm-tossed textures, based as they are on the whole-tone scale, sound as if they might have been borrowed from Richard Strauss—who was not even born when Liszt conceived them. It is strange to think of Liszt composing this futuristic music in the silence of his sanctuary in the heart of the Vatican.

It is in Part Three ("Passion and Resurrection") that Liszt reaches the greatest heights of emotional intensity. In the first number ("Tristis est anima mea") he presents us with a grief-laden picture of Christ's Agony in the Garden, a setting for baritone and orchestra, that in many ways is the core of the work. Liszt goes to the Gospel of St. Mark for the words: "My soul is exceeding sorrowful, even unto death," which he shrouds in a dark tapestry of sound drawn from muted strings. Some commentators have detected the influence of Act III of *Tristan,* and it is true that Liszt's music is informed by a similar kind of chromatic anguish. Yet this Garden of Gethsemane music, in which Christ drinks the cup of bitterness, has much more in common with *Parsifal,* on which Wagner had not yet begun work: in fact, the spiritual and musical connections between *Christus* and *Parsifal* have rarely been remarked, though they would make an absorbing study.

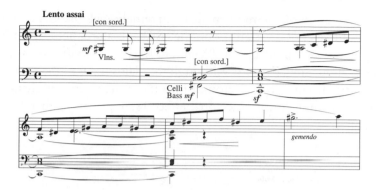

This is music of deep despair. Against the background of its inconsolable fabric Christ utters his prayer: "Father, if it be possible, let this cup pass from me." The movement then collapses into resigned passivity at the words: "Nevertheless not as I will, but as thou wilt."

After the wrenching depiction of the agony in the garden comes the monumental "Stabat mater dolorosa." We do not use the term "monumental" lightly. Liszt was truly inspired when he penned this movement, which offers some of the best choral writing to come out of the nineteenth century. It could easily stand as an independent composition, and it would make an overwhelming impression in the concert hall. The powerful climaxes are redolent of Verdi and Elgar, neither of whose choral masterpieces had yet been penned at the time of the first performance of *Christus*. Conceived for vocal quartet, mixed chorus, and full orchestra, Liszt's "Stabat mater" sets all ten verses of the venerable poem ascribed to Jacopone da Todi. (Whether or not Jacopone was the author, the words are of thirteenth-century Franciscan origin.) The anonymous plainchant melody has been associated with the poem since the fifteenth century, when the text crept into the liturgy. It was well known to Liszt through its inclusion in the *Liber usualis* and was traditionally sung on the first Friday after the Passion.

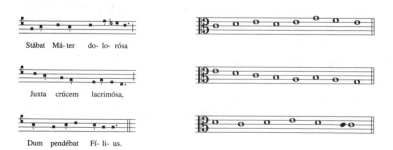

The architecture of the movement is supremely well planned. Liszt composes a set of free choral variations on the "Stabat mater" melody, reminiscent in their anguished mood of the "Weinen, Klagen" variations—and in the same key of mourning, F minor. Although the plainsong is in the major mode, Liszt shifts the harmonic background into the minor without changing the pitch of the chant, to great emotional effect. Here it is in its first, full choral harmonisation.

The throbbing, off-beat accompaniment provided by the orchestra (surely meant to depict a breaking heart) underlines the grief-laden picture of the mother of Christ mourning her dying Son. What raises the variation structure above the ordinary is the presence of contrasting episodes. A close inspection of the score reveals that these "contrasts" are themselves cast as free variations on the same plainchant material—thrust deep into the structural background, and which in consequence are now hardly recognizable. Highly developmental, intensely chromatic, remote in their key contrasts, these episodes always lead back to the grieving opening—as in a rondo. Liszt, in brief, has created "a form across a form." Consider the first episode, which introduces the words "O Mother, source of love, let me feel the strength of your sorrow. / Set my heart afire with love for Christ the Lord." Cast in Liszt's religious key of E major, it presents a musical texture of erotic beauty—and "erotic" is not too strong a word to describe the haunting chromaticisms with which Liszt clothes the old plainchant melody. His thematic material coils itself around the tune as if in a loving embrace. The following example makes the psychological connection clear. The image projected is that of a crucified Son drawing sustenance from his mother, whose silence happens to be the most articulate element in the texture.

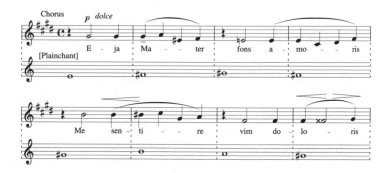

As if to assuage the emotional turmoil of the "Stabat mater," Liszt introduces a setting of the medieval Easter hymn "O filii et filiae" for female voices, softly accompanied by harmonium and woodwinds. He instructs that the choir be placed out of sight, off-stage. When properly performed, this music floats across the auditorium like an ethereal vision, as if coming from distant regions. Its message "Christ is risen" is a perfect preparation for the final movement "Resurrexit," an outbreak of jubilation. Liszt rarely composed fugues, but he provided one for the conclusion of this oratorio. The subject consists of a series of ascending fifths, as if to symbolize the ascent into heaven. "Christ has conquered, Christ commands, for ever and ever, Amen."

There is more to be written about this vast and strangely neglected work than has so far found its way into the literature. Perhaps we may leave the last word with Liszt: "The composition of *Christus* was an artistic necessity for me. Now that it is done, I am content."[8]

What were the reactions of Cosima and Richard Wagner as they listened to Liszt's choral masterpiece? Evidently they did not like it, and it must have cost them an effort to hide their true feelings from Liszt. According to Cosima's diary, the work aroused in them a "remarkable, peculiar impression, best summed up in the words R. said to me in the evening: 'He is the last great victim of this Latin-Roman world.' "[9] And two days later she added: "I write to my father, telling him of our feelings about *Christus* in detail, but I do not know if he will understand them properly."[10] The sentiments of that letter are at odds with the diary; and since it is somewhat long, we do not propose to reproduce it in full. The extracts which follow are sufficient to carry the burden of the situation. Better for it not to have been sent at all than to engage in this sort of duplicity.

---

8. GL, p. 5.
9. WT, vol. I, p. 689.
10. WT, vol. I, p. 681.

[30 May, 1873]

My Dear Father:

. . . It would be impossible for me to describe the torrent of impressions which overwhelmed me last Thursday, and the swarm of thoughts which arose from these impressions, because I was under the influence of an ever-increasing stupor which was like a "canto fermo" around which were grouped many emotions.

. . . Should I confess to you that I did not believe that Catholicism in our day was capable of producing a work of art which summed it up in such a vivid and striking way?

There can be nothing more different in appearance than your conception of the world and [Wagner's]; yet if anybody has managed to listen to, hear, and understand your work, it is him. . . . The elect recognize each other and greet each other across all the differences of language; and you would understand and like a *Christus* by Wagner as he understands and likes yours.

. . . I thanked Wagner effusively for having accompanied me (I know what it means to him to abandon his score).

. . . I do not know whether there is any joy for the artist once his work is finished, that is, detached from him and delivered up to the world of deceit and prostitution, except the echo of the thought of a peer; that is why the presence of Wagner in that church so delighted my heart. . . . May nothing mean or petty, however well-intentioned, come between you two geniuses, created uniquely to understand each other.

That is the wish of your daughter.[11]

When Cosima penned these dreadful lines, she had no idea that her diary might one day be published, and that Wagner's characterisation of Liszt as a "victim" of Catholicism would be there for all the world to see. And even if that remote possibility had ever entered into her thinking, she could never have imagined that the text of the letter itself would be preserved. A comparison of the two documents reveals a woman whose major preoccupation in life, in the year 1873 at any rate, was to ensure that Liszt was firmly allied with Wagner's cause. Nothing was to be allowed to stand in the way of their new-found rapprochement. Liszt was now central to the success of the struggling Bayreuth enterprise, and he must be kept on their side, even if it meant wrapping the Wagners' true opinion of his music in the language of distortion and falsehood.[12]

---

11. Hitherto unpublished. WA, Kasten 204, u. 2 (Abschrift).

12. It is not inappropriate at this point to remind the reader that on the very first page of her diary, Cosima recorded the fact that she was writing it for her children so that in later life they would understand her.

In one respect, Wagner's disappointment with *Christus* may have been justified, although on grounds that were different from the ones he gives. According to Eduard Lassen the performance was under-rehearsed.[13] Music had always laboured under difficult conditions at Weimar, as a study of Liszt's own Weimar years so readily shows. Evidently it was still impossible to mount a large-scale composition there without bringing in outside forces, with all the attendant musico-logistical problems. There was one other point about this first performance which ought also to be recorded. Although we traditionally call it "complete," Liszt introduced cuts which totalled 806 measures—or about twenty minutes of music.[14] These cuts were restored when Hans Richter conducted the oratorio a few months later in the great hall of the Budapest Vigadó, during Liszt's so-called Jubilee celebrations.

II

Although Liszt remained in Weimar for the next several months, he was far from idle. Even before his distinguished guests had dispersed, he had plunged into a busy round of teaching and was giving masterclasses in the Hofgärtnerei three times a week. Among his students during this spring of 1873 were Laura Kahrer, Martha Remmert, Kathie Gaul, Anton Urspruch, Georg Leitert, and the new pupil from Chicago, Amy Fay.[15] As the season progressed, the group swelled to about twenty people, and it was not unusual to find such notables as Grand Duke Carl Alexander, Olga von Meyendorff, and Eduard Lassen listening intently to the music, and then mingling with the young students on terms of equality as they consumed Pauline Apel's iced tea and cakes. Towards the end of June, Liszt undertook lightning trips to Dornburg, Berlin, and Leipzig (where he heard a performance of his Missa Choralis) and then resumed his teaching in Weimar. The following month he received a letter from Cosima, asking him to attend Bayreuth as a special guest at the Festspielhaus's roof-raising ceremony. Liszt gladly lent his presence to this event, and he remained in Bayreuth from July 26 to August 5.[16]

---

13. SNW, vol. 2, p. 245.

14. A complete table of these cuts, sanctioned by Liszt himself and published by him as a supplement to the full score, may be consulted in Volume Two of the present work, p. 323, n. 39.

15. FMSG, pp. 205–35.

16. WT, vol. 1, pp. 710–12. Cosima devotes some space in her diary to this visit and describes in loving detail her father's piano-playing of such works as the first three movements of Beethoven's *Hammerklavier* Sonata and the A-flat-minor Prelude and Fugue from Bach's "Forty-eight." She also reports that after they had taken their leave of Liszt at Bamberg, on his way back to Weimar, she gave way to melancholy and Wagner treated her to one of "those passionate outbursts with which I am confronted after every reunion with my father." While Wagner badly needed Liszt's support in building the Bayreuth theatre, it seems that he resented what he perceived to be the "loss" of Cosima to Liszt

Back in Weimar, Liszt found the city deep in preparations for the wedding of the grand duke's son and heir, Crown Prince Carl August, to Princess Pauline, which took place on August 26. Among the celebrations that followed in its wake were a number of concerts in which Liszt took part. On September 7 he appeared as a soloist with the Weimar Court Orchestra (conducted by Lassen), playing his arrangement of Weber's Polonaise Brillante and his own Fantasy on Hungarian Folk Themes. Amy Fay, who was present at the rehearsal of this concert, wrote:

> . . . He scarcely looked at the keys, and it was astounding to see his hands go rushing up and down the piano and perform passages of the utmost rapidity and difficulty, while his head was turned all the while towards the orchestra. . . . He did everything with the most immense aplomb, and without seeming to pay any attention to his hands, which moved of themselves as if they were independent beings and had their own brain and everything![17]

The following day Liszt conducted a performance of Beethoven's Ninth Symphony in the Court Theatre. It was an uncompromising choice, and a farewell of sorts: Liszt was not to mount the podium again in Weimar for another five years. After attending some further festivities in the Wartburg castle (where his Wartburg Lieder were given their first performance in honour of the young newlyweds), Liszt left Weimar en route for Rome.

He had no intention of lingering in the Eternal City for long. His main destination was Budapest, where the Hungarians were planning a Jubilee celebration for the fiftieth anniversary of his public career. While he was in Rome he stayed at Vicolo de' Greci 43, close enough to Princess Carolyne's residence to see her almost daily, and he also requested an audience of the pope. Pius IX received him in the Vatican on October 22, Liszt's sixty-second birthday, and they chatted alone for more than fifteen minutes. "There is something prodigious about his health and his spirits do not flag," observed Liszt.[18]

III

Fifty years had now elapsed since Liszt had embarked on his public career, and the Hungarians were determined to celebrate that event on a national

---

whenever her father was in the vicinity. The psychological undercurrents in this three-way relationship ran deep, and it is doubtful whether any of the principals fully understood the play of passions that held them in thrall.

17. FMSG, pp. 251–52.

18. WLLM, p. 99. Liszt was referring to the fact that Pius had by now been a prisoner inside the Vatican for more than three years. See p. 238.

scale.[19] The Jubilee celebrations, in fact, formed a chief highlight for Liszt in this year of 1873. He set out from Rome and crossed the Hungarian border by rail on October 30; he was met by delegations at Esztergom and Vác before continuing his journey to Budapest. When he got to the main railway terminal, another group of Hungarians were waiting for him, including the composer Henrik Gobbi, the sculptor Pál Kugler, and Baron Antal Augusz. The party drove directly to 4 Fischplatz, a building which had recently been purchased with a view to its becoming the site of the proposed Royal Academy of Music, and whose top floor contained a spacious apartment for Liszt's own use.[20]

Until Liszt arrived in Budapest he had little idea of the scope of the celebrations that had been prepared in his honour. It was only after his first meeting with Archbishop Lajos Haynald, the chairman of the recently formed "Liszt Festival Committee," that he grasped the fact that the festivities were to have a national dimension, and would include concerts in Esztergom and other cities besides Budapest.[21]

The festival began at six o'clock on the morning of November 8 when the combined bands of the 38th and 65th Regiments assembled in Fischplatz beneath the windows of Liszt's residence in order to serenade him.[22] This outdoor concert attracted crowds of people, and cries of "Éljen! Ferenc Liszt!" rang across the square, echoes of the ones uttered in 1839–40 when he had returned home for the first time as a national hero. Long after the bands had marched away, the crowds lingered in the hope of catching a glimpse of Liszt.

---

19. Liszt's public career was generally deemed to have begun in Vienna, at the famous "farewell recital" of 1823, which marked the commencement of the young prodigy's European tours. (See Volume One, pp. 79–80.)

20. The circumstances surrounding the acquisition of this building, and its importance in the musical life of Hungary, are described in detail in the chapter "Liszt and the Royal Academy of Music," pp. 289–90.

21. The *Aufruf* declaring Hungary's intention to honour Liszt's career, which bears the signatures of Kornél Ábrányi (sen.) and Archbishop Lajos Haynald, was dated September 10, 1873, and was circulated throughout the country. It proclaimed in ringing terms that a nation had a moral duty to honour its noblest sons, and listed many of the prominent Hungarians who had now rallied to the Jubilee celebrations of "Our Compatriot Franz Liszt." (An original copy of this rare document is preserved in WA, Kasten 166, u. 2.) Haynald and Ábrányi went on to circulate a printed invitation to the festivities; dated October 5, 1873, it referred to "our venerated countryman Franz Liszt." (WA, Kasten 166, u. 3) Both documents demonstrate yet again that Liszt was regarded as Hungarian by the leaders of his nation. Liszt and the "Hungarian question" was not yet the divisive topic it later became.

Incidentally, the final roster of the Festival Committee was: Haynald (chairman), Ábrányi (secretary), Imre von Huszár, Count Imre Széchényi, Ferenc Erkel, Ödön von Mihalovich, Baron Antal Augusz, Count Albert Apponyi, Hans Richter, Count Guido Karácsonyi, and János Nepomuk Dunkl. A photograph of the committee (from which Ábrányi is missing), taken to commemorate the occasion, is reproduced in BFL, p. 261.

22. According to the Hungarian press, two marches of Liszt were played: the *Ungarische Geschwindmarsch* and the Goethe Festival March, together with a specially composed serenade by the conductor W. Ludwig.

A proclamation of Liszt's Jubilee, November 1873: "Our Compatriot Franz Liszt."

On the afternoon of November 9 there was a performance of Henrik Gobbi's Liszt Cantata (a setting of a text by Emil Ábrányi), written in honour of the composer. At the conclusion of the concert Joseph Hellmesberger delivered a eulogy on behalf of the Gesellschaft der Musikfreunde in Vienna, and Liszt was presented with a golden laurel wreath on behalf of the Hungarian nation. The main celebration came in the evening, when Hans Richter conducted the augmented orchestra and chorus of the Hungarian National Theatre in an uncut performance of *Christus* in the specially illuminated great hall of the Vigadó. With intermissions the concert lasted for four hours, from five until nine.

On the last day of the Jubilee, the city of Pest gave Liszt a large banquet in the Hotel Hungária. About two hundred guests attended, among them three cabinet ministers (Ágoston Trefort, Tivabar Pauler, and Kálmán Tisza). Other prominent Hungarians also turned out in force, including his old compatriots Reményi, Baron Augusz, Count Albert Apponyi, and Count Guido Karácsonyi. There were also many out-of-towners present, such as Hellmesberger and Ludwig Bösendorfer from Vienna, Karl Pohlig from Dresden, C. F. Kahnt from Leipzig, Carl Lewy from St. Petersburg, Olga von Meyendorff, Marie von Mouchanoff, Countess Maria Dönhoff, David Popper, Sophie Menter, and newspaper correspondents from the *Moniteur Universel* and the London *Times*.[23] Merely to call the roll of such names indicates the significance attached to the celebration. But perhaps the most important deputation was the one from Weimar led by Baron August Loën, the intendant of the Court Theatre, whose attendance at the Jubilee was deemed by Grand Duke Carl Alexander to be so important for his city that he had paid for Loën's travel expenses himself.[24] In the middle of the banquet Loën got to his feet and delivered an eloquent speech in which he reviewed Liszt's long career. He reminded the audience of the pioneering work that Liszt had done as a conductor, especially of the music of Wagner, Berlioz, and Schumann. Then he brought forward the names of Tausig, Bülow, and Klindworth as examples of Liszt's teaching. At the conclusion of his address, Loën presented Liszt with an album whose cover was inscribed with the words "Weimars Gruss," and which contained the signatures of one hundred personalities associated with the Court Theatre.[25] Liszt also received many telegrammes and letters from around the world. That evening word also reached him that he had been appointed an honorary member of the Imperial Academy of Music at St. Petersburg. Perhaps the best-known legacy of the Jubilee celebration was the series of tableaux by István

---

23. The issue of November 19, 1873, covered the Jubilee in detail and gave English readers a retrospective account of Liszt's life.
24. WLLM, p. 111.
25. Ibid.

Halász depicting various episodes from Liszt's career, including the public "kiss of consecration" from Beethoven in April 1823, an event that never took place, but was already part of the Liszt mythology, and was to sow much confusion in the literature later on.

While Liszt was in Budapest, and still in a state of euphoria induced by the festivities, he visited the National Museum. This great depository of national treasures so impressed him that the idea occurred to him that there could be no better time than his Jubilee to make a gift to Hungary of some precious objects of his own. This was the context in which he made a commitment to the museum's director, Ferenc Pulszky, to bequeath to the nation such items as the Sword of Honour presented to him in Pest in 1840, Beethoven's Broadwood piano, the golden baton given to him by Carolyne in 1847, the golden wreath recently placed on his head by his compatriots, a solid silver music desk inscribed with the names of more than a hundred musicians, and a priceless vase that had belonged to Tsar Nicholas of Russia. Because some of these items were still in storage in Weimar, and were technically under the control of Princess Carolyne (who did not at first approve of such a generous bequest), the gifts were not handed over until after Liszt's death.[26]

Liszt actually lived in Budapest (with brief excursions to Vienna, Pressburg, Esztergom, Kalocsa, and elsewhere) for nearly seven months, from October 30 until May 17, on which date he finally returned to Rome. It was his longest sojourn in his native country since his childhood. During the days and weeks following the Jubilee, he lived on a tidal wave of national sentiment. He was swept along by the current of invitations which poured in from across the country pleading with him to participate in the musical life of the nation. And Liszt declared himself ready and willing to do so. In a letter to Prime Minister Andrássy he wrote of the "permanent link" that now existed "between a humble rhapsode of Hungary and his homeland," and he enclosed a dedicated copy of his arrangement of two national songs, the "Szózat" and "Hymnus."[27] His words were well chosen. At this time were forged the bonds that were to re-attach him to Hungary for the rest of his life, and make it necessary for him to return to his native land every year to fulfil his many commitments there.

Between November 1873 and May 1874, in fact, Liszt's itinerary became so crowded that simply to report it in all its glorious detail runs the risk of deflating one's prose to the flat language of a railway timetable. But certain events claim our attention. One well-publicised appearance took place on Sunday, November 23, when Liszt travelled to Pressburg for a performance of his "Gran" Mass, in honour of St. Cecilia. He called it "a last echo of the festival

26. LLB, vol. 7, pp. 44–45. Liszt's correspondence with Pulszky, and the subsequent fate of the bequests, will be found in GLMM, pp. 121–25.

27. LLB, vol. 8, p. 270.

at Pest, save for the crowns and banners."[28] An event of somewhat greater importance occurred on January 11, 1874, when Liszt was persuaded temporarily to vacate Budapest in order to appear in the Vienna Musikvereinsaal for the benefit of the Emperor Franz Joseph Foundation. This was an invitation he could hardly refuse, since it came from the imperial court. The Austro-Hungarian Compromise was now nearly seven years old, and Vienna and Budapest were bound together as never before by ties of culture, commerce, and above all royalty: Franz Joseph was emperor to the one country and king to the other, and as such was Liszt's reigning monarch. It was Liszt's first appearance in the imperial city as a solo pianist for almost thirty years; the last occasion had been in his heyday as a touring virtuoso, when Vienna lay at his feet. In the first half of the concert he played his own arrangement for piano and orchestra of Schubert's *Wanderer* Fantasy, and in the second his Fantasy on Hungarian Folk Themes. For both pieces the conductor was his faithful friend and supporter Johann Herbeck. Hanslick was present and wrote:

> His playing was free, poetic, replete with imaginative shadings, and at the same time characterised by noble, artistic repose. And his technique, his virtuosity? I hesitate to speak of it. It suffices to observe that he has not lost it, but has rather added to it in clarity and moderation. What a remarkable man! After a life incomparably rich and active, full of excitement, passion and pleasure, he returns at the age of sixty-two, and plays the most difficult music with the ease and freshness of youth.
>
> . . . Liszt brought the Rhapsody to a conclusion in a storm of octaves. The audience applauded, shouted, cheered, rose to its feet, recalled the master again and again, indefatigably. The latter in his turn, with the quiet, friendly, gracious bearing of the habitual conqueror, let it be known that he was not yet tired. For the Liszt of today it was a great accomplishment; and yet he went about it as if it were nothing and he himself still the Liszt of 1840. A darling of the gods indeed![29]

This concert was of more than passing interest because it also featured Johannes Brahms as a conductor in two short choral pieces by Mendelssohn and Bach. At the following banquet, also attended by Brahms, Liszt was presented with the Order of Franz Joseph.

---

28. WLLM, p. 105.
29. HCCV (n. 75), p. 123ff. It is one more proof that Hanslick was in the forefront of Liszt's admirers when it came to his piano playing. It was only towards Liszt's music that he generally experienced a strong aversion.

Back in Hungary Liszt showed no sign of cutting back on his activities. During the month of March 1874, for instance, he gave no fewer than five charity concerts in Budapest. The first of them was on March 4, when he appeared in the large hall of the Vigadó to raise money for the orphans of a recent cholera epidemic. A sea of two thousand faces greeted him with enthusiastic cheering as he and Ödön Mihalovich walked onto the specially constructed platform where two Bösendorfer grand pianos awaited them. They delivered a rivetting performance of Liszt's Fantasia on Motifs from Beethoven's *Ruins of Athens,* which created a pandemonium. After the applause had subsided there came a group of Liszt's songs, sung by a young English girl named Annie Wheelwright. Liszt then mounted the platform once more and launched into one of his Mélodies hongroises, followed by one of the war-horses of his early manhood, the *Sonnambula* Fantasie. The sheer polish and technical mastery of this last performance, coming as it did from an ageing Liszt who never practised, astonished all who heard it and evoked comparisons with Tausig and Rubinstein at their best. Liszt pronounced himself well satisfied with his playing, and even more pleased with the sum of nearly five thousand forints raised for the orphans. A similar concert, on March 23, was intended to raise money for the girls' school run by the Sisters of Mercy of Buda. This was not simply a token appearance of the kind that celebrities through the ages have made in order to part people from their money. It was a major musical contribution from Liszt, comparable with the full-blown recitals he had given during his years as a travelling virtuoso. He played the Beethoven Variations, op. 34; the Chopin Nocturne in B-flat minor, op. 9, no. 1; two mazurkas by Chopin; Weber's *Momento capriccioso;* and his own *St. Francis of Paola walking on the waters.* One newspaper review, after reminding its readers of the popular and oft-repeated notion that Liszt looked like a king, summed it all up by saying that "he is truly a king in the kingdom of art."[30] The assisting artists included the singer Josefine Ellinger and the faithful Mihalovich, the latter of whom joined Liszt in a four-handed performance of the Fantasy on Hungarian Folk Themes.

Even as Liszt was enjoying the homage of his nation, Grand Duke Carl Alexander was reminding him that Weimar, too, had a claim on his career. Carl Alexander had watched the Hungarian celebrations from afar and when, at the beginning of 1874, Liszt showed no sign of returning to Weimar, had reminded his royal chamberlain that the city awaited him. Liszt did not reply to this letter, but he told Rosa von Milde that the windows of the Hofgärtnerei would have to remain boarded over for the time being. The grand duke wrote again in some pique, telling Liszt that Weimar was willing to celebrate the fiftieth an-

---

30. WA, Kasten 266, u. 1.

niversary of Liszt's Vienna debut on April 13. But he added that if Liszt declined to attend because of commitments in Hungary, then he would have to take the view that a Hungarian celebration would be of as little concern to Weimar as a Weimar celebration would be to Hungary.[31] Again Liszt did not reply. It was not until April 1875 that he finally returned to the city of Goethe and Schiller, a lapse of more than eighteen months.

I V

Among the many guests who had assembled in the Herder Church for the first performance of *Christus* on May 29, 1873, none had listened to the oratorio more avidly than Lina Ramann, who had travelled from Nuremberg to experience it at first hand. She was already familiar with parts of the work, but not with all of it. Even before the last notes had died away she had resolved to write a detailed analysis of it, and asked Liszt for permission to do so. His laconic reply was that since the score was now published he could not prevent her. Within a year, her brochure "Franz Liszt's Oratorium *Christus*" was published, and Ramann herself was recognised as an authority on Liszt's music. She was forty years old, and had as yet no notion that her enthusiasm for Liszt and his compositions would one day turn her into his official biographer. Ramann ran a music school in Nuremberg in collaboration with Ida Volckmann, and her chief interest at this stage in her career was piano pedagogy. It was in the course of trying to put together a catalogue of Liszt's music in 1874 that Ramann first realised just how little biographical work of a serious kind had ever been done on him. Even the simplest chronology of his life and work was missing from the literature. By now she knew him well enough to write to him for information, and Liszt respected her well enough to respond with the details. Before long, an informal collaboration had been established, and in August 1874 Ramann sent him the first of a long series of questionnaires that slowly turned into the foundation for her official biography of him.

Ramann does not appear to have grasped at first the magnitude of the task before her. And Liszt soon realised that he himself had neither the time nor the means to unearth all the information she required. It was at this point that he turned to Princess Wittgenstein for assistance, and it was at this point too that the princess determined to take over the operation and direct Ramann's biographical work from Rome. The first step was for Ramann and the princess to meet. That encounter took place on June 12, 1876, when Ramann called on the princess in her apartments at the Via del Babuino. "I was with her for two

31. LBLCA, p. 159. The grand duke was slightly misinformed about Liszt's anniversary. To celebrate it in April 1874 would have been one year late.

hours," wrote Ramann. "What a woman! Her lively face, fluent intellect, her speech all soul." When it came time to take her leave, Ramann bowed and kissed the princess's hand with the remark: "Not that of the princess but that of the great lady." To which compliment the princess retorted: "Are you a democrat?"[32] Carolyne's reaction to Ramann was not at first flattering. She told Liszt that while Ramann had made a good impression, she was "a bit naively bourgeois . . . we'll have to see whether she is capable of becoming more sophisticated. If she is, she will produce a model biography—if not, she can do what she wants, and I will fill in the rest in my own way."[33]

This last sentence was an ominous portent of the troubles that lay ahead for Ramann as the princess tried to wrest control of the book away from her. Ramann remained in Rome for four weeks, and she saw Carolyne almost daily. Not only did Carolyne take her to locations of relevance to her biography (for instance, they visited the church of San Carlo al Corso together, where the princess unburdened the details of the débâcle of the thwarted marriage) but, more importantly, they had long meetings during which the princess reviewed the details of Liszt's life while Ramann took copious notes. In the course of one of these meetings, Ramann told her that Liszt had ceded to her the legal right to publish his collected writings in a German edition. "This news was a bit unexpected for me," the princess told Liszt, "but we will come to an understanding with her."[34] When she left Rome, in mid-July, Ramann was under few illusions as far as Princess Wittgenstein was concerned. She knew that she would have to fight every step of the way if she wanted to retain her independence. Sure enough, a crisis developed between the pair in 1878, and Ramann found herself in the painful position of having to tell the princess that she refused to become her mouthpiece.[35]

It will come as no surprise to students of this complex topic that within two or three years of its commencement Liszt had lost whatever enthusiasm he might at first have had at the prospect of reading a large-scale biography of himself. He observed the growing tension between Princess Carolyne and Ramann and became apprehensive. In April 1877 he told Carolyne:

> In my humble opinion, the best would be for Lina Ramann to restrict her work to a musical commentary on my compositions, of which a complete catalogue has just been published by Härtel.

---

32. RL, p. 74.
33. WA, Kasten 48, u. 1. Hitherto unpublished.
34. Ibid.
35. This crisis was touched on in Volume One (rev. ed., p. 7f), when we reviewed the place of Ramann's biography in the Liszt literature.

It would be enough for her in passing to touch on the biographical side—very far removed from her *deutsche Sittlichkeit*. If you
have no objection I would like you to advise her to restrict her
work to a single volume of about 400 pages—which will deal
with my individuality as a musician, pianist, and composer, such as
it is. In that way she will certainly obtain the serious success she
wants. Even if it were not sudden—it will increase in a few years!
Excuse this apparent fatuousness—closer to the truth than false
modesty.[36]

The fact is, Princess Carolyne had spoiled the project for Liszt, as she had
spoiled so much else for him in recent years. When he suggested that the situation might be redeemed by having Ramann concentrate on "musical commentary" rather than on biography, he knew that this was what Ramann did
best and Carolyne not at all. But it was better said than done. Ramann had invested time and money on the book, and the princess was not about to be deflected. So Liszt did not press his objections. Ramann often travelled over to
Weimar to see him, and he continued his habit of visiting her in Nuremberg
on those occasions when he happened to be in the vicinity. Meanwhile, he
good-naturedly continued to fill out her questionnaires.

It took Ramann four years to complete the first volume of her three-
volume biography. Liszt's response on reading it is well known: "Do not
entangle yourself in too many details,"[37] he advised her. By then it was too
late. The style and structure of the biography were already determined. As for
the accuracy of the "details," that is a matter over which scholars have wran-
gled for a hundred years.

Until recently, Ramann's work lay under a cloud of suspicion. Her text was
deemed to have been tainted by the constant interference of the princess, who
wanted the story of Liszt's life told from her own point of view. Indeed, Ramann was often dubbed in Liszt circles as "the creature of the princess," and
in the absence of solid information to the contrary the label stuck. Fortunately,
Ramann was fastidious in the matter of keeping notes, and she preserved a
mountain of material connected with her biographical research. When she
died, in 1912, she bequeathed her papers to the Goethe-Schiller Archive in
Weimar, with the proviso that they be placed under a fifty-year embargo. It was
only with the posthumous publication of her *Lisztiana* (1983), a collection of
private letters, diaries, and peripheral materials connected to her work, that the
world began to have a proper appreciation of the difficult position in which

36. LLB, vol. 7, p. 189.
37. WA, Kasten 351, no. 1.

Ramann found herself. We now know that she came into possession of much sensitive material that she was unable to use, because the principals involved were still alive.[38]

V

The arrival of Richard and Cosima Wagner in Budapest on March 6, 1875, less than a month after Liszt himself had got there from Rome, came at a time when he was deeply involved in the administrative and financial problems of the proposed Academy of Music. He was having regular discussions with Count Albert Apponyi and other Hungarian politicians regarding the presidency of the new institution, a title which was actually conferred on him by Minister Ágoston Trefort on March 30. Meanwhile, he deliberated daily with Ödön Mihalovich regarding the planning of the courses and the appointment of faculty. Liszt was nonetheless delighted to see the Wagners, and actually went out to Esztergom to meet them in the company of Baroness Meyendorff. Hav-

---

38. Although it takes us a little beyond our present chronology, it may be useful at this point to round off the chequered history of Ramann's life of Liszt. After the publication of the first volume, in 1880, she actively pursued the possibility of an English translation. She was not the first biographer to realise that a translation, when properly carried out, can be as good as a second edition since it is one of the very best ways to correct earlier mistakes. There is an interesting run of letters between Ramann and George Grove, who was then associated with the publishing firm of Macmillan in London, and was hard at work on the first edition of his famous *Dictionary of Music and Musicians*. Grove read the book and did not pull his punches:

> . . . In order to be successful in England, it will want a good deal of pruning. The taste of the English public with regard to Music is very different from that of the German public. We like facts, but have a horror of anything like rhapsody or eloquence. Now, your book seems to contain all the facts, but forgive me for saying there is a good deal in the mode of statement which the English reader would not care for, which it is almost impossible to translate accurately or effectively in our language, and which an English publisher would wish to see weeded out; and this I think would be the view of any publisher to whom it might be submitted. (WA, Kasten 322, u. 1, hitherto unpublished)

Ramann lost no time in looking elsewhere, and just over two years later her book was published by Allen & Co in an English translation by Miss M. E. Cowdery. To any student of the subject, it is evident that Ramann had taken much trouble to incorporate some revisions into the text, and she even wrote a new introduction to the book, in English. It is equally evident that her translator let her down, and that she could not have seen any proofs. Anxious to let Grove see the book that he had rejected, she despatched a copy to him in November 1882 and awaited his reply. She must have been devastated to read what he said.

November 20, 1882

Dear Miss Ramann:
    The copy of the English version of your book has just reached me, and I hasten to send you my warm thanks for it. I cannot resist saying that I wish you [had] a better translator. —Miss Cowdery, whoever she is, not only cannot write English, but knows

ing travelled back with them to Budapest, he installed them in the Hungária Hotel,[39] introduced them to his aristocratic friends, and arranged a number of lunches and dinners in their honour.

Wagner had not come to Budapest especially to see Liszt, but rather to take part in a fund-raising concert for the Bayreuth Festival project. In the event, Liszt proved to be crucial to the success of the enterprise. The idea came from Hans Richter, who from 1871 had been the chief conductor of the Budapest National Theatre, and who had already been selected by Wagner to conduct the complete *Ring* cycle when Bayreuth opened its doors in 1876. There was at first great opposition in Budapest to a benefit concert for Wagner, and it had taken on an unpleasant nationalistic flavour. Wagner was a German composer, so the argument ran, and Budapest was not a German city. Why should Hungary squander money to support German artistic enterprises when it did not have enough to support its own? The apathy was so great, and the tickets sold so slowly, that the organisers began to fear a fiasco. When Liszt was informed, he volunteered to play Beethoven's *Emperor* Concerto in the same concert. "On that day when this decision of the Master became known," wrote Count Apponyi, "all tickets were sold out."[40]

The concert took place in the Vigadó on March 10, 1875. Three works occupied the programme: the first performance of Liszt's recently completed can

---

nothing of music, and translated *dur* by sharp (instead of major), *moll* by flat (instead of minor), and commits the most dreadful blunders of the same kind. I am very glad to see my name in your book (p. 62) —even though "Mr. G. Grove—London" is rather an odd designation, but I wish she had not implied that I said the Variation was in C flat, which I certainly never did. It is in C *moll*. See also p. 132, 133; and fancy "42 composers keeping to C #." On that page and p. 134 there is such confusion as I never saw equalled. How easy for Miss Cowdery to have asked me, or one of the thousand English amateurs who understand German musical terms, and not do you the cruel injustice of sending you out to the English public in such a garb. (Ibid.)

Grove's hard words stood in sharp contrast to those of Ramann's English reviewers, who were generally kind to her, even though one or two of them gave no evidence of having read the book (one of them even going so far as to refer to her throughout as "Herr Ramann": in *Society Magazine,* June 10, 1883).

Although Ramann did not know it, an American writer named Sara Hershey Eddy had begun an independent translation of her work which was abandoned when Cowdery's version was published in England. One can only regret that the American did not make herself known to Ramann earlier, since her translation would probably have been a good deal more professional than Cowdery's. See the unpublished letter of Sara Hershey Eddy to Carl Lachmund on this topic, dated "Chicago, January 4, 1884." (CLC, JPB, 92-1, series 1, folder 30) In the event, Cowdery's translation was discontinued after the first volume. It nonetheless remains a salutary example of all the things that can go wrong in biographical work. Her text remained the basis for many of the biographies of Liszt that were to appear in English for the next thirty or forty years, sometimes with disastrous consequences.

39. Wagner was uncomfortable there. On the first night, a ball in another part of the hotel disturbed his slumbers, and he and Cosima moved in with Hans Richter and his family the following day.

40. AAM, pp. 82–88.

tata *The Bells of Strasbourg Cathedral*, conducted by Liszt himself; the *Emperor* Concerto, with Richter as conductor; and excerpts from *The Ring*, conducted by the composer. At the rehearsal on March 9 both Wagner and Richter were transfixed by Liszt's rendering of the concerto. Cosima observed: "My father absolutely overwhelms us with the way he plays the Beethoven concerto—a tremendous impression! Magic without parallel—this is not playing, it is pure sound. R[ichard] says it annihilates everything else."[41] Afterwards Wagner went up to Liszt and exclaimed: "My dear Franz, you have beaten me well and truly today! What can I do to compare with the playing we have just heard?"[42]

On the morning of the concert Count Apponyi and Mihalovich went to visit Liszt in order to discuss some details regarding Wagner's stay in the city. They were dismayed to see Liszt with a bandage on a finger of his right hand. Liszt informed them that he had just cut himself, and they assumed that the concert would have to be cancelled. Liszt would not hear of it, however. "But your injured finger?" exclaimed Apponyi. "Well, I'll just have to do without it," replied Liszt. The performance that he gave of the *Emperor* Concerto that evening has gone down in the annals of Liszt performance as one of his greatest.[43] Three thousand people filled the hall, the front rows being occupied by the Hungarian aristocracy—including Cardinal János Simor, the primate of Hungary. Neither *The Bells* nor *The Ring* enjoyed much public success. It was Liszt's rendering of Beethoven that lingered in the mind's ear. The following day, the newspaper *Pesther Lloyd* carried a long article which summed up the general feeling: "It was a full and complete triumph for Franz Liszt, the unparalleled pianistic interpreter of Beethoven, but for Richard Wagner no more than a *succès d'estime*."[44]

The Wagners left Budapest on March 11, and Liszt accompanied them to the station. "A sad parting!" wrote Cosima. "I should dearly have loved to have stayed another day in Pest with my father; I did not suggest it, but it was hard not to."[45]

V I

In retrospect, the chief aspect of the Vigadó concert that calls for comment was the one which was hardly noticed at the time: the first performance of *The Bells of Strasbourg Cathedral*.[46] The conspiracy of silence which still surrounds this re-

41. WT, vol. 1, p. 901.

42. AAM, p. 87.

43. AAM, p. 88.

44. Issue of March 11, 1875. To mark the occasion of the concert, the Budapest photographer György Klösz took a particularly fine photograph of Liszt, showing him in the dress of an abbé, holding a baton in his right hand, and with the full score of *The Bells* open before him on the music rack. (BFL, p. 265)

45. WT, vol. 1, p. 902.

46. As we now know, the presence of this work on the programme had at first upset Richard and Cosima Wagner. Unable to accept the fact that Wagner had no following at that time in Budapest, he

markable music is difficult to explain. True, the composition is not easy to bring off. It requires a large symphony orchestra, full choir, and two soloists. And its harmonic language is at times advanced. But that alone would not account for the neglect into which *The Bells* has fallen. Perhaps at first it had to do with the blending of the sacred and the profane, which early audiences found unusual. But none of these things is important today, and the time cannot be far distant when this arresting music will find its audience.

Ever since Liszt's encounters with Henry Wadsworth Longfellow in late 1868 and early 1869, the idea of setting the Prologue to his poem *The Golden Legend* had been much on his mind. The idea had originated with Princess Carolyne, who had even provided Liszt with a German translation of Longfellow's text. But Liszt's departure from the Eternal City in 1869, and the subsequent travels between Rome, Budapest, and Weimar that were now a regular feature of his itinerant life-style, had prevented him from rallying to the task. Despite a number of sharp reminders from the princess, it was not until July 19, 1874, that he was able to announce, from the tranquillity of the Villa d'Este, that he had at last brought his cantata to a conclusion.[47] On November 22 of that year he wrote to Longfellow, reminding him of their first meeting at the Santa Francesca Romana and seeking permission to dedicate his work to the celebrated poet. We do not have Longfellow's reply, but he must have agreed, since the next year the work was brought out by Schuberth bearing the inscription "Dedicated to the poet H. W. Longfellow."[48]

The Bells is divided into two parts: (I) Prelude, "Excelsior," and (II) "The Bells." The Prelude is a choral setting of the one word "Excelsior," an allusion to Longfellow's well-known poem of that name, and provides the context for what follows.[49] It begins with a theme that foreshadows the Prelude to Wagner's *Parsifal:*

---

and Cosima had blamed Liszt for the initially poor ticket sales. Cosima recorded glumly in her diary: "My father's composition will involve great expense and attract nobody to the concert." (WT, vol. 1, p. 893) Liszt actually volunteered to withdraw the work. Wagner appreciated the offer but refused to accept it. At that point Liszt resolved the matter by appearing as a piano soloist as well.

47. LLB, vol. 7, p. 78. "Yesterday evening I finished the orchestration of *The Bells*. It remains for me only to add the dynamic markings. . . ."

48. An extensive account of the creation of *The Bells* may be found in WLL, pp. 1–25. The holograph of Liszt's letter to Longfellow is today in the Library of Congress.

49. The poem "Excelsior" used to be required reading for every American schoolchild. But that was in yesterday's more literate world. It tells of a youth who braves a difficult Alpine pass carrying a banner bearing the single word "Excelsior!"

> The shades of night were falling fast,
> As through an Alpine village passed
> A youth, who bore, 'mid snow and ice,
> A banner with the strange device,
> 　　　　Excelsior!

As the youth crosses the difficult terrain, confronting avalanches, mountain torrents, and drifting snows, he tries to keep his banner constantly aloft. He expires at his journey's end,

Part II of *The Bells* is based on the Prologue to *The Golden Legend,* which Longfellow had recently incorporated as the second part of his *Christus* trilogy. The dramatic text concerns the spire and bells of Strasbourg Cathedral. It is night and a storm is raging. Lucifer and the powers of the air are trying to tear down the cross from the top of the steeple, but the bells sound out a warning and alert the saints and guardian angels before the deed can be accomplished. From time to time the chanting of monks may be heard through the continuous tolling of a deep bell.

> Laudo Deum Verum!
> Plebum voco!
> Congrego clerum!
>
> [I praise the true Lord!
> I summon the people!
> I gather the clergy!]

"Seize the loud vociferous bells," Lucifer urges the spirits. "Hurl them from their windy tower!" In vain do the powers of the air try to do his bidding. "These bells have been anointed and baptised with holy water!" they cry. "They defy our utmost power." Again and again Lucifer musters his dark forces, and each time the bells become articulate:

> Defunctos ploro!
> Pestem fugo!
> Festam decoro!

> Still grasping in his hand of ice
> That banner with the strange device,
> Excelsior!

The Latin word *excelsior* implies an incessant striving towards higher attainment, and it struck Liszt with force. For him it symbolized the Christian ideal of "onward and upward," whatever may be the adversities of life that block the way.

[I mourn the dead!
I chase away the plague!
I honour the festive days!]

At one point Lucifer makes a dramatic descent into the depths, enjoining his forces to "sack the house of God, and scatter wide the ashes of the dead!"

Still he is repelled by the clamour of the bells, and with the approaching day Lucifer abandons the struggle. "Craven spirits!" he commands, "leave this labour unto Time, the great Destroyer! Come away, ere night is gone!"

When Wagner first saw the score of *The Bells,* he claimed not to like the work. Liszt had sent an advance copy to Bayreuth, and after a preliminary run-through Cosima had recorded in her diary: "a curious work; done with great effect, but so alien to us."[50] But it is evident that after Wagner had heard it in the concert hall he was struck by both text and music, for elements from both were later to pervade *Parsifal,* the music drama that he had just begun to turn over in his mind as a relief from the rigours of *The Ring.*

After its first performance in Budapest, *The Bells* languished for five years. It was next performed in Vienna, on March 23, 1880, and again Liszt conducted. The work had an unfortunate effect on Eduard Hanslick, who wrote about its "horrible dissonances" and its "agonies of mistreated voices." His critique ended with the words "Music lay slain on the ground, and the Strasbourg bells were ringing out its burial."[51] When Liszt reported on the concert to Carolyne the next day, he told her in a masterpiece of understatement that "Dame Criticism took care to stir some muddy waters into my wine."[52] Although Longfellow was now associated with a highly controversial work, he does not appear to have minded, and remained proud of his connection with Liszt. On the occasion of Liszt's seventieth birthday he gave a large banquet in Boston, and sent the composer a telegramme.

---

50. WT, vol. 1, p. 891.
51. HCCV, p. 276.
52. LLB, vol. 7, p. 279.

Franz Liszt, Rome, Italy

> Illustrious master assembled at a banquet in your honour we re-
> spectfully offer congratulations upon your seventieth birthday.
>
> From: H. W. Longfellow, Lang, Appleton,
> Maas, Miss Cochrane, Sherwood,
> Petersilea, Bendix, Orth
> and 150 others.
>
> Boston, October 21[53]

VII

Liszt left Budapest on April 1, 1875, and routed his journey back to Weimar via
Vienna and Munich, in which latter city he attended a performance of his
Christus on April 12. The work so captured the interest of King Ludwig that
an additional command performance was arranged in the Court Theatre after
Liszt's departure from the city.

Two invitations were waiting for Liszt when he finally got back to the
Hofgärtnerei, on April 13. The first was from his former students Hans von
Bronsart and his wife, Ingeborg Starck. Bronsart, who was now the theatre intendant in Hanover, requested Liszt's presence at a performance of his oratorio *St. Elisabeth* on April 24. Liszt gladly consented. While he was in Hanover
he was also persuaded to take part in a Bach memorial concert on April 28 for
the purpose of raising money to erect a statue to the composer in his native
town of Eisenach. Liszt's solo contribution to the concert was a performance
of his "Weinen, Klagen" Variations. At the end he was joined by Starck for a
performance of his Prelude and Fugue on the name B–A–C–H in the arrangement for two pianos by Károly Thern.

The other invitation came from King Willem III of Holland at the royal castle of Loo, near Arnhem. This art-loving monarch was the brother of Grand
Duchess Sophie of Weimar, and Liszt felt a special obligation to accept. King
Willem had taken to surrounding himself annually with more than a dozen
painters, literati, and musicians, who were then formed into juries to judge
the artistic activities of the king's young "pensioners," as he called them—
scholarship holders who stood on the brink of artistic careers. It was an attempt
to place the arts on the map of his small country. Liszt stayed at Loo Castle for

---

53. WA, Kasten 22, no. 19. Although the telegramme was dated October 21, it was of course already
Liszt's birthday because of the six-hour time difference between Boston and Rome, where Liszt was
then staying.

ten days, from May 2 to 12. His fellow jurors included Ambroise Thomas and Henryk Wieniawski. Between-times everyone joined the monarch for banquets, indulged in animated conversations, and attended concerts and plays at the palace theatre. Liszt admired King Willem and was more than willing to support him in his royal patronage of the arts; besides, this two-week stay in Loo Castle came as a welcome respite from all Liszt's other activities. In his letter of thanks to Liszt,[54] King Willem spoke in glowing terms of his contribution and invited him back to Loo Castle the following year—an invitation Liszt duly accepted.

The next few weeks were tinged with sadness. For much of the early summer Liszt had been preoccupied with the task of organising a memorial concert for his old friend Marie von Mouchanoff, who had died the previous year after a long bout with cancer. Liszt felt that Weimar was the best place to honour her memory, and he assumed personal charge of the arrangements. The concert took place on June 17, 1875, at 3:00 p.m. in Weimar's Tempelherrenhaus. All the works were by Liszt, including his Requiem for Male Voices and the St. Cecilia Legend (1874). The concert also included the première of his First Elegy, in its version for cello and piano, which had been written in memory of Madame Mouchanoff shortly after her death and subtitled "Slumber Song in the Grave." Liszt himself described it as "more for dreaming than for playing."[55]

This is one of three versions of the piece (the others are for violin and piano and for the unusual combination of cello, piano, harp, and harmonium). The cello soloist for the Weimar memorial concert was Bernhard Cossmann.

Although Liszt was based in Weimar for the next several weeks, one would hardly guess it from his itinerary—which took him in turns on brief visits to Sondershausen, Wilhelmsthal, and the Wartburg. In the first half of August he was re-united with the Wagners in Bayreuth, where he attended rehearsals of

---

54. See LBZL, vol. 3, pp. 191–92.
55. WLLM, p. 147.

The Ring.[56] Among his other journeys was one to Leipzig, where he heard parts of his Missa Choralis. The trip was notable for an all-Liszt concert mounted in his honour by Julius Blüthner, the piano manufacturer. Liszt was gratified that this gesture took place in a city where his opponents, in his words, had done him all possible wrong for the past twenty years. The twenty-three-year-old Charles Villiers Stanford, who was at the concert, later put down his impressions of Liszt's piano playing:

> The moment his fingers touched the keys, I realised the immense gap between him and all other pianists. He was the very reverse of all my anticipations, which inclined me, perhaps from the caricatures familiar to me in my boyhood, to expect to see an inspired acrobat, with high-action arms, and wild locks falling on the keys. I saw instead a dignified composed figure, who sat like a rock, never indulging in a theatrical gesture, or helping out his amazingly full tone with the splashes and crashes of a charlatan, producing all his effects with the simplest means, and giving the impression of such ease that the most difficult passages sounded like child's play. . . . He had a magnetism and a charm which were all-compelling.[57]

It is clear that for these rare public appearances Liszt never practised, that he relied largely on his all-embracing memory. His technique was evidently still intact, and the richness and quality of his sound unsurpassed. The thing that mesmerized his listeners was his platform personality, and his ability to draw music from the keyboard without apparent physical effort.

One of his last public engagements for the city of Weimar took place on September 3, 1875, when Carl Alexander unveiled the equestrian statue of his distinguished grandfather Carl August, which still stands in the Fürstenplatz not far from the royal castle. Eighteen years earlier to the day, Carl Alexander had laid the foundation-stone, during the Carl August centennial celebrations, and the vast bronze monument which Adolf von Donndorff had meanwhile erected now dominated the square. As on that earlier occasion, Liszt provided the ceremonial music.[58] In many ways the unveiling of this monument was symbolic of a fact that everyone now recognised: that the shade of Carl August (whose statue was one of the last to be put into place—after those of Goethe, Schiller, Wieland, Herder, and others) hovered over the spiritual and intellectual life of the city. For this we have to thank his grandson, who

---

56. See pp. 346–47.
57. SPD, pp. 148–49.
58. The two pieces in question are the anthems for mixed chorus, brass, and organ entitled "Der Herr bewahret die Seelen seiner Heiligen" (R. 503) and "Carl August weilt mit uns" (R. 562).

all along had pursued his historical mission to turn Weimar into a shrine for the glorious dead.

As the autumn of 1875 approached, the time came for Liszt to leave Germany once more and set out on his annual pilgrimage to Rome. He stopped off in Nuremberg for two days (September 16 and 17) to help Ramann with her biography. As he walked into her study he was amazed to see her desk piled high with his compositions. "Is all that by me?" he exclaimed in disbelief, as he leafed through the pages with great curiosity to check the dates. After the evening meal, Ramann tells us, he sat down at the piano and played far into the night "the music of an entire century" from Bach to Beethoven. She was amazed at his tonal control, and observed that he could make the piano sound like a spinet in a Haydn sonata, while for a D-minor Gavotte by Bach it was as if one heard bagpipes.[59]

Liszt got to Rome on September 19, and shortly afterwards took up residence at the Villa d'Este in Tivoli. On October 22 he celebrated his sixty-fourth birthday on the Via del Babuino with Princess Carolyne and their old friend Adelheid von Schorn, who was on an extended visit to Italy. Afterwards he took Schorn for a long drive round the city in order to show her the various residences he had occupied across the years. For the next few weeks he remained quietly active at Tivoli, trying to concentrate on the creation of religious choral music. But there were heavier matters weighing on his mind. On November 17 he referred in mixed metaphors to "a millstone" around his neck and a "sword of Damocles" hanging over his head. These were the images he used when he told Carolyne that he was having difficulty in accepting the idea that the Royal Academy of Music in Budapest had finally been brought into existence, two days earlier, with himself as president.[60] Even allowing for the fact that he often told Carolyne what she wanted to hear, he knew that the new music academy would increase the burdens of his life. A far truer image, as we shall presently discover, was the one he had already enshrined in his music: "That banner with the strange device, Excelsior!"

59. RL, pp. 54–55.
60. LLB, vol. 7, p. 118.

The Royal Academy of Music, 1875

*I shall fulfill my duty conscientiously and to the
best of my ability, to the benefit and honour of my
country.*

FRANZ LISZT[1]

I

After the Compromise of 1867, Hungary began to determine much of its own
destiny through the Budapest legislature. There was increasing talk of the establishment of a national academy of music, but the matter always aroused dis-
sension and failed to muster the necessary majority. Hungary, it was argued, had
other priorities at this difficult juncture in its history. A low point had occurred
in 1872, when a sum of money that had been set aside for the express purpose
of founding a music academy was withdrawn for reason of economy. And
when this item was put back on the budget for 1873, it was threatened by the
same fate.

The turning-point came on February 8, 1873, when the twenty-seven-year-
old Albert Apponyi delivered a brilliant maiden speech in the Hungarian
legislature which he devoted entirely to the question of a national music academy.[2] Apponyi took the wise precaution of inviting Ferenc Deák ("the grand
old man of Hungarian politics") to hear it. Just before Apponyi rose to his feet,
Deák entered the chamber at the head of his cohorts, took his seat, and turned
very deliberately towards Apponyi in order to make it plain to the other par-
liamentarians that the young man would receive his full attention. Apponyi
spoke with an assured, resonant voice and in a polished style that was unusual

---

1. CLBA, p. 208.
2. "When I entered Parliament in 1872, I found this affair in a very bad way," wrote Apponyi. "I made
up my mind to speak publicly in its favour." (AAM, pp. 66–69)

in one so young. He stressed the importance of music in the cultural life of the people. He reminded his hearers that Prussia spent 500,000 florins a year on music; France spent 300,000 francs on the Conservatoire alone. Could Hungary afford to spend less when its brightest talents were leaving the country in order to study abroad? This loss could not be justified, he argued. A national academy of music must be given priority. There were sustained cheers at the end of Apponyi's speech, and Deák went over to congratulate him.[3] After adding a few public words of his own in support of the idea, Deák seized the opportunity to call a vote on the question of establishing a music academy, together with whatever funds were necessary to run it, and the idea was carried by a very large majority.[4]

On February 10, 1873, two days after Apponyi's speech, Liszt wrote to his cousin Eduard:

> Herewith I send you an extract from the sitting of the Chamber of the day before yesterday, the result of which is almost as unexpected as it is important. The deputies of the conservative party and of the opposition voted almost unanimously in favour of raising the funds for establishing a new *Music Academy*. And an unusual honour was conferred upon me on the occasion—for, although I have never come forward in the matter, it was nevertheless brought forward in my name, and this certainly puts rather a heavy burden upon me. I will endeavour conscientiously to do justice to the honour as well as the burden.[5]

A working committee was established to oversee the safe arrival of the academy. Twenty distinguished Hungarians with a special interest in music and the arts served on this group, which was chaired by Archbishop Lajos Haynald. Not long after the committee convened, however, it was discovered that only a third of the money allocated to it by Parliament was presently available; the rest had been appropriated for the newly formed School of Dramatic Art, under the direction of Count Leo Festetics. This caused much hand-wringing and cast a cloud over the proceedings. A sub-committee of seven members was formed to look at the problem: it consisted of Count Imre Széchenyi, Ferenc Erkel, Kornél Ábrányi, Robert Volkmann, Hans Richter, Ede Bartay, and Liszt.[6] It was clear that the academy would have to get off to a more modest start than

---

3. Apponyi's speech was reported in *Pesther Lloyd* on February 9, 1873.
4. LLC, pp. 171–72.
5. LLB, vol. 2, p. 184.
6. LLC, p. 179. Nor was Liszt's inclusion on the committee a mere formality. He actually attended the meetings. For example, we know that he was present at a meeting called by the Ministry of Education on March 26, 1873—that is, two years before he was nominated as president.

had at first been hoped. One of the committee's more urgent tasks was to find a suitable building. Eventually its choice fell upon a small, three-story house at 4 Fischplatz, which occupied a site on the Pest side of the present-day Elisabeth Bridge. The government would rent this building for six years (1873–79) from the owner, a fencing-master named Friedrich.

In March 1875 Liszt was formally named the first president of the Royal Academy of Music, and a decree was issued by the king. Ágoston Trefort, the minister of education, informed Liszt of his appointment in person, and presented him with the official documents on March 30, the day before Liszt left Budapest.[7] Liszt himself made only one stipulation before accepting: that invitations to occupy professorial chairs should be extended to Hans von Bülow (for piano) and Franz Witt (for choral and sacred music). In the event, neither appointment was realised. Bülow was on an American tour at that time, and when he returned he was disinclined to base himself in Hungary.[8] As for Witt, he was ill and unable to accept. Liszt had also hoped that Hans Richter might be persuaded to teach orchestration, but Richter was tied to Vienna by his conducting contract.

Liszt originally wanted to establish departments in piano, strings, voice, composition, and organ, but because of financial constraints only the piano and composition departments were ready when the academy opened its doors. Since it was understood from the start that Liszt would be able to reside in Budapest for only three or four months of each year, usually from December to April, Ferenc Erkel was appointed to the position of full-time director, a decision that removed much of the administrative burden from Liszt.[9] Other appointees were Kornél Ábrányi (secretary) and Robert Volkmann (composition). On the death of Volkmann, in 1883, the composition courses were taught by János Koessler. In place of Richter, the less effective Sándor Nikolits was appointed to teach orchestration. Liszt himself had already agreed to hold master-classes in piano-playing in collaboration with Erkel. Because of the large number of piano students, Henrik Gobbi was added to the faculty in 1879, together with Erkel's eldest son, Gyula. The string department was finally opened in 1882, headed by Károly Huber. (From 1886, it was taken over by his son, Jenő.) David Popper was to join the string faculty shortly after Liszt's death.

---

7. LLB, vol. 7, p. 94. Liszt told Carolyne that Trefort pressed him very hard to accept—a subtle pun on the minister's name: *très fort,* "very strong."

8. Bülow's refusal had deeper roots, however. By this time he was ambivalent about his entire relationship to Liszt. See p. 145 of the present volume.

9. Despite that, the affairs of the academy were never far from Liszt's thoughts. On December 11, 1878, for example, he wrote from Rome to Kornél Ábrányi, the secretary of the academy, nominating Aladár Juhász, Miklós Almássy, and Ilona Ravasz for the Liszt Scholarship. He also expressed the wish that Juhász should become a professor at the academy. Even though Liszt was hundreds of miles from Budapest, and leading a very different life, his letter proves that he took his responsibilities seriously.

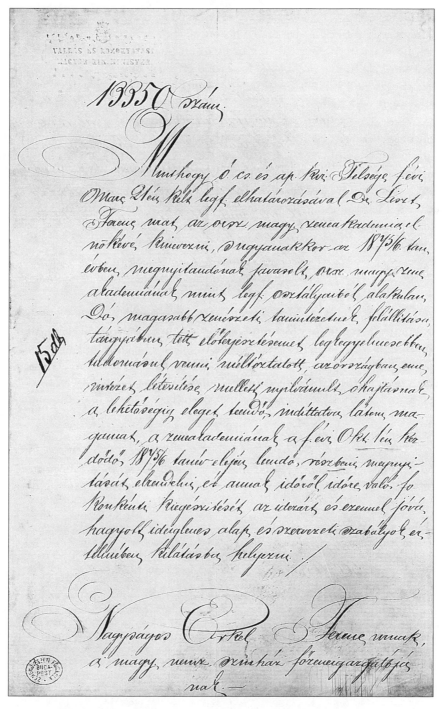

The Royal Academy of Music: a proclamation dated September 5, 1875,
signed by Ágoston Trefort, Minister of Education.

While every other faculty member received a salary, Liszt gave his services to the academy free of charge.[10] The only "fee" he ever received for all the work he did, whether in teaching or in administration, was the free use of the apartment that had been set aside for him on the top floor of the building. Liszt lived there with his new manservant, Spiridon Knežević, whose wages of course were paid by Liszt himself.[11] In the autumn of 1876 he arranged for five large crates of books to be sent from Weimar to Budapest, a collection he eventually bequeathed to the academy.[12] Shortly afterwards, the Hungarian publishing house of Táborszky followed suit and donated four hundred items from its own inventory. And then, a year or two later, the firm of Rózsavölgyi added some volumes of its own. In due course, the royal household sent the academy the monumental editions of both Mozart and Schubert. These gifts formed the basis of the academy's present-day collection.

II

The Royal Academy of Music opened its doors on November 14, 1875. The inauguration ceremony was attended by Ágoston Trefort, faculty, and students. Liszt himself was unable to be present and did not take up his duties until the following February. Ferenc Erkel delivered the opening address. He began by saying how privileged he felt at being named the first director of an institution that would have such far-reaching effects on the musical life of the nation. In fact, he declared, the first courses of the academy had already begun that very day. Then he went on:

> Besides its educational capacities, the Royal Academy of Music has
> an exceptional advantage not given to any similar institution in the

---

10. Erkel's professorial salary was 2,500 forints a year, which was supplemented by a director's stipend of 500 forints. Volkmann received 2,000 forints a year as a full professor, plus a housing bonus of 500 forints. Ábrányi's salary was 1,200 forints, at the rank of assistant professor, while Nikolits received 800 forints. These were generous payments. According to Dezső Legány (LLE, p. 29, n. 17) it was possible to stay in a downtown Budapest hotel in the 1870s for as little as one to three forints a day.

11. In anticipation of his new appointment, Liszt had taken up residence in his quarters as early as 1873. Some of his valuable possessions had already been moved there. To his consternation, when he and Spiridon arrived in Budapest in the first part of February 1875, they discovered that the flat had been robbed. The locks of several cupboards had been forced, and various items of jewellery, silverware, and linen had been taken. The police arrested the thieves and told Liszt they were hopeful of recovering most of the stolen property. Evidently his previous manservant, Miska Sipka, had boasted too loudly to one of his table companions of Liszt's possessions, and had unwittingly turned his master into a target. Liszt told Olga von Meyendorff that the only thing he really wanted back was a silver laurel wreath presented to him in Amsterdam in 1866. (WLLM, p. 183) At this time Miska was in the hospital of San Giacomo al Corso in Rome, where Liszt had left him, and where he was soon to die.

12. *Fővárosi Lapok,* October 7 and 11, 1876.

world. It is the presence of the great compatriot Ferenc Liszt, who has proved on innumerable occasions how readily he serves a patriotic cause. As president and spiritual leader of the Academy, he will become permanently linked to the country, and while in touch with the domestic talent in the field of the highest artistic interpretation and practical instruction, his creative and inspiring flame-like soul will illuminate, first and foremost, the altar of Hungarian art.[13]

For the first year of instruction, about seventy students had applied to the academy, and after an entrance examination thirty-nine were chosen. The age of those selected generally ranged from nineteen to twenty-four years, but some students were much younger: Olga Vaszilievits, József Weisz, and Margit Kun were only twelve years old at the time of their acceptance. The placement test itself was difficult, and became more so with the passing years. Fourteen-year-old Julia Bauholzer played Beethoven's Sonata in C major, op. 2, no. 3, while thirteen-year-old Eugénia Müller played Mendelssohn's Rondo Capriccioso. By the time that Béla Szabados applied to the academy, in 1881, at the age of fourteen, the examination had become highly structured. According to the boy's own account, given many years later, Erkel allowed the candidate to play a piece of his own choice. Erkel then set a piece for sight-reading, and whoever could not play it fluently was turned away. The ones who survived this ordeal were then subjected to an improvisation test by Volkmann. He would play a few measures on the piano several times; the candidate then had to repeat it from memory and improvise a continuation. Succesful candidates were enrolled as students. The unsuccessful ones were sent on to Gyula Erkel and subjected to one last trial: an unfigured bass, which he wrote on the blackboard, and which the student had to harmonize at sight. The ones who failed were shown the door.[14]

The generally high standard of piano-playing during the early years of the academy's existence can be explained by the fact that a number of the students had already completed the six-year piano course at the Pest Conservatory of Music, an institution that had been founded thirty-five years earlier, in 1840, with money donated in part by Liszt.[15] The relationship between the conservatory and the academy was always close, and the difference between the two might be defined in modern terms as undergraduate versus graduate education.

In the early days of its existence the academy's teaching faculty were expected to work very hard. This was particularly true in the case of Ferenc Erkel, who, in addition to his duties as the director, was obliged to accept a very large

---

13. *Zenészeti Lapok,* November 25, 1875.
14. LLE, p. 33.
15. See Volume One, p. 332.

number of piano students: by the third year he already had twenty-two, and by the fourth, more than thirty. He repeatedly called for an assistant, but this was denied him until the academy went into its new building on Sugár Street in 1879. Meanwhile, Erkel was expected to teach Liszt's students as well whenever Liszt was out of town. This caused him much frustration. It could not have been easy for someone of Erkel's stature to work in Liszt's shadow. This gifted composer and conductor had built up an enviable reputation as director of the National Theatre, where many of his nationalistic operas had been performed— including *Hunyadi László, Bánk bán,* and *Bátori Mária.* In 1875, he was sixty-five years old (a year older than Liszt), and he did not take kindly to the drudgery of teaching for so many hours a day. The academy robbed him of many opportunities to compose. And when confronted with students who wanted to transfer to the more glamorous environment of Liszt's classes—or, worse, a reluctant one who had worked with Liszt on repertory that he was now forced to bring to Professor Erkel for comment—what could poor Erkel do?

III

Liszt's apartment had been comfortably furnished for him, and he was able to do his private teaching there also. The windows on one side commanded a splendid view of the Danube, on the other a view of the Budapest parish church, where his music had so often been performed in the past, and where his good friend Mihály Schwendtner was the pastor. Now that the two men were neighbours, they often walked over to one another's homes to socialize. In fact, Liszt regularly held at-homes for his friends, colleagues, and pupils, which were an extension of the ones he gave in Weimar and Rome. Count Albert Apponyi, a frequent visitor, left a memoir of those occasions.

> Liszt then had a modest flat on the Fischplatz, which has completely disappeared in the course of town-planning. In the evening I would often meet a little group of friends there from the Budapest world of music. Sometimes they had come to supper, which at Liszt's always consisted of cold dishes, and which he called "cold treatment." There were always stimulating and instructive conversations. In the course of them, Liszt would often take his seat at the piano, perhaps to illustrate his words, and the enviable members of that circle would hear fragments of Beethoven or Mozart sonatas played in the most spontaneous manner, untrammelled by any thought of a public. Those were real courses in musical history. It was understood that we should not ask Liszt to play. Whoever did so, fell from grace and spoilt the atmosphere of the whole evening:

it had to be done at his own suggestion. I was a constant guest at
those gatherings, where I felt, to a certain extent, like Saul among
the prophets. Other famous artists used also to come there, musicians who had visited Budapest to pay their respects to Liszt, even
if they were not giving a concert. These naturally took an active
part in the musical performances, but they all sat as pupils at Liszt's
feet, and listened to his every word as if it were the saying of an
oracle. Among them were some of the greatest—Rubinstein,
Paderewski, and among famous violinists, Wieniawski and others.[16]

And Apponyi goes on to tell us that Liszt's own Hungarian pupils were often
present at these musical gatherings. "Liszt was plagued by talented and untal-
ented musicians, for the gift of ridding himself of the failures was never his."

IV

Liszt's teaching activities in Budapest fell into a somewhat different category
from those in Weimar, because as president of the Royal Academy he was supposed to be part of a wider curriculum, whether he liked it or not. Although he
himself had helped to set up that curriculum, he often chafed at the resulting bu-
reaucracy. He usually got to Budapest with only a few days to spare before the
winter term began, and there was often some uncertainty surrounding the exact
date of his arrival. His students therefore tended to register for their lessons as late
as possible, which caused some administrative headaches. In 1884 the Ministry of
Education issued a decree (no. 5672, February 13) to the effect that any student
who wished to enroll in Liszt's masterclasses must henceforth pay a registration
fee of thirty forints, to be settled in advance in the director's office, on pain of
exclusion from the curriculum. Liszt did his best to evade what he took to be
"administrative meddling" in his private activities. The academy yearbook for
1885–86 reported that the fee for that school term could not be collected "because the Maestro's students were declared by him to be his private students, and
as such they had been taught by him in his own apartment." This simple plan
also protected those of his foreign students who regularly followed him to Budapest and might otherwise have been charged for taking their lessons in the
academy building. Liszt could be forgiven for not recognizing the difference,
since his private apartments were actually inside the academy. Nor did Liszt's cir-
cumvention of the regulations end there. Many students continued to work with
him long after they had received their diplomas and were no longer required to
take lessons. Whoever they were, however, Liszt taught them all free of charge.

---

16. AAM, pp. 69–70.

There were also other sensitive issues arising from his work at the academy which set it apart from his teaching in Weimar and Rome. The two main piano teachers were Ferenc Erkel and Henrik Gobbi. Over the years they were responsible for the training of some formidable talents. Yet it was generally understood that once the student had reached a certain level, he or she would enter Liszt's masterclass. This meant that neither Erkel nor Gobbi ever received proper credit for their training, and they were perceived by some to be Liszt's assistants. The issue was a difficult one, especially since Erkel and Gobbi taught at the academy year-round, while Liszt was in residence for only three or four months. It could have led to an impossible situation had it not been for the dignity of the parties. It was tolerated because everyone knew that Liszt occupied a unique place in the history of piano playing, and that his presence in Hungary persuaded many local talents to enroll at the academy who might otherwise have pursued their training abroad.

The experiences of three of his academy students can stand for those of the others. Stefánia Forster entered the academy in 1880 when she was eighteen years old, and after working for two years with Gobbi she won a scholarship and was introduced to Liszt.

> He smiled at me benignly and kissed me on my brow. He sat on my right and asked me what I was to play. I was so confused that I opened my music but did not even glance at it. I played his *Au bord d'une source* from the *Années de pèlerinage.* My hands trembled so much that I hit several wrong notes with my left hand. When he saw that, the Maestro sat down and played two pages of the composition for me, so as to let me hear the tempos in which he wanted me to play it. After that, I listened to the playing of several of his students (I liked Bernhard Stavenhagen's performance. He was a smart looking blond youth of relaxed posture . . .) and after playing several pieces I thanked [Liszt] for being so kind as to listen to me and wanted again to kiss his hand; but he kissed me on my left cheek and bade me "Au revoir, mein Kind, baldiges Wiedersehen."[17]

Julia Bauholzer was still in her mid teens, and well on the way to becoming a polished player, when she auditioned for a place at the academy by playing Beethoven's Sonata in F minor, op. 2, no. 1. She was at once accepted as a pupil of Ferenc Erkel. After taking an accelerated programme of studies she became one of the youngest students to graduate, and included in her graduation recital Liszt's Second Hungarian Rhapsody and *Mazeppa*. During the course of her studies she was taken to a reception given in Liszt's honour. After she was in-

---

17. PLF, p. 56.

troduced to Liszt, he and Erkel each grasped her by the hand and went up to Count Apponyi, to whom Erkel remarked: "This is the girl about whom the Maestro and I argue. To whom should she belong?" The argument was evidently settled in Liszt's favour, and Julia became his student.

> How he appreciated and valued individual interpretation! On one occasion he let me play twice in a row his *Liebestraum* No. 3 saying: "Auf allgemeines Verlangen" [By popular request]. He was interested in the manner I played it, and afterwards he noted: "Sie haben eine ganz eigenartige und selbständige Auffassung, es ist viel Geist darin" [You have an entirely original and independent interpretation, and there is a lot of spirit in it]. On another occasion he acknowledged a well-executed passage in Schumann's *Etudes Symphoniques* as follows: "Servus! Kindchen, das nenn' ich gespielt" [Well served! Child, I call that played]. . . . When he sometimes demonstrated or played something, it was always a true revelation. Under his hands one could recognize neither the piano nor the piece, it appeared so magical. The softness of his touch—even in powerful playing—the variety of its colours, its astonishing expressiveness, bordered on the miraculous. There is no appropriate epithet to characterize the performance. He made all the beauty and value of a musical work understood by the listener; it acquired, so to speak, plasticity in front of us.[18]

Of special interest are the recollections of Ernesztina Kramer, who was Liszt's student for three years, from 1882 to 1885. Ernesztina had been an infant prodigy, and by the time she was ten years old she was a student of Erkel at the academy. The day dawned when she, like others before her, was introduced to Liszt. He asked her to play something, and since she had been specialising in the music of Schumann, he suggested one of the latter's sonatas. Nervous and trembling, the poor girl lost her composure and started to play the sonata a semitone high. Liszt did not interrupt her, but let her continue in the wrong key to the end of the piece. The girl then noticed what she had done and cried out: "My God! How unfortunate I am! I can play anything in any key, and that is what happened here." Liszt consoled her and said: "My child, thousands would be happy to be so unfortunate."[19]

---

18. PLF, pp. 41–42.
19. PLF, p. 73. Interview in *Pesther Lloyd*, October 18, 1932. Anyone who is even slightly familiar with the problems of piano-playing will appreciate how unusual was Ernesztina's natural ability to transpose at the keyboard. To do this kind of thing consciously usually requires years of work. To do it unconsciously, and for the length of an entire piece, suggests a natural (if undisciplined) talent at work.

On one occasion, Ernesztina brought a prelude and fugue by Mendelssohn
to the class, but she had no sooner begun it than Liszt interrupted her with the
words: "Can you read? It says here 'Allegro con fuoco' and you perform it in
a sentimental style!" "I learned it this way from Professor Erkel," replied Ernesztina defensively. "Ah!" growled Liszt. "Get up!" He then took her place at
the keyboard and played the entire piece—*con fuoco.* It was an eloquent reply.
The episode symbolized for Ernesztina the fact that Liszt and Erkel did not always agree on certain things. As she put it years later: "With Erkel I was a
Musikantin, but with Liszt I became a *Musikerin.*"[20]

Often when Ernesztina arrived for her lessons she would find a number of
Hungarian dignitaries in the same room—such people as Cardinal Lajos Haynald, Bishop Konstantin Schuszter, Bishop Lőrinc Schlauch, Count Géza
Zichy, Nándor Táborszky, and János Dunkl—who had gathered in the hope of
hearing Liszt play the piano and hold forth about music. No wonder that Ernesztina called Liszt's music classes "improvised house concerts" and his lessons
as "not so much piano instruction as remarks of the highest order about music
and musicians, or about some interesting artistic subject."

Ernesztina reminds us that Liszt was not above "playing the pedagogue" and
that he used to encourage his students to adopt a quiet posture at the keyboard.
If anyone kept moving his body to the left and right, in time to the music, he
would remark: "You 'metronomize,' just like the great Clara," a reproof of one
of Clara Schumann's mannerisms. At times he did not even allow the head to
nod back and forth, and would firmly hold the student's chin with his hand
during a performance. For the rest, the degree of contact that Liszt allowed
himself, particularly with his female students, sometimes caused comment.
There was much stroking of the hair, kissing of the cheeks, and embracing of
the entire person.

> My sister was watching all this [wrote Ernesztina], and could not help
> wondering. Of course, once we got home there followed the epi-
> logue. [My family] could not grasp what was happening: so many
> pretty girls and all in love with such an ugly old man? But his pupils
> were overjoyed if he only cast a glance at them, let alone commend
> one of them and kiss her upon the brow or cheek for recognition. . . .
> Now, half a century later, it is possible to think of, speak about, and
> judge this Liszt-kiss in many ways, but it is certain that we, his pupils,
> carry the memory of it for life as the greatest distinction.[21]

---

20. In German, a *Musikant* is someone who has acquired a lot of information about music, whereas a
Musiker is someone who feels it naturally and plays from the heart.
21. PLF, pp. 78–79.

For Liszt it was perfectly natural to express physical tenderness towards his students, male and female alike, for he regarded himself as their psychological father and often referred to them as "my children."

V

It has often been said that Liszt did not really want the position of president of the academy, that it was thrust upon him by his powerful Hungarian friends who saw in this appointment a way to "bind him to the country." Moreover, so the argument goes, Liszt feared that the job would be a drain on his time and energy at a stage in his life when he needed both for composition. After all, he was sixty-four years old and stood on the brink of old age; he suffered easily from fatigue, and he had permanent commitments in Weimar and Rome which involved him in travel. To add Budapest to his responsibilities was asking too much of him.

These are persuasive arguments, and they do not end there. Liszt's correspondence with Princess Carolyne contains a number of statements from him which voice his concern about getting drawn into the affairs of the academy; indeed, he had once referred to this institution as "a rope around my neck."[22] When considering this question, it is important to remember one thing. Liszt was always cautious when dealing with Carolyne; on all the important issues about which they disagreed his language was usually designed to placate her. Carolyne, in fact, was opposed to Liszt's plans to spend so much time in Budapest because she feared that a permanent commitment to the academy would take him away from Rome and, by implication, from her. She described the academy as "a swindle." "[Liszt] has become a *piano teacher* there," she exclaimed sarcastically. "A great and wonderful occupation indeed!"[23] Liszt was entirely familiar with her views and wrote to her accordingly.

Perhaps the most powerful arguments that he himself mustered against the founding of the academy are to be found in his letter to Ödön Mihalovich dated December 8, 1874, just two months before he received the king's nomination. There he asserted that (a) Hungary's precarious financial situation did not augur well for such an enterprise; (b) it would be better not to do it at all if it could not be done as well as in Vienna and Leipzig; and (c) the local difficulties, while minor, complicated matters unnecessarily.[24] But in the end Liszt's deeds spoke louder than his words. Once he had been appointed presi-

---

22. LLB, vol. 7, p. 9. August Stradal had also created much mischief when he asserted that the only reason that Liszt accepted the presidency was to keep his annual stipend of 4,000 forints that had been paid to him by the Hungarian government since 1871. But this stipend acknowledged his rank as a Royal Hungarian Counsellor and had nothing to do with the academy appointment. (SE, p. 45)
23. EKFL, p. 76.
24. LLB, vol. 2, pp. 214–15.

dent of the academy, he put the best of himself into the job. His final position is summed up in a letter he wrote to Baron Antal Augusz: "I shall fulfill my duty conscientiously and to the best of my ability, to the benefit and honour of my country. In all this, any fatigue or personal inconvenience I suffer are of no account: the only thing that matters is to do what must be done, the way it should be done, without bias or faltering."[25]

V I

After six years of existence, the academy had grown too large to conduct all its activities at no. 4 Fischplatz. The original idea had been for the government to buy this house and carry out some renovations, such as the addition of a small concert hall. But as the academy developed, and more and more students enrolled, the plan was shelved in favour of a more ambitious one: namely, the erection of a new, and much larger, building. An architect was hired, one Adolf Láng, and a prominent site was chosen at no. 67 Sugár Street. This building was opened in 1879, and like the first one it incorporated an apartment for Liszt's exclusive use, this time on the first floor.

In this building, too, the teaching activities of the academy were greatly expanded. To the faculties of piano and composition were now added those of singing, organ, and strings. This was the place in which three of Hungary's greatest musicians were to be educated: Dohnányi, Bartók, and Kodály. Less than twenty years after Apponyi's impassioned speech, his main goal had been realised: it was no longer necessary for the most promising Hungarian musicians to seek their fortunes abroad. The academy remained at Sugár Street for twenty-six years, after which it moved to its present location at Liszt Ferenc tér, in 1907. By then it was recognised throughout the world as one of the leading institutions of its kind; and since it contains what is still the best concert hall in Hungary, it remains the centre of much of the country's musical life. As for Liszt, his efforts were formally acknowledged by a grateful nation when the new building was re-named the Franz Liszt Academy of Music.

---

25. CLBA, p. 208.

The Last Years of Marie d'Agoult

I'm beginning my Mémoires *here. They will be
the Sword of Damocles over the heads of my
friends! Watch out, all of you!*

MARIE D'AGOULT (1865)[1]

I

Any attempt to re-write the life of Liszt must inevitably involve some small re-adjustments to the life of Marie d'Agoult as well. The sanitized version that came down to us[2] has long been in need of revision, for it contained certain features that could not be squared with reality. Some of her autobiographical utterances, in fact, are demonstrably false and may well have started out as fiction.[3] Many of the archival documents that might have served as a corrective to the narrative of her life—letters, diaries, scrapbooks, sketches, itineraries, and

---

1. VLR, p. 276.

2. Provided in large measure by Marie d'Agoult herself, first in her *Souvenirs* (1877) and then in her *Mémoires* (1927).

3. Consider Marie's novella *Episode de Venise,* with its later incorporation into her *Mémoires* as "fact" and the transformation of fictional characters into real ones. We devoted some attention to this difficult question in Volume One, pp. 259–63. Since that time, it has emerged that Marie also used another novella, entitled *Palma,* which relates the first years of her meeting with Liszt in fictional form. *Palma* (the pseudonym for Marie herself: Liszt is called "Walther") appears to have been written in the mid 1840s, possibly as a preliminary sketch for the novel *Nélida,* and some twenty-five years before the *Mémoires* themselves. (See DMSJ, pp. 257–65.)

When the *Mémoires* first appeared, more than fifty years after Marie's death, they were hailed as a remarkable and long-overdue "corrective" to the official account of her ten-year liaison with Liszt, between the years 1834 and 1844. It occurred to few people at the time to question their veracity, although we now know that there was good reason to do so. The *Mémoires* omit much that Marie d'Agoult wanted to hide from the world. The fact that they tarnished Liszt's image at the same time was considered on the whole to be a good thing, since this restored some balance to his life at a time when the figure of the "saintly" Liszt had come to dominate the literature.

the like—did not become available for general scrutiny until after World War II. By then it was the printed word that had beguiled posterity.

After Marie d'Agoult and Liszt went their separate ways, in 1844, her professional career had blossomed, despite the material difficulties she had encountered on her return to Paris. The rapprochement with her family, the Flavignys, one of the oldest dynasties in France, had been her chief concern, together with the delicate question of how she and they could live down the scandal of her elopement with Liszt. Later she had for years been tormented with the obstacles Liszt had placed in her way with regards to the upbringing of their three children. It is not our intention to traverse this familiar territory once again, since the ground has already been covered in earlier volumes. Yet there is one dark corner of it that deserves some illumination, because it explains much else that happened in Marie's subsequent life. After the death of her mother, Viscountess Marie-Elisabeth de Flavigny, in 1847, Marie had every expectation of receiving one half of the family fortune, the other going to her brother, Maurice. Instead, Marie had found herself involved in a long litigation as her brother fought for a greater share of the estate, a litigation that lasted for several years and which she lost. This simple fact explains many of her later problems, to which were added those of her daughter Claire. After the breakup of Claire's marriage to Count Guy de Charnacé, who had reduced the family coffers to naught by a reckless business investment, Claire had procured a legal separation from him in May 1855. The dissipation of the substantial dowry that Marie had settled on Claire at the time of her marriage to Guy in 1849, together with the sale of the family château at Croissy to settle some of the count's debts, had caused many difficulties for both mother and daughter.

That Madame d'Agoult had in the early 1840s no ambition to become a journalist, art-critic, and historian, let alone achieve prominence as a writer under the pen-name of "Daniel Stern" or any other, is borne out by something she wrote some years later in her *Mémoires:* "If [Liszt] had been what he should have been, I would have remained with him. My name would never have emerged from obscurity."[4] By the same logic, if she had remained with her husband, Count Charles d'Agoult, and had never become enamoured of Liszt in the first place, her obscurity would have been still more complete. The fact is that Madame d'Agoult had good reasons for wanting to credit Liszt with her "lack of obscurity." Her subsequent career, which attracted European attention, was an attempt to redeem what would otherwise have been the wasteland of her years with him. That was a noble effort for which she deserves praise. And the more prominent she became, the more the world was reminded of how it all began. Doubtless there were times when Liszt would have preferred her to fall back into the obscurity she had enjoyed before he met her.

---

4. AM, p. 184.

But life was not about to allow him to draw the veil of oblivion across their early years together. They were now too prominent for that.

One of the major surprises about Marie d'Agoult, and one that stands at odds with the received image of marbled beauty, lofty intelligence, and calm control that she presented to the outside world, was that she suffered all her life from suicidal tendencies. She succumbed to periodic outbreaks of uncontrollable violence, which not only put those in her vicinity at risk but also placed Marie herself in harm's way. Her behaviour lends a new meaning to her own famous description of herself as "six inches of snow covering twenty feet of lava."[5] On at least two occasions her physician Dr. Emile Blanche had to place her in a straitjacket, as much to protect her from herself as to protect those close to her.[6] The knowledge that suicide ran in her family (her nephew Léon Ehrmann had failed to drown himself when he jumped into the Seine, but her half-sister, Augusta Bussmann, had greater success when she threw herself into the Mainz) could not have helped her self-confidence, and it doubtless fed her lifelong fears that she was being pursued by demons that would drive her to the same fate—a belief that runs like a leitmotif through her private correspondence.

II

As early as 1832 Marie had been treated for mental illness by Dr. Jean-Charles Coindet when she was on a trip to Switzerland with her husband and their elder daughter, Louise—a piece of information that has only recently become available to us. While they were in Geneva the countess became suicidal and wanted to throw herself to her death. She was restrained by her frightened husband, who cried: "They will say that it is I who killed you!" Dr. Coindet admitted her to the city hospital, where her stay was sufficiently long to oblige Count d'Agoult and Louise to leave her behind and return with their servants to Paris.[7]

These suicidal depressions were frequent, and they were often followed by long periods of lethargy; in fact, "lethargy" hardly describes the trance-like stupor which overcame her and rendered her incapable of any activity—a condition that Marie feared might be mistaken for death and result in her being buried alive. She left instructions in her last will (1875) that Claire was to confirm her death before burial. As early as 1848 she had become a patient of Dr. Blanche, who regularly admitted her to his private clinic on the rue Berton in

---

5. AS, p. 349.
6. See OASE, pp. 151–52, and OJ, vol. 2, p. 362.
7. The confirmation of Marie's hospitalisation comes to us from her younger daughter, Claire, who tells us that her father had to restrain her mother from throwing herself into the river. (DMSJ, vol. 2, p. 288, n. 76)

Passy. One morning, not long after the death of her mother had plunged her into an emotional crisis, she suffered an attack of madness. Dr. Blanche found her in a fury, scratching and biting her chambermaid. She was taken to Passy in a straitjacket, where she was treated for "nerves."[8] Until we gain access to Blanche's medical notes, we may never know his final diagnosis of Marie's condition, or how he treated her. But the endless cycle of depression, lethargy, and remission, followed by more depression, makes compelling reading.

At first Marie described her symptoms as "spleen," a romantic appellation for melancholia. On June 26, 1857, for example, she told Charles Dollfuss: "I have been invaded by my mortal enemy, spleen. Since my earliest youth, when it appeared to me in the form of suicide, up to the present day when it slides into me surreptitiously, without naming itself, it has never given up making me its prey."[9] And she told the same correspondent on February 26, 1860: "The past year has been cruel for me. One could say that the disturbing force which has shaken my soul so violently and clouded my youth still has not finished its job of devastation."[10]

But with the passing of time it became clear to everyone that what was happening in Marie's tortured brain could not be described by such a term. During the period March to June 1863, Marie was confined to Blanche's clinic for treatment, but her "demons" gave her no rest. In September of that same year her old friend Juliette Adam describes a violent scene with Marie as symptoms of madness.[11] But it was in 1867 that her illness took a dramatic turn. One morning she had the horses harnessed to go for a drive. Upon reaching her destination she dismissed her coachman and went for a solitary walk along the Seine. When she failed to return, the servants raised the alarm but did not know where to look for her. Some hours later she got back to the house in a dishevelled state, without her coat, and out of breath from running. She was agitated and incoherent but managed to convey that she had been fleeing from

---

8. OASE, pp. 151–52. Louis de Ronchaud tells us that this little drama was repeated at more or less regular intervals. Dr. Blanche and informed friends were not upset by it, and the poor woman was locked up, treated, and when her faculties returned, resumed her social life with the same verve, as if nothing had happened.

Emile Blanche ran his clinic in collaboration with his father, Dr. Esprit Blanche, who was a noted physician for the treatment of the insane and wrote a standard work on the topic called *Du Danger des rigueurs corporelles dans le traitement de la folie* (Paris, 1839). Emile Blanche, who was not only a compassionate physician but also Marie's friend, became a member of the intelligentsia who frequented her salon in the 1850s and '60s. He had graduated from the Faculty of Medicine in the University of Paris in August 1848 with a thesis on "The Force-Feeding of the Insane by Catheter." What emerges from this study, beyond the clinical detail, is a genuine concern on Blanche's part not to harm or otherwise abuse his patients—a notable advance on the work of most of his colleagues in the field of mental health, who often brutalized the patients under their care.

9. VLR, pp. 111–12.

10. VLR, p. 141.

11. ASS, vol. 3, pp. 135–37.

the police for fear of being arrested. Her friends concluded that she had made an unsuccessful bid at suicide.[12] By 1868 her condition had become much worse. She sought refuge at the home of her friend Louis Tribert, at Puyraveau, but lay prostrate for days, seized by a terrible lethargy. When she was able to leave the house for short journeys, the coachman was obliged to stick to the wide roads, for she began to experience acute panic attacks whenever he turned into the narrow country lanes—a symptom of claustrophobia. The interesting thing is that Marie was able to observe her own symptoms—to watch herself losing her mind—for in calmer moments she recorded them.[13]

The climax to this catalogue of woes came in 1869. In April of that year Marie woke up raving mad. The commotion was so great that the neighbours summoned members of the family. When Maurice de Flavigny and Guy de Charnacé arrived at her home, the scene they witnessed was such that she was placed in the regulation straitjacket and transferred to Dr. Blanche's clinic. In her delirium Marie was obsessed with the thought of being cut up alive by the surgeon's knife. Her agitation turned to horror when her pious sister-in-law Mathilde (who had turned up in the company of Maurice) attempted to have the last sacraments administered.[14] Marie pushed her head violently back and forth (the only part of her body not constrained), as if to deliver blows against her imaginary adversaries. Claire de Charnacé intervened to moderate Mathilde's behaviour and reassure her mother. Claire, who had accompanied Marie to Blanche's clinic, stayed with her for a while before returning to Versailles. The scene was also reported by Emile Ollivier in his *Journal*.[15] Marie's fear of the surgeon's blade was not entirely the result of a fevered brain. While she was in Blanche's clinic he was obliged to operate on her for the removal of carbuncles.[16] As a direct result of this dreadful experience Marie became fearful not only of losing her reason permanently (and of therefore being denied the right to direct her own affairs) but of having her funeral presided over by a Catholic priest—a state of affairs which, as she herself put it, would have undermined the intellectual position of free thought that she had adopted throughout her entire adult life, and for which she was now widely admired.

---

12. DMA, pp. 292–93.

13. In a letter to her old friend Adolphe Pictet, she told him that her attacks were heralded by "gradual loss of sleep, loss of appetite, total languor, extreme tiredness, repulsion for work, nervous agitation during which I change my character, become angry, make wounding remarks, am filled with all sorts of terrors, haunted by the demon of suicide." The only remedies that she had discovered, she went on, were fresh air and silence. (DMA, p. 293)

14. Mathilde de Flavigny (née Montesquiou-Fezensac) appears to have been one of those doggedly devout individuals whose day's work remains undone until they have saved a soul from damnation. She had written a number of tracts on Catholic morality that must have filled the free-thinking Marie d'Agoult with dread.

15. OJ, vol. 2, p. 362.

16. DMA, p. 360.

In brief, she did not wish to leave her friends with the impression of a bedside conversion. This episode was a foretaste of death, and she learned from it. She subsequently gave instructions to Claire to ban all Catholic priests from her funeral.[17]

As soon as Marie was able to leave Blanche's clinic, in the spring of 1869, Louis de Ronchaud took her to his house at Saint-Lupicin in Jura, where she began a long convalescence. It was interrupted by the discovery of a breast abscess, which brought her back to Paris to consult a doctor. Although the tumour was benign, the stress told on her, and she had another mental relapse. Again Louis Tribert took care of her, as in the previous year. The doctor in attendance noticed that the slightest incident, however trivial, could plunge the patient into terror.

We may be sure that evidence of the kind that we have just reviewed represents but a small fraction of the observed incidents of Marie's erratic behaviour. These were the public crises, but there would have been many private ones which will probably never find their way into the literature. Maurice de Flavigny, Guy de Charnacé, and Emile Ollivier were unimpeachable witnesses to her sad decline, but they were usually called in when her violent conduct was already creating a spectacle. What was her behaviour like when her illness was supposed to be in remission, when she had as it were returned to "normality"? If we require testimony about her daily life, when much of what she did was hidden from the world's scrutiny, then her daughter Claire de Charnacé can provide it. Claire, who lived with her mother for long periods at a time, kept a diary from which we learn that she herself became convinced of her mother's madness as early as the winter of 1860–61.[18] The diary entry for that particular period includes a scrap of notepaper in Marie's hand on which are scribbled incoherent messages. Claire later observed that she had planned to destroy this piece of paper. "If anyone saw it, I said to myself, they would think that my mother was mad."[19] Claire herself relates how she came by it. Around New Year's Day, 1861, she and her mother were staying in Nice, occupying adjoining bedrooms. "That morning," wrote Claire, "she opened the communicating door and appeared in her nightdress, her eyes wild, with this piece of paper in her hand, saying to me with an anguished expression (mental, not physical): 'I cannot speak, read it.' I felt strangely afraid . . . that she intended to throw herself out of the window, and I put my arms around her

---

17. "I give you the absolute right to oppose a Catholic priest being brought to my bedside." (Charnacé Archives F 859, carton 1, unpublished letter dated July 18, 1869) These instructions were later embodied in Marie's will (1875), and Claire carried them out.

18. Charnacé Archives, F 859, carton 11, unpublished. Dark red notebook with entries which begin on February 12, 1855. On the inside cover is written the phrase "Unpublished and incommunicable documents."

19. Ibid., p. 36.

gently and led her to her bed."[20] The paper in question contained nothing but vague ramblings and a request that Claire give her some eau de Cologne, a supply of which Marie already possessed. Years later, Louis de Ronchaud said that he too had received such notes. In 1867, according to Claire, and presumably while she was still in Blanche's clinic, Marie used to address her nurses and servants as "tu," while Claire herself was addressed in the third person—forms of communication that Claire was not wrong to call "strange."[21] Claire also added that her mother was obsessed with selectively burning some of the things that she had written. "It was always with the idea of posturing for the public, to get the public interested, to arrange her past."[22]

"To arrange her past . . ." That is a common enough desire, especially among writers who have left a lot of it lying around. The story of Madame d'Agoult's life took her an unconscionable time to write, and Claire is doubtless correct when she implies that it passed through flame and fire before the sanitized version of which we spoke at the beginning of this chapter achieved a readable form. But Marie could not consign to the flames what others knew about her and preserved for posterity. In any case, such matters raise a question of fundamental importance to any biographer of Liszt: Was Liszt himself aware of Marie's mental instability? He never talked about it, much less wrote about it. Yet we are confident that he knew, although he may not have realized the extent to which it would one day devastate her life. After all, he lived on terms of intimacy with her for the better part of ten years. It would be unthinkable that she would not have confided her suicidal tendencies to him during that time, for she had certainly confided them to others. And there had been a number of occasions when the scenes between them, involving verbal violence, must have given him pause to reflect on the character of the woman with whom he lived.

When the pair eloped to Switzerland, in the spring of 1835, one of the first people to join their circle of friends in Geneva was the same Dr. Coindet who had admitted Marie to hospital there just three years earlier. It is hardly possible that she could have kept the circumstances of that first encounter from Liszt. An even more difficult question arises from such considerations: Is this why Liszt, after ten increasingly desperate years, after the true nature of Marie's volatile and unpredictable mood-swings had impressed itself upon him, "abandoned" her (to use her language)? To that we can give an unequivocal reply. The contemporary evidence shows that it was actually Marie who finally broke off the relationship, in April 1844, and refused to see him again.[23] She

---

20. Ibid., pp. 37–38.
21. Ibid., p. 38.
22. Ibid., p. 45.
23. The letter in which she dismissed him is dated "April 1844, at Paris." ACLA, vol. 2, p. 337.

was doubtless right to do so, given the depths to which their relationship had by that time sunk. But posterity must regard that final rupture as a godsend for Liszt. If the pair had stayed together, Marie's subsequent history suggests, his existence could well have been filled with the daily anguish of those condemned to watch their closest companions walking with phantoms.

III

In 1871, fearing that her hold on life was at best uncertain, Marie had named Louis de Ronchaud as her literary executor. This was a wise precaution, since during her long life of literary activity Marie had amassed many valuable manuscripts, letters, and papers from a large variety of distinguished people. Nonetheless, the existence of a letter from her to Ronchaud repeating what was already in her will suggests that she was apprehensive about her future.

Geneva, March 1, 1871

To Monsieur Louis de Ronchaud [her underlining]

Dear Friend,
    If I were prevented through illness from taking care of my affairs, I want what I ask for in my will to be done: that is, that all my papers, manuscripts, correspondence, notes, etc. should be given to you to dispose of as you see fit. These are my express wishes.
Countess d'Agoult[24]

The choice of Ronchaud as her literary executor was no accident. She had first met him in the mid-1830s, when he was barely twenty years old, and he had followed her and Liszt around Europe with dog-like devotion.[25] After her permanent return to Paris their acquaintance had ripened into a firm friendship, and Ronchaud became her confidant, travelling companion, and general factotum. She often turned to him at times of personal stress, and during the 1860s she was a frequent guest at his home in Saint-Lupicin. It was there, in fact, that she returned to her *Mémoires* and also worked on her *Souvenirs,* which are dedicated to Ronchaud.

---

24. Hitherto unpublished. NAF 16440 f. 7.
25. See the *Letters of a Bachelor of Music* that Liszt addressed to Ronchaud from Italy in the autumn of 1837. The one from Bellagio begins: "When you write the story of two happy lovers, place them on the shores of Lake Como." (RGS, vol. 2, p. 172; CPR, p. 164)

IV

It would be wrong to assume that Marie d'Agoult succumbed without a struggle to her physical and mental indignities, exhausting though they were. She
fought back with the best weapons at her disposal: she continued to write, she
cultivated a wide circle of friends within the arts and sciences who regularly
gathered in her salon, and she travelled extensively. Her chief scholarly work,
written during the early 1850s, was the three-volume *Histoire de la révolution de
1848,* widely regarded as the definitive book on this subject. Then came her
historical dramas *Marie Stuart* (1855) and *Jeanne d'Arc* (1857), and her *Dialogues*
on Goethe and Dante (1866). As for her friends, they included Louis de
Ronchaud, Ernest Havet, Louis Tribert, Juliette Adam, Emile de Girardin,
Théodore de Banville, Henri Bouchet, Félix Henneguy, and Louise Ackermann. During the Second Empire, in fact, Marie's salon became well-known
as a centre for the Republican opposition party. One of its political newspapers
came to life there (the *Revue de Paris*), and the founder-editors of two others
were often to be seen in her circle (Adolphe Guéroult of *L'Opinion Nationale*
and Auguste Nefftzer of *Le Temps*). She had a variety of addresses during those
years; but wherever she happened to be located, her presence acted like a mag-
net on the brightest and best in Paris. After her main home, La Maison Rose,
was demolished in 1857 to make way for the new boulevards being driven
through Paris by Georges Haussmann, she moved to the avenue de l'Impératrice. Later she lived on the rue Circulaire near the Arc de Triomphe. And from
1869 she lived on the rue Malesherbes, where she died.

Marie's salon was regularly graced by her daughter Claire, who proved to be
almost as brilliant a hostess as her mother. Louis de Ronchaud often observed
Claire in Marie's salon, where she managed to keep "a distinct personality beneath her daughterly affection and deference" and aroused admiration with
her lively conversation, "which came from an independent and alert mind."[26]
Claire soon discovered that she had a taste for literature and art, and like her
mother before her she began to write under a *nom de plume,* "C. de Sault."[27]
Her first article, about the German architect Gottfried Semper, appeared in *La
Presse* in October 1856. Between the years 1861 and 1870 she published more
than fifty articles of art criticism in *Le Temps*.

Everyone who observed Madame d'Agoult at this time commented on her
dignity, sharp intelligence, and natural charm. Her low, harmonious voice had
become a vehicle for the expression of serious philosophical reflection. Louis

---

26. SEM, p. 54.
27. "Sault" was the name of one of the estates of the d'Agoult family.

de Ronchaud talks of her "natural majesty to which no one refused to pay homage."[28] To some of the younger personalities in her group Marie was now an establishment figure, with direct links to a glorious past, including Goethe. By the mid-1850s Marie's golden hair had turned snowy white, a fact of which she was at first unduly conscious, since she thought it made her look prematurely aged. Yet the contemporary photographs of her reveal a woman of commanding beauty and striking personality. Years of close reading and writing gradually weakened her eyesight, and she consulted oculists, who provided reading-glasses her vanity did not always allow her to wear.

Travel became a chief source of comfort. Every summer she set out for such places as Brittany, Switzerland, Italy, and Germany. This was not merely to escape the rigours of daily life in Paris, nor even to find a better climate for her increasingly precarious health. Those who knew her well realized that she was overcome by nostalgia, and that her trips to Geneva, Florence, Turin, and Nonnenwerth were an attempt to re-live her past, and in particular that part of it she had shared with Liszt. Her face was often bathed in tears at the recollection of their earlier visits to these old haunts. As late as 1862, eighteen years after her final rupture with Liszt, we find her writing in her diary that she is pre-occupied with him and thinks of him constantly.[29] These journeys into the past acted as a therapy on her ravaged emotions, and they prompted her to resume work on her abandoned *Mémoires;* the first part (which she had begun in 1836) was finished by 1866.[30]

Her travelling companion on many of these trips was Louis Tribert, a senator, whose knowledge of art and literature was unrivalled. He had long been an habitué of Marie's salon, and he eventually became one of her literary executors. According to Ronchaud, he was a traveller by vocation, "who preferred the dust of the highway to the ashes of the fireside."[31] Marie valued Tribert's familiarity with languages, and she was stimulated by the erudite stream of conversation that flowed from him during their visits to castles, churches, museums, and ruins. The closeness of their relationship is evident from the fact that in her will she left to Tribert half her furniture and books.

It gave her tremendous pleasure to see her former son-in-law, Emile Ollivier, catapulted to high office in the French legislature. He had begun life as her protégé and she had followed his rising political star with close attention. When he became prime minister of France, in 1870, she had no compunction about asking him for a number of political favours, including the Cross of the Legion of Honour for Dr. Emile Blanche.[32]

---

28. SEM, p. 54.
29. VCA, pp. 229–30.
30. The second part of the *Mémoires* was begun in 1866, but never finished.
31. SEM, p. 29.
32. OAAL, pp. 104–05.

The Franco-Prussian War, and with it the political downfall of Emile Ollivier, was a difficult experience for Marie. Yet she had foreseen the conflict for some time. To another young protégée, Juliette Adam, she wrote: "I am afraid that we are going to have a horrible war in our United States of Europe; and I will add that in my opinion . . . the Empire is lost."[33] She was correct on both counts. To be sure, it was the downfall of Napoleon III and the Second Empire that she as a lifelong Republican had always sought; but if the cost of achieving that goal was another bloodbath in France, then the price was too high. She had always stood for internationalism in her intellectual work, and really believed that the pen was mightier than the sword. That is why, in 1858, she had been delighted to collaborate with two youthful journalists, Charles Dollfuss and Auguste Nefftzer, in the creation of their new magazine, *Revue Germanique,* for which she wrote a number of articles. Marie herself was half German and half French, and when the war finally came she was torn. But not for long. Her ancestral ties to Germany were not so strong as her cultural ties to France. She rallied to the cause, like many other prominent Republicans, and expressed her bitterness at the defeat of the French army and the subsequent siege of Paris and the horrors of the Commune. Marie did not have to endure the ordeal of starvation, unlike many of her friends who remained behind in Paris. She was staying in the home of Louis de Ronchaud at Saint-Lupicin when the war broke out. In November 1870 she moved to Divonne and then settled for a while in Geneva. She wrote two powerful articles against Bismarck under her pseudonym Daniel Stern, which appeared in *La Liberté* and *Le Journal de Genève;* and she also dealt with the question of the republic versus the monarchy in *Le Temps.* It probably frustrated her beyond endurance to receive letter after jingoistic letter from Cosima gloating over the defeats of the French and glorifying the Prussians. Cosima was by now so thoroughly imbued with Wagner and German nationalism that she even likened the war to "a Beethoven jubilee." Beethoven had been born on December 17, 1770, a preponderance of the number seven. War had been declared on the seventeenth day of the seventh month of the year 1870. "I only hope to God that there is a lucky seven in all this!" To which Wagner added another mindless comment: "War is something noble."[34]

Cosima's attitude must have made a rapprochement with her mother difficult, but a rapprochement nonetheless took place. In the spring of 1871 Marie received an invitation from Cosima to visit Triebschen. Cosima had not seen her mother for seven momentous years, during which time her life had undergone a complete transformation. She was apprehensive at first about whether Madame d'Agoult would even bother to make the journey, let alone approve of her recent marriage. Her diary reveals something of her agitation. The entry for

---

33. HGL, p. 217.
34. WT, vol 1, p. 246.

March 23 reads: "The day passes in preparations for my mother. I sort out papers and read old letters from my father, which show me once again that I had neither a father nor a mother."[35] Marie arrived the following day and stayed at Triebschen for ten days. Cosima need not have worried about her mother's blessing, which had never been in doubt. Marie had always been ambivalent towards Hans von Bülow, whom she had once called "a little man," and she had never approved of his marriage to Cosima, which had gone ahead without her consent. Besides, Wagner fascinated her, and this was her first real chance to get to know her new son-in-law. She and Cosima spent much time reminiscing. Cosima confided to her diary that she felt "very strange towards her, but she is pleasant company because of her wide education."[36] Although the one topic on which they could not agree was the Franco-Prussian War, and the recent humiliation of the siege of Paris, this did not prevent Cosima from delivering herself of the opinion that the French had brought it largely on themselves. One wonders what Marie thought, as she sat there listening to a tactless performance of Wagner's *Kaiserlied* sung by his children in her honour. It did not seem to have occurred to either Cosima or Wagner that her mother was at that moment an exile from France, and that many of her friends were either starving in Paris or were prisoners of the Prussian army. Cosima's thoroughly Prussian outlook, in fact, distressed Marie, but she tried not to let it destroy her new-found relationship with her daughter. Her grandchildren Isolde, Eva, and Siegfried delighted her, and her enthusiasm for Wagner and his music increased daily. She got Hans Richter (who was also a house-guest at Triebschen) to play a number of Wagner's things at the piano. She could not fail to observe how contented both Cosima and Wagner were in these peaceful surroundings. And the striking parallel between her own life and that of Cosima did not escape her. Cosima had abandoned husband, hearth, and home to be with the man she loved. She had borne him illegitimate children. She had endured the slings and arrows of an offended society. In the eyes of the world she was now the chief muse of a composer of genius. Cosima was indeed the daughter of her mother. What were Marie's feelings as she saw her own shattered ideals being redeemed by her daughter? Before she left Triebschen she told Cosima that it was the life that she herself had always dreamed of.[37] On April 2 Marie departed for Geneva. As Cosima embraced her mother for the last time, she said that she felt as if all the sorrows of the world had overcome her.[38]

---

35. WT, vol. 1, p. 351.

36. WT, vol. 1, p. 352.

37. TBCW, vol. 1, p. 72.

38. WT, vol. 1, p. 353. Note that this rapprochement with her mother came at a time when Cosima had had no dealings with her father for two years because of the Bülow-Wagner scandal. Marie d'Agoult may have derived some small satisfaction from knowing that she had moved back into Cosima's orbit at a time when Liszt had moved out of it.

Whatever peace Marie d'Agoult had found at Triebschen did not last long. Only a few weeks after her reunion with Cosima, she became ill again and suffered a violent attack of "spleen." Cosima's diary contains the terse entry: "Letter from Claire, my mother has become deranged again"[39]—a sentence that speaks volumes and tells us that Cosima was quite familiar with her mother's fight against mental illness. Marie travelled to Puyraveau in search of peace of mind, but to little avail. She would be pursued by her "phantoms" for the rest of her life. As her end drew close she received a number of reminders of her mortality. In 1873 her brother, Maurice, passed away. Despite their many differences, she found the breaking of this "dear link" horrible.[40] Two years later, in March 1875, her husband, Charles d'Agoult, died at his modest lodgings on the rue du Colisée, in his eighty-fifth year. That was an even more severe loss to her; even though they had not lived together for many years, she retained a lifelong affection for him. In the letter she wrote on April 5 of that year from which we have already quoted she eulogized him and confirmed that "I wear mourning for him with respect."[41] By November 1875 her life was again darkened by depression and we find her meditating in the Montmartre cemetery;[42] the dead at such times seemed to offer her better comfort than the living.

V

Marie d'Agoult died on March 5, 1876, of pulmonary disease, after a short illness. Louis de Ronchaud was at her bedside when she passed away. A photograph was taken of the body on its deathbed before it was placed in the coffin.[43] The funeral took place two days later, on March 7. A large group of mourners gathered in Marie's drawing-rooms at 38, rue Malesherbes to pay their last respects and to hear the funeral oration delivered at her express wish by a Protestant pastor, M. Fontanès, president of the Consistory of the Reformed Church of Le Havre. The cortège then wended its way to the cemetery of Père-Lachaise, where the body was interred in a temporary vault until the permanent monument which today marks her grave could be erected.[44] It was a mark

---

39. WT, vol. 1, p. 383, diary entry dated June 29, 1871.
40. VLR, p. 282.
41. VAMA, p. 16. See also Volume One, p. 205.
42. Diary entry for November 2, 1875.
43. DMA, facing p. 193.
44. The monument, designed by the French sculptor Henri Chapu, won a Medal of Honour in the Exhibition of 1877. It depicts "Thought," in the poetical words of Louis de Ronchaud, "rising from its veils like dawn and radiating the pure glow of beauty." (SEM, p. 101) On the tombstone are engraved the titles of all those literary works—*Essai sur liberté, Esquisses morales,* and *Nélida*—through which the name of "Daniel Stern" is best remembered. The carved figure of Goethe gazes down in admiration at her idealized form. Goethe, who had once placed his hands on her head as a child, now

of the respect in which she was held by the literary world that her pallbearers included the historian Henri Martin, Baron de Viel-Castel, and both Alfred Mézière and Charles Blanc of the French Academy. The mourners included Louis de Ronchaud, Emile Blanche, and Michel Lévy and Emile de Girardin, respectively the publisher and the chief editor of *La France*. On the day of the funeral Madame d'Agoult's obituary notice appeared in *La Presse*.

> We regret to announce the death of Mme la Comtesse d'Agoult, who died yesterday morning, after a chest infection which progressed very rapidly.
>
> Mme d'Agoult, aside from the position she occupied in society, had gained another, no less important one in the world of letters, under the pseudonym Daniel Stern; she had made for herself the most distinguished name. She was seventy-one years old.
>
> Her literary début goes back to 1841. She contributed to the *Revue des Deux-Mondes,* the *Revue Indépendante,* the *Courrier Français, Le Temps,* and *La Presse.*
>
> Her claim to fame, her lasting work, is her *Histoire de la Révolution de 1848.*

Knowing that her end was not far off, Marie had drawn up a fresh will in December 1875:

The Last Will of Marie d'Agoult

This is my Will   Paris,
                                                    10 December 1875

> Thinking myself predisposed to long states of lethargy, I beg my daughter and the people present at my last moments to have the most careful precautions taken to confirm death.
>
> In the event that I have not given in my lifetime to Madame Cosima Wagner the forty thousand francs I have promised her, I hereby bequeath them to her officially, making a special request to my daughter Claire d'Agoult, Comtesse de Charnacé, to acquit this sacred debt.[45]

---

appears to give her his benediction in death: a touch of vanity perhaps, but one which no one who reviews the contribution Marie d'Agoult made to the intellectual life of the Second Empire would begrudge her.

45. It will be recalled that Madame d'Agoult's non-payment of Cosima's wedding dowry, in 1857, had been the cause of great tension between her and Liszt. See Volume Two, p. 439, for a summary of this affair. Marie's will makes clear that the matter was still outstanding in 1875.

I bequeath to Daniel Ollivier, in memory of his mother, my literary property, under the express condition not to publish anything from my works without the collaboration and express authorisation of my two friends Louis Tribert and Louis de Ronchaud.

I give, without any preconditions, to my friend Louis de Ronchaud, all the papers, manuscripts, notebooks, diaries, which are at my home after my death. I except a copy of my *Mémoires* which forms part of the legacy of literary property given to Daniel Ollivier.

I give and bequeath to Louis Tribert and Louis de Ronchaud to share as they see fit my books and furnishings, except the souvenirs which will be discussed.

Having been born into the Protestant religion and having been raised in the Catholic faith, without being consulted, and contrary to the law on mixed marriages agreed to by my parents, I ask that a pastor of the Protestant sect called Nonconformist, Mons. Fontanès, Mons. de Magnier, pastor in Rotterdam, or any other in their absence, be requested to accompany my remains to the cemetery and to say a few edifying words.

I enclose here the list of objects I wish to leave as mementos to various people.[46]

Signed:

MARIE DE FLAVIGNY,
COMTESSE D'AGOULT

An inventory of all Madame d'Agoult's household and personal effects was carried out on the initiative of Claire de Charnacé on March 26, 1876, in the presence of Marie's lawyer, Félix Morel d'Arleux.[47] From an examination of this inventory it is clear that she was not particularly wealthy at the time of her death. The value placed on her personal effects was just over 26,000 francs. There were as well approximately 20,000 francs in shares and bonds, most of

At the moment of Marie's death, Cosima was in Berlin with Wagner, and she learned of her mother's passing from the newspapers.

46. No such list of legatees was found attached to the will (hitherto unpublished), and Claire signed a release to that effect. From documents filed together with the will, it emerges that Madame d'Agoult was given the right to receive a war widow's pension of 975 francs per annum following the death of Count Charles d'Agoult in March 1875, although she may not have collected it. The count had been twice wounded during the Napoleonic wars: the first time was when he received a sword cut on September 19, 1812, in Spain; the second was when he led a cavalry charge against Russian infantry at the Battle of Nangis, on February 17, 1814, and was shot in the left leg. He also had a horse shot from under him during the latter battle. For these and other military exploits he was eventually made a Commander of the Legion of Honour on September 22, 1823.

47. The meticulously detailed document (which runs to more than forty pages) may be consulted in the Archives Nationales: call no. cx, 1064.

them issued by the Paris Gas Company and the Paris-Lyon-Méditerranée Railway Company; and a further 25,000 francs from investments in the state of Virginia. The figures prove that she must have inherited less from her own mother than we have generally been led to believe. Indeed, she used to observe ironically that her brother, Maurice de Flavigny, had "arranged matters well" in this regard.

And what of Marie's "sacred debt," the payment to Cosima of her long-postponed wedding-dowry? This sum was paid three months after Marie's death, and twenty years after it had been promised. There is an unpublished document in the Bibliothèque Nationale, a legal contract between Claire and Emile Ollivier, that throws a ray of light on this vexed question.[48] It will be re-called that when Cosima and Blandine had married, in 1857, Marie had promised them each a dowry of 40,000 francs. This money was not at first forthcoming, and the matter became a sore point between Marie and Liszt, who had himself agreed to put up matching sums for his daughters. Eventually Marie had managed to set aside a capital sum of 80,000 francs, the interest on which she regularly paid out to them. The capital, however, remained under her control. Although Blandine had died in 1862, her son, Daniel, was legally entitled to the dowry, and his lawyer father, Emile, now came forward to look after his interests. Because of the modest circumstances in which Marie had died, Claire was unable to find significant capital to pay both dowries. The contract between her and Emile authorised her to pay Cosima the sum of 40,000 francs immediately[49] and to pay him (as the fourteen-year-old Daniel's guardian) twenty-five percent of all future royalties from Marie d'Agoult's published writings, an arrangement made all the more logical by the fact that Marie had already left some of her literary papers to her grandson, which could one day be published and yield still further income. The incentive for Claire to agree to this arrangement was simple: she was to receive the remaining seventy-five percent of the royalties. There is little doubt that Claire needed the money. She was not a direct beneficiary of Marie's will for the obvious reason that she had received the bulk of Marie's patrimony at the time of her wed-ding to Count de Charnacé. The fact that her husband had left her living in a

---

48. NAF 16440. Contract signed by Emile Ollivier and Claire Christine d'Agoult, Comtesse de Char-nacé, and dated "June 17, 1876, Versailles." See also the letter that Ollivier wrote to Carolyne von Sayn-Wittgenstein on this subject, less than two weeks after Marie d'Agoult's death. (TOS-W, p. 146)
49. As early as November 1869 Cosima had pressed her mother for payment of this debt. It was at the height of the Bülow-Wagner entanglement, and she needed money. Marie could offer her daughter nothing but a dignified reply, in which she told her that she had asked her brother, Count de Flavi-gny, to try to arrange matters in Cosima's favour. (See Marie d'Agoult's unpublished letter to Cosima dated January 14, 1870, in the Richard Wagner Archives, Bayreuth.) The Franco-Prussian War fol-lowed soon afterwards and prevented all currency transactions. Later Marie declared herself unable to discharge the debt during her lifetime. That explains why she had made it a priority in her will.

condition of genteel poverty must have made Ollivier's proposition all the more attractive to her.[50]

Liszt learned about Marie's death from the newspapers. He was in Budapest, teaching at the newly opened Academy of Music. What were his thoughts at the passing of his old lover? After doubtless silently contemplating the turmoil, confrontation, and bitter quarrels that had characterised their ill-starred relationship across the years and had left lasting scars on both of them, he delivered this blistering verdict to Carolyne:

> Barring hypocrisy, I could not bring myself to weep any more after her passing than during her lifetime. . . . Mme d'Agoult had a great liking, nay, a real passion, for falsehood—except at certain moments of ecstasy, which she subsequently could not bear to remember!
>
> Moreover, at my age condolences are as embarrassing as congratulations. *Il mondo va da sè*—one lives one's life, occupies oneself, grieves, suffers, makes mistakes, changes one's views, and dies as best one can! The sacrament most to be desired seems to me to be that of extreme unction![51]

To Emile Ollivier he delivered a softer (and perhaps more truthful) response: "The memory that I retain of Mme d'Agoult is a secret sadness; I confide it to

---

There was an unexpected coda to this saga. Shortly after Cosima received her money, the first Bayreuth Festival was mounted, in August 1876, and almost immediately incurred a large deficit. Cosima's "wedding dowry" went to settle some of the bills. The entry in Cosima's diary for March 14, 1878 (WT, p. 59), makes a glancing reference to this matter.

50. This was surely one reason why Daniel Ollivier waited so long before publishing his grandmother's *Mémoires,* to say nothing of her correspondence with Liszt. Not until his aunt Claire died, in 1912, were many of the legal constraints removed with regards to what he could and could not do with the material. Moreover, Claire's rights in the matter would have passed to her son Daniel de Charnacé, who did not die until 1942.

51. LLB, vol. 7, p. 131. "Extreme unction" was also his response to a suggestion of Carolyne's, sent to him a day or two earlier from Rome, that he should have "a lot of masses" said for Marie. Until now, Carolyne's response to the death of her nemesis has gone unrecorded. In a letter to Liszt, preserved in the Weimar Archive, she told him: "[Countess d'Agoult] ended by renouncing her God, to die like an animal, without hope and without a priest! Poor, poor soul!" (WA, Kasten 48, u. 1) And a month or so later she added:

> I have received a few private details about the sad end of Mme d'Agoult. It seems that her raving madness[es] had left her a year ago, and they thought that she was cured. When one fine day she was so violently seized by them again that she died—perhaps she strangled herself? In any event, what a horrible end! Ah, let us pray for her—how she must repent bitterly now her faults and mistakes! The chest infection and the Protestant minister were for the sake of decorum! They say that Cosima learned this news from a Berlin newspaper . . . the poor child. (Letter dated April 24–27, 1876. Hitherto unpublished. WA, Kasten 48, u. 1)

God, and beseech Him to grant peace and light to the soul of the mother of my three dear children."[52]

He was unable to mourn. Whatever passion Marie had once aroused within him had long since been extinguished. He had not seen her for ten years, and during their last conversation in Paris he had told her of the "poses and lies" that her forthcoming *Mémoires* would represent. He had buried her then in his mind. Her actual burial now was but a formality for him.

---

52. LLB, vol. 8, p. 309.

"External Weaknesses—
Interior Causes"

*The great burden of my old age is to find myself op-
posed to you in my opinions. It was not like that
from '47 to '62!*
LISZT TO CAROLYNE VON SAYN-WITTGENSTEIN[1]

I

And what of Marie's nemesis, Princess Carolyne? A comparison between the
two ladies is instructive and deserves attention. If Liszt was fortunate to have
escaped the misery of a permanent bondage with Marie d'Agoult, it was nothing short of providential that he was prevented from putting on the yoke of a
marriage to Carolyne. Carolyne may not have been suicidal, but her behaviour
was at times very bizarre; she would have made him an equally difficult companion. Even Lisztians who are otherwise favourably disposed towards her are
hard-pressed to know why he maintained their friendship after the débâcle of
the wedding service. Merely to ask the question, however, is to show scant
knowledge of the depth of the relationship. The lives of Liszt and Carolyne
continued to be connected at a hundred different points. Consider the purely
material factors. Their wills named each of them as the other's chief beneficiary; moreover, in Liszt's case Carolyne was his executrix.[2] Carolyne had always managed Liszt's financial portfolios, and that continued: much of the
money he had invested with Rothschild's in Paris, and with Eduard Liszt in
Vienna, had been sent there at Carolyne's instigation in order to protect their
future. Nor should we forget that many of Liszt's personal effects—pianos,
books, ornaments, paintings, manuscript collections, etc.—were still in storage

---

1. LLB, vol. 7, p. 171.
2. As late as 1879 we find Liszt writing to Carolyne: "I have never thought of withdrawing or alter-
ing this will—when death comes to me I shall add to it my last blessing for you!" (LLB, vol. 7, pp.
245–46)

in Weimar, where the rent continued to be paid by Carolyne. These ties could have been undone, of course, but the fact that they were not speaks volumes. Liszt and Carolyne were comfortable with the legal provisions they had made while planning their marriage. The fact that they would now never celebrate their nuptials changed nothing, for they trusted one another implicitly. And if the material ties were strong, the emotional ones were still stronger. The mutual respect and affection that had withstood the trials of the Weimar years, to say nothing of the machinations of the Hohenlohes, were still in place, as the correspondence confirms. It was not merely a sense of duty that prompted Liszt to visit Carolyne whenever he was in Rome, to live near her and often take his meals with her, but a genuine desire to see her again and share the remembrance of things past. She remained close to the centre of his moral and ethical outlook, and he to hers. The pair by now had formed a union that survived every crisis of their old age, even the most serious.

Carolyne continued to live in Rome, on the third floor of Via del Babuino 89, an address she had occupied since shortly after the days of the wedding fiasco. Here she allowed her many eccentricities full play. Thick velvet curtains were perpetually drawn against the daylight, and the gloomy interior was lit by flickering candles. No fresh air was allowed to penetrate the apartment for fear she might catch a chill. Her visitors were kept waiting in the anteroom until they had been "de-ventilated," and the cold air trapped inside the folds of their garments had gradually warmed up to the temperature of the room. Only then was her bearded footman allowed to usher them into the Presence. And what a presence it was! Carolyne has been likened to a spider sitting in the centre of its web awaiting its prey, her visitors. She harangued them on a wide variety of subjects—theology, politics, history, and philosophy—matters on which she could more than hold her own. She dressed in multi-coloured silks and wore a small bonnet from which streamers of ribbons in all the colours of the rainbow flowed down to her waist, enhancing the image of threads in a web. It was only towards the end of her life that she switched to black and covered her shoulders with a shawl—the picture that posterity prefers to remember. Her tobacco-stained fingers were rarely without one of her long, specially made cigars, from which she inhaled heavily in order to sharpen her concentration. (A separate essay could be written about these cigars, which were of the Minghetti type, double the length and double the strength of ordinary ones, and said to have been dipped in iron-filings to give them a powerful metallic taste.) A bowl of chocolates stood on a nearby table and she frequently munched them whenever she was not smoking. A grand piano was positioned by one wall, the lid open, the mute keys waiting to be stroked into life whenever Liszt was there. Pictures and busts of Liszt adorned every room—icons to the memory of their lost life together—which evidently assuaged some of the pain. From this heart of darkness there emerged the first, faint glimmer of her psychological salvation. Carolyne became obsessed with canon law, and she began to fill her rooms with theological tomes over which she pored incessantly. The occasional visitor took away a memory of walls and corridors lined with volumes, like a library. There were even piles of books stacked around the bed—a place in which she sometimes liked to read and write. The atmosphere was claustrophobic, and many a guest must have left the Via del Babuino gasping for breath in the hot Roman summer, eyes watering from the princess's exhalations.

This familiar picture is not false, but as far as the early days are concerned it is not complete, either. Carolyne was not at first the recluse she later became. She often went out by carriage on shopping expeditions, to attend mass in the church of San Carlo al Corso, to visit the Vatican, or to go to various galleries and exhibitions. She was a frequent visitor to the Villa Medici, whose director, Antoine Hébert, liked to invite her to his receptions. But the princess never left Rome.[3] Even in the summer, when others departed from the Eternal City to escape the heat, Carolyne sought a change of air simply by moving up one floor to the fourth level of Via del Babuino 89, which she imagined to be cooler. Gradually, however, she abandoned her social activities, withdrew into herself, and concentrated her energies almost exclusively on her work. Her eccentricities made her vulnerable; in December 1868 thieves broke into her apartment and stole some of her jewelry. They also took away some of the orders and decorations which Liszt had left with her for safe-keeping.[4]

Some of the best images of Carolyne in old age come from Dora Melegari, who tells us that she first met Carolyne in Rome when the princess was fifty-seven years old—that is, in 1876. When Pius IX died, she went into mourning for him and wore a long black crepe veil, which covered her bonnet and went down to her feet. She was quite oblivious to the ridicule to which this strange apparel exposed her, for she thought it natural to pay her respects to the dead pontiff in this manner. It was to Pius that she attributed the "miracle cure" of her failing eyesight. By the mid-1870s, in fact, Carolyne's eyes had become so weak that she could no longer read and write without difficulty. One day, she attended a papal audience at the Vatican with several other people. As the pontiff came close to her, she was seized by a sudden impulse. She took his two hands in hers and said: "Holy Father, I suffer so much with my poor eyes! You must cure me." She then placed his hands on her eyelids for a few moments and Pius IX gave her his blessing. That evening, after she had returned to her

---

3. The only exception was a short visit she once made to the Villa d'Este. Cardinal Hohenlohe had invited her to spend a summer there. She left after twenty-four hours, claiming it was only in the Via del Babuino that she found the atmosphere right for her work. (LLB, vol. 4, p. xix)

4. The police arrested no fewer than twelve people in connection with this robbery—one or two of them directly concerned with the theft, and the others with receiving goods they knew to have been stolen. The matter is documented, together with the names of the suspects, in the Vatican Secret Archive under "Rubrica 93, Anno 1870." (HLC, pp. 262–63 and note)

apartment, she picked up a newspaper and read it without difficulty. "Since then," she told Melegari, "I have been cured."[5]

Among Carolyne's more peculiar ideas was the notion that her living room was filled with benevolent spirits. They kept her company, she said, and prevented her from becoming lonely. Once, when she attended mass at Sant' Andrea delle Fratte, she saw clouds of angels fluttering around her.[6] Such images do not flatter Princess Wittgenstein; they made her an easy target for her critics.

The German writer Richard Voss visited Carolyne in Rome in 1877 and came away with the impression that she was not only a convinced Catholic but a convinced spiritualist as well. Voss also reported that Carolyne felt that she was surrounded by "ghostly visitants"; she regularly conversed with them and also introduced them to her earthly visitors. It is difficult to imagine the fretted feelings of her callers who sat in her darkened rooms at Via del Babuino while the names of the departed were announced to them "with ecstatic cheerfulness." "Unlike the living," Voss adds ironically, "whom she received one at a time, the dead were allowed to come to her *in corpore*. . . ."[7]

II

It was in these airless, darkened rooms that Carolyne did most of her voluminous writing. She loved painting and sculpture, and her first extended essay was on the Sistine Chapel. Later came such books as *Buddhism and Christianity,* and *Practical Conversations for the Use of Society Ladies.* But then she fell under the spell of canon law and began to write almost exclusively on theological subjects. There is circumstantial evidence that she published more than forty-five volumes in the twenty-six years she spent in the Via del Babuino, but that evidence is clouded by the fact that Rome had no commercial publishing houses, and she printed many of her titles privately at her own expense, often in limited editions which have meanwhile vanished.[8] In 1870 she began her monumental *Causes intérieures de la faiblesse extérieure de l'Eglise en 1870*—a work which eventually ran to twenty-four volumes and which she managed to complete just before her death, in 1887. Today the book is known largely for being known.[9] We shall only come to understand this strange work if we regard it as

---

5. MAL, p. 185.
6. MAL, p. 192.
7. VAPL, pp. 95–97.
8. Nonetheless, we have assembled a list of fifteen titles in Appendix IV, some of them containing a number of different volumes, whose authenticity can be confirmed.
9. Copies of *Causes intérieures* are extremely difficult to locate. The Library of Congress acquired one in 1965 which had originally been in the personal library of Cardinal Gustav von Hohenlohe. It may be consulted in the Rare Books Division of the library under the call number BX 1751. S19. See also Appendix IV, where the structure of the book is described in detail.

a gigantic rationalisation of Carolyne's differences with the Church. To express it another way, it was really a therapy for her to write it, an attempt to seek release from the pent-up frustrations which still lingered from her battles with the clergy. Its main point is that the Church had made a grave historical error in not coming to grips with modern society and in not taking a lead in shaping it. Dogma, canon law, Church history, politics, and morals are all a part of the provocative mixture. The book is dedicated "to all Christian believers," a challenging phrase. Her great model was Lamennais, one of the Church's most celebrated outcasts.

Although the book was published anonymously, it got Carolyne into difficulty with the Church hierarchy, and two of its volumes were placed on the *Index Librorum Prohibitorum*.[10] Several people had seen this coming, including Emile Ollivier and Liszt himself. Ollivier warned her that she had gone too far: "It is Lamennais's brand of Catholicism and you will be put on the Index."[11] By February 1877, when the threat of official sanction had become imminent, Liszt told Princess Marie Hohenlohe that he regretted not having warned Carolyne more emphatically about where she might be heading at the time of the Vatican Council in 1869–70, but "I wasn't able to combat her arguments."[12] As early as May 1873, Liszt had spoken candidly to the princess about her latest work. He told her that the title was "almost rash," that the book was not op-

---

10 One need read no further than Carolyne's preface to understand the provocative nature of her words. She informed her readers that Jesus ("the Man-God"), who founded the Church, had not entrusted it to angels but to imperfect human beings "who can never do a good deed without involving a bad deed in it." The weaknesses of the Church, she went on with that stubborn determination so typical of her thinking, are therefore the result of human error and can be cured. The "cure" was what the twenty-four volumes were basically about.

11. TOS-W, p. 106.

12. HLSW, p. 213. The correspondence between Carolyne and Liszt makes it clear that by 1877 their relationship had declined to the level where she was reluctant to reveal to him any part of her work-in-progress before it was published, and he chided her more than once about her secretiveness in the matter. He had always included Carolyne in his own work and he could not understand why she now wished to exclude him from hers. In the event, this was a blessing for him; he was a bystander to the misfortune that descended on Carolyne's book. On April 26, 1877, he told her: "Formerly, in better days, in Weimar and even in Rome, you were more generous towards me, and did not entrench yourself in a sort of Thabor, inaccessible to fools of my kind!" (LLB, vol. 7, pp. 190–91) And on July 14, two days after Volume Five had been placed on the Index, he wrote to her: "As you have excluded me from your almost superhuman work for the past ten years, because of my ignorance and unworthiness, I do not dare speak to you about it any more." (LLB, vol. 7, pp. 197–98)

It was Liszt's decision to leave Rome in 1870 that lay at the heart of Carolyne's exclusion of him from her intellectual life. It was the only way she could think of to punish him for what she regarded as a kind of desertion. "Since '70 what has happened?" she cried out despairingly to Baron Augusz in March 1877. "What is Liszt doing, far away from me, since the time that his letters began to resemble a correspondence that one would be prepared to drop?" She knew that her missives often upset and agitated Liszt, and she confessed to Augusz that she had become embittered by the thought that Liszt would rather not hear from her. "But," she went on, "I have not promised God to be nice to him, I have promised to be useful to him." (From a letter dated March 27, 1877, National Széchényi Library, Budapest, shelf mark Li-II)

portune when one considered the sort of people who now surrounded the pope and rightly thought that the business of running the Church belonged to them. And he told her bluntly: "Since you have the additional misfortune of being a woman, you must resign yourself in this case to the role of silence which St. Paul imposed upon your sex."[13] Doubtless the advice was well-meant, but Carolyne was not about to heed it. In any case, her book was already at the printers. On July 18, 1873, the first two volumes were delivered to Weimar, and Liszt accepted reality. "*Eljen, Hoch et Vivat,*" he exclaimed, "to your volumes of nearly a thousand pages each!"[14] At first the work attracted praise from liberal clerics such as Gustav Hohenlohe and the famous Munich theologian Ignaz Döllinger (to whom she had sent copies), who remarked that it contained so much learning that "only someone who had studied the history of the Church in depth could understand it."[15] But Liszt himself remained deeply concerned. In an attempt to influence the future direction of her thinking, his letters to Carolyne ran the whole gamut of praise, criticism, flattery, irony, and caution. He urged her at least not to send the book to clerics, to keep the circulation confined to friends—all to no avail. Carolyne's intellectual obsessions had become a form of sickness, and the patient could not be cured. The axe fell on July 12, 1877, when Pius IX signed a decree which placed Volume Five on the *Index Librorum Prohibitorum*. This was the book that dealt with the nature and the constitution of the Vatican Council.[16] Carolyne refused to heed warnings from either friend or foe and ploughed on with her work. The axe fell again on February 3, 1879, when Volume Three—in which the princess had delivered some unwelcome opinions on the methods whereby the clergy elected themselves to higher office—joined its companion on the Index, this time by a decree of Leo XIII.

Such matters were discussed all the time in Rome, especially among the clerics. Why was Carolyne singled out for chastisement? And more importantly, why did the Vatican wait four years before moving against her? In order

---

13. LLB, vol. 7, p. 19.

14. LLB, vol. 7, p. 25.

15. SZM, p. 314. Döllinger had refused to accept the doctrine of papal infallibility at the First Vatican Council. In 1869 he had published a treatise called *The Pope and the Council* (under the pen-name "Janus"), which Bishop William Ullathorne of Birmingham called "the greatest and severest attack on the Holy See and the Jesuits . . . for a thousand years." His book was placed on the Index, and Döllinger himself was excommunicated in 1871.

16. The news was brought to Carolyne by Cardinal Hohenlohe "in the most tactful way." On July 23 she wrote to Liszt:

> Well, mon bon, Cisiamo! Whether I publish or do not publish, my *Causes* are already on the Index. My heart regrets it sincerely. I would really have liked not to have to go through all that fanfare of publicity! For at this moment, for such a work, condemnation will sooner or later end by becoming the best publicity, *since the book is good,* which you will allow me to say without false modesty! (Hitherto unpublished, WA, Kasten 207, Abschrift)

CAUSES INTÉRIEURES

DE LA

FAIBLESSE EXTÉRIEURE

DE L'EGLISE

EN

1870.

————◆————

Première Partie

————◆————

ROME,

IMPRIMERIE DE J. AURELI
Place Borghèse 89.

————◆————

Title page of Princess Carolyne's twenty-four-volume magnum opus
Causes intérieures, *1872–1887.*

to answer these questions we have to consider the religious and political turmoil that was Rome. Carolyne could not have chosen a worse time to write
her books. For there was a dark side to life in the Eternal City which today is
all but forgotten, especially in biographies of Liszt. When Carolyne and he had
first taken up residence in Rome, the Catholic Church was in the middle of
the gravest crisis of its long existence. The Vatican itself was hopelessly divided
into factions whose manner of doing business with one another included conspiracy, violence, assassination, and suicide. Papal Rome was a battlefield in
which Franciscan strove against Domenican, Jesuit against liberal, "Blacks"
against "Whites." When Carolyne picked up her pen and started writing
about the Church, she knew that she would henceforth be regarded as an active participant in that war, but probably thought that she could overcome the
opposition. In fact, she had a better chance of walking through a minefield at
night and arriving safely at the other side.

III

Pius IX had been elected pope on June 16, 1846, and his elevation to the Holy
See had been greeted in Italy with an outpouring of joy. The restrictive policies of his predecessor, Gregory XIV, and the latter's secretary of state, Cardinal Luigi Lambruschini, had brought the Papal States to the verge of
revolution.[17] "Young Italy," in particular, saw in Pius its last, best hope, a national leader who would succeed in untying the bonds that had fettered the
Italian states to the House of Habsburg for centuries. The cry "Viva Pio
Nono!" was soon on everyone's lips; the drive towards a unified Italy appeared
to carry the pope's sanction. It was the first time in history that a "liberal" pope
had occupied St. Peter's, and the heads of state in France, Austria, Prussia, and
England trembled to think of the consequences. They did not have to wait
long to find out. One of Pius IX's first political acts was the granting of a general amnesty to political prisoners and exiles, on July 16, 1846, less than three

---

17. Giovanni Maria Mastai-Ferretti (1792–1876) had never wanted to be pope. Nor was he considered
to be the strongest candidate for the pontificate. He had only received the red hat in 1840, and through
his charitable work as cardinal priest of Santi Pietro e Marcellino he had become known as a friend
of the common people. This made him suspect at a time when the "common people" were toppling
thrones all over Europe. Everyone remembered that it was Mastai-Ferretti who, as archbishop of Spoleto, had persuaded four thousand Italian revolutionaries who were fleeing before the Austrian army
to lay down their arms and had then induced the Austrian commander to pardon them for their treason. In consequence of this act, Mastai-Ferretti had made many friends among the revolutionaries,
whose cause he appeared to support. After Gregory XIV's death the mounting frustration of the Italian nationalists, and the fear that Gregory's repressive secretary of state, Cardinal Luigi Lambruschini,
might be elected as his successor, prompted a group of liberal cardinals, headed by Bernetti, to block
his election. On June 14, 1846, fifty cardinals assembled in the Quirinal Palace for the conclave. They

weeks after his coronation in St. Peter's. He naively supposed that this would have a healing effect, and utterly failed to realise that these same revolutionaries, some of whom pursued assassination as political policy, would simply continue their fight to have the Vatican itself swept aside and establish a democratic government in its place. Within a short time Pius found himself besieged by problems and had to act against the very people he had so recently pardoned. In his encyclical *Qui Pluribus,* of November 9, 1846, he lamented the intrigues against the Holy See, the machinations of the secret societies, the emergence of communism, and the calumnies of the press. One of the most powerful of the secret societies was the fanatical Circolo Romano, which, under their leader, Ciceruacchio, instituted mob rule and brought Rome to the brink of riot. They demanded a constitutionally elected government, a lay ministry, and a declaration of war against Austria. To this last demand Pius was unable to accede, whereupon he was denounced as a traitor to Italy and marked for death.

Nothing better sums up these turbulent times than the assassination of Pellegrino Rossi, the prime minister to Pius IX. On November 15, 1848, Rossi was on his way to the legislative assembly in the Palazzo della Cancelleria to explain the pope's new programme of administrative reform. He had just seated himself in his carriage when an assassin's dagger was plunged through his neck, and he expired almost at once. The killing was carried out at the behest of one of the secret societies. Rossi's murder triggered an attack on the Quirinal Palace the next day. Monsignor Palma, a papal prelate who was standing at a window, was shot, and Pius was forced to escape the palace in disguise. He and many of his cardinals fled the city and assembled in Gaëta, in the kingdom of Naples, from where he issued appeals for help to France, Austria, and Spain. Mazzini and his followers proclaimed a Roman Republic, but it was short-lived. On June 29, 1849, French troops entered Rome and restored order. When Pius himself returned to the Vatican, on April 12, 1850, he was no longer a liberal.

After his return to Rome, Pius clung tenaciously to his waning authority. Since he was unwilling to give up any of his temporal possessions, they were taken from him one by one, by force. The King of Sardinia Victor Emmanuel II and his anti-papal prime minister, Camillo Cavour, wanted a united Italy

---

were divided roughly into the absolutists, who favoured a continuance of the temporal powers of the pope, and the liberals, who wanted greater flexibility in the Church's dealings with Italian national aspirations. At the first scrutiny Lambruschini acquired more votes than Mastai-Ferretti, but not enough for the necessary majority. It was not until the fourth scrutiny that Mastai-Ferretti emerged as the clear candidate. Even then, he would never have been elected pope if Cardinal Gaysruch of Milan had not arrived too late to make use of the right of exclusion vested in him by the Austrian government. Had that happened, the subsequent history of the papacy might have been entirely different. But with the elevation of Mastai-Ferretti to St. Peter's, the dramatic confrontation between Church and State, which was to characterise so much of his reign, began to unfold. It was also the longest papacy in the history of the Roman Catholic Church, lasting for thirty years.

with Rome as its capital. They worked unceasingly towards the dissolution of the pope's domains, an objective that was difficult to achieve so long as the house of Habsburg supported Pius and kept its military garrisons within the Papal States.[18] But in 1859 Austria and Sardinia (supported by the provinces of Piedmont) went to war with one another; and France, in fulfillment of its treaty obligations, came to the assistance of Victor Emmanuel. The armies clashed at Magenta on June 4 and then at Solferino on June 24. During this latter battle, in which the two armies were led by their respective monarchs, Emperor Franz Joseph and Napoleon III, approximately 150,000 soldiers on each side confronted one another. At the end of the day the Austrians had sustained 23,000 casualties, while the French and the Piedmontese had suffered 12,000 and 5,500, respectively. The carnage on the Austrian side obliged that army to withdraw not only from the field of battle but from all its garrisons as well. Napoleon III, shocked by the number of French casualties, rushed to sign an armistice with the Austrians, under the terms of which Lombardy was ceded to the Piedmontese. Plebiscites in favour of unification with Piedmont added Romagna and Tuscany to Victor Emmanuel's territories. In the meantime, Garibaldi, with a small army of volunteers, proceeded to conquer the south. In order to prevent him from attacking Rome, which was still protected by the French, Victor Emmanuel crossed into the Papal States. Pius IX refused to yield any of his domains (he called them "the robe of Jesus Christ"), so Victor Emmanuel waged a military campaign against him. He defeated the newly raised papal army at Castelfidardo on September 12, 1860, and again at Ancona on September 30. Meanwhile, on September 26, Victor Emmanuel had met Garibaldi, who had proclaimed him king of Italy. For the next ten years it was the French garrison in Rome that protected the patrimony of St. Peter's—all that was now left of Pius IX's temporal possessions. In 1870, when France was preoccupied with its disastrous war against Germany, Victor Emmanuel marched into Rome and made it the capital of a united Italy.

Church and state were now officially separated. Although the so-called Law of Guarantees recognised Pius as a sovereign, and made him a financial provision of more than three million lire annually, Pius refused the conditions and remained a self-imposed prisoner in the Vatican for the rest of his life—as, for that matter, did his successor, Leo XIII. Thereafter, it was the official policy of the Vatican to have no formal diplomatic ties of any kind with the government of Italy, many of whose members were excommunicated; indeed, the Church sometimes excommunicated its own clergy if they breached this rule. It was not until 1929, with the arrival of Mussolini, that the Concordat between the Vatican and Italy was signed and the Roman question was settled.

---

18. The Papal States included the following domains: Romagna, Umbria, The Marches, Sabina, and Emilia, over which the popes had ruled as sovereign monarchs for centuries.

I V

The enormous political pressures that were exerted on Pius IX during his long and tragic pontificate help to explain some of his doctrinal reforms, which were designed to help the Church during its crisis. His celebrated encyclical *Quanta Cura* (December 1864) was an attack against liberalism and was issued with a *Syllabus Errorum* which listed eighty of the "principal errors of our times." And at the First Vatican Council (1869–70), which took Pius and his advisors several years to plan, the doctrine of papal infallibility was adopted, although not without acrimonious debate. Henceforth, the pope was empowered to make *ex cathedra* statements on all matters involving the interests of the church and claim that his authority came from God.

Some of the liberal cardinals who had been swept into office with the election of Pius IX now found themselves isolated—and (for such was the temper of the times) physically endangered. They included Cardinals Franchi, Schiaffino, and Hohenlohe, all of whom died under mysterious circumstances and were generally believed to have been poisoned. Their enemies the Jesuits were known to be expert in the preparation of the *acquetta*.[19] Their most famous victim was Father Antonio Rosmini-Serbati, one of the greatest religious leaders the Catholic Church has ever produced, a man who incurred the implacable hatred of the Jesuits for his support of a unified Italy and the clear separation of church and state. His central thesis was that the true business of the Church was the saving of souls, not the pursuit of political power. The Jesuits eventually denounced him and condemned his ideas through the Inquisition. The last entry in Rosmini's *Diario della Carità* is dated February 25, 1852:

> Ash Wednesday. A man, dressed in black, with a blue overcoat, came into the garden at Stresa, and inquired of Antonio Carli [Rosmini's lay-brother] if he looked after the Abate Rosmini. He answered that he did and the man said that he had a small request to make, which if agreed to would be rewarded with a great sum of money. He took out of his pocket a small phial, and asked him to pour its contents into the coffee or chocolate that the Abate Rosmini took in the morning. Astounded, Carli refused, and the stranger at once replied that it was no matter, and coolly walked out of the garden and went straight to the shore opposite the house, where there was a boat waiting with three or four boatmen. He boarded it and was gone.[20]

---

19. The *acquetta di Perugia* was a cup of slow-acting poisoned chocolate, possibly with an arsenic base.
20. LR, p. 466.

During the months that followed Rosmini suffered from intestinal pains, vomiting, and haemorrhages. After developing jaundice and dropsy, he died a lingering, painful death in 1855.

V

Gustav von Hohenlohe is an interesting case because of his special connection with Liszt and Carolyne. The best information about his private life comes from his longtime friend and colleague Primo Levi, the editor of Rome's *Tribuna*.[21] Hohenlohe was a liberal who was given a cardinal's hat in 1866 thanks in part to his powerful family connections in a largely Protestant Germany— connections which Pius hoped to manipulate to his advantage.[22] But Hohenlohe's profound disillusionment with Pius caused him to leave Rome for extended periods between 1871 and 1876. Indeed, his liberal views created a solid wall of opposition within the Vatican's secretariat, and it became impossible for him to function there. It was not until Leo XIII was elected pope, in 1878, that Hohenlohe returned formally to the Eternal City. In that year he was appointed archbishop of Santa Maria Maggiore, one of the most important dioceses in Rome, and a year later he became bishop of Albano. These distinctions were possible for him only because it was Leo XIII's official policy to indulge in window-dressing: that is to say, Leo decided to adopt the outer trappings of liberalism while remaining true to the conservative traditions he had inherited from Pius IX. But he reckoned without Hohenlohe's outspokenness and readiness to resist him. Hohenlohe had many connections within the new Italian government, and he used them constantly, in defiance of the papal injunction forbidding any diplomatic contacts with these arch-enemies of the Vatican. He found it hypocritical that Leo censured him for this while doing exactly the same thing himself, albeit surreptitiously. Several times Hohenlohe was reprimanded by Leo through the latter's intermediary Cardinal Mariano Rampolla. The conflict between the pair is symbolized in the famous letter that Hohenlohe wrote to Leo on July 24, 1889.

> Today we can no longer isolate ourselves in Chinese fashion from the personages of the Italian Government. God has so ordained that the Church can never again get back her temporal power. The salvation of souls requires that we resign ourselves to this fact, that we

---

21. LK.

22. It was Hohenlohe who helped to negotiate the treaty between Bismarck and the pope, which ended the *Kulturkampf*—the conflict between the Roman Catholic church and the newly unified German state.

keep quietly within the ecclesiastical sphere and perform charity by giving of our substance and by teaching the faithful.

There is talk of quitting [Rome]. Now His Excellency [Francesco] Crispi [minister for external affairs] told me the other day to inform Your Holiness that, if you wish to go, he will not oppose it and will have you escorted with all honours, but that Your Holiness will never return to Rome; that if your departure should stir up a war—for example on the part of France—religion would lose immensely thereby; that Italy would not make war unless France attacks her; that in the case of war the Italian Government guarantees the safety of the pope at Rome, but that the pope must cherish no illusions: let him depart, and he shall never return to Rome, and the Holy See will suffer a terrible shock.

. . . We cardinals have the strictest right to speak the truth to the pope; therefore listen. In the time of Pius VI the five million crowns stored by Sixtus V [reigned 1585–90] in Castel Sant' Angelo were lost, and nevertheless, up to 1839, every new cardinal had to swear to preserve those five millions which no longer existed. It was only Cardinal Acton who in 1839 protested against that oath, and Pope Gregory found Acton's reasons just. Likewise, today also, cardinals are made to swear things which they cannot perform. Therefore it is time to find a remedy.[23]

This last point must have been deeply resented by Leo. What Hohenlohe was complaining about was the fact that every new cardinal was still made to swear an oath to preserve intact the inheritance of the Holy See, which theoretically included those temporal powers which had been lost nearly twenty years earlier and would never be restored. It took courage to write such a letter, and Hohenlohe himself believed that he might well fall victim to the assassin's dagger or the equally deadly *acquetta*. On December 5, 1891, the newspaper *Il Messagero* carried a notice that he was ill, although this was not true. Hohenlohe told Primo Levi that the news had been inspired by the secretariat of the Vatican in order to prepare the public for his death.[24] Not long afterwards, Hohenlohe was summoned to his family home at Rauden, where his eldest brother, Viktor, Duke of Ratibor, lay on his deathbed. He refused to travel with the priests that the Vatican wished to appoint as his aides (whose job was ostensibly to protect him), because he could not trust them, and asked Levi, a Jew, to recommend someone else—a situation that one of his biographers has rightly characterised

23. LCH, pp. 11–12.
24. LK, p. 12.

as "dramatic."[25] Levi selected for this purpose Monsignor Bignani, priest at the royal villa in Monza, whom he knew to be above suspicion.[26]

Hohenlohe believed that his particular enemies were the Jesuits, and with good reason. At the time of their unremitting assault on the teachings of Rosmini, it had been Hohenlohe who had emerged as one of that priest's strongest champions. As long as Pius IX lived, this had caused him no real harm; Pius had been sympathetic to Rosmini, to the extent of promising him a cardinal's hat, although the Jesuits had blocked the nomination. But with the accession of Leo XIII, the Jesuits suddenly found in the occupant of St. Peter's one of their staunchest allies. In 1892 the Vatican press issued a posthumous attack against Rosmini[27] which the *Osservatore Romano,* the official organ of the Jesuits, praised without stint. When he read it, Cardinal Hohenlohe wrote a satirical reply to the *Osservatore,* in which he told Rosmini's anonymous accusers that they were doing harm to the Church and that, in the unlikely event that the criticisms came from Leo XIII himself, the episcopate "would find itself in the hard necessity of deposing him," since the utterances of Pius IX on these matters would make Leo guilty of propagating a false doctrine.

VI

But what made Hohenlohe such a perceived threat to Pope Leo and his cohorts was his deep friendship with Francesco Crispi, minister for foreign affairs in the new Italian government. It was well known that Hohenlohe entertained Crispi in his private apartments in the Santa Maria Maggiore, and that the two talked politics. Hohenlohe did nothing to quell the gossip. Once, at a wedding reception for one of Crispi's lieutenants at the Foreign Office, Hohenlohe playfully removed his crimson beretta and placed it on Crispi's head. "When I am pope," joked Hohenlohe, "I will make you my secretary of state." Not long afterwards, Hohenlohe was present at a reception given by Crispi in the magnificent Sciarra Palace. In the course of the dinner, Hohenlohe caught Crispi's eye, lifted his glass, and silently toasted him with champagne. The whole of Rome talked about that incident the following day.[28]

---

25. TCH, p. 295.

26. LK, p. 13.

27. *Rosminianarum propositionum, quas S.R.U. Onquisitio, approbante S.P. Leone XIII, reprobavit, proscripsit, damnavit, Trutina theologica,* 1892.

28. What added fuel to the fires of speculation was that Hohenlohe was considered to be a possible candidate for pope by some of the cardinals. The playful exchange of words with Crispi masked a deadly game.

Incidentally, the implacable hatred of the Jesuits towards Gustav Hohenlohe can only be understood within a wider context. Even before Gustav's brother Chlodwig became chancellor of Germany, his public utterances against the Jesuits and the influence they had on public life in Germany

Such behaviour, however good-humoured it was meant to be, created consternation at the Vatican,[29] and Leo was obliged to administer a severe rebuke to his renegade cardinal. In his defence, Hohenlohe pointed out that he was the brother of Prince Chlodwig, vice-president of the German Reichstag, and this made it impossible for him to evade certain social responsibilities. The interview, according to Levi, "was not absolutely pacific," and Hohenlohe left Rome for several months. The displeasure of the pope was not diminished when he learned that Hohenlohe had sent a personal representative to Milan to attend the unveiling of Luca Beltrami's monument to Rosmini. Had Hohenlohe been well enough to make the trip in person, he would have done so, but he had meanwhile succumbed to a mysterious sickness. When Levi saw him at Tivoli in August 1896, he was already in a strange cycle of illness and health. First he was unwell, then he would recover, and his doctors could not say what was wrong with him. But nothing prepared his friends for the shock of the announcement from Santa Maria Maggiore that he had suddenly expired "of a heart attack" on October 30, 1896. Levi hints at poisoning, but he refused to elaborate because the Hohenlohe family declined to order an autopsy. They had good reason to make this decision, according to Levi, because two earlier attempts to poison Hohenlohe had convinced them that on this occasion he might well have become a victim.[30] And had that been proved, they would have been obliged to launch an inquiry into the identity of his enemies. The impact that such an inquiry would have had on the Catholic Church in Germany and Austria would have been incalculable.

Hohenlohe was laid to rest in the little German cemetery at Santa Maria Maggiore. Over his tomb was placed a marble slab bearing an inscription from Chlodwig.

---

had made him famous. On May 15, 1872, Chlodwig made a speech in the Reichstag which proposed the introduction of a bill whose chief purpose would be to outlaw the order throughout Germany. Its principal assertions ran:

> (a) The order of Jesuits, and orders standing in connection with that order, are prohibited in Germany;
>
> (b) Every German who enters the Jesuit order loses thereby his rights as a citizen of the state;
>
> (c) No German who has been educated in a Jesuit teaching establishment may be installed in the service of the state or of the Church in Germany.

The Reichstag passed its anti-Jesuit bill the following month, although in a somewhat watered-down version. (MHS, vol. 2, pp. 75–78)

29. TCH, pp. 299–300.

30. LK, p. 142; and LCH, pp. 49–50. It had long been taken for granted within the Hohenlohe family circle that Gustav was a marked man. His niece Princess Marie von Thurn und Taxis wrote in her memoirs that whenever he visited their home Gustav would refuse even a glass of water, "because he was convinced that the Jesuits wanted to poison him. He hated them and they returned the compliment." (MP, p. 51) If the absence of an autopsy made it impossible to prove that they had succeeded, it also made it possible to keep alive the rumour that they had.

HERE RESTS IN PEACE
MONSIGNOR GUSTAV HOHENLOHE,
CARDINAL OF THE HOLY ROMAN CHURCH
AND TITULAR PRIEST OF ST. CALLIXTUS,
PRINCE OF THE GERMAN EMPIRE
AND A PRIEST OF THE BASILICA LIBERIANA.
BORN OF A NOBLE FAMILY WITH AN EVEN NOBLER MIND,
LOYAL TO CHURCH, COUNTRY AND FRIENDS,
HE WAS A LOVER OF THE ARTS AND A FATHER TO THE POOR.
HE DIED IN THE LORD, AGED SEVENTY-TWO
ON OCTOBER 30, 1896 IN ROME
CHLODWIG, PRINCE VON HOHENLOHE AND
CHANCELLOR OF THE GERMAN EMPIRE
ERECTED TO THE WORTHY MEMORY OF HIS BROTHER.

V I I

It is now much easier to understand why Carolyne's relations with the Church rested on shifting ground. She had jumped straight into the simmering cauldron of religion, politics, war, and history, and had been badly scalded. Moreover, her much-publicized annulment had made her highly visible. She was already notorious for her ceaseless disputations, for her letters, her briefs, and her memoranda, and most of all for the cultivation of clerics within the Vatican's inner circle whom she pumped for favours. And now she had set herself up as an authority on Church affairs. When *Causes intérieures* first began to appear, in 1872, Pius IX was a prisoner inside the Vatican, and no one could tell what the outcome of negotiations with the new Italian government in Rome would be. But as the years passed, and it became clear to Pius and his circle that they had lost their temporal powers, they fought back with the only weapons at their disposal and began to purge the Church of all its theological impurities. Paradoxically, the pope's temporal weakness gradually became his spiritual strength. Carolyne and her books were now a valid target. By placing her tomes on the Index the Vatican made an example of her and of her "liberal" ideas, and the clergy was banned from reading her on pain of excommunication.[31]

---

31. In trying to understand why this was so, we must not forget the full title of Carolyne's work: *Causes intérieures de la faiblesse extérieure de l'Eglise en 1870*. That last phrase "in 1870" is often overlooked. It announced to everybody that the book took as its starting-point that fateful year in which the Church received a mortal blow. Moreover, it reviewed such little matters as the method of electing cardinals

Carolyne also had other problems. During her early years in Rome she had mixed exclusively with the so-called Blacks—that is, the group around the pope who favoured the retention of Rome's temporal powers. She did this not only because the Blacks were the ones with the power to help her with her annulment, but because she was at that time a highly conservative Catholic. Later she consorted with the Whites—those who favoured giving up the political control of Rome to King Victor Emmanuel.[32] Among her White contacts were Baron Robert von Keudell, the German ambassador to Rome, and the statesman Marco Minghetti. Nor did it help Carolyne's cause in the mid-1870s to be related by marriage to the "banished" Cardinal Hohenlohe. Carolyne, in fact, was placed in the same delicate position as millions of Catholics whose loyalties were deeply divided. Many of the prominent ones were excommunicated for refusing to give up their "modern" views. Carolyne was at least spared that prospect. Nonetheless, her friends trembled for her and her unrepentant ways.

And where did Liszt stand in all this? When he first took up residence in Rome, in October 1861, many of these cataclysmic upheavals were just beginning. It remains a fact that he wrote very little about them, even though they held the city in thrall. Liszt, in short, behaved like the proverbial diplomat who thinks twice before saying nothing. He was a fervent supporter of Pius IX, however, and accepted without question the findings of the First Vatican Council, and in particular the doctrines of papal infallibility and the Immaculate Conception. He expressed it thus: "Our Church is only so strong because she exacts total obedience. We must obey, even if we hang for it. . . . That is why all the princes of the church will adhere to it: not one of them can remain outside."[33] (This prediction turned out to be absolutely correct. Those cardinals who had left Rome because of the dispute over papal infallibility did eventually submit to the authority of the Church.) And on another occasion he wrote: "I submit and give my support [to the *Syllabus Errorum*], as Catholics are duty-bound to do."[34] When Pius died, Liszt described him as "a saint." All this makes Liszt sound like a conservative. Yet he sided with the liberals on a num-

to high office, the composition of conclaves and congregations, and the separation of powers. Stripped of its external strength, the last thing the Vatican now needed was a gadfly princess to sting it into exposing its internal weakness. For an overview of the contents of Carolyne's *magnum opus,* see p. 554.

32. The deep split between Blacks and Whites ran along social lines as well, and this affected the musical life of Rome. There were two rival concert societies in the city, the Neri and the Bianchi, whose membership reflected the burning theological disputes of the day. Liszt attended the concerts of both societies. See WLLM, p. 361.

33. SZM, p. 258.

34. LLB, vol. 7, p. 171.

ber of fundamental issues, including the separation of church and state. And his admiration for such revolutionary figures as Lamennais and Rosmini was unbounded, although he was far less sympathetic to their followers, whom he accused of wanting to destroy the Church from without, rather than change it from within. In fact, it was Liszt's liberal ideas that linked him to Hohenlohe, and which help to explain the friendship that developed between the pair in the 1860s and 1870s—their earlier differences about Carolyne's annulment notwithstanding. Liszt genuinely admired Hohenlohe's liberal stance, and his willingness to stand up and be counted.

Liszt kept up his visits to Carolyne even though canonical storms raged around her. Nonetheless, he found these occasions increasingly irksome. He understood and loved Carolyne better than any other person alive, yet he also saw that she was turning into a truculent recluse, with strange ideas and few friends. There were many subjects on which they disagreed, and Liszt soon learned to keep quiet if he wished to avoid an unpleasant confrontation. Theology, Hungarians, and the "Jewish question" were all topics on which he had to bite his tongue in order to avoid a verbal confrontation. And sometimes he failed. Cosima Wagner tells of a violent argument that once broke out between Carolyne and her father. He was beside himself with rage and rushed out of her apartment to his own lodgings not far away, where one of his relatives was at that time staying with him. After he had calmed down, he turned to his visitor and said: "And yet she has a great heart."[35] Adelheid von Schorn also witnessed such scenes. She reports that on one occasion Liszt became so agitated that he smashed a window-pane with his fist. This brought them to their senses and they both broke down and wept.[36] Such confrontations rarely lasted long, for Liszt and Carolyne had long since agreed to disagree on all the major issues that separated them—a mark of any mature friendship.

Behind these scenes lay a complex tapestry of mutual complaints and reproaches, which were by now woven into the very weft and weave of their voluminous correspondence. One of the more disagreeable aspects of the relationship at this time was Carolyne's readiness to share with others her catalogue of grievances against Liszt. In May 1875 we find her haranguing Eduard Liszt about sexual liaisons that Liszt was supposed to have had with Emilie Genast, Olga Janina, and Olga von Meyendorff. These allegations arouse our curiosity simply because there is no evidence that Liszt had affairs with any of these ladies, although he was certainly guilty of another crime in the eyes of the princess: he had spent much time in their company.[37]

---

35. WFLG, pp. 44–45.
36. RL, p. 189.
37. EKFL, pp. 66–69. Aficionados of the topic of Liszt and the ladies are unlikely to get far with such material. Liszt did not leave a paper trail with these women—as he did, for example, with Agnès

But a much more serious breach of that trust which is supposed to exist between two people who love one another occurred in March 1877, when Carolyne heard from Antal Augusz that Liszt was finding it increasingly unpleasant to write to her. This provoked the outburst in which she informed Augusz that Liszt's letters resembled "a correspondence that one would be prepared to drop." She went on to utter some amazing accusations. She complained that the pontiff had betrayed Liszt by paying him private visits, "an unprecedented honour," and dangling before him the prospect of an important musical position within the Church; that after he had taken holy orders nothing happened ("They said 'Come,' and they opened for him neither church nor choir!"); that he had then sought to better his lot by leaving Rome and going to Budapest and other places, but it had ended badly; that Liszt was now far away from her and was not writing anything worthwhile, that he was "sterilising his genius before his time." Warming to her theme, she touched on more personal matters. She told Augusz that while she had never promised to marry Liszt, she had sworn not to abandon him either. She was wounded to think that Liszt found her letters disturbing, that he would prefer not to receive them. ("But I have not promised God to be nice to him, I have promised to be useful to him, not to abandon him, but to support him in word and deed. The deed is always welcome, but not always the word!") After describing herself as a woman who had made immense sacrifices for Liszt, she informed Augusz that even after they had settled in Weimar in 1848, he "was breaking off" a liaison with the prima donna (Hermine Haller) who created the role of Venus in the Court Theatre's production of *Tannhäuser.* And she ended: "It is understood, dear Baron, that this letter is for you alone; Liszt especially must never know of it."[38]

Once we cut through the bluff and bluster of such letters, one conclusion emerges with crystal clarity: Carolyne could never accept Liszt's departure from Rome, and by implication his "abandonment" of her. She hugged this imagined harm to her person all the way to the grave. So long as she and Liszt had been together, either in Weimar or in Rome, she could control their destiny. But in 1869 he had done an unforgivable thing by leaving the city and putting down roots in Weimar and Budapest. For nine months of the year he

---

Street-Klindworth, whom Carolyne does not even mention—and in the absence of paper, scholarship is wise to remain mute. Perhaps the most spiteful sentence in her letter to Eduard Liszt is the one in which she quotes the famous advice that Liszt's father is supposed to have uttered to his son on his deathbed: "Beware of women, they will bring about your ruin." We recall that this *cri de coeur* had been wrenched from Liszt the previous summer, shortly after Olga Janina's novel *Souvenirs d'une cosaque* had been published, and Carolyne had not even heard the phrase until then. But we find her passing it across to Eduard Liszt as if it were common currency instead of the intimate disclosure that it was. On the subject of Adam's deathbed "prophecy," see Volume One, p. 127.

38. This letter, from which we already quoted on p. 323, n. 12, raises so many questions of fact, fancy, and downright falsehood that we can only suppose that in her near-isolation in Rome, Carolyne was simply trying to make the present more comfortable for herself by re-arranging the past—a familiar

was beyond her reach, and what she could not accomplish in person she had to try to accomplish by correspondence—often with disturbing consequences. This way of life, marked as it was by long separations, was only accepted by the princess with difficulty. But then the two old companions found a bone of contention that would not go away. They gnawed over it ceaselessly, they exchanged wounding words about it, and on one or two bruising occasions they came perilously close to breaking a relationship that neither church nor state had so far been able to sunder.

---

enough occupation in the history of human nature. Thus, it has been proved a hundred times over that Liszt's entry into the clerical state was not even remotely connected with a promise to let him take over the direction of Catholic church music. As for his work in Weimar and particularly in Budapest (by now he was the president of the Royal Academy of Music there), it was regarded by everybody as a triumph. That leaves the "sterilisation of his genius." During the very year in which Carolyne penned that phrase, Liszt had embarked on the composition of the last book of his *Années de pèlerinage*—a gateway to modern music.

It is worth recording here that a good many of Carolyne's letters to Liszt during the seventies and eighties contain some pithy marginal annotations by him—his spontaneous reactions to her thoughts. They are of interest to the biographer because they occasionally reveal to us what Liszt really thought, as opposed to the neutered responses he so often gave her. Carolyne never saw them, of course; but had she ever discovered Liszt's references to her "Roman thinking" scrawled across her letters, a correspondence that "one would be prepared to drop" might well have been—dropped.

BOOK FOUR

De Profundis
1876 · 1886

Liszt and Bayreuth

To Bayreuth I am not a composer, but a publicity agent.

FRANZ LISZT[1]

I

The greatest problem facing Liszt in September 1872 was how to explain his rapprochement with Cosima and Richard Wagner to Princess Carolyne, whose implacable dislike of them both had grown with the years and had never been disguised from him. Within a day of the Wagners' return to Bayreuth early that month, he told Carolyne of their historic visit to Weimar and of the invitation they had extended to him to come to Bayreuth—an invitation that he had every intention of accepting. "In all the circumstances," he wrote,

> I could not refuse [Wagner], it was against my nature, which I do not separate from my conscience! . . . On the topic of my daughter I recall particularly your admirable solicitude for my three children, and I bless you for all you did for them during the long years of your frustrations and sorrows. Cosima is indeed my terrible daughter, as I used to call her in the old days, an extraordinary woman of great merit, far above the criticisms of the vulgar and perfectly worthy of the admiration she inspires in those who know her—beginning with her first husband Bülow! She has devoted herself with absolute zeal to Wagner, like Senta to the *fliegende Holländer*—and will be his salvation, for he listens to her and follows her clear-sightedly.[2]

---

1. PEMH, p. 535.
2. LLB, vol. 6, pp. 359–60.

This was something that Carolyne was unable to accept. Liszt's rapprochement with Wagner and Cosima was to her a form of betrayal which gnawed at her heart and gave her no peace. In order to understand why this was so, we have to look at the situation through her eyes. Carolyne was quite incapable of accepting the fact that Cosima and Hans had been granted a Protestant divorce and that Cosima had gone on to marry Wagner in a Protestant church. To her this was a form of blasphemy, a wicked way for Catholics to resolve their matrimonial difficulties. But Cosima had not stopped there. She was now actively considering converting to Protestantism itself.

Shortly before she took this final step, Liszt returned the Wagners' visit; he stayed in Bayreuth as their guest from October 15 to 21, 1872. He there unburdened himself to Cosima about his growing problems with Carolyne, and Cosima unburdened them in turn to her diary.

> Long talk with my father; Princess Wittgenstein is tormenting him on our account—he should flee from Wagner's influence, artistic as well as moral, should not see me again, his self-respect demands this, we murdered Hans from a moral point of view, etc. I am very upset that my father should be tormented like this—he is so tired and is always being torn about! Particularly this wretched woman in Rome has never done anything but goad him—but he does not intend to give me and us up.[3]

Nonetheless, Liszt was careful not to spend October 22, his sixty-first birthday, at Bayreuth, because he knew that Carolyne would hear about it and create yet more difficulties for him. On October 21 he travelled to Regensburg, where he spent the following day alone. In Bayreuth he and Cosima must have discussed something else: her forthcoming conversion. This step caused him distress; but since he knew that she had thought it through, and since he had been expecting the move for a long time, he resigned himself to the inevitable.

Ten days after his departure, on October 31, Cosima took communion in the Protestant church of Bayreuth, in the company of Wagner, and was formally received into the faith of Martin Luther. That placed her beyond the pale in Carolyne's eyes. Henceforth the princess talked about "pagan Bayreuth," while she said of Liszt's visit that it was "as if St. Peter were going to visit Judas Iscariot."[4] Before we condemn Carolyne's attitude as both cruel and unyielding, let us remember that she of all people had earned the right to hold it. She and Liszt had steadfastly refused to turn Protestant merely to make it easier to regularize their own union, despite some powerful urgings to do so. Moreover,

---

3. WT, vol. 1, p. 581.
4. Hitherto unpublished letter, dated September 14, 1872. (WA, Kasten 59, u. 45, letter no. 71)

she too had been divorced by a Protestant husband, but had found the "solution" of conversion beneath contempt, and she found Cosima's "solution" beneath contempt, too.[5]

At first Liszt turned aside her criticisms of Cosima as wife and mother, but as they persisted he was obliged to come to his daughter's defence. To one of Carolyne's tirades he replied: "The children are . . . perfectly well brought-up and remarkably charming. Cosima is surpassing herself! Let others judge and condemn her—for me she remains a dignified soul of the *gran perdone* of St. Francis and admirably my daughter!"[6] Matters reached a new low between them in September 1876. Carolyne, beside herself with anger that the Wagners had once again visited Liszt in Weimar and that she had been powerless to prevent it, vented her wrath on the topic and succeeded in wounding him deeply. He replied on September 6:

> In all humility I do not think I deserved the letter you administered to me today. With the most sorrowful sincerity I maintain what I told you in Rome—you are seriously mistaken about your daughter, about mine, and about me. God knows that lightening your suffering was my only care for many years! I did not have much success it seems! As for me, I want to recall only the times when we wept and prayed together, with a single heart! After your letter today I am abandoning my trip to Rome.[7]

Carolyne's letter, which was evidently filled with recriminations against him, is not with her other correspondence to Liszt in the Weimar Archive, and with good reason: Liszt returned it to her, together with marginal comments

---

5. Cosima's diary plots the progress of her conversion, and records her worries about how this change in her religion would affect her children.

February 25, 1871: "Heavy thoughts in connection with the children's change of religion one day; I wish to assume the responsibility for this myself."

March 2, 1871: "Prince Pückler has succeeded in having his body cremated, and his ashes will be preserved in an urn; I wish this also for R[ichard] and myself, and that is one reason why I want to become a Protestant, so that I can be cremated and buried with him." (In the event, neither Cosima nor Richard was cremated.)

March 13, 1871: "My resolve to change to the Protestant faith is growing ever deeper; I shall do it in Bayreuth. But Bayreuth—when?"

March 30, 1871: "Great disturbances in church and state: the priest Egli in Lucerne, who will not recognize the dogma [of infallibility], and the nuncio, whom Bern is expelling."

October 31, 1872. "We set out at 10 o'clock for the dean's house, where my conversion is recorded in front of witnesses . . . then to the vestry, where I receive the sacrament with R. . . . For me it has seemed more significant almost to have gone with R. to Communion than to the marriage altar."

While Cosima may well have adopted the faith of Martin Luther under pressure from Wagner, the diary proves that her decision to do so was taken in the full knowledge of what it meant.

6. LLB, vol. 6, p. 366.

7. LLB, vol. 7, p. 155.

and corrections.[8] Moreover, he told her that as a result of the things she had said to him, he would not be returning to Rome that year. When she realised the harm that she had done, she wrote him a conciliatory letter in which she told him that "no one will ever understand you as I understand you, and no one will love me as you have loved me." And it ended with the sentence: "Come, for I await you with open arms."[9] This attempt to pacify Liszt for the wounds she had inflicted on him did not work; he thanked her for her soft words, but ignored her offer to return to her open arms. His decision to put off his return to Rome was the most powerful weapon at his disposal. Thoroughly alarmed at the prospect of not seeing him again for many months, Carolyne softened her words still more, but Liszt remained steadfast: "Your latest letter is full of kindness and indulgence. I thank you for it from my heart, which is still bleeding from recent wounds. Allow me to cure myself alone, without further discussion of my faults and wrongdoings!"[10]

Carolyne's remorse was genuine, for on October 22, his sixty-fifth birthday, she consoled herself in his absence by reminiscing about the first of his birthdays they had spent together.

> On this day twenty-nine years ago, we were in Woronince in the oak-wood where there was the big celebration for the peasants. That morning I had given you your gold conductor's baton! What did I not give you? And for twenty-nine years I would have liked to own a fairy's wand to evoke before you here below everything the sky above contains! I was not granted the wish to be a fairy, but I am a Christian and, even if I have no wand, I have prayer. May God grant that we meet each other next October to celebrate together our thirtieth anniversary of October 22.[11]

But their quarrel deepened still further when Carolyne had a falling out with her daughter, Princess Marie, and Liszt took Marie's part. A crisis of sorts was reached in January 1877 when Liszt told Carolyne with candour: "Basically, and very sadly for me, four cardinal points keep me from Rome. Shall I list them? Yes—they are: you and me, your daughter and mine."[12]

---

8. This, at any rate, is the information vouchsafed to us by the General Catalogue of Liszt holdings in the Goethe-Schiller Archive, in the section on Carolyne's letters to Liszt for the year 1876.
9. WA, Kasten 205, u. 1.
10. LLB, vol. 7, p. 155.
11. Hitherto unpublished. WA, Kasten 206, Abschrift.
12. LLB, vol. 7, p. 171. Liszt sent a copy of this letter to Princess Marie Hohenlohe in Vienna, with whom he was still in fairly constant touch. Out of her inflamed imagination Carolyne had produced a whole catalogue of "crimes" that Marie had committed against her, and had set them out in a

Franz Liszt, a photograph taken in Hungary, 1876.

11

Among Liszt's "faults and wrongdoings" had been his attendance at the first Bayreuth Festival in the summer of 1876, when he witnessed all three cycles of *The Ring*. These epic performances, which marked a turning-point in Wagner's career, were widely reported in both the European and the American press. Even his most virulent opponents had to admit that they were dealing with a figure of historical dimensions. The technological wonders alone which were required to depict such things as fire, water, and the Rhinemaidens floating around the stage without visible means of support, rivetted the attention of the artistic world. But these onstage "miracles" were matched by one offstage which went almost unnoticed. It was the first time that the new transatlantic cable was used for the transmission of music criticism, which went straight from Bayreuth to the offices of *The New York Times*. Never before in music history had the readers of any journal been able to read criticism of an event that had taken place the previous evening in a different hemisphere. As the *Times* itself declared: "Is it altogether beyond anticipation that the time may come when we shall record and judge the production of an opera in another planet . . . ?"[13]

As early as the previous summer the preliminary trials for *The Ring* had already begun in the still-unfinished theatre. Although there were workmen, stage-technicians, and scaffolding all over the place, Wagner had expressed a desire to hear a part of *Das Rheingold;* so on July 24, 1875, his three Rhinemaidens had scrambled onto the stage from the auditorium and had sung their trio

---

letter to Marie which she in turn had passed across to Liszt—who was now a go-between. When he saw it he told her: "The incredible letter from Rome stuns me." (HLSW, p. 212) This letter, alas, does not appear to have survived, so the precise nature of the quarrel remains obscure. But we get some idea of what it may have contained from an unpublished letter of Carolyne to Liszt, mailed to him shortly afterwards, in which she tells him:

> For me there is one thing which surpasses success, and that is honour! As long as Mme my daughter and Mons. my son-in-law have not reached the point *at which they should be,* and according to the laws and principles which I represent, the struggle will continue, either hidden or in the open. I am well aware of what I want. There will not be *perfect peace* among us except on *my* conditions. Until then, a few or many truces, which risk at any moment turning into open warfare. . . . (January 26–28, 1877; WA, Kasten 48, u. 2)

A week later, Liszt received another of these missives, more astonishing than the last, in which Carolyne described herself as "eine kinderlose Mutter"—a childless mother—something, she told Liszt, that she had felt in her heart for more than ten years. (Unpublished letter dated February 5–8, 1877; WA, Kasten 48, u. 2) We surmise that such letters were touched off by the still-unresolved matter of the 70,000 roubles which Marie had promised to pay in order to secure Carolyne's annulment, in 1859, and on which promise Konstantin, her son-in-law, had constantly reneged after he had secured

for him. These were the first musical sounds ever heard in the Bayreuth theatre, and Wagner expressed great satisfaction with the acoustics. The orchestra
played there for the first time on August 2; it numbered 115 players, including
64 strings, was led by August Wilhelmj, and had had intermittent rehearsals
ever since. The conductor was the thirty-three-year-old Hans Richter, who
was closely supervised by Wagner himself. His singers, who had been hand-
picked by Wagner from the best opera houses in Germany, had also begun to
arrive in Bayreuth, curious to inspect a theatre which was already the talk of
Germany.[14]

Liszt had been present at these preliminary rehearsals as well. He arrived in
Bayreuth on the overnight train at 5:30 a.m. on July 29, 1875, specifically to
hear the theatre's acoustics for himself. He stayed with the Wagners for more
than two weeks and became identified as a major supporter of the Bayreuth
project. He and Wagner, who saw one another daily, must have spent much
time talking about musical matters, for in an unpublished diary-entry for August 6, 1875, Liszt compares two definitions of music by Leibniz and Schopenhauer respectively, a clear indication that these philosophers had come up for
discussion between the two composers.[15] On August 13 Wagner gave a small
party for the orchestral players, during which he invited Liszt to play the piano
for the benefit of those who had never heard him. Liszt chose his Legend *St.
Francis of Paola walking on the waters,* and the players left Bayreuth with this musical benediction ringing in their ears.

By May 1876, rehearsals of *The Ring* had begun in earnest, and by the end of
July Bayreuth had started to overflow with guests. Since the small town only

---

control of Marie's fortune. For the background to this tangled question, see Volume Two, pp. 517 and
521–22.

By now the letters of Liszt and Carolyne were characterised by real anger and sarcasm. To their
differences over Wagner and Cosima, Carolyne kept adding those of theology. She had sent him her
latest tome, which rejoiced in the strange title of *Simplicité des colombes, prudence des serpens* (Simplicity
of Doves, Prudence of Serpents) Under different circumstances Liszt might have tempered his words,
but he now lit into her with a vengeance. "Excuse me for not being wonderstruck by the symbolic
menagerie of lions, eagles, bears, wolves, foxes, serpents. The roaring and dissonance of some of them
delight me no more than do the howlings and whistlings of the rest. May I say in total Catholic submission: the wisdom of the serpents could do without venom, and the simplicity of the doves without bile." (LLB, vol. 7, p. 173) What he received from Carolyne in return were words to the effect that
she did not need his respect for her work since she had enough respect of her own—to which he
replied that her attitude "surpassed moderation." (LLB, vol. 7, p. 270)

13. *The New York Times,* August 20, 1876.

14. A complete list of the singers, together with much information about the difficult beginnings of
the Bayreuth Festival, will be found in NLRW, vol. 4, pp. 445–46 and 478.

15. WA, Kasten 216, u. 5. The two definitions are: "Music is an unconscious exercise in arithmetic in
which the mind does not know that it is counting" (Leibniz) and "Music is an unconscious exercise
in metaphysics in which the mind does not know that it is philosophizing" (Schopenhauer).

possessed four modest inns, demand for the rooms drove up prices, with the result that most of the visitors were quartered on the inhabitants. Talk was of nothing but Wagner and his works. The shops were filled with Wagner mementos, including cigar cases bearing his image, pipes with their heads carved in his likeness, prints of Valhalla, and suchlike. One ingenious hatter had designed a travelling cap called a *Nibelungen-Mütze,* which sold in vast quantities. In short, it was the beginning of the Wagner industry which is still a characteristic of the town to this day. Even domestic pets had to suffer the burden of names drawn by their owners from the dazzling lexicon of Wagnerian mythology, perhaps the prize example being a small and peace-loving dog whose master had proudly dubbed him Fafner, after the terrifying dragon in *Siegfried.*[16] Of greater interest than the *Ring* cycle to many people was the theatre that had been designed to contain it—a temple in which the faithful could congregate in order to worship the genius of Wagner on hallowed ground. The auditorium, which held more than two thousand people, had been designed in such a way that the curved, descending amphitheatre gave everyone a clear line of vision to all parts of the stage.[17] But its most novel feature was the "invisible" orchestra, placed beneath the stage and hidden from view. The orchestral music rose like some majestic, metaphysical commentary on the action taking place on the stage above.

Even during the soil-turning ceremony of 1872, the building had been dedicated to the German nation. In the inaugural speech Wagner had told his audience that his theatre merely outlined an idea. "It is up to the German nation to make of it a worthy monument." But the German nation had shown scant interest. Wagner had tried to finance the venture by floating his Patrons' Vouchers, and he had appealed to Germans to buy them. The scheme was a failure; by the end of 1874 less than a third of the required amount had been raised. Meanwhile, the citizens of Bayreuth had seen the theatre on the hill slowly rising like a cathedral towards the sky. And still it was not finished. As Wagner surveyed the scaffolded building, for which he had no idea how to pay, he called it "a fool's caprice," and almost abandoned it as an artistic folly. King Ludwig finally came to the rescue and headed the list of subscribers with a donation of 300,000 marks—a sum which was later repaid by the Wagner family.

The Ring had finally gone into full dress-rehearsals in June 1876. Wagner fell into one depression after another as he struggled to reduce the distance that

---

16. The canine was patted on the head by *The New York Times'* special correspondent to the Bayreuth Festival, who reported that it meekly returned to its master when summoned by name. (Issue of August 26, 1876)

17. The basic design of the theatre was the work of Gottfried Semper, whom Wagner had known from the Munich days; but modifications to Semper's plans were the work of the Leipzig architect Otto Brückwald.

separated his idealized performance from the imperfect spectacle that greeted him daily on the stage. It was at such moments that his true genius shone forth. Somehow he rallied the players, galvanized the singers, and taught the stage-hands the craft of moving their props around the stage on cue. He acted all the parts himself, was everywhere at once, and became all things to all men. Even so, the production was not without the occasional touch of comedy. When *Das Rheingold* went into rehearsal at the beginning of June, the three Rhinemaid-ens—Lilli and Marie Lehmann and Minna Lammert—were fearful of mount-ing the machines that had been designed to carry them through the air. The prospect of three reluctant maidens with feet firmly planted on terra firma filled Wagner with foreboding. Marie was finally persuaded to try the ride, and amid many cries and squeaks she was strapped into her seat and borne aloft. As she flew around the stage she gradually lost her anxiety, and that seemed to in-spire the others. Soon all three of them were flying through the air with shouts of joy.

With the design of the mechanical dragon in *Siegfried* Wagner was not so lucky. This huge monster was made from *papier-mâché*. Its long tail was sup-posed to produce a caterpillar-like motion, and its head to roll back and forth on its specially constructed neck. It was built in London by the famous maker of pantomime props, Richard Keene of Wandsworth; but by one of those strange quirks of misfortune that seemed to dog so many of Wagner's high-minded efforts, some of the parts, including the neck, were sent by mistake to Beirut in Lebanon. The beast was meant to terrify the audience, but at the first performance the dragon just stood there with a downcast head (an appendage that had arrived at the last moment and had been hastily stitched onto the body, minus the neck), with the result that when Siegfried slew the animal he appeared to be putting it out of its misery, and the audience laughed. Small wonder that in a moment of despair Wagner should exclaim: "Now that I have made the orchestra invisible, I should like to invent an invisible stage!" But these were minor matters when set beside the overwhelming experience of the music itself. *Der Ring* forever changed the language of music, and the few thou-sand people who were fortunate enough to attend its Bayreuth premiere knew that they were ear-witnesses to history.

III

Liszt arrived in Bayreuth on August 1 and stayed until September 2. His at-tendance at all three cycles of *The Ring*, as well as the public dress rehearsals leading up to them, deserves acknowledgement.

REHEARSALS IN PROGRESS

Wednesday, August 2	*Siegfried*
Thursday, August 3	*Götterdämmerung*
Sunday, August 6	*Das Rheingold*
Monday, August 7	*Die Walküre*
Tuesday, August 8	*Siegfried*
Wednesday, August 9	*Götterdämmerung*

First Cycle

Sunday, August 13	*Das Rheingold*
Monday, August 14	*Die Walküre*
Wednesday, August 16	*Siegfried*
Thursday, August 17	*Götterdämmerung*

Second Cycle

Sunday, August 20	*Das Rheingold*
Monday, August 21	*Die Walküre*
Tuesday, August 22	*Siegfried*
Wednesday, August 23	*Götterdämmerung*

Third Cycle

Sunday, August 27	*Das Rheingold*
Monday, August 28	*Die Walküre*
Tuesday, August 29	*Siegfried*
Wednesday, August 30	*Götterdämmerung*

To produce a list of the many guests who turned up to witness this epoch-making production would be to unfold a Who's Who of contemporary civilization. More than five thousand people were turned away from the theatre on the first night. Statesmen, aristocrats, composers, and music-lovers from around the world all converged on the small Bavarian town. Andrássy and Apponyi were there from Hungary, and Reichstag Minister Franz Duncker from Berlin. Saint-Saëns journeyed from Paris, Sir George Henschel from London, Franz von Suppé from Vienna, and Tchaikovsky from St. Petersburg.[18] The critics were there in abundance, headed by Eduard Hanslick from Vienna, Karl Fren-

---

18. Liszt and Tchaikovsky met for the first time at this festival. Tchaikovsky described Bayreuth as "a small, unimportant town. . . . The *service* is very bad." (WDS, p. 238) And to his brother, Modest, he wrote: "Visited Liszt, who was most kind." Their subsequent relations were not marked by great cordiality, however, although Liszt did transcribe the Polonaise from *Eugene Onegin* some three years later.

zel and Gustav Engel from Berlin, and J. W. Davison from London. Generally speaking, they gave *The Ring* a highly positive reception, although the French newspaper contingent, still smarting from the war of 1870, found much to complain about. Albert Wolff of *Le Figaro* led the charge and called *The Ring* "the dream of a lunatic." Among the many friends and colleagues of Wagner who also joined the Bayreuth throng were Judith Gauthier, the Wesendoncks, the Bronsarts, Friedrich Nietzsche, Olga von Meyendorff, and Adelheid von Schorn. Grand Duke Carl Alexander also turned up; many years ago he had had the chance to mount *The Ring* at Weimar and had been too fainthearted to proceed.[19] What were his feelings as he surveyed Wagner's triumph? Despite the glittering array of special visitors to Bayreuth, there were some notable absentees. Brahms and Joachim and Clara Schumann failed to attend. The "War of the Romantics" was still alive and well.

Kaiser Wilhelm arrived in Bayreuth on August 12, accompanied by the Grand Duke of Schwerin and the Grand Duchess of Baden, among others. He only stayed for *Rheingold* on August 13 and *Walküre* on the 14th, and then dashed away in order to attend military manoeuvres, but his visit was of enormous symbolic importance to Bayreuth. Wagner had always insisted that in his music dramas he was trying to create a truly German national art-form, and here was the Kaiser himself to lend visible support to that endeavour. Wagner, who cancelled a rehearsal and went to the railway station to meet the sovereign, was gratified beyond measure when he heard Wilhelm say that he regarded Bayreuth as "a national matter." He gave the Kaiser a guided tour of the Festspielhaus; when Wilhelm observed the concealed orchestra, by which he was greatly struck, he remarked: "If I were a musician I would not burrow myself down in there."[20] Sir George Henschel spotted Wagner driving to the station in an open landau, wearing evening-dress and white tie, in order to receive yet another reigning German prince, and could not help remarking how times had changed since 1848: "Truly a wonderful illustration of the all-conquering power of genius."[21] King Ludwig of Bavaria was there for a few days at the beginning of August but left the city after the dress rehearsals of August 6–9, which were, in fact, specially mounted for him. He deliberately stayed away until the third cycle, in order to avoid mixing with royal dignitaries he preferred not to meet; but he was back from August 27 to 30 for the last cycle, which he attended incognito.

For the duration of his stay Liszt lived with the Wagners in Wahnfried.[22] The house was luxurious beyond anything that he was used to. His own entourage

---

19. See Volume Two, pp. 234–35n.
20. LL, p. 142.
21. HMMM, p. 133.
22. The Wagners had lived there since April 1874. The house had been specially built to Wagner's own design, on land he had purchased from the local Stahlmann brothers for 12,000 gulden. It was the first permanent home that Wagner had ever had, and, as with the theatre being built at the same

gathered around him in Bayreuth, and he continued to hold court. Among the many friends and acquaintances who socialized with him were Count Albert Apponyi and Count Gyula Andrássy; among his pupils and disciples were Lina Ramann and Berthold Kellermann; and among his Weimar colleagues were Eduard Lassen and Adelheid von Schorn. Wahnfried was alive with visitors from morning till night, and there were a number of parties in which Liszt inevitably came into his own. The jokes flew thick and fast in such vivacious company. One of the best was a pun by Wagner, which Liszt later recorded in his diary. Evidently Wagner had just received the gift of an organ from a noted American firm, which wheezed and coughed when anyone played it. When he heard the dying strains he paraphrased the saying "One should not look a gift-horse in the mouth" into "Einer geschenkten Orgel schaut man nicht in die Gorgel"—which may be loosely translated as "One should not look a gift-organ in the windpipe."[23] But it was the informal music-making that made these social gatherings so memorable. Standing in the centre of the great music room was Wagner's new Steinway grand piano, a gift from the American firm to mark the inauguration of the festival.[24] It was on this piano that Liszt delivered a memorable performance of the slow movement of Beethoven's *Hammerklavier* Sonata, which moved Wagner to tears. Count Apponyi's graphic description of the scene has already been quoted, but his last few words are worth recalling: "This experience still lives within me, and has confirmed and deepened my innermost conviction that those three great men [Liszt, Wagner, and Beethoven] belonged to one another."[25]

There were many who agreed with Apponyi. The origins of the Liszt-Wagner story had never been kept secret from those musicians who formed the wide circle of their friends and acquaintances. From the moment that Liszt had lifted his baton in the service of Wagner, more than a quarter of a century ear-

---

time, he supervised every stage of its construction. Wagner regarded it as a refuge from the woes of the world, and he symbolised that fact by having engraved across its portals the following lines:

Hier, wo mein Wähnen Frieden fand
WAHNFRIED
Sei dieses Haus von mir genannt.

(Here where my illusion found peace
PEACE FROM ILLUSION
Be this house named by me.)

23. LL, p. 143.
24. It bears a commemorative plate on which are inscribed the words:

Fest-Gruss aus Steinway Hall
Richard Wagner
Steinway and Sons, New York, 1876
no. 34,304.

25. See Volume One, p. 317, n. 41.

lier, and had introduced *Lohengrin* to the world, they had followed the fortunes of the two musicians with keen interest. Many people were well aware that Wagner might not have survived the long years of exile without the constant support of Liszt, who was perceived even then to have rescued his old friend from oblivion. But the Wagnerians gradually became uncomfortable with such a thought. They did not like to think that their hero had ever depended on Liszt for material and inspirational help, and they now began a conspiracy to change history. In this they were assisted by the many "Wagner Societies" that sprang up in the 1870s and '80s, and also by the founding of the *Bayreuther Blätter,* the festival's official propaganda sheet. The Lisztians naturally pressed the case as they had always understood it. They argued that Wagner had, in fact, received far too much support from Liszt, that he was ungrateful for it, and that he never made proper acknowledgement after the tide of history had begun to turn in his favour. It has been well said that the only thing wrong with masters are the disciples they attract. The facts illustrate that both sides overstated the matter. There were at least two occasions when Wagner made public speeches in which he went out of his way to thank Liszt for his many sacrifices. One of them was at the Bayreuth Festival of 1876, and we may briefly consider it here.[26]

On the evening of August 18, at the end of the festival, there was a great banquet in the Festspielhaus restaurant, attended by about five hundred people. A series of long tables had been set up in parallel lines, twenty guests to each table. At the specially decorated head table sat Wagner, Cosima, Liszt, Richter, the violinist August Wilhelmj, and others. Nearby were Saint-Saëns, Adelheid von Schorn, Apponyi, and Berthold Kellermann. After the first course Wagner got up and thanked his artists, the members of the festival committee, and the burghers of Bayreuth. "But for their aid," he exclaimed, pointing to the various groups, "I could have accomplished nothing!" As one course succeeded another, various dignitaries got up to speak, including Reichsminister Duncker, and Apponyi, who made a poetical speech in which he likened

---

26. The other was at the festival of 1882, after the premiere of *Parsifal* (see p. 417). Nor should we forget the "open letter" that Wagner wrote to Marie von Sayn-Wittgenstein in April 1857:

> Do you know a musician who is more musical than Liszt? who holds within his breast the powers of music in richer, deeper store than he? who has felt more sensitively and more tenderly, who knows more and who can do more, who is more gifted by Nature and who, by educating himself, has developed his potential more forcefully than he? If you cannot name a second one like him, oh, you may confidently place your trust in this unique individual, a man who, moreover, is far too noble a human being ever to think of deceiving you. (WGSD, vol. 5, p. 197)

These are not the words of someone who is ungrateful, but rather the words of someone who wants to put something on the record. And when we remember that they were reinforced by the public tributes of 1876 and 1882, we must conclude that the case concerning Wagner's "ingratitude" may have been overstated by the Lisztians.

Wagner to a latter-day Siegfried who had awakened a new national art-form, just as Siegfried had awakened a sleeping Brünnhilde, by passing through clouds of fire. By now, Wagner was in an expansive mood, and he got up to make a second speech in which he paid a special tribute to Liszt.

> For everything that I am and have achieved, I have one person to thank, without whom not a single note of mine would have been known; a dear friend who, when I was banned from Germany, with matchless devotion and self-denial drew me into the light, and was the first to recognize me. To this dear friend belongs the highest honour. It is my sublime friend and master, Franz Liszt![27]

As the two musicians embraced one another, a hush fell across the hall. After a brief moment of silence, which seemed to contain an eternity, great waves of cheering broke out, and Liszt, who appears to have been taken by surprise at Wagner's speech, turned to the audience and said simply: "For those deeply appreciated words of recognition I thank my friend, to whom I remain humbly devoted."[28]

Liszt's attendance at the festival was generally interpreted as granting an important seal of approval to Bayreuth, which was still in its infancy, with no guarantee of a future. He had been one of the earliest patrons, and he had given concerts in benefit of the Festspielhaus.[29] Carolyne was convinced that the Wagners were simply using Liszt for publicity purposes, and that his association with the festival would divert attention away from his own work as a composer. In this she showed herself to be immensely shrewd and perceptive. By placing himself in Wagner's proximity, Liszt did indeed unwittingly invite a comparison between them, and it slowly worked to his disadvantage. As Wagner's star waxed, his own waned. And this change in their fortunes can be traced back to Bayreuth and the year 1876.

If Carolyne had not pressed her anti-Bayreuth crusade on Liszt with such determination, it is entirely possible that he might not have resisted her to the extent that he did, in which case his relationship with the festival would have been of a different order. But she was by this time incapable of calm debate, so he took the opposite tack and practically fell into Bayreuth's arms. Carolyne

---

27. KE, p. 195. The details of the banquet itself were reported quite extensively in *The New York Times*, September 4, 1876.

28. Ibid.

29. These benefit concerts have not been well documented, and they remain among the best-kept secrets in the Liszt literature. Adelheid von Schorn mentions one which was given jointly by Liszt and Ingeborg von Bronsart in Hanover. (SZM, p. 325) On May 9, 1876, Liszt also appeared in that same city as soloist in Beethoven's *Emperor* Concerto, conducted by Hans von Bronsart, the proceeds going to Bayreuth.

thus helped to bring about the very situation that she had dreaded. Liszt became an artistic subordinate of Wagner in Bayreuth; the secondary role he
played there was remarked by all. Even he was eventually obliged to admit it.
When he wrote that "to Bayreuth I am not a composer, but a publicity agent,"
he was merely recording the unvarnished truth and describing the role that
Cosima and Wagner had assigned to him.[30]

I V

Whatever artistic triumphs Wagner achieved as a result of mounting *Der Ring,*
the reality was that he was left with a festival deficit of 120,000 marks and an
uncertain future. The liquidation of this debt now became an urgent priority
for him and his supporters. Until the books were balanced there could be no
question of arranging another festival (the second Bayreuth Festival did not
take place until 1882). Utterly exhausted, Wagner left Bayreuth with his family
for a holiday in Italy, during which he pondered his future. Of all the ways he
might raise money, by far the one most likely to succeed was for him to appear
as a conductor of his own music. With the encouragement of August Wilhelmj
and Edward Dannreuther, Wagner was persuaded to visit London in the spring
of 1877 and conduct a series of concerts in benefit of the Bayreuth Festival
Deficit Fund. Wilhelmj especially was convinced that the Londoners would
turn out in great numbers to see Wagner and hear his music. Several halls were
considered, including Exeter Hall and St. James's Hall, but the choice eventually fell upon the Royal Albert Hall because of its superior seating capacity of
nearly eight thousand people. Wagner arrived in London on May 1, 1877, in
the company of Cosima, and they remained as guests of Dannreuther in his
comfortable home in Bayswater.

Eight concerts took place in the cavernous hall throughout the month of
May.[31] Constituting a remarkable overview of Wagner's music, they consisted
of authorised selections from *Rienzi, Holländer, Tannhäuser, Lohengrin, Meistersinger,* and *Tristan* in the first half of the programme, and selections from *The
Ring* in the second. The conducting was divided between Wagner (part one)
and Richter (part two). A huge orchestra of 170 musicians was amassed (105 in
the string section alone), and several singers who had sung leading roles at
Bayreuth were engaged as well, including Amalie Materna, Friederike von
Sadler-Grün, Elisabeth Exter, Karl Hill, Max Schlosser, and Georg Unger.

---

30. PEMH, p. 535.
31. Six concerts were originally announced, but the official festival brochure shows that eight actually
took place (May 7, 9, 12, 14, 16, 19, 28, and 29), the last two having been planned at the last moment,
when it became clear that Wagner was going to lose money. At the conclusion of the concert on the
19th, there was a speech in Wagner's honour, and a laurel-wreath was placed on his brow.

There had been nothing like this to enliven the London music season within living memory. As Bernard Shaw put it, "Not since King Nebuchadnessar set up the golden image . . . was such an assemblage of musical instruments . . . ever collected together."[32] Although the attendances were large, they were not large enough to show much profit.[33] After Wagner had paid the singers and the players, he returned to Germany with little more than seven hundred pounds in his pocket—a derisory sum when set beside the figure of five hundred pounds' profit for each of the eight concerts he had been led to expect. When the result became known, a number of public-spirited individuals came forward "determined to wipe off the stain on the English artistic character,"[34] and opened a subscription list which resulted in a further sum of five hundred and sixty pounds. This money Wagner refused to accept because it came, as he put it, from a group of total strangers. So "the stain" remained.

---

32. SMC, vol. 1, p. 122.

33. Incredibly, the firm of London concert agents hired to arrange the event, Hodge and Essex, had failed to build into their calculations the all-important fact that a good third of the seats at the Albert Hall were privately owned and could not therefore be used to generate revenue. When Dannreuther came to write his *Grove* article on Wagner, he mentioned the London benefit concerts in some detail, but played down his own part in arranging them. But the unpublished correspondence between him and Cosima Wagner on this topic shows beyond doubt that Dannreuther played a very large role in the enterprise, and that without his urging it is unlikely that Wagner would ever have gone to London believing that "das Land ohne Musik" was capable of solving his financial woes. (ENC, Folder 132)

34. KSB, p. 286. *The Times* carried extensive coverage of the Wagner concerts; see especially the issues of May 8 and May 14, 1877.

Wanderer Eternal, 1876–1881

In life one has to decide whether to conjugate the
verb "to have" or the verb "to be."

FRANZ LISZT[1]

I

Simply to keep track of Liszt's movements during the late 1870s and early 1880s confronts the modern biographer with major difficulties. Liszt is here, there, and everywhere. His footprints criss-cross their way across Europe, not once but many times. There are moments when his peregrinations become so complex that all one can do is to follow the main trails and hope that they do not lead one astray. It has been well said that "the Devil lies in the details"—a cautionary phrase that Liszt's chroniclers do well to heed. Liszt teaches, composes, conducts, administrates, and corresponds. And he does all this not just in one city, but in four or five at the same time. For to his regular activities in Weimar, Rome, and Budapest are now added important visits to such cities as Paris, Vienna, and Brussels. To save time, he usually travels at night, and to save money he travels third-class. This is less comfortable, but he does not sleep much anyway. In fact, as the train moves through one darkened city after another, Liszt spends much of his time scribbling in his so-called *Konzeptbuch,* the notebook in which he jots down the first drafts of his letters, to be polished, refined, and then mailed to their recipients when he has arrived at the end of his journey.[2] It is easy to see how posterity, confronted by this whirlwind of activity, can

---

1. WFLG, p. 117.
2. These *Konzeptbücher* have become an important tool of Liszt research. Liszt often discloses ideas—such as opinions about others, or thoughts on the problems of the day—that were suppressed when he came to write out the finished version of the letters.

wash its hands of the problem and dismiss Liszt as a compulsive itinerant, a trav-eller for travel's sake. That is not really good enough, for behind the ceaseless movement there is much to be understood.

Naturally he could not have undertaken so much unless he had been able to work quickly and easily. He had the knack of being able to drive out those daily distractions which often overwhelm other people in order to complete the task in hand. While there is a dearth of studies on Liszt's composing meth-ods, we know that he often worked on several compositions at the same time. Berthold Kellermann, who studied with him between 1873 and 1879, tells us that Liszt "wrote full scores with fluent speed, from the bottom to the top, as fast as someone else would write a letter." On one occasion Kellermann and his young wife, passing through Munich, decided to call on Liszt in his hotel. Although Liszt was working on a new composition he made them welcome. He then returned to his writing-table, explaining that the work was urgent. He refused to let the Kellermanns go, however, "but continued to talk to us for a long time in the most friendly way, while continuing to write uninterruptedly at his score. . . ."[3]

Nor was procrastination in Liszt's nature. He had nothing in common with those human beings who daily devote their lives to doing nothing. The really busy ones are capable of not doing two or three things simultaneously. Liszt early discovered that by reversing the process he could live three lives instead of one. And what he himself called his "threefold life" offers striking proof of that fact. We propose to review the highlights here, for they reveal a diversity of activity that is the quintessential Liszt.

II

Liszt arrived in Budapest from Rome on February 15, 1876, and took up resi-dence at his apartment in the Royal Academy of Music building. He had no inkling that within a week his wonderful view of the Danube would be trans-formed into scenes of devastation. In a replay that was reminiscent of the great flood of 1838, the river began to swell from the melting winter snows, and in a few days it burst its banks—this time on the Buda side. A vast tract of west-ern and northern Hungary was inundated, and the towns of Komárom, Esz-tergom, Ujpest, and Óbuda lay beneath a lake of icy flood-water. More than fifteen thousand refugees abandoned their homes and converged on Budapest, whose resources were quickly overwhelmed. By February 24 the river threat-ened to wash over the Pest embankment, which had been specially reinforced

---

3. KE, pp. 31–32.

after the 1838 disaster. Cannon were fired from the fortress on Gellért Hill to warn the population of possible danger. Liszt kept a lunch appointment with Baron Augusz, but it was interrupted by further cannon salvos booming across the city telling the residents that a disaster was at hand. Buildings were hurriedly evacuated, and Liszt was transferred at Ábrányi's insistence to Albert Apponyi's apartment (which had withstood the flood of 1838) until the danger to Fischplatz could be properly assessed. Liszt took with him some manuscripts of works-in-progress and a bundle of private correspondence, and sat out the crisis. As daylight broke the following morning an awe-inspiring sight greeted the citizens. A raging torrent of water was flowing near the top of the embankment at great speed, carrying with it chunks of ice the size of houses, together with boats, trees, smashed furniture, and the debris of homes from miles up-river. The torrent raged for three days until it finally subsided into a vast lake of ice and mud.

The whole of Hungarian society rallied to the help of the victims, including the king and queen, who came forward with large charitable donations; about sixty thousand forints were collected for the homeless.[4] Schools and public buildings were appropriated and used as emergency refugee sites. One hundred families who had lost everything were given sanctuary in the monasteries of the Franciscans and the Capuchins, who were themselves impoverished.[5] It was unthinkable that Liszt would stand idly by and not volunteer to help. He wrote a letter to the minister of education, Ágoston Trefort, offering to appear as a pianist for charity, which was published in the newspapers together with Trefort's letter of acceptance. It ended with the patriotic words: "I remain until the grave Hungary's true and grateful son."[6] While the offer violated Liszt's long-standing decision never to give solo recitals, he felt that the gravity of the crisis warranted it. As he told Princess Carolyne, he really had no alternative but to place "my old fingers" in the service of the needy.[7] The concert took place in the Vigadó, on March 20, in the presence of Prime Minister Kálmán Tisza, Ágoston Trefort, cabinet minister Tamás Péchy, various dignitaries from the city of Budapest, and a packed audience that surged "like the waves of the sea." Two Bösendorfers stood on the great platform, and as Liszt walked out promptly at 7:00 p.m. he was greeted by waves of cheering. His programme had been specially selected to symbolize both the tragedy of the disaster and the triumph in overcoming it.

---

4. LLC, vol. 2, p. 47.
5. WLLM, p. 235.
6. See the *Pesther Lloyd* for March 1, 1876; also LLB, vol. 2, pp. 236–37.
7. LLB, vol. 7, p. 129.

Pathétique Sonata	Beethoven
St. Francis of Paola Walking on the Waters	Liszt
Mélodies hongroises	Schubert-Liszt
La Charité	Rossini-Liszt
Hungarian anthems "Szozat" and	Liszt
"Hymnus" Paraphrases	

Liszt then walked over to where the Liszt Society Choir was situated,[8] and conducted a performance of his choral prayer *An den heiligen Franziskus von Paula,* for soloists, male-voice chorus, and organ. Although the piece had been composed many years earlier in Weimar (in 1860), it had only been heard once before, in Budapest the previous year.

> St. Francis!
> You walk across the ocean storm
> And are not afraid
> In your heart is love, and in your hand a glowing ember
> Through the clouded heavens God's light appears.[9]

The text goes on to draw a moral, and urges us to walk like St. Francis across life's tempests, to preserve the glowing ember of love, and to walk towards the everlasting light. The musical connection between the choral prayer and the piano Legend *St. Francis of Paola walking on the water* (which was written later, in 1863) emerges towards the end of both pieces.

---

8. Between the items of Liszt's recital, the recently formed Liszt Society Choir, conducted by Mátyás Engeszer, interposed the "Reapers' Chorus" from Liszt's *Prometheus Unbound* and his *Hymne de l'enfant à son réveil,* accompanied by Antal Siposs and Liszt, respectively.

9. We now know that the words of Liszt's prayer to St. Francis were written by his pupil Martha von Sabinin, the daughter of the Russian Orthodox priest in Weimar, who had herself taken holy orders and had meanwhile become the abbess of the Order of the Annunciation, in the Crimea. Martha Sabinin's poem describes the scene of Steinle's drawing *St. Francis of Paola,* which used to hang in Liszt's music room at the Altenburg and which she must have observed many times. She wrote the prayer for Liszt's name-day on April 2 in either 1855 or 1856. (See PALP.) For the Budapest première the text was translated into Hungarian by Count Albert Apponyi.

SOLO-QUARTETT
Inbrünstig betend

Pianists might like to compare the above example with the one on page 59. They would do well to become aware of Liszt's musical self-quotation; otherwise, they deny themselves access to the deeper meaning of the Legend. When Liszt forged its connection with his choral prayer ("Let us keep Love whole") he revealed the Legend's true character. We are free to ignore the link, of course; but if we do, our wider understanding of the piano work will remain defective.

III

Liszt spent the spring and summer of 1876 in Weimar, where he resumed teaching and composing at the Hofgärtnerei. Among his new students was twelve-year-old Alfred Reisenauer, whose parents had travelled with their prodigy son from Königsberg to place him in Liszt's charge, and who remained Liszt's pupil for the next ten years. Also much in evidence at this time was the American Max Pinner, who had turned up in Rome a short time earlier bearing a letter of introduction from Leopold Damrosch.[10] Damrosch had already done much to spread Liszt's name and fame since settling in the United States, with the result that the first large wave of American pupils had already swept into Weimar, including William Sherwood (Boston), Kathie Gaul (Baltimore), and Anna Bock (New York). Other new pupils included the German Karl Pohlig, the Russian Vera Timanova, and the Pole Juliusz Zarembski. From this time Liszt's Weimar masterclasses were truly international. Under his guidance both Pinner and Zarembski had already given public concerts in Rome. They

10. LLB, vol. 2, p. 238.

were among the best of the present crop of his pupils, while Timanova was a virtuoso whom Liszt described as having fingers of steel.

Excursions to various towns and cities in Germany interrupted Liszt's daily routine. On April 29 he set out for Düsseldorf for three days in order to attend the Lower Rhine Music Festival, which featured performances of his symphonic poem *Prometheus,* the *Prometheus* Choruses, and the "Gran" Mass, conducted by his old pupil Theodor Ratzenberger. He had not planned to go, but when he heard that the tickets were not selling very well he volunteered to be present at the concerts and even to appear as a soloist—a publicity coup for Ratzenberger that assured the financial success of the festival. The visit was enlivened by chance encounters with Clara Schumann and his old rival Ferdinand Hiller, both of whom complimented him on his indestructible youth.[11] Hiller heard Liszt play an arrangement of Schubert's Hungarian March in C minor which brought tears to his eyes. "That old man . . . makes me feel like a schoolboy. I want to shut my piano and never open it again!" he exclaimed.[12] Liszt was invited round to Hiller's for a dinner-party. He wrily described the spice in the anecdotes (or rather the lack of it) as the culinary equivalent of "cold jellied chicken."[13]

In the second half of May we once more find Liszt in Holland as a guest of King Willem III at Loo Castle, whence he had wended his way for the purpose of judging the king's scholarship students. This year the musicians on the jury included Henri Vieuxtemps, Alexandre Batta, Eduard Hartog, and Saint-Saëns. After a lightning trip back to Weimar on May 26, he left after one day for the town of Altenburg in order to attend the annual festival of the Allgemeiner Deutscher Musikverein, an event he rarely missed. He was well represented, with performances of his *Prometheus Unbound, Hunnenschlacht,* the "Weinen, Klagen" Variations, and the Fantasy for Piano and Orchestra on Motifs from Beethoven's *Ruins of Athens.*

One of the more interesting forays for Liszt was his excursion to Sondershausen on July 2. There he attended the first performance of his symphonic poem *Hamlet,* under the direction of Max Erdmannsdörfer, a work that—astonishingly—he had not yet heard.[14] At the end of July he paid a visit to Wilhelmsthal as the guest of Carl Alexander, and from there he travelled to Bayreuth, as we have seen.

From Wahnfried Liszt travelled once more to Hanover, to visit Hans von Bülow, who had been taken seriously ill shortly after returning from his first

---

11. WLLM, p. 239.
12. CFL, p. 110.
13. WLLM, p. 240.
14. We have this information from Liszt himself. The chief work in the programme, which was devoted to "The Music of the Future," was Berlioz's *Harold in Italy.* But Liszt also asked the enterprising Erdmannsdörfer to include Wagner's new Festival March, Bülow's *Nirvana,* and, "in case there

American tour—a marathon undertaking during which Bülow gave more than 140 concerts in less than eight months. Liszt found his former son-in-law in the grip of a paralysing depression. Bülow was suicidal and had only just been prevented from taking his own life.[15] "To find Bülow in such a state of suffering distressed me," wrote Liszt. The rumour had spread that Bülow had lost his mind, and during the journey to Hanover Liszt had been fearful of what might confront him. He was relieved to find Bulow "most markedly lucid . . . he retains that great nobility of character with a heroic touch, which I admire and love in him." According to Liszt, Bülow's great mistake was to have ignored a light stroke which afflicted him before setting out for America—a piece of medical information which has not found its way into the standard literature about this musician. His gargantuan programmes did the rest. Liszt claimed that had Fasolt and Fafner (the giants in Wagner's *Ring*) given such concerts, they would have killed themselves without assistance from anybody. For two weeks (from September 24 to October 5) Liszt stayed with Bülow, offering emotional support and practical advice. The irony of the situation will not be lost on the reader. Elation prevailed at Wahnfried, depression at Hanover. Liszt was expected to partake of both at the same time, and he did so at no small cost to his own psychological well-being. He must have felt as if he were being torn between God and the devil. Once more we are struck by the profound links that connected his art to his emotional life: for it was at Hanover that he composed his piano transcription of Saint-Saëns's *Danse macabre,* a fitting symbol of his fretted feelings.[16]

He was in an uncertain frame of mind when he moved on to Nuremberg (October 6 to 9) in fulfillment of a promise he had given to Lina Ramann to make himself available for more interviews. Ramann treasured these visits and wrote about them extensively in her *Lisztiana.* On this occasion Liszt played a number of his compositions to her, including *St. Francis of Paola walking on the waters.* He worked up a tremendous storm, and when he had finished, wrote Ramann, his brow was covered in perspiration and his hands were cold and trembling. "Everything that lay in this storm," she added in a flash of biographical revelation, "was sealed in the past."[17]

---

should be room for one of my shorter things, I would modestly suggest the symphonic poem *Hamlet,* which I have never heard." (LLB, vol. 2, p. 241) About eighteen years had elapsed since Liszt composed the work.

15. See p. 144.

16. He sent a copy of the manuscript to Saint-Saëns on October 2. "I beg you to excuse my unskilfulness in reducing the marvellous colouring of the score to the possibilities of the piano." And he added, in a masterpiece of understatement: "No one is bound by the impossible. To play an orchestra on the piano is not yet given to anyone." (LLB, vol. 2, p. 243)

17. RL, pp. 100–01.

IV

Altogether Liszt spent nearly five months in Hungary during the winter of 1876–77, one of the longest periods of residence in his native land since his childhood. After catching the night train from Vienna (where he had spent a few days with cousin Eduard in the Schottenhof) he arrived in Budapest at dawn on October 16 in the company of his manservant Spiridon, and did not leave until March 11—apart from a few brief forays into provincial Hungarian towns. He was caught up almost immediately in a busy round of teaching and administration at the Royal Academy of Music, which was now one year old and growing rapidly. One of the first decisions he had to make was to select three winners for the newly established Liszt Scholarship, the money for which had come from the interest on a capital sum of 10,000 forints set aside by the city of Budapest three years earlier for the creation of a Liszt Foundation. His choice fell upon three of his most gifted Hungarian piano students: Károly Agg-házy, Aladár Juhász, and Ilona Lépessy. This year he had fifteen students at-tending his piano classes, which were held four times a week, between 4:00 and 6:00 p.m. The sessions were not unlike the masterclasses conducted in Weimar, with their strong emphasis on interpretation and hardly any mention of tech-nique. Despite the fact that they were given in the more formal setting of the academy building, they attracted an audience of prominent musicians who simply wanted to see (and hear) Liszt working with his students.

Liszt attended many concerts in Budapest during the months of November and December, irrespective of whether his own music was featured. Nor did it much matter to him whether the music-making was professional or amateur. He went to the opera and the philharmonic concerts in exactly the same spirit as to school concerts or to struggling choral societies: he was interested chiefly in the musical life of the country, and he knew that his presence was an en-couragement to local musicians.

Three of Liszt's best female pianists accepted his invitation to join him dur-ing this winter of 1876–77—Martha Remmert, Vera Timanova, and Sophie Menter—so that he might introduce them to Hungarian concert-goers. Rem-mert and Timanova stood on the threshold of their careers and still needed his help; Menter was already a finished artist (Liszt described her as "the greatest woman pianist of her generation") but was doubtless happy to receive Liszt's support. He took a personal interest in arranging their concerts, selecting their programmes, and generally smoothing a path through the bureaucratic jungle of hall-rentals, ticket-sales, and advance newspaper publicity—things that were easier for him to do in Budapest than in other major European cities. By mak-ing this gesture, he not only brought his students to prominence but also introduced Hungary to some fine piano playing. In those days there was far less competition in the field than was later to be the case. Until the Compromise of 1867 Hungary's cultural life had been in the doldrums. But in January 1877 Liszt's students gave the citizens of Budapest a feast of piano music the like of which had rarely been heard. Since he also arranged for these pupils to present concerts in provincial towns elsewhere in Hungary, he was helping to fulfil one of the goals he had outlined to Minister Trefort: that the purpose of the Royal Academy was to stimulate not only the cultural life of Budapest but that of the entire country.

His daily life was complicated somewhat by two accidents he suffered at this time. On December 18, 1876, as he was getting out of his carriage outside the Hungária Hotel, he missed his footing and fell headlong onto the cobblestones beneath, striking his right arm and chest against the kerbstone. The accident left him with some bruising, and for several days he had difficulty in breathing. His pupil Géza Zichy saw him a few days later and expressed concern for his health. Liszt, who never thought ill-health a worthy topic of conversation, told him, "It's nothing, just a small bruise on my right arm," and joked that he would be ashamed to complain in the presence of Zichy, who had only one arm. But even as he spoke, Zichy saw him bite his lip to keep back the pain.[18] The other accident had occurred a short time earlier. One morning, as he was being shaved by Spiridon, Liszt raised his left hand in order to make a point in the conversation, and the razor accidentally cut his index finger.[19] Most pianists who had sustained a severe blow to the right arm, following a razor cut to the left hand, would have withdrawn from public life for a time, fearful that their handicaps might result in inferior playing and tarnish their reputations. But Liszt seemed impervious to such setbacks; he played the piano a lot to his fellow Hungarians during the next few weeks—albeit with nine fingers. It is one more proof that for Liszt, piano playing was hardly a physical activity. The spirit rather than the flesh brought music into being. As for his reputation, even with nine fingers he was still the standard by which other pianists were judged.

---

18. ZLEF, vol. 2, pp. 23–30. Count Géza Zichy had just been appointed president of the National Conservatory of Music in Budapest, at the early age of twenty-six, and he became an increasingly prominent figure in the musical life of Hungary. When he was fourteen he lost his right arm in a hunting accident. He himself tells the dramatic story of how that happened in his *Das Buch des Einarmigen* (1915). An animal sprang at his horse, and his gun went off at half-cock. The bullet blew off the right arm above the elbow. His brother got him home with difficulty, a doctor was summoned, and the arm was amputated after Zichy had been given ether. Zichy's love of the piano was such that he went on to develop considerable skill with the left hand, and he arranged a number of pieces for himself to play.

19. LLB, vol. 7, p. 168.

V

The year 1877 marked the fiftieth anniversary of Beethoven's death. As on similar occasions in the past, a number of European cities vied with one another to offer their homage to the master. No tribute was more fitting than the one mounted in Vienna, Beethoven's musical home for nearly forty years. Liszt was invited to participate in recognition of the half-century of service he had devoted to Beethoven's cause. Ironically, Vienna still did not have a public statue to Beethoven, and the proceeds of Liszt's concert were intended for that purpose. Unlike the one hundredth birthday festival of 1870, from which Liszt had been effectively excluded amidst a good deal of back-biting and recrimination, this celebration was surrounded by goodwill. In his letter of acceptance, dated "Budapest, December 10, 1876," he told the Beethoven Monument Committee that he intended to "work with a full heart and with both hands" to help them in their task.[20] And he kept his word, despite his physical afflictions.

He set out from Hungary and arrived in Vienna on March 11, where he stayed as usual with his cousin Eduard in the Schottenhof. For the past several years Eduard had placed a large room at Liszt's disposal whenever he was in the city. It was furnished with items taken from the Altenburg and brought into the Schottenhof by Eduard in 1868—carpets, furniture, paintings, and a piano, so Liszt was not wrong to call it a second home. Here he was looked after by Eduard and his second wife, Henriette, and here too he regularly met his friends and entertained them when time and opportunity allowed. At the Beethoven memorial concert, on March 16, he played the *Emperor* Concerto and the Choral Fantasy for piano, orchestra, and chorus. He also accompanied Caroline Gomperz-Bettelheim in Beethoven's Scottish Songs. The great Musikvereinsaal was specially illuminated for the occasion, and the piano was festooned with flowers. Liszt was sixty-five years old and he no longer practised. Yet according to Hanslick his playing "delighted his audience" and was characterised by "nobility and refinement."

In comparing Liszt's playing with his performances in Vienna in 1874, Hanslick perceived some lack of strength, which he described as "old age knocking at the artist's door." But he added generously: "The younger generation should not rejoice too loudly; they still will not catch up with the old man."[21] Hanslick was unaware that Liszt had injured a finger and was redistributing the

---

20. LLB, vol. 2, p. 250.
21. HCCV, n. 75, pp. 202–03.

notes among the ones remaining.[22] In any case, Liszt may well have been tired by the time that Hanslick heard him, since the concert was actually given three times, being preceded by two public rehearsals for which the audience was charged admission.

The concert forged an important link with history. Sitting in the audience was the ten-year-old Ferruccio Busoni, who would one day become a champion of Liszt. After the concert the boy was taken by his mother to the Schottenhof to play for Liszt, but no record of the meeting has survived.[23] At the gala dinner following the concert, which was given in Liszt's honour at the Hotel Imperial by the Beethoven Monument Committee, Liszt encountered Brahms among the guests. Alas, no record of their conversation has come down to us. The following day, March 17, Liszt was presented with the gold Redeemer Medal by the mayor of Vienna in recognition of his contribution to the Beethoven Jubilee.

From Vienna Liszt travelled to Bayreuth, where he stayed with the Wagners from March 24 to April 3. They celebrated his name-day (April 2) in fine style. Wagner gave him a signed copy of his newly published autobiography, *Mein Leben,* and in the afternoon he read aloud the text of the first act of *Parsifal.* In the evening Liszt reciprocated and gave a performance of his B-minor Piano Sonata. Cosima wrote in her diary of "a lovely cherished day, on which I can thank Heaven for the comforting feeling that nothing—no deeply tragic parting of the ways, no malice on the part of others, no differences in character— could ever separate us three." To which she added the painful sentences: "Oh, if it were possible to add a fourth [Bülow] to our numbers here! But that an inexorable fate forbids, and for me every joy and every exaltation ends with an anxious cry to my inner being!"[24]

---

22. The story of Liszt's cut finger has come down to us in two versions. According to Göllerich, Liszt later told him that the cut occurred on the morning of the concert, and was to the fourth finger of the right hand. In his personal copy of Ramann's biography, however, Liszt made a marginal note to the effect that it was to the second (index) finger of the left hand (RLKM, vol. 1, p. 166; WA, Kasten 352)—not the first time that Göllerich's recollections were disproved by the primary documents. Moreover, in a letter to Princess Carolyne (dated December 27, 1876), Liszt confirmed that it was indeed to the left hand. Since that letter was written ten weeks before the concert took place, either the finger healed very slowly or there is a discrepancy that scholarship cannot resolve. Of course, it is entirely possible that there were two injuries, at two different times, but that raises the unlikely spectacle of Spiridon wielding such an indiscriminate razor as to pose a daily threat to Liszt's very survival.
23. See DFB, p. 24. Evidently this meeting was arranged by Caroline Gomperz-Bettelheim. Although Liszt was pleased with the young boy's playing, he refused to give him a testimonial when Busoni's father requested one. Liszt wrote from Rome that he had long since ceased to give testimonials. (DFB, p. 26)
24. WT, vol. 1, p. 1041.

VI

Much of the spring and summer of 1877 Liszt spent in Weimar, composing and teaching. Even though he had bound himself to the city for three months of each year, he was never constrained from making short excursions to nearby destinations, and this summer was no exception. He was present in Leipzig when Carl Riedel conducted portions of *Christus* on June 17; and in Eisenach for a performance of *St. Elisabeth* on June 29. A few days later, on July 2, he turned up in Jena to hear a concert containing some of his shorter sacred choral compositions, arranged by Carl Gille ("my untiring friend of many years standing"),[25] an event that Gille now mounted annually.

Liszt's main summer commitment, whenever he was in Germany, was to the annual festival of the Allgemeiner Deutscher Musikverein, which this year was held in Hanover. The moving spirits behind the festival of 1877 were Hans von Bronsart and his wife, Ingeborg Starck, two of Liszt's former pupils. In his capacity as the Royal Theatre intendant, Bronsart enjoyed much latitude in musical matters, and with Liszt's help he had arranged one of the more ambitious festivals of recent years. Liszt stayed in Hanover from May 15 to 30. Among the large-scale orchestral performances were Berlioz's *Fantastic* Symphony, Lassen's newly composed incidental music to Goethe's *Faust,* and Tchaikovsky's Second Symphony—a work that Bronsart had not at first wanted to perform but had included at Liszt's insistence.[26] Ingeborg Starck also appeared as a soloist in Saint-Saëns's *Variations on a Theme of Beethoven* and Liszt's *Concerto Pathétique*. Liszt himself was represented by his Legend of Saint Cecilia and *St. Elisabeth,* in which latter work the role of Landgräfin Sophie was sung by Marianne Brandt, who later achieved fame as Kundry in Wagner's *Parsifal*. Brandt was in glorious voice that evening, May 20, but she was completely upstaged by the court conductor, Jean-Joseph Bott, who fell off the podium and crashed to the floor in a state of intoxication. There was a stunned silence, and the performance stopped in its tracks. As the insensible Bott was removed from the carpet, Liszt came forward, picked up the baton, and directed the rest of *St. Elisabeth* himself. While Bott suffered no serious bodily harm, his reputation was irretrievably damaged. He was forced to resign from his position at Hanover and seek temporary refuge in Magdeburg as director of the local music conservatory.

---

25. LLB, vol. 2, p. 253.
26. WLLM, p. 277. Tchaikovsky's Second Symphony was still in manuscript.

VII

Anyone observing Liszt's manifold activities at this time would have been struck by his boundless energy. They would have seen a man of powerful action and unlimited enthusiasm, a man who pursued his goals with an almost fanatical determination. It was a common enough complaint among his friends and pupils that they had a hard time just keeping up with him, and they often fell by the wayside, exhausted by a crushing round of activity which seemed to leave Liszt himself refreshed and energized. They would have been astonished to learn that the opposite was the case: that he stood on the brink of nervous collapse, and had entered the first of a series of mental depressions that characterised his old age.

The initial symptoms had announced themselves in 1876, and took the form of melancholia: "Sometimes sadness envelops my soul like a shroud," was his mournful way of describing it. It became a physical effort for him to get through certain hours and days.[27] Liszt had almost burnt himself out; it was at this time that he first entertained thoughts of suicide. One of his few confidantes was Baroness Olga von Meyendorff, to whom he wrote: "I feel that I am reaching the end and even succumbing—and no longer want an extension."[28] By the spring of 1877 his melancholia was producing severe bouts of lethargy in which he was unable to bring himself to work. On one occasion he spent two whole days in bed for no other reason than that he saw no point in getting up. On April 25 he told Carolyne that his pen was "paralysed," that even a short letter to her cost him more than four hours, and that he sometimes sat for a whole day, pen in hand, waiting for ideas to come.[29] By June 15 his apathy had become worse, and he wrote to her: "My difficulty in writing is increasing and is becoming excessive—as is my weariness of living! Without feeling sorry for myself, I often suffer from [merely] existing—physical health remains, that of the spirit is lacking! *Tristis est anima mea!*"[30] The Latin quotation ("My soul is exceeding sorrowful") comes from Mark 14:34–36; Liszt refrained from completing it, since he knew that Carolyne would do that for him: "*usque ad mortem*"—"even unto death." Such outcries become a common occurrence as Liszt approaches old age.

It was in this sad frame of mind that Liszt returned to the Villa d'Este at the end of August 1877. He used to sit throughout the warm summer nights, con-

---

27. WLLM, p. 244.
28. WLLM, p. 299.
29. LLB, vol. 7, p. 188.
30. June 15, 1877. LLB, vol. 7, p. 193.

templating the great cypresses and listening to the play of the fountains. The experience brought him closer to nature and helped to calm his troubled spirits. His mortal sadness sought expression in two of the best piano pieces of his old age: the "Cypress" Threnodies. Liszt himself gives an account of their gestation: "I have just written a hundred or so measures for the piano. It is a fairly gloomy and disconsolate elegy; illumined towards the end by a beam of patient resignation. If I publish it, the title will be *Aux cyprès de la Villa d'Este*."[31] A short time later, and still with the cypresses as his nocturnal companions, he confessed that the word "elegy" (his first choice of title) hardly summed up the character of this music, and that he had substituted the more powerful "threnody."

> For the last two weeks I've been absorbed in *cypresses*. . . . I have composed two *groups* of cypresses, each of more than two hundred bars, plus a *postludium,* to the cypresses of the Villa d'Este. These sad pieces won't have much success and can do without it. I shall call them *Thrénodies,* as the word *élegie* strikes me as too tender, and almost worldly.[32]

And by November 9 we find him writing:

> A few more leaves have been added to the cypresses—no less boring and redundant than the previous ones! To tell the truth I sense in myself a terrible lack of talent compared with what I would like to express; the notes I write are pitiful. A strange sense of the infinite makes me impersonal and uncommunicative.[33]

He eventually placed his two "Cypress" Threnodies within the third and final volume of the great collection of pieces he called *Years of Pilgrimage* (1867–77). The titles run:

1. *Angelus!* Prière aux anges gardiens
2. *Aux cyprès de la Villa d'Este:* Threnodie I
3. *Aux cyprès de la Villa d'Este:* Threnodie II
4. *Les jeux d'eaux à la Villa d'Este*
5. *Sunt lacrymae rerum,* en mode hongrois
6. *Marche funèbre*
7. *Sursum corda*

---

31. WLLM, p. 292.
32. WLLM, p. 293.
33. WLLM, p. 297.

These seven pieces show a strong stylistic departure from the ones in the two earlier volumes. There is an unmistakably modern ring to this music. It has often been remarked that Threnodie II casts a backward glance at the third act of *Tristan*. But it would be just as true to say that it represents the future towards which Liszt's own "Die Lorelei" (1840) and "Ich möchte hingehn" (1859) had already pointed. Liszt, in short, was more than capable of fulfilling his own prophecies.

In any case, once Liszt begins to metamorphose this material, it moans with that special anguish unique to his later years.

The two examples are worth comparing; the "contrasts" they reflect spring from a single source. If we wish to reveal their common background, all we have to do is to re-express them, thus:

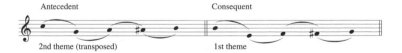

To put the relationship in simple analytical terms: the one theme declares itself to be the Antecedent of the other's Consequent—a piece of musical logic that is in no wise diminished through being both reversed and postponed. Liszt's name is rarely associated with notions of "deep structure," yet proponents of the Schoenbergian *Grundgestalt,* to say nothing of the Schenkerian *Urlinie,* would find in his music a rich supply of material to support their theoretical models. For the rest, anyone interested in the psychopathology of the musical mind will marvel that the creation of the "Cypress" pieces aroused in Liszt a sense of his own inadequacy. Despite his gloomy forecast that this music would not have much success, it has entered the standard repertory, admittedly a century after its first publication in 1883.

The undoubted masterpiece of the set is *Les jeux d'eaux à la Villa d'Este,* which dates from that same melancholy summer of 1877. Liszt used to sit for hours gazing at the fountains, spellbound by the play of their cascading waters. The result was a piece of musical impressionism so advanced for its time that for thirty years it had no successor until Ravel composed his own *Jeux d'eau.* We have already had occasion to mention the profound effect on Ravel of a much earlier piece of "water music" by Liszt, *Au bord d'une source,* whose cascading rivulets feed the d'Este fountains as well. But whereas Ravel, the master impressionist, merely composed a piece of water music, Liszt transcended simple visual imagery and turned his streaming fountains into mystical symbols, associating them with the well-known verse from the Gospel According to St. John (4:14) which he quotes in Latin in the score: *Sed aqua quam ego dabo ei, fiet in eo fons aquae salientis in vitam aeternam* ("But whosoever drinketh of the water that I shall give him, shall never thirst [but the water that I shall give him shall be in him a well of water springing up into everlasting life]"). As if to confirm that this is really a religious piece, Liszt enshrines it in his "divine" key of F-sharp major.[34] And when we hear such passages as the following, it is difficult to disagree with Busoni's observation that the piece has remained the model for all musical fountains which have flowed since then.[35]

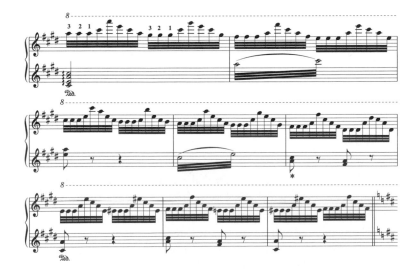

---

34. See Volume Two, p. 154.
35. BEM, p. 138.

VIII

Liszt left Rome on November 17. After pausing briefly at Lamporecchio as a guest of Prince Rospigliosi, he continued the long journey back to Budapest. It took him thirty-six hours of non-stop travel; he arrived in the City of the Magyars on November 21. He brought with him a heavy cold, as well as the mental depression that had cast such a dark pall over his life at the Villa d'Este. As in the previous year, he poured most of his energy into the Royal Academy of Music and his masterclasses, which helped to dispel his gloom; mingling with his young Hungarian students restored him to life. He was not isolated in Budapest, as he had been at the Villa d'Este, and had much less time to sink into himself.

By now Liszt's annual visits to Hungary had taken on the trappings of national ritual. People from all walks of life approached him to pay their respects, and he was routinely invited to lend his reputation to a variety of different organisations. He was honoured by the Society of Israelite Women, who put on a concert in his honour on the morning of December 6 in the presence of the mayor of Budapest, Károly Ráth, and the leaders of the Jewish religious community. It was meant as a token of thanks for a benefit concert he had given for the Israelite orphanage the previous spring. The children's choir sang for him, and a speech was delivered by Dr. Samuel Kohn. A commemorative tablet was then unveiled, which bore the inscription:

> To Ferenc Liszt, the world-famous composer, generous patron and noble benefactor of our orphans, as token of our gratitude for the concert to benefit our Society on March 10, 1877, and of our esteem, the Israelite Women's Society of Pest.[36]

Such examples prove that Liszt enjoyed excellent relations with the Jewish community in Hungary at this time. Malice and stupidity had not yet poisoned the connection; Princess Carolyne had not yet begun work on the revised Israelite chapter of Liszt's book *Des Bohémiens et de leur musique en Hongrie*.

He also continued his practice of attending as many concerts as possible in order to encourage local artists. One such concert deserves mention. On January 3, 1878, Léo Delibes conducted a performance of his ballet *Coppélia* at the National Theatre. Liszt was charmed by the score and the following

---

36. LLC, vol. 2, p. 85. This same source offers the best information about Liszt's daily itinerary in Hungary during the winter of 1877–78. See especially LLC, vol. 2, pp. 88–96.

evening he gave a reception for Delibes at Fischplatz, and invited Zichy, Apponyi, Ábrányi, Sándor Erkel, and other members of Hungary's intelligentsia to join them. The climax of the evening came when Liszt sat down at the piano and in the subdued lighting of his music salon gave a performance of Beethoven's *Moonlight* Sonata. He then repaired to the next room to play a game of whist with his friends, but it was the memory of his playing of Beethoven that lingered.

Liszt also attended the celebrations mounted for the Hungarian violinist Károly Huber, to mark the latter's twenty-five years of service as a teacher at the National Conservatory of Music. A concert of Huber's works took place in the large hall of the Hungária Hotel on January 6; but it was his twenty-year-old son, Jenő, who captured the limelight with his violin playing. This young man would later go on to found a Hungarian school of violin playing that included Jelly d'Arányi and József Szigeti. Forty-one years later he would also occupy Liszt's position as director of the Liszt Academy of Music. The threads that form the rich tapestry of Hungary's present-day musical life were already being woven during Liszt's visits to his native land.

A violinist of a somewhat different stamp visited Budapest at this time. Ole Bull, the Norwegian virtuoso and friend of Liszt's early manhood, had come from Vienna for the specific purpose of seeing Liszt. Bull and his wife, Sara, spent two days in Liszt's home (January 16 and 17), and the two old colleagues played Beethoven together. More than forty-seven years had elapsed since they had last played the *Kreutzer* Sonata, in London, but they attempted a performance now. According to Liszt's pupil Ilka Horowitz-Barnay, all did not go well, since the largely self-taught Bull played out of time and blamed Liszt for the frequent derailments. In her recollections of that evening, Horowitz-Barnay has the two white-haired musicians quarrelling over the musical mishaps. We take leave to doubt that Liszt threw a temper-tantrum and smashed a chair on the floor to express his anger, especially in front of an audience of his colleagues and pupils.[37] In any event, he attended the wayward Scandinavian's recital the following day, and before Bull left Budapest on February 19 he received an invitation from Liszt to pay a farewell visit to his "old colleague and devoted friend."

It goes without saying that Liszt was in constant demand for charitable causes. One such appearance was at the Institute for the Blind on February 23, when he heard its chamber ensemble play the slow movement from Beethoven's Fifth Symphony, and the sixteen-year-old blind pianist Attila Horváth attempt some of Liszt's own pieces. He was touched by the boy's playing and promised to accept him as a student at the academy the following year. Two other appearances were at the so-called Institute for Young English Ladies, on March 3 and 21; on

---

37. *Deutsche Revue* (Stuttgart), July/September 1898, pp. 82–83.

the second occasion he played among other pieces his transcription of Schubert's "Frühlingsglaube."

In view of Liszt's prominence in the national life of Hungary it would be easy to conclude that his genius was everywhere recognised and fêted by a grateful country. But this was not entirely true, for there were those among his compatriots who admired him neither as a man nor as a musician. An anti-Liszt faction had already emerged in Budapest. It was led for a time by Adolf Ágai, the editor of the weekly journal *Magyarország és a Nagyvilág* (Hungary and the World), which had printed a number of hostile reviews of Liszt's music. Ágai now used the occasion of an obituary notice he had written about the Hungarian song-composer János Palotásy to attack Liszt. In the absence of anything original to say, Ágai revived the old chestnut that Liszt thought the Gypsies had created Hungarian folk-music. Liszt's melodic gift was thin, wrote Ágai, like the Gypsies'; while he might be able to weave from those thin threads a cloak that was fit for a king, and even overlay it with gold, pearls, and gems, the threads nevertheless remained thin. That is why his larger original works, such as *St. Elisabeth* and the "Gran" Mass, would hardly outlast him. His true value, the article concluded, lay in his transcriptions of Hungarian folk-songs (namely the Hungarian Rhapsodies).[38]

Liszt was stunned. This was a criticism he felt deeply wherever it was brandished, but he never thought that he would encounter it in Hungary. Was the image of the impotent painter Guermann Regnier, unable to fill his blank walls, to pursue him even to his native land? In his depressed state of mind Liszt may have over-reacted. He struck back in a way that harmed not only his own best interests but those of the musical life of Budapest as well. To Katalin Engeszer, a director of the Budapest Liszt Society, he wrote that he absolutely forbade a performance of the "Gran" Mass shortly to be given in the city—a blow that hurt those of his friends and supporters who had already begun to rehearse the work. More than that, he told her, he would have absolutely nothing to do with any Budapest concerts in which he was to be featured, either as a composer or as a pianist. And because he knew that there were those in the Philharmonic Society who sided with Ágai, he instructed Ábrányi to ask Sándor Erkel to cancel a performance of the *Dante* Symphony already scheduled for March 27.[39] Erkel refused to comply, so Liszt shunned that concert as well. From Liszt's point of view these were not extreme reactions. He felt betrayed by Ágai's public attack. He was exhausting himself in Hungary's cause, only to be told that he was not a real composer. Of course, Liszt's many friends rallied to his side, and he appreciated their devotion. But the fact remains that when he promised to spend three or four months out of each year in his native land, he had not bargained

---

38. *Magyarország és a Nagyvilág,* February 24, 1878.
39. PBUS, p. 195.

on the emergence of an opposition party, one which would get stronger with the passing years. As the date of his departure from Hungary drew closer, Liszt may have reflected on the wisdom of linking himself so securely to his country, but he never changed his mind about the essential correctness of the decision itself. In the end he recognised that the swirl of controversy that had marred his recent sojourn would always be a part of his existence, but the good he could do for Hungary far outweighed the harm. On April 1 he was accompanied to the railway station by a large group of friends and supporters—Ábrányi, Zichy, Mihalovich, Augusz, Apponyi, and his pupils from the academy. As he exchanged farewells with them, he could take satisfaction from the knowledge that the academy was now firmly established, and that the array of talent before him had no need to go to Vienna, Berlin, or Paris in order to be "finished," but could stay at home and enrich the life of the nation.

Liszt spent the first week of April with his cousin Eduard in Vienna, where he celebrated his name-day; he then proceeded to Bayreuth once more to join the Wagners in Wahnfried, from April 8 to 17. Cosima's diary carries a report of the visit. Liszt played to Wagner some of his recent piano compositions, including *Les jeux d'eaux,* the "Cypress" Threnodies, and the *Angelus!* While Wagner evidently liked these pieces, he saw in them only impressions of the Villa d'Este, a somewhat superficial response; their deeper psychological significance was lost on him. Wagner then showed Liszt the first act of *Parsifal,* in which, as Liszt later told Ábrányi, "are revealed the most wondrous depths and the most celestial heights of Art."[40] At Cosima's request Liszt played some selections from Bach's "Forty-eight," which he did "to the amazement and delight of us all."[41] From Bayreuth Liszt touched down briefly in Weimar, where he worked with his masterclasses. But he was there for barely a month before moving off to Hanover to see Hans von Bülow. He was determined to find room in his crowded itinerary for his former son-in-law whenever he was in Germany, even though he felt helpless in the face of Bülow's depressions. A performance of Wagner's *Rienzi* (on May 26) under Bülow's incomparable baton gave Liszt considerable heart. A year or two earlier Bülow had been at his lowest ebb. He had meanwhile made this fundamental discovery about himself: that the only way to heal his wounded personality and rise above Wagner was by continuing to conduct Wagner's music in public. It was a supreme gesture of aristocratic detachment. From anyone else it would have amounted to contempt. But Bülow's superlative performances (he was still the greatest Wagnerian of his generation) were shining gifts for which the master of

40. LLB, vol. 2, p. 267.
41. WT, vol. 2, p. 83.

Bayreuth could only mutter his thanks. *Noblesse oblige!* On such occasions the
victim turned victor. Whatever the rest of the world may have thought, these
moments gave Bülow a great psychological advantage and were for him a part
of the dignity of being human. He had begun the long road to recovery.[42]

IX

By now Liszt was well entrenched in his "threefold life." It is reasonable to
suppose that he travelled an average of four thousand miles a year on his peregrinations from Rome to Budapest, from Budapest to Weimar, and from
Weimar back to Rome, with fleeting trips to Vienna, Bayreuth, and occasionally Paris thrown in. That is an exceptional figure for a man in his twilight
years, exposed to the rigours of rail and road in the 1870s. And it increases dramatically when we add those long journeys he made in pursuit of the annual
festivals of the Allgemeiner Deutscher Musikverein, which, as we have seen,
were held at such widely scattered places as Hanover, Erfurt, Karlsruhe, and
Leipzig. The popular biographies often depict Liszt at this stage of his life as
someone pushed from behind, in the grip of forces he does not understand but
has no alternative but to obey; the ceaseless travel, so we are constantly reminded, was part of his complex psychology, and were we but to unravel it we
would see a man of deep insecurities who had to keep moving in order to live
with himself. It is a commonly held notion, and one that has taken a deep hold
on the literature. Yet it does not withstand careful scrutiny. Anyone who is remotely acquainted with the facts of Liszt's life, at least in his later years, knows
that far from being pushed from behind he was drawn from in front. It was the
demand on his time and talent by others that created his itinerant life-style.
What is of psychological interest is why he acceded to those demands in the
first place. With hardly an exception, it was to serve the needs of others. In
Weimar it was to support the artistic pride of Carl Alexander and his court; in
Budapest to help the fledgling Royal Academy of Music; in Bayreuth to help
publicise Wagner's grandiose vision; and in Rome to maintain his personal loyalty to Princess Wittgenstein. Remove these causes and you remove the need
for Liszt to have travelled at all. There was no monetary or material gain for

---

42. About the performance of *Rienzi* Bülow told his mother: "Thirty-four years ago, in Dresden, after
a performance of *Rienzi,* I made the acquaintance of Liszt, and through him I was introduced in the
Saxony Hotel to—Lola Montez!!!! Today, in Hanover, son-in-law no. 1 conducted for the magician
of Rome, Pest, and Weimar that same firstborn work of his son-in-law no. 2, solemnly attired in a
white cravat with his six orders, and the performance went superbly, intoxicatingly, as if shot out of a
pistol." (BB, vol. 5, pp. 503–04) Both the language and the imagery suggest a man who could once
more look at himself and his life with amused detachment, a man who was once more capable of
mocking himself—and others.

him in any of these places, and since he invariably paid his own and his manservants' travel expenses, he was often out of pocket. He sometimes had to send urgent requests to Cousin Eduard in Vienna to forward from his dwindling account five hundred florins here, a hundred marks there, and dozens of francs everywhere to settle the bills that were generated in his wake—even such a modest wake as the one created by the frugal life-style he imposed on himself.

It is the Franciscan element in Liszt's nature that comes to the fore during these years and helps to explain his behaviour. The moral imperative had always been there, but now it was mingled with self-abnegation. "Caritas!" was the cry that drew him forward, the notion to which he was most deeply attached. That he was generous to a fault is self-evident; but this very generosity was the despair of his friends and the bewilderment of his foes. For every time he helped someone—in cash or in kind—he was giving himself away, one piece at a time. These were his declining years, and time was no longer on his side. The emergence of the "saintly" Liszt has provoked mirth among the composer's detractors, most of whom would never be caught boarding a train in order to travel a thousand miles to help others for absolutely no remuneration. The very fact that such people would consider this behaviour bizarre (while at the same time being happy to find themselves at the receiving end of similar benefactions) is sufficient commentary on a cramped view of human nature that prevails in the arts to this day.

Typical of his time-consuming journeys was his trip to Paris in June 1878. He went not because of any particular urge to see Paris but in response to a request by minister Ágoston Trefort to represent his native country at the World Exhibition. His chief duty, Trefort informed him, would be to serve on the international jury which judged musical instruments—a prospect that Liszt found less than appealing. He did not relish the idea of hearing several hundred musical instruments, including "pianos and pianinos," "languorous flutes," "exterminating trumpets," as well as a variety of tubas and guitars.[43] He could only convince himself that the trip was worthwhile by regarding it as a "*patriotic* concession" to Hungary, as he put it to Baron Augusz.[44]

Of all Liszt's trips to Paris this one was the least publicised. He arrived in the company of his manservant Spiridon almost without notice on June 9 and remained in the City of Light until June 18. It was not until two days before his departure that *Le Ménestrel* carried a brief announcement of his presence in the city, from which we learn that shortly after he got there the international jury elected him its honorary chairman—a suggestion that evidently came from Eduard Hanslick, who was also a jury member. Hanslick, in fact, provides us with a number of charming details about Liszt, and the tactful manner in

---

43. LLB, vol. 7, p. 218.
44. CLBA, p. 220.

which the composer approached his task. As the party walked from one booth to another, Liszt studiously avoided getting too closely involved in the judicial process. He seemed to cultivate a diplomatic detachment when confronted by the various piano manufacturers, and praised them all equally. "Towards midday," Hanslick tells us, "he stopped in his tracks, somewhat weary, and confessed that he was now ready to award first prize to a knife and fork." Liszt then invited the entire jury to accompany him across the exhibition park and have a meal in the Hungarian "Czarda," with a Gypsy band in attendance. "Rarely have I seen Liszt so good-humoured and so communicative," said Hanslick, "I might even say so amiable, if I had ever known him to be other than amiable."[45]

Throughout his stay in Paris, Liszt was a guest of the Erard family at 13, rue du Mail. Spiridon was especially impressed with the luxury of the Erard home, which he thought compared with that of King Willem of the Netherlands. Liszt met Ollivier and his new wife, Marie-Thérèse, together with his sixteen-year-old grandson, Daniel, and the trio joined him at the Erards for dinner. He also saw his old friend Saint-Saëns, who was still in a state of shock from the recent deaths of his two small children.[46] Liszt was prevented from attending concerts by the flood of social invitations that poured in towards the end of his stay, but he did manage to visit the Opéra and hear the last two acts of Gounod's *Faust*. He also attended high mass at Notre Dame in the company of Father Joseph Mohr, a Jesuit, where he was impressed by the singing of the plainchant.

Back in Weimar, Liszt hardly had time to shake the dust from his feet before he was off again for the annual festival of the Allgemeiner Deutscher Musikverein, held this year in Erfurt (June 21 to 26). Liszt was represented chiefly by his Psalm 13, but he was also billed to conduct the Bronsart Piano Concerto, with Bülow as soloist. This latter engagement seemed to give him cause for concern, for in his later years he rarely appeared as a conductor of other composers' music. In a revealing letter to the director of this year's festival, Carl Riedel, he requested that some of his compositions be dropped (including the often-heard Hungarian Fantasy) and that his name not be advertised as a conductor. "I could not bear the false appearance of making use of the Tonkünstler-Versammlung for bringing forward my compositions," he wrote.[47] Because he was a founding member of the Musikverein, he did not want to give

45. HAML, vol. 2, pp. 184–86. Although the two men had exchanged sharp differences of opinion across the years, and were to do so again, their meeting in Paris is one more proof that they got on well enough on a personal level.

46. WLLM, pp. 314–15. On May 28, Saint-Saëns's two-and-a-half-year-old son, André, had fallen from the fifth floor of the family apartment and was killed outright. Six weeks earlier his infant son had succumbed to a childhood fever. Saint-Saëns was ravaged by this domestic tragedy, for which he blamed his young wife. Three years later he deserted her.

47. LLB, vol. 2, pp. 272–73.

his enemies the chance to declare that he was abusing his position to promote his own career. Better to yield the platform to younger musicians. It was entirely due to his urging, for example, that Riedel was persuaded to put Borodin's Symphony No. 2 in B minor into this year's festival. When it was learned that the orchestral parts had not yet been copied, because of insufficient funds, Liszt refused to accept this as a good enough reason for not performing the work, and he volunteered to pay the copyist himself.[48]

Liszt spent the rest of the summer in Weimar. His new pupils included sixteen-year-old Moriz Rosenthal, Adèle aus der Ohe, Ilona Ravasz, and Bertrand Roth. These and other gifted young pianists regularly took part in Liszt's Sunday-morning concerts, together with a number of distinguished local musicians. The violinist August Kömpel was a frequent guest at the Hofgärtnerei, as was the cellist Leopold Grützmacher, and both artists joined Liszt in performances of chamber music by Saint-Saëns, Raff, Rubinstein, and Sgambati. And in early July, when Bülow arrived unexpectedly in Weimar, he too was happy to grace one of Liszt's at-homes with his playing.

X

Liszt arrived in Rome on September 3, 1878, and by the twelfth he had returned to the Villa d'Este and his "sad companions" the melancholy cypresses. As usual, his routine was very simple. He rose before dawn, went to early-morning mass at the Tivoli church, and then got down to composing. After lunch he attended to his voluminous correspondence, received the occasional visitor, and gave a lesson to whichever of his pupils was hardy enough to endure the bone-jolting journey along the rough roads that linked Rome with Tivoli. During that autumn the only student he saw at the villa was Moriz Rosenthal, who had followed him to Rome. Rosenthal used to turn up every afternoon and find Liszt composing in his study or sitting on the terrace gazing across the campagna towards the distant horizon, absorbed in his thoughts. When Rosenthal later reflected on those halcyon days, it appeared to him that Liszt had been a "great magician." He recalled "the sparkling Roman autumn, the picturesque beauty of the place, the Master's lofty teaching—everything merged within me into a bliss which I can still feel today."[49] Liszt's daily round was enlivened by occasional encounters with Cardinal Hohenlohe, who sometimes joined him for lunch.

It was at the Villa d'Este that news of the death of Baron Antal Augusz was brought to Liszt, in September 1878. "The loss of Augusz touches me most

---

48. Ibid.
49. *Die Musik,* xii, 1911–12, pp. 46–47.

painfully," he wrote. "Since the first performance of the 'Gran' Mass, more than twenty years ago, we have been *one in heart*. He also confirmed me in my wish to settle myself in Budapest."[50]

The passing of his old friend placed Liszt once more under the shadow of depression. And once more he searched for a world of sound with which to express his gravity. Among the compositions that emerged was *Via Crucis,* one of the most uncompromising of his choral works. Its fourteen short movements depict the Stations of the Cross. The texts had earlier been selected by Princess Carolyne from the Bible and from various hymns and chorales. Scored for mixed chorus, soloists and organ, the titles of the movements are:

> Prelude: "Vexilla Regis"
> 1. Jesus is condemned to death
> 2. Jesus takes up his Cross
> 3. Jesus falls for the first time
> 4. Jesus meets his blessed Mother
> 5. Simon of Cyrene helps Jesus to carry the Cross
> 6. St. Veronica wipes Jesus' face with her veil
> 7. Jesus falls for the second time
> 8. The Women of Jerusalem mourn for Jesus
> 9. Jesus falls for the third time
> 10. Jesus is stripped of his clothing
> 11. Jesus is nailed to the Cross
> 12. Jesus dies on the Cross
> 13. Jesus is taken down from the Cross
> 14. Jesus is laid in the Tomb

In a hitherto unpublished first sketch of his official foreword to *Via Crucis* Liszt revealed his affinity with this time-honoured ceremony.

> Devotion to the "Way of the Cross" is very widespread among Catholics. Many churches feature the images of the fourteen Stations of the Cross, which on Good Friday the faithful follow with the officiating priest.
>
> I have participated in this ceremony, notably at the Colosseum in Rome, steeped in the blood of the holy martyrs. In the pages of

---

50. LLB, vol. 2, p. 276.

music which follow I have attempted humbly to express my devout emotion.

O crux, ave, spes unica! [Hail, O Cross, our single hope!][51]

It is safe to say that never before had the traditional story of the Crucifixion been clothed in such innovative sounds. The piece contradicts all our expectations of what the Passion is supposed to represent. Even Liszt confessed that he was "quite shaken by it."[52] He wanted to bring home to his listeners not only the agony of the Cross but the pain of those in Christ's circle who witnessed it. In order to do that, he had to jolt his listeners from their complacency and use a harmonic language that would have been quite literally shocking to those who heard it.

The Prelude with which the work begins is based on the plainchant "Vexilla Regis prodeunt" ("The royal banners forward go, the Cross shines forth in mystic glow").[53]

Vexíl- la Ré- gis pród- e- unt :

Liszt's realisation:

Liszt's simple realisation of the old plainchant melody gives no idea of the advanced harmonic language that is to follow. Consider the movement entitled "Jesus meets his blessed Mother."

---

51. WA, Kasten 96, u. 2.

52. WLLM, p. 320.

53. This ancient processional hymn was written by the cleric Venantius Fortunatus and was first sung on November 19, 569, when the Relics of the Cross were brought to the monastery at Poitiers in solemn procession. Traditionally it has been used at the office of the Vespers, in which context it would have been familiar to Liszt.

The so-called "Madonna chord" is an emotional blend of pain and love, tinged with eroticism. It cannot be explained in terms of traditional harmony, and Liszt himself would have been the last to insist on such an explanation. A later age would call it a "tone-cluster" and perhaps wonder how it came to be introduced into music as early as 1878. But by now Liszt was standing on the brink of the extraordinary music of his old age, and all things were possible for him. His music not only made history; it had a history of making history.

The movement called "The Women of Jerusalem mourn for Jesus" wails in a chromatic language that can find no repose. When the voice of Jesus enters and enjoins them, "Do not weep for me, But rather weep for yourselves and for your children,"

the grieving reaches a new level of intensity.

Liszt offered *Via Crucis* and two other late religious works composed at this time (*Septum Sacramenta* and the *Rosario*) to the publisher Friedrich Pustet of Regensburg. "The question of the honorarium is quite irrelevant," wrote Liszt. "I do not write such compositions for monetary gain, but from the inner necessity of a Catholic heart."[54] Pustet turned the pieces down, thereby creating a niche for himself in musical history. It was a rare experience for Liszt to be rejected by a publisher, but he took the rebuff with good grace. He had already told Marie Lipsius: "Their publication is of little concern to me, for they

---

54. LLB, vol. 8, p. 415.

do not fit into the usual music business routine. . . . So why bargain over them?"[55] *Via Crucis* did not receive its first performance until Good Friday 1929, in Budapest, more than fifty years after it was written. A work of outcries and asides, whispers and laments, it has meanwhile come to enjoy a high status among students of Liszt's later music. When it is placed in a sacred setting, and given a performance of high calibre, the effect can be stunning.

From time to time Liszt broke his routine at the Villa d'Este in order to keep up his Roman connections. Whenever he visited the Eternal City he occupied his old rooms on the Vicolo de' Greci, not far from the Accademia Santa Cecilia. Here he saw much of Sgambati, who was just about to publish his Piano Quintet in F minor, a work he dedicated to Liszt, who esteemed it highly. He also mingled with some of his other pupils, including Nadine Helbig, Bertrand Roth, and Karl Pohlig, and gave them occasional lessons in the Sala Dante. Liszt celebrated his sixty-seventh birthday in Rome in the company of Princess Carolyne. It could not have been a happy occasion for either of them, for the issues that separated them continued to gnaw at their hearts.[56] Nor could Carolyne have found much cause for rejoicing in the fact that Liszt had taken to dining with her former adversaries at the Russian embassy and with her old opponent Gustav Hohenlohe, who was now installed in magnificent apartments attached to the Santa Maria Maggiore which he had furnished in sumptuous style at a rumoured cost of twenty thousand francs. In her fretful condition she doubtless feared that she was a topic of conversation between Hohenlohe and Liszt. That Hohenlohe kept Liszt informed of his brother Konstantin's negative attitude towards Carolyne goes without saying. One matter in which Carolyne was able to find some consolation was the interest shown in Liszt's Roman visits by Pope Leo XIII. On All Saints' Day, November 1, the new pontiff granted him a private audience at the Vatican. Liszt found in Leo a somewhat austere personality, one with whom he was unable to enjoy the same feelings of warm cordiality that had existed with Pius IX. While there is no record of the beleaguered pontiff asking Liszt to play the piano for him, the meeting was nonetheless an important experience for Liszt to have had. He was probably the only musician of his time to have been received not by one Vicar of Christ, but by two.

He got back to the Villa d'Este on November 5 and resumed work on *Via Crucis*. One welcome interruption occurred about the middle of the month when Liszt was invaded by a group of friends from Rome, including Nadine Helbig and her husband, the sculptor and diplomat Count Joseph-Arthur de

---

55. LLB, vol. 2, p. 282.
56. For a fuller account of their quarrels, see pp. 336–38.

Gobineau, Countess Latour, and Count Metternich. Laughter and merrymaking were unusual sounds at the villa, and Liszt enjoyed the brief ray of sunlight they brought into his life. Hohenlohe also turned up, and provided lavish hospitality for the unexpected visitors. The mood of warm conviviality did not last long, however. It was shattered by one of those venomous letters that Carolyne had got into the habit of sending Liszt whenever there was something about him she wished to attack. She told him pointedly that there were things of which he should repent, doubtless referring to her long-standing quarrel with her daughter, Marie, and Liszt's support of Marie's point of view. She also objected to the social life that Liszt led on his fleeting visits to Rome, and even more to the friends (her enemies) with whom he consorted while there. Liszt told her on December 23 that the "logical honour" of his life was one she invariably overlooked and one that he was duty-bound to pursue, and that while repentance was not at all foreign to his nature, it also carried with it the corollary of forgiveness, which, he implied, was lacking in her. Her Roman ways, he told her bluntly, had given her a measure of "absolutism." After such an exchange of letters, he was chagrined to receive from Carolyne a note of consolation and a large bouquet of flowers that were sent to the Villa d'Este on Christmas Eve. He replied on Christmas Day that her gift had made him almost ashamed of the lines that he had despatched to her two days earlier.[57]

XI

From Rome the weary itinerant wended his way back to Budapest (via Florence, where he stayed for a few days with his old friend Jessie Laussot), arriving in the City of the Magyars on January 17, 1879. His life in Hungary during the next three months was much the same as before, with one dramatic exception.

On the night of March 11, 1879, the river Tisza overflowed its banks. Swollen by storms and melting ice, a wall of water rushed with force towards the southern city of Szeged and broke through the dam. Within one hour it had flooded the centre of the city and destroyed the power supply. In total darkness both man and beast were swept away by the torrent, while the gales continued to lash the area for two days. When the waters at last subsided, they revealed a devastating scene. This once-prosperous city of 77,000 inhabitants had been inundated. Of its more than 6,000 houses, only 384 were left standing. More than 35,000 people were evacuated by train and coach to Temesvár and other communities. There are no accurate figures for the number of people who drowned.

News of the disaster was slow to spread because the storms had knocked out the telegraph system, but when the response came it was world-wide. Kossuth

---

57. LLB, vol. 7, pp. 237–38.

Mittwoch, den 26. März 1879, Abends ¹⁄₂8 Uhr

im grossen Redoutensaale

CONCERT

zu Gunsten der

Szegediner und Altölder Überschwemmten

veranstaltet durch den

Künster- u. Schriftsteller-Verein.

PROGRAMM:

1. „Die Wiege", Gedicht . . . . *M. Jókai,*
   gesprochen von Frau **JÓKAI.**
2. Trauermarsch . . . . *F. Schubert.*
   Pianoforte: **FRANZ LISZT.**
3. a) „Es blinkt der Thau" . . . . *A. Rubinstein,*
   b) „In Liebeslust" . . . . *F. Liszt,*
   c) Ungarisches Lied . . . . *C. Ábrányi,*
   gesungen von Frl. **ALWINE BUSSE.**
4. a) „Dem Andenken Petőfi's" ⎫ . . . . *F. Liszt.*
   b) „Cantique d'amour" ⎭
   FRANZ LISZT.
5. a) Lied . . . . *Ch. Gounod,*
   b) „Die Rose" . . . . *R. Wagner,*
   gesungen von Herrn **LEHEL ODRY.**
6. Fantasie, für zwei Pianoforte . . . . *F. Schubert.*
   FRANZ LISZT und **EDMUND v. MIHALOVICH.**

Die Pianoforte sind aus der Fabrik Bösendorfer.

Preise der Plätze: Logen à 50 fl., Cercle-Sitze à 15 und 10 fl., Numme-
rirte Sitze à 5 fl, Gallerie-Sitze à 5 fl, Entrée à 2 fl. sind in der Musikalien-
handlung von **Táborszky & Parsch,** Krongasse Nr. 1, und am Tage des Concertes
Abends an der Cassa zu haben.

☛ An diejenigen verehrlichen Besucher des Concertes, welche erst erschei-
nen, nachdem die Production bereits begonnen, wird die höfliche Bitte gerichtet,
ihren Eintritt in den Saal, im Interesse des Auditoriums, bis nach Beendigung
eines Satzes oder einer Nummer zu verzögern.

*A Liszt benefit concert in aid of the flood victims of Szeged and the
Hungarian Plains, given in Budapest,
March 26, 1879.*

sent 350 francs from his Italian exile; Verdi sent 200. The Vienna Philharmonic donated the proceeds of one of its Budapest concerts to the flood victims. In Paris there was a great outpouring of sympathy, and some of its leading musicians (including Saint-Saëns, Delibes, and Massenet) donated their services. Until the river had swept through Szeged's town square, most of Europe had never heard of the place. A week after the disaster it was world-famous.

Liszt was on a brief visit to Klausenburg, in the company of Géza Zichy, when he heard the news. "Nothing will be achieved by lamenting," he exclaimed, "we must do something to help."[58] Within hours he and Zichy had drawn up a joint programme and posters were scattered throughout the city announcing a concert for March 14. Thirty-three years had passed since Liszt had last played in Klausenburg. When he walked onto the platform, he was greeted by a standing ovation. According to Zichy, the flowers rained down on the stage until it resembled a flower-garden. At the end of the programme Liszt and Zichy played the *Rákóczy* March, which Zichy had arranged for three hands. As the performance came to a close, the hall erupted and students rushed to the platform to lift the sixty-seven-year-old Liszt onto their shoulders. It was a triumphal return to that concert platform after so many years.

Liszt gave two other charity concerts for the victims of the Szeged floods, which remain under-reported. On March 26 he appeared in the Budapest Redoute, under the aegis of the Artists and Writers Society. It was a collaborative effort in which Liszt shared the platform with several other artists, including Róza Jókai (the wife of Hungary's greatest living author, Mór Jókai), who opened the concert with a rendering of Jókai's poem "Die Wiege" ("The Cradle"), especially written for the occasion. Liszt then took his place at the keyboard and played his arrangement of a funeral march by Schubert—a symbolic coupling of the cradle and the grave which would not have been lost on an audience in mourning for their compatriots. After a group of songs sung by Alwine Busse, Liszt returned to the stage and played two pieces of his own: the still-unpublished *To the Memory of Sándor Petőfi* and *Cantique d'amour* from the early cycle *Harmonies poétiques et religieuses*. The concert ended with a performance of his two-piano arrangement of Schubert's *Wanderer* Fantasy, played by Liszt and Ödön Mihalovich.[59]

XII

The Szeged victims were still much on Liszt's mind when he set out on his annual trek to Vienna. From April 2 to April 9 he made a number of well-

---

58. ZLEF, vol. 2, p. 57.
59. A copy of the original handbill is reproduced opposite.

publicised appearances in the imperial city, one or two of them in benefit of the dispossessed Hungarians. This week-long sojourn in Vienna was a veritable triumph for Liszt, all the more remarkable since it happened in a city that was typically hostile towards him. The details were captured for posterity by an unusually affable Eduard Hanslick, whose chronicle is probably the best that we have.[60]

Liszt's first appearance occurred at a concert given by the Hellmesberger Quartet on the evening of April 3. As they were nearing the end of the Schubert E-flat-major Quartet, Liszt entered the back of the hall and stood unobtrusively near the door until the work had ended. He then walked down the aisle to take his seat near the front of the hall. The audience recognized him at once, and the whole assembly began to applaud and would not cease until he had stepped forward to acknowledge it.

> It was a delightful, unforgettable moment [wrote Hanslick]. We know of no other instance when an artist has entered a concert hall, neither as a composer nor as a performer but merely as a listener, and been welcomed as loudly and as unanimously by the entire assembly. If Bismarck and Gambetta, Richard Wagner and Verdi, the youngest and prettiest *prima donna* and the oldest virtuoso were to appear at a concert or in the theatre, they could none of them boast of such a scene. No one in the whole of Europe could, indeed except for Liszt. The feeling that flared up instinctively in the majority of the listeners, that it was right to welcome Liszt, was transmitted as though by an electric cable, until almost simultaneously the entire hall erupted in thunderous acclaim. . . . What magic still surrounds the elderly man![61]

A veritable Liszt festival took place during the next few days. On April 4 and 5, we find the composer attending two concerts in his honour in the *Saal* of Ludwig Bösendorfer, the well-known piano manufacturer. Among the performers at the second concert was his Austrian pupil Toni Raab. Then on April 7 he appeared in the Viennese salon of Count Gyula Andrássy, in benefit of the Szeged victims, before an audience which included Emperor Franz Joseph; he shared the honours with the soprano Caroline von Gomperz-Bettelheim and her accompanist, the fledgling conductor Felix Mottl. Liszt had first met Mottl a day or two earlier when the young man had been brought to his lodgings by the publisher Albert Gutmann. The meeting would hardly be worth reporting were it not for the fact that Mottl had brought with him some of his newly

---

60. See Hanslick's detailed review in the *Neue Freie Presse* for April 10, 1879; also BFL, pp. 342–43.
61. BFL, pp. 342–43.

composed songs. Before he had time to present them, Liszt had snatched them away and placed them on the music rack of the piano upside-down, from which position he sight-read them fluently. In Gutmann's memoir of the occasion, the publisher recalled that he had seen Liszt perform similar feats with orchestral scores a number of times.[62] The episode reminds us that even as he entered old age, Liszt's unsurpassed ability to sight-read from full score remained intact. Only his failing eyesight was to cause him problems in the years still remaining to him.

The climax of this visit to Vienna came on April 8, when Liszt conducted a performance of his "Gran" Mass under the aegis of the Gesellschaft der Musikfreunde. The podium was specially garlanded for the occasion, and Liszt mounted it wearing his abbé's cassock. From his neck was suspended a cluster of orders. Again Hanslick was present, and although he continued to dislike the mass, which he had first heard many years earlier, he was struck by the image Liszt created while conducting. Liszt did not beat time but marked the shape of the phrases, a fairly usual practice with him, so that there were times when his arms hovered motionless over the players and singers. It seemed to Hanslick that Liszt in his priestly garb was offering up a benediction, and he reminded his readers of Liszt's well-known dictum to conductors: "We are steersmen, not oarsmen."[63]

Altogether this visit was one of the most successful that Liszt had ever enjoyed in the imperial city. It was marred for him by only one thing. The death of his cousin Eduard on February 8, less than two months before his arrival, had plunged the Liszt family into mourning, and the house in the Schottenhof seemed empty without Eduard's engaging presence. He visited Eduard's grave and bade a silent farewell to his oldest relative. The last remaining link with his childhood was broken. Eduard's widow, Henriette, and their two young children, Hedwig and Eduard, remained on the friendliest terms with Liszt, and he continued to regard them as his family and stay with them whenever his journeys took him through Vienna. As Liszt packed his bags and set out once more on his ceaseless travels, he carried away some mingled feelings. More than a year later we find him writing to Henriette: "It is for me a constant sorrow of the heart that Eduard is no longer with us."[64]

From Vienna Liszt journeyed to Hanover, where on April 13 Hans von Bülow conducted his *Prometheus* and Beethoven's Ninth Symphony. Bülow was fast approaching the apex of his career as a conductor. After this concert Liszt described him as "the most eminent of the Kapellmeisters" except for Wagner[65]—a comparison that had less to do with Bülow's technical mastery of

62. GAWM, vol. 1, p. 51.
63. *Neue Freie Presse,* April 10, 1879.
64. LLB, vol. 2, p. 279.
65. WLLM, p. 344.

WEIMAR,

Donnerstag, den 10. Juli 1879, Abends 7¹|₂ Uhr:

in der Stadtkirche

Geistliches Concert.

Sämmtliche Compositionen von Dr. FRANZ LISZT

unter persönlicher Leitung desselben.

PROGRAMM.

1) Einleitung zur Legende von der heiligen Elisabeth, für Orgel übertragen von *Müller-Hartung,*
   gespielt von Hrn. Stadtorganist Sulze.

2) Ave maris stella für Altsolo, Frauenchor und Orgel, übertragen von *B. Sulze,*
   gesungen von Frl. Agnes Schöler.

3) 2 Consolations für Cello und Orgel,
   Hr. Kammermusikus Friedrich's und Hr. Sulze.

4) Der 137. Psalm für Sopran, Violine, Harfe und Orgel,
   gesungen von Frl. Mina Sciubro.
   Violine: Herr Kammermusikus Freyberg.
   Harfe: Frau Covacsics.

5) Fantasie und Fuge über B A C H,
   gespielt von Hrn. Stadtorganist Sulze.

6) **Die sieben Sacramente** für Chor, Soli und Orgel,
   Frl. A. Schöler und die Herren Thiene, Ickel, Schnell und Denstedt.

   1. Baptisma. 2. Confirmatio. 3. Eucharistia. 4. Matrimonium. 5. Ordo.
   6. Poenitentia. 7. Extrema unctio.

   Texte umstehend.

A concert of Liszt's sacred choral music in Weimar, conducted by the composer, July 10, 1879.

the baton than with Wagner's newly achieved status as a world-renowned composer. Frankfurt came next, where Liszt attended a performance of *Christus* under Julius Kniese. While such trips were physically exhausting for Liszt, they were not otherwise unpleasant. The fact is that in defiance of certain opinions coming out of Berlin, Vienna, and Leipzig, Liszt was regarded in some quarters as the Grand Old Man of Music, and he found it a pleasant change to be fêted as a composer. In Hanover, as in Frankfurt, nothing more was asked of him than that he attend and that he let his admirers pay their personal tribute to him.

XIII

In July 1879 Liszt was informed by Cardinal Hohenlohe that he intended to make him an honorary canon of Albano. This distinction lay within Hohenlohe's gift by virtue of the fact that he himself was bishop of Albano and titular head of the chapter of canons there. The ancient town lay about twenty-five miles southeast of Rome, nestled on a hillside overlooking Lake Albano. In those days it was not easily accessible; the journey from Rome took two and a half hours by carriage. Liszt's clerical duties were minimal, however, involving little more than sporadic appearances at the cathedral, for which he received a small stipend. His letter of acceptance, written in Italian, was dated "Weimar, July 18, 1879," and was addressed to the Chapter of the Cathedral of Albano.

> I have just received from His Eminence the Bishop [of Albano] the most gratifying news that this Most Reverend Chapter has appointed me Honorary Canon.
>
> This most ancient Chapter is, even today, as it ever was in the past, distinguished for the presence of so many learned Churchmen of paramount virtues. It is, then, for me a genuine pleasure and an honour to belong to such a worthy assembly and I beg you to accept my most heartfelt thanks for the distinction conferred upon me. I hope to be able to express my gratitude in person in the near future.
>
> With feelings of the highest esteem and consideration I confirm myself the Most Reverend Chapter's
>
> most obliged servant,
> FRANCESCO DI LISZT[66]

---

66. PFLA, p. 8. The official certificate of nomination for Liszt's appointment as honorary canon of Albano is dated August 1879. (WA, Kasten 127, Überformate 159)

From the correspondence concerning this matter between Hohenlohe and Monsignor del Frate, the vicar-general of Albano, we learn that in September 1879 Liszt bestowed the sum of two thousand lire on the cathedral "for the acquisition of sacred objects" and for the setting up in perpetuity of a mass to be celebrated each year on April 2, the day of his patron saint, Francis of Paola.[67]

During the second week of October, Liszt and Hohenlohe travelled together from Rome in the latter's personal coach through the rolling countryside towards Albano. The composer stayed as Hohenlohe's guest in the episcopal palace, a building that dated back to the time of Benedict XIII. On Sunday, October 12, Liszt was formally inducted into his honorary canonship within the great basilica of San Pancrazio di Albano. The rarely reported ceremony began at 10:30 a.m. and was conducted in the presence of Hohenlohe himself.[68] Shortly before the appointed hour, Liszt and Hohenlohe arrived at the cathedral vestry, where the other members of the chapter were assembled. There Liszt donned the surplice and the rochet. Accompanied by two of the canons of the cathedral, the Most Reverends Pietro de Angelis and Lorenzo Ginobbi, Liszt walked down the aisle towards the side altar of the Most Holy Sacrament and knelt before it in silent worship. He then proceeded to the main altar, kissed it, and offered a short prayer. Afterwards he took possession of his stall, flanked by de Angelis and Ginobbi. After the service he returned to the vestry, where he received the "kiss of peace" from Hohenlohe and from various other members of the chapter. Then followed a high mass conducted by Monsignor del Frate, during which "some ten canons loudly intoned Gregorian plainchant in unison."[69]

At 1:00 p.m. there followed a lunch in the episcopal palace for about thirty people, while the brilliantly uniformed municipal band, wearing head-plumes, played music in the town square. Liszt tells us that he himself rounded off this musical offering "with a few *sonatinas* as a *chasse-café*" (literally, a "coffee-chaser").[70]

Liszt's title of honorary canon of Albano made little difference to his lowly status within the Church, and none at all to the way he conducted his life. While it may have represented a modest advancement in his career as a cleric, he remained firm in his resolve not to enter higher orders.[71] But he used the appellation, he kept in touch with the chapter, and he even visited the city whenever he was in the vicinity. A chief result of the Albano episode was to

---

67. Letter dated September 6, 1879. PFLA, p. 9.

68. The details are culled from the eye-witness description left by Francesco Giorni, canon and historian of Albano. (PFLA, p. 9)

69. WLLM, p. 354. There was also an indifferent organist of whose playing Liszt remarked, "our friend Gottschalg would not much approve."

70. WLLM, p. 355.

71. LLB, vol. 7, p. 258.

strengthen the ties of friendship that bound him to Hohenlohe. For the rest, the eternal wanderer not only kept on wandering but even extended his boundaries as he began to answer the calls that soon came in from more distant horizons.

XIV

Even as they were journeying back to Tivoli, Hohenlohe and Liszt must have discussed the topic that was on everybody's lips. The harvest of 1879 had been a disaster, and the region of the Sabine mountains had been struck by famine. Local populations were already facing starvation, with the worst of the winter weather yet to come. Hohenlohe volunteered to put on a benefit concert, and open the great hall of the Villa d'Este for that purpose. Would his new canon of Albano agree to participate? Liszt needed no prompting, and together the two men laid their plans, relying heavily on their Roman connections for an audience. The concert was announced for December 30, and once it was learned that Liszt would play, the tickets sold out. Many of them were distributed by the foreign embassies to their nationals visiting Rome, who scrambled for a chance to see and hear the living legend. Nadine Helbig reports that the newly installed steam trams were quadrupled and ran between Tivoli and Rome repeatedly. Alongside the railway line ran the country road, which was covered with carriages stretching in a black line through the Campagna. Never before had Tivoli swarmed with so many people. Liszt shared the concert with other artists, including his pupils Reisenauer and Helbig. His own solo contribution was billed as a "Fantasia" on *Ave Maris Stella*.[72] There was great applause from the audience, curiosity was satisfied, the hungry were fed. For Liszt it was an ideal use of his talent. It was one more example of his belief that the artistic impulse was mis-directed unless it was driven by a moral imperative.

XV

As Liszt entered his declining years, it was mainly at the Villa d'Este that he found peace and seclusion from the hurly-burly of his "threefold life." The twenty-mile journey from Rome, across some rugged terrain, protected him from the casual visitors who besieged him in other parts of Europe. However, he was rarely inhospitable when uninvited guests succeeded in penetrating his

---

72. HLR, p. 176. Liszt left three settings of *Ave Maris Stella*, and it is impossible to determine whether he worked with material he had already composed or whether he "fantasized" on new ideas derived from the old plainchant theme.

solitude. One such occasion occurred in November 1880, when he was visited by the English cleric Hugh Reginald Haweis. Haweis was the incumbent at St. James's Church in Marylebone, London, where he was renowned as a preacher. An admirer of Wagner, he spent much time travelling on the Continent, recording his impression of people and places. Although Haweis had seen Liszt from a distance on his earlier travels, he had never met him, and he never dreamed that he would have the pleasure of hearing him play the piano. When he got to the Villa d'Este, he found that the only other person present, apart from the manservant, was Liszt's pupil Karl Pohlig. After an introductory conversation, in which Liszt inquired about some of his old friends, the pair roamed around the terraced gardens, pausing from time to time to admire the fountains, or to allow Liszt to point out the spectacular views of St. Peter's dome and the general direction of Hadrian's Villa. As they were climbing back to their starting-point, the bell from the tower of Santa Croce rang out a quarter to one. "It was a bad bell," recalled Haweis, "like most Italian bells," and he remarked on the superiority of the bells he had heard in Belgium. Whereupon a discussion on bells got underway. Liszt took his guest indoors and made for the keyboard.

> "As we were talking of bells," he said, "I should like to show you an 'Angelus' which I have just written";[73] and, opening the piano, he sat down. This was the moment which I had so often and so vainly longed for. . . .
> "You know," said Liszt, turning to me, "they ring the Angelus in Italy carelessly; the bells swing irregularly, and leave off, and the cadences are often broken up thus": and he began a little swaying passage in the treble—like bells tossing high up in the evening air:

it ceased, but so softly that the half-bar of silence made itself felt, and the listening ear still carried the broken rhythm through the pause. The Abbate himself seemed to fall into a dream; his fingers fell again lightly on the keys, and the bells went on, leaving off in the middle of

---

73. Although Haweis does not identify the piece, there can be little doubt from his general description that Liszt played the *Angelus!* from the third volume of the *Années de pèlerinage.* We have provided the two music examples to illustrate his memoir.

a phrase. Then rose from the bass the song of the Angelus, or rather, it seemed like the vague emotion of one who, as he passes, hears in the ruins of some wayside cloister the ghosts of old monks humming their drowsy melodies, as the sun goes down rapidly, and the purple shadows of Italy steal over the land, out of the orange west!

We sat motionless—the disciple [Pohlig] on one side, I on the other. Liszt was almost as motionless: his fingers seemed quite independent, chance ministers of his soul. The dream was broken by a pause; then came back the little swaying passage of bells, tossing high up in the evening air, the half-bar of silence, the broken rhythm—and the Angelus was rung.[74]

Lunch was served, and the conversation continued with a review of Liszt's past connections with many of the leading composers of the Romantic era— Meyerbeer, Mendelssohn, and Wagner, among others. When it came to Chopin, Liszt mentioned that his book on the composer had recently appeared in a new edition. He disappeared and returned with a copy that he specially inscribed for Haweis; whereupon Haweis decided to seize a golden opportunity. "Chopin always maintained that you were the most perfect exponent of his works. I cannot say how grateful I should be to hear, were it only a fugitive passage of Chopin's, touched by your hand." Liszt was evidently in an expansive mood. Relaxed by the lunch and the wine and by a conversation that he was evidently enjoying, he returned to the piano and played two of Chopin's nocturnes, the ones in G major, Op. 37, and in C minor, Op. 48. Haweis was struck by the manner in which Liszt held his hands,

> the first finger and thumb drawn together to emphasize a note, or the fingers doubled up, then lifted in a peculiar manner, with a gentle sweep in the middle of a phrase . . . and the caressing touch which seemed to draw the soul of the piano out of it almost before the finger reached the keyboard.[75]

74. HMML, pp. 652–54.
75. HMML, pp. 665–66.

The stormy octaves in the middle of the C-minor Nocturne called forth all Liszt's old vigour. Yet all was perfect, wrote Haweis; not a note was missed. When he later reflected on the episode, Haweis recalled that over the years he had heard Clara Schumann, Bülow, Rubinstein, Menter, and Essipova. But what echoed in his memory after the last tones had died beneath Liszt's fingers were the words of Tausig: "No mortal can measure himself with Liszt. He dwells upon a solitary height."[76]

It was about this time that Liszt renewed his acquaintance with the American sculptor Moses Ezekiel, who produced one of the most realistic busts of the composer in old age. The pair had met about ten years earlier in Weimar, during the Beethoven festival of 1870, when the sculptor had heard Liszt conduct the Ninth Symphony and had met Tausig. Ezekiel recalled that on that earlier occasion Liszt was "very tall and thin and wore a long priestly garment, buttoned up to the throat."[77] Liszt's face had changed with the years; it was now heavy and deeply lined, and Ezekiel was struck by the difference. The sculptor had lived for about four years in Rome, and his studio in the Baths of Diocletian had brought him some celebrity. When, towards the end of 1880, he was commissioned to make a life-size bust of Liszt, he decided to reproduce reality and present Liszt's face as it was. He tells us that he followed the composer to the Villa d'Este, whither Liszt had gone to see Cardinal Hohenlohe, in order to begin his work.

> There sat the old Master, his face jovial and lion-like, his grey hair brushed off his forehead and cut straight round his neck, his close-fitting clerical coat buttoned down the front. He was sitting at a desk in what seemed to me a poorly decorated, circular room. His genial smile gave me a ready welcome. He at once offered me one of his Tuscan cigars and said: "I am just making some notes on one of my compositions, and you are not disturbing me in the least."[78]

Ezekiel stayed on at the villa for a week during the month of January 1881, and Liszt sat for him every day, "glad of having an opportunity of being made . . . as God Himself made me!"[79] The bust was eventually cast in bronze; but when Ezekiel got it back to the Baths of Diocletian he made a provisional plaster-cast and took it round to show Princess Carolyne. She was indisposed and in bed when Ezekiel got to her apartment, but she roused herself and viewed it in her candlelit parlour. After approaching it very closely, the better to view it

---

76. HMML, p. 646.
77. EMBD, p. 144.
78. EMBD, p. 220.
79. Ibid.

Franz Liszt, a photograph taken in Baden-Baden, May 1880.

in the subdued light, she almost put her nose in contact with the bust and peered all the way round it, as if smelling it, all the time exclaiming: "C'est un très bon buste! C'est un très bon buste!"

XVI

By the winter of 1880–81, Liszt's private apartment in the new Royal Academy of Music building in Budapest was ready for occupancy, and he moved in on January 20, 1881. This salon had been designed by the architect Sándor Fellner in such a way that it adjoined the platform of the academy's great hall, thus enabling him to walk straight out of his rooms into the concert hall. It was furnished with carpets, armchairs, and sofas especially embroidered by about a dozen volunteer ladies from Budapest. Although not luxurious, it was to prove one of the most comfortable homes of his old age. His windows overlooked Sugár Street, one of the main thoroughfares of Budapest, and offered him excellent views of the bustling city. From this coign of vantage he felt central to whatever was taking place around him.

Hans von Bülow gave two memorable concerts in Budapest during February 1881. The first was an all-Liszt recital (February 14), which began with his master's B-minor Piano Sonata, then continued with selections from the Années de pèlerinage (the "Swiss" volume), four études (Paysage, Feux-follets, Waldesrauschen, and Gnomenreigen), the Second Polonaise, and St. Francis of Paola walking on the waters—fifteen Liszt pieces altogether. No other pianist then appearing before the public would have dared to put on such an uncompromising recital. Four days later (February 18) Bülow surpassed himself when he mounted the platform again, this time in an all-Beethoven recital consisting of the last five piano sonatas. Liszt was uplifted to see his former son-in-law and to observe the immense strides forward his piano-playing had taken since he had emerged from the refining fire of his mental breakdown. The letter Liszt wrote to Dénes Pázmándy, the editor of the Gazette de Hongrie, has been widely quoted:

> You want to know my impression of yesterday's Bülow concert? Certainly it must have been the same as yours, as that of us all, that of the whole of the intelligent public of Europe. To define it in two words: admiration, enthusiasm. Twenty-five years ago Bülow was my pupil in music, just as twenty-five years earlier I myself had been the pupil of my respected and beloved master Czerny. But to Bülow it is given to do battle better and with more success than I. His admirable Beethoven edition is dedicated to me as the "fruit of my teaching." Here, however, the master learned from the pupil, and

Bülow continues to teach by his astonishing virtuosity at the keyboard, as well as by his exceptional musical learning, and now too
by his matchless direction of the Meiningen orchestra. There you
have the musical progress of our time!

Cordially,
F. LISZT

Budapest,
February 15, 1881[80]

The fact that Bülow carried so many Liszt works in his repertory, and that
within the space of eight weeks he gave major Liszt recitals in Vienna, Budapest, Prague, Weimar, and Berlin, does not support the idea, first put forward
by his widow, Marie Schanzer, that during the seventies and eighties Bülow
was in revolt against Liszt's music.[81] Everybody knew that he had asserted his
independence by refusing the academy professorship that Liszt had offered him
six years earlier; they also knew that his tastes in orchestral music had become
much more conservative with the passing years, since the two composers
whom he consistently featured in his Meiningen orchestral concerts were
Beethoven and Brahms, and Liszt hardly at all. But that did not mean that he
bore hostility towards his former master. We do well to bear this context in
mind when considering why Liszt would bother to write to the newspaper at
all in praise of his pupil, whom he here compliments with the special phrase
"the master learned from the pupil."

As in previous seasons, Liszt's sojourn in his native land during this winter and
spring of 1881 was enlivened by several forays into nearby cities.

   On Sunday, April 3, accompanied by Géza Zichy, Liszt went to Pressburg in
fulfillment of a promise he had made to take part in a concert to raise funds for
the erection of a Hummel monument in that composer's native city. Although
Liszt was hardly on speaking terms with the Hummel family, who still lived almost directly opposite his house in Weimar, this was no reason for him to refuse
to help such a worthy cause, for he was the first to acknowledge the importance
of Hummel in the history of piano playing.[82] At the railway station he and

---

80. LLB, vol. 2, p. 306.
81. BBLW, p. 169. She quotes Bülow as describing the *Faust* Symphony (which he had conducted so
memorably on earlier occasions) as "unmusic, quack-music, antimusic," without disclosing any context. When was Bülow right about this work, which he had earlier smothered in praise—before or
after he was supposed to have uttered the criticism? Naturally, the words were gratefully received by
Ernest Newman, coming as they did from so seemingly unimpeachable a source as the widow, and
were used as ammunition in his ongoing crusade against Liszt and his music. (NML, pp. 208–09)
82. See Volume Two, pp. 97–98.

Zichy were met by a deputation of dignitaries, including the lord lieutenant, the mayor of the city, and friend Ludwig Bösendorfer. The hall was packed, the atmosphere expectant. A hush then descended on the audience. It was announced that Zichy had recently broken a finger-nail, and that the lion's share of the piano-playing that evening would be taken by Liszt—news that was greeted with a storm of applause. Apart from playing two piano solos (*Mélodies hongroises* and *La Charité*), Liszt also joined his pupil Aladár Juhász in a performance of Hummel's Piano Sonata in A-flat major for piano duet. The concert ended when Zichy appeared on the platform with Liszt to perform a three-handed arrangement of the *Rákóczy* March, at the conclusion of which the pair stood on the platform while the audience showered them with flowers.

From Pressburg Liszt passed through Vienna, tarrying just long enough to have dinner with Princess Marie von Hohenlohe in the Augarten. Within a few hours he and his nephew Franz von Liszt had boarded the train to Oedenburg, the site of his first public triumph as a boy of nine. Here he was met by a deputation of city dignitaries (a protocol to which he was entitled, since he had been made a freeman of Oedenburg in 1840 and had later become a city magistrate), and by delegates of the local Literary and Artistic Circle, the organisation which had arranged the trip. He was wined and dined by the Benedictine monks, and he played once again in an evening concert with Zichy and other artists, ending as before with the three-handed arrangement of the *Rákóczy* March. The frequent choice of the march was deliberate. It was a defiant echo of Liszt's own performances of this "forbidden" music during his first Hungarian tour of 1839–40, when he had roused the audiences of Pressburg and Oedenburg with the strains of this national song. The political climate was different now, but there were those in the audience who were old enough to recall Liszt's sensational appearances in their country forty years earlier, when he had expressed their national aspirations through his piano playing. And history was about to repeat itself in another way, too.

X V I I

On April 7, 1881, Liszt paid a nostalgic visit to his birthplace in Raiding, where plans had been made to unveil a marble memorial plaque inscribed in his honour. He had at first resisted the effort "to make me illustrious before my death,"[83] but gave in to the pressure of his friends. He travelled in a long caravan of sixteen coaches from Oedenburg, in the company of Géza Zichy, the composer Adalbert von Goldschmidt, Ludwig Bösendorfer, and his nephew, Franz von Liszt. At the outskirts of Raiding they were met by a line of

---

83. LLB, vol. 7, p. 313.

mounted horsemen who escorted them into the village. Liszt could not help reflecting on the prophecy made by the Gypsies sixty years earlier, just before he and his family had left Raiding for good: that he would one day return as a famous man in "a glass coach." It seemed that the entire village had turned out to welcome its distinguished son, for hundreds of people milled around him as he was taken to the places associated with his early childhood. He saw again the old school where he had been a pupil of Johann Rohrer, and the tiny church where he had attended mass as a boy. The climax of the visit came when he entered the house in which he was born, an experience which released a flood of memories. He observed that many features of the interior had remained unchanged, including the remains of the old kitchen stove which had blown up when as a small boy he had emptied the contents of his father's gunpowder-pouch into the flames in order to enjoy the explosion.[84] "Already it was apparent that I had a feeling for mass effects," he joked.[85] As he emerged from the old house, and mingled with the crowds outside, the senior notary of the region, József Hannibál, mounted the hastily assembled podium, addressed a few words of homage to Liszt, and dedicated the marble plaque which had been mounted above the front door. It bore a simple inscription in gold letters: "Franz Liszt was born here on October 22, 1811." This historic scene, which was captured by a local photographer, expresses better than words the excitement generated in Raiding that day.[86] After his return to Vienna Liszt wrote a letter to the *Vizegespam* expressing his gratitude for the warmth of the reception extended to him. He enclosed a bank-note for 200 gulden to help towards the upkeep of the school and the village church.[87]

The pace of Liszt's travels increased dramatically during the spring and early summer of 1881. We calculate that in addition to the usual journeys that linked the cities of Budapest, Rome, and Weimar, he was to add during the next few weeks a further two thousand miles to his ceaseless peregrinations. The reason for this additional burst of activity is easy to explain, and it is one that gratified him: there were Liszt performances taking place all over Europe, and he was invariably asked to attend. After getting back from Raiding he spent several days in Vienna. Then, towards the end of April, we find him in Berlin, where Benjamin Bilse conducted an all-Liszt concert in his honour. On April 25 he attended the first Berlin performance of *Christus,* which was followed two days later by an all-Liszt concert conducted by Bülow. At the beginning of May he

---

84. The episode is recounted in Volume One, p. 61.
85. ZLEF, vol. 2, 101–04.
86. The photographer was M. Rupprecht from Sopron (see BFL, p. 282). Liszt gave a brief account of the day's events to Princess Carolyne, LLB, vol. 7, pp. 313–14.
87. PBUS, p. 242.

was in Freiburg to attend another performance of *Christus;* he then moved on to Karlsruhe and Baden-Baden, where Felix Mottl honored him with performances of *Mazeppa, Hunnenschlacht,* and the Second "Mephisto" Waltz. After the briefest of touch-downs in Weimar, Liszt took off again, this time to the music festivals of Antwerp (for the "Gran" Mass and *Totentanz*) and Brussels (for the *Faust* Symphony, *Tasso,* and the Concerto Pathétique). Even those who had reservations about the value of his compositions saw merit in having the Grand Old Man himself present. And so Liszt travelled, drawn forward by an ever-beckoning circle of admirers. At Brussels he was especially touched to be received by the King of the Belgians, who on May 31 invested him with the Order of Leopold.

It was clear to those who followed his progress across Europe that the sheer physical effort of it all could not be sustained. Liszt daily showed signs of fatigue. When he got back to Weimar in June 1881, friends and colleagues who were in a position to observe his daily life were concerned by the ominous swelling in his feet and legs, which made walking a real effort for him. These were dangerous symptoms, but he did not seek medical advice. "If one does not enjoy good health, one must create some," he often joked.[88] It was a remark that would soon come back to haunt him, for within four weeks of his return to Weimar his world collapsed about him, and his life-style was henceforth seriously curtailed.

---

88. WFLG, p. 120.

Unstern!

A man is in reality worth only what he is consid-
ered to be in the eyes of God!

FRANZ LISZT[1]

I

On July 2, 1881, Liszt fell down the stairs of the Hofgärtnerei. It was his traumatic entry into old age. Not quite seventy years old, he had until then enjoyed
reasonably good health, and his body had retained much of the slimness and
suppleness of his youth. The accident changed all that. Although Liszt made
light of the incident, he agreed to let a local physician, Dr. Richard Brehme,
examine him. Brehme was concerned enough to seek a second opinion and
brought in Dr. Richard von Volkmann, the head of surgery at Halle. They prescribed complete rest and a regimen free of alcohol—the sort of advice that
Liszt always accepted with difficulty. He dutifully took to his bed, thinking that
he would be up and about within a few days. In fact, he was immobilized for
nearly eight weeks. For the first few days Hans von Bülow and his daughter
Daniela, who were enjoying a brief holiday with Liszt at that time, kept him
company and sat by his bedside. Adelheid von Schorn was also a frequent visitor, and when the Bülows left (on July 9), she took over the tasks of reading
to him and taking dictation for his correspondence. Whenever he left his bed
he moved with difficulty. He stubbornly insisted on resuming his teaching, but
could only do so while reclining in an armchair, almost immobile. From this
episode Liszt's decline into the infirmities of old age can be traced. The accident seemed to trigger a number of ailments that until then had been lying
dormant within him—including dropsy, asthma, insomnia, a cataract of the left

---

1. LLB, vol. 6, p. 69.

eye, and chronic heart disease. This latter illness would kill him within five years.[2]

Although Liszt disliked discussing his symptoms, to Princess Carolyne he confessed that he had an unpleasant pain in his right side, and an overwhelming feeling of nausea when he got up in the mornings. One of the remedies prescribed by his doctors was a series of hot baths to make him perspire. "To this end," he told Carolyne, "I have been sent a bath tub from the palace."[3] She followed the progress of Liszt's slow recovery every step of the way, and was kept informed through a steady supply of "health bulletins" from Adelheid von Schorn. In one of her tactful letters to Liszt, Carolyne showed that she had a perfect understanding of his arrogant disregard for illness, and that unless he started to take better care of himself, he might become infirm before his time. Moreover, based on thirty years of intimacy with him, she knew that she was the only one to whom he would listen about such matters.

> I have confidence in the doctor, but the doctor only concerns himself with the accident and the fall. On the other hand, I learned quite by chance that from the time of your trip to Belgium, your legs began to swell after you got tired. This is a very serious matter, because it presages a condition. In itself it may not be dangerous, and in Rome they call it "jambe de cardinale." But this condition, if it is not treated very carefully, can easily change into dropsy, which, as you know, is horribly painful. Your plumpness, quite unnatural for your type of constitution, which is congenitally lean, could lead one to fear a disposition towards this illness, provoked by

---

2. Since the medical details of Liszt's accident have never before found their way into the literature, we give them here. Dr. Brehme listed the main symptoms as follows:

    1. Inflammation of the middle toe
    2. Swelling of the ankles
    3. Loss of appetite
    4. Feelings of nausea in the mornings
    5. A serious open wound in the right thigh, for which Brehme recommended
       frequent cleansing with a five-percent solution of carbolic acid in water
    6. Two fractured ribs with the possibility of bruising of the lungs
    7. Pleurisy

Brehme had a sample of Liszt's urine analysed, but it came back negative. He therefore concluded that the swelling of Liszt's tissues was the result of his age and his "life-style" (i.e., his alcoholic intake) rather than the onset of disease.

    Brehme recorded these symptoms on October 27, 1881, nearly four months after Liszt became his patient. (WA, Kasten 100, u. 1) Clearly, Liszt's accident was far more serious than anyone realised. Adelheid von Schorn gives a long account of his illness in SZM, pp. 390–91. Another visitor was La Mara, who wrote that "suddenly he had become older. . . . This episode announced the first symptoms of dropsy." (LDML, vol. 1, p. 355)

3. LLB, vol. 7, p. 326.

excessive efforts. I shall say no more about it, for I think that is enough to make you take some care of your health.[4]

The dropsy was a particularly difficult burden for Liszt to bear. "The cataract I probably deserved," he used to say, doubtless thinking of the many years of strain to which he had subjected his eyes in the writing and reading of music at all hours of the day and night. "But the dropsy I did not deserve at all."[5] Indeed, the swelling of his legs and feet made it so difficult for him to get around that it was at this time he took to wearing as his permanent footwear a pair of loose-fitting leather slippers, without supporting heels.

II

The period 1881–1884 was one of the most difficult that Liszt was called upon to bear. It was not only a matter of declining health; he was willing to suffer that in silence. But there were other problems of magnitude building up around him, whose consequences now started to impress themselves on his daily life. He seemed at a loss to know how they had occurred and how they might be resolved.

In November 1881 there appeared a revised edition of his book *Des Bohémiens et de leur musique en Hongrie,* and it created a storm of protest in Budapest. The chapter on the Israelites, especially, enraged the Jews and turned them against Liszt wherever he travelled. From Rome to Budapest, from Budapest to Weimar, from Weimar to Vienna, he was labelled an anti-Semite, a charge which wounded him deeply. We now know that the revisions were carried out by Carolyne, and that she alone was responsible for the chapter on the Israelites. When a new edition of this notorious book had been proposed to him, Liszt was happy enough to leave the proof-checking to Carolyne, for she herself had contributed to this work when it had first appeared, in 1859, a fact reported to us by her daughter, Princess Marie. But what Carolyne now did was a major piece of re-writing, without Liszt's knowledge or consent. She had never bothered to conceal her anti-Semitism, which had been reinforced by more than twenty-five years of mixing with the higher clergy in Rome, among whose members she found many allies on this topic. Particularly sensitive to Jews was her view that they be given their own state in Palestine, by force of Western arms if necessary. Palestine belonged to the Jews, she said, just as Italy belonged to Italians, Poland to the Poles, France to the French, England to the English. Why should not the Jews recover their homeland, as the Italians had

4. Hitherto unpublished letter dated August 5, 1881. WA, Kasten 50, u. 2.
5. RL-B, p. 23.

recovered theirs?[6] Many thousands of Jews of the Diaspora were uncomfortable with the notion of Zionism and were quite content to remain where history had placed them. By referring to Poland, her native country, the princess had tipped her hand. Poland had been removed from the map, having been absorbed by Russia, and the only way it would be recovered was by bloodshed. As Carolyne pored over her maps in the Via del Babuino, deciding the fate of peoples with the stroke of a pen, Liszt was a thousand miles away, unaware that his name was being used for this nefarious purpose. Carolyne wove other tainted threads into her racial narrative, too, and talked about people who refused to assimilate and preferred to work for four-hundred-percent profit. And there were plenty of insults left over for Hungarians. She told them that the old Magyar folk-songs had actually been stolen from the Gypsies and had had Hungarian words attached to them to make them sound authentic. That this farrago of nonsense, some of it with sinister ethnic overtones, should have been attributed to Liszt is a biographical problem of the first magnitude. All his actions contradicted Carolyne's statements. At the very least, we can say that he blundered by not taking charge of the project himself, or better still, by forbidding yet another edition of a book from which he had already suffered greatly. But by allowing Carolyne to control matters, he guaranteed a public-relations disaster from which he never entirely escaped.[7]

The response came quickly. In Budapest the fires of hostility were fanned by such newspapers as *Pesther Lloyd* and the *Neues Pesther Journal*. Then the flames spread to Vienna and flickered in the columns of the *Neue Freie Presse* and other journals. Perhaps the worst consequence for Liszt was the publication of the pamphlet *Franz Liszt über die Juden* by Miksa Schütz, the critic of *Pesther Lloyd*, who wrote under the pen-name "Sagittarius."[8] Schütz proved himself to be as despicable as Carolyne, by fighting back with language and ideas to match her own. But the damage was done. Liszt was branded as an anti-Semite, a charge that was preposterous to anyone who knew his life and work. The seething resentment that was felt for a time by the Hungarian Jews came out in a variety of ways. The Association of Jewish Law Students made it known through their newspaper *Függetlenség* that they would physically assault Liszt the moment he alighted at the Budapest railway station if he visited the city again.[9] One unfortunate consequence of this threat was that the Budapest Philharmonic Society, fearing public unrest, cancelled a performance of the *Faust* Symphony that was scheduled to take place in December 1881. On the surface, Liszt took

6. RGS, vol. 6, p. 66.
7. The background to the writing and publication of *Des Bohémiens* has been dealt with at some length in Volume Two, pp. 380–90.
8. For our earlier comments on "Sagittarius" and his response to the 1881 edition of *Des Bohémiens,* see Volume Two, pp. 388–90.
9. Issue dated November 26, 1881.

it all calmly, and he continued to enjoy excellent relations with his Jewish friends and pupils. Deep down, however, he had been spiritually harmed.

Where Budapest led, Vienna was not slow to follow. The day after he was threatened with physical violence by Hungarian Jews, he was pilloried in the Viennese satirical journal *Der Floh* in an article entitled "Der allerneueste Messias der Juden." It is clear from this piece that it was the idea of a Jewish homeland that brought more censure down on Liszt's head than anything else. The front cover of the journal carried a caricature of the Entry into Jerusalem, with Liszt as the Messiah seated on a donkey, Wagner and Bülow at his side, and behind them a multitude of Jews surging towards the Holy City. The accompanying verse drove home the message: "Hosannah! Beat the drums, sound the cymbal, blow the trombones, the Messiah has appeared who will lead the Jews from Exile into the Promised Land. . . . His name is Liszt."[10]

His friends and colleagues rallied to his defence, and so did some of the press. One of the most perceptive articles, published in *Fővárosi Lapok,* ended with the revealing sentence: "We would not be at all surprised if someone should come forward to affirm that somebody from the land of Anti-Semitism has smuggled these pages into this book by the good old Liszt."[11] This is a clear indication that those within his inner circle suspected the truth. Of course, no one came forward. The fact is that Carolyne's attempts to cloak herself in anonymity whenever she picked up her pen were always pathetic, for her arguments gave her away. Her name does not appear on any of the twenty-four volumes of her *Causes intérieures* either, although the whole world knew that the text was being churned out at Via del Babuino 89.[12]

Something else lay behind the hullabaloo created by *Des Bohémiens,* and we do well to consider it here. In 1882, not long after the appearance of Liszt's book, a potentially explosive issue arose that caused the Jewish community in Hungary great anguish. This was the year of the so-called "blood trial" of Tiszaeszlár, a small village in the hinterland. Briefly, the local kosher butcher and his partners were accused of killing a young girl in order to use her blood in the unleavened Passover bread. The charges were eventually thrown out of court, but not before the story had worked its way around Europe and provoked loud protests from prominent individuals—including the exiled Kossuth. The "blood trial," which lasted for more than a year, gripped the imagination of the nation and created tension between Jew and Gentile. When Carolyne, safe in the haven of her rooms in the Eternal City, decided to com-

---

10. Issue of November 27, 1881.
11. Issue of November 25, 1881.
12. Significantly, the last part of Carolyne's *Causes intérieures* (published in 1887) contains a section on Judaism. It is clear from the dates that she must have been expanding the Israelite chapter in *Des Bohémiens* at about the same time. Nor do we require any particular forensic gifts to see that the same hand penned both pieces.

mandeer the text of *Des Bohémiens* and use it for her own purpose, she had no idea that she was about to throw Liszt into a boiling ocean of racial discontent.

By February 1883, the turmoil surrounding the book had grown to such a degree that it had become imperative for Liszt to make a public response. By remaining silent, he appeared not only to accept the poisoned chalice, but to drink deeply and willingly from it as well. This put him in a false position with regard to his friends, a number of whom realised that the chapter on the Jews was the work of Carolyne and waited in vain for him to disown it. He chose a French-language Budapest newspaper to reply to his critics, the *Gazette de Hongrie,* which published the following letter on February 8.

> Dear Editor:
>
> It is not without regret that I address these lines to you; but as there has been some report spread here about my supposed hostility towards the Israelites, I must rectify the error of this false account.
>
> Many illustrious Israelites of good repute in the musical world, with Meyerbeer at their head, have given me their esteem and friendship; the same in the world of literature, Heine among others.
>
> It seems superflous to me to enumerate the many proofs I have given, over a period of fifty years of active loyalty, towards Israelites of talent and ability, and I likewise abstain from talking about my voluntary contributions to the charitable Jewish institutions in various countries.
>
> The motto of my patron saint St. Francis of Paola is "Caritas!" I will remain faithful to this throughout my life!
>
> If, through some garbled passages taken from my book on the *Gypsies* [Liszt's italics] in Hungary, the idea has been to make me the object of controversy, and to make what is called in French *une querelle d'Allemand,* I can affirm in good conscience that I do not regard myself as being guilty of any other misdeed than that of having feebly reproduced the argument put forward by Disraeli (Lord Beaconsfield), George Eliot (Mrs. Lewes),[13] and Crémieux, three outstanding Israelites, concerning the Kingdom of Jerusalem.
>
> Accept, Sir, etc.[14]
>
> 6 February, 1883, Budapest

---

13. Liszt was mistaken in thinking that George Eliot (Mary Ann Evans) was Jewish.

14. LLB, vol. 2, pp. 345–46. Liszt enclosed with this letter a private one to the editor, M. Saissy, asking his frank opinion about the wisdom of printing anything at all. "As the proverb goes: 'Silence is golden,' " wrote Liszt. Saissy printed not only Liszt's official statement but the private one as well. See LLB, vol. 2, pp. 344–45.

There are two things to observe about this letter. The first is the perfectly correct statement that the idea of a Jewish homeland was not his, but was originally a Jewish idea; he had merely "feebly reproduced" it. The second, and far more important, thing is what Liszt did not say. Why did he not tell his readers that this chapter was really the work of Princess Carolyne? The true answer is that despite his anger and frustration he wanted to protect her. Richard Wagner put it best of all. He was in Venice when he read Liszt's letter to the *Gazette,* and he saw at once what had happened. He told Cosima on February 12 (the day before he died): "Your father goes to his ruin out of pure chivalry!"[15]

Of all Liszt's friends and admirers, none was more troubled by what had happened than Lina Ramann. She was in the middle of her German translation of Liszt's *Collected Writings* in six volumes (1880–83), and people on all sides now started to ask her what she intended to do when she got to the Gypsy book. Would she use Carolyne's revised edition? "Wait and see," was her reply. Privately she declared: "The chapter [on the Israelites] does not belong in the *Bohémiens.*" Nonetheless, when her translation of the book appeared in this very year of 1883, Carolyne's chapter on the Israelites was there, albeit stripped of excess.[16]

III

The most severe blow was yet to fall. Even as Liszt was fighting for the restoration of his public reputation, his enemies in Hungary began to plan a further humiliation. By early 1884, the arrangements for the inauguration of the newly built Budapest Opera House were well advanced. The site was on Sugár Street, one of the main thoroughfares of the city, and no effort had been spared to turn the building into an architectural showpiece, both in its external aspect and its

---

15. WT, vol. 2, p. 1112. Wagner actually uses the word "Cavalerie"—a triple pun on chivalry, cavalry, and Calvary.

16. For Lina Ramann's strong protests against Carolyne's work, see RL, pp. 183–85. Ramann later reported a conversation with Liszt on the topic of the dilemma she faced as his translator. He reminded her that Cornelius had dropped a chapter on the Jews from the first German edition. She did not think that this was a correct solution to the problem, however, but felt that the text would have to be retained. Liszt agreed with her. "What has been uttered, has been uttered," he remarked. "You are right, Master," replied Ramann. "However, I regret the matter—the abusive language. The Jews strongly influence the press. Your compositions will be heard less often." To which Liszt retorted: "I can wait." (RL, p. 195) This conversation took place on November 14, 1882. It is clear that only the decision to translate Carolyne's text into German had Liszt's approval, not the text itself. Ramann came to the same conclusion as Wagner was to come to a few weeks later: that Liszt was defending Carolyne and was willing to destroy himself in the process. "At that moment," she said, "he was a Cavalier from head to toe." (p. 197)

interior beauty. Ferenc Erkel was appointed the first music director, and Baron
Frigyes Podmaniczky the first theatre intendant. The sculptor Alajos Stróbl had
already cast a large statue of Liszt which dominated the façade of the building.
(Liszt and his pupils would have observed it each time they walked along Sugár
Street towards the Royal Academy of Music, built a few years earlier on the
same street.) As for Liszt himself, he had been invited to compose a work for
the opening ceremonies—a gesture which genuinely pleased him. The inaugural concert was to be given in the presence of Emperor Franz Joseph and Empress Elisabeth on September 27, and many of the leaders of the political
establishment of Austro-Hungary. Liszt accordingly began to compose a patriotic piece for chorus and orchestra "in the wake of an old Hungarian song," as
he put it—that is, the *Rákóczy* Song. He took it to be an entirely appropriate
thing to do on this national occasion. The text, by Kornél Ábrányi, saluted the
emperor as "the king of Hungary" ("Blessed be the king of Hungarians!"). Liszt
submitted his new composition, the *Ungarisches Königslied,* well in advance of
the concert so as to allow sufficient time for rehearsal. On September 17, ten
days before the building was to be opened, he was distressed to receive a formal
letter from Baron Podmaniczky which informed both him and Erkel that "an
insurmountable obstacle stands in the way of the performance of the *Ungarisches
Königslied.*"[17] What was that obstacle? A melody, no less. It seems that Podmaniczky was fearful that the royal couple might be offended at the inclusion of a
Hungarian national song reminding them of Rákóczi, an enemy of the Habsburgs; therefore, Liszt's composition would have to be removed. Liszt replied
that there was nothing revolutionary about the *Rákóczy* Song, that he had found
it in the old Bartalus anthology, and it must not be confused with the *Rákóczy*
March, which was indeed a call to arms.[18] These arguments fell on deaf ears: in
brief, Emperor Franz Joseph and his court could not be expected to appreciate
the difference. It is possible that Podmaniczky was being manipulated by Prime
Minister Tisza and his political cohorts, who did not like the notoriety that had
gathered around Liszt and his Gypsy book. The very threat of a public demonstration against Liszt on that earlier occasion must have raised the spectre in this
politician's mind of something similar happening inside the opera house on this
infinitely more important occasion. For the rest, Tisza had never been a supporter of Liszt, as a later speech in parliament was to prove—a speech in which
the "scandal" of Liszt's book on the Gypsies was a chief issue.[19]

---

17. LLC, vol. 2, p. 248. See also Liszt's reply to Baron Podmaniczky, dated September 21, 1884, in LLB,
vol. 2, pp. 368–69.
18. The *Rákóczy* Song is not as well known as the march. A song of exile, it has nothing to do with
rallying the nation and toppling thrones. The Bartalus anthology had been published fifteen years earlier under aegis of the Hungarian National Academy of Sciences. That fact alone gave it the stamp of
official approval and made Podmaniczky's present attitude all the more perplexing.
19. See pp. 524–25.

And so the Budapest Opera House was opened without either Liszt or his score. There were even attempts to prevent the dissemination of Liszt's composition, which did not succeed. The first performance may well have been the one that was given less than three weeks later on October 16, by the orchestra of the 83rd Infantry Regiment at Fehértemplom.[20] But when at last it was heard in Budapest the following year, all that the music critic of *Pesther Lloyd* could find to say about it was that it was "a mockery of human song," and that it could "put to flight a cavalry division."[21]

The tensions arising from the *Königslied* affair, following so hard on the heels of the controversy surrounding the Gypsy book, threw Liszt into despair. He perceived himself to be rejected by his native Hungary, something he neither expected nor thought he deserved. It was against this background of personal disaster, both public and private, that he uttered a cry of anguish that has reverberated across the generations, and gives us pause for thought even today.

> Everyone is against me. Catholics because they find my church music profane, Protestants because to them my music is Catholic, Freemasons because they think my music is too clerical; to conservatives I am a revolutionary, to the "futurists" an old Jacobin. As for the Italians, in spite of Sgambati, if they support Garibaldi they detest me as a hypocrite, if they are on the side of the Vatican I am accused of bringing the Venusberg into the Church. To Bayreuth I am not a composer but a publicity agent. The Germans reject my music as French, the French as German; to the Austrians I write Gypsy music, to the Hungarians foreign music. And the Jews loathe me, my music and myself, for no reason at all.[22]

I V

In the midst of this sea of troubles, those nearest to Liszt noticed a marked increase in his drinking. From the late summer of 1882 he began to drink absinthe, a lethal mixture of grape alcohol and wormwood. Achille Colonello, his manservant, feared it would harm him, but was powerless to stop it. In a suppressed passage from the diary of Carl Lachmund we read:

---

20. LLC, vol. 2, p. 310, n. 240.
21. Issue of March 26, 1885.
22. Although the holograph of this letter to Ödön Mihalovich has never been found, it is considered by all Liszt scholars to be genuine. It is quoted by Emile Haraszti, without date or source, in the *Pléiade Encyclopedia of Music History*, vol. 2 (Paris, 1963), p. 535.

I hear through Achille, the gentlemanly secretary of Liszt, that the Master drinks much so as to keep himself strong. But I fear he will kill himself, as already he looks "dropsy-bloated." Liszt drinks daily one bottle of cognac and two or three bottles of wine. Sometimes in fact he drinks two bottles of cognac and as much wine. Now, while at Bayreuth [July 1882] he has taken it into his head that he must have absinthe. Where will this end. He cannot stand that terrible stuff very long.[23]

Whether Liszt was by now an alcoholic in the medical sense of that term, we cannot be sure. But his consumption of wine and liquor in the course of a single day had become considerable. Nonetheless, he was never seen to be inebriated, and alcohol seemed to impair neither his piano-playing nor his speech.

Increasingly, he had to rely on others to get out and about. But the most frustrating thing was his failing eyesight, which made it very difficult for him to read and write. It affected his composing and to a limited extent his piano-playing. This caused him such concern that in February 1884 he consulted "a celebrated oculist" who reassured him that he had nothing to fear from cataracts, and that he ought to try to save his eyes by cutting down on reading and writing.[24] Just over two years later, however, this diagnosis had to be reversed, for when he finally became a patient of Alfred Graefe, the world's leading expert on the removal of cataracts, a surgical operation was recommended. Liszt had always made it a rule never to complain about his health, which often gave people the mistaken impression that he was physically fit. But the "iron constitution" of his youth, which was always something of a myth, was slowly being eroded.

Whatever the crisis, his pupils rallied round; they were an extended family and supported him in a multitude of ways. Nonetheless, one or two of them caused him personal grief. A long-standing rivalry between Dori Petersen and Lina Schmalhausen spilled over into an unpleasant scandal. Matters reached a point where it began to affect the morale of the class, and Liszt felt that he had

---

23. CLC, series 2, folder 5, pp. 166–67. Absinthe had been introduced in Paris in the 1850s and was by now a "fashionable" drink among the intelligentsia. There were devastating consequences attached to drinking this milky-green fluid on a regular basis, including blindness, loss of memory, and paralysis. Nonetheless, the dreamy euphoria associated with the beverage led to the introduction of "Absinthe hour" in the cafés and restaurants of the Left Bank, where it was popular among artists in search of inspiration. Van Gogh was said to have cut off his ear while under its influence, while Toulouse-Lautrec became so addicted to it that he blended it with cognac—a beverage to which he attached the appellation "the earthquake," for it did indeed change one's centre of gravity, sometimes permanently. During World War I absinthe was finally banned by the French government, which attributed the poor showing of their army against the Germans to its widespread use among the troops.
24. LLB, vol. 7, p. 400. We presume that the "celebrated oculist" was Alfred Graefe of Halle, who gave Liszt a much more extensive examination in the summer of 1886.

no alternative but to intervene. He wrote Dori a sharp note in which he told her that unless she stopped the intrigues she had mounted against the Schmal-hausen family, things would go badly for her.[25] The quarrel continued to smoulder, however, so Liszt suspended her from the class. Then Lina furnished her nemesis with some sensational ammunition: in the spring of 1884 she was charged with shoplifting in Weimar. While making some purchases she had slipped some lace into her basket without paying for it and had been appre-hended by the shop-girl. The matter went to law and Lina went to Liszt. After convincing himself of her innocence, Liszt sought the advice of Hofrath Carl Gille, and together they went to the judge and managed to have the charges dropped.

The matter must have been an unpleasant one for Liszt, because at the very time he took up Lina's cause there were also some thefts of money from his desk in the Hofgärtnerei. Again, Lina Schmalhausen was the prime suspect. Pauline Apel, his housekeeper, had walked into Liszt's bedroom only to find Lina with her hand in the desk drawer. When the matter was reported to Liszt, he again refused to believe Lina guilty of theft, and absolutely forbade that any action be taken.[26] These matters were common knowledge among the other students. Xaver Scharwenka, who was in the masterclass of 1884, wrote some witty lines about Lina's pilfering.

> Andern etwas wegzumausen
> In der Kunst recht schmal zu hausen[27]
> Ohn' Begriff von Noten, Pausen
> Nur zu klimpern—oh, welch Grausen!

> [To pilfer from others
> To rummage shallowly in art,
> Without an inkling of notes or rests
> Merely tinkling—oh, what horror!]

Naturally, Dori Petersen (who had meanwhile been taken back into the class) stoked the fires of scandal and made life utterly miserable for her rival. She went to the Weimar shopkeeper and got her to sign a statement to the effect that

---

25. A run of unpublished letters from Liszt to both pupils is preserved in the Ramann Bibliothek, WA, Kasten 380, u. 3. On July 8, 1883, Liszt made it clear to Petersen that as a result of her aggressive be-haviour, she was temporarily banned from his circle. He wrote to her: "Following your recent behav-iour towards the Schmalhausen family, you will understand that I cannot receive you now or in the future. The whole intrigue was stirred up by you in a mean-spirited way, and was unfortunately con-tinued."
26. LL, pp. 319–20.
27. Ibid. Scharwenka's word-play on the name "Schmalhausen" confirms that it was the luckless Lina who was embroiled in charges of petty theft.

Schmalhausen was indeed guilty of theft, which she then showed to Liszt. Again Liszt chastised her, and added a threat that she could not ignore: unless she abandoned her crusade against Schmalhausen, "her former friend," he would break off their connection.[28] That would have put a permanent end to Petersen's career as a Liszt student.

Many people wondered why Liszt kept Schmalhausen in his circle, since she not only was one of his least talented pupils but was now tainted by gossip. Two reasons suggest themselves. Lina had come to him with a letter of recommendation from Empress Augusta of Prussia, the sister of Carl Alexander, and if he dismissed her he would have to say why; the conclusion is that he did not want to embarrass his royal benefactor. More important, Lina, who had pressed herself on him like a daughter, was now an indispensable part of his household, reading to him, helping him with his correspondence, and generally looking after his welfare. Unlike the other students, she accompanied him from one town to another not merely to continue taking lessons from him but to help make his life softer. To expel her in the face of so many kindnesses would have seemed like base ingratitude; so Lina stayed.[29]

The thefts of money from Liszt compounded the financial problems with which he was beset in the second half of 1884. No one could understand why he was impoverished at this particular time. Earlier in the year he had received 7,300 marks for various compositions—2,000 for the Third "Mephisto" Waltz, an unusually large sum of money for a late work of Liszt. The truth came to light when it was learned that he had contributed 3,000 thalers towards the Bach monument in Eisenach, which was unveiled in September of that year. This made him one of the largest benefactors; it also beggared him for several months. All the more surprising, then, that the committee in charge of the unveiling ceremonies failed to send a delegation to the railway station to meet Liszt and the other dignitaries from Weimar, who included Eduard Lassen and Olga von Meyendorff. When the grand duke heard about this discourtesy to

---

28. See the unpublished run of letters in the Ramann Bibliothek, WA, 204, u. 5.

29. Gossip about Schmalhausen's brush with the law appears to have been rife. Did it reach Bayreuth? It would go a long way to explain Cosima Wagner's loathing of Schmalhausen and of her adamant refusal to have the young woman in the house during the last few days of Liszt's life. It would also explain why Liszt, having given Lina the holograph score of *Christus* shortly before his death, felt constrained to add to the manuscript a sentence to the effect that it was his *gift* to her.

Towards the end of her life Schmalhausen fell upon terrible times. In the summer of 1927 she had her right leg amputated in a Berlin hospital. She was so poor that she was admitted as a "third-class" patient and shared a ward with 30 other patients. Since the cost of the artificial limb came to 300–400 marks, it was beyond her means to pay for it. Emma Grosskurth, one of her fellow class-members, heard of Lina's plight, visited her in hospital, and contacted a number of Liszt's students with a request that they make donations to the hospital in Lina's name to pay for her treatment. (CLC, JPB 92–1, series 1, folder 49)

Liszt, his court chamberlain, he was displeased, since it came from the officials of his own "Wartburg Stadt."[30]

Liszt was now in his twilight years. But instead of being allowed to recollect his life in proverbial tranquillity, he was weighed down with impossible burdens. Carolyne had betrayed him by depicting him as an anti-Semite; Hungary had humiliated him over the *Königslied* affair; one or two of his pupils were causing him distress; he was subject to frequent bouts of depression; and his physical health was failing. He was seventy-one years old, and there were times when he must have thought that his life had become void. But still worse things were pressing down on him. Wagner had died; and for reasons which were as inexplicable to Liszt as to everyone else, his daughter Cosima had withdrawn into perpetual widowhood and had broken off all contact with him. His life was cloaked in a shawl of sorrow. *Unstern!* Unlucky star indeed!

---

30. LL, p. 337. Joachim was among the distinguished soloists at the Eisenach festival, and he took part in a performance of Bach's Double Concerto for two violins. Since the rapprochement between Liszt and Joachim was not yet complete, even though the break between them was now more than twenty-five years old, the committee may not have known how to handle this delicate situation. Of that break Liszt used to say good-humouredly: "Es hat ihm genutzt" ("He has profited from it"). Shortly after the Bach festival, and doubtless prompted by the knowledge that Liszt had been slighted, Joachim called at the Hofgärtnerei (a thing he had not done for years) in order to apologise. Liszt immediately cut him off and turned the conversation to some pleasant matters concerning Joachim himself. "This was the magnanimous Liszt!" observed Lachmund.

Perhaps this is the place to remark that Joachim, too, had identified himself with the Bach monument project, and, like Liszt, he had given a number of rarely reported fund-raising concerts across the years. One of them had taken place in the unlikely location of Rugby School, in England, on March 23, 1875. Among the works Joachim played on that occasion were Bach's Violin Concerto in A minor and his Sonata in A major (pieces which were hardly known until Joachim revived them) together with Beethoven's Romance in G major, and an unspecified work of Brahms. (These details are culled from an extant programme in the British Library, call no. L. 23, c.11 [74].)

Nuages gris

Ever since the days of my youth I have considered
dying much simpler than living.

FRANZ LISZT[1]

I

When Liszt and his small entourage of pupils arrived in Bayreuth on July 15, 1882, for the première of *Parsifal* later that month, the town was again in the grip of a Wagner craze. Thousands of guests had converged on the small community in readiness for an event that had been advertised across the Western world. The streets were decked out with bunting, and the local business people, sensing that the Wagner festival was about to turn the place into a gold-mine, albeit for only one month of the year, had gone to work with a will. The waitresses in the restaurants were called "Kundry," the gift-shops were pushing "Wagner pens" and "Wagner neckties," and there was a fast-selling wine called "Klingsor's Magic Drink." Hotel rooms were at a premium. As the theatre was outside the city limits, the cabmen did a brisk trade, and a long line of carriages stretched all the way up the hill from the town to the theatre door. In brief, the festival laid down the model for that strange mixture of God and Mammon which has come to characterise all such festivals today. There had been fifty rehearsals of *Parsifal,* including separate ones for soloists, chorus, and orchestra, with two alternating casts and two conductors, Hermann Levi and Franz Fischer. Not even Bayreuth's first performance of *The Ring,* in 1876, had aroused such world-wide anticipation.

On the afternoon of July 25 a *Liebesmahl* was arranged for Wagner in the large hall of the theatre restaurant. More than four hundred guests were seated at three

---

1. LLB, vol. 2, p. 348.

long tables. Wagner sat at the centre of the first table, with Liszt on his left and Marianne Brandt (one of three singers alternating in the role of Kundry) on his right. Cosima sat facing them, with other singers clustered around them. Wagner, in a jovial mood, left his place from time to time to chat with his friends. Someone joked that the courses were moving slowly, to which Wagner retorted: "Yes, they move as slowly as the transformation scene in the second act."[2] When someone else observed that his recent stay in Italy appeared to have done him good, he replied: "No, it is my good heart that keeps me well"—a fateful comment when we recall the heart-attack to which he succumbed less than seven months later. Wagner then caught sight of Liszt, who had got up to stretch his legs, and invited him to make a speech, which Liszt declined to do since he thought it inappropriate in such company. He had no idea that Wagner was planning a speech of his own. Wagner waited until the next course had been cleared away, got to his feet, and addressed the sea of faces turned towards him. His first words were to his faithful artists, telling them that without their loyalty and devotion the production of *Parsifal* could not have taken place. The gist of his thoughts was that through this enterprise they had lifted themselves above the commonplace taste of the masses. "We do it through you, our artists!" he exclaimed. It was an emotional re-play of similar speeches he had made in the past, and on similar occasions, notably before the first performance of *Tristan*. He then turned to Liszt, and began a long review of their musical friendship and of Liszt's value and significance to him. The importance of this speech (which Cosima described as "wonderful") was not lost on the many musicians present, and the Liszt contingent was especially pleased to see Liszt's contribution to the Wagner cause acknowledged in so public a fashion.[3]

The first performance of *Parsifal* took place the following day, July 26. The distinguished cast included Hermann Winkelmann (Parsifal), Amalie Materna (Kundry), Theodor Reichmann (Amfortas), Emil Scaria (Gurnemanz), and Karl Hill (Klingsor), with Levi conducting the Munich chorus and orchestra, which had been expanded to 107 players for this occasion. Liszt, as a chief guest-of-honour, attended not only at least four of the performances, but some of the rehearsals as well. Moreover, he did much socializing at Wahnfried,

2. Wagner's joke may require some explanation for the modern reader. During the final rehearsals it was discovered that the stage designer, Carl Brandt, had somehow miscalculated by many yards the length of the painted landscape required to unroll across the back of the stage, and so create the illusion of Parsifal's journey towards Monsalvat. It was now too late to modify the mechanical rollers required to produce this visual miracle. In order to prevent the activities on the stage from going in one direction and the musical score in another, Wagner had been obliged to repeat one of the orchestral interludes—with generous ritardandos along the way.

3. Cosima's terse diary-entry (WT, vol. 1, p. 893) differs in a number of details from the longer account given by Carl Lachmund, who was present at this dinner. (LL, pp. 121–22) See also Lachmund's serialized review of the *Parsifal* production, published in seven consecutive issues of *Music and Drama*, from August 19 through September 30, 1882.

where he willingly took his place at Wagner's Steinway grand piano and played excerpts from *Parsifal* to the assembled guests.[4] His knowledge of the score, in fact, was probably unrivalled; it was at this time that he came out with his transcription of the Ceremonial March of the Holy Grail.[5]

The Ceremonial March is the least known of all Liszt's piano transcriptions of Wagner. Unlike the others it poses no serious technical problems; yet its glowing sonority, which encircles it like a halo, can fill a concert hall. A life, somewhat like history, is full of might-have-beens, about which it is usually better not to speculate. But the Ceremonial March arouses our curiosity as to what Liszt might have achieved with other sections of *Parsifal*—above all, Kundry's seduction music in Act Two, which would surely have succumbed to his all-encompassing fingers. Alas, it was not to be.

During the last performance of *Parsifal,* on August 29,[6] Wagner waited until the final act and then descended the steps under the stage and took over the baton from Hermann Levi, bringing the work to a moving conclusion. It was his farewell to the Bayreuth opera house. Somewhat to Wagner's chagrin, Liszt had already left town and hurried back to Weimar.[7] Before he departed, on August 5, he accepted an invitation to spend the coming winter with the Wagners in Venice.

---

4. The famous oil-paintings by George Papperitz and Wilhelm Beckmann capture the atmosphere of the Wahnfried soirées better than verbal description. (BFL, pp. 288–29)

5. A public performance of this transcription had already been given in Weimar by the eighteen-year-old Eugène d'Albert, on September 29, 1882. (LL, p. 174) This may well have been its première. See p. 423, where the programme of the young man's recital is given in full.

6. Altogether there were sixteen performances of *Parsifal* during this four-week period.

7. Cosima's diary puts it more strongly: "My father's departure . . . arouses very great anger in him." (WT, vol. 2, p. 987) Evidently Wagner had expected Liszt to stay on in Bayreuth. It did not occur to him that Liszt might have a life to lead beyond the confines of the Wagner festival. Even so, Liszt made a swift return trip to Bayreuth at Cosima's request in order to be present at the wedding of his granddaughter Blandine, who married Count Biagio Gravina there in a civil ceremony on August 25, 1882, and a religious one the following day. When Liszt returned once more to Weimar, Wagner was again swept by "a great outburst of anger." (WT, vol. 2, p. 995)

11

One reason Liszt had returned to Weimar was to take charge of his master-classes, since many students had meanwhile descended on the small town and were awaiting his return. An unusually large contingent of American students had assembled at the Hofgärtnerei this year, and these friendly young men and women formed a circle within a circle. Already Liszt had had several encounters with American hospitality. Carl and Caroline Lachmund had invited him over to their apartment on Breitestrasse for an at-home, and Liszt had been happy to climb the three flights of stairs in order to reach their cramped quarters. Wilhelm Posse, the Berlin harpist, was there, and delighted Liszt with his playing. The day was unusually hot, so they placed "ice-cakes" at strategic points in the room in order to bring down the temperature. Liszt was much amused by the stratagem, and sat next to one of these miniature icebergs while one of the guests fanned the cool air in his direction. Even in those days, it seems, the Americans were obsessed with air-conditioning. On September 7 they even gave him an "American dinner" in the garden of Armbrust's restaurant. Liszt arrived from the Hofgärtnerei in a droshky, accompanied by Martha Remmert. When he entered the garden, he saw before him a long banquet table decorated with the American and Hungarian flags, and a group of Americans including Arthur Bird, William Dayas, May Hoeltge, and the Lachmunds. Others in the group included Walter Bache, Alfred Reisenauer, and Alexander Gottschalg. The menu consisted of typical American dishes, including roast beef with Saratoga potatoes and cauliflower, followed by co-conut cake and whipped cream. Various toasts and speeches were given, and a telegramme from Wilhelm Posse (whose professional duties had detained him in Berlin) was read. This gave Liszt a chance to respond. After thanking America for having received so much of his music with an open mind when other countries had rejected it, he glanced at the Stars and Stripes fluttering from one of the trees and remarked: "May there arise for each one of the young artists here a 'Glücks-Stern' [lucky star] to ascend higher and higher." The banquet concluded with a performance of Bach's Fugue in A minor (known to every one of Liszt's students through his piano transcription), with each participant taking one note of the angular subject in turn as it moved around the table, the point of the game being to see how far the melody could be taken before everything collapsed. Liszt enjoyed the game and even joined in.

Edward MacDowell was the most prominent American student to make his way to Weimar during the summer of 1882. He had been introduced to Liszt by Eugène d'Albert, and played to the master his newly composed Piano Concerto in A minor with d'Albert at the second piano. Liszt was delighted with this concerto, which MacDowell eventually dedicated to him. The American composer's music for solo piano appealed to Liszt no less, and he arranged for MacDowell to play his first "Modern" Suite for piano at the Allgemeiner Deutscher Musikverein in Zurich, in July 1882. This gesture was well within Liszt's gift, for he had just recently been appointed honorary lifetime president of the Verein.

At one of the classes, held towards the end of August, Liszt's students noticed that he was in an uncharacteristically angry mood. He paced the music-room of the Hofgärtnerei incessantly while listening to Katharina Ranouchewitsch play Chopin's Ballade in A-flat major in a performance that would normally have garnered some praise. When she defended herself against some of Liszt's minor criticisms, telling him and the class that her previous teacher, Henselt, had directed her to play the work in that manner, he flared up and accused her of impertinence. "Halten Sie's Maul, ich habe genug naseweise Bermerkung!" ("Hold your tongue—I have had enough of your smart remarks!") The class was stunned, and quite unable to account for Liszt's dark humour. It later transpired that earlier in the day a deputation had knocked on his door asking for a contribution to commemorate "Sedan Day." Ever since the Franco-Prussian War, September 2 had been set aside to celebrate the victory of Sedan. It was now regarded as one of the most important dates in the German calendar, a day on which money was raised each year for the wounded veterans of that conflict. Liszt's generosity was well-known, and whenever donations were sought the Hofgärtnerei could usually be counted on to help. On this occasion, however, the local committee had received short shrift. Liszt identified with France, and he regarded it as an indelicacy to be invited to celebrate the defeat of his friends. Moreover, the committee showed scant regard for his family history. The request for a donation was obtuse, and Liszt was offended.[8]

Such dark clouds could not hover for long. Soon afterwards, Liszt arranged a special outing for his students and friends. Early on the morning of September 24 he and a small contingent of supporters boarded the train for Arnstadt in order to attend an organ recital by his disciple Ernst Schilling.[9] The weather had turned wet and chilly, and Liszt had developed a cold. But he insisted on making the journey because he had learned that the local musicians were already pooh-poohing Schilling's announcement that Liszt would be there, and that they wanted to see him cut down to size when Liszt failed to show up at

---

8. LL, pp. 135–36.
9. Liszt had met Ernst Schilling in Rome, where the young man was the organist at the English church there, a post previously held by Walter Bache. After hearing him play, he had invited Schilling to Weimar to attend the summer masterclasses.

the small church. Liszt, in short, was determined to arrive with a real cold, rather than be prevented from doing so by a diplomatic one. Carl Gille travelled with the party, and so did Gottschalg—which meant that these worthies were obliged to travel third-class, Liszt's usual mode of locomotion. The train journey was slow, with a change at the village of Dietendorf. Liszt suddenly remembered that the place was famous for its *Pfeffermünzschen,* and sent Gille to buy some. The dignified Hofrath happily went off in pursuit of his mission, and got back with not one, but half-a-dozen of the familiar blue oval boxes. As the train moved off, Liszt handed them round to his companions, who continued their journey munching these delicacies. By the time they got to Arnstadt, the air of the carriage was filled with the aroma of mint.

Although they did not know it, it was to be their last meal for several hours. Schilling, preoccupied with the details of his recital, had neglected to order lunch for his guests, so the carriages waiting at the railway station took Liszt and his group straight to the church, instead of to the restaurant and the hearty meal they had all expected. Liszt took the oversight in good part, and doubtless received some satisfaction from arriving at the church a little early, thus confounding Schilling's critics. The two main works in Schilling's recital were a Mendelssohn sonata and Liszt's own Fantasy and Fugue on the name B-A-C-H. It is difficult for the modern observer to appreciate how these two pieces might have sounded on a small two-manual instrument that had remained basically unchanged since Bach played it. There were, in fact, very few organs in Germany at that time capable of showing the full resources of the B-A-C-H Fantasy (the great five-manual organ at Merseburg, for which the work was originally composed, being an obvious exception). However, Liszt pronounced himself well pleased at the result, and the recital helped to launch his young protégé's career in Germany.[10] By the time the recital had ended the Weimar contingent was ravenous, and the *Pfeffermünzschen* had all been consumed. They hurried out of church and down to the railway station, where Liszt had somehow made good on Schilling's earlier forgetfulness and had prevailed on the railway staff to provide a fish dinner for the entire party before they boarded the train back to Weimar.[11]

III

Another event to which the Weimar students looked forward with uncommon enthusiasm was the début recital of Liszt's young pupil Eugène d'Albert. The

---

10. See the brief account of this recital in *Music and Drama* (New York), November 18, 1882, p. 11. Also, LL, pp. 170–73.
11. LL, pp. 168–71.

eighteen-year-old pianist had arrived in Weimar earlier that season[12] and had bowled everyone over with the brilliance of his playing. Liszt called him "a second Tausig," referred to him affectionately as "Albertus Magnus," and foretold a shining future for him. He frequently called on the young man to play in front of the other students, and d'Albert won high praise for his playing of Chopin, Beethoven, and Liszt—to whose Second Hungarian Rhapsody he had already composed a clever cadenza which, much to Liszt's delight, combined two of the rhapsody's main themes:

Grand Duke Carl Alexander attended the class on June 27 at Liszt's invitation, in order to hear the prodigy for himself, and proclaimed him to be "wonderful! Astounding!"[13] Since the young man bore more than a passing physical resemblance to Tausig, with whom Liszt was constantly comparing him, the Weimar gossip-mills started to grind out the story that d'Albert was an illegitimate son of the great Pole. Such tales never harmed anyone in the profession of piano-playing, and the aura of romance that had already been placed around d'Albert by his admirers glowed all the brighter because of this one.[14]

D'Albert's début concert in Weimar took place on September 29 before a packed house which included Liszt; Eduard Lassen; the young crown prince,

---

12. His first appearance at a Weimar masterclass was on May 27, 1882. Young as he was, d'Albert was already covered in laurels. He had appeared as a soloist with Richter, and had even been represented as a composer in the St. James's Hall concerts in London two or three years before that.

13. LL, p. 97.

14. In fact, d'Albert was the son of the dancing master and composer of light music Charles d'Albert, who was also his first music teacher. Born in Glasgow, d'Albert never liked to be described as British, although he received much of his early education at the National Training School in London, which later became the Royal College of Music. He was a pupil of Max Pauer for piano and of Ebenezer Prout and Sir Arthur Sullivan for theory. He was only seventeen when he appeared at the Crystal Palace in a performance of the Schumann Piano Concerto, and this event was followed a year later by a sensational début in Berlin. D'Albert was one of those artists who never have to practice, yet he had an enormous repertoire—kept alive by his phenomenal powers of sight-reading. In later life he deliberately neglected his piano-playing in order to concentrate on composing; the world in turn neglected his composing. His output is considerable, though, and includes several operas.

D'Albert's private life was a stormy one. He was much married—so much married, in fact, that Dr. Johnson's description of second marriages as "a triumph of hope over experience" ceased before long to have any meaning for him. His fourth wife was Teresa Carreño; he was her third husband. She is supposed to have remonstrated with him once: "Your children and my children are quarrelling again with our children." When d'Albert decided to marry for the seventh time, the witty Heinrich Grünfeld told him: "I congratulate you, my dear friend. You have seldom had so charming a wife." (LL, p. 276)

Carl August; the painter Paul von Joukowsky; Martha Remmert; and a galaxy of Liszt pupils. It was an audience that would have paralysed most seasoned performers, but d'Albert took it in his stride. His programme was formidable:

Kaisermarsch	Wagner–Tausig
Sonata in E major, op. 90	Beethoven
Berceuse	Chopin
Polonaise in A-flat, op. 53	Chopin
Fantasie on motifs from *Halka*	Moniuszko–Tausig
Ceremonial March of the Holy Grail from *Parsifal*	Wagner–Liszt
Soirée de Vienne no. 6	Liszt
Les jeux d'eaux à la Villa d'Este	Liszt
Hungarian Rhapsody	Liszt
Ride of the Valkyries	Wagner–Tausig

The piano aficionado will not fail to notice two works which at that time were still new. Liszt's arrangement of the Holy Grail music from *Parsifal* had only just been published, and although Liszt himself had played the work privately, this public performance by d'Albert was probably a world première. So, too, was the performance of *Les jeux d'eaux à la Villa d'Este,* which d'Albert must have learned from the manuscript, since it was not to appear in print until 1883. By public demand this recital had to be repeated one week later.[15]

Nor did d'Albert's success end there. As part of the celebrations surrounding Liszt's seventy-first birthday on October 22, a concert was mounted in the Court Theatre, conducted by Carl Müller-Hartung. Although it included the Prelude to *Parsifal* and Liszt's symphonic poem *Ce qu'on entend sur la montagne,* it was the young iron-eater who stole the show with performances of Liszt's E-flat-major Piano Concerto and a group of Liszt's virtuoso pieces, including the *Pesther Carnival* Rhapsody.

The presence of Paul von Joukowsky at d'Albert's début reminds us that this artist, who was still basking in praise for his stage designs for *Parsifal,* had followed Liszt from Bayreuth in order to paint his portrait. The picture had been commissioned by Liszt himself as a gift to the piano manufacturer Vincent Risch, who had recently met Liszt and had presented him with one of the first grand pianos made by his Toronto-based firm, Mason and Risch.[16] Liszt had

---

15. See the review in *Music and Drama,* November 18, 1882, p. 11.
16. Although the firm of Mason and Risch had long been making upright and square pianos, they had never made grands. At Liszt's encouragement they produced their first model in April 1882. Risch was delighted with the result, and he told Liszt that it was notable for its richness, breadth, and power. When Liszt expressed interest in testing the instrument, Risch sent him a second model, which was delivered to Weimar on September 19, 1882. After playing on it for more than two months, Liszt told

already granted Joukowsky a number of sittings. By the end of the year the picture was finished, and all who saw it were struck by its vivid likeness to the
composer. Joukowsky was prevailed upon by Carl Alexander to make a copy
for deposit in the Weimar art gallery, which necessitated a short delay before
the original could be despatched to Toronto. When it arrived, Risch had it
hung in his showrooms, where it generated intense local interest.[17]

I V

At the beginning of November 1882, Liszt's thoughts began to turn to Venice
and the promise he had given to the Wagners to spend the coming winter with
them at the Palazzo Vendramin. He had wanted to set out earlier but was detained at Weimar by a mild indisposition; and then, just as he was recovering,
Anton Rubinstein unexpectedly turned up in the company of the conductor
Arthur Nikisch, and Liszt felt obliged to entertain them. It was November 14
before he was able to pack his bags and bid farewell to the Hofgärtnerei for a
few months. Even then, he was unable to travel directly to Venice. He went via
Nuremberg, where Lina Ramann was expecting him for further consultations
about her biography of him.[18]

Risch: "The Mason & Risch grand piano you forwarded to me is excellent, magnificent, unequalled.
Artists, Judges, and the Public will certainly be of the same opinion." (This letter, which is dated November 10, 1882, is reproduced in a Mason & Risch advertisement in the *Toronto Globe* for December 18, 1883.) Liszt eventually gave the instrument to Carl Gille. (See LL, pp. 156–57.)
   17. The picture arrived in Toronto on September 5, 1883. Vincent Risch told Liszt: "For weeks
Toronto society came in their thousands to our hall, with their hats off and as serious as if they were
in church. Men come and gaze on those well-known, admired, and venerated features. . . . This portrait, so strikingly natural, established the talent of the artist, and makes us all feel that you, dear master, are in our midst; and Canada feels richer and happier at the thought of possessing you. . . ."
(WFLR, pp. 189–90) See also Liszt's letter on this topic to Risch. (LLB, vol. 2, p. 346)
   The firm of Mason and Risch continued to make capital out of the Liszt portrait for a number of
years. At the Toronto Exhibition of 1887 their booth was dominated by the painting, given to them
"in acknowledgement of the excellence of a pianoforte sent to [Liszt] at Weimar by these gentlemen."
(*Toronto Daily Mail*, September 10, 1887)
   The portrait remained in the Toronto showroom until after World War II, when the firm went
into liquidation. Meanwhile, the painting has passed into private ownership in America. (It was often
wrongly attributed to the Toronto Conservatory of Music, who were never its owners.) Fortunately,
the firm of Alfred Krupp, in Essen, made a good likeness of the picture which has made its way into
many of the Liszt iconographies (see BFL, p. 286). And what became of the second canvas that
Joukowsky painted for the grand duke? This, too, found its way to Vincent Risch in Toronto, and was
exhibited by him at the Colonial Exhibition in London in the summer of 1886. This painting, which
is now in the possession of a private owner in southern Ontario, was only identified in 1993.
   18. Lina Ramann had spent a part of the summer in England, where she had stayed in the home of
her friend Louisa Martindale of Lewes, Sussex, working on Volume Two of her biography of Liszt.
Her visit also coincided with the publication of Volume One in its English translation by Miss
E. Cowdery, to which Ramann had written a new introduction in English. When Liszt was informed

Liszt finally arrived in Venice on November 19. The journey was not without incident. He was recognized by the proprietor of his Zürich hotel, who refused to accept any payment for his room, dinners, and wines, a gesture which delighted Liszt. (He urged Adelheid von Schorn to make such munificence known to the owners of the Erbprinz Hotel in Weimar, in the vain hope that the place where he had given so many parties in years past might follow suit.) The rest of the journey was not so pleasant. He was apprehended as he passed through customs at Milan, and fined seventy francs for bringing fifty cigars across the border. As he ruefully put it: "Stricter people than myself would call it a regular fleecing."[19] Liszt was to stay in Venice until January 13. It was the first winter for many years that he had not spent at the Villa d'Este.

The Wagners had taken a lease on the Palazzo Vendramin for one year. It belonged to Duke della Grazia, who had kept the original furnishings, paintings, and carpets in luxurious condition. No fewer than eighteen rooms had been set aside for the use of the Wagner entourage—Richard, Cosima, their four children, three tutors, three or four domestic servants, and two gondoliers. These last were a vital part of the household, since the only access to the palazzo was along the waterways, and the gondoliers provided a continuous ferry-service for the Wagners and their guests. A spacious apartment had been set aside for Liszt's own use, and he was free to come and go as he pleased. He had not known a real family life for many years; he often joined the Wagners for their meals, and enjoyed relaxing among his grandchildren and generally being looked after by Cosima. A bond of affection grew up between him and his grandson Siegfried, who was now thirteen years old. Liszt used to allow "Sigius," as he dubbed him, to visit him in his apartment, and the boy used to rummage in his grandfather's wastepaper basket looking for foreign stamps and discarded manuscript paper. Sigius once accompanied Liszt to church and sat next to him during high mass. When the organist began playing, Liszt became visibly disturbed. It was a time when the most commonplace music could be heard accompanying services, and on this occasion the congregation was treated to a medley of polkas and galops, culminating in a rendering of the popular song "I Would Like to Kiss Your Beautiful Black Eyes" during the consecration. Liszt handed young Sigius a prayerbook and told him to read it. After the service he grasped the boy by the hand and hurried out of church, only to be confronted by the organist, who had the temerity to ask Liszt what he thought of the music. "To tell you the truth," Liszt replied, "it was an ob-

---

of this development, he exclaimed: "So! England, sea air, and an English edition of *our* biography! Always better and better!" (RL, p. 193) At this moment, too, the sixth volume of Ramann's "collected edition" of Liszt's writings was about to appear. Liszt's visit to Nuremberg, then, was propitious, for it gave him an opportunity to go over a number of professional concerns with his "dear, kind biographer."

19. LLB, vol. 2, p. 338.

scenity, an indecency," and he kept repeating these words under his breath as they travelled back home by gondola.[20]

Wagner did not "receive" in Venice. After the rigours of the recent *Parsifal* production he was determined to preserve a quiet domesticity. Liszt tried to follow suit, but he found it impossible to avoid invitations from some of the more prominent families then living there. Venetian society in those days was still somewhat provincial. One evening he attended a party given by Princess Pauline von Metternich. While Liszt was engrossed in conversation with the princess and the painter Wolkov-Mouromtzov, a young lady approached him and said: "Sir, I have been asked to sing something. Will you accompany me?" This was a gaffe of the first order, and the young woman did not appear to understand what she had done. Without even turning to her, Liszt sank to the occasion and replied tersely: "No, madam." What followed was typical of him. After two or three minutes had elapsed, he called out to Prince Philip Hohenlohe: "Come and sing Schumann's 'The Two Grenadiers' I'll accompany you."[21] The moral was not lost on those present. One never pressed Liszt to play; one could only allow him to *volunteer* to play.

Wagner and Liszt had long since learned to respect each other's independence, and they tried not to get in one another's way. In the evenings they often played whist. Wagner was outclassed, and Liszt had to let him win from time to time in order to keep him in good humour, for he was subject to fits of irritability. Liszt went on composing throughout his stay in Venice; in fact, he ran out of manuscript paper and had to send for more from Leipzig.[22]

V

The Palazzo Vendramin faced the Grand Canal, and Liszt's room had wonderful views of the waterways leading away from it. He had been haunted by the magic of Venice ever since his first visit, in 1837, and the city stirred many memories. But there was a dark side to the visit. The Palazzo Vendramin lay under the shadow of death; Wagner was ill, his days already numbered. The funeral processions by gondola along the canals came to fascinate Liszt, and the thought that Wagner himself might die and his corpse float across the lagoons in this way began to exercise his mind. Liszt's premonition of Wagner's death came out in two extraordinary funeral elegies, which he called *La Lugubre Gon-*

---

20. WE, pp. 20–22.
21. Prince Philip Hohenlohe (1864–1942), a nephew of Cardinal Gustav Hohenlohe, was also spending the winter in Venice. (W-MM, pp. 205–10)
22. LLB, vol. 2, p. 343.

dola I and II, composed in Venice in December 1882. This was two months before Wagner died and his funeral procession glided down those same canals, en
route for the railway station and the long, mournful train journey back to
Bayreuth.[23]

Although we talk conventionally of "two" funeral elegies, these pieces are
really different aspects of one another, and it makes musical sense to play them
in succession.[24] The same rocking movement in the left hand, depicting a swaying gondola, provides the irregular accompaniment over which the right hand
floats two contrasting threnodies.

One wonders whether Wagner ever heard these pieces. It is a good question,
prompted by a censored entry in Cosima's diary. "Today [Wagner] begins to
talk about my father again, very blunt in his truthfulness; he described his new
works as 'budding insanity' and finds it impossible to develop a taste for their

---

23. Liszt later told the Hungarian music publisher Nándor Táborszky: "I wrote this elegy [No. 1] by
some premonition in Venice, six weeks before Wagner's death." (LLB, vol. 2, p. 381)
24. This idea of "two in one" is borne out by a comment that Liszt made to Princess Marie Hohenlohe: "The oars of a Gondole Lugubre beat on my brain. I have tried to write them and had to re-
write them twice, whereupon other lugubrious things came back to mind. . . ." (WLLM, p. 441)

dissonances."[25] Wagner was certainly within earshot of Liszt's room, and there would have been times when the sound of Liszt's piano came ringing through the spacious building. In theory, then, Wagner could have overheard his own funeral elegy—a quixotic thought. As for his description of Liszt's grinding dissonances as "budding insanity," it is harsh. Wagner was not the first musician to lack the courage of Liszt's convictions.

Even in Bayreuth the heart spasms from which Wagner suffered had alarmed Cosima, and in Venice they had grown worse. Wagner usually paid a penalty for any physical exertion with "cramps" of the heart and could not walk for any reasonable distance without suffering from shortage of breath. Nor was his general condition helped by a hernia of the right groin which he had neglected in earlier years and which was now difficult to contain. A local German doctor, Friedrich Keppler, ordered a special truss for him and showed him how to secure it, which eased this condition somewhat. Keppler also kept in touch with Wagner's Bayreuth physician, Dr. Landberg, and together they prescribed valerian with occasional doses of opium. Cosima was tense with worry and lived in daily fear of Wagner's demise. She had been told far more about the seriousness of his condition than he had been told himself, and she had to find ways and means of devoting herself to his needs both night and day without arousing his suspicion. For this she often received verbal abuse when he was in pain, an experience she found only slightly less devastating than the contrition he expressed to her when the crisis had passed. He could not bear her to be in the same room when he suffered a spasm, and she was condemned to agonise over his condition behind closed doors, while he sat at his desk moaning and clutching his heart.

In all these circumstances, the effort that Wagner took to celebrate Cosima's birthday was little short of heroic. He arranged for the local orchestra of students and professors at the Venice Conservatoire to resurrect his youthful Symphony in C Major, which he had composed in 1832, the parts of which had turned up in Dresden a few years earlier. He had tried to persuade Anton Seidl, who had reconstructed the score, to come to Venice and conduct it; but when that proved impossible he brought in Engelbert Humperdinck from Paris. This delay meant that Wagner himself had to supervise some of the preliminary rehearsals, with the consequence that he was unable to keep the concert a secret from Cosima. On December 22 he conducted the final rehearsal in the foyer of the Teatro La Fenice, in the presence of Cosima, the children, Paul von Joukowsky, and Liszt. The occasion was marred when Wagner suffered a heart

---

25. WT, vol. 2, p. 1059. The diary-entry is dated November 29, 1882. The sentence was crossed out after Cosima's death, possibly by her daughter Eva Chamberlain, who doubtless wanted to obscure Wagner's negative comments. While part of it was restored when the diaries were published, twelve additional words in that sentence remain illegible.

spasm and a long pause ensued before he was able to continue.[26] For the performance proper, on December 24, the Teatro La Fenice was decked out with Christmas festival lights and Wagner was received with cheers by a large audience. At the end of the performance the orchestral players crowded round Cosima and toasted her health. There then occurred one of those scenes which typified the entire Liszt-Wagner relationship. Anxious to reward the players, Wagner suddenly turned to Liszt and whispered in his ear: "Do you love your daughter?" Liszt looked startled, and before he could respond Wagner added: "Then sit down at the piano and play."[27] Without hesitation Liszt went over to the keyboard and held the orchestral musicians in thrall. He would not have obeyed such a command from anyone else. Kings and princes had been snubbed for asking less.

V I

Liszt set out from Venice in mid-January 1883. Wagner accompanied his old friend to the gondola, and the parting was a particularly painful one. After he had taken his leave and began to mount the steps back to the palace, he turned impulsively and wrapped his arms around Liszt in a last, emotional embrace.[28] Liszt then got into the gondola and moved slowly along the Grand Canal towards the railway station, as Wagner disappeared in the distance. The two composers never saw one another again. Wagner died a few weeks later, on February 13. Liszt had meanwhile resumed his duties as president of the Royal Academy of Music in Budapest, and news of Wagner's passing was brought to him in his study by Kornél Ábrányi the following day. He paused for a moment, then whispered to himself: "He today, I tomorrow!"[29] At first he refused to believe the newspaper reports, but then came the cable from Cosima, which put an end to all speculation. He offered to return to Venice in order to accompany Cosima and the coffin back to Bayreuth. Through Daniela he learned that his offer was declined. Truth to tell, he was not sorry, for the publicity that he knew Wagner's funeral cortège would generate as it wended its way from Venice to Bayreuth would have been for him a wrenching experience. He told Princess Carolyne that it was enough for him to go to Bayreuth in six weeks' time and pay his respects to Cosima in person.[30]

Nothing prepared him for the wall of seclusion that Cosima now built around herself. She refused to see anyone, including her father. They had at first

26. WT, vol. 2, p. 1079.
27. Ibid.
28. GL, p. 25.
29. Ibid.
30. LLB, vol. 7, p. 375.

been unable to part her from Wagner's body, and for twenty-four hours she had held him in her arms, whispering words of devotion into his ear. As they placed Wagner in his coffin Cosima cut off her hair and laid it alongside his body. Then the funeral cortège set out along the Grand Canal and glided silently towards the Venice railway station. From there the party of mourners (which included as well as the Wagner family Joukowsky, Hans Richter, and Adolf von Gross) boarded a specially chartered train. Cosima travelled alone in a separate compartment with the body. She refused all nourishment and would not be comforted; she wanted nothing more than to die with the man to whom she had devoted her life. The train made several stops along the way. At Innsbruck it was boarded by Hermann Levi and Heinrich Porges; and at the tiny Bavarian border town of Kufstein, King Ludwig's personal emissary, von Bürstein, was waiting to hand over a letter of condolence to Cosima from the sovereign. When the train arrived at Munich, the silent crowds were lined along the railway platform bearing torches and floral wreaths. Numbed with grief, Cosima refused to alight and acknowledge this demonstration of respect. The last stop, Bayreuth, was reached shortly before midnight. A guard of honour stood vigil at the train until the following day. On Sunday afternoon, February 18, public tributes were read, a military band played Siegfried's Funeral Music, and the cortège set out for Wahnfried, its final destination. The coffin had been transferred to an open hearse drawn by four horses; and as the procession made its way through the streets, which were packed with silent citizens, from every window fluttered a black flag. A light snow had started to fall; it was bitterly cold. At twilight Wagner was laid to rest in the family vault in that part of the garden which he himself had set aside years earlier for this purpose. Cosima was the last to leave the tomb. In a deep and profound sense she was never to leave it, for in the years that followed her thoughts rarely strayed from her dead husband and his music. Not long after the funeral, Hans von Bülow (who had himself been shattered by the death of Wagner) heard of Cosima's wasted condition and her unwillingness to emerge from seclusion. He sent her a terse telegramme: "Soeur, il faut vivre" ("Sister, it is necessary to live"). It was a prophetic message. Cosima showed every sign of becoming a permanent recluse until the flagging fortunes of the Bayreuth Festival eventually forced her out of mourning, compelled her to take charge of the theatre, and made it "necessary to live." For nearly three years she cut herself off from the world, and she brought much sadness to Liszt through her refusal to maintain contact with him.[31]

---

31. No one has been able satisfactorily to explain why Cosima deliberately cut herself off from Liszt, and occasionally even rebuffed him; perhaps even Cosima herself did not fully understand her actions. At the very least it indicates a deep ambivalence towards her father, and its unbridled expression was only made possible for her by the death of his rival, Wagner. There are some unfortunate gaps in the

It was under the immediate shadow of Wagner's death that Liszt composed his third "Wagner elegy," *R. W.—Venezia*. It rises from the black depths of the keyboard thus:

This is the music of catastrophe. It is void and without form. For thirty-one measures this hopeless, keyless music strives to find the light. It arrives at a "Wagnerian fanfare," which ascends through B-flat and D-flat and reaches a plateau on E major (Liszt's "religious" key), only to collapse and fall back into the abyss.

On May 22, 1883, a memorial concert was held in Weimar to mark Wagner's birthday. He would have been seventy years old. Carl Müller-Hartung was the conductor of the all-Wagner programme, and Liszt was in the audience. At a pre-arranged moment, Liszt walked down the aisle, mounted the podium, and conducted the orchestra in music of his personal choice: the Prelude and Good Friday Music from *Parsifal*. That evening was notable for something else, too. Before he arrived at the theatre, he had composed another

---

published correspondence between Liszt and Carolyne which obscure our understanding of this perplexing matter. From an unpublished letter that Carolyne wrote to Liszt in the first half of May 1883, however, we gather that he had made a serious attempt to seek a reconciliation with his daughter, which had been rejected. Princess Carolyne told him:

> I am upset by Cosima's actions towards you, for your sake. I would have liked to spare you. But it does not surprise me. She has always been more the daughter of her mother than of you. When she married Bülow I was opposed to it because I could see that she would live neither for him nor for you! . . . Everything you do is well done with regards to her, as it was with regards to her mother. Why was it necessary that you had to see her again? (Hitherto unpublished, WA, Kasten 51, u. 1)

In another letter, written shortly afterwards, Carolyne expressed matters more succinctly: "Since her widowhood [Cosima] has become a bad daughter for you." (Hitherto unpublished, WA, Kasten 51, u. 2) This bleak state of affairs persisted until 1886, when Cosima finally realised that she needed her father's help if the Bayreuth Festival was to be kept alive. (See p. 503.)

Wagner elegy, his evocative *Am Grabe Richard Wagners* (At the Grave of Richard Wagner), whose manuscript bears the inscription:

> Wagner once reminded me of the likeness between his *Parsifal* theme and my previously written *Excelsior!* May this remembrance remain here. He has fulfilled the Great and Sublime in the art of the present day.
>
> F. LISZT.
>
> May 22, '83, Weimar

Throughout most of that day, in fact, *Parsifal* and *Excelsior!* must have haunted Liszt's imagination, for the two become mixed and mingled in this composition. The *Parsifal* theme (the motif of the Sacrament) rises from the depths of the keyboard, but in a strangely tortured form.

The model for this theme, as Wagner himself acknowledged, was *Excelsior!* (the prelude to Liszt's cantata *The Bells of Strasbourg*). Wagner had heard a performance of that work in Liszt's company when the two composers were together in Budapest for a joint Liszt-Wagner concert in March 1875. Much has been made of this particular thematic connection, which rests on more than mere externals.[32]

After being cast in a variety of different tonal contexts, this *Parsifal-Excelsior!* reminiscence gives way to an ethereal transformation of the bell motif from *Parsifal*—surely a benediction on the Liszt-Wagner relationship itself.[33]

---

32. See Arthur W. Marget, "Liszt and Parsifal," *Music Review* 14, no. 2, 1953.
33. Liszt simultaneously made two transcriptions of this composition, which are rarely heard today: one for string quartet and harp and the other for organ.

August Göllerich was not wrong to call *Am Grabe* a "personal greeting of the spirit" whose other-worldly character, he maintained, almost forbade its being made public.[34] It is an indication of the general lack of interest in Liszt's late music that Göllerich's prediction almost came true. The piece was neither played nor published until 1952, nearly seventy years after its composition.

Not surprisingly, the mantle of neglect settled on the manuscripts themselves. It is a minor miracle that any of them survived. Liszt himself was rather careless in this regard, because he often gave such pieces away as souvenirs to friends and pupils, who did not always understand the value of what they had. Several of them (including one of the *Gondola* pieces and *Am Grabe Richard Wagners*) came into the possession of Lina Schmalhausen. Within a few years of Liszt's death, having fallen on hard times, she offered to sell these pieces to the British Museum, including the oratorio *Christus*. Although the trustees bought *Christus*, they were evidently not interested in the piano pieces:

> Wallnertheaterstrasse 41
> bei Bernstein
> Berlin
> April 9, 1892

Dear Sir:

Having sent you Liszt's manuscript of *Christus* last Wednesday the 6th, I should be very glad to know whether it has safely reached you. In 1889 you offered to buy it for the sum of 30 pounds. I had not then been able to decide to sell it, but as I am at present in a little money difficulty, I should now take that amount which you then offered for it. I should be very much obliged and grateful if you could kindly do so.

I should also like to ask you if the Museum would buy two small manuscripts which have never yet been published, *Die Trauergondel* and *Am Grabe Richard Wagners*. Although I possess these writings [sic], they were given me by Liszt, I have not the right to edit them, as the heirs of Liszt would have that right. I have no wish to consult them about this matter, and should prefer the Museum to have them.[35]

While there are a number of further letters between Schmalhausen and the museum, the sale of the two manuscripts did not go through. She sold them to other buyers.

---

34. GL, p. 23.

VII

After Wagner's death in February 1883, pressure was brought to bear on Liszt
to return all the letters and autograph documents of Wagner that he had accumulated across the years. It was a sizable legacy, and the letters in particular revealed the close contact between the two composers, especially during the
1850s. Cosima was now anxious that these materials be returned to the Wagner archive, but Liszt refused to comply.[36] The letters belonged to him, and he
was not about to part with them. For many years the correspondence had been
stored in Weimar, together with other priceless manuscripts, and Princess Carolyne had long since assumed the burden of the monthly storage fees. Even a
communication on this topic from Paul von Joukowsky, which was inspired by
Cosima, failed to move Liszt, who replied through his granddaughter Daniela
on March 9, 1883.

> Dear Daniela:
> I reply directly to the three questions forwarded to me through
> our excellent friend Joukowsky.
> 1. When Princess Carolyne Wittgenstein left the Altenburg (in
> October '60)[37] the objects, the library, the pictures, the jewels and
> the valuable correspondence were transferred to the premises I
> showed you in Weimar. Wagner's letters have been there for 22
> years, under lock and key, in the same premises for which Princess
> Wittgenstein has been paying regularly, every year, together with
> the salary of the inspectress, Madame Pickel.
> 2. The draft of Wagner's "Christ" drama will be either among
> the letters or the other manuscripts, none of which I would dare
> touch without the explicit orders of the Princess which she will
> probably not give since she still reserves to herself the right to con-
> trol the Weimar relics. I myself have committed only a single intru-
> sion into these rooms which contain so many rare souvenirs. It was

---

35. Hitherto unpublished; British Library, M.S. folio 87.
36. It is just as well that he did. Had he gone along with Cosima's wishes, the Liszt-Wagner correspondence would have been "edited" from the Bayreuth perspective. In 1888, two years after Liszt's
death, these letters were published in their entirety. They revealed to the world the full extent of the
support, both financial and moral, that Liszt had given Wagner across the years.
37. Liszt's memory is slightly at fault here. It was actually in May 1860. The "premises" to which Liszt
goes on to refer was the home of Frau Rosina Walther to whom Princess Carolyne was evidently still
paying rent for the privilege of storing what still remained of the Altenburg effects after the auction
of 1867. See Volume Two, p. 552.

to give your mother the autograph score of *Lohengrin* and the scores of *Tannhäuser* and the *fliegende Holländer* which Wagner gave me more than 25 years ago. Princess Wittgenstein also selected at that time a fine music-cabinet to fit them, which should be in Bayreuth.

It is not to my liking to repeat the intrusion, nor would I encourage you to write to Rome on this matter.

3. To avoid all kinds of indiscretion and indignity, I send you, by today's mail, my copy of the three volumes of *Mein Leben*. Please send a telegraph every week, my dear Daniela, to your loving-hearted Papa,

F.L.[38]

The letter reveals something of the psychological underplay which now governed the relations between Cosima, Carolyne, and Liszt. Liszt "owned" the letters, Carolyne "controlled" them, and Cosima wanted them "returned" to Bayreuth. Cosima writes indirectly to her father through Joukowsky; Liszt replies indirectly to Cosima through Daniela; neither can summon up the courage to write directly or indirectly to Carolyne—who doubtless drew some satisfaction from the three-way standoff. This minuet was danced for three years; it ended only when Liszt's death put a stop to the music and paved the way for the publication of the correspondence.

VIII

The twin spectres of depression and death stalked Liszt throughout his declining years and began to make deep inroads into his personality. He contemplated suicide, but rejected the idea as running contrary to his innermost religious beliefs. Although it is a rarely reported aspect of his personality, he was by now morbidly superstitious. Carl Lachmund relates that during the summer of 1883, when Liszt was nearly seventy-two years old, his wife, Caroline, persuaded Liszt to take part in a game of "magnetic mind-reading." Evidently she was adept at reading the thoughts of others, and could even pick out objects in the room blindfolded, while holding the hand of the person generating the thought. Liszt entered into the game with reluctance, and seated himself in such a way that he was partly hidden from view—as if to protect himself from the proceedings. Everybody was amused by his apprehension, and took it to be feigned, but in deference to his feelings they stopped the game. "That we had acted wisely in discontinuing it," Lachmund wrote,

---

38. HLFG, p. 128. [BA, Hs 51/1–12]

I was to learn accidentally, but not until twenty-five years later. It was during Reisenauer's last tour in America, on one of our evenings of retrospections that the pianist recalled this affair. "You know," said he, "Mrs. Lachmund's mind-reading incident caused much talk among the Hofgärtnerei habituées at the time." "How so?" I replied, rather puzzled. "It was even said," Reisenauer continued, "that had it been anyone else but the Lachmunds it would have cost them their position and pleasant relations at the Liszt home." "I do not comprehend. What in the world was there improper about that?" I interrupted. "Well, Liszt considered it a spiritualistic experiment—*ein falsches Eindringen in das Ueberirdische*," a false searching into things supernatural—which, according to his mystic and religious beliefs he considered an unpardonable sin.

"I was dumbfounded!" Lachmund concluded.[39]

Shortly afterwards, Lachmund had another chance to observe Liszt's leaning toward the superstitious. The scene again took place in the dining-room of the Hofgärtnerei. As the company was about to be seated, Liszt stood for a moment contemplating the table; evidently something disturbed him. He summoned Pauline Apel with the words: "Pauline, this will not do—there are thirteen plates! We must have one removed." Only when plate number thirteen was taken away did the meal begin. Nor was this the only bad omen that evening. While the supper was in progress, Caroline Lachmund had the misfortune to upset her wine-glass. Liszt's face darkened; a spilt wine-glass was a bad omen. Mrs. Lachmund's anxiety only increased when she saw that the glass was also chipped. "And I have broken the glass, too, *lieber Meister!*" she said sorrowfully. At that Liszt's face brightened, and he replied: "*Nun*, that is very well, for then it is a *good* omen, you know."[40]

Omens, premonitions, and portents: such things had always been respected by Liszt, but during his final years they began to dominate his psychology. It has been well said that Liszt loved God but feared the Devil. A cynic might argue that his profound religious beliefs were there to contain his fear of those dark forces which lie deep within each one of us, and are poised to overwhelm us in unguarded moments. There is much to the idea that "beneath the greatest saint lies the greatest sinner," that the one has been put into place in order to control the other. Such speculation has no end. Liszt's superstitious behaviour was no different than that which drives the rest of mankind, and it served the same function: it was a defence mechanism which helped to get him through the day.

---

39. LL, pp. 245–46.
40. LL, p. 285.

The Music of Liszt's Old Age

And be advisèd
Love not the sun too much,
nor yet the stars,
Come, follow me to the realms of Night!
GOETHE[1]

I

It is only against the deepening shadows of his life that we shall come to understand the true meaning of the music of Liszt's old age. There have been many attempts to discuss this strange repertory, some of them of merit.[2] But almost without exception, the path-breaking compositions of Liszt's later years have been treated by theorists and analysts as if their chief importance were to make a contribution towards the history of harmony. Liszt is often described as "the father of modern music" on the basis of this repertory. It is a seductive idea. From the vantage-point of the twentieth century, everything seems to have flowed from him. His experiments in harmony, his audacious handling of form, his unparalleled ability to draw strange sonorities from his instruments—all confirm that his was one of the truly revolutionary spirits in music. Yet this is but one side of a complex picture. We make a mistake when we detach his late music from the disturbed emotions from which it emerged. By the early 1880s Liszt was often ravaged by a universal sadness which would descend on him without warning and threaten to overwhelm everything that he did. He told Lina Ramann, "I carry a deep sadness of the heart which must now and

---

1. *Faust*, Part Two.
2. The pioneering studies by Bence Szabolcsi (STL) and Humphrey Searle (SLFP) remain among the best introductions to the topic. A more technical discussion has been undertaken by Lajos Bárdos in his *Ferenc Liszt, the Innovator*, 1975 (see BLI).

then break out in sound."[3] He wrestled daily with the demons of desolation, despair, and death, and brought forth music which utterly failed to find its audience. In retrospect, we now know that his contemporaries were offered a glimpse into a mind on the verge of catastrophe. Small wonder that they shrank from the view. It was at this point that what Bence Szabolcsi called a "conspiracy of silence" descended on the late pieces, which was not lifted until modern times.

Broadly speaking, the music of Liszt's old age falls into three categories: (1) the music of retrospection; (2) the music of despair; (3) the music of death. The first category contains pieces in which a troubled spirit seeks consolation in the memories of the past. Liszt referred to this music as his "forgotten" pieces, a sardonic reference to compositions that were forgotten before they were even played, because they often went by such appellations as *Valse oubliée, Polka oubliée,* and *Romance oubliée.*

The second category, the music of despair, is much more important. It is easy to select at random a series of titles which when placed side by side alert us to the presence of a troubled mind:

> *Schlaflos! Frage und Antwort*
> *Unstern! Sinistre, Disastro*
> *Nuages gris*
> *Ossa arida*
> *Csárdás macabre*
> *Farewell*

These pieces (and there are others) are best understood as fragments broken off from a greater whole, each one offering a glimpse of the pathology of despair. Although there are no overtly musical connections among them, they nonetheless seek one another's company, like the members of a large family who never assemble in one place at the same time but nonetheless become acquainted through chance encounters at smaller gatherings. In fact, performers may create whatever random groupings they like; the pieces will always hang together.

Finally, there is the large branch of elegiac music in which Liszt raised grief to the level of a high art form. Memorials, funerals, eulogies, and other aspects of the grieving process all find their home in the music of Liszt's old age. Again, a random selection tells its own tale.

---

3. RLKM, vol. 2, p. 470.

Funeral March for Emperor Maximilian
Seven Hungarian Historical Portraits

> Széchenyi István (Lament)
> Eötvös József
> Vörösmarty Mihály
> Teleki László (Funeral Music)
> Deák Ferenc
> Petőfi Sándor (In Memory of)
> Mosonyi Mihály (Funeral Music)[4]

Funeral Prelude
Elegy in Memory of Mme Mouchanoff
Und wir dachten der Toten
> (And We Thought of the Dead)

Liszt once referred to such compositions as his "mortuary pieces." The joke was doubtless intended to deflect criticism, but it is a fact that what could once have been called a pre-occupation with death had now become transformed into an obsession.[5]

The technical aspects of this music have long held theorists in thrall. There is no other composer of the late nineteenth century who offers the thinking musician such a cornucopia of compositorial devices. This has nothing to do with the "value" of the music. Take it or leave it, the devices are there, and they point to the future. Yet we do a disservice to these compositions if we regard them merely as fragments of sonic history, there to be held up for particular scrutiny by admiring theorists. (A strange fate for music, this, to be relegated to the level of a "sound bite"!) These pieces reveal a soul in turmoil; and since that too is a part of the human condition, there is something here for all of us.

I I

Liszt never lost interest in the problem of tonality. The means that he employed to stretch it—and even, on a few remarkable occasions, to suspend it altogether—

---

4. The pieces are listed here in their published order. However, it does not coincide with the one intended by Liszt himself, which originally ran: Széchenyi, Deák, Teleki, Eötvös, Vörösmarty, Petőfi, and Mosonyi. (LLB, vol. 7, p. 427) Evidently the manuscript remained in the possession of Göllerich for many years. At the invitation of Breitkopf and Härtel the *Historical Portraits* were prepared by Göllerich for the ongoing Complete Liszt Edition, but work on that edition stopped before the *Portraits* could be published. We now know that the pieces were mixed up by Göllerich, whose faulty proof became the basis of the first publication of the cycle in 1956. (See LHHP.)

5. In this connection it is interesting to note that the first title he gave to his last symphonic poem, *From the Cradle to the Grave* (1881–82) was *From the Cradle to the Coffin*. (LLB, vol. 7, p. 327) The softer title was substituted at the suggestion of Princess Carolyne.

form an unwritten chapter of musical history.[6] Unusual scale formations (including the whole-tone scale and the "Gypsy" scale), chords built out of fourths and sevenths, chains of so-called functional chords, and the simultaneous clash of major and minor intervals—all these things find a home in his music.

As early as 1832 Liszt is known to have attended a series of lectures on the philosophy of music given by Fétis in Paris, from whom he derived the idea of an *ordre omnitonique* whose purpose would be to replace tonality (much like the Schoenbergian tone-row). Liszt regarded it as a logical outcome of the historical process which from a "unitonic" (tonality) moved to a "pluritonic" (polytonality) and ended in an "omnitonic" (atonality), where every note is, so to speak, a tonic. In his marginal corrections to Ramann's biography, made when he was seventy years old, Liszt called the "omnitonic" an *Endziel,* or final goal of the historical process.[7] He is known to have composed a "Prélude omnitonique" to illustrate the theory, but the manuscript of that work has meanwhile disappeared.[8] A similar fate also attended the sketches of Liszt's treatise on modern harmony, on which he worked until at least 1885. Arthur Friedheim tells of seeing it among Liszt's papers at Weimar:

> In his later years the Master had formed the habit of rising at five o'clock in the morning, and I paid him many a solitary visit at that hour, even playing to him occasionally. Jokingly, he would inquire whether I were still up, or already up. On the last of these matutinal visits I found him poring over books and old manuscripts. With his permission I joined him in this very interesting occupation. Catching sight of one manuscript which particularly drew my attention I picked it up saying: "This will make you responsible for a lot of nonsense which is bound to be written someday." I expected a rebuke for my remark, but he answered very seriously: "That may be. I have not published it because the time for it is not yet ripe." The title of this little book was *Sketches for a Harmony of the Future.*[9]

While the "sketches" may have disappeared, there is enough music from this period to tell us what they might have contained. The little piano piece *Nuages gris* (1881) could well be described as the gateway to modern music. Not the least of its intriguing features is its ending, which drifts away into keylessness and foretells the coming of impressionism in music.

---

6. It is not that this topic has not so far been addressed. The problem runs deeper than that. Rather it has not been properly integrated into the history of harmony. It still languishes in the realm of special pleading.

7. RLKM, vol. I, p. 207.

8. It was last exhibited in London in 1904.

9. FLL, p. 161.

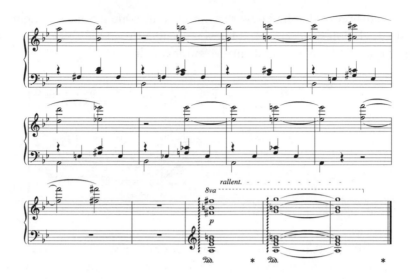

The "grey clouds" of the piece were evidently autobiographical in origin. The manuscript bears the date August 24, 1881. This was a bleak month for Liszt. Seven weeks earlier he had fallen down the stairs of the Hofgärtnerei and had sustained severe injuries.[10] He had expected to make a swift recovery, but the healing process was slow, and it was compounded by his other difficulties, which now included dropsy and failing eyesight. By late August he was still moving about with difficulty. The night was closing in, and *Nuages gris* was the soundscape that symbolised his feelings of desolation.

III

The music of Liszt's old age is marked by an unusual economy of means. Gone are the days of creative abundance. It is almost as if he were trying to starve his compositions of the very notes they require to achieve their identity. His works frequently collapse into monody, and then into silence. Sometimes the piece is open-ended; that is, it just vanishes. The composition called *Schlaflos! Frage und Antwort* expires with a melodic line that ends on the dominant degree of C-sharp minor.[11] For the faint-hearted, Liszt provided an *ossia* ending that is

---

10. See pp. 403–05 for their full extent.

11. *Schlaflos! Frage und Antwort* (Sleepless! Question and Answer) was written in March 1883, not long after Wagner's death, and is a typical product of Liszt's old age. While the restless, ever-striving Question is in E minor, the Answer is in E major. The symbolism is too obvious to require detailed comment: E major is Liszt's "religious" key. Since the note E is sustained as a pedal-point throughout the entire Question, Liszt is suggesting that the Question actually contains the Answer. The piece might be described as a musical equivalent of the biblical text "Come unto me all ye who are heavy laden,

harmonized—proof that he knew that some of his contemporaries might find his first conclusion unacceptable. He even changes the mode, so that they may hear the final G-sharp as a mediant—a softer conclusion.

The practice of "abandoning" a work in mid-air was not introduced by Liszt. There are some intriguing examples in both Chopin and Schumann which pre-date his efforts by a number of years.[12] But Liszt's contributions are more radical than theirs. When he sets sail on his sea of sonority we are not always certain where the voyage will end, for he can come dangerously close to navigating his craft right over the edge. At such moments we can only invoke John Donne's lines "At the round Earth's imagined corners" and suggest that it is only the timid voyager who requires the safety of "imagined corners" for the completion of his journey—an attitude that was, admittedly, part of the historical baggage of the times. For the true explorer, however, borders are there to be broken. Witness the "Mephisto" Polka (1883), which continues to surprise us more than a century after Liszt penned it. The piece is simply deserted, without explanation:

In the song "Go not, happy day" (1882) we come to rest on a dominant seventh chord in its second inversion, which melts away into silence.

---

and I will give ye rest." In brief, its subject is redemption. As with so many of the other pieces of the period, there was no thought in Liszt's mind to publish this music. It was sufficient for him to have written it, and it was only printed by default, as it were, in 1927.

According to the title-page, *Schlaflos!* was based on an original poem by Liszt's pupil Toni Raab which has remained unpublished and has never been traced.

12. Among them are Chopin's Mazurka in A minor, Op. 17, no. 4, and Schumann's "Entreating Child" from *Kinderscenen,* which drift away into silence, their final chords unresolved.

At such moments we are almost persuaded that the difference between sound and silence is illusory, that music may go on sounding long after silence has begun.

And what are we to make of that fateful piece to which Liszt gave the title *Unstern! Sinistre, Disastro*? The play of tritones with which it begins evokes the "devil in music":

and forms the basis of a terrifying climax in which two mutually exclusive chords are pitched in battle against each other. Peter Raabe put it well when he remarked that it is as if a prisoner were hammering on the walls of his cell, well knowing that nobody would hear him.[13]

In a letter to his pupil Ingeborg Starck, Liszt once wrote with mock serious-ness about the dissonances of the "Music of the Future." He told her that the following twelve-note chord would soon become the basis of harmony, and that all chords would be formed by the arbitrary exclusion of certain intervals:

---

13. RL, vol. 2, p. 63.

"In fact," he went on, "it will soon be necessary to complete the system by the admission of quarter- and half-quarter-tones until something better turns up! Behold the abyss of progress into which abominable *Musicians of the Future* precipitate us!"[14] While Liszt was writing tongue-in-cheek, his comments show a shrewd insight into the future of music, for not only did a twelve-note system emerge (albeit not quite the one he envisaged) but quarter- and half-quarter-tones also enjoyed their brief immortality.

More striking still is the way that *Unstern!* draws to its conclusion: it withers on the vine, so to speak. Like other pieces of the period, this one disintegrates into monody, and in the sepulchral depths of the keyboard it once more describes the "devil's interval" before it is finally extinguished on the degree of the sub-dominant.

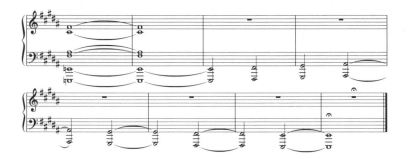

Anyone who had mounted the concert platform in the late 1880s in order to play this music in public would have been considered insane. Small wonder that Liszt himself went out of his way to discourage it; he knew that his pupils might harm their careers by doing so. As for him, he was by now used to the hail of criticism that regularly descended on his music, and his reply had long been to hand: "I calmly persist in staying stubbornly in my corner, and just work at becoming more and more misunderstood."[15]

IV

Nonetheless, there were performances of some of the late pieces, albeit not sanctioned by Liszt himself. This meant that the students had to take extraordinary pains to make sure that Liszt did not find out ahead of time and raise objections—no easy task. The Bagatelle Without Tonality (1885) was one such piece. The unusual title is Liszt's own. It describes music which hovers on the

14. LLB, vol. 1, p. 363.
15. LLB, vol. 3, p. 170.

brink of atonality, some twenty-five years before Schoenberg felt "the breath of another planet."

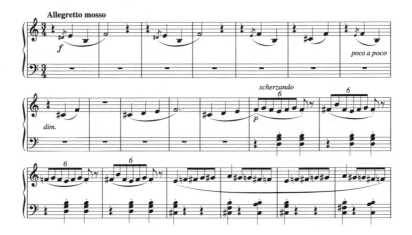

The Bagatelle is not to everyone's taste. But Liszt's aphorism on the topic of taste cannot be bettered: "Taste is a negative thing. Genius affirms and always affirms."[16]

Hugo Mansfeldt gave the first public performance of the Bagatelle shortly after hearing Liszt himself play it to the students gathered at the Hofgärtnerei during the first week of July 1885. This is how he reports the occasion.

> One evening the following were invited to Liszt's house: Friedheim, Rosenthal, Hugo Mansfeldt, Emil Sauer, and A. v. Siloti. When we arrived, we found Liszt finishing his last piano composition—the fourth Mephisto Waltz *ohne Tonart*. He then went to the piano to play it for us. . . . When Liszt had finished it we stood in respectful silence. I dare say none of us were very enthusiastic about the piece. . . . Liszt turned to us and said: "Let's play whist." Two of us sat down and Liszt turned to me saying: "Mansfeldt, take a hand." I replied that I did not know the first thing about cards. Liszt then said to me: "Then you can be a critic." (You remember what opinion he had of critics.) Liszt and three others sat down to play whist, while Rosenthal and I sat on the divan in front of the grand piano, where Liszt had left on the music rack that new composition. While conversing with Rosenthal the thought struck me to copy

---

16. LLB, vol. 4, p. 7. It is always tempting to pursue such wisdom, only to have it evaporate in the chase. What Liszt was saying was that "taste" is defined by what it excludes, whereas genius is defined by what it includes.

that piece then and there and play it as an encore at my recital three days hence . . . as a surprise for Liszt. I went to Liszt's desk to procure some music paper, and returned to the piano and began copying that piece, Rosenthal often prompting me to hasten my writing. . . . When Liszt and the other three whist players had finished their game, I had copied three-fourths of that piece, unknown to Liszt whose whist table was in another part of the room where he could not see me write. The next day at the class meeting I went to Liszt's desk where, fortunately for my plan, I still found that Mephisto Waltz. I hid it under my coat, went into an adjoining room, and finished copying it, after which I returned Liszt's copy to the desk.[17]

Mansfeldt tells us that he learned the piece in a few hours and played it at his début recital in Weimar on July 10. Gottschalg was present, and wrote of the Bagatelle that it was "a highly capricious tone picture which whirls through all the keys and then ends abruptly on a chord of the diminished seventh." He must have told Liszt about this "unofficial" performance, because next day, when Mansfeldt turned up at the Hofgärtnerei as usual, Liszt entered the room and said: "Where's Mansfeldt?"

"Riesberg pushed me forward," said Mansfeldt. "I heard that you played magnificently yesterday," said Liszt, "come and play for me" . . .
    "Liszt led me to the piano and insisted on my playing his last composition. [Mansfeldt tells us that he included some "improvements" which caught Liszt's keen attention.] It is naturally gratifying to me that there is a Liszt composition that has only been played by Liszt and myself."[18]

Liszt often suspended tonality by creating chains of so-called functional chords, a device that later became a hallmark of Debussy's music. The internal structure of a functional chord remains unchanged while its pitch-level varies. There is a good example in *Unstern!*

---

17. CLC, box 2, folder no. 93. Hitherto unpublished letter, dated "San Francisco, March 6, 1917."
18. Ibid. When Mansfeldt penned these lines, his statement was still true. The Bagatelle Without Tonality was not even published until 1956. Mansfeldt gives a slightly different version of the incident in his autobiographical typescript *Liszt, My Life in Europe in 1884*, parts of which were published in the *Journal of the American Liszt Society*, vol. 21 (January–June 1987) and vol. 22 (July–December 1987). See especially pp. 28–31 in the latter issue.

This ascension of augmented chords is matched by another in *R.W.—Venezia.*

Nor was Liszt's interest in the "keyless" augmented chord confined to instrumental music. It also invaded his sacred choral music with telling effect. During the last five or six years of his life Liszt composed a number of small-scale religious choral pieces whose painful brevity lends them the stature of aphorisms. These miniatures frequently last a mere two or three minutes each. They seem to drift toward heaven and vanish, like a cloud of incense. And on occasion the melodic and harmonic material is remote from its time. Take the opening of the second number of the little-known *Le Crucifix* (1884). The de-rhythmicized melodic line uncoils through an augmented triad:

A ravishing example of tone-painting occurs in Liszt's setting of words from Psalm 125 (1884). The text runs: "Qui seminant in lacrimis, in exsultatione metent" ("They that sow in tears shall reap in joy"). On the word "lacrimis" the harmony mingles both the bitter and the sweet in a combination of notes that had rarely reverberated in the hallowed spaces of a church:

A similar example of word becoming tone occurs in the Requiem for Male Voices (1868–69). In the Offertorium Liszt rivets his listeners with the word "tartarus" (i.e.=inferno), which he clothes with two tritones (F–B and G–C#) played simultaneously. The result is a musical inferno, so to speak, a grinding dissonance which comes across with startling force. "Let them not be consumed in hell, let them not fall into eternal darkness." And the music lapses into B major, as if in supplication.

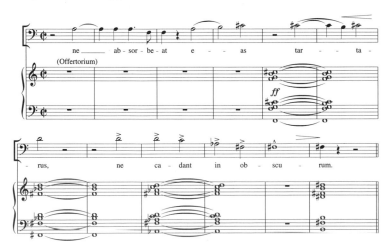

By allowing his texts to determine the character of his musical vocabulary, Liszt was often led to produce some striking effects. In his late setting of *De Profundis* ("Out of the depths," 1881) the opening rises literally from the depths, the words being graphically depicted as two ascending sevenths which are then presented in an audacious harmonic combination. The result is uncompromising, but not without precedent in Liszt's output:

V

A work like *Ossa arida* (1879) could not have been foreseen from anything that Liszt had so far written. It comes like a bolt from the blue, and upsets all our notions about the logical development of music. The evocative words are taken from Ezekiel 37:4—"O ye dry bones, hear the word of the Lord"—and they drew a powerful response from Liszt. His setting calls for a male-voice chorus with four-handed organ accompaniment.

The pile-up of thirds is meant to illustrate the raising up of the flesh from dust. It reaches an overpowering climax when all the notes of the diatonic scale have been accumulated and are sounding simultaneously, at which point the male voice chorus enters in unison with the words "Ossa arida."

The dramatic biblical text recounting the vision of Ezekiel seems to have exerted a spell over Liszt. Ezekiel is set down in a valley of dry bones, and the Lord prophesies that they will take on flesh. "I will open your graves, and cause you to come up out of your graves, and bring you into the land of Israel." Liszt was under no illusions as to the difficulty of performing this music. He told Princess Marie Hohenlohe:

The vision of Ezekiel would be revolting to all the reigning critics; I don't know whether I'll ever risk showing "these dry bones" at a public concert. It's only 50 or 60 slow measures; but they are frightful, and move in a progression of dissonant chords such as have never been written before.[19]

Ossa arida could only have sprung from the mind of a genius; a mere talent would have been too fainthearted, too bound by the conventions. By such words as "genius" and "talent" we do not mean anything vague. The clearest description of these two quite distinct creative types was offered by Schopenhauer. "Talent is like a marksman who hits a target the others cannot reach; genius is like a marksman who hits a target the others cannot even see."[20] In his efforts to hit "a target the others cannot even see" Liszt frequently jettisoned the structure of the normal triad, and built his chords from "forbidden" intervals, as the just-quoted passage from *Ossa arida* reminds us. Its piled-up thirds has a counterpart in the piled-up fourths in the Third "Mephisto" Waltz (1883):

The chord on which this passage is based—

—is difficult to explain in terms of traditional harmony. It is best regarded as a "fourths" chord in its last inversion.[21]

---

19. Letter of January 1, 1880; HLSW, p. 236. He was more forthright still to Princess Carolyne: "Unfortunately, my composition is almost impossible to execute, and it will not fail to make the critics grind their teeth." (LLB, vol. 7, p. 393)

20. SWWV, vol. 2, p. 391.

21. I first drew attention to this remarkable passage in my Liszt Symposium of 1970, p. 360, when the Third "Mephisto" Waltz was barely known, and not yet recorded. Humphrey Searle later reproduced these examples in his Liszt article for *The New Grove* (1980), in which context they have become familiar.

Theorists today might describe such examples as contributions towards a "rising norm of consonance," whereby the dissonances of one generation devolve through repetition into the consonances of the next. According to this view, consonance will eventually spread its loving mantle across the whole of music and draw dissonance into the folds of a universal embrace. Liszt was no stranger to the modern concept of "the emancipation of the dissonance," although he never used the phrase. It is hardly necessary to add that he did not allow it to encumber him either. He simply went where his musician's ear led him, and left it to others to explain his eventual place in the general scheme of things.

Throughout his life Liszt's music had flirted with unusual scale formations. The "Gypsy" scale, the pentatonic scale, and the whole-tone scale had left their exotic imprint on his music long before he entered old age. During the final years, however, Liszt's attachment to these colourful sounds took on the force of an obsession, for they lie everywhere to hand. One of the more intriguing examples is the four-note pattern

which is drawn from the "Gypsy" scale, with its augmented seconds and fourths,

and which becomes the ground bass of the Funeral March for *László Teleki* (1884)—one of the aforementioned *Hungarian Historical Portraits.*

Liszt once said that this motif (which, incidentally, he borrowed from Mosonyi's own funeral music for István Széchenyi) should sound "like the tolling of bells." We called it "intriguing" because of its tonal ambiguity. Do you hear it in G minor, starting on the leading-note? Or do you hear it in B minor, starting on the dominant? As the march rises to its climax, the bells toll in conflict with the roaming tonalities above them, producing a feeling of exceptional violence.

László Teleki remains one of the most powerful utterances of Liszt's old age. Together with the other *Historical Portraits,* it remained unpublished until 1956, when it became part of Liszt's musical "afterlife," as he called it—that growing body of music that did not exist for his contemporaries but which he believed our time would make its own.

VI

To take an overview of the music of Liszt's old age is to marvel afresh at its historical location. It does not belong to its time and place—and yet it is there, in defiance of all the laws of musical chronology. What such pieces teach us is that history can occasionally produce a time-warp in which, without warning, we may find ourselves in distant galaxies. Gesualdo, Stravinsky, and Liszt make strange bedfellows, but they have this one thing in common: they are time-travellers who ignore temporal frontiers when the spirit moves them. There is nothing in the chord-structures from the aforementioned Third "Mephisto" Waltz that Schoenberg was not to introduce in his First Chamber Symphony (1906); but Liszt had already travelled into the future and shown a familiarity with this work, even though it was not composed until twenty-one years after his death. The notion of the genius-composer as a time-traveller, stealing from composers as yet unborn, has had a good run; if it is no longer so fashionable today, it has nonetheless provided some of the deepest insights into the life of the mind. It is what led Goethe to deliver one of his best aphorisms: "A genius is invariably linked to his times through some weakness," a thought that takes on the power of revelation when we consider its opposite: namely, that since a genius's strengths are timeless, they cannot belong to his times, nor can they possibly have been learned from them. The times, in brief, transmit weakness. For the rest, the connections between late Liszt and the music of Schoenberg have often been remarked. Whether or not the ties were casual or causal, it was nonetheless a happy symbol of the musical relationship between the pair when Schoenberg was awarded the Liszt Prize for his *Gurrelieder* in 1901 by the influential Richard Strauss, the historical link between them both.[22]

If further proof were required of Liszt's lifelong interest in the theoretical foundations of harmony, it is to be discovered in his correspondence. He exchanged a long series of letters with the Berlin theorist Carl Weitzmann across the years which was frequently characterised by technical discourse. Weitzmann's ideas on harmony proved to be a stimulus, and some of his letters carry intriguing music examples (one of them even proffers a set of puzzle-canons to be solved) that must have given Liszt pause for thought. As early as 1869 Weitzmann had submitted to Liszt the following example from a *Valse noble* by Tausig to show how chords could be built in fourths rather than thirds.[23]

The bare fifths with which the *Csárdás macabre* (1881–82) begins are audacious and without precedent in the music of Liszt's contemporaries. It is unlikely that they were written to provoke Hanslick, a view that has enjoyed common currency of late: Liszt surely had better things to do with his time. In any case, only a small handful of people knew of the work's existence, and Hanslick would hardly have been one of them.

A more intriguing topic for debate is the second-subject stage of the structure. Is it a parody of the *Dies Irae* in which death lurks just beneath the surface of

---

22. The Liszt Prize was awarded annually by the Allgemeiner Deutscher Musikverein, of which organisation Liszt had been made lifelong honorary president in 1882.

23. Unpublished letter to Liszt dated February 11, 1869, WA, Kasten 32, no. 17. Liszt had been impressed with Weitzmann's dissertation on the augmented triad, *Der übermässige Dreiklange,* when it had first appeared in 1853.

a dance with the devil? Or is it a quotation from the old Hungarian folk-song "*Ég a kunyhó, ropog a nád*"?[24] Both theories have their contenders. Liszt himself is silent on the matter.

When Liszt had finished work on the *Csárdás macabre* he scribbled on the manuscript: "May one write or listen to such a thing?"[25] It was a pointed question. The loneliness of his artistic position had struck him with force, and he was assailed by doubt. The *Csárdás macabre* remained unplayed and unpublished until 1951. That is a remarkable fact, and it may serve as a paradigm for so much of the neglect endured by the late Liszt. A more dramatic way to bring out the historical anomaly is to point out that the *Csárdás macabre* was composed during the year of Bartók's birth but not published until the year of Schoenberg's death.

---

24. The words of the folk-song run:

> The little hut is burning,
> The thatched roof is crackling.
> You should embrace the brown-haired girl,
> And while you are embracing her, the blond-haired girl
> Will run away.

25. It used to be thought that these words were first uttered by August Göllerich, since he included them in his catalogue entry for this work (see GL, p. 289). An inspection of the Weimar manuscript confirms that they come from Liszt. (WA, ms. I, 11)

VII

Perhaps it was because of the blank incredulity which greeted some of Liszt's later music that he eventually came to the conclusion that he would never be accepted as a major composer in his lifetime. Even during the most difficult days of the Weimar period he had never lost hope. But the setbacks of his old age were of a different order, and there were times when defeat stared him in the face. The critics were not prepared to let him forget that he was first and foremost a pianist, the leading member of a profession which (according to them) he should never have abandoned, and they generally remained hostile to his compositions. Already, fifteen years earlier (1865), he had summed up his plight thus:

> . . . it seems to me that Mr. Litz [sic] is, as it were, always welcome when he appears *at the piano* (especially since he has made a profession of the contrary) but he is not allowed to have anything to do with thinking and writing according to his own fancy . . . The result is that for some 15 years, so-called friends, as well as indifferent and ill-disposed people on all sides, sing, enough to split your head, to this unhappy Mr. Litz, who has nothing to do with it: "Be a pianist, and nothing but that. *How is it possible for you not to be a pianist?*"[26]

"How is it possible for you *not* to be a pianist?" The question now recurred like a leitmotif to haunt his old age. The degree of negative criticism that Liszt endured for the last twenty years of his life, because he had abandoned his public in order to write a kind of music that they did not like, left a deep mark on him. Self-abnegation is an unexpected aspect of his personality, but it is the best term to describe the profound changes that were taking place in his character in the 1880s.

VIII

Liszt once told Princess Carolyne that his only remaining ambition as a musician was to "hurl my lance into the boundless realms of the future."[27] The sen-

---

26. LLB, vol. 2, p. 78.
27. LLB, vol. 7, pp. 57–58. To which Carolyne added the observation: "Liszt has thrown his lance much further into the future [than Wagner]. Several generations will pass before he is fully understood." (SZM, p. 242)

tence has been much-quoted, for the image is compelling. That lance was soon picked up—by Bartók and Schoenberg among others, who hurled it in turn to a generation not yet conceived. Liszt's late music proves the truth of the old adage that there are no difficult composers, only difficult listeners. And they can be cured.

Towards the end of Liszt's life—it was the spring of 1885—his pupil August Stradal was reading passages from Schopenauer's *Parerga und Paralipomena* to his old master, who was by then nearly blind. When Stradal came to the famous passage in which the maker of fireworks discovers that he has arrived at the wrong place, and that the spectators before whom he has just displayed the most beautiful illuminations are all inmates of an institution for the blind, Liszt was reminded of his own historical plight. His own "blind spectators," he re-marked, would one day be blessed with the power of sight.[28] He knew that he was not the first composer in history to have outrun his audience. Meanwhile, he had a phrase to sum up his general attitude whenever his uncertain place in the scheme of things was a topic of conversation: "Ich kann warten"—"I can wait." Liszt had faith in his musical "after-life," as he called it. We know today that his trust in posterity was not misplaced.

---

28. SE, p. 71. The passage from Schopenhauer will be found in SPP (2), vol. 2, p. 459. It is worth pro-viding the ending (omitted by Stradal) because Liszt would surely have appreciated the philosopher's biting humour. "And yet perhaps he is better off than he would be if his public had been none but makers of fireworks; for in that case it might have cost him his head if his display had been extraordi-narily good."

Harmonies du soir,
1881-1885

*I exist, after a fashion—and as long as this lasts my
only worries concern another world.*

FRANZ LISZT[1]

I

When Liszt arrived in Italy in the autumn of 1881, it was not to his beloved
Tivoli and the Villa d'Este that he ventured. Instead he took up residence in the
heart of Rome, at the Hotel Alibert. He checked in on October 16 and remained there until January 28 the following year—a fifteen-week period that
was broken only by short journeys to nearby places. The reason for this change
of address had to do with his declining health. Not yet properly recovered from
his fall, he still needed support when walking long distances. His swollen legs
and crushed toe made the rugged terrain of the Villa d'Este a serious handicap
for him, and he hardly went there, except for brief visits. Moreover, the place
often became cold and damp during the bleaker weeks of the Roman winter.
His fingers had been susceptible to chilblains in the past,[2] and even the heaters
that Cardinal Hohenlohe had recently installed at the villa did not seem to keep
him warm. By contrast, the Alibert offered modest comforts and a central location that provided Liszt a good base from which to conduct his social activities.
Situated just off the Via del Babuino, near the Piazza del Popolo, it was within
easy distance of Princess Carolyne's apartments. The church of San Carlo al
Corso also lay nearby, and Liszt frequently attended mass there, despite the spirits of times past that haunted the place. The Alibert had one other advantage
too. His students found it easier to visit him for their piano lessons, and one or

---

1. WLLM, p. 478.
2. HLR, pp. 175–76.

two of them even rented rooms there. Arthur Friedheim was a frequent resident; it was at the Alibert that he became Liszt's secretary and took on the task of helping his master deal with his voluminous correspondence. We would not be wrong to describe the Alibert as "the Erbprinz of Rome," for it began to take on much of the hubbub associated with the Weimar years. The pupils whom Liszt taught at the Alibert, apart from Friedheim, included Alfred Reisenauer, Henryk van Zeyl, Giuseppe Ferrata, Ernst Schilling, and István Thomán.

There were disadvantages, of course. Once it became known that he was a resident at the Alibert, the invitations began to pour in, often from people whom it was difficult to turn down. On October 22, 1881, for example, a gala concert was arranged in honour of Liszt's seventieth birthday at the German embassy in Rome. It consisted entirely of his works and was given before a large audience. The event was of more than passing interest since Tchaikovsky was present. He observed: "One could not but feel emotion at the sight of this genius, now an old man, so touched and moved by the ovations of the enraptured Italians." But he added that the performances were mediocre and that Liszt's music left him cold.[3]

During his sojourn in Rome Liszt was deluged with letters from friends and well-wishers. He tells us that he received well over one hundred letters during a six-week period in November and December 1881. "I should have to give ten hours a day to letter-writing if I were to attempt to pay my debts of correspondence," he remarked.[4] Instead, he gave way to what he called his old mania for composition, and left much of the drudgery of acknowledging the letters to Friedheim. It was in the Alibert Hotel that he transcribed his pupil Zarembski's *Galician Dances* for full orchestra; he also checked the proofs of the *Christmas-tree Suite* and put the final touches to his Second Mephisto Waltz. The psalm *De Profundis* also dates from this time, as does the ballade *St. Christopher* for baritone and piano, a work which is still unpublished. Because of Liszt's frail condition, his granddaughter Daniela had accompanied him to Rome, where they were joined at the Alibert by Adelheid von Schorn. Schorn tells us that she and Daniela did their best to persuade Liszt to take some exercise and get some fresh air, but to little avail. Liszt had never been in the habit of taking walks, an activity he considered useless unless there was a clear destination in mind; he preferred to remain closeted in the hotel, working. When it was impossible for him to resist Daniela's pleas, he would don his hat and coat, pick up a walking-stick, stroll a short distance with the two ladies, and then park himself on a bench behind a newspaper, telling them to pick him up when they returned. From his hotel window Liszt could see the Villa Medici, the home of the French Academy, nestling on the side of the Monte Pincio, and he was not averse to accepting an occasional

---

3. BBF, p. 414.
4. LLB, vol. 2, p. 315.

invitation from the director, Ernest Hébert, to attend dinner parties and mix with the intelligentsia; but that was after the day's work was done. He went to a number of concerts given in his honour. On December 6 the Società Orchestrale Romana put on a concert of his works, which included the A major piano concerto (with Sgambati as soloist) and the *Dante* Symphony conducted by Ettore Pinelli. As Liszt entered the hall he got a standing ovation. At the end of the concert he was presented by the directors of the Società with a specially bound edition of the *Divine Comedy,* and a letter signed by all the leading musicians of Rome.

Christmas Day he celebrated quietly, his chief "present" being a surprise performance of his *Christmas-tree Suite,* which took place in Daniela's hotel room. The title page bears the inscription: "First performed on Christmas Day, 1881, by amateurs in Rome."

He saw less of Princess Carolyne than on previous visits, and this fact may have prompted her to "punish" him by indulging in a tactic that can be charitably described as meddlesome. She had never reconciled herself to Liszt's long absences in Budapest. She sent a telegramme to Kornél Ábrányi at the Music Academy, telling him that Liszt's poor health, which had improved in Italy's mild climate, might not be able to withstand the shock of a Budapest winter. "If you wish to hasten his death, then urge him to undertake the journey in Winter. [It] would be a veritable suicide for patriotism."[5] The message sowed confusion and uncertainty among Liszt's colleagues in Budapest, as it was intended to do. Nobody knew when to expect him, or whether he would even turn up. It was not until Liszt arrived in the City of the Magyars, on the evening of February 4, 1882, that the Hungarians knew for sure that there had never really been any question of his staying in Rome. Whenever his duties at the Academy beckoned, Liszt was always there to fulfil them.

II

Of all the varied activities of the last five or six years of Liszt's life, none shows him in a more consistent light than his work in behalf of the Allgemeiner Deutscher Musikverein. It is an untold tale; his manifold duties have yet to find their chronicler. Liszt became involved in much correspondence, in committee meetings, in long journeys, at a time when he was becoming increasingly frail, and above all in a search for new talent. Ever since he had helped to found the parent organisation, in 1859, under the title of the Tonkünstler-Versammlung, he had attended the annual festivals quite faithfully, irrespective of the particular city in which they happened to be held or the great distances he had to travel in order to get there. And after he was appointed lifetime honorary president in

5. PBUS, p. 419.

1882, he felt a greater duty than ever to lend this national organisation his personal prestige. The reason he was happy to make such a commitment is very simple to explain. The Verein was devoted to the promotion of modern music, and Liszt was able to help many struggling young musicians find a national platform, either as composers or as performers. It was one of those happy circumstances in which his public persona matched his private one.

In many ways the festival of 1883 stood out from the others. Held in Leipzig between May 3 and May 6, and celebrating the twentieth anniversary of the Verein's existence, it contained an unusually impressive array of new music, much of which was hardly known in Germany or anywhere else. The opening concert, which was given in the Thomaskirche, consisted of a performance of Felix Draeseke's Requiem under the direction of the ever-faithful Carl Riedel. On the second day the festival moved into the Gewandhaus for chamber music: a string quartet by Eduard Hartog, a piano quintet by Friedrich Kiel, and songs by Peter Cornelius, Reinhold Becker, and Mór Vogel among others. Alfred Reisenauer also played some Liszt pieces.

The afternoon of the second day (May 4) was also devoted to chamber music—this time by Rimsky-Korsakoff, C. P. E. Bach, Schumann (the four "Mignon" Lieder), and J. S. Bach (an unaccompanied cello sonata). In the evening there was a full-scale symphony concert, in three parts, conducted by Max Staegemann:[6]

PART I

Symphony No. 1 in E-flat major	Borodin
Violin Concerto in D major	Brahms
(soloist: Adolf Brodsky)	

PART II

Two Songs for Male Chorus	Cornelius
(directed by Hermann Langer)	
Piano Concerto No. 1 in E-flat major	Liszt
(soloist: Eugène d'Albert)	

PART III

A *Faust* Overture	Wagner
Prelude and Finale to Act I of *Parsifal*	

---

6. Both the NZfM (issue of May 11, 1883) and *Music and Drama* (issue of June 23, 1883) give a full account of this anniversary festival. Among the best of the organisation's early histories is Arthur Seidl's *Festschrift,* which was published in celebration of the fiftieth anniversary of the Verein and is dedicated to Liszt. Seidl gives some useful statistics in his brief study, including the names of all the composers whose works were performed during the first fifty years of the Verein's existence. (See SADM.)

D'Albert, who was now nineteen years old, was received tumultuously, and delivered as an encore Rubinstein's famous "Staccato" Study, op. 23. (The next day, the young man lay sick in hospital with the measles!)

This programme seems unbearably long by modern standards, yet it is almost parsimonious when set beside the one with which the festival ended, on May 6.

PART I

March from *King Hiarvel* (played from manuscript)	Ingeborg von Bronsart
Romance, Hamerik, and Serenade (soloist: Anton Hekking)	Benjamin Godard
A *Faust* Fantasy	Ödön von Mihalovich
Song of Destiny, for Chorus and Orchestra	Brahms
Les Ombres, valse étude (soloist: Marie Jaëll)	Saint-Saëns

PART II

Prometheus, symphonic poem with choral obbligato	Liszt

PART III

Die Liebesfee, character piece for violin and orchestra	Raff
Prelude and Love Scene from *Die sieben Todsünden*	Adalbert von Goldschmidt
Kaisermarsch, with closing chorus	Wagner

The entire audience stood up at the end of the concert and joined in the rendering of the old Lutheran chorale "Nun danket alle Gott," with which the *Kaisermarsch* concludes. According to a report in *Music and Drama,* this particular concert lasted from 11:00 a.m. until 3:30 p.m.—that is, four and a half hours. Could anyone sit through it today? The magazine tells us that at least one person did, and sat through all the others as well: "The beloved honorary President, Franz Liszt, attended every concert, sitting in the audience, showing no sign of fatigue no matter how long the concert! And this at seventy-one!"[7]

---

7. *Music and Drama,* June 23, 1883, p. 13.

III

Liszt's annual departure from Germany was delayed during the autumn of 1883. For one thing, he was depressed by Cosima's continued refusal to see him, and he did not want to set out for Italy as long as there was a chance that she might invite him to make his usual pilgrimage to Bayreuth. He lingered in vain; and when he heard that he was not welcome to stay in Wahnfried, his gloom deepened.[8] For another, his daily life was also complicated by the fatal illness of his manservant, Achille Colonello. This treasured valet, who had become indispensable to Liszt during the past three years, was now an invalid in the Hofgärtnerei. Liszt did not want to abandon him there, and that was the chief reason he spent Christmas in Weimar—his first in many years. Adelheid von Schorn visited daily and took temporary charge of Liszt's affairs. Achille finally entered hospital in the new year, and it was only then, when there was nothing more to be done for his old factotum, that Liszt decided not to go to Italy at all this year, but travel directly to Budapest instead. He set out in the company of a young manservant named Carl Lehmann, who was loaned to him by Olga von Meyendorff, and whom he quickly discovered to be a highly intelligent conversationalist and an ideal travelling companion. The pair were with Lina Ramann in Nuremberg when news reached them of Achille's death on February 1, 1884. Liszt sent a cable to Adelheid von Schorn and asked her to be sure to have the Catholic priest offer a prayer over Achille's coffin, since Achille was a devout Catholic. He also arranged to reimburse the costs of the hospital, the funeral service, and the burial. "I should like a stone cross to be placed over his grave with the inscription: 'Achille Colonello, Manservant to Franz Liszt, Honorary Canon.' "[9]

Liszt arrived in Budapest on February 4. No one was at the railway-station to meet him, since his colleagues were not sure when, or even whether, he would come. But he quickly got back into his usual stride—administering, teaching, and lending his presence to the more important concerts. He heard Rubinstein give a piano recital in the auditorium of the Hungária Hotel on February 16; and the following month he attended a Philharmonic concert especially to hear Vladimir de Pachmann play Chopin's F-minor Piano Concerto. Pachmann never knew that he was in the audience, since Liszt had

---

8. In May Cosima had made it known to her father that she did not wish to see him (SZM, p. 441), and by the end of the year it had become painfully obvious that she was shutting herself off from everyone. Liszt wrote to Carolyne that his daughter was doing her best not to survive Wagner. "From what I am told—for I neither receive nor request any direct news—she passes hours each day at Wagner's grave, ignoring all appeals to the contrary. A decisive vocation!" (LLB, vol. 7, p. 395)
9. SLG, p. 73.

hidden himself in a box at the back of the theatre; he had long since stopped making official appearances at the Philharmonic concerts, with which organisation he was still in contention.[10] Both Pachmann and Rubinstein paid tribute to Liszt by performing some of his solo pieces, including *Au bord d'une source,* which was in the repertoire of both men.

As usual with Liszt, there were many ancilliary activities stemming from his stay in Hungary. We will confine ourselves to mentioning only his trip to Pressburg Cathedral, where he conducted his Hungarian Coronation Mass on February 25, and his visits to Gran (on March 5) and Kalocsa (in mid-April), where he was the guest of Cardinals Simor and Haynald, respectively. He crossed the Hungarian border on April 20 and stayed in Vienna for five days, during which time he attended the first performance in that city of his symphonic poem *Tasso.* Back in Weimar on April 25, he was poised to begin yet another annual circuit of his endlessly revolving "three-fold life."

I V

On May 18, 1884, Liszt travelled to Leipzig in the company of a group of students in order to hear a performance of *Christus,* under the direction of Carl Riedel. The event was really an unofficial curtain-raiser for the next Allgemeiner Deutscher Musikverein festival, which was held in Weimar from May 23 to May 28. Because it was in his "native city," Liszt had to play a more demanding role than usual, for he was both president and host-in-residence as well. Among the many guests who descended on the town were Pauline Viardot-Garcia, Felix Weingartner, and Camille Saint-Saëns. Louis Held captured the 1884 festival for posterity in a remarkable group photograph of more than one hundred of the assembled delegates, taken outside the old Weimar shooting gallery, with Liszt sitting in the centre.[11]

The festival opened on May 23 with a staged performance of *St. Elisabeth,* given in the opera house under the direction of Eduard Lassen. As Liszt entered, the grand duke stood up in the royal box in homage to Liszt, and the entire audience followed suit. To be treated like royalty had become a common enough experience for Liszt, but we cannot help reflecting that before his time such a reversal of protocol was unheard of. Other works featured in the festival were the "Gran" Mass (May 26) and the twenty-one-year-old Weingartner's opera *Sakuntala* (May 28), which the young man had brought to Weimar earlier in the year at the insistence of Liszt. The opera's first performance, under

---

10. See pp. 375–76.
11. It is reproduced in BFL, p. 298.

Lassen, had not been a success,[12] so Lassen had agreed to relinquish the baton and allow Weingartner himself to conduct this performance, with much improved results.

The festival of 1884 was the last occasion on which Liszt appeared as a conductor. On May 25 he led the orchestra through performances of Bülow's symphonic poem *Nirvana* and the "Salve Polonia" from his own unfinished oratorio *St. Stanislas*. As he walked towards the podium in his flowing abbé's robes, he was greeted with great applause. He turned towards the royal box, bowed slowly in the direction of the grand duke, and then began the performance. According to Weingartner, the orchestral playing was insecure, and at one point the players broke down. The cellist Leopold Grützmacher saved the situation by playing an easily recognizable passage, and the rest of the orchestra took their cue from him. As the performance resumed, Liszt bowed towards Grützmacher in acknowledgement of his help.[13]

The reunion with Saint-Saëns gave Liszt particular pleasure. He not only put on a special reception for his old friend in the Hofgärtnerei,[14] but also invited him into the piano masterclasses, where Saint-Saëns played to the students a piano transcription from his recently composed opera *Henry VIII,* and then gave a rivetting performance of Mozart's Rondo in A minor. Liszt's eyes lit up during the playing. "That is real piano playing," he remarked as the two colleagues embraced one another.[15]

Liszt's piano classes were enlivened in 1884 by the arrival of a number of newcomers, whose ranks included Emil von Sauer from Hamburg, Clothilde Jeschke from Berlin, and Victoria Drewing from Russia. There was also a large colony of Americans: Edwin Klahre (Brooklyn), Carlyle Petersilia (Boston), Hugo Mansfeldt (San Francisco), and William Dayas (Manhattan). Early on the morning of July 4, they sent a large floral arrangement to the Hofgärtnerei— a mass of red, white, and blue flowers mounted on a bed of moss—in the form of the American flag. That evening Liszt joined them for a celebration at the Chemnicus restaurant, and they all wore American badges in their lapels, including Liszt.[16]

---

12. Weingartner gives details of the débâcle that occurred on the Weimar stage in his memoirs, WLE, vol. 1, pp. 189–90.

13. WLE, vol. 1, p. 194. Apart from the widely recognised fact that the Weimar Court Orchestra had declined since Liszt had been in charge of the ensemble in the 1850s, both compositions were also being performed from manuscript, a state of affairs which carried its own hazards. "Over this unforgettable scene," Weingartner later wrote, "there lay a feeling of leave-taking. . . . No one could fail to see that here was a tired old man whose clock was running down." (Ibid.)

14. LL, p. 323.

15. WLE, vol. 1, p. 195.

16. LL, p. 331.

V

Liszt's visit to the Bayreuth Festival in the summer of 1884 was one which in retrospect it would have been better for him not to have made. The festival itself still lay under the shadow of Wagner's death, its future uncertain. Cosima had assumed direction of the enterprise in a determined attempt to save Wagner's legacy. But she was still struggling with the emotional burdens of her widowhood, and as yet she barely understood the magnitude of the task before her. Ten performances of *Parsifal* were planned this year, and they attracted large audiences, but Cosima lacked the professional experience to direct an opera house. She supervised everything from a concealed box, which allowed her to see the stage but kept her from public scrutiny. At first she passed hastily scribbled notes on small scraps of paper to Hermann Levi, which contained detailed instructions on such matters as tempi, the balance of orchestra and singers, and the niceties of the stage action. No detail seemed too small to escape her attention, and there was no question that she had an intimate knowledge of the scores. Liszt had assumed that at a time of crisis he would have been useful to his daughter, but he was badly mistaken. He was not invited to stay at Wahnfried and had to take lodgings with the Fröhlich family in nearby Siegfriedstrasse. He attended all the rehearsals, sitting in the darkened theatre following the score with the aid of a lamp, which did not help his poor eyesight. But Cosima avoided him. His grandson Daniel Ollivier saw him there and reported that Liszt was so fatigued that he often fell asleep during the apotheoses, "much to the indignation of the holy family [the Wagners]."[17] From this same source we learn that on the one occasion he encountered Cosima, Liszt addressed a few words to her and was met by "a spectral silence." It was after a rehearsal, when the theatre was almost deserted. Liszt saw his daughter advancing towards him along one of the empty corridors, and she passed him like a ghost.[18]

V I

By the beginning of 1885 the rapid deterioration in Liszt's eyesight was noticed by everybody. It was a difficult affliction for him to bear, since he could no longer notate music with the ease and certainty of previous years. Several months earlier he had told Olga von Meyendorff: "My eyes are growing so

---

17. TOS-W, p. 311.
18. See also p. 462, n. 8.

weak that it is becoming almost impossible for me to use them for more than a few hours in the day. Too much time spent on music sheets affects my sight."[19] And he added that he intended to give himself a big negative Christmas present: that of writing no more music. This was one promise that he did not keep, but from this time his creative output was curtailed.

One of the people most distressed by Liszt's physical deterioration was Princess Carolyne, for their long separations made it more noticeable to her. When he got back to Rome at the beginning of 1885, for example, she was deeply shaken by his decline. He appeared to her to be physically and mentally worn out. He was so fatigued, his body so swollen, that she did not think he would last out the week.[20] The warmer Italian climate revived him, so she claimed, for his underlying constitution remained strong. Carolyne was probably justified in complaining that people insisted on treating Liszt as if he were still a young man, that there were times when all the hospitality and social invitations that were showered on him represented a form of abuse. Insofar as he accepted them, however, he had only himself to blame if they brought unpleasant consequences in their wake. One of the symptoms that had plagued him for a long time was nausea and occasional vomiting when he got up in the mornings. Liszt was the worst of patients, not because he complained but because he never complained. By carrying on his daily life as if he enjoyed perfect health, he probably shortened it.

Since it was cumbersome for him to read books and newspapers, to say nothing of responding to the mountains of correspondence that still reached him every week, he had to rely increasingly on his students to help him in such tasks. Several of them became indispensable to him. Apart from Friedheim and Lina Schmalhausen, who had assisted him with the daily routine of his personal life for several years and had regularly accompanied him on his journeys, there now appeared Bernhard Stavenhagen and August Stradal, who took it in turns to read aloud to him. Stradal had joined Liszt's masterclass in Weimar the previous September and had followed him to Budapest. He tells us that among Liszt's favourite newspapers, from which Stradal had to read out the news every day, were the Budapest *Tageblatt* and the Munich *Allgemeine Zeitung* (his fondness for this latter newspaper, Liszt joked, was something he had in common with Beethoven). Stradal also read aloud from religious and philosophical works, including Schopenhauer's *Parerga und Paralipomena*. Liszt particularly approved of the passage in which Schopenauer classes writers into "meteors," "planets," and "fixed stars," and he approved of Schopenhauer's notion that because the fixed stars were so distant, their

---

19. WLLM, p. 459.
20. SZM, p. 456.

light took many years to reach the earth[21]—likewise with great composers who must await their success.

One of Liszt's last piano compositions emerged during the spring of 1885: his Hungarian Rhapsody No. 19, in D minor. The piece attracts our attention because it goes against the general trend of his last compositions, with their sparse textures and experimental harmonies. Based on themes from Kornél Ábrányi's *Csárdás nobles,* this rhapsody blazes with colour and demands exceptional virtuosity; it is almost as if Liszt were seized with nostalgia and were trying to recapture the days of his youth. After some cascading cembalom effects, based on the "Gypsy" scale,

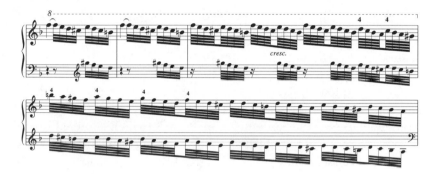

the main theme of the *lassan* emerges with solemn dignity, as if to declare: "The Rhapsode speaks!"

The grave tones of the Rhapsode fall silent, and the *friss* takes over. The music reaches a real paroxysm of excitement, and exhibits a level of delirium rare in the compositions of Liszt's old age; it has the pianist's hands racing back and forth across the keyboard with abandon, as if in emulation of the Gypsy dance itself.

---

21. SE, p. 71.

August Stradal walked into Liszt's study in the Royal Academy of Music at the very moment that Liszt had completed work on the rhapsody. "Copy out the manuscript for the publisher immediately," said Liszt, "and play it from memory at the music teachers' concert in eight days' time." Stradal was taken aback by the request, and asked Liszt if he would first play the rhapsody through and show him how it went. Thereupon Liszt went through the dining room, walked into the academy's concert hall (which adjoined his apartment), and began to play. Stradal described the performance as matchless, made all the more astonishing by the fact that Liszt had probably never played it before, and had certainly not practised it. Yet the true revelation for Stradal was the fact that under Liszt's fingers the piano seemed disembodied, the music arising from an instrument that had lost everything material. As he brought the taxing coda to its frenzied climax and finished the piece, Liszt arose from the keyboard exhausted. It was already dusk and the light had started to fade in the hall. The occasion burned itself into Stradal's memory, and in later years spoiled all other piano playing for him. He summarized his feelings in the lines of Dante: "There is no greater pain than the remembrance of past joys in times of misery."[22]

VII

On April 13 and 14, 1885, Liszt was in Pressburg in order to attend a concert given by Anton Rubinstein in aid of the Hummel monument. From there he went to Vienna to attend the dress-rehearsal of Rubinstein's opera *Nero* at the Court Theatre. At a morning matinée put on in Liszt's honour by Adalbert von Goldschmidt, he met Johann Strauss II, Károly Goldmark, and his old

---

22. SE, pp. 53–54.

friend Joseph Hellmesberger. There was also a rare encounter between Liszt and Anton Bruckner. Bruckner, who held Liszt in near idolatry, caused some amusement by turning up wearing an old-fashioned overcoat, a pair of large boots, and buttoned leggings of the kind worn by country folk, which lent him a rustic appearance. He held his hat in his hand, and insisted on addressing Liszt as "Your Grace, Herr Canon."[23] He had come to request that his Seventh Symphony be performed at the forthcoming festival of the Allgemeiner Deutscher Musikverein, to be held at Karlsruhe in a few weeks' time. This request he pressed on Liszt with such fervour that those in the group observed Liszt's patience wearing thin. Bruckner did not seem to realise that it was impossible to accommodate a work of such vast proportions at relatively short notice; but Liszt did arrange that the Adagio be played, and he later expressed a favourable opinion of it.

Having been invited to visit the Brussels World Fair in June 1885, Liszt spent several days there and at Antwerp. Many artists converged on the city for this event, including Jenő Huber, Zarembski, and Servais. Liszt attended a performance of his "Szekszárd" Mass at St. Joseph's Church in Antwerp on June 8; it was conducted by Peter Benoit, whom Liszt dubbed "the Rubens of Antwerp." It was during this trip to Belgium that he was decorated by the king with the Order of Leopold. Liszt later remarked that this honour gave him more pleasure than any other he had ever received.

On July 18 Liszt travelled to Halle in order to meet his old friend Robert Franz. By now Franz was somewhat frail, completely deaf, and was suffering from a nervous disability. He had long since ceased to compose on a regular basis, and even the act of listening to music was sometimes physically painful for him. Liszt was accompanied by August Göllerich, who later recorded that Franz poured out his gratitude for all the help that Liszt had given him, which he was convinced had saved him from destitution. Conversation was difficult since everything had to be written down. But Franz informed Göllerich that he was well aware that Liszt had made some handsome donations to the Robert Franz Fund across the years, and that it was Liszt who had prevailed upon the Beethoven Foundation to award Franz an honorarium. After the meal Liszt retired for a short rest, and while Göllerich and Franz were taking coffee together, Franz confided: "I have *him* to thank for everything . . . without him I could have starved!" At the end of the visit there was an emotional farewell, and Franz renewed his thanks to his old friend. Both men well understood the notion that the pain of parting, in its deepest sense, is a foretaste of death. And so it was here; they never met again.[24]

---

23. SE, p. 90.
24. GL, pp. 111–12.

VIII

Our chronicler-in-chief for the Weimar masterclasses of 1885 is August Göllerich, whose diary records an impressive total of forty-one lessons held between June 28 and September 9, in which more than 180 works were played—a diversity of composers ranging from Bach and Beethoven, through Chopin and Schumann, to Raff, Smetana, and Tchaikovsky.[25] Nor were these classes foreshortened to save Liszt from fatigue; some of them lasted for more than four hours. They also attracted exceptionally large numbers of visitors: on August 10, for instance, we learn that forty people were crowded into the music room of the Hofgärtnerei in order to witness the lesson. All the while, Liszt was on his feet, shuffling back and forth across the room, commenting and criticising as he went, and occasionally even playing excerpts when the spirit moved him. Amy Fay was a return visitor to the class this season. She had been re-united with Liszt at the Brussels World Fair earlier in the year, and had suddenly taken it into her head to travel down to Weimar and stay there during August. Fay was by now a well-known teacher in the States, in part because her book *Music Study in Germany,* published some four years earlier, had gained her a following as an authority on Liszt. Among other things Liszt heard her play was Beethoven's *Pastorale* Sonata.[26]

Newcomers to the class of 1885 included Frederic Lamond, Conrad Ansorge, and José Vianna da Motta. Hugo Mansfeldt also returned after a brief visit the previous year. Mansfeldt, who hailed from San Francisco, had for many years given annual piano recitals of Liszt's music in his home city, to celebrate the composer's birthday, and he had written to Liszt as early as 1880 to inform him of that fact.[27] Two other Americans crossed Liszt's path at this time. The

---

25. GLK, pp. 61–103.
26. GLK, p. 93.
27. Mansfeldt's first letter to Liszt was dated "San Francisco, California, September 22, 1880." In light of its inherent charm and straightforward honesty, and the fact that hardly any information about Mansfeldt's relationship with Liszt is available in the standard reference books, we include a few extracts from it here.

> Franz von Liszt, Reverend Sir,
>   . . . I am 35 years old. My parents came to this country from Germany when I was a mere child. I never saw a piano until I was 13 years old; then I received 3 months instruction, and as my parents were too poor to continue my music lessons, they were stopped, and ever afterwards my own intelligence and talent were the only teachers I had. My only drawback has been that I never had time to practice to any extent; but a fortunate hand, quick reading, good memory and talent enabled me to accomplish a great deal with little practice. Up to my 16th year my entire time was taken up with school studies; after that I had to help to support our family by teaching piano; then I married very young, at the age of 19, and had to support a growing family. I soon

first was Morris Bagby, who later became a well-known impresario in New York, and who left an indispensable account of the visit in his "Summer with Liszt in Weimar."[28] Bagby was present at the Jena "Sausage Festival" of '85, an event that fell this year on June 26. Liszt and his students travelled to Jena, first for the annual choral concert (this time it was to hear Bach's St. John Passion) and thence to the garden of the Zum Bären. Pyramids of sandwiches were consumed, speeches were made, and healths drunk. Bagby's vivid account of the Fourth of July celebrations in Weimar the following week, and Liszt's insistence on a performance of Rubinstein's Variations on "Yankee Doodle" to celebrate the occasion, have already been detailed.[29]

The other American in Weimar at this time was the young violinist Arma Senkrah. She derived her unusual name by reversing the letters of the one with which she was born—Mary Harkness.[30] She had already played in a number of German towns when she arrived in Weimar in the summer of 1885, in the hope of boosting her career. Chamber music was regularly featured at Liszt's matinées, and Senkrah performed frequently. On one occasion Liszt arranged for her to play Beethoven's *Spring* Sonata with Arthur Friedheim as her accompanist. A mutual dislike had grown up between these two young people, and Liszt heard about it. He waited until just before the performance was about to start, then leaned across to where Friedheim was sitting and whispered: "I find it advisable to take your place at the piano." What followed was a performance which delighted everyone. According to Friedheim, Emil von Sauer was so overjoyed that he performed somersaults in the next room.[31] Stradal tells us that Senkrah wasted no time in capitalizing on the situation. She dragged

---

became a well-known teacher and my entire time was taken up in teaching; at this moment I am teaching every day for 10 hours; so you can imagine I have very little time for practice. I was 20 years old when I was electrified by seeing a few of your compositions for the first time. I commenced practising them and am so carried away by them that everything else seems tame after them. Their fire and magical effects seemed to suit me exactly. (I have been called your apostle in this far-off country, California; I am the only one in this state who plays your compositions.) . . . (Hitherto unpublished, WA, Kasten 59, u. 23)

Four years after writing this letter Mansfeldt fulfilled his life's ambition, travelled to Weimar, and became a trusted member of Liszt's circle. As we have seen, he gave the first public performance of Liszt's Bagatelle Without Tonality (see pp. 445–46).

28. BSLW, pp. 655–69.
29. See p. 242.
30. According to Morris Bagby, Miss Senkrah had refused to give up her American name in favour of a European one, and the backward-running version was a compromise. She once met Hans von Bülow in the offices of their Berlin concert manager, Hermann Wolff. When she showed Bülow one of her recent reviews from Leipzig, he wrote beneath it "Bravo!" When she pointed out that this sign of approval was not complete without his signature, Bülow wrote beneath it "Snah nov Wolüb." The bewildered Senkrah may not have been amused when she pressed Bülow to explain his strange signature, and he replied that he was only exercising the same privilege as she herself.
31. FLL, pp. 146–47.

Liszt to Louis Held's studios in order to pose with him at the piano, a copy of the *Spring* Sonata on the music rack. These photographs adorn every modern Liszt iconography.[32] Liszt good-naturedly inscribed one of them: "To the distinguished violin virtuoso—her most devoted accompanist F. Liszt."[33] Senkrah sent this picture from town to town, with the result that she always played to full houses. In the later 1880s Senkrah entered into a disastrous marriage with a Weimar lawyer named Hoffman. Within two or three years she had committed suicide. Today she lies buried in a remote corner of the Weimar Stadtfriedhof, beyond the area that would have been consecrated ground at that time. Inscribed on her modest tombstone of black marble are the simple words "Arma Senkrah Hoffman," without any dates.

I X

The year 1885 was also notable for a sharp rise in the number of performances of Liszt's music. Perhaps the best explanation for this unexpected surge in its popularity is also the simplest. The struggle of the 1850s, in which Liszt had to fight to secure performances of the new music at the expense of his own, was now thirty years old and had become enshrined in the annals of history. A new and largely unprejudiced generation of gifted performers had emerged who, brought up with the legend, saw in Liszt a battle-scarred survivor from the past, someone who had walked into the future without flinching and ought to be welcomed. Whatever the case, it was the younger generation who carried things forward. His *Dante* Symphony was conducted by the twenty-nine-year-old Felix Mottl at the Karlsruhe Festival on May 31, while his *Bells of Strasbourg* was performed in Strasbourg itself on June 3. Then followed no fewer than three all-Liszt concerts: the first in Antwerp on June 7, conducted by the thirty-eight-year-old Franz Servais; the second in Aachen, under the direction of the thirty-six-year-old Julius Kniese; and the third in the Gewandhaus in Leipzig, given by a group of his pupils on September 3. The day before this particular concert, Liszt's American pupil William Dayas had delivered a rare performance of the B-minor Piano Sonata, an interpretation which gave Liszt enormous pleasure. As if to crown this season of success, there was an attempt to start a "Liszt-Verein" in Weimar, at the instigation of Siloti. It was quashed by Liszt himself,[34] who was, however, unable to prevent a similar movement from developing in Leipzig under the direction of his pupil Martin Krause—

---

32. This famous performance of the *Spring* Sonata took place on July 20, 1885. The photograph was taken by Louis Held on July 31. (GLK, pp. 87 and 90)
33. SE, p. 112.
34. "In Weimar," Liszt had told Siloti, "it is wisest to keep oneself *negative* and *passive*. Therefore, dear Siloti, attempt *no* 'Liszt-Verein.' " (LLB, vol. 2, p. 379)

no mean achievement in a city that was traditionally hostile towards Liszt. It was the only such society formed in Germany during Liszt's own lifetime.

By mid-October his German peregrinations had come to an end, and Liszt set out on his annual trek to Rome in the company of Friedheim, Stavenhagen, and István Thomán. The party made a number of stopovers along the way. They travelled first to Munich in order to hear Cornelius's *Barber of Bagdad* under Mottl. For this particular production, Liszt had suggested various modifications which Mottl had accepted, including a cut towards the end of the first act and a re-orchestration of the second overture by Liszt himself. From Munich the group ventured on to Itter Castle, Sophie Menter's fairy-tale retreat in the Austrian Tyrol. Menter was now a piano professor at the St. Petersburg Conservatory, and it was doubtless during this visit that Liszt agreed in principle to visit the imperial capital the following year if he received an official invitation to do so.[35] Innsbruck was the next stop on his leisurely perambulations towards Italy. He spent his seventy-fourth birthday there and was honoured with a celebration concert put on by the local male-voice choir.

X

Liszt and his group of students arrived in the Eternal City on October 25. He moved into the Alibert Hotel once again (this time for a period of eleven weeks), and resumed work on a composition that had occupied him intermittently for many years: his oratorio-in-progress, *St. Stanislas*. Liszt had begun to nourish the idea of writing an oratorio on the life and death of the first Polish saint as early as 1869, after reading the account of St. Stanislas in a poem by Lucien Siemienski. Carolyne herself had arranged the text, but Liszt was unhappy with the result, and across the years he had engaged a number of writers to make changes, the most recent being K. E. Edler in 1883, who had incorporated some newly discovered chronicles from the monastery of Ossiach, near Klagenfurt. *St. Stanislas* was conceived in six tableaux, on a scale that might have placed it alongside *Christus* and *St. Elisabeth* had it ever been completed.[36]

1. The Cry of the Oppressed
2. The King's Banquet
3. The Miracle of the Resuscitation

---

35. This invitation was actually issued less than three months later by Grand Duke Constantin, and Liszt promised to travel to Russia in April 1886. (See Liszt's letter to Menter on the topic, LLB, vol. 2, pp. 387–88.) The trip never materialized, however; Liszt extended his visits to Paris and London instead. (See p. 477.)

36. See RLS, vol. 2, pp. 141–44, for an account of the genesis of this oratorio.

4. The Curse

5. Martyrdom

6. Gloria in Excelsis

Liszt saw in the life of St. Stanislas one of the great themes of history: the struggle between church and state. He was particularly well fitted to deal with the topic, but it was not to be. Carolyne badgered him constantly about this work and blamed what she saw as the disruptive life-style he led in Weimar and Budapest as the reason for its non-appearance.[37] As early as the spring of 1884 Liszt had told Marie Hohenlohe that he hoped to have the score ready "by Pentecost of '85. . . . I write slowly—cross out three-quarters, and then do not know whether the fourth part can stand by itself."[38] But Pentecost came and went, and *St. Stanislas* remained nailed to his desk, fragmented. (The only sections that have ever been performed are the "Salve Polonia" [which began as a separate composition, in 1863], and a setting of Psalm 129 ["De Profundis," 1881], which Liszt planned to include as a requiem for King Boleslaw.)[39] Since it was unusual for him to experience "creative blocks," even in old age, we attribute his inability to complete this score not so much to the infirmities of the spirit as to those of the body. At the time of this sojourn in the Alibert Hotel he wrote to Olga von Meyendorff, "My weakness of sight is going from bad to worse. Soon I shall no longer be able to write."[40] An equally serious problem was his dropsy, which for the past three years had followed its relentless course. The build-up of fluids had changed the shape of his body, which had by now acquired the barrel-chested form so typical of this disease. Breathing had become laboured, and movement slow. Sufferers may carry up to twenty pounds of additional body weight, and this results in one of the worst symptoms of all: a feeling of fatigue at the slightest exertion, and the need to rest.

---

37. One can understand Carolyne's obsession with St. Stanislas, because his life was intertwined with Poland's destiny at a crucial point in its history. Appointed bishop of Cracow in 1072, Stanislas excommunicated the tyrannical King Boleslaw II, the Bold, was accused in turn by the royal court of treason, and was condemned to death by dismemberment. Because the knights who had been ordered to carry out the execution hesitated, Boleslaw killed Stanislas himself, and was eventually forced to flee to Hungary. Stanislas, whose alleged remains rest in Cracow cathedral, was canonized by Pope Innocent IV in 1253.

38. HLSW, p. 272. Liszt confided more details about his oratorio-in-progress to Marie Hohenlohe than to anyone else, perhaps because it appears to have been Marie who arranged for the scholar K. E. Edler to revise the libretto in light of the new discoveries at Ossiach. (See especially letters 196–98 in HLSW.) Marie received a private hearing of what Liszt called the "definitive" *Stanislas* on April 4, 1883, when Liszt passed through Vienna. It may well have been the case that much more of the oratorio was composed in his head than he had written down. It may also be the case that many more sketches exist than the few we presently know about.

39. What remains of the unpublished sketches may be consulted in the Weimar Archives. See Raabe no. 671.

40. WLLM, p. 489.

Liszt nonetheless continued to teach his pupils at the Alibert. The last time that Nadine Helbig heard him play was at one of these lessons. A young Neapolitan pupil, Luisa Cognetti, had just plodded her way through his transcription of Schubert's "Serenade." The performance was accurate, and even had bravura, but was dull. "Not like that!" he called out. "It must be simpler!" He then sat down and played the work himself. "It was simple, quiet and clear, like a beautiful moonlight night," wrote Helbig. "Then he let himself go for the last time, and we heard the cadenza like nightingales who burst into songs of longing and joy, of love, and exultation."[41] His own music seemed to be burdened with memories for him, some of them too painful to bear. He had long resisted hearing his *Vallée d'Obermann,* and whenever a student brought the piece he declined to hear it. But on one occasion, after he and his entourage had returned from a performance of Spontini's *Olympia* at the Sala Dante, he asked Göllerich to play it for him. As he listened, his emotions got the better of him and he broke into tears—as if the memories of experiences long repressed could no longer be contained.[42]

In January 1886 Liszt met the young Claude Debussy, who was at that time residing at the Villa Medici, enduring a reluctant incumbency as the winner of the Grand Prix de Rome. It was one of those moments in history about which so little is known that André de Ternant found it easy to fabricate some "memories" of the occasion which were widely accepted as genuine until recent times. But the following is certain. Ernest Hébert, the director of the French Academy, invited Liszt to dine with him at the villa on January 8, 1886 (the menu was "dictated" in advance to the kitchen staff by the ever-watchful Princess Carolyne). Present with Hébert were three scholars-in-residence: Paul Vidal, Odilon Redon, and the twenty-three-year-old Claude Debussy. Four days earlier a piano had been installed at the villa in readiness for the occasion, and after dinner Debussy and Vidal performed for Liszt his *Faust* Symphony, during which, we learn, Liszt fell asleep![43] The following day, Debussy and Vidal, in the company of Hébert, went over to see Liszt at the Hotel Alibert, which lay conveniently close to the villa. This may have been the occasion on which they played Chabrier's *Trois Valses romantiques* for two pianos to Liszt, who at that time had heard no keyboard music by this composer.[44] On January 13, Liszt returned once more to the villa for dinner, and this time Debussy and the others had the pleasure of hearing him play his *Au bord d'une source* and his transcription of Schubert's "Ave Maria."[45] In later life Debussy recalled that

---

41. HLR, p. 180. Helbig's reference to a cadenza suggests that the piece was "Hark, Hark, the Lark!," also described as a "Serenade."
42. GL, p. 119.
43. LAV, p. 21.
44. RGPR, p. 60.
45. LAV, p. 21.

Liszt used the pedal sparingly, "like a form of breathing." The connection between the young Debussy and the elderly Liszt rested on at least three substantial meetings and was not the fleeting encounter we are sometimes led to
believe. And Liszt's prescience in electing to play his *Au bord d'une source* to Debussy, the later master of musical impressionism, provides historians with a further, happy proof that one thing may indeed lead to another.

Liszt had celebrated New Year's Eve with a whist-party for his pupils in
Rome. In the middle of the game the clock in his study had stopped ticking.
"That is a bad sign," Liszt remarked. "One of us will certainly die next year!"[46]
The day following, New Year's Day, 1886, fell on a Friday. Liszt observed that
his next birthday would also be celebrated on a Friday. Always superstitious, he
regarded this coincidence of days and dates as a bad omen, and greeted Göllerich with the words: "This will be an unlucky year for me."[47] These premonitions weighed heavily on him. A farewell concert was given by his pupils at
the Palazzo Barca, and Liszt set out for Budapest on January 21. As the train
pulled out of Rome's railway station, and his Italian students waved goodbye,
he leaned out of the window of his second-class compartment and raised his
arm as if in a benediction. It was his final parting from the Eternal City.

---

46. GL, p. 122.
47. Ibid.

Liszt's Last Visit to England, April 1886

For years [Walter Bache] has sacrificed money for the performance of my works in London. Several times I advised him against it, but he answered imperturbably: "That is my business!"

FRANZ LISZT[1]

I

As the year 1886 approached, and with it the seventy-fifth anniversary of Liszt's birth, concerts were arranged in various parts of the world to celebrate the event. It became clear to him that he could not possibly accept all the invitations which were showered on him, some of which came from as far away as St. Petersburg. But one invitation he did accept. His English pupil Walter Bache had long been pressing him to come to London, and Liszt felt that he must repay the great debt that he owed to Bache by returning to the English capital. For years Bache had been mounting annual Liszt concerts at his own expense, and Liszt knew that whatever standing he had in London as a composer was due in large measure to this disciple. In November 1885 there was an exchange of correspondence in which Liszt told Bache that his invitation took precedence over all others; and on November 26, in a further letter, he informed Bache: "It is fixed then: Thursday, 8 April, *Ricevimento* at Walter Bache's house."[2] That was all that Bache required to begin arranging what would turn out to be three weeks of festivities the following April, with two strikingly successful performances of *St. Elisabeth* as the centrepiece.

As word spread of Liszt's decision to come to London, various invitations flowed in—from the Philharmonic Society, from the Royal Academy of

---

1. LLB, vol. 7, p. 438.
2. LLB, vol. 2, published only in Constance Bache's English translation of Liszt's letters, p. 478.

477

Music, from Buckingham Palace. There was talk that Liszt might even consent to give a recital, but he soon scotched that idea in a further letter to Bache.

> My very dear friend:
>   They seem determined in London to push me to the piano. I cannot allow this to happen in public, as my seventy-five-year-old fingers are no longer suited to it, and Bülow, Saint-Saëns, Rubinstein, and you, dear Bache, play my compositions much better than what is left of my humble self.
>   Perhaps it would be opportune if friend Hueffer would have the kindness to let the public know, by a short announcement, that Liszt only ventures to appear as a grateful visitor, and neither in London nor anywhere else as a man with an interest in his fingers.
>   In all friendship yours,
>
>   F. Liszt
>   Budapest,
>
>   February 11, 1886[3]

Liszt left Budapest one month later. On March 11 he was accompanied to the railway station by a group of his students and caught the night train to Vienna. It was an emotional parting, since several of them seemed to realise that they might not see their master again. Liszt's long, leisurely journey to London took him through Liège and Antwerp, and thence to Paris, where he arrived on March 20. He stayed at the Hôtel de Calais, in rooms that were buried beneath floral bouquets from friends and well-wishers across the city. For much of the time he was a guest of Mihály Munkácsy and his wife, Cécile, at their palatial residence on the avenue de Villiers, and it was here that Munkácsy began painting his celebrated portrait of Liszt seated at the keyboard. On March 22, Madame Munkácsy gave a dinner for Liszt whose guests included distinguished representatives from the ranks of politics, society, and the arts. One of the chief reasons for his visit to Paris was to attend a performance of his "Gran" Mass, which took place in the church of Saint-Eustache on March 25, under the direction of Edouard Colonne. He also spent time with Emile Ollivier; on March 27 they attended a performance of Massenet's opera *Le Cid* in the company of Ollivier's twenty-three-year-old son, Daniel. Sitting in the audience was Giuseppe Verdi. It would be pleasant to record that history was made that evening. Alas, because of other social engagements Liszt's party only arrived in time for the last act, and since the two great composers occupied different boxes they were not introduced; they may not even have seen one an-

---

3. LLB, vol. 2, p. 389.

ÉGLISE SAINT-EUSTACHE

Jeudi 25 mars 1886, à midi très précis

MESSE DES ÉCOLES

CHRETIENNES LIBRES DU 2ᵉ ARRONDISSEMENT

Entrée (Grand Orgue).— PRÉLUDE ET FUGUE sur le nom B.A.C.H.

Ces lettres correspondent aux notes si *b,* la, do, si. — **Franz LISZT**
exécutée par M. HENRY DALLIER.

MESSE SOLENNELLE DE GRAN
COMPOSÉE PAR

Franz LISZT

1.		**Kyrie**	Andante solenne.
2.	A	**Gloria in excelsis.**	Andante ma non troppo.
	B	**Qui tollis**	Adagio ma non troppo.
	C	**Quoniam.**	Allegro mosso.
3.		**Credo**	Andante maestoso.

Offertoire (grand orgue). - MARCHE PAPALE - (Franz LISZT)
Exécutée par M. HENRI DALLIER

4.	**Sanctus**	Andante solenne.
5.	**Benedictus.**	Andante con pieta.
6.	**Agnus Dei.**	Adagio non troppo.

Sortie (Grand Orgue).- MARCHE DES FIANÇAILLES de LOHENGRIN
Transcription par **Franz LISZT** exécutée par M. HENRI DALLIER

L'Orchestre et les Chœurs composés de 400 exécutants seront dirigés
par M. Ed. COLONNE

Les soli seront chantés par MM. **ESCALAIS, AUGUEZ,** VEYRET, DELAHÈGUE, DAGENY

L'orgue d'accompagnement sera tenu par M. BLONDEL

CHEFS DE CHANT :

MM. STEENMAN,	maître de Chapelle de Saint-Eustache.	
BELNOT,	—	Saint-Sulpice.
MINART,	—	Saint-Germain-des-Prés.
PÉRON,	—	Saint-Roch.
PICKAERT,	—	Notre-Dame-des-Victoires.
SCHMELTZ,	—	Saint-Lambert de Vaugirard.
ALFRED FOCK, chef des chœurs des concerts Colonne.		

Franz LISZT présidera cette cérémonie.

Pour se procurer des entrées dans les nefs on peut s'adresser à la
Loueuse des chaises de Saint-Eustache et aux éditeurs de musique.

PARIS. — IMP. CHAIX. — 6870-6.

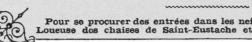

Liszt in Paris, a handbill for a performance of the "Gran" Mass, March 25, 1886.

other in the darkened theatre. This was the closest that they came to making a personal acquaintance. After promising to return to Paris on his way back from London, Liszt resumed his journey to the British capital. When he came to settle the hotel bill, he was touched to learn that his account had already been paid by the firm of Erard.

11

Liszt set out from Paris on April 3 at 11:00 a.m., accompanied by Bernhard Stavenhagen and Cécile Munkácsy. By early afternoon they had reached Calais, where they were met by the conductor Alexander Mackenzie and Alfred Littleton of Novello and Co. Together the little party crossed the English Channel to Dover, where they found Walter Bache awaiting them. There they boarded the Continental express train, which normally travelled non-stop to Victoria Station, London. On this occasion, however, the train was brought to a halt at Penge in order to allow Liszt and his party to alight.[4] Crowded into the waiting-room of the tiny railway station was a group of his friends and admirers. As Liszt entered, one of the ladies strewed the floor with flowers, and Ferdinand Ráth, the vice-chairman of the London Hungarian Association, came forward and made a short speech of welcome in French and Hungarian,[5] to which Liszt replied "in appropriate terms," as one newspaper put it. Liszt and his friends then got into their carriages and proceeded to Westwood House, Sydenham, where he stayed as a guest of Henry Littleton (head of the music-publishing firm Novello & Co.) for the duration of his sojourn in London. Although it was already 8:00 p.m. by the time Liszt reached Westwood House, a great reception was held in his honour that same evening, at which several hundred guests were assembled to meet him. As he entered the large music-room he was greeted by a burst of applause. Many of England's best-known musicians were present—Sir George Grove, Sir Arthur Sullivan, Charles Hallé, August Manns—as well as Alexander Mackenzie, John Stainer, Carl Rosa, Edward Dannreuther, and many others. Among the aristocracy present were Count Moritz Esterházy, Count Metternich, and the German ambassador to England.[6] After mingling with the crowd in the friendliest fashion, and renewing some of his old acquaintances, Liszt settled himself in a chair near the platform to enjoy the concert that had

---

4. This, in the words of *The Musical Times,* was accomplished through "the great kindness of Mr. Forbes, the Chairman of the London, Chatham and Dover Railway." (Issue of May 1, 1886, p. 253)

5. *The Times,* Monday, April 5, 1886. From this article we learn that the reception arranged for Liszt at Victoria Station had been cancelled at the last minute, because he had alighted unexpectedly at Penge. Not to be outdone, Ráth and a few Hungarian supporters had rushed from Victoria to Penge and had greeted Liszt there instead.

6. A larger guest-list may be found in the *Times* article of April 5, cited above.

been arranged in his honour. Several artists took part, including Walter Bache and Frederic Lamond. Everyone longed for Liszt himself to play, but he refused on grounds of fatigue, and shortly after ten he retired to his room. He had been up for sixteen hours and was exhausted.

III

Liszt had last set foot on Albion's shores in 1841, some forty-five years earlier. England was now a vastly different country, and London a vastly different city. At the time of his earlier visit, the British capital was little more than a conglomeration of villages—Hampstead, Chelsea, Chalk Farm, Swiss Cottage, and Battersea—linked by a network of charming country lanes across open fields. The railways were still in their infancy, and travel through the provinces was problematic. (Liszt's colourful tour of the British Isles in 1840–41 had provided plenty of evidence of that.) Queen Victoria had only recently ascended the throne, her glorious reign still before her. As for music, the profession was held in low esteem, its practitioners regarded as little better than social misfits.[7] The Germans were not wrong to describe the England of that time as "das Land ohne Musik." Forty-five years later, Britain was the most powerful nation in the world, and London the wealthiest and largest capital. The city's population had more than doubled in size and stood at nearly five million souls. Moreover, its musical life had been transformed. It now boasted several very good orchestras and choirs, a permanent opera house, and no fewer than five colleges of music.[8] England was also an increasingly literate society with a large number of national newspapers and professional journals, in which musical events were often given a lot of coverage. It is thanks to the English newspapers, in fact, that Liszt's last visit to London remains one of the best-documented periods of his career. Long before his arrival it had been turned into a "media event," and there was a great deal of false speculation about what he would do. Much of it centred on his piano-playing, which in England, as elsewhere, had long since passed into legend. One journal had confidently announced that Liszt was to give "seven pianoforte recitals of an historic character. The programmes will include music illustrative of olden times and later ones."[9] There

---

7. See Volume One, pp. 353–63, and Volume Two, p. 250, n. 74, for a fuller account of musical life in England during the 1840s and '50s.
8. The Royal Academy of Music (1822), the London Academy of Music (1861–1939), the Trinity College of Music (1872), the Royal College of Music (1883), and the Guildhall School of Music and Drama (1880).
9. *The Musical Opinion*, January 1, 1886, p. 181. Perhaps the writer was confusing Liszt with Anton Rubinstein, whose famous "historical recitals" took place in London one month after Liszt had left the city.

was not a word of truth in the report, but it had helped to fan the flames of curiosity. Needless to add, Liszt *did* play the piano while he was in London, and he played it frequently. Nor was there any great contradiction here; whenever he played, it was not because he was obliged to, but because he wanted to. His piano-playing, in brief, had to remain within his gift, a privilege to be offered or withdrawn as he liked. It was his way of repaying the kindness of the many people he met, both in public and in private.

There was a great deal of his music to be heard during this visit. But more than one newspaper voiced the view that the very fascination that the great public had with Liszt's personality could well divert attention away from his works, and to a large extent that is what happened. Whenever he appeared in the concert hall he was fêted and cheered, but the various performances of his music, so laboriously arranged by Walter Bache and others, tended to be eclipsed by his presence. On April 12, *The Times* already noted that "ovations such as those offered to Liszt have never before been witnessed in musical England. . . . Even outside the hall the composer's arrival was always waited for by crowds who raised their hats to him as if he were a king." In such an atmosphere of hero-worship, which at times bordered on hysteria, that calm assessment of his music so long denied him in England was not really possible.

IV

It is only when we follow Liszt's English itinerary in detail that we really appreciate what a major physical effort it involved for him, one that would have put many a younger man to shame. There were some who questioned the wisdom of subjecting the ageing composer to so much stress; Bache himself came under criticism for not taking Liszt's frail health into account.[10] It is true that Liszt tired easily; moreover, his swollen legs made it impossible to move around with his former agility. On the other hand, he had no set duties, and he could have withdrawn from his social engagements at any time. His sole function in England was to show himself to the great public and bask in the adulation of his many admirers.

Liszt's first public appearance took place on Monday, April 5, when he attended the final rehearsals of *St. Elisabeth* in St. James's Hall, at the invitation of Alexander Mackenzie. For several weeks this young Scottish conductor had been rehearsing the choir and the orchestra, and he was anxious to get Liszt's opinion of his interpretation of the oratorio. By the time Liszt got to the hall, more than fifteen hundred people had crowded into the auditorium to catch a glimpse of the living legend. It was an augury of things to come. The British

---

10. HME, p. 136.

public, it seemed, was determined to compensate for the disastrous reception they had accorded Liszt the last time he was in their capital, in 1841. Despite the presence of so many people in the hall, Liszt managed to find a coign of vantage near the platform, from which he offered words of advice and encouragement to Mackenzie. That same evening, Liszt went to Neumeyer Hall in order to observe an additional rehearsal for the choir alone. He then journeyed back to Westwood House in the horse and carriage that Henry Littleton had placed at his disposal.

V

Tuesday, April 6, was one of Liszt's busiest days. In the afternoon he visited the Royal Academy of Music in order to attend the inaugural ceremony for the newly established Liszt Scholarship, which was intended to help young composers and pianists and was to be awarded through an open competition. Thanks largely to the efforts of Walter Bache, the very large sum of eleven hundred pounds had been raised.[11] As Liszt entered the academy's concert hall in the company of the principal, Sir George Macfarren, the assembled students raised a cheer, and Liszt was presented with a large floral lyre arranged in the national colours of Hungary. In the concert that followed, which was played entirely by the students, Liszt's music was combined with that of British composers associated with the academy. The programme began with Liszt's Goethe Festival March; Miss Dora Bright then played Sterndale Bennett's Caprice for Piano and Orchestra; then came Mackenzie's Violin Concerto, played by Miss Winifred Robinson; while Mr. William Shakespeare conducted the academy orchestra in a performance of Macfarren's Overture to *John the Baptist*. A key-

---

11. Mention has already been made of the pioneering work that Bache did in helping to secure Liszt's reputation in England, work that covered a span of almost a quarter-century. A complete set of his annual concert programmes is preserved in the Bodleian Library (17402, e. 59). These concerts ran for twenty-three years, from 1865 to 1888. They are a tribute to his devotion to the Liszt cause; in fact, they are indispensable to anyone interested in the history of "Liszt reception" in Britain in the nineteenth century. At first Bache held his concerts in the Queen's Concert Rooms, Hanover Square. As they gained a following, they were transferred (in 1873) to the more imposing St. James's Hall. Since their primary purpose was to introduce the British public to the music of Liszt, they featured not only his piano music but his orchestral, choral, and solo vocal music as well.

The cost of these concerts was borne entirely by Bache himself. He paid for the hall, for the orchestral players, for the soloists, for the programmes, and for newspaper advertisements. The evangelical zeal which he brought to his task was worthy of this son of a Unitarian minister, and it took a variety of forms. First there were the lavish programme notes, illustrated with copious music examples. These were not the usual sort of pamphlets into which the audience might gently retreat whenever it got bored with whatever was happening on the platform. Rather they were major analytical tracts which were meant to drive out ignorance and prejudice, and which were there to be studied at leisure, long after the programme was over. On at least two occasions, these "notes" took the form of

board work of Liszt was also included: the Concert Study in D-flat major ("Sospiro"), played by one Septimus Webbe.

At the end of the programme the applause showed no signs of abating, so Liszt got to his feet to acknowledge it, hesitated for a moment, and then walked slowly towards the platform. Flowers rained on him from all sides, with the consequence that when he got to the piano he found it half full of blossoms and had to wait until the strings were cleared. Liszt then began to caress the keys of the instrument, and out of his preliminary improvisation there arose a performance of one of his *Chants polonaises,* followed by his *Cantique d'amour.* The audience was mesmerized by his playing, which was mostly soft, rarely rising in volume above *forte,* but crystal clear and without any affectation. Many a young student who heard Liszt that afternoon took the memory of his playing to the grave. In the words of one of them, the composer and writer Orsmond Anderton: "No piano has ever sounded the same to me, before or since."[12]

After Liszt had finished playing there followed a short presentation ceremony, in which Sir George Macfarren made a speech of thanks. Liszt, he told the audience, had retired at the zenith of his powers. In this, he went on, he was like another famous man, the Duke of Wellington, who, when he had no more battles to fight, had gone on to prove himself as great a statesman as he had been a warrior. After that, Walter Bache handed an envelope to Liszt (which contained details of the Liszt scholarship), who in turn handed it to Sir George, to the accompaniment of sustained cheering from the students. With that, the ceremonials were concluded.[13]

---

a major essay about Liszt by Frederick Niecks; the famous Berlin theorist and Liszt enthusiast Carl Weitzmann also contributed an essay. Second, there were the distinguished "supporting artists" hired by Bache to arouse the curiosity of the public and make it easier for them to swallow the music of Liszt: personalities of the calibre of Hans von Bülow, Karl Klindworth, August Manns, and Edward Dannreuther. Finally, there were the frequent edicts to the public itself, which throw a good deal of light on the Philistine nature of the London audiences of those days. On February 25, 1875, for example, Bache found it necessary to remind his audience that there would be "an interval of three minutes, during which all who do not wish to hear the last piece are requested to leave the hall." The "last piece" on this occasion was the Overture to Wagner's *Tannhäuser.* Perhaps it was the failure of his audience to avail themselves of this pause, and to continue to regard the music itself as a noise which would drown out whatever disturbance was created as people made for the doors, that led Bache to issue some further instructions:

> The time-honoured custom of treating as an "out-voluntary" whatever may have the misfortune to stand last on a concert programme, is most discouraging to those interested in its worthy performance. It is therefore respectfully suggested that those who do not wish to remain until the end of the concert, should leave during any of the intervals which necessarily follow each piece.

Deserters, in short, would be closely watched.

12. WLC, p. 87.

13. The full significance of Liszt's visit to the Royal Academy of Music is generally forgotten today. At that time, his name was not held in particularly high esteem there, and Sir George (a musical conservative) had often gone out of his way to attack the progressive elements in Liszt's music. The fact

VI

From the Royal Academy Liszt went over to Bache's home just off Dorset Square, for a quiet dinner with him and his sister, Constance.[14] This gave him a chance to rest before the evening performance of *St. Elisabeth,* the centre-piece of the London festivities. Constance had turned up at her brother's house with a large basket of roses, tied together with the Hungarian colours— an allusion to the "Miracle of the Roses" scene from *St. Elisabeth.* After din-ner, the little party went over to St. James's Hall to hear Alexander Mackenzie direct the first complete performance of this oratorio in England.[15] As the composer entered the hall, the audience burst into applause, and many stood on their seats to get a better glimpse of the venerable figure. Such spontaneous behaviour had not been witnessed in a Victorian concert-hall within living memory. A combined chorus and orchestra of 350 performers had been as-sembled for this event, which had been eagerly awaited for several weeks. Since this was one of the popular "Novello Oratorio Concerts," the text was sung in English, in a translation by Constance Bache. Among the distin-guished principals were Emma Albani (St. Elisabeth), Pauline Cramer (Landgravine Sophie), and Charles Santley (Landgrave Ludwig). By the inter-mission it was clear that the performance was going exceptionally well. The Prince of Wales went round to Liszt's box to congratulate him and took him away to introduce him to the princess. At the end of the evening Liszt re-ceived one of the greatest ovations of his career. He stood in the middle of the orchestra while players, singers, and listeners created a storm of applause. Liszt was especially impressed with Albani, whom he showered with compliments. Everyone agreed, however, that the true hero of the evening was Mackenzie,

---

that the ceremony took place at all, and did so with the blessing and full support of Macfarren, was due in no small measure to the tireless efforts of Walter Bache, who was a professor of piano there.

Incidentally, the competition for the first Liszt Scholarship took place the following year. The jury consisted of Macfarren, Mackenzie (who was soon to take over Macfarren's job as principal), and Ed-ward Dannreuther. The first prize-winner was Grace Mary Henshaw, a pupil of Bache. After Bache's unexpected death in March 1888, a sum of 500 pounds was collected by his friends and added to the parent fund. The fund was further enriched by money left by Bache in his will, and the scholarship was thenceforth known as the Liszt-Bache Scholarship.

14. Constance Bache, like her brothers, Edward and Walter, had been trained as a pianist (under Klind-worth), but after sustaining an injury to her hand she had to abandon all thought of a concert career. With great determination she turned herself into a musicologist, and later became well known as the English translator of letters by Hans von Bülow and Liszt. Her book *Brother Musicians,* about the ca-reers of Edward and Walter, contains many useful descriptions of Liszt's last visit to England.

15. There had been two earlier performances of *St. Elisabeth* in London, both of them incomplete. The first took place in 1870, at a New Philharmonic Concert under the direction of Dr. Henry Wylde; and the second on February 24, 1876, directed by Walter Bache.

who had worked wonders with the forces at his disposal. (In his memoirs, written many years later, the only thing that Mackenzie could clearly recall about the performance was that "the unusual height of one of the soloists caused my baton to come into contact with her headgear with unexpected consequences.")[16] Mackenzie realised that such a success could not be allowed to go by default, and a second performance of *St. Elisabeth* was hurriedly planned for April 17, this time at the Crystal Palace.

VII

The next day, April 7, Liszt set out for Windsor Castle in answer to a summons from Queen Victoria. They had first met forty-six years earlier, at Buckingham Palace, during his heyday as a touring virtuoso. Not long afterwards, it will be recalled, he had met her again, at the unveiling of the Beethoven Monument in Bonn. Both of them had retained a vivid recollection of these earlier encounters. The queen herself left the following account of the reunion.

> After luncheon we went to the Red Drawing-room, where we saw the celebrated Abbé Liszt, whom I had not seen for 43 years [sic], and who, from having then been a very wild phantastic looking man, was now a quiet benevolent looking old Priest, with long white hair, and scarcely any teeth. We asked him to play, which he did, several of his own compositions. He played beautifully. He is 76 [sic], and before leaving England in a few days, is going to sit to [Edgar] Boehm for his Bust.[17]

Liszt began with an improvisation on themes from *St. Elisabeth*. As his hands wandered up and down the keyboard, he may have thought back to the last occasion he had played in that room, to King George IV, in 1824. He had been a boy of twelve then, in the company of his father, and on the brink of a shining career. Now he was a venerable abbé, and almost at the end of his life. At the queen's request, he played "The Miracle of the Roses"; then he launched into a Hungarian Rhapsody, and concluded his little concert with a performance of Chopin's Nocturne in B-flat minor, Op. 9. Later that day the queen wrote: "We have just heard Liszt, who is such a fine old man. He came down here and played four pieces beautifully. What an exquisite touch!"[18] Before he

---

16. MMN, p. 151.
17. RA. Unpublished diary entry for April 7, 1886.
18. RA. Unpublished letter to Crown Princess Victoria (later Empress of Germany), dated April 7, 1886.

left Windsor, the queen presented him with a marble bust of herself, sculpted by Edgar Boehm. It bears the inscription: "Presented to Dr. Fr. Liszt by Queen Victoria, in remembrance of his visit to Windsor, April 7, 1886."

VIII

The biggest reception of Liszt's sojourn in London took place on Thursday, April 8, at the Grosvenor Gallery. This event was put on at the personal expense of Walter Bache, who had planned it with care. About four hundred guests had been invited to the "Conversazione," as Bache termed it, representing music, art, literature, medicine, and the Church.[19] Bache had also arranged an informal concert of Liszt's music, consisting of the following programme:

> "Angelus" for stringed instruments
> Chorus of Angels from *Faust* (sung by female students of
> the Royal Academy)
> Settings of Liszt's Schiller songs
> *Bénédiction de Dieu dans la solitude* (played by Bache)

All the musicians donated their services, including the orchestral players, who were the pick of the best London orchestras. This, too, was Bache's doing. The previous month, he had sent out a circular letter appealing to them for support, and they had responded generously.[20] At the end of the concert, Liszt acknowledged the musicians, turned to the assembled company with a bow, and then made his way towards the piano. He sat down and played his arrangement of Schubert's *Divertissement hongroise* and one of his own Hungarian Rhapsodies. Sir George Grove, who was in the audience, later wrote:

---

19. Constance Bache gives a fairly comprehensive guest-list in BBM, pp. 298–99. She was indignant that a number of people behaved as though it were a public concert instead of a private-invitation party, and she noted that there were some gate-crashers.
20. Bache wrote the musicians:

> For the performance of the "Angelus," the cooperation of twelve violins (1st and 2nd), four violas, four violincelli and four contrabasses is desirable. The necessary rehearsal will take place at the Grosvenor Gallery, New Bond Street, at *one o'clock* on Thursday, April 8.
>
> I now venture to suggest to yourself that it will be a *very great compliment* to the composer of the "Angelus"—and one which he will not fail to appreciate—if you will take part in its performance.
>
> My suggestion is an unusual one: but so is the cause prompting it: neither one nor the other is likely to recur. I do not ask a favour on my own behalf—but desire to ascertain whether you are able and willing to give this important help to our efforts to receive Liszt with that heartiness and cordiality which have invariably marked his treatment of others. (BBM, p. 285)

I went to Liszt's reception on Thursday and was delighted (1) by his playing, so calm, clear, correct, refined—so entirely unlike the style of the so-called "Liszt School," (2) by his face. Directly he sat down he dismissed that very artificial smile, which he always wears, and his face assumed the most beautiful serene look with enormous power and repose in it. It was quite a wonderful sight.[21]

A crowning event of the evening occurred when Liszt was re-united with Joseph Joachim, who was giving concerts in London and had been invited by Bache to the reception. Their historic handshake, witnessed by the artistic elite of London, was published in *The Graphic* a few days later. It symbolised for everyone present that the old enmities between them were now dead.[22]

The following evening the composer was back at St. James's Hall for an all-Liszt concert conducted by Albert Randegger. Emil Bach appeared as soloist in the E-flat-major Concerto, while Liza Lehmann sang a selection of songs; the purely orchestral items consisted of the symphonic poem *Orpheus* and the "March of the Three Holy Kings" from *Christus*. Although the hour was late, Liszt accepted an invitation from the Prince of Wales to go over to Prince's Hall for the last of the so-called "smoking concerts" of the Royal Amateur Orchestral Society. Liszt sat next to the prince and heard the orchestra play pieces by Beethoven and Rossini. From the standpoint of posterity, the most interesting event of that "smoker" was the appearance of Vladimir de Pachmann playing piano solos by Henselt and Liszt himself. It was, in the words of one reporter, a jovial evening in which the abbé "showed himself thoroughly smoke-proof."[23]

One of the most notable all-Liszt concerts took place on Saturday afternoon at the Crystal Palace, under the direction of August Manns. As Liszt arrived at the hall, a group of cab-drivers doffed their hats and addressed him as "Habby Liszt." As *The Times* noted a day or two later, these characters had never heard a note of his music, and would probably be none the wiser if that privilege had been accorded to them.[24] But they were rivetted by the mesmeric personality of the old man with the white hair and clerical collar, who was now the talk of London. Manns was no stranger to Liszt's music. For several years he had in-

---

21. GLL, pp. 311–12.

22. *The Graphic,* April 17, 1886, p. 415. The divisions created by the "War of the Romantics" were not yet entirely bridged, however. By one of those strange coincidences, Clara Schumann was also in London at this time giving concerts of her own, and she did not come to this reception. "It would have been [pleasant] to see the two great pianists in amicable converse together, or to watch Herr Joachim leading the violins in the *Angelus* at Mr. Bache's conversazione," remarked one observer (HME, pp. 145–46), an indication that the poisoned relations between Liszt and Madame Schumann were common knowledge in England.

23. *Musical Times,* May 1, 1886, p. 257.

24. April 12, 1886.

cluded Liszt's orchestral works in his popular Saturday-afternoon concerts, but on this occasion he surpassed himself.

> *Rákóczy* March
> Symphonic Poem *Les Préludes*
> Ballade: "Die Lorelei"
>   (soloist: Liza Lehmann)
> Piano Concerto No. 1 in E-flat major
>   (soloist: Bernhard Stavenhagen)
> Symphonic Poem *Mazeppa*
> Songs
>   "Es muss ein Wunderbares sein"
>   "Angiolin dal biondo crin"
>   (soloist: Liza Lehmann)
> Piano solos
>   *Liebestraum* No. 1 in A-flat major
>   Fantasy on *Les Huguenots*
>   (soloist: Stavenhagen)
> Hungarian Rhapsody No. 4 in D minor
>   (orchestral version)

This concert featured the London debut of Stavenhagen, who, according to *The Times,* played with "sensational brilliancy of execution."[25] Certainly, it aroused great expectations for the young man's solo recital in Prince's Hall the following Friday.

IX

On Sunday, April 11, Liszt was fêted by the English aristocracy. Auguste, Duchess of Cambridge (who was now eighty-eight years old, yet still retained a lively recollection of her first encounter with Liszt, in 1841), insisted that he call on her at St. James's Palace, and she sent her household comptroller, Major-General Fulke-Greville, to invite him in person. One of her entourage recorded some details of the visit.

> Liszt came in at a quarter-to-eight. He had been here but five min-
> utes when came P.T, P.M, & May.[26] Liszt must indeed be strangely

---

25. Ibid.
26. P.T. = the Duke of Teck; P.M. = the Duchess of Teck (formerly Princess Mary of Cambridge); and May = Princess Mary of Teck, the future Queen Mary of England.

altered from when he was young! He has now grown large, & his rugged massive face is disfigured by *several very* large warts! Yet undoubtedly a clever, interesting head! The abnormally *long* (quite down on the shoulders) thick snow-white hair, & therewith quite black eyebrows make a very curious effect—he was very pleasant and agreeable & played two pieces—to *perfection* is but half to express it!—with the most exquisite & *delicious* softness! unutterably lovely. At a quarter-past eight he and the Tecks went off to dine at Marlborough H[ouse]![27]

At Marlborough House Liszt was greeted by the Prince and Princess of Wales, and joined about twenty other guests mostly from the upper aristocracy, for dinner. Afterwards he again charmed everybody with his piano-playing.[28]

The following afternoon, Monday, April 12, the Hungarian Association of London arranged a reception for Liszt in the home of their president, Dr. Theodore Duka, at Nevern Square. Duka had been a political refugee from the 1849 uprising and was now an English citizen. Once again Liszt was prevailed upon to play, although his programme remains unknown. The audience contained many Hungarians, however, and *The Musical Times* noted that "his playing was listened to with almost greedy satisfaction."[29] From there, Liszt found his way to the so-called Monday Popular Concerts, where he heard his compatriot Joachim take part in performances of Beethoven's *Kreutzer* Sonata (with Charles Hallé at the piano) and the first "Rasoumowsky" quartet. Although Liszt was there simply to listen, he was, in the words of *The Musical Times,* as much a part of the entertainment as the music itself.

One of the most interesting engagements took place on Wednesday, April 14, when he was taken to see the actor Henry Irving in *Faust* at the Lyceum Theatre. He was accompanied by Mr. and Mrs. Littleton, Cécile Munkácsy, and Stavenhagen. Since Liszt was now the object of universal curiosity and had become the target of autograph-hunters, interviewers, and plain publicity-seekers, some extraordinary precautions were taken to protect him from their attentions. He and his party were given a box whose door was nailed shut; en-

27. RA. Unpublished journal of Lady Geraldine Somerset, lady-in-waiting to the Duchess of Cambridge.
28. According to the engagement diary of the Prince of Wales (later King Edward VII), the guests included the following: the Duchess of Teck and the Princess Mary of Teck; the Duke of Connaught; Louise, Princess of Wales; the Russian ambassador and Madame de Staal; the Italian ambassador, Count Corti; Lord and Lady Gosford; Lord and Lady de Grey; Lady Cadogan; Lady Suffield; Baron F. Rothschild; Mr. A. de Rothschild; the Hon. H. T. Wilson and Mr. Boehm. (RA, unpublished) The information that Liszt played the piano during this dinner-party comes to us from the engagement diary of the Princess of Wales, although she fails to tell us what he played. (RA, unpublished)
29. *The Musical Times,* May 1, 1886, p. 258.

Liszt with his pupil Bernhard Stavenhagen in London, April 1886.

trance and exit could be made only via the Royal Box next door, the key to which was held by Littleton. Nevertheless, word soon spread through the darkened theatre that Liszt was present, and during an entr'acte the orchestra played one of his Hungarian marches. At the end of the play, Irving took him to the famous Beefsteak Room for supper, where Liszt sat next to Ellen Terry. Irving had arranged to have some of Liszt's favourite dishes served—lentil pudding, lamb cutlets, and mushrooms in batter. Afterwards, Stavenhagen played the piano. Bram Stoker, the author of *Dracula*, was present and left a memoir of the occasion.[30] Apparently, the uncanny likeness between Liszt and the much younger actor (Irving was forty-eight at the time) was remarked by all. Even though they knew very little of one another's language, an animated conversation broke out between the pair, reinforced by much gesticulation, which the others found fascinating, and the party did not break up until four in the morning. But Liszt was up and about a few hours later, joining Irving and some other friends at Baroness Burdett-Coutts's residence in Stratton Street for lunch.[31]

X

From Stratton Street Liszt must have gone straight to Frederic Lamond's recital in St. James's Hall, which we know he attended on the afternoon of Thursday, April 15. The seventeen-year-old Lamond had recently returned from his studies with Liszt in Weimar, and he was now in the middle of a series of recitals which were making the critics sit up and take notice. *The Musical Times* had described the first of them (on March 30) as "so fairly astounding that if reason rocked upon her throne there would have been plentiful excuse for it. To find such a mere lad in the possession of such Herculean powers was sufficient to make musicians believe that the millennium was at hand." At the request of all his friends Lamond had moved into St. James's Hall for his fourth concert, which he had invited Liszt to attend. His recital was made up of a formidable series of pieces:

---

30. SPR(2), pp. 145–48.
31. Lady Burdett-Coutts had thoughtfully arranged to have the piano removed from her reception room so that Liszt would not be burdened with requests to play. Liszt could not help observing its absence. "I see that you have no pianos in these rooms!" The baroness explained to her famous guest that she only wanted to protect him from trivial requests. "But I would like some music," Liszt insisted; so the piano was wheeled back into its usual place by the servants. A singer, Antoinette Sterling, sang some ballads, to everybody's delight. " 'Now I will play!,' said Liszt. And he did! It was magnificent and never to be forgotten." (SPR(2), pp. 147–48)

Toccata and Fugue in D minor	Bach–Tausig
Sonata in F minor, Op. 57	Beethoven
(*Appassionata*)	
Fantasy in F minor, Op. 49	Chopin
Klavierstücke, Op. 76	Brahms
Transcendental Studies	Liszt
Harmonies du soir	
Feux-follets	
Mazeppa	
Liebestraum	
Hungarian Rhapsody No. 9	
("Pesther Carnival")	
Fantasia and Fugue	Raff
Impromptu in F major	Lamond
Valse	Nicholas Rubinstein

Unfortunately, Liszt arrived at the hall late, and Lamond was already well into the middle of the programme as the master took his seat. When they spotted the familiar white-haired figure, the audience rose and cheered. In the words of one newspaper reporter, it "disturbed the smooth sequence of events. . . . Fortunately, Mr. Lamond did not lose his nerve, though he certainly looked anxiously round at the master at the conclusion of each piece." At the end of the recital Lamond was recalled twice, and Liszt stood up and bowed towards his young protégé.

    A similar scene took place the following evening, April 16, in Prince's Hall, when Bernhard Stavenhagen made his London début. Once again Liszt was in the audience to lend his blessing to the occasion. Unlike Lamond, Stavenhagen had chosen an all-Liszt programme.

> *Funérailles (October 1849)*
> *Sposalizio*
> Fantasy and Fugue on the name B–A–C–H
> Two Franciscan Legends
> Two "Paganini" Studies
>   in G-sharp minor (*La campanella*)
>   in E-flat major
> Petrarch Sonnet No. 3 in A-flat major
> Grand Fantasy on Meyerbeer's *Les Huguenots*

Such a recital would tax the mind and muscles of the most seasoned virtuoso today, so it is worth recalling that Stavenhagen was only twenty-three years old at the time of his concert. There is no question that this all-Liszt programme was meant as an homage to his master; but that very fact prevented Stavenhagen from equalling the success of Lamond the previous evening. *The Musical Times* put it best when it reported that while Stavenhagen was an accomplished player, "the misfortune of appearing only as an expositor of Liszt's music prevents any accurate judgement being formed as to his calibre as an artist." But it went on to observe that "Herr Stavenhagen obtained every possible encouragement from his hearers, and may be assured of a high place in our esteem whenever he thinks fit to revisit our shores."[32]

These recitals remind us once again of the fatherly interest Liszt took in the artistic welfare of his students. His presence in the audience was meant to set the seal of approval on their careers. As a matter of fact, this character-trait had led, a few days earlier, to a little confrontation between him and the board of the Philharmonic Society. Apparently Liszt had urged the society to engage Walter Bache as a soloist at one of its concerts, but his request had fallen on deaf ears. On April 10, Arthur Sullivan had noted in his diary: "Received letter from Liszt declining to come to a Phil: Concert as the Directors had taken no notice of his recommendation of Bache." Four days later, on April 14, Sullivan noted: "Received letter from Liszt—unable to dine with me, engaged every evening."[33] We may be sure that Liszt was making a point, since he accepted every other invitation offered to him during his London sojourn.

XI

The repeat performance of *St. Elisabeth* (arranged at eleven days' notice by popular demand) took place at the Crystal Palace on Saturday, April 17. By a happy coincidence, the work that it displaced from the regular Saturday Palace Concerts was Beethoven's *Choral* Symphony, which meant that the Novello Choir was already in place. August Manns gladly yielded the baton to Alexander Mackenzie, and the principals were the same as before. Prior to the concert Liszt joined the Crystal Palace directors for lunch, during which he was presented with a "valedictory address" from the London branch of the Richard Wagner Society.

As Liszt entered the auditorium of the Crystal Palace on the arm of Walter Bache, he was mobbed by the crowd of well-wishers, and a path had to be cleared for him by two policemen. "Liszt was fêted as no artist has ever been in this country," observed one newspaper. The performance that followed

---

32. *The Musical Times*, May 1, 1886, p. 259.
33. The unpublished diaries of Arthur Sullivan, 1886. Yale University Library.

Liszt in London, a photograph from April 1886.

was, by all accounts, even better than the one in St. James's Hall eleven days earlier.[34]

Liszt's sojourn in London was fast drawing to a close. On Sunday, April 18, Constance Bache drove with him from Sydenham to London so that he could worship at Brompton Oratory and hear a mass by Palestrina. Afterwards he went over to Wimpole Street to join Baron Bódog Orczy for lunch. Naturally a large crowd was in attendance and he was pressed to play the piano. Good-naturedly he allowed himself to be led to the instrument and played part of his *Dante* Symphony and one of his Hungarian Rhapsodies. Afterwards, Walter and Constance Bache took Liszt round to the studio of Edgar Boehm, who was making a bust of him. The sitting was a long one, Liszt smoked and chatted as Boehm moulded the clay. "It was a most delightful hour," wrote Constance, "and you can fancy how interesting it was to watch Mr. Boehm at his work. Boehm also is a Hungarian, but has lived in England since he was quite a young fellow, and has been naturalized."[35]

That evening a farewell dinner was given for Liszt at Westwood House, at which Henry Irving and Ellen Terry were present. Liszt may have sensed that he would never see his English friends again, for after dinner he treated the guests to a miniature recital in the music room. Constance Bache has documented the programme for us.

Variations in F major, Op. 34	Beethoven
Soirées de Vienne	Schubert-Liszt
Polonaise	Weber
Momento Capriccioso	Weber
Study in D major	Cramer
Fugue in D major, Book One,	Bach
The Well-Tempered Clavier	

At first he forgot nearly half the Bach fugue; "but do you suppose he made a mistake?" wrote Constance. "Not a bit of it! He simply joined on the end of the fugue to the beginning most beautifully, and this second time played it all through complete."[36] These were the last sounds Liszt drew from the piano in England.

His last public appearance was on Monday, April 19, when he attended a concert of his own music in Prince's Hall, organized by Countess Sadowska

---

34. Apart from these two official performances of *St. Elisabeth,* there was a third that went virtually unnoticed. The students of the London Academy of Music, under the direction of their principal, Dr. Henry Wylde, mounted the first part of the work on the afternoon of April 7, in St. James's Hall. What distinguished their effort was the fact they sang it in the original German.

35. BBM, p. 293.

36. BBM, p. 294.

and a group of supporting artists. It included Saint-Saëns's chamber-orchestral arrangement of the symphonic poem *Orpheus,* his own two-piano version of Weber's Polonaise brillante, together with some of his smaller piano pieces and songs. At the conclusion of the concert Charles Fry, "the well-known elocu-tionist," mounted the platform and delivered an ode entitled "Farewell to Liszt," written by William Beatty-Kingston, which was later published in *The Theatre* magazine.

The following morning Liszt took his leave of his friends at Westwood House and travelled to Dover, where he was greeted by the mayor of that town, W. J. Adcock, together with the town clerk and the borough surveyor. After these civic dignitaries had offered their respects, the composer boarded the cross-Channel steamer to Calais. As the white cliffs of Dover receded into the distance, Liszt might well have reflected that his seventeen days in London had turned into a personal triumph, unmatched by anything he had experienced since his halcyon days as a touring virtuoso.

Approaching the End

*I am already more than half blind; perhaps I shall
not have to wait long for the rest . . . ,*

FRANZ LISZT[1]

I

When the boat docked at Calais, Liszt and Cécile Munkácsy, who had travelled with him across the Channel, temporarily parted company. She now hurried back to Paris to prepare for his arrival there the following week, while Liszt and the faithful Stavenhagen boarded the train for Antwerp, where they had arranged to stay for a few days with Victor Lynen, the publisher. The rigours of his English trip had thoroughly exhausted Liszt, and he was badly in need of rest. That was difficult for him in Antwerp, however. Not only was he the guest-of-honour, surrounded as usual by friends and curiosity-seekers; it was also Easter, so he spent much of his time in church, fulfilling "my duties as an abbé at the Holy Week services," as he told Princess Carolyne.[2] From Antwerp he went to Brussels, where he spent a couple of days sightseeing. He called on Monsignor Ferrata, the papal nuncio, and they chatted about their old days in the Eternal City. Ferrata expressed his gratitude to Liszt for the interest he had always taken in the musical career of his nephew Giuseppe, who was now one of Sgambati's best pupils at the Santa Cecilia Academy in Rome.[3] In Brussels Liszt also paid his respects to the painter Gouffens, in whose studio he admired some large murals depicting the Way of the Cross. He would have liked to linger a day or two longer, but he was determined to fulfil his promise, made at the beginning of March, to return once more to Paris.

---

1. LLB, vol. 2, p. 392.
2. LLB, vol. 7, p. 438.
3. See p. 231, n. 8, for more information about Giuseppe Ferrata.

He arrived in the City of Light on April 27 and stayed with the Munkácsys at their luxurious home on the avenue de Villiers.[4] The chief reason he returned to the French capital was to attend a performance of *St. Elisabeth,* conducted by Auguste Vianesi, which was to be given at the Trocadéro on May 8. The Munkácsys lived in the parish of Saint François de Sales, so that is where Liszt attended mass while he was in Paris. During his stay there, the newspapers announced that his Hungarian Coronation Mass would be performed in that local church, which was consequently filled to overflowing. Unfortunately, the parts failed to arrive from Leipzig in time; but the curé, with great presence of mind, urged his disappointed parishioners to go to the Trocadéro, where they could compensate for their loss by hearing *St. Elisabeth* instead.[5] That immense auditorium held seven thousand people, and it was nearly full. Although some details were inevitably lost in the vast space, the music was received with enthusiasm. Gounod sat next to Liszt and observed: "This work is built with holy stones."[6]

Two other Liszt concerts that took place at this time were equally successful. For the first time in his life Liszt felt that he was being given his proper recognition as a composer. "I hardly expected such successes in Paris and London," he wrote to Olga von Meyendorff, "but since they come to me spontaneously I cannot grumble."[7] While he was in the French capital, Liszt did the usual rounds. He saw the Olliviers and his old factotum Gaëtano Belloni and had dinner with Prince Napoleon. A social engagement with Princess Mathilde had to be cancelled because he suffered a last minute indisposition. In fact, this was much more serious than Liszt made it out to be; on one occasion he had gone out without his overcoat and had succumbed to a cold. The last four days of his sojourn in Paris were spent in bed, and he was unable to shake off the effects of this illness. Before he left Paris, the Munkácsys made him promise that he would join them at Castle Colpach in Luxembourg in a few weeks' time.

---

4. Liszt wrote of the Munkácsy residence: "The luxury of the Munkácsys' house surpasses by far that of Wahnfried, Bayreuth. Few princes are set up as dazzlingly and run a household on the scale of Munkácsy." (LLB, vol. 7, p. 439) Mihály Munkácsy's wealth came not from his paintings but from the estate of Cécile's first husband, Baron Eduard de Marsches, who not only left her his entire capital but also the Castle Colpach in Luxembourg. The house was one of the first in Paris to be equipped with electric lighting, which created a sensation at Madame Munkácsy's dinner parties.

5. LLB, vol. 7, p. 439. The performance was helped by the presence of some distinguished soloists. According to the *Revue Musicale* they were MM. Faure and Soum and Mmes Schroeder and Masson. M. Guilmant officiated at the organ.

6. LLB, vol. 7, p. 440. This performance was reported by the Paris press, including *Le Ménestrel* (May 16), and *L'Art musicale* (May 15). From these sources we learn that Liszt shared a box with the Munkácsys, Saint-Saëns, Pauline Viardot-Garcia, and Marie Jaëll. The musical forces, as vast as the ones assembled in London, consisted of an orchestra of 120 players and a choir of 150 singers, with an "Angels' Chorus" of twelve singers from the Conservatoire. Among the soloists were Jean-Baptiste Faure (the leading baritone of the Paris Opéra) and Madame Schroeder.

7. WLLM, p. 496.

II

Liszt got back to Weimar on May 17, having been away for more than six months. A small deputation of his students—including Göllerich, Goepfart, and Stradal—had assembled on the railway platform to greet him in anticipation of another round of masterclasses. As the train drew to a stop and the carriage doors opened, Miska, the manservant, indicated to them that something was wrong. Liszt was so weak and ill, and his legs were so severely swollen, that he was unable to leave the train, and the students had to lift him from the carriage.[8] With difficulty they got him back to the Hofgärtnerei, where they tried to make him as comfortable as they could. His housekeeper, Pauline Apel, was shocked to see how frail he had become.

Liszt's physical condition had deteriorated rapidly during his time in Paris and London. His swollen legs made movement uncomfortable, and his eyes had grown so weak that he was forced to dictate all his letters. A month earlier he had instructed Olga von Meyendorff: "In view of the growing weakness of my eyes, please write large."[9] To Malwide Tardieu he was even more direct: "My sight is going, dear friend, and I can no longer write without difficulty."[10] The most serious setback was the fact that he was now unable to compose, since he could not focus on the manuscript paper. It was evident to everybody that he would have to seek medical attention. This was a disagreeable prospect for Liszt, who could never bear conversations about illnesses, and tried to make light of them.[11] On June 1 he travelled in the company of Olga von Meyendorff to Halle, where he consulted "two illustrious doctors," Alfred Graefe and Richard von Volkmann. The latter confirmed the disease of dropsy and prescribed a cure in Bad Kissingen, while Graefe advised Liszt that after the cure he would have to undergo an operation for the removal of a cataract on his left eye. Graefe noted that the cataract was a "grey cataract," most likely of the dense nuclear senile variety.[12] When,

---

8. RL, pp. 313–14. In a typical understatement he told Princess Carolyne: "I arrived peacefully here on Monday evening, May 17, with no other travelling companion than my Mihal." (LLB, vol. 7, p. 440)

9. WLLM, p. 496.

10. LLB, vol. 2, p. 392.

11. Because he dismissed his own illnesses, Liszt probably felt that that entitled him to dismiss the illnesses of others. But the results were sometimes unfortunate. When his pupil Karl Pohlig started to tell him about the symptoms of his smallpox, Liszt cut him off with the remark: "A very healthy illness!" (WFLG, p. 121)

12. Some years earlier, Graefe had opened a private clinic in Halle, for which he was now famous. His chief claim to medical fame was his pioneering use of antiseptic techniques in the field of eye surgery. Before him, the loss of the eye through post-operative infection was commonplace. By the

two or three weeks earlier, Liszt had told Lina Schmalhausen to write to him in large letters and in red ink, he was providing clear proof of Graefe's diagnosis. A "grey" cataract tends to filter out blue, while red remains visible. The fact that Graefe recommended an operation at all suggests that Liszt's vision in that eye must have been very poor, and would soon have been reduced to light perception only. This news had a depressing effect on Liszt, but he faced up to his uncertain future with stoicism. The hardest part for him was to follow the advice of his doctors and give up alcohol. Wine and brandy had been his lifelong companions, and he found it difficult to part with them. In the end he compromised: with his meals he started to drink a mixture of Tokaj wine and water.

I I I

From Halle Liszt travelled to Sondershausen, where he had promised to attend the annual festival of the Allgemeiner Deutscher Musikverein between June 3 and 5. A large crowd of friends and colleagues converged on the town for the event: Göllerich, Friedheim, Damrosch, Siloti, Draeseke, Stavenhagen, Martin Krause, and Alexander Ritter were all in attendance. There were also a number of distinguished foreign musicians, including the twenty-one-year-old Alexander Glazunov, who was on an extended visit to Germany. When Liszt got off the train, he was met by a small deputation of artists, who accompanied him to his hotel. Two all-Liszt concerts had been arranged in honour of his forthcoming seventy-fifth birthday, which were to be directed by Carl Schröder, the resident Kapellmeister.

---

time that Liszt consulted him, Graefe was claiming a phenomenal success-rate. Between November 1884 and July 1889, Graefe performed 1,074 cataract operations under an ongoing antiseptic programme, and lost only 0.93% cases to infection. He had also removed much of the pain and unpleasantness of this operation through his exploratory use of cocaine as a local anesthetic and he assured Liszt that the procedure was "quite anodyne." Alfred Graefe should not be confused with his equally illustrious cousin, Albrecht von Graefe, who had invented the "Graefe knife" for the removal of cataracts, which had made that difficult operation much simpler. For confirmation that it was Liszt's left eye on which Graefe proposed to operate, see Liszt's letter to Carolyne dated June 14, 1886. (LLB, vol. 7, p. 442), and also Carolyne's letter to Emile Ollivier dated July 26, 1886) (TOS-W, p. 352).

One endearing characteristic of Graefe deserves to be better known: evidently he believed in the healing power of prayer, and made a practice of saying the Lord's Prayer with his patients in the operating room before commencing his work. That indicates humility, a refreshing contrast to the godlike omnipotence sometimes encountered in the medical profession. (See "Die Augenheilkunde an der Universität Halle," by Hans-Heinz Eulner and Rudolf Sachsenweger, *Wissenschaftliche Zeitschrift* de Martin-Luther-Universität Halle-Wittenberg, July 1958, pp. 398–99.)

The first consisted of a programme of instrumental works:

Ce qu'on entend sur la montagne
Die Ideale
Hunnenschlacht
Hamlet
Totentanz
    (soloist: Siloti)
Hungarian Historical Portraits
    (four numbers only, orchestrated and conducted by
    Arthur Friedheim)

On June 5 there came a performance of *Christus* in the Stadtkirche. By all accounts Schröder was an efficient conductor but not an inspired one. During
the rehearsal of the oratorio Liszt expressed dissatisfaction with the interpretation of the tempest scene and the despairing cries of the disciples, which were
not agitated enough for him. When the singer of Christ came in with the
words "O ye of little faith!" as if he were singing some lyrical *bel canto* aria, Liszt
rounded on him and exclaimed: "You must reproach them bitterly, as if to say
'What cowards you are!' " That same day Louis Held travelled down from
Weimar, set up his camera, and persuaded Liszt and nearly a hundred of his admirers to pose for a photograph.[13] It was destined to become one of the most
famous pictures in the Liszt iconography, and happens to be one of the last
photographs of the composer.

After the festival Liszt returned to Weimar in the company of Walter Damrosch, Adelheid von Schorn, and Paul von Joukowsky. He was in high spirits
throughout the journey and kept the company in fits of laughter as he bom-
barded them with puns and amusing comments on certain episodes of the
festival, in particular a long and boring debate that had taken place between
Dr. Hugo Riemann and another eminent theorist on the science of harmony.
This debate had lasted for more than two hours, in a crowded room in which
people were nearly suffocated for want of fresh air, while Liszt sat in the front
row, under the very noses of the protagonists, trying not to go to sleep. When
they got back to Weimar, Joukowsky invited everybody to dine with him.
Champagne was served, and Liszt held the company spellbound as he remi-
nisced about the old Weimar days.[14] It was midnight when they all accompanied him through the Goethe Park back to his house. As they walked beneath
the trees, silhouetted against the moonlight, Liszt paused and exclaimed: "Lis-

13. BFL, p. 319. Among the distinguished group are August Göllerich, Carl Gille, Alexander Ritter,
Alexander Siloti, Martin Krause, Lina Ramann, Arthur Seidl, and Alexander Glazunov.
14. DMML, pp. 47–48.

ten!" It was the sound of a nightingale. Damrosch, who had never heard one before, was transported by the sound. Thirty-five years later he captured the scene for posterity in his memoirs.[15]

IV

Liszt had already made up his mind not to attend the Wagner festival in Bayreuth, which was scheduled to begin during the last week of July. Despite the importance of the occasion (both *Parsifal* and *Tristan* were to be staged, the latter for the first time in Bayreuth), Liszt felt that the festival could manage without him. But on May 18, the day after he had got back to Weimar from his long trips to Paris and London, Cosima had unexpectedly turned up at the Hofgärtnerei. The visit took Liszt completely by surprise; he had been rebuffed by his daughter for three years. Her ostensible reason was to invite him to attend the forthcoming marriage of her eldest daughter, Daniela, to the art historian Dr. Henry Thode, which was to take place in Bayreuth at the beginning of July. But Cosima had much else on her mind besides the wedding of her daughter. Liszt was struck by the change in her character, and particularly by her fanatical determination to perpetuate her husband's memory. We have no record of their conversation, but it is clear that Cosima impressed on her father the idea that his presence in Bayreuth was vital if the Wagner festivals were to survive. So Liszt gave in and agreed to come. To Carolyne all he would say was: "I shall be a Bayreuthian again from the end of July to August 23, but without living in Wahnfried, as I did in Wagner's lifetime."[16]

Liszt said farewell to his Weimar students at the end of June. Did he sense that this would be the last time he would see them gathered together in the Hofgärtnerei? Arthur Friedheim felt something of the sort, for in his memoir of the occasion, written many years later, he tells us that for no apparent reason Liszt seated himself at the piano and played a solitary piece, very softly. It was Chopin's A-flat-major Study, the second of the Trois Nouvelles Etudes. Although everybody in the room was well used to the ethereal sounds Liszt could draw from the keyboard, Friedheim reports that the performance seemed to come from mystical regions where time and space are merged.[17] The tears flowed freely that day, and it was right that they should do so. Everyone sensed that a musical era was about to come to an end.

On July 1, Liszt arrived in Bayreuth for the wedding. Since he had not been invited to stay at Wahnfried, which was filled with guests, he rented a private

---

15. DMML, p. 49.
16. LLB, vol. 7, p. 440.
17. FLL, p. 169. It is a small point, but Friedheim places this occasion in July 1886, which cannot be correct. Since it occurred after the Sondershausen festival but before Liszt's departure for Bayreuth, it must have taken place at the end of June.

room in the home of Frau Fröhlich at Siegfriedstrasse 1, on the opposite side of
the road. On July 3, he witnessed the signing of the marriage contract at Wahnfried. Afterwards there was a grand reception for more than eighty guests, at
which the burgomeister made a speech in honour of the young couple. The religious ceremony itself took place on Sunday morning, July 4, in the Protestant
church, which was packed with guests. (Rehearsals for *Parsifal* were already in
full swing, and a large number of visitors had descended on the small town
early.) The wedding-party had lunch in the Festspielhaus restaurant, and Liszt
was seated between Daniela and Princess Marie Hatzfeldt. What were his
thoughts at that time? A week or two earlier he had expressed some private misgivings about the marriage. "I hope that [Thode] is the right man for Daniela,
who was not born for everyone, having too much of the uncomfortable mixture of her father."[18] These were prophetic words. Daniela was twenty-six;
Thode was thirty-one and a *privat Dozent* at the University of Bonn. On the
face of it, this was a brilliant match. Unfortunately, the marriage caused the couple much unhappiness, remained childless, and ended in divorce in 1914. The
grounds cited in the legal action were that the union was unconsummated.

V

From Bayreuth Liszt set out on July 6 for Colpach Castle, where he had been
invited to enjoy a fortnight's rest in the company of the Munkácsys.[19] We
know from a report in the *Luxemburger Wort* (July 7) that he broke his journey
at the city of Luxembourg, where he was met at the station by Stavenhagen
and one M. Papier, the nephew of Cécile Munkácsy. After the station-master
had presented the distinguished passenger with a bouquet, the party went into
the waiting room, where Liszt took some refreshments.

> A crowd of onlookers had gathered to see the illustrious visitor, and
> many did not leave the station until his departure, so that they might
> see him again. . . . His head is bowed, his long hair snow-white; yet
> his eyes are still bright, his voice still powerful, and taken all in all he
> gives a pleasing impression of an otherwise really healthy man, who,
> we hope, will survive for Art and its admirers for many years.[20]

After relaxing for about an hour, Liszt and Stavenhagen boarded the train
and travelled on to Arlon in Belgium (the only way to get to Colpach in those

---

18. LDML, vol. 2, p. 129.
19. This visit was very well documented by the local newspapers, in particular the *Luxemburger Wort*
and the *Luxemburger Zeitung*. The material has been ably dealt with in BLSJ, vol. 9, pp. 45–53.
20. BLSJ, vol. 9, p. 47.

days) and thence by carriage to the castle. The Munkácsys had invited about eight house guests (including Liszt's old friend Cardinal Lajos Haynald) to join them at their country retreat. The simple routine suited Liszt. In the mornings he would dictate his letters to Stavenhagen; then he would walk around the beautiful park, join the others for meals, and play two or three hands of whist in the evenings. He was usually in bed by 10:30 p.m. He also had to undergo certain prescribed massages, infusions, and bathing of his eyes to alleviate his physical condition. ("Not very effective" was his laconic verdict.)[21] In one of his last letters Liszt described Colpach as "an ancient and roomy house of two floors, rather than a castle. The rooms are well laid out and richly and elegantly furnished. The principal charm of the countryside lies in forests of oak, beech, ash, and pine. In the old vaulted chapel on the ground floor, Cardinal Haynald celebrated mass yesterday and today."[22]

Liszt had no intention of playing the piano in public during his stay in Luxembourg. But when the Société de Musique heard that the famous pianist was in the vicinity, they invited him to honour them with his presence at their next concert at the Luxembourg Casino, one of the largest auditoriums in the city, on July 21. Liszt told them that that would be impossible, since he was due to set out for Bayreuth on July 20. The Société was not to be so easily rebuffed, however. If Liszt would agree to come, they said, the concert could be brought forward to July 19. Liszt was not really in any condition to make public appearances. He was half blind, he shuffled about with difficulty, and to add to his other problems he had developed a hacking cough, for which he was taking mustard plasters. But he doubtless felt that he owed it to the Munkácsys to accept, since they had social and artistic links to the Société, and so he agreed.

On the morning of July 19, Liszt and Cécile Munkácsy set out for Luxembourg[23] and went straight to the music shop of Guillaume Stomp (who in the past had provided pianos for Colpach Castle), where Liszt inspected several instruments before selecting one for his concert. The *Luxemburger Wort* (July 20) picked up the story.

> The renowned piano virtuoso, the Abbé Franz Liszt . . . arrived here from Castle Colpach at one o'clock yesterday afternoon on the Belgian train and put up at the Hotel de Cologne. In the course of the afternoon he paid a visit to the Bishop and then accompanied him to the Cathedral, to pay homage to the comfortress of the afflicted. On leaving the Cathedral, he became aware of the silvery

---

21. WLLM, p. 499.
22. WLLM, pp. 498–99.
23. One of the very last photographs we have of Liszt was taken at this time. It shows Liszt and Cécile Munkácsy arm-in-arm, setting out from Colpach Castle. (BFL, p. 321)

voices of the pupils of the Saint Cecilia Society, who in an adjacent
hall were having their choir practice under the direction of Herr
Barthel, master of the choristers. Liszt could not resist visiting the
little musicians, to their delight, and getting them to perform a
piece for him. It earned his full approval, and he said that not even
in Paris had he found such beautiful and well-trained voices.[24]

Liszt then repaired to his hotel, where he rested before his concert. A full description of this event was published in the *Journal de Luxembourg* and *L'Indépendance Luxembourgeoise* in their issues of July 20. By 8:00 p.m. the casino was
already full to overflowing. "All lovers of the arts had gathered to see the king
of the piano and to listen to the music to be played in his honour." The orchestra was assembled, the conductor was ready, and an expectant hush descended on the audience. A carpet of flowers was arranged around the foot of
the podium. Nearby was a row of empty armchairs, awaiting their distinguished
occupants. In the corner, almost out of sight, was the grand piano that Liszt had
selected from Stomp's warehouse. At 8:40 p.m. there was a stir, and the entire
audience rose as Liszt entered the hall accompanied by the Munkácsys, Stavenhagen, and representatives of the board of directors. Liszt was holding a large
bouquet of flowers presented to him by the members of the board just before
he entered the auditorium, and he smiled at the audience as he was led to his
seat. "Liszt is a fine-looking old man," wrote the *Journal,* "with long, silver hair
and distinctive features, slightly stooping; his eyes are bright and a kindly smile
plays around his lips; his long delicate hands seem to be caressing something."
When Liszt was settled comfortably in his armchair, the conductor, Henri
Weber, mounted the podium and the concert began. The programme included
Weber's *Freischütz* Overture, Haydn's Symphony No. 6, Hamm's Polonaise de
Concert for clarinet and orchestra, and excerpts from *Lohengrin.* It is clear that
at the conclusion of the concert, the general audience still had no idea that Liszt
had agreed to play. But when they saw the piano being moved to the centre of
the stage, and Liszt advancing towards the platform, there was frantic applause
from all sides, only "to give way to the most profound silence." Among the
pieces he played was his first *Liebestraum* ("Hohe Liebe"), one of his arrangements of Chopin's *Chants Polonais,* and the sixth of his *Soirées de Vienne.* This
was not only the last time that Liszt played in public, but it may also have been
the last time that he ever touched the keys of a piano. With these three pieces,
as La Mara later expressed it, Liszt's magical playing fell silent for ever.

---

24. BLSJ, vol. 9, p. 49.

VI

After spending the night at the Hotel de Cologne, Liszt attended early-morning mass in Luxembourg cathedral on July 20.[25] He then set out for Bayreuth in the company of Stavenhagen. The first leg of the journey took them to Frankfurt, where they caught the overnight train to Bayreuth. Everyone begged Liszt not to undertake the journey, but he insisted: "Cosima wants it, and I promised her that I would go." He was not really fit to travel. His throat was inflamed, he coughed incessantly, and he had a fever which made him perspire. On the overnight journey the window of the carriage was left open at the request of the other passengers, and he did not complain. But the cold night air pierced his lungs and precipitated the final illness from which he never recovered.

---

25. BLSJ, vol. 9, p. 53.

The Death of Liszt

I have never wished to live long. In my early youth,
I often went to sleep hoping not to awake again
here below.

FRANZ LISZT[1]

I

When Liszt arrived in Bayreuth July 21, he had difficulty in breathing, and he was obliged to take to his bed with a high fever and a racking cough. Once more he rented rooms at the Fröhlich house, where he had stayed two weeks earlier. Cosima, who was heavily involved in the Wagner festival, brought his coffee across from Wahnfried at six o'clock every morning and chatted with him for an hour or so; she would then leave for the Festpielhaus and remain there for the rest of the day. She had also arranged to have Liszt's meals prepared at Wahnfried. The idea was that he could walk across the road for them; but as he was ill, that proved to be impossible, so they were sent over to him.

For the first day or two Liszt confined himself to his room, and scarcely anybody knew that he had arrived. His pupils Göllerich, Siloti, Thomán, and Stavenhagen tried to keep him amused with games of whist, but his hands trembled so badly that he could hardly hold the cards, much less order them. He often lapsed into fitful slumber from which he was aroused by yet another bout of coughing. Lina Schmalhausen had arrived in Bayreuth the same day as Liszt, in response to his telegramme asking her to join him there, and she was shocked when she observed his condition. It is from her unpublished diary, in fact, that we have our best account of what took place during his final days.[2]

---

1. WLLM, p. 384.
2. She gives a closely detailed account of the twelve days from July 22 to August 3, which covers Liszt's final illness, his death, and his funeral in Bayreuth. It was written at the request of Lina Ramann, who was at work on the last volume of her "official" life of Liszt at the time of his death, but it proved to

She reported that whenever he coughed, his whole body shook, his face turned bright red, and he brought up large quantities of phlegm. Liszt told Schmalhausen that Dr. Richard von Volkmann of Halle had confirmed the earlier diagnosis of dropsy, and she now worried that he was drinking too much fluid; his feet and legs were bloated and he moved around his room with difficulty. Because alcoholic spirits were forbidden him, he consumed glass after glass of wine mixed with water in a vain attempt to quench his raging thirst.

On Friday, July 23, he attended the first of the *Parsifal* performances. As the guest of honour he knew that he had to show himself at the theatre, lead the applause, and generally act the role of diplomat among the festival visitors. It taxed his strength to do so, and for most of the next day he lay on a sofa propped up with pillows. He was lucid enough to discuss the performance, however; and when Otto Lessmann started to rhapsodize about it, he brought him down to earth: "It goes without saying that after having rehearsed for so many years, the singers and the orchestra can perform [the work] in their sleep." The conversation then switched to Bülow's genius for punning on people's names, which the young students found amusing. "I don't like twisting people's names around; that is cheap," responded Liszt. Siloti offered Liszt a new kind of cigar, which he had jokingly dubbed "the Liszt Society cigar," but Liszt had to decline it, for by now he was quite unable to smoke.[3] Another fit of coughing ensued, and Göllerich was despatched for some gum-drops, the sugar from which had to

be such a harrowing description that Ramann did not use it (see RL–B). One can understand Ramann's reservations. Schmalhausen was highly critical of Cosima's neglect of Liszt during his last days, and of the boisterous behaviour of some of the young acolytes who surrounded him, and Ramann evidently did not want to risk offending these people, all of whom were still alive when her final volume appeared in 1894. When Ramann herself died, in 1912, her archives went to Weimar and an embargo was placed on their use until fifty years after her death. Julius Kapp knew about the existence of Schmalhausen's account and interviewed her for his own Liszt biography, which appeared in 1909; while there are some discrepancies between the oral account that Schmalhausen gave to Kapp and the written account she had given to Ramann years earlier, Kapp's second-hand account was the best that could be achieved until the embargo on Ramann's archive was lifted. A highly curtailed version of Schmalhausen's eye-witness report was published in 1983, in Ramann's posthumous *Lisztiana* (RL, pp. 370–78), but the document has never been used in full until now.

Schmalhausen does not emerge from the Liszt literature as a particularly attractive character, and the present life of Liszt has done nothing to tilt the balance in her favour. The question arises: Why should we place any credence at all on her recollections of the last few days of Liszt's life in light of her questionable conduct earlier? There is one chief reason. Other students who were there at the time of Liszt's death also left their recollections, and they confirm the essential truth of the Schmalhausen narrative. But while theirs are sporadic, hers are complete, and no one contradicts her. In fact, the Schmalhausen account runs not only on a daily but sometimes on an hourly basis. Quite simply, it is irreplaceable.

The account which follows, the result of a careful inspection of the original eighty-four-page diary, gives many details of Liszt's illness and death that will strike even the well-informed Lisztian with force. Far from dying "without pain," as the popular biographies invariably seem to put it, Liszt suffered a cruel and tormented end. His death remains a standing indictment against those who were in a position to ease his last moments.

3. RL–B, p. 23.

be scraped off by Lina Schmalhausen before Liszt could take them. From time to time the pupils would take turns to give Liszt a spoonful of the cough medicine his doctor had prescribed for him. Since it contained morphine, it not only helped to suppress the cough but also exacerbated the chronic drowsiness from which he now suffered. At one point Lina heard him complaining to Göllerich about his weak eyes and his swollen body. And Lina added that a look of inexpressible gloom passed across his face as he made the remark.[4]

This picture of the dying master surrounded by his disciples, hardly any of whom had grasped the fact that he was so seriously ill he was soon to pass away, etched itself deeply on the mind of Adelheid von Schorn, who arrived in the middle of that scene, which took place on July 24.

> [Liszt] was sitting on the sofa holding his cards in his hand and surrounded by a number of his pupils who were playing whist with him. . . . He coughed, fell asleep for a moment, then went on playing. He hardly knew who was there and could scarcely sit upright. Deeply depressed, [I] left knowing that there was nothing we could do for the master we loved.[5]

On Sunday, July 25, came the Bayreuth premiere of *Tristan,* which Liszt had promised Cosima he would attend. His coughing was by now so chronic that he feared that he would be unable to get to the theatre. A local physician, Dr. Karl Landgraf, was summoned. He subjected Liszt to a thorough examination and had the manservant, Miska, show him the chamber-pot so that he could inspect Liszt's urine and stool. "It is considerably better than before," the doctor told Liszt. "The urine is much lighter, and in a few days you will have overcome this little cold." Lina, who was also present, later reported that she was thoroughly alarmed to see what looked like ink in the chamber-pot, an indication that Liszt was passing blood. But Miska told her that it meant nothing: "It has been like that for three weeks already."[6] Lina caught up with the doctor in the hallway. He reassured her that there was nothing to worry about, that Liszt should not speak too much or meet too many people, otherwise the illness could turn into pneumonia. When she reported that conversation to Liszt, he remarked ironically, "But I thought that I already *had* pneumonia."[7] From that moment they lost faith in his medical treatment.

---

4. Liszt had fallen once more into a deep depression, and there is some circumstantial evidence to suggest that he may have entertained thoughts of suicide. According to Gottschalg, one of the Stahr sisters told him that Liszt broke a window-pane with a seltzer glass so that the cold night air would hasten his end. (GLW, p. 157)
5. SZM, p. 466.
6. RL–B, p. 27.
7. RL–B, p. 28.

Liszt's problems were further compounded by the fact that no one seemed to understand that he could not eat the food prepared for him at Wahnfried. His dentures caused him discomfort, so he never wore them, with the consequence that he could not chew meat or solid foods.[8] Some smoked veal cutlet covered in apricot sauce had been sent across, but Liszt gave it to Lina's dog, and Lina prepared some clear broth, which seemed better suited to his condition. In order to get some rest, Liszt instructed Miska not to admit anyone to his rooms except Lina and Göllerich, whom he now wanted to read to him. Göllerich chose some passages from the literary works of Wagner, and Liszt was soon asleep. He was disturbed by a visit from Henriette Liszt, the widow of his cousin Eduard, who insisted on seeing him, brushed Miska aside, and, according to Lina, bent his ear with idle chatter for an hour or so. No sooner had Frau Liszt departed than Sophie Menter arrived in the company of friends. It was an impossible situation for Liszt; he needed to be left alone, but he knew that as long as he was in Bayreuth he would be expected to hold court and remain a centre of attention. That evening, at the performance of *Tristan,* he withdrew into the shadows of his box, a handkerchief clasped to his mouth, and moved forward only to show himself during the intermissions and lead the applause.

11

The next day, Monday, July 26, Liszt's condition became worse. He sat slumped on the sofa coughing, his forehead mottled blood-red with the effort. Every five minutes or so he drifted off to sleep. Since Göllerich was also ill (he had taken to his bed the previous day), and since Miska had disappeared on some errands, Liszt was alone for much of the time. Then word was sent across from

---

8. Liszt had suffered from chronic dental disease for much of his adult life. He had had a partial set of upper false teeth made in Paris in 1864 by the famous American dentist Thomas Evans. It contained five teeth, including the two front ones. Liszt evidently had pyorrhoea, and his teeth often loosened and fell out. His condition was aggravated by the fact that he often unconsciously ground his teeth, possibly because of excitement while playing the piano, and some teeth were impacted. (This first denture came into the possession of Henrik Gobbi in the 1870s.) Liszt's gum disease progressed, and during the next fifteen years he lost still more teeth. He had a second upper denture made, this time in Budapest by Professor József Árkövy, in the period 1879–80. It contained eight teeth, including five in the front, with a supporting metal brace. Liszt was friendly with the Árkövy family and often visited them at their home in Franciscan Square. According to Frau Árkövy, her husband made Liszt a complete set of false teeth in 1883.

It is clear that dental disease was a difficult burden for Liszt to carry with him into old age. It affected many aspects of his daily life and resulted in a highly restricted diet of soft foods. Liszt's friends and pupils understood his problems, and whenever they entertained him to a meal were careful to supervise the cooking. But there were times, as at Bayreuth, when Liszt was at the mercy of people who were too busy or too indifferent to care. During his last ten days, Liszt complained of extreme soreness of the lower jaw. (For a detailed account of the history of Liszt's dental problems, see Henrik Salámon's article "Liszt Ferenc Fogai" in *Fogorvosi Szemle,* vol. 31, no. 3 [Budapest, 1938], pp. 3–20.)

Wahnfried that in future, broth would only be served twice a week, so Liszt had nothing to eat. Lina finally arrived, and Liszt begged her to keep watch on Wahnfried, and then, when everyone "over there" had left for the theatre, to come and keep a vigil beside him. This was a revealing statement, which indicated that he wanted to place some distance between himself and the Wagners. Lina did his bidding, kept watch until the Wagners had left, and then returned to Liszt. He asked her to help him to bed. With difficulty she got him to his feet.

> His body was as heavy as lead. Finally I had him standing up. He embraced me, with a thankful gaze that was both heavenly and *deeply sad*. Then he pressed a long kiss on my neck. I carried him closer to the bedroom (he could hardly place one foot in front of the other from weakness), and he immediately fell onto the chair in front of his bed.[9]

Liszt called for Miska to undress him and put him to bed, but the house was deserted and his servant was nowhere to be found. Lina offered to undress him, but Liszt muttered: "That is exactly why they hate you and gossip so much about us; they begrudge your help." When Lina protested that he was ill, and that no one could possibly object, Liszt replied: "The whole of Bayreuth would be full of gossip tomorrow."[10] He was right. Liszt's inner circle had not failed to notice the little attentions that he and Lina had given one another ever since the young woman had served as his housekeeper in Budapest. Liszt knew that the outside world might easily misunderstand their arrangement, and he was nervous of compromising her reputation at this moment. So Lina left in search of Miska, tracked him down in the neighborhood, and had him put his master to bed. Lina then sat by Liszt, holding his hand, and read to him. At 8:00 p.m. Miska returned with Liszt's supper, chicken and rice, but Liszt could hardly touch it. Lina noticed that his whole body was boiling hot and that he was intermittently delirious. He would abruptly wake up and tell her: "I know that I'm saying a lot of confused things; I have a high fever. I always feel as if a wave is coming and I am in the water, and yet I know that I'm lying in bed."[11] Later that evening the doctor came, and after declaring that there was nothing wrong with Liszt except a severe cold, he departed. Lina wanted to sit up with Liszt all night, but he would not allow it. At eleven she put out his night light ("Extinguish it, I am not used to it," he told her) and departed with a promise that she would come back at seven-thirty the following morning.

---

9. RL-B, p. 40.
10. Ibid.
11. RL-B, p. 43. Such fears of drowning are not uncommon in patients suffering from advanced pneumonia, where the lungs are overwhelmed with fluid.

III

When Lina returned after breakfast on Tuesday, July 27, she found Miska in a highly nervous state. Liszt had hallucinated the whole night, no one had been to see him, and Miska did not know what to do. In a lucid moment Liszt had said: "If only I had fallen ill somewhere else! But to have to be ill just here, where everything throngs around me, is really too stupid."[12] Cosima then arrived and spent more than an hour in Liszt's room. For the first time, she seemed to realise the full seriousness of her father's condition. When she walked out, she looked neither at Stavenhagen (who had meanwhile returned to the house) nor at Lina Schmalhausen, but went straight up to Miska and firmly instructed him to forbid anyone to see her father.[13] This was easier said than done; Cosima put no one in charge of her father's welfare, and since the students were now the only contact he had with the outside world, they continued to minister to his needs in defiance of Cosima's ban. At 4:00 p.m., however, as Lina came back to Siegfriedstrasse from some small errand, she encountered Miska, who told her that everybody—Stavenhagen, Göllerich, and Lina herself—had been formally excluded from Liszt's presence, that Cosima herself was now nursing her father.

In fact, after seeing her father's poor condition earlier in the day, Cosima had called in one of the best physicians from Erlangen University, Dr. Fleischer, who examined Liszt the next day and diagnosed pneumonia. The students hovered outside the house, offended by Cosima's ban but uncertain what to do next. A great reception was held at Wahnfried that afternoon, at which Cosima played the hostess while her father lay dying across the street. To do her justice, however, she had left instructions that a bed be set up for her next to Liszt's room so that she could start to keep watch over him during the night. On July 29, she carried blankets, sheets, and pillows across the road and established herself in a room next to Liszt's. Frau Fröhlich, the landlady, was highly critical of this move; she complained to Lina that Liszt's illness had already caused her enough inconvenience. Moreover, Frau Fröhlich went on, she herself could not sleep at night. Her bedroom was directly above Liszt's and his moaning and rattling cut her to the quick: "Last night he moaned terribly, and I wept un-

---

12. RL-B, p. 46.
13. Cosima's ban on visitors to her father's bedside was in Liszt's best interests, but her motive in banning Lina, who had acted as Liszt's nurse and who could have gone on tending him, appears to have sprung from extreme dislike of this young lady. Lina's diary tells us why. While Cosima was in Liszt's bedroom, her father had lapsed once more into delirium and had mistaken her for Lina. His failing eyesight had done the rest. Unable to see Cosima properly, he addressed some intimate remarks to her that were really intended for Lina. Cosima resolved there and then to dismiss her.

controllably. One would be inclined to believe that he was *your* grandfather," she told Lina, "and not [the grandfather] of those over there," as she pointed toward Wahnfried. Frau Fröhlich privately accused Cosima of putting on an "act": Cosima, she claimed, closed the adjoining door at night, could not hear her father, and left for the theatre first thing in the morning. So what was the point of her being there?[14]

Since Lina was now barred from the house, she decided to wait until Cosima had left for the theatre, and then slip in and out of Liszt's room surreptitiously. However, on July 30, when she arrived at Siegfriedstrasse, she found herself locked out of the house. Nothing daunted, she took up her vigil behind some bushes in the garden, and it was from this unusual outpost that she continued to observe Liszt on his sickbed, which was positioned close to the window. In fact, Lina could see everything that went on inside his room and even identify his visitors. The Stahr sisters—Anna and Helene—came for ten minutes and left weeping. "He doesn't recognize us anymore and rattles terribly," they said. "If only it would end quickly for him—he suffers dreadfully!"[15] While Miska was distracted by the presence of these ladies, Lina seized the chance to force her way into the room. Liszt's eyes were tightly shut and he was moaning. His whole body was shaking and ice-cold. Between clenched teeth he called out to Miska: "What time is it?" "Nine o'clock," replied the servant. And then after a pause Liszt said: "Today I feel so ill. Is today Thursday?" "No, Your Grace," replied Miska, "it's Friday." Liszt sank back into his pillows. "Friday," he echoed.[16] He was always superstitious. While this scene was unfolding, the Wagner family were attending another performance of *Parsifal*. Lina noted bitterly that they were capable of being moved by a puppet-theatre, but not by a living Amfortas who was struggling with death.

At 9:30 p.m. Lina resumed her vigil in the garden, dressed in a thick coat and armed with a flask of cognac. Dr. Landgraf arrived about 11:30 p.m. and waited for Cosima, who got back from the theatre at midnight. She conferred with the doctor for ten minutes and then, without approaching her father's

---

14. RL-B, p. 53. Schmalhausen was further incensed by the fact that while she and the other students had been banned from Liszt's room, his grandchildren were allowed unrestricted access to him, and they showed him scant respect. When eighteen-year-old Eva turned up in the sickroom, he begged her to help him get up because he was suffering from bedsores. But she admonished him in mock-severe tones: "Just wait until Mama comes, she will tell you what to do." Liszt then tried to get out of bed himself, but Eva got Stavenhagen to force him back in, which caused him to sob with frustration. Liszt then called Miska and asked him for a shave, thinking that this way he would at least be allowed to sit in an armchair. But Miska shaved him in bed, and then, to make sure that his master stayed there, he removed Liszt's shoes from beside the bed, under the pretext of cleaning them, making it impossible for him to leave the room. At this point, everybody was treating Liszt like a small child; he knew it and felt humiliated. Lina observed him lying on his pillows weeping, completely exhausted. "At that moment, I felt that he was King Lear," she observed.

15. RL-B, p. 65.

16. RL-B, p. 66.

bedside, closed the door and retired to her room. At 2:00 a.m. there was a dramatic scene. Liszt suddenly leaped up in a frenzy, clutched his chest, and shouted "Luft! Luft!" He was gasping for air. Miska tried to restrain him, but Liszt had incredible reserves of energy and hurled him aside. His cries of pain lasted for half an hour and could be heard across the neighborhood. Cosima dressed hurriedly and called Dr. Landgraf, who did not appear for an hour and a half, by which time Liszt had collapsed diagonally across the bed. Landgraf at first declared: "He is dead." But he massaged Liszt's ice-cold body until the limbs warmed up, and gave him Hoffmann's drops. From then on Liszt remained in a coma.[17]

The next morning, Saturday, July 31, Cosima wired Dr. Fleischer, who got to Bayreuth in the early afternoon. The whole Wagner family was gathered in the salon outside Liszt's room—Cosima, Daniela, Eva, Isolde, and Siegfried. Fleischer informed them that the coming night would be crucial. He now considered it to have been a mistake to forbid Liszt all alcohol, and he prescribed a cocktail of heavy wines and champagne in an attempt to revive the patient. As the mixture was forced into Liszt's mouth he came to for a few seconds. He tried to speak, but although Cosima bent over him she could not catch the words. The Wagners then left, since Cosima had arranged a supper party at Wahnfried in the evening.

Dr. Fleischer was now joined by Dr. Landgraf. Throughout the evening, Fleischer sat by Liszt's bed, continually taking his pulse with one hand and checking it against a pocket-watch in the other. At 10:30 p.m. Liszt stopped moaning but continued to breathe heavily. About 11:00 both doctors leaned over the bed, holding two large silver candelabras, and examined Liszt closely. At 11:30 Liszt was given two injections in the region of the heart.[18] The effect was dramatic; Liszt's body was shaken by convulsions; the bed covers flew violently up and down; and then he became still, his left arm falling by the side of the bed. Once more the doctors bent over him, then left the room without exchanging a word. Liszt was dead.[19]

---

17. RL–B, pp. 69–70.

18. Some sources say that these were injections of morphine; others say camphor. Lina, from her vantage-point just outside the open windows of Liszt's room, smelled the aroma of the injections as it drifted towards her, and morphine has no perceptible smell. Camphor was sometimes used to counter the effects of hypothermia, and shallow injections beneath the surface of the skin, followed by massage, were known to warm the body. But an accidental injection of camphor into the heart itself would have resulted in a swift infarction, and death.

It is a small detail, but the death register puts the official time of death at 11:15 p.m., while Lina observed the two doctors give the injections at 11:30.

19. RL–B, pp. 71–72. Let us note that there is not a shred of evidence to support the statement that the last word Liszt uttered just before his death was "Tristan." After the heart attack that led to his coma, in the early hours of July 31, he was unable to speak. It doubtless suited the Bayreuth circle to think that even in death Liszt had been thinking of Wagner's masterpiece.

A facsimile page from the unpublished diary of Lina Schmalhausen,
entry for July 31, 1886: "At 11:30 the Master received
2 morphine injections in the region of the heart."

IV

Cosima entered the room shortly afterwards and knelt before the bed. Completely calm, showing no trace of emotion, she gazed for a long time at the body and lovingly caressed Liszt's left arm. She then laid herself diagonally across his feet, and remained in this position for several minutes, as if in prayer. Isolde came in, knelt before the bed, embraced her mother, and left the room. Cosima then sat down on a chair at the foot of the bed and remained there for a long time, looking at her father; she eventually drifted off to sleep. Lina, who had observed every detail of this dramatic scene from just outside the window, did not know at that moment that Liszt was dead. In fact, she was convinced that he was resting, else why would Cosima be sleeping? She stood in the garden observing this strange tableau until 4:30 a.m., and crept back to her lodgings, chilled to the bone, just as the first grey light of dawn was breaking. It was not until breakfast that her landlady came to arouse her with the news "So Liszt is dead."[20]

Lina rushed back to Siegfriedstrasse, pushed her way past Miska, and entered Liszt's room. He lay fully clothed on his bed, dressed as an abbé, a rosary in his right hand; his face was a waxen yellow, his body like a shell. The face wore a strange expression, but it looked ten years younger, gaunt but peaceful. Liszt had often asked Lina to pray for him after his death. This she now did as she knelt at his bedside. Cosima then entered and gave her Liszt's prayer-book. She also gave her permission to remove a lock of Liszt's hair. Whatever hostility Cosima had shown the young woman on previous occasions was forgotten in the trauma of her father's death. After Lina had returned to her lodgings, she went into the garden, picked a small bunch of forget-me-nots, ran back to

---

20. RL-B, p. 73. At this point Miska sent out many telegrammes to Liszt's friends and colleagues, informing them of the master's death, and word spread quickly. Alexander Siloti, who had temporarily left Bayreuth a few days earlier, rushed back to the city and got there about 9:00 p.m. on July 31. He wrote:

> It was twilight, and just as I entered the street [Siegfriedstrasse] I heard the mournful howl of a dog. It proved to be Wagner's dog, who after his master's funeral had lain down beside the grave, neither howling nor moving from that time forward. This dog at the moment of Liszt's death had suddenly started howling. When I heard it I began to tremble all over. I do not remember how I got to the house; how I entered the room and saw him lying dead. . . . (SML, pp. 73–74)

Arthur Friedheim was in Leipzig when he received news on July 31 that Liszt was gravely ill and was not expected to live. He and his mother, in the company of William Dayas, caught the night train to Bayreuth and arrived there shortly after 9:00 a.m. on August 1. They were met at the station by Stavenhagen and Martin Krause. "We read it on their faces before we could get out of the wagon. Too late . . . ," wrote Dayas. (WDC, hitherto unpublished) The little party went straight to Siegfriedstrasse to pay their respects to the deceased master, and took turns standing vigil by the body.

Liszt's room with them, and placed them in his left hand. It was a hot day, and some flies had started to attach themselves to Liszt's face. Lina went out and got a small bottle of pine-essence, which she rubbed onto his face, throat, and hands. She closed his left eye, which had remained partially open, kissed him for the last time, and then covered the body with muslin. Although Liszt was a Roman Catholic cleric, no priest had been called in during his illness, and he had not been given extreme unction. It was only now that the local priest was summoned and a service held at the bedside for the Wagner family alone; Liszt's friends, pupils, and close associates were excluded. After the service a death-mask was taken by the sculptor Weissbrod, in the presence of Paul von Joukowsky and Wagner's old factotum Bernhard Schnappauf.[21] While this was happening, Lina went off in search of a photographer and returned with Hans Brand, who took three pictures. The first one did not come out very well, because the warm wax used for the death-mask had raised the features, but the other two were excellent; they are to be found in all the major Liszt iconographies.[22] At 10:00 a.m., Cosima gave permission for the corpse to be viewed. Word spread quickly throughout the small town that Liszt had died the previous night, and crowds of people turned up at the house. Some were legitimate mourners who wanted to pay their last respects; others were morbid sightseers—a few of whom even trooped into the room with their small children.

Later in the day there was an attempt to embalm Liszt's body. We have few details, but according to Schmalhausen's account the procedure was bungled, and the corpse was cut apart so badly that the body and face were bloated almost beyond recognition. Consequently, it was forbidden to view the distorted remains, which were covered in gauze. Cosima locked the door to the death-room and the body remained in darkness all night.

The following day, August 2, Lina went back to Siegfriedstrasse. All round the deathbed stood bowls of chlorine, and the doors were wide open to ensure a supply of fresh air. A young man was scrubbing the floor around the body in an attempt to clean the area around the bed. As Lina left the house she encountered a boy rolling the coffin along the street on a handcart. The coffin was made of brown metal and bore the inscription "The Lord Jesus Christ." Frau Fröhlich insisted that the corpse be put into the coffin at once, since the body was starting to decompose and her other tenants objected to the odour. Cosima was so angered by this that she and Schnappauf put Liszt's body into

---

21. This death-mask was later sent to Weimar, where it was photographed by Louis Held. See BFL, p. 324.
22. RL-B, pp. 74–75. See also BFL, pp. 322 and 323. These two photographs provide us with a piece of evidence that is impossible to ignore, for it conclusively supports Lina's testimony. They show Lina's forget-me-nots in Liszt's left hand, and the lock of Liszt's hair, just as she described them. In the brief interval separating the taking of these images, the hands were moved in accordance with Lina's request to feature them more prominently in the picture, and this change of position is also reflected in the photography.

the coffin themselves; with Cosima at one end and Schnappauf at the other, they transported it on the handcart across the street to Wahnfried.[23] She then sent her daughters back to the Fröhlich house to have his clothes packed into baskets and brought to Wahnfried. For the rest of the day the coffin lay in state in the entrance hall to Wahnfried and Liszt's pupils stood vigil.

V

The funeral took place on Tuesday morning, August 3. A large crowd assembled at Wahnfried for the ceremony, including the Wagner family, some friends and pupils of Liszt, and a number of town officials. After a brief service, during which the body was blessed by the town priest, Father Karzendorfer, the funeral cortège set out for the Bayreuth municipal cemetery. The coffin rode on a catafalque covered in flowers and drawn by four horses. The pallbearers were Felix Mottl, Hans von Wolzogen, Baron August von Loën, and Ödön Mihalovich. Cosima had at first refused permission to Liszt's students to join the procession, but thanks to the indignant protests of Friedheim and Siloti, she relented, and a group of them marched on each side of the coffin as torchbearers—Reisenauer, Weingartner, Thomán, Stavenhagen, Göllerich, Krause, Klindworth, Bache, Dayas, Friedheim, and Siloti. Walking behind the hearse were Siegfried Wagner, Henry Thode, Adolf von Gross, and, representing Grand Duke Carl Alexander, the Weimar court chamberlain Count Oskar von Wedell. Then came the carriages, in the first of which sat Cosima and Daniela, Princess Marie Hatzfeldt, and Olga von Meyendorff, who had arrived in Bayreuth a day or two earlier to take Liszt to the spa of Kissingen and now found herself a mourner at his funeral. As the cortège moved slowly down Maximilianstrasse, a distant cemetery bell tolled in the Stadtfriedhof. The road was lined with spectators, many of whom were in festive mood because of the Wagner celebrations; two days earlier the same crowd had turned out along the same route, which had been decked out with flags and multi-coloured bunting, to welcome Crown Prince Friedrich of Germany to the Wagner festival. Everything had been hastily removed, and even as the funeral cortège was turning the corner, the lighted gas-lamps were still being draped with makeshift black crepe.

At the graveside the mayor of Bayreuth, Dr. Theodor von Muncker, gave an oration. He fastened on words from *Tristan:* "Doomed head, doomed heart." He referred to Liszt in fulsome terms as "a master of sound, the devoted friend and promoter of the Wagner cause," and he promised that Liszt's burial site would always be preserved and kept sacred. After the mayor had finished speaking, Eduard Reuss came forward and delivered a eulogy on behalf of Liszt's students. He

23. RL–B, p. 78.

was followed by Martin Krause, who spoke on behalf of the Liszt-Verein. The last speaker was Liszt's old colleague Dr. Carl Gille, but as he recalled his longtime friend he broke into tears and his words were lost on the crowd. Liszt's body was then lowered into the ground while Muncker laid down a laurel wreath from the city of Bayreuth; a second wreath from "the loyal town of Vienna" was placed by its side. Dozens of other tributes buried the grave beneath a mountain of flowers, including one from Anton Bruckner ("To the great master Franz Liszt") and one laid by Alfred Littleton on behalf of Queen Victoria.[24]

The day after the funeral, August 4, a requiem mass was held for Liszt in the local Catholic church. Much dissatisfaction was expressed at the musical part of the service, and the general feeling was that it would have been better to have had no music at all than the nasal chanting of two or three priests responding to the discordant singing of an indifferent choir. Bayreuth was filled with some of the world's greatest musicians, but with one exception they remained mute. Anton Bruckner played the organ, but he improvised on themes from *Parsifal*. Not a note of Liszt's own music was heard.

V I

Liszt's friends and supporters suffered greatly from the indifference surrounding his death. Walter Bache, who had dashed from London to Bayreuth in forty-eight hours to be present at the funeral, got to Wahnfried just as the coffin was being taken out of the house, and he joined the cortège in his dusty travelling clothes.[25] The crowd that milled around the graveside was so large that Bache could not hear the speeches, and he was appalled at the levity of the hangers-on. Everybody was in a gay mood, many of the "mourners" being casual visitors to the Wagner festival. Felix Weingartner observed that not even the flag on the Festspielhaus was hung at half-mast; nor did the Wagner family give any outward sign of grief. Not a single reception at Wahnfried was interrupted. Wrote Weingartner: "Everything was made to look—as if on purpose—that Franz Liszt's passing was not of sufficient importance to dim the glory of the festival even temporarily by a veil of mourning. . . . From that time on I never entered the portals of Wahnfried again."[26]

---

24. BBM, p. 306. A complete list of floral tributes was published in the *Bayreuther Tageblatt* on August 9, 1886. They included wreaths from a large number of associations, including the Allgemeiner Deutscher Musikverein, the Liszt-Verein, the Wagner-Verein, and the theatres of Weimar, Leipzig, and Vienna, as well as from the Royal Academy of Music in Budapest, and prominent individual artists such as Amalie Materna, Sophie Menter, and Robert Franz.

25. BBM, p. 307.

26. WLE, vol. 1, p. 276. William Dayas made a similar observation when he wrote to his sister Emma a few days after the funeral. "On Tuesday morning he was buried—in the common graveyard—among common people—and that by his daughter. Why? Because it would ruin the opera business

Immediately after the funeral Cosima hurried back to the theatre to supervise that evening's performance of *Tristan*. Such unseemly conduct was to cost
Cosima dear in the years ahead, as she was pursued by a growing chorus of criticism from Liszt's admirers. Yet when we look at the situation from her point
of view she faced a terrible dilemma. The Wagner festival of 1886 had been
planned far ahead. The town was filled with important guests from around the
world, many of them there at Cosima's personal invitation. Hundreds of musicians, singers, and artisans had been imported to help her mount the produc-
tions of *Parsifal* and *Tristan*. It was not only an important turning-point in the
history of Wagner's fortunes but of Cosima's as well, for it marked the end of
her three-year period of mourning. The entire festival enterprise was fraught
with risk, both artistic and financial. Was all this to be abandoned because of
the death of her father? The answer was clearly no; it could not be otherwise.
Simply put, the timing of Liszt's death was unfortunate, and Cosima became
its chief victim. Even under normal circumstances she would have been placed
under tremendous pressure by the daily business of running the festival. But her
behaviour became stoic as she struggled to keep the festival going on the one
hand while shouldering the responsibility of nursing her father and supervis-
ing the funeral arrangements on the other.

So all Bayreuth celebrated Wagner while Liszt was lowered into the ground.
And perhaps this is how Liszt, in his deepest moments of self-abnegation,
would have wished it. Not so his dearest friends, however. A few days after the
funeral Princess Wittgenstein wrote a blistering letter which summed up the
anger and frustration they all felt.[27]

> I sent for the Bayreuth newspapers from July 28 to August 10. Just
> think—*not once* is Liszt's illness mentioned, as in a bathing resort
> where illness and death are hushed up in order to arouse no painful
> sensitivities among the bathers. I send you the paper of August 2 in
> which his death is then announced straight away. Then, the fact that
> he was a Catholic is kept quiet, or kept dark. Every reader will think
> that he was buried in this nest of atheists by some free-thinking
> Protestant clergyman! In the issue of August 11 you can see that she

---

in Bayreuth to make as much of Liszt her father as of Wagner her husband. It was sad. . . ." (WDC,
hitherto unpublished)

27. Typical of the haste with which the *Bayreuther Tageblatt* churned out the news of Liszt's illness and
death was the potted biography published in the issue of August 1. Its second paragraph began with
this gaffe: "Liszt wurde den 11. Oktober 1811 in Raiding bei Oedenburg gestorben" ("Liszt died on
October 11, 1811, in Raiding, in the district of Oedenburg"). A somewhat more damaging error appeared in the obituary published in the London *Times* on Monday, August 2: "Franz Liszt died last
night at Bayreuth." This led many people to assume that the date of death was August 1, a piece of
misinformation that crept into Sacheverell Sitwell's Liszt biography, among others.

who for three years would not see her own father [after Wagner's death] was staying ten days later in the public house called "The Gaiety" [Zum Frohsinn]. On both the last two evenings she was in the theatre, for the show must go on, and Cosima was so fond of playing the producer that she remained there day and night.[28]

Six weeks after the funeral Lina Schmalhausen returned to Bayreuth and visited the house in which Liszt had died. She hardly recognized it. The old wallpaper had been torn down, the floor had been waxed, new furniture had been installed, and the deathbed had been sold. In short, everything had been changed. Frau Fröhlich, who had never ceased to complain about the inconvenience that Liszt's death had caused her, had been mollified only when Princess Carolyne promised to send her an expensive gift in recompense. The cleaning expenses and the cost of the new furniture had been borne by Cosima, who gave Frau Fröhlich one hundred marks for her trouble. That, remarked Lina, was the *true* end of the great Liszt.[29]

Lina then visited his grave. No stone yet marked it. There was only a simple cross of ivy, surrounded by dark blue flowers. Everything looked temporary. Indeed, no one yet knew whether the body would remain in Bayreuth. Within days of his death a monumental quarrel had broken out about the site of his last resting-place.

---

28. KFL (edition of 1924 only, p. 297).
29. RL-B, p. 80.

Aftermath

I will not have any other place for my body than
the cemetery . . . in use in the place where I die.
FRANZ LISZT[1]

I

Even as the mourners were leaving the Bayreuth cemetery, there were murmurs of discontent about the choice of Liszt's burial-place. Everybody realized that it was a misfortune for the master to have died in Bayreuth. And Liszt himself seemed to have had a premonition of the trouble it would cause.[2] Had he known that he would die in the city of Wagner, the chances are that he would never have set out on that last, fatal journey. In the event, the drama that began to unfold even as his coffin was being lowered into the ground equalled anything he had experienced during his lifetime. The struggle for possession of Liszt's remains is a little-known chapter of his posthumous fate, though the dispute was kept going by the press for three generations. One file in the Weimar Archives contains newspaper clippings on this topic that cover a span of forty years.[3] Both Weimar and Budapest had a strong claim to the body, and in due course they came forward. There was also a suggestion that Liszt should be buried at the foot of the Wartburg, in the Elisabeth Church, because of its deep connections with Hungary and the fact that Liszt's oratorio *St. Elisabeth* had been performed there. Even the village of Raiding wanted to have Liszt's body brought back to his birthplace, an idea that the village elders were still pressing as late as 1906. But Cosima overruled them all; and she had her reasons, as we shall see.

---

1. LLB, vol. 6, pp. 228–29.
2. RL–B, p. 46.
3. WA, Kasten 270/4.

The Hungarian case was particularly strong. Mihalovich, who had been a pallbearer at Liszt's funeral, was adamant that Liszt had told him many times that he wished to be buried in Hungary; and this view was confirmed by other prominent Hungarians, including Kornél Ábrányi and Cardinal Haynald. Princess Carolyne, his executrix, also wanted the body brought to Hungary and could not tolerate the thought that Liszt's remains might be abandoned in "pagan Bayreuth." The Franciscans of Hungary added their voices to the general clamour and requested that Liszt be returned to them for burial in Budapest. On August 5, just two days after the funeral, the *Neue Freie Presse* voiced the opinion that it would be "an insult to educated Europe" if Hungary left its great son lying on foreign soil. By November 18 this same newspaper reported that there had been great agitation in Budapest over the question of transferring Liszt's remains from Bayreuth to his native land. Cardinal Haynald had procured a copy of Liszt's will (written in 1860) from Princess Carolyne, it reported, and he revealed that Liszt's wish to be buried in the habit of the Franciscan order had not been carried out. Liszt's desire to be buried simply, "without pomp, and if possible at night," had likewise been ignored. Haynald also revealed that the will contained no definite instructions about a burial-place. From the Hungarian point of view, then, that meant that no legal obstacle need be placed in the way of returning the body to Budapest.

Cosima meanwhile made it known that she had no objection to her father's remains being transferred to Hungary, providing the request came from both houses of the legislature and Liszt was accorded national honours. A petition was now got up from the citizenry of Hungary requesting that Liszt be brought home. On February 26, 1887, the Hungarian legislature received the petition and debated the question. Prime Minister Kálmán Tisza got up and made an unfortunate speech, the burden of which was that Liszt was not a patriotic Hungarian, and that Liszt had made a gift of Hungarian music to the Gypsies.[4] It was an unpardonable gaffe, one which re-opened old wounds at a difficult

---

4. The debate was printed in full in the *Képviselőházi Napló* (Proceedings of the House of Representatives), 1884–87, vol. 16, 332nd sitting, February 26, 1887. The speakers included the eminent historian Kálmán von Thaly, Kornél Ábrányi, Ödön Steinacker, and Prime Minister Tisza.

Thaly spoke first. He said that he would support the *idea* behind the petition to bring Liszt home. But he recalled that there was already a petition before the Committee for Petitions from more than fifty Hungarian municipalities requesting the return of the body of Prince Ferenc Rákóczy II (who had been buried in Turkey for a hundred and fifty years). Rákóczy was an infinitely greater patriot than Liszt, Thaly went on, and the petition to bring him home was rotting somewhere in the archives of the Ministry of the Interior. Had Rákóczy not taken up arms, there probably would be no Hungarian nation today, Thaly continued. Without wishing to diminish the merits of Franz Liszt, he concluded, Rákóczy's case was far stronger. Liszt had only transcribed the march of a great man who really was worthy of having his remains brought home! At that, Kornél Ábrányi rose to his feet and delivered a flaming speech in defence of Liszt. Music, too, was a national language, declared Ábrányi, and Liszt had made Hungarian music known throughout the world. Every nation placed great weight on

time. More to the point, it incensed Cosima and ensured that whatever the outcome, she would never allow her father to be buried on Hungarian soil. In 1906, when Cosima was almost seventy years old, Lajos Karpath raised the question afresh and contacted officials in both Budapest and Bayreuth. He reported that the Hungarian government had communicated to him in writing the view that "now is not the time to ventilate this question."[5] Cosima herself went to her grave in 1930, and she never wavered. In 1936, the fiftieth anniversary of Liszt's death was celebrated across the world, and once again there was a move in Hungary to have his remains brought home. Viktor Papp even suggested that a symbolic grave be erected in Budapest, but the idea came to nothing. Four generations of Hungarian heads have grown grey over this problem, but Liszt's grave remains in Bayreuth.

The Weimar case was also compelling. Liszt had spent thirteen of his most productive years in the city. For the last seventeen years of his life he had maintained a home there; his masterclasses in the Hofgärtnerei had become an institution. And his links with Weimar's royal household were strong. When Carl Alexander heard that Liszt was to be buried in Bayreuth, he offered to have the remains transferred to Weimar. His view was that if Hungary had a claim, then

---

the fact that after the death of their great men, their bodies should rest in the soil of their fatherland. He reminded the House that Rossini had been brought home to Italy, Weber had been brought home to Germany, and Byron to England, and he begged the government to work towards a similar end in the case of Liszt. Steinacker agreed, and reminded his colleagues of Liszt's patriotic deeds, including his help when the Danube had overflowed its banks in 1838. Steinacker was interrupted at this point by a voice from the back-benches: "He enjoyed a pension!" "That was not a pension," Steinacker retorted, and he reminded his colleagues that Liszt devoted far more in material goods to his country than the return of his remains would cost.

Prime Minister Tisza now got up to reply. He first told the assembly that, in principle, he too accepted the idea of bringing distinguished artists home, and that the government had a moral duty to heed such petitions as the one now brought before it. Tisza asked the honourable delegates not to demand more than was possible. "There is a well-known saying," he remarked: "*De mortuis nil nisi bene*" ["Do not speak ill of the dead"], and he begged his colleagues not to press their case so hard that he would be obliged to break this rule. In the interests of truth, he went on, he had to point out that everything the House understood by Hungarian music had been popularized abroad by Liszt. But at a time when Hungary owned practically nothing but its music, Liszt told the world that it really belonged to the Gypsies. A voice then interrupted: "This has been refuted!" Tisza then turned to his heckler and said: "With respect, I have recently checked the brochure where [Liszt] said this." And Tisza concluded with the reassurance that he accepted the petition in principle, but repeated his warning: "Do not stretch the strings too tightly, because they are liable to snap."

It is clear today that the timing of the petition was not ideal. Thaly's recommendation that Prince Rákóczy be given priority was a powerful one. Nonetheless, it was a lamentable performance on the part of the prime minister. Leaving aside all the charitable contributions that Liszt had made towards Hungarian causes across the years, he was also the president of the Royal Academy of Music and a Royal Hungarian Counsellor, with the right to sit in the legislature. Any or all of these things would have entitled him to better national consideration than he actually received. We are not wrong to assume that Tisza personally disliked Liszt, whom he had once privately described as "a common comedian."

5. Lajos Karpath, *Der Kampf um die Asche Franz Liszts. Neue musikalische Presse*, no. 19, Vienna, 1906.

Weimar had an even stronger one. On October 14 he wrote to Cosima to say that Weimar wanted to build for her father a mausoleum worthy of his name. But Cosima attached an impossible condition: she requested that Liszt's body be buried in the royal vault, side by side with Goethe and Schiller.[6] To this request the grand duke was unable to accede, and a moment's reflection will tell us why. When his grandfather Carl August had commanded that the bodies of Goethe and Schiller be brought into the royal vault to sleep with him and his ancestors in perpetuity, the honour was without precedent. The whole of Germany still stood in awe of that remarkable gesture. Liszt would have had no place in such surroundings. Unlike Goethe and Schiller, he symbolized nothing for the German nation, and his presence in the vault would have struck a jarring note.[7]

Liszt himself was partly responsible for starting the controversy which still swirls around his burial-place today. During his lifetime he expressed contradictory views about where he wished to be buried. In 1863 he said he would like to be interred in Rome.[8] A few years later, in 1866, he told Emile Ollivier that he wanted to be buried in Saint-Tropez.[9] In 1869 he assured Carolyne that he wanted no other place for his remains than the cemetery nearest to the place of his death.[10] Later still he told Cardinal Hohenlohe that he would like to be buried in the Tivoli cemetery.[11] In the face of such contradictions it is difficult today to know what Liszt wanted; a hundred years ago it was impossible. He could quite easily have left instructions in his will, but although this complex

---

6. Some of the correspondence between Cosima and the grand duke on this question will be found in the Staatsarchiv, Hausarchiv Carl Alexander, Abt. A XXVI, no. 1182. In a letter dated October 23, 1886, Cosima thanked the grand duke for the honour he had done her father in asking for the remains to be transferred to Weimar. And then, in a masterpiece of diplomacy, she added that the request alone was honour enough; there was no need to add to it by returning the body as well. In this same letter, she makes clear that of all the voices now clamouring to have a say in the disposition of Liszt's remains (including Carolyne's, to whom she refers icily as "her, the sole executrix") the only one she considers truthful is that of the manservant Miska, who has told her himself that Liszt wanted to be buried where he fell. All the others, according to Cosima, were suffering from "a mirage of the imagination."

7. Today the entire family of the once-powerful house of Sachsen-Weimar lie in leaden caskets in the royal vault. This family, whose patronage of the arts did more than anything else to lift Weimar out of petty provincialism and make of it a centre for European culture, succeeded so completely in its noble aim as to obscure its own remembrance. And this becomes painfully evident the moment one visits the royal chapel in the Weimar churchyard and descends the spiral steps into the burial chamber beneath. The coffins of Sachsen-Weimar have been pushed aside into dark recesses, where they jostle for space beneath crumbling arches, while those of the two literary giants whom Carl August brought to his city lie on a raised dais in the centre of the chamber, illuminated both day and night as the world files past in homage. It is not for artists to complain about this reverence of genius, but the extent to which the patrons have become the patronized would require a Goethe to explain the paradox.

8. LLB, vol. 3, p. 161.

9. OJ, vol. 2, pp. 246–47.

10. LLB, vol. 6, pp. 228–29.

11. LLB, vol. 8, p. 319.

document mentions many other details of a profound and personal nature, including the sort of funeral service he wanted, the question of his burial-place is not broached. In the event, it was his letter of 1869 to Carolyne, written nine years after the will itself, that emerged as the most authentic document. "Let my body be buried, not in a church, but in some cemetery, and let it not be removed from that grave to any other. I will not have any other place for my body than the cemetery . . . in use in the place where I die. . . . The inscription on my tomb might be: 'Et habitabunt recti cum vultu tuo.' "[12] Liszt, in short, wanted to be buried where he fell.

But the matter cannot be allowed to rest there. While Liszt may at various times have expressed a wish to be buried in various places, he never once expressed a preference for Bayreuth. Quite the opposite, in fact. From the standpoint of Liszt's posthumous reputation, there were more appropriate places for him to have been interred. Apart from Budapest and Weimar, there were Rome and Paris, both of which cities had far stronger artistic attachments to Liszt than Bayreuth. Even the village of Raiding would have been better than Bayreuth, where he lies beneath the shadow of Richard Wagner. And this is surely the crux of the matter. There is no doubt that it suited the Wagner family to have Liszt's grave in Bayreuth. In 1886 Wagner's reputation was by no means as secure as it is today, and Cosima saw in her father a threat to the posthumous reputation of her husband. This highly intelligent woman was not content to leave the final judgement to history. History would have to be created, and it would have to be created from Wagner's point of view. There could be no better solution than to have Liszt and Wagner side by side, as it were, so that a comparison could be made, and visitors to the festival could see for themselves just how much more Wagner had achieved. This policy has been enormously successful. In Bayreuth, the Wagner legacy is omnipresent, and

---

12. LLB, vol. 6, pp. 228–29. Liszt's Latin tag comes from Psalm 140, v. 13: "The upright shall dwell in Thy presence." The timing of this letter was significant. Liszt had been offended by the ostentation surrounding the funeral of the German painter Overbeck, who had died earlier that year, and he did not want a similar fate for himself. In this letter Liszt urgently entreated and commanded "that my burial take place without show, and be as simple and economical as possible. I protest against a burial such as Rossini's was. . . . Let there be no pomp, no music, no procession in my honour, no superfluous illuminations, or any kind of oration." None of Liszt's wishes was heeded, of course, since no one in Bayreuth was aware of the existence of this (as yet unpublished) letter to Carolyne.

In 1911, the one-hundredth anniversary of Liszt's birth, the question of his last resting-place once more became a topic for discussion in Hungary. Marie Hohenlohe, who had discovered the letter in her mother's legacy, regarded it as a binding document. She told Count Géza Zichy: "I believe that in her great grief, and already seriously ill, [my mother] no longer remembered this letter. . . . Her first impulse was to have him moved from *pagan* Bayreuth and, in defiance of all the intentions of her dear one, to entrust [his remains] to the faithful care of the Franciscans. . . ." But she went on: "Whatever scruples remain today would appear to me to be petty if the united will of the [Hungarian] nation felt that it had the authority to set aside the wishes of the master." (*Akadémiai Értesítő* 42, fasc. 451, October–November 1932)

Liszt counts for very little. Moreover, there were details about the Liszt-Wagner relationship to be revealed, brushed aside, and even suppressed, if Wagner's cause was to prevail. This process could take a long time; meanwhile, it was best controlled by having Liszt's body in the place where he was remembered as "Wagner's father-in-law."

That Cosima had come to regard Bayreuth as her father's last resting-place even while negotiations for the removal of the body were still taking place is borne out by a small but telling piece of evidence. On October 25, 1886, less than three months after Liszt's death, she announced a competition for the design of a memorial chapel to be erected over the burial-site. The commission went to the Munich architect Gabriel Seidl, who obligingly incorporated certain features outlined by Siegfried Wagner, and by September 1887 the structure was in place.[13] Above the entrance was inscribed a phrase from the New Testament: "I know that my Redeemer liveth." The structure suffered bomb damage in the final weeks of World War II (as did Wahnfried), and Liszt's coffin was temporarily exhumed and re-buried on the same site, this time with a simple tombstone. In 1978 the city of Bayreuth restored the original mausoleum, which remains there today.

I I

While the struggle over Liszt's remains unfolded, another one began over his will. A few days after his death a copy of this document was sent from Weimar to Hungary, and a summary of the contents was published in the newspaper *Pesther Lloyd* on August 19, 1886. For the first time it became clear to everyone that Princess Carolyne was the sole "residuary legatee."[14] Unfortunately, the will left no instructions as to the disposal of his Hungarian possessions. Apart from his personal belongings (the books, pianos, and furniture in his Budapest apartment, of which more later), it was known that Liszt had left 1,000 forints in a Hungarian bank-account. In January 1887, the newspaper *Fővárosi Lapok* reported that the matter looked as if it were about to become a court case.[15] Apparently, the Hungarian courts had refused to hand over the bankbook to Princess Carolyne, even though she was Liszt's executrix. The position of the court was that she was not a relative, and there might be those who had a prior claim to the money. When they read about this legal impasse, Ludwig Lager and his four brothers (the Austrian nephews of Anna Lager, Liszt's mother) applied to the courts as the legitimate beneficiaries. Eventually these

---

13. The matter is briefly touched on in MCW, vol. 2, pp. 119 and 177.
14. The complete text of this will, together with a codicil, was published in Volume Two, Appendix I.
15. *Fővárosi Lapok,* January 25, 1887.

"relatives" were turned down on the grounds that their petition was drafted in the form of a letter, not a legal document, and it was not written in Hungarian.[16] This claim of the Lagers on the estate was truly brazen; Liszt had never dealt with their branch of the family, and he had often expressed disinterest in them. Moreover, they were not his nearest relatives. Cosima was still alive, and if the blood tie meant anything at all it surely meant that she, as his next-of-kin, had a prior claim on his estate. Actually, the "blood tie" meant nothing at all in this case, as we shall see.

The bulk of Liszt's estate was held by Rothschilds bank in Paris. Liszt had made it clear in his will that whatever money remained after his death was to be divided equally between his two daughters. It will be recalled that at the time of their marriages in 1857, he had settled on each of them a capital sum of 100,000 francs, the interest of which they would draw until his death, after which the capital itself would be transferred to them. He had also given them substantial dowries. In recognition of these bequests, Blandine and Cosima had relinquished all further claims on Liszt's estate. Moreover, since he had named Princess Carolyne as his "residuary legatee," anything left over was hers to dispose of as she wished.[17] In the event, everything was left over. Blandine had died, so her share remained in the estate; as for Cosima, she was divorced from Hans von Bülow, and the marriage contract drawn up at the time of her wedding was void.

Across the years, the balance of Liszt's money (invested partly in North American railway shares) had grown substantially, and his accounts at Rothschilds showed that he left the sum of 207,733 francs at the time of his death. As the rightful owner of this money, Carolyne decided to release 40,000 francs to Emile Ollivier and 10,000 francs to his son, Daniel, thinking that this would have been Blandine's share of the interest had she lived. There were difficulties, however, in prying this money away from Rothschilds, who placed many legal obstacles in Carolyne's way. So she engaged the services of Dr. Johann Brichta, the Viennese lawyer who had handled all Liszt's business affairs since the death of cousin Eduard in 1879. Rothschilds wanted a copy of Liszt's will, a copy of his birth and death certificates, proof of domicile, and letters from legal experts on such a wide variety of topics that the princess despaired of ever getting the will executed. Ollivier had already asked her to give him power of attorney, and Carolyne signed the necessary authority on August 13, 1886. He rightly sensed a disaster-in-the-making. The will was in Weimar, Brichta was in Vienna, Carolyne was in Rome, and Ollivier himself was at La Moutte, in the south of France. He asked his brother, Adolphe, to represent him in Paris

---

16. Liszt's estate was represented by the well-known Hungarian advocate Dr. Mór Stiller, who worked on this matter with Liszt's financial adviser in Vienna, Dr. Johann Brichta.

17. See Volume Two, p. 563.

and demand that Rothschilds comply with Carolyne's wishes. "Everything will fall to Daniel," he assured Adolphe.[18]

Now followed a series of delays which began to exhaust Carolyne's patience. On October 30, 1886, she wrote to Baron Rothschild setting forth the legal position, and chastising his firm for the long delays. "It would just be acceptable if it were a question of some fellow or other who had died in the depths of Russia, or a young tradesman killed in the middle of Africa. But when it is a question of a death, the dazzling news of which occupied both hemispheres only a few weeks ago, such pettiness becomes quibbling."[19] Rothschilds were not to be hurried, however, and the case dragged on for months. On February 25, 1887, Adolphe Ollivier wrote a nervous note to Rothschilds, asking them to explain the exact situation with regards to Liszt's estate. "I am leaving this evening and would like to take to my brother the information you will be good enough to give me."[20] The thing that Emile most feared now happened. Princess Carolyne died on March 9, and with her passing the Olliviers lost whatever legal advantages they had hitherto possessed. Everything that Carolyne owned, including all the monies due to her from Liszt's estate, passed by default to her only beneficiary, Princess Marie von Hohenlohe. And so, by a supreme twist of fate, the family that had wrought so much mischief in the life of Liszt eventually came into possession of every franc that he owned. The Rothschild archives prove it.

After Carolyne's death, Dr. Brichta began to act for Marie Hohenlohe, and he provided Rothschilds with a new power-of-attorney. Liszt's will was finally executed on August 31, 1887, thirteen months after he died.[21]

III

While these dramatic proceedings were taking place, Grand Duke Carl Alexander took the first positive step towards honouring Liszt's memory. Since he had been denied the privilege of erecting a mausoleum, he suggested the creation of a *Stiftung* whose primary task would be to launch a number of projects to ensure that Liszt's name and fame were properly acknowledged,

---

18. Hitherto unpublished letter to his brother, Adolphe, BN NAF 25192, vol. 18. Aside from the fact that Blandine was dead and no longer drew her interest, Emile himself had signed away all claims on Liszt's property in January 1858, when he, Liszt, and Blandine had drawn up the latter's marriage contract in Weimar.

19. AN, Rothschild Archives, Box 3V47, item 4.

20. AN, Rothschild Archives, Box 3V47, item 13.

21. AN, Rothschild Archives, Box 3V47, item 16. Marie Hohenlohe signed the document releasing Rothschilds from all further responsibility, and Konstantin Hohenlohe counter-signed it, thereby giving the necessary legal permission for his wife to receive Liszt's estate.

and he gave permission to turn the Hofgärtnerei into a permanent Liszt Museum. The building was inseparably associated with Liszt by the mere fact of his having lived there for so many years. Moreover, it was already world-famous because of his masterclasses, and it housed many of his most precious belongings. But where to find the funding? Princess Marie Hohenlohe, who, as we have seen, inherited much of Liszt's estate on the death of her mother in March 1887, very generously gave to the *Stiftung* all of Liszt's treasures, which form the basis of the collection today: manuscripts, diplomas, gold medallions, decorations, and priceless objects from his early concert tours (the silver breakfast-service presented to him by the Philharmonic Society of London in 1840, the valuable jade-and-gold clock from his admirers in St. Petersburg in 1842, and a bejewelled casket from Maria Pawlowna). Princess Marie herself travelled to Weimar in May 1887 to supervise the arrangements.[22] She also gave the *Stiftung* 70,000 gulden to pay for its operations. Without in any way detracting from such generosity, it needs to be said that this was almost precisely the amount of money that she had inherited by default from Liszt's estate; in brief, through yet another irony, Liszt had become his own posthumous beneficiary.

The first requirement was to appoint a curator, and Carl Gille agreed to serve in this capacity. The housekeeper, Pauline Apel, who had continued to live in the Hofgärtnerei after Liszt's death, became the official in-house tourist guide to the exhibition.[23] The Liszt Museum was opened on May 22, 1887. The simple inauguration ceremony was attended by Carl Alexander and Grand Duchess Sophie, Marie and Konstantin Hohenlohe, and a hundred or so friends, pupils, and disciples, who filled the small rooms and spread onto the garden outside. Professor Adolf Stern of Dresden delivered the inaugural address.[24] Cosima had been invited, but she did not attend. May 22 happened to be Wagner's birthday, and nothing was allowed to mar this hallowed anniversary.

This was the first such retrospective exhibition of Liszt's life and work ever to have been assembled in one place, and it spanned a career of more than sixty years. Cosima visited the Liszthaus only once, in the company of her daughter Eva. According to Pauline Apel, who showed them round the museum, the occasion was not a particularly happy one. After viewing the various objects which symbolised her father's artistic life, Cosima paused before a showcase that contained some precious relics of his concert tours. She stared

---

22. SZM, pp. 470–71.
23. Pauline Apel remained the curator for the rest of her life. She kept in touch with all the *Lisztianer*, received them cordially whenever they visited Weimar, and even corresponded with many of them. They in turn came to regard her as an institution until her death in 1926, aged eighty-eight. As Pauline neared her end, her sixty-three-year-old daughter, Frau Theodora Beck, moved into the Hofgärtnerei and showed the visitors around the house in her mother's stead.
24. It was re-printed in NZfM on June 2, 1887.

at it for a long time through her lorgnette, and then turned to her daughter and said in French, so as not to be understood by Frau Apel: "All these beautiful things are lying around here doing no good. I would like to know why my father didn't leave them to his family."[25] The comment suggests that Cosima may have lacked a true comprehension of the meaning of her father's life. Presumably a more useful function for all those gold medals would have been to melt them down and use the money to support the Wagner festival in Bayreuth.

After the death of Carl Gille in 1899, the Hofgärtnerei was directed by three outstanding curators who looked after the collection until modern times: Carl Müller-Hartung (1899–1902), Aloys Obrist (1902–10), and Peter Raabe (1910–44). During the long years of Raabe's custodianship the first serious attempt was made to catalogue Liszt's compositions and the many thousands of letters that formed his epistolary legacy. Between the two world wars the collection was greatly increased in size when those who had known Liszt bequeathed their letters and other memorabilia to the museum. (Three of the most impressive collections to be added to Liszt's were those of Müller-Hartung, Lina Ramann, and Martha Remmert, which made Weimar by far the most significant centre for Liszt research in the world.) After World War II most of these manuscripts and letters were removed to the Goethe-Schiller Archive in Weimar, which offers superior research facilities and which is where scholars consult them today. The historical objects remained in the Hofgärtnerei.[26]

In 1907 the *Stiftung* announced that it would embark upon the publication of Liszt's Collected Edition. This project was long overdue. One of the difficulties facing those who wanted to come to grips with Liszt's huge output was that his legacy was scattered. Many different publishers had brought out his music during his lifetime, and much of it was now out of print or otherwise unobtainable. One of the most distinguished editorial teams ever assembled took part in the reclamation. Ferruccio Busoni was given the task of editing the études, Eugène d'Albert the symphonic poems, the young Béla Bartók the lesser orchestral works, Peter Raabe the songs, Philipp Wolfrum the choral works, and Vianna da Motta the *Années de pèlerinage* and a great deal of the miscellaneous piano music besides. This monumental edition was known as "The Grand Duke Carl Alexander Edition" in memory of the founder of the *Stiftung,* who had died in 1901. The enterprise was overseen by Aloys Obrist

25. "Liszt's Pauline." Cuk, *Neues Wiener Journal,* September 26, 1926.
26. The fullest account of the contents of the Liszt Museum as they existed at the end of the nineteenth century may be found in *Das Liszt-Museum zu Weimar und seine Erinnerungen* by Adolf Mirus (Weimar, 1892).

and Otto Taubmann. Between 1908 and 1936 the *Stiftung* succeeded in bringing out thirty-four volumes of Liszt's music, at which point the project stopped for lack of money. During this very long period of time the editorial team encountered many setbacks. (Obrist died in 1910, Wolfrum in 1919, and Busoni in 1924.) Despite the fact that many worthy items were never included (the Schubert song-transcriptions, for instance, and such large-scale choral works as *Christus*), the edition continued to do yeoman service until modern times.

The one-hundredth anniversary of Liszt's birth, which fell in 1911, produced the first real test of the composer's posthumous reputation. How would Liszt's name be celebrated? What sort of judgement would history now render? Among the crop of Liszt festivals to break out across Europe that year, the ones in Budapest, Weimar, and Heidelberg stand out in importance. A galaxy of Liszt pupils descended on Budapest between October 21 and 25, including Emil Sauer, Eugène d'Albert, Moriz Rosenthal, Arthur Friedheim, Sophie Menter, Vera Timanova, and Frederic Lamond. They were all there at the special invitation of the Liszt Festival Committee, whose president was Count Géza Zichy. The special guests of honour included two of Liszt's grandchildren—Siegfried Wagner and Countess Blandine Gravina von Bülow—and Princess Marie Hohenlohe. Siegfried Wagner, in fact, had been invited to conduct a performance of the *Faust* Symphony, which turned out to be a memorable one.

Much of the Hungarian festival took place in the new building of the Liszt Academy of Music, whose strikingly attractive concert hall provided a superior venue for the star-studded cast of performers. That is where a historic piano gala took place, during which some of Liszt's pupils walked onto the platform in succession to place their musical tributes at the altar of his memory: d'Albert's Polonaise in E major, Friedheim's Sonata in B minor, Juhász's *Cantique d'amour* and *Mazeppa,* and Lamond's *Don Giovanni* Fantasy were just a few of the blooms in this bouquet.[27] These pianists were vastly different from one another—one poetic, another heroic, a third philosophic—and they were a tribute to Liszt's respect for artistic individuality. D'Albert played with so much power, in fact, that by the time it was Lamond's turn to appear, the piano had collapsed and had to receive some first-aid.

While this celebration was taking place in Budapest, a similar one was being held in Weimar. On October 22 there was another performance of the *Faust* Symphony, under Peter Raabe, while Frederic Lamond played *Totentanz* in the same concert.[28] Then on October 24 came a staged performance of *St. Elisabeth.*

---

27. By far the most detailed report of this festival was printed in New York's *Musical Courier,* in the issue of November 15, 1911. See also the account given by La Mara in LDML, vol. 2, pp. 442–49.
28. As far as we can discover, Frederic Lamond was the only artist to take part in both festivals.

But it was left to the Allgemeiner Deutscher Musikverein to mount the biggest Liszt festival of the centennial year when it transformed its annual meeting, held this time in Heidelberg, into a vast celebration of the composer's life and work. This was due in large measure to the advocacy of Richard Strauss, who added much lustre to the event when he invited the seventy-six-year-old Camille Saint-Saëns to come out of semi-retirement and appear as a soloist. The veteran pianist delivered a stunning recital of Liszt's music, which included *Au bord d'une source,* Liszt's transcriptions of Saint-Saëns's own *Danse macabre,* and Glinka's Tscherkessen March. After six curtain calls, a beaming Strauss himself led Saint-Saëns back onto the platform for an encore. The Heidelberg celebrations were also notable for a full-scale performance of *Christus.*

The thing to command our attention in the midst of all this jubilation is that most of it was generated by Liszt's own students and disciples. These individuals were members of a world-wide family, and although many of them were now musicians of distinction in their own right, they were a family nonetheless. And when they dispersed, the rest of the world retained but a fleeting recollection of the event—a temporary disturbance on the otherwise placid waters of one more concert season. The Liszt centennial year, in fact, was not unlike a snapshot album which contains pictures of interest only to those relatives who are depicted in them. Contrary to all the hopes and expectations, the exposure of so much of Liszt's music in so brief a period of time did little to shift the burden of critical debate in his direction. Liszt was still perceived to be a "cause" pursued by crusaders. But crusaders in turn arouse suspicion. And that is still the case today.

Of all the countries with a claim to honour Liszt's memory, Hungary remained paramount since it was rooted in history, in biography, and in national pride. Not long after the composer's death, plans were made for a Liszt Memorial Museum at the Academy of Music in Budapest, in his old suite of rooms at no. 67 Sugár Street. Liszt had bequeathed the contents of these rooms to the academy in perpetuity.[29] Among the items were the Chickering grand piano, an Alexandre-Erard harmonium-piano, some furniture, and a library of several hundred books or more. Unfortunately, there were some setbacks. The academy was filled with students, and Liszt's rooms were required for teaching. And there were other difficulties. Since Liszt's will did not cover his Budapest possessions, Princess Carolyne diplomatically suggested that they be returned to their original donors (much of what Liszt had owned in Hungary had been given to him by Hungarian admirers). This was a pity, since many items were

---

29. He had done so in a letter to Kornél Ábrányi, the secretary of the academy, dated May 22, 1881. For the biographical circumstances in which Liszt made the decision to make these bequests to Hungary, see p. 272.

thus lost.[30] The *Pesther Lloyd* reported that a mere three weeks after his death Liszt's flat looked as if a removal were in progress.[31] Some things were eventually returned by the donors to the museum, including his prayer-stool. In 1907 the academy was transferred to its present building in Liszt Square, but it was not until 1925, the fiftieth anniversary of the founding of the academy, that a Liszt Memorial Room was opened, where the collection remained on permanent exhibition for more than sixty years. As part of the Liszt centennial celebrations in 1986, the old academy building on Sugár Street was re-opened and turned into an official Liszt Museum and Research Centre. The Liszt memorial collection had finally come home.[32]

Even during Liszt's lifetime it was understood that the task of publishing an edition of his letters would fall to La Mara. A month before Liszt died, in fact, La Mara had come out with her *Musikerbriefe aus fünf Jahrhunderten,* a collection of musicians' letters across five centuries which contained nine by Liszt— to Czerny, Brockhaus, Draeseke, and Brendel. Liszt was pleased with their inclusion and told La Mara: "You have my permission to print whatever you like by me."[33] This was the beginning of a publishing project that was to occupy La Mara for the rest of her long life. Her *Franz Liszt's Briefe* runs to eight volumes, and La Mara edited additional volumes of Liszt's letters as well—to Carl Alexander and to his mother, for example. La Mara has been criticised elsewhere in this study for censoring Liszt's prose. But it has to be said in her defence that if Princess Carolyne had had her way the results might have been far worse. When La Mara sent Carolyne a copy of her newly published *Musikerbriefe* in November 1886, the princess was not particularly impressed. She was, in fact, perturbed to see that Liszt's letters had been served up, as she put it, "like so many raw vegetables," and felt that a certain amount of dressing up would have been in order. She recalled that when she had first arrived

---

30. In light of this action of the princess, we can see how fortunate it was that Liszt himself had already given to the Hungarian nation certain items of value—including the Sword of Honour, the golden goblet given to him by the women of Hungary in 1840, the golden conductor's baton given to him by Carolyne herself, and the Broadwood grand piano that had belonged to Beethoven. These gifts had been made in November 1873, and we know that the princess did not entirely approve of them going to Hungary. (GLMM, pp. 121–25; also Liszt's letter to Carolyne on this topic, dated "Budapest, March 18, 1879," LLB, vol. 7, pp. 245–46) They are now on permanent exhibition in the Hungarian National Museum.
31. Issue of August 22, 1886. More than a year later the journal *Zenelap* complained that no Liszt museum had so far been established in Hungary to match the one in Weimar. In fact, it went on, every vestige of the master's memory appeared to have been carried off within a few months of his death.
32. For the most comprehensive account of the present holdings of the Budapest Liszt Museum and Research Centre see ELF and EFLE.
33. LDML, vol. 2, p. 127.

in Weimar, "in the good old days of 1848," a commission had been set up to scrutinize every word that Goethe had written in his letters, according to the rules of grammar, even when it was a mere matter of sending asparagus to a friend or receiving pineapples, and she felt that Liszt deserved no less. "I would like people to see him *properly dressed* in his letters," Carolyne observed, and reminded La Mara that it was better to see someone with a decent toilette, washed, combed, and properly groomed, rather than lounging around in a dressing-gown.[34] What this meant, of course, when all the flowery euphemisms had been swept aside, was that Liszt's letters would have to be censored. The choice of letters to be published was also important, Carolyne insisted. Liszt, she said, had been quite indignant at the large number of thoroughly routine letters that had been included in the Goethe collection, in which the ones of genuine importance tended to get buried. La Mara probably did the best that she could in all the circumstances. While a good many letters were edited and others were suppressed, the damage could have been greater. For better or worse, the influence of La Mara's work on modern Liszt scholarship cannot be denied.[35]

IV

And what of Princess Carolyne herself? When news of Liszt's death was brought to her, she took to her bed and never left it.[36] She appears to have suffered a seizure which partially immobilized her. Her mental energies also began to decline, and she succumbed to dropsy and intermittent fevers. Her friend Malwida von Meysenbug, one of the few people to visit her, reported that life appeared to have lost its value for Carolyne.[37] However, her will to work was indomitable. She continued to write a mass of correspondence, as we have seen, on such matters as Liszt's last resting-place and the disposition of his will. This cost her a great deal of physical pain, for she had difficulty in holding the pen in her swollen hand, which was ravaged with rheumatism, her old enemy. She also managed to complete work on her *magnum opus;* the twenty-fourth and final volume of her *Causes intérieures* was finished just two weeks before her death. It concludes with the date "February 23, 'Ash Wednesday,' Rome, 1887."

Carolyne drew her last breath on the evening of March 9, 1887, only a few months after Liszt himself had expired. Princess Marie described her mother's

---

34. LDML, vol. 2, pp. 136–37.
35. For further commentary on La Mara's place in the scheme of things, see Volume One, pp. 11–14.
36. LDML, vol. 2, p. 136.
37. MLEI, pp. 103–04.

last days on earth.[38] At the beginning of March, Marie had come down from Vienna in response to an urgent summons from friends to look after her mother at Via del Babuino. She was shocked when she entered the stifling sickroom and saw that Carolyne was suffering from dropsy. A doctor was summoned, but he could do little except to ease her last moments. On the evening of March 8 Cardinal Hohenlohe called on his sister-in-law, and he and Marie began to discuss the possibility of sending for Carolyne's confessor. As they were chatting, the chambermaid entered and said: "There is a deathly silence in the bedroom." When they opened the door, they saw Carolyne's head slightly inclined, an expression of great calm on her face. She had slipped into the arms of death without a sound. It was 1:30 a.m.[39]

For two days the body lay in state in the apartment, and mass was celebrated there by special permission of the cardinal vicar of Rome. On the evening of March 11, Carolyne's corpse was placed in a coffin, and the body was brought to the church of Santa Maria del Popolo, her parish church, and ceremoniously placed near the altar.[40] The next day, March 12, a requiem mass was celebrated by Monsignor Luigi Meurin, assistant to Cardinal Hohenlohe: during the service Liszt's Requiem for Organ was played. Afterwards Cardinal Hohenlohe himself provided absolution at the bier. At 6:00 p.m. the funeral cortège set out for the German Cemetery inside the Vatican, not far from St. Peter's Basilica. There the body was buried in a niche in the wall and covered over with a tombstone which bears the following inscription:

---

38. In a letter to Emma Herwegh, Princess Marie mourned the fact that with the death of her mother all the "heroes" of the Altenburg years were gone, and that she herself felt like a hyphen between a vanished past and future which was yet to take shape. "After Liszt's death," she wrote,

> my mother asked to remain alone. She was afraid that my visits would upset her too much. From then on, she only wanted to be isolated in her sorrow and silence. She hardly saw anyone all winter, complained a great deal about little things; but we were used to that. It was only in February that her complaints became more sorrowful, and some friends in Rome wrote to me that they were fearful about her condition.
>
> I rushed to Rome and was frightened to find her suffering from dropsy, when nothing had prepared me for that. The enormous affection that she had formerly felt for me revived then; she greeted me, radiant with joy. The doctor predicted a long illness, but God was merciful to her. A high fever broke out and managed to burn up her feeble resistance in a few days. She was not aware of death's approach and fell gently asleep, without suffering, during the night of March 9.

> Vienna, Easter Saturday, 1887 (HSD, p. 125)

39. See the hitherto unpublished account of Carolyne's burial in the Register of Deaths for the Parish of Santa Maria del Popolo, March 9, 1887, Appendix I, p. 541.

40. Because certain parts of the *Causes intérieures* had been placed on the Index, there was some question about Carolyne receiving the last rites. As it happened, the funeral services for such people were traditionally held in her own parish church of Santa Maria del Popolo, which took a lenient view of the "liberal aristocrats" of Catholicism.

HERE RESTS IN PEACE
CAROLYNE
PRINCESS VON SAYN–WITTGENSTEIN
OF THE IWANOWSKA LINE
BORN FEBRUARY 8, 1819
DIED MARCH 9, 1887
PER ANGUSTA AD AUGUSTA[41]

Beneath this inscription lies a simple marble slab bearing the epitaph "Jenseits ist meine Hoffnung"—"Eternity is my hope."

---

41. "Through suffering to greatness."

Appendixes
Sources
Index

Appendix I:

PRINCESS CAROLYNE'S DEATH NOTICE,
FROM THE REGISTER OF
SANTA MARIA DEL POPOLO, ROME

No. 36. Iwanowska Wittgenstein, Carolyne

A.D. 1887 9 March.

Her Most Illustrious Highness Princess Carolyne Iwanowska, born in Podolia in Russian Poland, daughter of the late Peter Iwanowski and the late Countess Pauline Podowska, and the widow of the late Nicholas, Prince von Sayn–Wittgenstein, died with the comfort of the Sacraments at Via del Babuino no. 89, at 1:30 a.m. She was 68 years old. For two days, her remains lay in state at her home, where, by permission of the Most Eminent Cardinal Vicar of the City, several masses were celebrated. From there, on the evening of the 11th, the body was brought to this church in a solemn funeral cortège and, on the following day, in accordance with the custom extended to Princes, it was ceremoniously placed on the ground with the celebration of many masses. After the Office for the dead, a Pontifical High Mass was celebrated by His Most Illustrious and Reverend Excellency Monsignor Luigi Meurin, of the Society of Jesus, Archbishop of Ascalon among the infidels and Apostolic Vicar in Bombay, and assistant to the Most Eminent Cardinal of the Holy Roman Church Monsignor Gustav Hohenlohe, who later provided absolution at the bier. Then, around 6:00 p.m. of the 12th, the body was brought to the German Cemetery close to the Vatican Basilica and was buried there in a special niche. In faith etc.

Pastor: Friar Guglielmo Maria D'Ambrogi of the Augustinian Order.

[original text]

No. 36. Iwanowska Wittgenstein, Carolina

Anno D[omi]ni 1887. Die 9 Martii.

In Via Babbuino [sic] no. 89, hora 1½ a.m. Sacramentis munita obiit aet[atis] suae anno 68 Ill[ustrissi]ma Altitudo Principissa Carolina Iwanowska e Podolia Poloniae Russae, filia q[uondam] Petri, et q[uondam] Comitissae Paulinae Podoska, et Vidua q[uondam] Nicolai Principis Sayn–Wittgenstein. Per duos dies Cadaver expositum fuit domi, ubi nonnullae Missae de Licentia Eminant[issimi] Cardinalis Vicarii Urbis celebratae sunt. Hinc sub vespaere diei 11ae solemnissima pompa funebri ad hanc Ecclesiam translatum fuit, et sequenti die solemniter, more principum, in terra expositum cum celebratione plurimarum missarum. Post Officium Defunctorum, celebrata est Solemnis

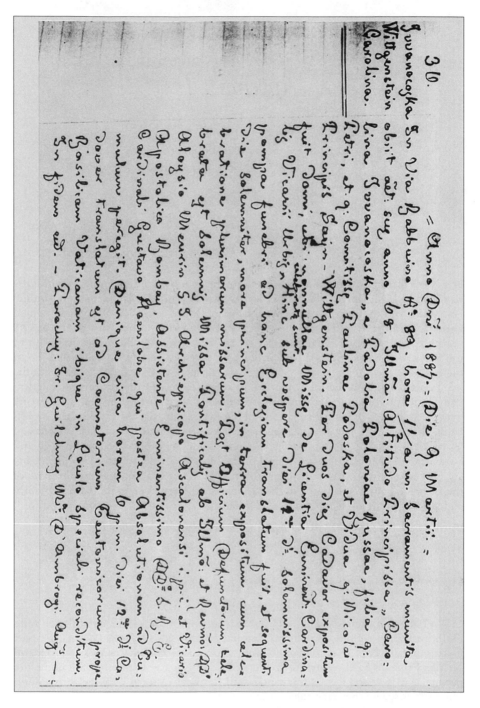

A facsimile of Princess Carolyne's entry in the Register of Deaths for March 9, 1887,
at the church of Santa Maria del Popolo, Rome.

Missa Pontificalis ab Ill[ustrissi]mo et Rev[erendissi]mo D.D. Aloysio Meurin S[oci-etatis] J[esu], Archiepiscopo Ascalonensi i[n] p[artibus] i[nfidelium] et Vicario Apos-tolico Bombay, Assistente Eminentissimo D[omino] D[omino] S[antcae] R[omanae] E[cclesiae] Cardinali Gustavo Ho[h]enlohe, qui postea Absolutionem ad Tumulum peregit. Denique circam horam 6 p.m. diei 12ae diei Cadaver translatum est ad Co-emeterium Teutonicorum prope Basilicam Vaticanam ibique in Loculo Speciali re-conditum. In fidem etc.

Parochus: Fr[ater] Guilelmus M[ari]a D'Ambrogi Aug[ustinianu]s.

Appendix II:

LISZT ENTERS THE MINOR ORDERS
OF THE PRIESTHOOD:
ENTRIES FROM THE *LIBER ORDINATIONUM*
FOR 1863-1872, VICARIATO DI ROMA

[p. 114]

On April 25, 1865, in a private chapel in Rome, Monsignor Gustav Adolf von Hohenlohe, Archbishop of Edessa, elevated M. Franz Liszt to the First Clerical Tonsure,
having received from the Most Holy Father, Pope Pius IX, on the force of assurances
given by the same archbishop, dispensation from presenting episcopal letters of permission, undergoing formal examination and providing the other attestations that are
normally to be presented to the office of the Secretariat in the Vicariate.

[Original text]

Gustavus Adolphus de Hohenlohe Archiep[isco]pus Edessen[sis] die 25 Aprilis 1865
promovit Romae in privato sacello ad primam clericalem Tonsuram D[ominum]
Franciscum Liszt . . . dispensatis a S[ancti]s[i]mo D[omi]no N[ost]ro P[a]p[a] Pio IX
dimissoriis, examine aliisque attestationibus in Secretaria Vicariatus de more exhibendis, prout in fide eiusdem Archiep[isco]i.

[p. 131]

On July 30, 1865, the eighth Sunday after Pentecost, in a private chapel in Tivoli, in the
exercise of his prerogatives and after consideration of all that needs to be considered,
the Most Illustrious and Reverend Monsignor Gustav von Hohenlohe, Archbishop of
Edessa, elevated to the four minor orders M. Franz Liszt, born in the district of Tyr-
navia, and now a member of the Roman clergy.

[Original text]

Ill[ustrissi]mus ac R[everendissi]mus P[ater], D[ominus] Gustavus de Hohenlohe,
Archiep[iscop]us Edessen[sis] Tibure in oratorio privato die 30 Julii ann[i] 1865
Dom[inica] octava post Pent[ecostem] de licentia promovit ad quartos minores ordines
D[ominum] Franciscum Liszt origine Taurinen[sem] et in romanum clerum coopta-
tum servatis servandis.

Romæ in privato sacello de licentia promovit D. Silvestrum Szczepan-
kiewicz Cincinnaten. D.? die 17. Aprilis Fer. II post Pascha ann. 1865
ad subdiaconatum tit. missionis, die vero 23 eiusdem mensis Dom.
in albis ad Diaconatum præviis dimissoriis, publicat. sp. exercitiis,
examine, dispensa Aplica super extra tempora.

Gustavus Adolphus de Hohenlohe Archiepus Edessen. die 25
Aprilis 1865 promovit Romæ in privato sacello ad primam clericalem
tonsuram D. Franciscum Liszt — dispensatus a ssmo
Dno nro SS. Pio IX dimissoriis examine absque attestationibus
in secretaria Vicariatus de more exhibendis, prout in fide eiusdem
Archiepi.

Liszt receives the tonsure from Monsigner Hohenlohe, April 25, 1865. A facsimile page from the
Liber Ordinationum *for 1863–1872, Vicariato di Roma.*

Liszt enters the minor orders of the priesthood on July 30, 1865. A facsimile page from the
Liber Ordinationum *for 1863–1872, Vicariato di Roma.*

Appendix III:

LISZT'S TITLES AND HONOURS

It has often been said that in the course of his long life Franz Liszt received as many orders and titles as a prince. The following list goes some way toward proving the point. It is by no means complete, but all the major titles are here. The many gifts and tokens that he received, especially during his career as a virtuoso, have been omitted, although they were sometimes more exotic than a medal. Thus, there is no mention of such things as the silver breakfast service presented to him by the Philharmonic Society of London in June 1840, or of the inscribed baton he received from the mayor of Vienna after he had directed the Mozart Festival there in January 1856, to say nothing of the pair of performing bears sent to him by Tsar Nicholas I after he had played in Moscow in May 1843.

What is left would be an impressive enough catalogue of honours for an aristocrat. For a musician it probably remains unmatched in history.

January 15, 1824	Honorary member of the Société Academique des Enfants d'Apollon, Paris
January 25, 1826	Gold medallion of the Bordeaux Philharmonic Society
1839	Academician of the Accademia di Santa Cecilia
January 4, 1840	Hungarian Sword of Honour
February 18, 1840	Honorary Citizen of Oedenburg
July 1841	Danebrog Order
January 22, 1842	Honorary Member of the North German Music Association
March 1842	Prussian order "Pour le Mérite"; a member of the Prussian Academy of Arts
March 1842	Honorary doctorate from the University of Königsberg
July 18, 1842	Order of the Lion of Belgium from King Leopold I
October 1842	Freedom of the City of Jena
October 13, 1843	Honorary Member of the Albrecht Dürer Society
October 14, 1843	Honorary Member of the Mozart Society of Nuremburg
November 1843	Court Councillor to Prince Konstantin von Hohenzollern-Hechingen

November 7, 1844	Cross of Carlos III from Queen Isabella of Spain
February 1845	Order of Christ, from Queen Maria II of Portugal
August 3, 1846	Magistrate of the County of Oedenburg
September 25, 1846	Freedom of the town of Köszeg
November 11, 1846	Freedom of the city of Arad
July 1847	Order of Nichan-Iftikhar from the Sultan of Turkey, Abdul-Medjid Khan
February 13, 1854	Order of the White Falcon (Second Class) from Grand Duke Carl Alexander of Weimar
June 12, 1857	Member of the Royal Swedish Academy of Music in Stockholm
April 1858	Confrater of the Order of St. Francis
April 10, 1859	Order of the Iron Crown of Austria
August 1859	Commander of the Order of St. Gregory the Great, from Pope Pius IX
October 30, 1859	Elevated to the Austrian nobility (Thereafter, he is entitled to use the prefix "von" before his name, but does not do so. He allows this title to pass to his cousin Eduard and the latter's heirs.)
February 16, 1860	Order of the Noble Cross of the House of Hohenzollern-Hechingen, Second Class
August 1860	Officer of the French Legion of Honour
October 26, 1860	Freedom of the city of Weimar
May 1861	Commander of the French Legion of Honour
August 17, 1861	Chamberlain of the Weimar Court
April 15, 1864	Order of Pius IX, Third Class
April 25, 1865	Receives the tonsure in the Vatican
May 19, 1865	Elected to the Congregazione Pontifica dei Virtuosi al Pantheon
July 30, 1865	Minor orders of the priesthood (Doorkeeper, Lector, Exorcist, and Acolyte)
December 1, 1865	Honorary membership of the Mexican Philharmonic Society
April 4, 1866	Cross of the Order of St. Michael of King Ludwig II of Bavaria
June 7, 1867	Commander's Cross of the Order of the Emperor Franz Joseph
June 13, 1871	Royal Hungarian Councillor, with an annual pension of 4,000 forints
November 9, 1873	Honorary member of the Imperial Academy of Music, St. Petersburg
January 11, 1874	Order of the Emperor Franz Joseph

February 26, 1874	Honorary member of the Provident Society of the Factory Workers of Old Buda
March 30, 1875	President of the Royal Hungarian Academy of Music
March 17, 1877	Presented by the Mayor of Vienna with the city's gold Redeemer Medal
April 29, 1879	Honorary Member of the Società Musicale Romana
October 12, 1879	Installed as Honorary Canon of Albano by Cardinal Gustav von Hohenlohe
May 31, 1881	Order of Leopold from the King of the Belgians

Appendix IV:

CATALOGUE OF PRINCESS CAROLYNE'S WRITINGS

The extent of Princess Carolyne's literary activity is hardly recognized today. Yet after she and Liszt parted, in 1861, and she picked up her pen in earnest, she published at least forty-four volumes of prose. The sheer quantity of her output beggars the imagination, and it is all the more remarkable for having emerged during the last twenty-five years of her life.

Boudhisme et Christianisme, 1 volume. Rome, 1868, pp. 254.

De la prière par une femme du monde, 1 volume, Rome, 1869, pp. 370.

Entretiens pratiques à l'usage des femmes du monde, 1 volume.

Religion et monde, 1 volume.

L'Amitié des anges, 1 volume.

La Chapelle sixtine, 1 volume, Paris, 1867, pp. 39.

"L'istoria religiosa e civite dei papi scritta dal prof.–G. Audisio–per la principessa C. di Sayn-Wittgenstein," *Rivista universale,* 1867, pp. 21.

"Il Monumento di Pio VIII," *Annali Catholici,* 1866, pp. 7.

La Mathière dans la dogmatique chrétienne, 3 volumes, 1871.[1]

L'Eglise attaquée par la médisance, 1 volume, Rome, 1869, pp. 252.

Petits entretiens pratiques à l'usage des femmes du grand monde pour la durée d'une retraite spirituelle, 8 volumes.

Simplicité des colombes, prudence des serpens: Quelques reflexions suggérées par les femmes et les temps actuels, 1 volume, n.p., n.d.

Souffrance et prudence, 1 volume, Rome, 1869, pp. 38.

Sur la perfection chrétienne et la vie intérieure, 1 volume.

"L'Exposé de la musique de l'Eglise," 1872, pp. 117.

---

1. Dedicated to Liszt. The flowery inscription runs: "A Monsieur l'Abbé Liszt, Grand-Croix de hautes Ordres, etc."

Causes intérieures de la faiblesse extérieure de l'Eglise en 1870, 24 volumes, Rome, 1872–87.[2]
  Divided into nine parts:

Part One (1 vol., 1872):
  I. De l'état actuel de l'Eglise, moral et intellectuel

Part Two (1 vol., 1872):
  Des biens de l'Eglise. Du culte. De l'entretiens du clergé. De l'administration des biens ecclésiastiques.

Part Three (1 vol., 1873):
  Du principe de l'élection et de la nomination dans le clergé hiérarchique

Part Four (4 vols., 1875): De l'épiscopat
  I. Situation de l'épiscopat dans l'Eglise. Caractère de l'épiscopat.
  II. Premières conditions d'un bon gouvernement épiscopal. Exemption des ordres religieux de la juridiction épiscopale. Séminaires.
  III. Administration épiscopale
  IV. Qualités épiscopales. Relations épiscopales.

Part Five (3 vols., 1876): Des conciles
  I. Leur nécessité
  II. De la tenue des conciles
  III. De ce qui regarde les conciles particuliers

Part Six (5 vols., 1881): Du cardinalat
  I. Considerations générales
  II. Du conclave. Des cardinaux en particulier. Des consistoires.
  III. Des congrégations
  IV. Suite des congrégations
  V. De l'élection des cardinaux. Costume et étiquette.

Part Seven (4 vols., 1883): De la papauté
  I. La papauté dans Rome
  II. La papauté dans l'Eglise (De Maistre, Lamennais, Rosmini)
  III. La papauté dans la chrétienté
  IV. L'aristocratie dans les sociétés et l'Eglise

Part Eight (2 vols., 1884): Des ordres religieux
  I. De la vie religieuse, de son but et de ses moyens
  II. Du gouvernement des ordres religieux

Part Nine (3 vols., 1885–86–87): Considérations sans titre
  I. Contains sections on Buddhism, Judaism, Luther, the Old and New Testaments
  II. Contains sections on socialism and on Napoleon III
  III. A hypothetical interpretation of the Apocalypse According to St. John

---

2. This work was published anonymously. Two of its volumes were placed on the *Index librorum prohibitorum:* volume nine by a decree of Pius IX dated July 12, 1877; and volume three by a decree of Leo XIII dated February 3, 1879. These volumes were never removed from the Index, as a glance at the last edition of 1961 will show.

Sources Consulted in the Preparation of Volume III

AAM	Apponyi, Count Albert. *Memoirs.* London, 1935.
AAT	Ábrányi, Kornél. *Az élet tarkaságaiból* [Diversities of Life]. Budapest
ABB	Ambros, A. W. *Bunte Blätter: Skizzen und Studien für Freunde der Musik und der bildenden Kunst.* Leipzig, 1872.
ACLA	Agoult, Marie d'. *Correspondance de Liszt et de la Comtesse d'Agoult.* Edited by Daniel Ollivier. 2 vols. Paris, 1933, 1934.
AE	Adelburg, August Ritter von. *Entgegnung auf die von Franz Liszt in seinem Werke "Des Bohémiens et de leur musique en Hongrie" aufgestellte Behauptung: Dass es keine ungarische Nationalmusik . . . gibt.* Vorwort von Alexander von Czeke. Pest, 1859.
ALUK	Ábrányi, Kornél, Sr. *Franz Liszts Ungarische Krönungsmesse. Eine musikalische Studie.* Aus dem ungarischen, von H. Gobbi. Leipzig, New York, 1871.
AMZSZ	Ábrányi, Kornél, Sr. *A magyar zene a 19-ik században* [Hungarian Music in the Nineteenth Century]. Budapest, 1900.
AN	Archives Nationales de France, Paris.
AS	Agoult, Marie d' ("Daniel Stern"). *Mes Souvenirs (1806–33).* Paris, 1877.
ASS	Adam, Juliette. *Mes Souvenirs, mes sentiments et nos idées avant 1870.* 7 vols. Paris, 1902–10.
ASVR(1)	Archivio Segreto Vaticano, Rome. Documents from the archives of Cardinal Antonino de Luca, papal nuncio to Vienna, and from the diocese of Fulda (1860–61). "Special annex: The Matrimonial Case of Wittgenstein versus Iwanowska." Cited by folio number.
ASVR(2)	Archivio Segreto Vaticano, Rome. Documents from the Holy Congregation of the Council of Cardinals (1860–61). Z-60. Cited by folio number.
AVR	Archivio Storico del Vicariato di Roma, St. John Lateran, Rome. Documents pertaining to the marriage of Liszt and Princess Carolyne von Sayn-Wittgenstein (1861). N.4477, L/41.
BA	Bayreuth Archive. Nationalarchiv der Richard Wagner Stiftung, Bayreuth.
BB	Bülow, Hans von. *Briefe.* Herausgegeben von Marie von Bülow. 7 vols. Leipzig, 1899–1908.
BBF	Bowen, Catherine Drinker, and Barbara von Meck. *Beloved Friend: The Story of Tchaikovsky and Nadejda von Meck.* London, 1937.
BBLW	Bülow, Marie von. *Hans von Bülow in Leben und Wort.* Stuttgart, 1925.

BBM   Bache, Constance. *Brother Musicians: Reminiscences of Edward and Walter Bache.* London, 1901.

BBRC   Barzun, Jacques. *Berlioz and the Romantic Century.* 2 vols. 3rd ed. New York, 1969.

BBW   *Bayreuther Blätter: Deutsche Zeitschrift im Geist Richard Wagners.* Herausgegeben von Hans von Wolzogen. Bayreuth, 1901.

BDD   Barker, Nancy Nichol. *Distaff Diplomacy: The Empress Eugénie and the Foreign Policy of the Second Empire.* Austin, Texas, 1967.

BDLL   Robert Bory. "Diverses Lettres inédites de Liszt." *Schweizerisches Jahrbuch für Musikwissenschaft* (Aarau) 3 (1928).

BEM   Busoni, Ferruccio. *The Essence of Music.* London, 1957.

BFL   Burger, Ernst. *Franz Liszt: A Chronicle of His Life in Pictures and Documents.* Translated by Stewart Spencer. Princeton, 1989.

BFLE   Bertha, Alexandre de. "Franz Liszt: Etude musico-psychologique." *Mercure musical* S. I. M. (Paris) 3, nos. 9 to 11 (September 15 to November 15, 1907).

BFM   Bettelheim, Anton, ed. *Fürstin Marie zu Hohenlohe und Ferdinand von Saar: Ein Briefwechsel.* Vienna, 1910.

BGM   Banister, Henry C. *George Alexander Macfarren: His Life, Works and Influence.* London, 1892.

B-KMCE   Beatty-Kingston, William. *Men, Cities and Events.* London, 1895.

BLI   Bárdos, Lajos. "Ferenc Liszt, the Innovator." *Studia Musicologica Academiae Scientiarium Hungaricae* (Budapest) 17 (1975).

BLSJ   *British Liszt Society Journal.* Cited by issue.

BMC   Brassai, Sámuel. *Magyar- vagy czigány-zene? Elmefuttatás Liszt Ferencz "Czigányokról" irt könyve felett* [Hungarian or Gypsy Music? Reflections on Franz Liszt's Book "On the Gypsies"]. Kolozsvár, 1860.

BN   Bibliothèque Nationale, Paris.

BNB   Bülow, Hans von. *Neue Briefe.* Herausgegeben und eingeleitet von Richard Graf du Moulin Eckart. Munich, 1927.

BNCE   Bierman, John. *Napoleon III and His Carnival Empire.* New York, 1988.

BSLW   Bagby, Morris. "A Summer with Liszt in Weimar." *Century* Magazine (New York) 32 (September 1886), pp. 655–69.

BVL   Bory, Robert. *La Vie de Franz Liszt par l'image.* Geneva, 1936.

BWL   *Briefwechsel zwischen Wagner und Liszt.* 2 vols. Leipzig, 1887.

CE   The Breitkopf and Härtel *Collected Edition* of Liszt's works, in thirty-four volumes. Leipzig, 1901–36.

CFL   Corder, Frederick. *Ferencz Liszt.* London, 1925.

CLBA   Csapó, Wilhelm von, ed. *Franz Liszts Briefe an Baron Antal Augusz, 1846–78.* Budapest, 1911.

CLC   Carl Lachmund Collection. Special Collections Department of the Performing Arts Division of the New York Public Library. Call no. JPB 92-1.

CLW   Cornelius, Peter. *Literarische Werke.* 4 vols. Leipzig, 1904–05.
       1–2: *Ausgewählte Briefe,* nebst Tagebuchblättern und Gelegenheitsgedichten, herausgegeben von seinem Sohne Carl Maria Cornelius. 2 vols. Leipzig, 1904–05. 3: *Aufsätze über Musik und Kunst,* zum erstenmal gesammelt und herausgegeben von Edgar Istel. Leipzig, 1905.

4: *Gedichte,* gesammelt und herausgegeben von Adolf Stern. Leipzig, 1905.

CMW   Chanler, Mrs. Margaret Winthrop. *Roman Spring.* Boston, 1934.

CWHSC   *Cosima Wagner und Houston Stewart Chamberlain im Briefwechsel, 1888–1908.* Herausgegeben von Paul Pretzsch. Leipzig, 1934.

DA   Darmstadt Archive. Originale der Briefe Liszts an eine Freundin. Hessische Landes- und Hochschulbibliothek, Darmstadt.

DAF   De Angelis, Alberto. *Francesco Liszt a Roma.* Rivista Musicale Italiana, vol. 18. Turin, 1911.

DFB   Dent, Edward J. *Ferruccio Busoni; A Biography.* London, 1933.

DGG   Dörffel, Alfred. *Geschichte der Gewandhausconcerte zu Leipzig vom 25. November 1791 bis 25. November 1881.* Leipzig, 1884.

DHP   Darimon, Alfred. *Histoire d'un parti: Les Cinq sous l'empire.* Paris, 1885.

DMA(2)   Dupêchez, Charles. *Marie d'Agoult, 1805–1876.* Paris, 1989.

DMML   Damrosch, Walter. *My Musical Life.* New York, 1923.

DMSJ   Dupêchez, Charles, ed. *Mémoires, souvenirs et journaux de la Comtesse d'Agoult.* Paris, 1990.

EFLE   Eckhardt, Mária. *Franz Liszt's Estate.* 2 vols. I: *Books.* Budapest, 1986. II: *Music.* Budapest, 1993.

EHC   Eubel, Konrad. *Hierarchia Catholica medii et recentioris aevi.* Vols. 7–, Patavii, 1979.

EKFL   Eckhardt, Mária P., and Knotik, Cornelia, eds. *Franz Liszt und sein Kreis in Briefen und Dokumenten aus den Beständen des Burgenländischen Landesmuseums.* Eisenstadt, 1983.

ELF   Eckhardt, Mária. *Liszt Ferenc Memorial Museum Catalogue.* Budapest, 1986.

EMBD   Ezekiel, Moses Jacob. *Memoirs from the Baths of Diocletian.* Edited by Joseph Gutmann and Stanley F. Chyet. Detroit, 1975.

ENC   Ernest Newman Collection. Juilliard School of Music Library, Special Collections, New York.

FLL   Friedheim, Arthur. *Life and Liszt: The Recollections of a Concert Pianist.* Edited by Theodore L. Bullock. New York, 1961.

FMG   Fay, Amy. *Music Study in Germany, from the Home Correspondence of Amy Fay.* Edited by Mrs. Fay Pierce. New York, 1880.

GAWM   Gutmann, Albert. *Aus dem Wiener Musikleben: Künstler-Erinnerungen, 1873–1908.* 2 vols. Vienna, 1914.

GCAF   *Grossherzog Carl Alexander und Fanny Lewald-Stahr in ihren Briefen, 1848–1889.* Eingeleitet und herausgegeben von Rudolf Göhler. 2 vols. Berlin, 1932.

GFLF   Gajdoš, Vševlad. *František Liszt a františkáni* (Frantiskansky Obzor) [Ferenc Liszt and the Franciscans]. Bratislava, 1936.

GL   Göllerich, August. *Franz Liszt.* Berlin, 1908.

GLK   Göllerich, August. *Franz Liszts Klavierunterricht von 1884–1886.* Dargestellt an den Tagebuchaufzeichnungen von August Göllerich, von Wilhelm Jerger. Regensburg, 1975.

GLL   Graves, Charles L. *The Life and Letters of Sir Charles Groves, C. B.* London, 1903.

GLW   Gottschalg, A. W. *Franz Liszt in Weimar, und seine letzten Lebensjahre: Erinnerungen und Tagebuchnotizen.* Berlin, 1910.

GMR   Goethe, Johann Wolfgang von. *Maximen und Reflexionen*. Nach den Handschriften des Goethe- und Schiller-Archivs, herausgegeben von Max Hecker. Goethe-Gesellschaft, Weimar, 1907.

GRT   Gregorovius, Ferdinand. *Römische Tagebücher (1852–74)*. Herausgegeben von Friedrich Althaus. Stuttgart, 1892.

GRW   Gutman, Robert W. *Richard Wagner: The Man, His Mind and His Music*. London, 1968.

GSE   Garets, Comtesse de. *Souvenirs d'une demoiselle d'honneur auprès de l'impératrice Eugénie*. Paris, 1928.

GWLF   Gadjoš, Vševlad. "War Franz Liszt Franziskaner?" *Studia Musicologica* (Budapest) 6 (1964), pp. 299–310.

HA   Hecker, Jutta. *Die Altenburg: Geschichte eines Hauses*. 2nd ed. Berlin, 1983.

HAML   Hanslick, Eduard. *Aus meinem Leben*. 2 vols. Berlin, 1911.

HCCV   Hanslick, Eduard. *Concerte, Componisten und Virtuosen der letzten fünfzehn Jahre: 1870–1885*. Berlin, 1886.

HCS   Hooper, George. *The Campaign of Sedan: The Downfall of the Second Empire, August–September, 1870*. London, 1897.

HF-PW   Howard, Michael. *The Franco-Prussian War. The German Invasion of France, 1870–71*. London, 1961.

HGC   Hanslick, Eduard. *Geschichte des Concertwesens in Wien. Aus dem Concertsaal: Kritiken und Schilderungen aus den letzten 20 Jahren des Wiener Musiklebens 1848–1868*. 2 vols. Vienna, 1869, 1870.

HGL   Haldane, Charlotte. *The Galley Slaves of Love: The Story of Marie d'Agoult and Franz Liszt*. London, 1957.

HJH   Herbeck, Ludwig. *Johann Herbeck: Ein Lebensbild von seinem Sohne Ludwig*. Vienna, 1885.

HL   Haraszti, Emile. *Franz Liszt*. Paris, 1967.

HLC   Hamburger, Klára. "Franz Liszt et Michelangelo Caetani, duc de Sermonta." *Studia Musicologica Academiae Scientiarum Hungaricae* (Budapest) 21 (1979).

HLEO   Hamburger, Klára. "Liszt and Emile Ollivier." *Studia Musicologica Academiae Scientiarum Hungaricae* (Budapest) 28 (1986).

HLFG   Hamburger, Klára. "Liszt, Father and Grandfather." *New Hungarian Quarterly* (Budapest) 32, no. 121 (Spring 1991), p. 128.

H-LL   Hegermann-Lindencrone, Lille de. *In the Courts of Memory, 1858–1875, from Contemporary Letters*. New York, 1925.

HLR   Helbig, Nadine. "Franz Liszt in Rom." *Deutsche Revue* 32 (January–March 1907) and 33 (April–June 1907). An expanded English version appears in certain editions of Raphaël Ledos de Beaufort's *The Abbé Liszt*. London, 1886.

HLSW   Hugo, Howard E., ed. and trans. *The Letters of Franz Liszt to Marie zu Sayn-Wittgenstein*. Cambridge, Mass., 1953.

HME   Hueffer, Francis. *Half a Century of Music in England, 1837–1887: Essays Towards a History*. London, 1889.

HMML   Haweis, H. R. *My Musical Life*. London, 1886.

HMMM   Henschel, Sir George. *Musings and Memories of a Musician*. New York, 1919.

HSC   Harding, J. *Saint-Saëns and His Circle*. London, 1965.

HSD   Herwegh, Marcel. *Au Soir des dieux*. Paris, 1933.

HSMM   Hadow, Sir W. H. *Studies in Modern Music.* First Series. London, 1892.

ICF   d'Indy, Vincent. *César Franck.* Paris, 1906.

JBB   *Johannes Brahms: Briefwechsel.* 16 vols. Deutsche Brahms Gesellschaft Edition. Berlin, 1907–22.

JLB   Jung, Hans Rudolf. *Franz Liszt in seinen Briefen.* Berlin, 1987.

JSC   Janina, Olga ("Robert Franz"). *Souvenirs d'une cosaque.* Paris, 1874.

JSP   Janina, Olga. *Souvenirs d'un pianiste: Réponse aux Souvenirs d'une cosaque.* Paris, 1874.

KBWP   Karpath, Ludwig. *Zu den Briefen Richard Wagners an eine Putzmacherin: Unterredungen mit der Putzmacherin Berta.* Berlin, 1907(?).

KE   Kellermann, Berthold. *Erinnerungen, ein Künstlerleben.* Herausgegeben von Sebastian Hausmann und Helmut Kellermann. Zürich, 1932.

KFL   Kapp, Julius. *Franz Liszt.* Berlin, 1909.

KFW   Ernst Kreowski and Eduard Fuchs. *Richard Wagner in der Karikatur.* Berlin, 1907.

KJB   Kalbeck, Max. *Johannes Brahms,* 4 vols. Berlin, 1904–14.

KLB(2) Kopf, Josef von. *Lebenserinnerungen eines Bildhauers.* Stuttgart and Leipzig, 1899.

KLRWB *König Ludwig II und Richard Wagner Briefwechsel.* Bearbeitet von Otto Strobel. 5 vols. Karlsruhe, 1936, 1939.

KSB   Kerr, Caroline V., ed. and trans. *The Story of Bayreuth as Told in the Bayreuth Letters of Richard Wagner.* London, 1912.

KWL   Kloss, Erich, ed. *Briefwechsel zwischen Wagner und Liszt.* 2 vols. Leipzig, 1910.

LAG   La Mara [Marie Lipsius], ed. *Aus der Glanzzeit der Weimarer Altenburg.* Leipzig, 1906.

LAV   Lesure, François. *Achille à la Villa (1885–1887).* Cahiers Debussy, 12–13, 1988–1989. Paris, 1990.

LBCW   La Mara, ed. *Briefe von Hector Berlioz an die Fürstin Carolyne von Sayn-Wittgenstein.* Leipzig, 1903.

LBLB   La Mara, ed. *Briefwechsel zwischen Franz Liszt und Hans von Bülow.* Leipzig, 1898.

LBLCA La Mara, ed. *Briefwechsel zwischen Franz Liszt und Carl Alexander, Grossherzog von Sachsen.* Leipzig, 1909.

LBSW   La Mara, ed. *Bilder und Briefe aus dem Leben der Fürstin Carolyne von Sayn-Wittgenstein.* Leipzig, 1906.

LBZL   La Mara, ed. *Briefe hervorragender Zeitgenossen an Franz Liszt.* 3 vols. Leipzig, 1895–1904.

LC   Levi, Primo. *Il Cardinale d'Hohenlohe nella vita italiana.* Torino-Roma, 1907.

LCS   Litzmann, Berthold. *Clara Schumann: Ein Künstlerleben.* 3 vols. Leipzig, 1902–08.

LDML   La Mara. *Durch Musik und Leben im Dienste des Ideals.* 2 vols. Leipzig, 1917.

LFLW   Legány, Dezső. *Franz Liszt: Unbekannte Presse und Briefe aus Wien, 1822–1886.* Budapest, 1984.

LHHP   Legány, Dezső. "Hungarian Historical Portraits." *Studia Musicologica Academiae Scientiarum Hungaricae* (Budapest) 28 (1986), pp. 79–88.

LK   Levi, Primo. "Kardinal Prinz Hohenlohe: Persönliche Erinnerungen
           eines Italieners." *Deutsche Revue* 32 (January–March 1907).
LL   *Living with Liszt: The Diary of Carl Lachmund, an American pupil of Liszt,*
           1882–1884. Edited, annotated, and introduced by Alan Walker. Stuyvesant,
           N.Y., 1995.
LLB   La Mara, ed. *Franz Liszts Briefe.* 8 vols. Leipzig, 1893–1905.
               1: *Von Paris bis Rom*
               2: *Von Rom bis ans Ende*
               3: *Briefe an eine Freundin*
               4, 5, 6, 7: *Briefe an die Fürstin Carolyne Sayn-Wittgenstein*
               8: *Neue Folge zu Band I und II*
LLBM   La Mara, ed. *Franz Liszts Briefe an seine Mutter.* Leipzig, 1918.
LLC   Legány, Dezső. *Liszt and His Country.* 2 vols. Budapest, 1983, 1992.
LLE   Legány, Dezső. *Liszt's and Erkel's Relations and Students.* Studia Musico-
           logica Academiae Scientiarum Hungaricae (Budapest) 18 (1976), pp.
           19–50.
LLF   La Mara. *Liszt und die Frauen.* Leipzig, 1911.
LLFM   Legány, Dezső. *Liszt Ferenc Magyarországon, 1874–1886.* Budapest, 1986.
LLR   Legány, Dezső. "Liszt in Rom, nach der Presse." *Studia Musicologica*
           Academiae Scientiarum Hungaricae (Budapest) 19 (1978).
LM   Lamond, Frederic. *The Memoirs of Frederic Lamond.* Glasgow, 1949.
LMM-K   La Mara, ed. *Marie von Mouchanoff-Kalergis (geb. Gräfin Nesselrode) in*
           Briefen an ihre Tochter. Leipzig, 1911.
LR   Leetham, Claude. *Rosmini: Priest, Philosopher and Patriot.* With an intro-
           duction by Giuseppe Bozzetti. London, 1957.
LSJ   La Mara, ed. *An der Schwelle des Jenseits: Letzte Erinnerungen an die Fürstin*
           Carolyne Sayn-Wittgenstein, die Freundin Liszts. Leipzig, 1925.
MAL   Melegari, Dora. "Une amie de Liszt, la Princesse de Sayn-
           Wittgenstein." *La Revue de Paris,* September 1, 1897.
MCW   Moulin Eckart, Richard Graf du. *Cosima Wagner, ein Lebens- und Charak-*
           terbild. 2 vols. Munich, 1929.
MGGE   Metternich-Winneburg, Princess Pauline Marie von. *Geschehenes, Gese-*
           henes, Erlebtes von Metternich-Sándor. Berlin, 1920.
MH-S   *Memoirs of Prince Chlodwig of Hohenlohe-Schillingsfürst.* Edited by
           Friedrich Curtius, translated by George W. Chrystal. 2 vols. London,
           1906.
M-JEG   Monrad-Johansen, David. *Edvard Grieg.* Oslo, 1934.
MLEI   Meysenbug, Malwida von. *Der Lebensabend einer Idealistin.* Berlin and
           Leipzig, 1898.
MLMW   Mirus, Dr. Adolf. *Das Liszt-Museum zu Weimar und seine Erinnerungen.*
           Weimar 1892.
MMN   Mackenzie, Sir Alexander Campbell. *A Musician's Narrative.* London,
           1927.
MMS   Massenet, Jules. *Mes Souvenirs (1848–1912).* Paris, 1912.
MP   *Memoirs of a Princess: The Reminiscences of Princess Marie von Thurn und*
           Taxis. Translated and compiled by Nora Wydenbruck. London, 1959.
MRR   Merrick, Paul. *Revolution and Religion in the Music of Liszt.* London,
           1987.
MRSE   Molloy, Fitzgerald. *The Romance of the Second Empire.* London, 1904.

NLE   *New Liszt Edition, Complete Works.* Edited by Zoltán Gárdonyi, István Szelényi, Imre Sulyok, and Imre Mező. Kassel-Budapest, 1970–.

NLRW   Newman, Ernest. *The Life of Richard Wagner.* 4 vols. London, 1933–47.

NML   Newman, Ernest. *The Man Liszt: A Study of the Tragi-comedy of a Soul Divided Against Itself.* London, 1934.

NWB   Nietzsche, Friedrich. *Werke in drei Bänden.* Edited by Karl Schlechta. Munich, 1966.

NZfM   *Neue Zeitschrift für Musik* (Leipzig). Edited by Robert Schumann (1834–44) and Franz Brendel (1845–68). Cited by issue.

OAAL   Ollivier, Daniel, ed. *Autour de Mme d'Agoult et de Liszt (Alfred de Vigny, Emile Ollivier, Princess de Belgiojoso): Lettres publiés avec introduction et notes.* Paris, 1941.

OASE   Ollivier, Marie-Thérèse Emile. *J'ai vécu l'agonie du Second Empire.* Text selected and presented by Anne Troisier de Diaz. Paris, 1970.

OCLF   Ollivier, Daniel, ed. *Correspondance de Liszt et de sa fille Madame Emile Ollivier, 1842–1862.* Paris, 1936.

OJ   Ollivier, Emile. *Journal, 1846–1869.* 2 vols. Text selected and edited by Theodore Zeldin and Anne Troisier de Diaz. Paris, 1961.

PALP   Pocknell, Pauline. "Author! Author! Liszt's Prayer an den heiligen Franziskus von Paula." *Journal of the American Liszt Society* 30 (July–December 1991).

PBUS   Prahács, Margit, ed. *Franz Liszt: Briefe aus ungarischen Sammlungen, 1835–86.* Budapest-Kassel, 1966.

PEMH   *Pléïade Encyclopedia of Music History.* Paris, 1963. Vol. 2, article on Liszt by Emile Haraszti.

PFLA   Pinto, Giuseppe del. "Francesco Liszt ad Albano." Estrato della rivista *Roma. Anno II. fascicolo 12.* Rome, 1924.

PGS   Pohl, Richard. *Gesammelte Schriften über Musik und Musiker.* Leipzig, 1883–84.
         1: *Richard Wagner: Studien und Kritiken*
         2: *Franz Liszt: Studien und Erinnerungen*
         3: *Hektor Berlioz: Studien und Kritiken*

PHB   Payzant, Geoffrey. *Eduard Hanslick and Ritter Berlioz in Prague: A Documentary Narrative.* Calgary, 1991.

PHZ   Pukánszky, Béla. "Hohenlohe Mária hercegnő levele gróf Zichy Gézahoz" [A letter of Princess Marie Hohenlohe to Count Géza Zichy]. *Akadémiai Értesítő* 42 (October–November 1932), pp. 287–92.

PLF   Papp, Viktor. *Liszt Ferenc élő magyar tanítványai* [Living Hungarian students of Ferenc Liszt]. Budapest, 1936.

PW   Panofsky, Walter. *Wagner, a Pictorial Biography.* London, 1963.

RA   Royal Archives, Windsor Castle, England.
         (a) Queen Victoria's Journal
         (b) Correspondence between Queen Victoria and her relations in Germany

REL   Rohlfs, Gerhard. *Erinnerungen an Franz Liszt, Weimar, 1871–1886.* Hanover, 1993.

RFLEG   Rabes, Lennart. *Franz Liszt and Edvard Grieg.* Liszt Saeculum, vol. 1, no. 52, 1994.

RGPR   Rebois, Henri. *Les Grands Prix de Rome de musique à l'Académie de France.* Paris, 1932.

RGS   Ramann, Lina, ed. *Franz Liszts Gesammelte Schriften.* 6 vols. Leipzig, 1880–83.

     1: *Friedrich Chopin*
     2: *Essays und Reisebriefe eines Baccalaureus der Tonkunst*
     3: *Dramaturgische Blätter*
       (a) *Essays*
       (b) *Richard Wagner*
     4: *Aus den Annalen des Fortschritts*
     5: *Streifzüge: Kritische, polemische und zeithistorische Essays*
     6: *Die Zigeuner und ihre Musik in Ungarn*

RL   Ramann, Lina. *Lisztiana: Erinnerungen an Franz Liszt in Tagebuchblättern, Briefen und Dokumenten aus den Jahren 1873–1886/87.* Herausgegeben von Arthur Seidl. Textrevision von Friedrich Schnapp. Mainz, 1983.

RL-B   Ramann, Lina. Liszt-Bibliothek, no. 362. "Lina Schmalhausen: Liszt's letzte Lebenstage." Unpublished. Goethe- und Schiller-Archiv, Weimar.

RLKM   Ramann, Lina. *Franz Liszt als Künstler und Mensch.* 3 vols. Leipzig, 1880–94.

RL-P   Ramann, Lina. *Liszt-Pädagogium: Klavier-Kompositionen Franz Liszts nebst noch unedirten Veränderungen, Zusätzen und Kadenzen nach des Meisters Lehren pädagogisch glossirt von Lina Ramann.* Leipzig, 1901.

RLS   Raabe, Peter. *Franz Liszt: Leben und Schaffen.* 2 vols. Stuttgart, 1931; rev. ed., 1968.

RWBB   *The Diary of Richard Wagner, 1865–1882: The Brown Book.* Presented and annotated by Joachim Bergfeld; translated by George Bird. London, 1980.

RWJK   *Richard Wagner-Jahrbuch.* Herausgegeben von Joseph Kürschner. Stuttgart, 1886

SADM   Seidl, Arthur. *Festschrift zum fünfzigjährigen Bestehen des Allgemeinen Deutschen Musikvereins.* Berlin, 1911.

SE   Stradal, August. *Erinnerungen an Franz Liszt.* Berne, 1929.

SEM   Stern, Daniel (Marie d'Agoult). *Esquisses Morales: pensées, réflexions et maximes suives des Poésies de Daniel Stern et précédes d'une étude biographique et littéraire par L. de Ronchaud.* Paris, 1880.

SFLJ   Sagittarius [Miksa Schütz]. *Franz Liszt über die Juden.* Budapest, 1881.

SLAB   Suttoni, Charles. "Franz Liszt's Published Correspondence: An Annotated Bibliography." *Fontes Artis Musicae* (Kassel) 26, no. 3 (1979). Revised and expanded edition, Journal of the American Liszt Society 25 (January–June 1989).

SLFH   Sylvain, Charles. *Life of the Reverend Father Hermann.* New York, 1925.

SLFP   Searle, Humphrey. "Liszt's Final Period (1860–1886)." *Proceedings of the Royal Music Association* (London) 78 (1951–52).

SLG   Stern, Adolf, ed. *Franz Liszts Briefe an Carl Gille.* Leipzig, 1903.

SMC   Shaw, George Bernard. *Shaw's Music: The Complete Musical Criticism in Three Volumes.* Edited by Dan H. Lawrence. London, 1981.

SML(2)   Siloti, Alexander. *My Memories of Liszt.* London, 1913.

SMW(2)   Sauer, Emil. *Meine Welt.* Stuttgart, 1901.

SNW	Schorn, Adelheid von. *Das Nachklassische Weimar.* 2 vols.
	1: *Unter der Regierungszeit Karl Friedrichs und Maria Paulownas.* Weimar, 1911.
	2: *Unter der Regierungszeit von Karl Alexander und Sophie.* Weimar, 1912.
SPD	Stanford, Sir Charles Villiers. *Pages from an Unwritten Diary.* London, 1914.
SPP(2)	Schopenhauer, Arthur. *Parerga und Paralipomena.* 2 vols. Berlin, 1851. Translated by E. F. J. Payne, Oxford, 1974.
SPR(2)	Stoker, Bram. *Personal Reminiscences of Henry Irving.* London, 1906.
SPRL	Strelezki, Anton. *Personal Recollections of Chats with Liszt.* London, 1893.
SRB	Schlözer, Kurd von. *Römische Briefe, 1864–1869.* Herausgegeben von Karl von Schlözer. 2nd ed. Stuttgart and Berlin, 1913.
STL	Szabolcsi, Bence. *The Twilight of Ferenc Liszt.* Translated by András Deák. Budapest, 1959.
SWWV	Schopenhauer, Arthur. *Die Welt als Wille und Vorstellung.* Leipzig (?), 1819; 3rd ed., 1859. Translated as *The World as Will and Representation,* by E. F. J. Payne. Oxford, 1958.
SZM	Schorn, Adelheid von. *Zwei Menschenalter: Erinnerungen und Briefe.* Berlin, 1901.
TBCW	*Die Briefe Cosima Wagners an Friedrich Nietzsche.* Herausgegeben von Erhart Thierbach, vol 1. (1869–1871). Weimar, 1938.
TCH	Thayer, William Roscoe. *Cardinal Hohenlohe—Liberal.* Italica. Cambridge, Mass., 1908.
TOS-W	Troisier de Diaz, Anne, ed. *Emile Ollivier et Carolyne de Sayn-Wittgenstein: Correspondance, 1858–1887.* Paris, 1984.
VAMA	Vier, Jacques. *Marie d'Agoult—son mari—ses amis: Documents inédits.* Paris, 1950.
VAPL	Voss, Richard. *Aus einem phantastichen Leben.* Stuttgart, 1920.
VCA	Vier, Jacques. *La Comtesse d'Agoult et son temps, avec des documents inédits.* 6 vols. Paris, 1955–63.
VDS	Vier, Jacques. *Daniel Stern: Lettres républicaines du second empire. Documents inédits.* Paris, 1951.
VFL	Vier, Jacques. *Franz Liszt: L'artiste, le clerc. Documents inédits.* Paris, 1951.
VLES	Vendel-Mohay Lajosné. *Liszt-Emlékek Szekszfárdon.* Szekszárd, 1986.
VLKN	Végh, Gyula. "Liszt Ferenc kiadatlan naplója [Franz Liszt's Unpublished Diary]: Memento Journalier, 1861–1862." *Muzsika* (Budapest) nos. 1–2 (January–February 1930).
VLR	Vier, Jacques. *Lettres républicaines du Second Empire. Documents inédits.* Paris, 1951.
VMA	Versailles Municipal Library Archive. The unpublished legacy of Claire de Charnacé (*née* d'Agoult), including her letters, notebooks, and memoirs. F. 859, cartons 1–30.
WA	Weimar Archives. Liszt Collection held by the Nationale Forschungs- und Gedenkstätten der klassichen deutschen Literatur in Weimar. Goethe- und Schiller-Archiv, Weimar.
WBB	*Richard Wagners Briefe an Hans von Bülow.* Jena, 1916.
WCN	Wellesley, Sir Victor, and Robert Sencourt. *Conversations with Napoleon III.* London, 1934.

WCWB	Waldberg, Max Freiherr von, ed. *Cosima Wagners Briefe an ihre Töchter Daniela von Bülow, 1866–1885.* Stuttgart and Berlin, 1933.
WDC	William Dayas Collection. Special Collections Department, McMaster University, Hamilton, Canada.
WDS	*Wagner: A Documentary Study,* compiled and edited by Herbert Barth, Dietrich Mack, and Egon Voss. London, 1975.
WE	Wagner, Siegfried. *Erinnerungen.* Stuttgart, 1923.
WELC	Walker, Alan, and Gabriele Erasmi. *Liszt, Carolyne, and the Vatican: The Story of a Thwarted Marriage.* Stuyvesant, N.Y., 1991.
WEW	Weissheimer, Wendelin. *Erlebnisse mit Richard Wagner, Franz Liszt und vielen anderen Zeitgenossen.* Stuttgart, 1898.
WFLG	Wagner, Cosima. *Franz Liszt: Ein Gedenkblatt von seiner Tochter.* 2nd ed. Munich, 1911.
WFLR	Wohl, Janka. *François Liszt: Recollections of a Compatriot.* Translated by B. Peyton Ward. London, 1887.
WGSD	Wagner, Richard. *Gesammelte Schriften und Dichtungen.* 3rd ed. 10 vols. Leipzig, 1897–98.
WLC	Westerby, Herbert. *Liszt, Composer, and His Piano Works.* London, 1936.
WLE	Weingartner, Felix. *Lebens-Erinnerungen.* 2 vols. Zürich, Leipzig, 1928, 1929.
WLL	Waters, Edward N. "Liszt and Longfellow." *The Musical Quarterly* 41, no. 1 (January 1955).
WLLM	Waters, Edward N., ed. *The Letters of Franz Liszt to Olga von Meyendorff, 1871–1886.* Translated by William R. Tyler. Dumbarton Oaks, 1979.
WLWP	Wallace, William. *Liszt, Wagner and the Princess.* London, 1927.
WML	Wagner, Richard. *Mein Leben.* Munich, 1911. Authorized English translation, London, 1912.
W-MM	Wolkoff-Mouromtzoff, A. *Memoirs.* London, 1928.
WMME	Walker, Bettina. *My Musical Experiences.* London, 1890.
WT	Wagner, Cosima. *Die Tagebücher.* 2 vols. Ediert und kommentiert von Martin Gregor-Dellin und Dietrich Mack. Munich, 1976, 1977. Translated as *Cosima Wagner's Diaries* by Geoffrey Skelton. London and New York, 1978 and 1980.
WTS	Winterberger, Alexander. *Technische Studien für Pianoforte von Franz Liszt, unter Redaktion von Alexander Winterberger.* Leipzig, 1887.
WZL	Wagner, Cosima. *Das Zweite Leben: Briefe und Aufzeichnungen, 1883–1930.* Munich, 1980.
ZAC	"Zorelli, Sylvia" (Olga Janina). *Les Amours d'une cosaque par un ami de l'Abbé "X."* Paris, 1875.
ZEO	Zeldin, Theodore. *Emile Ollivier and the Liberal Empire of Napoleon III.* Oxford, 1963.
ZLEF	Zichy, Count Géza. *Aus meinem Leben: Erinnerungen und Fragmente.* 3 vols. Stuttgart, 1911–20.
ZRPC	"Zorelli, Sylvia" (Olga Janina). *Le Roman du pianiste et de la cosaque.* Paris, 1875.

Index

Page numbers in italics refer to main entries.

Abendzeitung (Augsburg), 120
Ábrányi, Emil (1851–1920), 271
Ábrányi, Kornél Sr. (1822–1903), 5, 91,
    227, 256, 290, 359, 374, 376, 410,
    429, 459, 524 and *n*.4
  Csárdás nobles, 467
  description of Liszt, 237–38
Ackermann, Louise, 309
Acton, Cardinal Charles (1803–1847), 331
Adam, Juliette (1836–1936), 304, 311
Adcock, W. J. (Mayor of Dover), 497
Ágai, Adolf (1836–1916), 375
  anti-Liszt faction, 375
Agénor, Antoine, 214
Aggh ázy, Károly von (1855–1918), 364
Agoult, Count Charles d' (1790–1873),
    302, 313, 315*n*.46
Agoult, Countess Marie Catherine
    Sophie d' (1805–1876), 104, 319
  Claire (1830–1912) (daughter), *see*
    Charnacé, Claire Christine de
  Cosima and, 311–13
  as "Daniel Stern," 302, 311
  death of, 313–14
  illnesses of, 304–06
  last Will, 308, 314–15
  Louise (1828–1834) (daughter), 303
  suicidal tendencies of, 303 and *n*.7,
    305*n*.13, 307, 313
  WRITINGS:
    Correspondance, 53*n*.19
    Épisode de Venise, 301*n*.3
    Esquisses morales, 313*n*.44
    Essai sur la liberté, 313*n*.44
    Histoire de la révolution de 1848, 309
    Jeanne d'Arc, 309
    Maria Stuart, 309

    Mémoires, 53*n*.19, 301*n*.3, 302, 308,
      310, 317*n*.50, 318
    Nélida, 104–05, and *n*.28, 301*n*.3,
      313*n*.44
    Souvenirs, 104–05, 308
Akadémiai Ertesítő (Budapest), 527*n*.12
Albani, Emma (1847–1930), 485
Albano (Italy), xvii, 69, 391–93
  Liszt is made honorary canon of,
    391–92
Albert, Prince Consort of Victoria
    (1819–1861), 155
Albert, Eugène d' (1864–1932), 228, 240,
    248, 418*n*.5, 419, 422*n*.14, 532,
    533
  cadenza to Liszt's Second Hungarian
    Rhapsody, 422
  Charles (father), 422*n*.14
  debut recital, 421–23
Alexander II (1818–1881), Tsar of Russia
    (1855–1881), 22–23, 25, 155,
    156–57 and *n*.18
Allegri, Gregorio (1582–1652), *42*
  Miserere, 42, 43
Allgemeiner Deutscher Musikverein, 362,
    368, 377, 379, 420, 533–34
  festival of 1883, *460–61*
  festival of 1884, *463–64*
  festival of 1886, *501–02*
  Liszt becomes honorary president of
    (1882), 420, 460, 461
Allgemeine Zeitung (Munich), 466
Almássy, Miklós (1860–1920), 290*n*.9
Altenburg, The
  Blue Room, 21, 77
  Liszt's departure from (1861), 21
  Liszt's return to (1864), 76–77

Amberg's Theatre (New York), 242
Ambrogi, Father Guglielmo Maria D',
        541, 543
Ambros, Dr. August Wilhelm
        (1816–1876), 88
American Civil War (1861–1865), 217*n*.10
American Independence Day (4 July),
        241–42
Amsterdam (Netherlands), 103, 292*n*.11
    Moses and Aaron Church, 103
    Zaal van het Park, 103
Ancona (Italy), 24
Ancona, Battle of (September 30, 1860),
        328
Anderton, Orsmond (1863–1934), 484
Andrássy, Count Gyula (1823–1890), 227
        and *n*.42, 272, 350, 352
Andrea, Cardinal Gerolamo De (d. 1868),
        30*n*.32
Angelis, Canon Pietro De, 392
Angelus ad pastores ait plainchant, 260–61
Ansorge, Conrad (1862–1930), 470
Antonelli, Cardinal Giocomo
        (1806–1876), 11, 25*n*.19, 80
Antonio (Hohenlohe's manservant), 86
Antwerp (Belgium), 402, 469, 472, 478, 498
Apel, Pauline (1838–1926), 195–96, 242,
        267, 413, 436, 500, 531–32 and
        n.23
Apponyi, Count Albert (1846–1933), 256,
        297, 350, 359, 360*n*.9, 374, 376
    his descriptions of Liszt, 294–95, 352
    Royal Academy of Music and, 288–89,
        300
d'Arányi, Jelly (1895–1966), 374
Árkövy, József (1851–1922), 511*n*.8
Arlon (Belgium), 504
Arnhem (Netherlands), 284
Arnim, Count Harry von (1824–1881), 38
Arnstadt (Germany), 420, 421
Art musicale, L' (Paris), 101, 102, 499*n*.6
Athens (Greece), 22, 24, 25
Auber, Daniel-François-Esprit
        (1782–1871), 98–99, 102
Audisio, Monsignor, 88*n*.12
Augsburger Allgemeine Zeitung, 93
Augusta (maid at Altenburg), 77 and *n*.56,
        151
Augusta, Empress of Prussia (1811–1890),
        414

Augusz, Baron Antal (1807–1878), 92,
        170, 174, 178, 179, 187, 211, 225,
        300, 323*n*.12, 337, 359, 376, 378
    death of, 380–81
Aus der Ohe, Adèle (1864–1937), 235, 380
Avenir national (Paris), 180*n*.21

Bach, Carl Philip Emmanuel (1714–1788),
        460
Bach, Johann Sebastian (1685–1750), 39,
        103, 210, 273, 470
    Liszt plays "48," 267*n*.16, 376, 496
    monument (Eisenach), 414
    WORKS:
        Cantata "Weinen, Klagen," 51
        Double Concerto, for two violins,
            415*n*.30
        Gavotte in D minor, 287
        Mass in B minor, 51–52
        Organ Fugue in A minor, 419
        St. John Passion, 471
        Sonata in A major, for violin and
            piano, 415*n*.30
        Violin Concerto in A minor,
            415*n*.30
Bach, Leonhard Emil (1849–1902), 488
Bache, Walter (1842–1888), 38–39, 54, 60,
        100, 419, 420*n*.9, 477
    Constance (sister) (1846–1903), 38, 485,
        496
        Brother Musicians, 485*n*.14
        as translator, 38*n*.16, 485*n*.14
    establishes Liszt Scholarship (1886),
        483–84
    Francis Edward (brother) (1833–1858),
        485*n*.14
    Liszt concerts (1865–1888), 477, 483*n*.11
    reception for Liszt (1886), 487–88
Bad Kissingen (Germany), 500
Baden-Baden (Germany), 176, 402
Baden Gazette, 70
Bad Reichenhall (Germany), 113
Bagby, Albert Morris (1859–1941), 241, 471
Balakirev, Mily (1837–1910), 239
    Islamey, 239
Banville, Théodore de, 309
Barbey d'Aurevilly, Jules (1808–1889), 189
Bárdos, Lajos (1899–1986), 437*n*.2

Bartalus, István (1821–1899), 410 and *n*.18

Bartay, Ede (1825–1901), 289

Bartók, Béla (1881–1945), 17, 300, 454, 456, 532

Basel (Switzerland), 23, 120, 122, 123, 125

Batta, Alexandre (1816–1902), 362

Batthyány, Count Lajos (1806–1849), 148

Bauholzer, Julia (1863–1942), 293, 296, 297
    description of Liszt, 297

Bayreuth (Germany), 14, 354, 377, 503, 507
    festival deficit, 144*n*.26, 355–56,
    foundation-stone, 256
    Wagner festivals
        (1876), 346–55
        (1882), 416–18
        (1884), 465
        (1886), 503, 521

Bayreuther Blätter, 353

Bazaine, Marshal Achille-François (1811–1888), 217

Beatty-Kingston, William (1837–1900), 205, 497

Bechstein, Carl (1826–1900), 114, 123*n*.23, 114, 144, 229*n*.5

Beck, Theodora, 531*n*.23

Becker, Reinhold (1842–1924), 460

Beckmann, Wilhelm (painter), 418*n*.4

Bedegh (Hungary), 93

Beethoven, Ludwig van (1770–1827), 37, 287, 466, 470
    Beethoven festivals
        (1870), 173, *205–09*, 311
        (1877), 366
    Beethoven Foundation, 469
    Beethoven monument (Bonn), 486
    Beethoven monument (Vienna), 366, 367
    Broadwood piano of, 272, 534*n*.30
    Liszt's performances of, 205, 352
    Liszt's piano transcriptions of, *62–68*, 89
    WORKS:
        Piano concertos
            in G major, op. 58, 103
            in E-flat major (*Emperor*), op. 73, 208–09, 279, 354*n*.29, 366
        Piano Trio in B-flat major (*Archduke*), op. 97, 209*n*.36
        Piano sonatas
            in F minor, op. 2,, no. 1, 296
            in C major, op. 2, no. 3, 293

        in C minor (*Pathétique*), op. 13, 360
        in A-flat major, op. 26, 188*n*.36,
        in C-sharp minor (*Moonlight*), op. 27, no. 2, 374
        in D major (*Pastorale*), op. 28, 470
        in C major (*Waldstein*), op. 53, 246, 247
        in B-flat major (*Hammerklavier*), op. 106, 267*n*.16, 352
        in E major, op. 109, 231
    Symphonies
        no. 3, in E flat major (*Eroica*), 37, 64–65
        no. 5, in C minor, 63–64, 374
        no. 8, in F major, 65
        no. 9, in D minor (*Choral*), 209, 242, 269, 389, 396
    Violin Concerto in D major, 226
    Miscellaneous
        Egmont Overture, 124
        Choral Fantasy, 366
        Kreutzer Sonata, 225, 374, 490
        Missa Solemnis, 149, 206
        "Rasoumowsky" Quartet no. 1, 490
        Romance in G major, for violin and orchestra, 415*n*.30
        Scottish Songs, 366
        Spring Sonata, 471, 472

Beirut (Lebanon), 349

Bellagio (Italy), 308*n*.25

Bellini, Vincenzo (1801–1835), 56
    Norma, 56

Belloni, Gaëtano (c. 1810–1887), 499

Beltrami, Luca (1854–1933), 333

Benedetti, Count Vincente (1817–1900), 213

Benedict XIII, Pope (1649–1730), 392

Bennett, Sir William Sterndale (1816–1875), 483
    Caprice for piano and orchestra, 483

Benoit, Peter (1834–1901), 469

Berardi, Monsignor Giuseppe (1810–1878), 25*n*.19

Berlin (Germany), 24, 391, 399
    Hochschule für Musik, 200

Berlioz, Hector (1803–1869), 23, 101*n*.18
    Fantastic Symphony, 368
    Harold in Italy, 362*n*.14

Bernard, Marie, 40n.23
Bernini, Gian Lorenzo (1598–1680), 35
Bertha, Alexandre de (1843–1912), 96n.3
Bessel, Colonel Karl von (d. 1870), 152, 173
Beust, Count Friedrich Hermann
        (1809–1886), 77, 152
Bignani, Monsignor, 332
Bilse, Benjamin (1816–1902), 401
Bird, Arthur (1856–1923), 419
Birkenbühl, Karl (pseud. for Hans
        Grasberger) (1836–1898), 161
Birmingham (England), 39
Bismarck, Prince Otto Eduard Leopold
        von (1815–1896), 155, 156, 212
    Chancellor of Germany (1871–1890),
        221, 330n.22
    Franco-Prussian War and, 213, 214, 217,
        219, 218–19
Bissing, Henriette von (1798–1879),
        73n.42
Blanc, Charles, 314
Blanche, Dr. Antoine Emile (1828–1893),
        303–04 and n.8, 310, 314
    Esprit (father), 304n.8
Blodék, Vilem (1834–1874), 172
Blüthner, Julius (1824–1910), 286
Bock, Anna (Liszt pupil), 361
Boehm, Edgar (1834–90), 486, 487, 496
Bofondi, Cardinal Giuseppe (1797–1867),
        30n.32
Boisselot, Louis (1809–1850), 34, 52
Boleslaw II (1039–1081), King of Poland
        (1058–1081), 474n.37
Bonn (Germany), 206, 486, 504
Bonnechose, Cardinal Henri Marie
        Gaston de (1800–1883), 100
        and n.15
Borodin, Alexander (1833–1887), 380
    Symphony no. 2, in B minor, 380
Bory, Robert (1891–1960), 187n.34
Bösendorfer, Ludwig (1835–1919), 271,
        359, 388, 400
Boston (America), 158
    New England Conservatory, 243
Bott, Jean-Joseph (1826–1895), 368
Bouillerie, Monsignor de la, 40n.23
Boulogne-sur-mer (France), 189
Brahms, Johannes (1833–1897), 206, 351,
        399
    meeting with Liszt (1874), 273

"Paganini" Studies, op. 35, 235
Brand, Hans (photographer), 518
Brandes, Herr (tenor), 71
Brandt, Carl (1828–1881), 417n.2
Brandt, Marianne (1842–1921), 368, 417
Bree, Herman van (1836–1885), 103
Brehme, Dr. Richard (1826–1887), 403
    medical report on Liszt (1881), 404n.2
Breithaupt, Rudolf (1873–1945), 230
Breitkopf and Härtel, 65–66, 439n.4
Bremen (Germany), 200n.16
Brendel, Karl Franz (1811–1868), 35, 38,
        70, 71, 75n.49, 93, 94
Breslau (Germany), 73
Brichta, Dr. Johann, 529, 530
Bright, Miss Dora, 483
British Medical Journal (London), 230n.6
Brockhaus, Max (1867–1957), 535
Brodsky, Adolf (1851–1929), 460
Bronsart von Schellendorf, Hans
        (1830–1913), 70, 144, 228, 284
    Piano Concerto, 379
Bronsart von Schellendorf, Colonel Paul
        (1832–1891), 218 and n.15
Bruckner, Anton (1824–1896), 114, 256,
        469, 520
Brückwald, Otto (1841–1904), 348n.17
Brussels (Belgium), 103, 357, 402, 498
    Conservatory of Music, 230
    World Fair (1885), 469, 470
Bucquet, Monsignor, 81, 95
Budapest (Hungary)
    Capuchin monastery, 359
    Chain Bridge, 150
    Elisabeth Bridge, 290
    flood of 1876, 358–59
    Franciscan monastery, 359
    Hungária Hotel, 188, 271, 278, 365, 374,
        462
    Institute for English Ladies, 374
    Liszt Society Choir, 360n.8
    Matthias Church, 148, 150
    National Academy of Sciences, 410n.18
    National Theatre, 278, 294, 373
    National Conservatory of Music, 90,
        293, 365n.18, 374
    National Széchényi Library, xix, 323 n.
        12
    Philharmonic Society, 375, 494, 531
    railway station, 90, 406

Redoutensaal, 92, 387
Royal Academy of Music, 13–14, 145, 234, 287, 338n.38, 358
Royal Opera House, 409, 411
Vigadó, 271, 359
Bülow, Cosima Francesca Gaetana von (1837–1930). *See* Wagner, Richard
Bülow, Baron Hans Guido von (1830–1894), xix, 22n.5, 24, 70, 94, 103, 190, 194, 200, 228, 234, 341–42, 389, 398–99
 Beethoven playing of, 103, 144, 267n.16, 398–99
 Blandine Elisabeth (daughter) (1863–1941), 74, 106, 418n.7
 Daniela Senta (daughter) (1860–1940), 74, 129, 245, 403
 Marie (second wife, *née* Schanzer) (1857–1941), 144 and n.25, 399 and n.81
 caricatures of, 114
 concert tours of, 146
 conducting of, 124, 210, 376–77, 389–91
  first performance of *Meistersinger* (1868), *130–31*
  first performance of *Tristan* (1865), *112–14*
 Court Pianist in Munich, 79–80, 107
 depressions of, 3–4, 72–73, 107n.3, 144, 362–63, 376–77
 Liszt and, 145, 244
 Nirvana (symphonic poem), 362n.14, 464
 Royal Kapellmeister in Munich, 123–24
 as a teacher, 244, 245–46
 Wagner and, 131
Bülow, Franziska Elisabeth von (mother) (1800–1888), 106, 131
Bull, Ole (1810–1880), 374
 Sara (wife), 374
Bunzlau (Germany), 22
Burdett-Coutts, Baroness Angela Georgina (1814–1906), 492 and n.31
Bürstein, von, 430
Busoni, Ferruccio Dante Michelangiolo Benvenuto (1866–1924), 17
 meeting with Liszt (1877), 367

Busse, Alwine (singer), 387
Byron, Lord George Gordon Noel (1788–1824), 46, 524n.4
 Childe Harold, 35n.1

Cadogan, Lady, 490n.28
Caetani, Duke Michelangelo of Sermoneta (1804–1882), 37
Cagiano de Azevedo, Cardinal Antonio Maria (1797–1867), 30n.32
Calais (France), 480, 497, 498
Calm-Podowski (Carolyne's cousin), 28, 31
Cambridge (Massachusetts),168n.42
Cambridge, Duchess of (1797–1889), 489–90
Canzi and Heller (photographers), 91n.19
Carl Alexander (1818–1901), Grand Duke of Weimar (1853–1901), 21–22, 32–33, 80, 161, 193, 286, 362, 414, 424, 525–26
 Carl August, Crown Prince (1844–1894) (son), 269
 correspondence with Liszt, 32, 194, 197, 274–75
 Franco-Prussian War and, 211, 217n.10
 Sophie (1824–1897) (wife), Grand Duchess of Weimar (1853–1897), 22, 198, 531
Carl August (1757–1828), Grand Duke of Weimar (1775–1828), 151, 526
Carmen Sylva (1843–1916), Queen of Rumania (1881–1914), 42 and n.25
Carreño, Teresa (1853–1917), 422n.14
Castano, Dr. F., 70n.31
Castelfidardo (Italy), 328
Castel Gandolfo (Italy), 69
Caterini, Cardinal Prospero (1795–1881), 28, 30
Cauvin, Désiré, 50n.10
Cavaillé-Coll, Aristide (1811–1899), 103
Cavour, Count Camillo (1810–1861), 327–28
Cézano, Paul Guy (b. 1843). *See* Zielinska-Piasecka, Olga
Chabrier, Emmanuel (1841–1894), 475
 Valses romantiques, 475

Chamberlain, Houston Stewart
(1855–1927), 76*n*.54
Eva (wife) (1867–1942), 428*n*.25
Chapu, Henri (1833–1891), 313*n*.44
Charles V, Holy Roman Emperor
(1500–1558), 153
Charnacé, Claire Christine de (*née*
d'Agoult) (1830–1912), 95*n*.3
"C. de Sault," 309
Count Guy de (husband) (1825–1909),
101, 302
unpublished letters of, 133–34, 136–43
Chauvet, M. (organist), 103
Cheramateff, Princess Olga, 232*n*.8
Cherubini, Luigi (1760–1842), 38*n*.15
Chicago (America), 166*n*.40
Chickering, Frank (1827–91), 158–59
Legion of Honour, 158
prize-winning piano, 128, *158–59,
161–63,* 166, 168, 534
Chislehurst (England), 222
Chorley, Henry Fothergill (1808–1872),
71
Chopin, Frédéric François (1810–1849),
442
Ballade in A-flat major, op. 47, 420
Ballade in G minor, op. 23, 174
Barcarolle, op. 60, 247
Concerto no. 2, in F minor, op. 21,
462
Mazurka in A minor, op. 17, 442*n*.12
Nocturne in B-flat minor, op. 9, 274,
486
in C minor, op. 48, 395–96
in G major, op. 37, 395
Polonaise in A-flat major, op. 53, 229
Scherzo in B-flat minor, op. 31, 237
Sonata in B minor, op. 58, 236, 237
Study in A-flat major, op. 25, no. 1, 233,
246
Study in F minor, op. 25, no. 2, 233
Trois nouvelles études, 503
Christian Inquirer, 68–69
Cicero, Marcus Tullius (106–143), 48*n*.3
Ciceruacchio (pseud. for Angelo
Brunetti) (1800–1849), 327
Clement XI, Pope (Albani Giovanni
Francesco) (1649–1721), 55
Cognetti, Luisa (Liszt pupil), 475

Cohen, Father Hermann ("Puzzi")
(1821–1871), 40 and *n*.23,
219*n*.16
Coindet, Dr. Jean-Charles (1796–1876),
303, 307
Cologne (Germany), 200
Colonello, Achille (d.1884), 5, 6, 411
death of, 462
Colonne, Edouard (1838–1910), 478
Colpach Castle (Luxembourg), 499 and
n.4, 505
Compromise, The (of 1867, between
Austria and Hungary), 147–48
Connaught, Duke of, 490*n*.28
Constitutionnel, Le (Paris), 189
Corazzo, Monsignor, 86
Corder, Frederick (1852–1932), 14
Cornelius, Peter (1824–1874), 26*n*.21, 116,
129, 201, 255, 409*n*.16, 460
Barber of Bagdad, 473
Cornelius, Peter von (painter)
(1783–1867), 23
Cossmann, Bernhard (1822–1910), 285
Cotta publishers (Stuttgart), 166*n*.38
Couperin, François (1668–1733), 57
Cousin-Montauban, General Charles de
(1796–1878), 217
Cowdery, Miss E., 278*n*.38, 425*n*.18
Craigie House (Cambridge, Mass.),
168*n*.42
Cramer, Pauline (singer), 485
Crémieux, Adolphe (1796–1880), 408
Crispi, Francesco (1819–1901), 331–32
Croissy (France), 302
Cromwell, Oliver (1599–1658), 7
Curschmann, Karl Friedrich (1804–1841),
39
Czerny, Carl (1791–1857), 45, 63*n*.21, 398,
535

Daily Mail (Toronto), 424*n*.16
Dalkau (Germany), 22
Damcke, Berthold (1812–1875), 102
Damrosch, Leopold (1832–1885), 207,
361
Damrosch, Walter (1862–1950), 152, 177,
243–44, 501, 502

Dannreuther, Edward (1844–1905), 355,
    356n.33, 480, 485n.13
Dante Alighieri (1265–1321), 459, 468
    Divine Comedy, 459
Danube River, 150, 294, 358
David, Ferdinand (1810–1873), 65, 152,
    200, 207, 209
Davison, James William (1813–1885), 351
Dayas, William Humphrys (1863–1903),
    419, 464, 472, 517n.20, 519
Deák, Ferenc (1803–1876), 288–89
Deauville (France), 219
Debussy, Achille-Claude (1862–1918),
    446
    meetings with Liszt (1886), 475–76
Delibes, Léo (1836–1891), 373–74, 387
    Coppélia, 373
Denis, Ferdinand (1798–1890), 96
Deppe, Ludwig (1828–1890), 230
Der Floh (Vienna), 407
Del Frate, Vicar General of Albano, 392
Devrient, Eduard (1801–1877), 71
Diderot, Denis (1713–1784), 233
Dies irae plainchant, 453
Dietendorf (Germany), 421
Dietz, Sophie, 152, 153n.13
Dillon, Patrick, xx
Dingelstedt, Franz von (1814–1881),
    77–79
Disraeli, Benjamin (1804–1881), 408
Dohnányi, Ernő von (1877–1960), 300
Dollfuss, Charles (1827–1913), 311
Döllinger, Johann Joseph Ignaz von
    (1799–1890), 324 and n.15
Dönhoff, Countess Maria (c. 1848–1886),
    271
Don Marcello, 86
Donndorff, Adolf von (1835–1916), 286
Donne, John (1572–1631), 442
Doré, Gustave (1832–1883), 104
Dornburg (Germany), 267
Douglas, Mr. (Vice-Consul), 61
Dover (England), 480, 497
Draeseke, Felix August Bernhard
    (1835–1913), 114, 460, 501, 535
    Requiem Mass, 460
Dresden (Germany), 112, 113, 115, 377,
    531
    Saxony Hotel, 377

Drewing, Victoria, 464
Dreyschock, Alexander (1818–1869), 172
Dwight's Musical Journal (Boston), 86n.3
Dufour, M. (Mayor of Paris), 97
Duka, Dr. Theodore, 490
Duncker, Franz (Reichsminister), 350, 353
Dunkl, János Nepomuk (1832–1910), 298
Düsseldorf (Germany), 362

Eddy, Sara Hershey, 280n.38
Edler, Carl Erdmann (b. 1844), 473
Edward, Prince of Wales (1841–1910), 485
    Alexandra, Princess of Wales
        (1844–1925), 485
Eisenach (Germany), 80, 81, 211, 284, 368,
    414, 415n.30
Eisenstadt (Austria), 205
Egger, Dr. Franz, 206
Egli (Lucerne priest), 343n.5
Ehrmann, Léon (1822–1845), 303
Elgar, Sir Edward (1857–1934), 255n.2, 263
Eliot, George (pseud. for Marian Evans)
    (1819–1880), 408
Elisabeth (1837–1898), Empress of Austria
    (1854–1898) and Queen of
    Hungary (1867–1898), 148
Ellinger, Josefine (1852–1920), 274
Ems (Germany), 214
Engel, Gustav (1823–95), 351
Engeszer, Mátyás (1812–1885), 360n.8
    Katalin (wife), 375
Eptacorde (Rome), 151
Erard family, 379, 480
Erasmi, Dr. Gabriele (b. 1942), xviii, xx,
    30n.32
Erdmannsdörfer, Max (1848–1905), 362
Erfurt (Germany), 377, 379
Erkel, Ferenc (1810–1893), 91, 289, 290,
    293–94, 410
    Bánk bán, 294
    Bátori Mária, 294
    Hunyadi László, 294
    speech at the inauguration of the
        Academy of Music, 292–93,
        296, 298
Erkel, Gyula (1842–1909), 290
Erkel, Sándor (1846–1900), 375

Erlangen (Germany), 513
Ernst, Heinrich Wilhelm (1814–1865), 92*n*.24
Escudier, Léon (1821–1881), 101
Essen (Germany), 424*n*.17
Essipova, Anna Nikolaievna (1851–1914), 396
Este, Cardinal Ippolite d' (1509–1572), 165
Esterházy, Count Moritz, 480
Esztergom (Gran, Hungary), 92, 270, 272, 358, 463
Ettersburg (Germany), xvii
Eugénie (1826–1920), Empress of the French (1853–1870), 212–13, 215 and *n*.6, 216, 217, 221*n*.20
Evans, Dr. Thomas, 219
Evening World, The (New York), 243*n*.37
Exter, Elisabeth, 355
Ezekiel, Book of (Old Testament), 449
Ezekiel, Moses Jacob (1844–1917), 396–98
  bust of Liszt, 396–98

Faure, Jean-Baptiste (1830–1914), 499*n*.6
Fay, Amy (1844–1928), 7, 199, 234–35, 241*n*.34, 267, 470
  descriptions of Liszt's playing (1873), 234–35, 238, 269
  Music Study in Germany, 470
Fehértemplom (Hungary), 411
Fellner, Sándor (1857–1944), 398
Fenili, Count, 164
Ferrari, Father Giacinto de, 28*n*.24, 86
Ferrata, Cardinal Domenico, 232*n*.8, 498
Ferrata, Guiseppe (1865–1928), 231*n*.8, 458, 498
Festetics, Count Leo (1800–1884), 92 and *n*.24, 289
Fétis, François-Joseph (1784–1871), 440
Figaro, Le (Paris), 351
Fischer, Franz (1849–1918), 416
"Five Weeks' War" (1866), 213
Flavigny, Viscountess Marie-Elisabeth (1772–1847), 302
Flavigny, Count Maurice Adolphe Charles de (1799–1873), 305, 306
  Mathilde (wife), 305
Fleischer, Dr. 513, 515

Floh, Der (Vienna), 407
Florence (Italy), 122, 144, 196, 310, 385
Fontanès, M. (pastor), 313, 315
Forbes, Mr., 480*n*.4
Forster, Stefánia (1862–d. after 1936), 296
Fortunatus, Venantius (c. 540–c. 600), 382
Fővárosi Lapok (Budapest), 407, 528
France, La (Paris)
Franchi, Cardinal, 329
Franciscans of Hungary, 90–91
Franck, César (1822–1890), 102–03
  Piano trio in B minor, 102*n*.21
Franco-Prussian War (1870), 206, 211, *212–27,* 311, 312, 420
Frankfurt (Germany), 23, 391, 507
Frankfurter Europa (Frankfurt), 56*n*.10
Franz, Robert (1815–1892), 469, 520*n*.24
  response to "La Cosaque," 187–88 and *n*.36
  "Robert Franz Fund," 469
Franz Joseph I (1830–1916), Emperor of Austria (1848–1916) and King of Hungary (1867–1916), 155, 273, 328, 410
  Coronation of (1867), *147–48*
  Dual Monarchy, 147–48, 154
  Elisabeth (1837–1898), Empress of Austria and Queen of Hungary (1867–1898), 410
Freiburg (Germany), 401
French Foreign Legion, 199
Frenzel, Karl (critic), 350
Friedheim, Arthur (1859–1932), 13, 228, 234, 240, 253, 445, 458, 466
  arrest and arraignment of, 242 and *n*.37
  describes Liszt's playing (1886), 503
  paraphrase on "Yankee Doodle," 242
Fröhlich, Frau von, 465, 504, 513–14, 518, 522
Fry, Charles, 497
Függetlenség (Budapest), 406
Fulke-Greville, Major-General, 489

Galliffet, Marquis Gaston Auguste de (1830–1909), 218
Gambetta, Léon (1838–1882), 220, 221
Garets, Comtesse de (1848–1927), 215*n*.6

Garibaldi, Giuseppe (1807–1882), 155, 328, 411

Gaul, Kathie Cecilie (Liszt pupil), 267, 361

Gauthier, Judith (1846–1917), 351

Gaysruch, Cardinal (d. 1848), 327*n*.17

Gazette de Hongrie (Budapest), 398, 408, 409

Gemenos (France), 48, 49, 50

Genast-Merian, Emilie ("Mici") (1833–1905), 153*n*.13, 196, 208*n*.35

Geneva (Switzerland), 117, 189 and *n*.42, 190, 303, 307, 310, 311

George IV (1762–1830), King of England (1820–1830), 486

Gersdorff (Germany), 22

Gesualdo, Don Carlo (1560–1613), 452

Gevaert, François (1828–1908), 159

Gille, Dr. Carl (1813–1899), 6, 71, 94, 164, 196, 240, 368, 413

Ginobbi, Canon Lorenzo, 392

Giorni, Canon Francesco, 392*n*.68

Girardin, Emile de (1802–1881), 101*n*.17, 309, 314

Glazunov, Alexander (1865–1936), 501

Glinka, Mikail (1804–1857), 534
  Tscherkessen March, 534

Gobbi, Henrik (1842–1920), 270, 271, 290, 296, 511*n*.8

Gobineau, Count Joseph-Arthur de (1816–1882), 385

Godard, Benjamin (1849–1895), 461

Goepfart, Karl (1859–1942), 178*n*.16, 500

Goethe, Johann Wolfgang von (1749–1832), 203, 210, 240, 286, 310, 452, 526, 536
  "Erinnerungen," 194*n*.2

Gogh, Vincent van (1853–1890), 412*n*.23

Goldmark, Károly (1830–1915), 207, 468

Goldschmidt, Adalbert von (1848–1906), 400, 468

Goldwag, Bertha, 109 and *n*.5

Göllerich, August (1859–1923), 7, 235, 433, 439*n*.4, 454*n*.25, 469

Gomperz-Bettelheim, Caroline von (1845–1926), 366, 367*n*.22, 388

Gosford, Lord, 490*n*.28

Gottschalg, Alexander Wilhelm (1827–1908), 79 and *n*.63, 178*n*.16, 200

Götze, Franz Carl (1814–1888), 79

Gouffens (painter), 498

Gounod, Charles François (1818–1893), 379, 499
  Faust, 379
  Roméo et Juliette, 104

Graefe, Dr. Albrecht von (1828–1870), 500*n*.12

Graefe, Dr. Alfred Carl (1830–1899), 412 and *n*.24, 500–01 and *n*.12

Grand Prix de Rome, 475

Graphic, The (London), 488

Gravier, Marie-Thérèse (1850–1934), 53*n*.19, 379

Gravina, Count Biagio (1850–1897), 418*n*.7, 533

Grazia, Duke della, 425

Gregorovius, Ferdinand (1821–1891), 40 and *n*.24, 41, 69*n*.27, 97, 209*n*.36
  description of Liszt (1865), 86 and *n*.3, 90
  Werdomar and Wladislav, 41*n*.24

Gregory XVI, Pope (Capellari, Bartolomeo Alberto) (1765–1846), 326 and *n*.17

Grieg, Edvard Hagerup (1843–1907)
  meetings with Liszt, *168–70*
  Piano Concerto in A minor, 169–70
  Sonata in F major, for violin and piano, 168*n*.45
  Sonata in G major, for violin and piano, 169

Grillparzer, Franz (1791–1872), 116

Gross, Adolf von (1845–1931), 430, 519

Grosse, Eduard, 77

Grosskurth, Emma, 245, 414*n*.29

Grotta Mare (Italy), 163, 164

Grove, Sir George (1820–1900), 163, 278*n*.38, 480, 487–88
  Dictionary of Music, 163, 278*n*.38, 356*n*.33

Grünfeld, Heinrich (1855–1931), 422*n*.14

Grützmacher, Leopold (1835–1900), 380, 464

Guépin, Dr. Ange (1805–1873), 105*n*.28

"Guermann Regnier," 104, 375

Guéroult, Adolphe (editor), 309
Gutmann, Albert, 388–89
Gutt, Bernhard (1812–1849), 60*n*.15
Gutzkow, Carl (1811–1878), 79

Hadow, Sir William Henry (1859–1937),
    14
Hadrian's Villa (Italy), 165*n*.36, 394
Hague, The (Holland), 103
Halir, Carl (1859–1909), 200 and *n*.18
Halle (Germany), 187, 403, 500 and *n*.12,
    501, 509
Hallé, Sir Charles (1819–1895), 480, 490
Haller, Hermine (singer), 337*n*.37
Hamburger, Dr. Klára (b. 1934), xx, 225
Handel, George Frederick (1685–1759),
    39
Hannibál, József, 401
Hanover (Germany), 144, 176*n*.11,
    354*n*.29, 362, 363, 368, 376
Hanslick, Eduard (1825–1904), 14, 350,
    378–79, 388, 453
  criticisms of Liszt, 59*n*.15, 203, 283
  descriptions of Liszt
      (1874), 273
      (1877), 366–67
      (1878), 379
      (1879), 388
  as plagiarist, 59*n*.15
  Vom Musikalisch-Schönen, 59*n*.15
Haraszti, Emile (1885–1958), 104, 224,
    411*n*.22
Hartog, Eduard (1829–1909), 460
Hatos, Brother Hubert, 91
Hatzfeldt, Princess Marie (1820–1897),
    504, 519
Hauptmann, Moritz (1792–1868), 200
Haussman, Baron Georges-Eugène
    (1809–1891), 154–55, 309
Havet, Ernest, 309
Haweis, Rev. Hugh Reginald
    (1839–1901), 394–96
Haydn, Joseph (1732–1809), 287, 506
Haynald, Cardinal Lajos (1816–1891), 71,
    225, 270, 289, 298, 463
Healy, George Peter Alexander
    (1813–1894), 166–68

Hébert, Antoine Auguste Ernest
    (1817–1908), 177*n*.15, 179, 321,
    459, 475
Hegel, Georg Wilhelm Friedrich
    (1770–1831), 41*n*.24
Heidelberg (Germany), 534
Heine, Heinrich (1797–1856), 408
Helbig, Nadine (*née* Princess
    Shahavskaya) (1847–c. 1923),
    36, 162 and *n*.28, 166, 384, 393,
    475
Helbig, Wolfgang (1839–1915), 162 and
    n.28, 173*n*.4, 384
Held, Louis (1851–1927), 7–8 and *n*.9,
    463, 472, 502
Hellmesberger, Joseph (1828–1893), 150,
    204, 207, 209, 469
Henneguy, Félix, 309
Hennig, Father Alois (1826–1902), 93 and
    n.25
Henschel, Sir George (1850–1934), 350,
    351
Henselt, Adolf (1814–89), 22, 237, 488
Henshaw, Grace Mary, 485*n*.13
Herbeck, Johann Franz von (1831–1877),
    15, 94, 204, 207, 273
Herder, Johann Gottfried (1744–1803),
    286
Herwegh, Georg (1817–1875), 255
  Emma (wife) (1817–1901), 537*n*.38
Herz, Henri (1803–1888), 98, 172
  Salle Herz, 172*n*.3
Heymann, Karl (1854–1922), 239
Hill, Karl (1831–1893), 355, 417
Hiller, Ferdinand (1811–1885), 362
Hoch Conservatory (Frankfurt), 200
Hodge and Essex, 355*n*.33
Hoeltge, May, 419
Hoffmann von Fallersleben, August
    Heinrich (1798–1874), 79
Hohenlohe-Schillingsfürst, Cardinal Gus-
    tav Adolf von (1823–1896), 55,
    69, 88, 159*n*.23, 165, 320, 324,
    330–34
  Prince Chlodwig (brother)
      (1819–1901), 332, 333
  death of, 329, 333–34
  Jesuits and, 332 and *n*. 20, 333
  Liszt and, *86–89*

opposition to Carolyne's marriage,
    28–30
Prince Philip (nephew) (1864–1942),
    426 and *n.*21
Vatican and, 330–333
Prince Viktor (brother) (Duke of Rati-
    bor) (1818–1893), 331
Hohenlohe-Schillingsfürst, Princess
    Marie von (*née* Sayn-
    Wittgenstein) (1837–1920), xix,
    30*n.*35, 31, 323
Franz Joseph (son) (1861–1871), 31
Konstantin (husband) (1828–1896), 384,
    530*n.*21
quarrels with her mother, 30*n.*35,
    31*n.*38
Wagner's "Open Letter" to, 353*n.*26
Hohenschwangau (Germany), 74
Hohenzollern-Hechingen, Prince Con-
    stantin von (1801–1869), 22,
    87
Hohenzollern-Sigmaringen, Prince
    Leopold, 214
Höhle, G. (piano maker), 229*n.*5
Hohmann, Father Anton (1811–1886),
    77
Horowitz-Barnay, Ilka, 374
Horpács (Hungary), 180*n.*24
Horváth, Attila (1862–1921), 374
Huber (later Hubay), Jenő (1858–1937),
    290, 374, 469
Huber, Károly (1828–1885), 290, 374
Hueffer, Francis (1843–1889), 478
Hugo, Victor (1802–1885), 49, 221
    Les Misérables, 49
Hummel, Johann Nepomuk (1778–1837),
    63*n.*21, 399
    Elisabeth (wife) (1793–1883), 195*n.*5
    monument to, 399, 468
    Piano sonata in A-flat major (piano
        duet), 400
Hungarian Association of London, 480
Hurand, M. (music director), 99
Huszár, Imre von (1838–1916), 270

Ibach (piano maker), 229*n.*5
Illustrierte Zeitung (Leipzig), 91

Indépendance Luxembourgeoise, L', 506
Index Librorum Prohibitorum, 323, 324
Indicator, The (Chicago), 201*n.*19
Irving, Sir Henry (1838–1905), 490, 496
Isnard, Dr. Charles, 48 and *n.*3, 49, 50
Israelite Women, Society of (Budapest),
    373
Itter Castle (Austrian Tyrol), 473
Iwanowsky, Dyonis (Carolyne's uncle),
    28*n.*27

Jacopone da Todi (c. 1228–1306), 263
Jaëll, Marie (1846–1925), 499*n.*6
Jámbor, László (b. 1935), xx
Janina, Olga. *See* Zielinska-Piasecka,
    Olga
Jena (Germany), 94, 211, 240
    "Sausage Festival," 240–41, 471
Jeschke, Clothilde, 464
Jewish Law Students' Association
    (Budapest), 406
Joachim, Joseph (1831–1907), 71, 200,
    206–07, 351, 415*n.*30, 488
Johnson, Dr. Samuel (1709–1804),
    422*n.*14
Jókai, Mór (1825–1904), 387
    Róza (wife) (1817–1886), 387
    Die Wiege, 387
Joseffy, Rafael (1853–1915), 203*n.*23,
    231*n.*8
Joukowsky, Paul von (1845–1912), 423,
    428, 430, 434, 435, 502, 518
    portraits of Liszt (1882), 423–24
Journal des Débats (Paris), 101
Journal de Genève, (Geneva), 311
Journal de Luxembourg, 506
Juhász, Aladár (1856–1922), 290*n.*9, 364,
    400, 533

Kahn, Dr. Samuel, 373
Kahnt, Christian Friedrich (1823–1897),
    94, 271
Kahrer, Laura (1853–1925), 267
Kalkbrenner, Friedrich (1785–1849),
    63*n.*21, 67, 230

Kalocsa (Hungary), 93, 225, 272, 463
Kant, Immanuel (1724–1804), 41*n*.24
Kapp, Julius (1883–1962), 509*n*.2
Karácsonyi, Count Guido (1817–1885), 271, 379
Karlsruhe (Germany), 198, 377, 402, 469, 472
   Tonkünstler-Versammlung Festival (1864), 70–72, 74, 75*n*.49
Karpath, Lajos (1866–1936), 525
Karzendorfer, Father, 519
Keene, Richard, 349
Keil, Dr. (Weimar lawyer), 79
Kellermann, Berthold (1853–1926), 16, 244, 352, 353
   description of Liszt (1879), 358
Keppler, Dr. Friedrich, 428
Kepviselöhazi Napló (Budapest), 524*n*.4
Keudell, Baron Robert von (1824–1903), 335
Kiel, Friedrich (1821–1885), 460
Kiev (Ukraine), 181
Klagenfurt (Austria), 473
Klahre, Edwin, 243, 464
   description of Liszt's playing, 248
Klausenburg (now Cluj, Rumania), 387
Klindworth, Karl (1830–1916), 114, 232, 271, 519
Knežević, Spiridon (manservant), 5–6, 292, 364, 367*n*.22, 378, 379
Kniese, Julius (1848–1905), 391, 472
Kodály, Zoltán (1882–1967), 300
Koessler, János (1853–1926), 290
Komárom (Hungary), 358
Kömpel, August (1831–91), 196, 209, 380
Königsberg (now Kaliningrad, Russia), 41*n*.24, 361
Konopacka, Anna (Liszt pupil), 9*n*.12
Kopf, Josef von (1827–1903), 173*n*.4
Kossuth, Lajos (1802–1894), 385, 407
Kramer, Ernesztina (b. 1864–after 1936), 297
   description of Liszt, 298
Krainer, Mihály ("Miska"), 6, 500, 510, 512–15
Krause, Martin (1853–1918), 472, 501, 517*n*.20, 519, 520
Kreutzer, Léon (1817–1868), 102
Krivácsy, Ilona, 236

Krupp, Alfred (1812–1887), 424*n*.17
Kryzanowicz Castle (now Krizanovice, Poland), 424*n*.13
Kufstein (Germany), 430
Kullak, Theodor (1818–1882), 11–12 and *n*.19, 230, 239
Kun, Margit (Liszt pupil), 293
Kurtz, Father Vilmos, 91*n*.19

Lachmund, Carl Valentine (1853–1928), 4, 7, 8, 13, 202, 411–12
   Caroline (wife) (1854–1889), 8, 419, 435–36
   defence of Liszt, 244 and *n*.40
   descriptions of Liszt's playing (1883), 232–33, 246–47
   Ladies' Home Journal, The (New York), 244*n*.39
   Living with Liszt: 1882–84, xviii, 236–37 and *n*.22
Lager, Ludwig (1830–after 1886), 528–29
Lagos (Africa), 199
La Mara (pseud. for Marie Lipsius) (1837–1927), 210, 383, 404, 409, 506
   as editor of Liszt's letters, 535–36
   Musikerbriefe, 535
Lambruschini, Cardinal Luigi (1776–1854), 326
Lamennais, Abbé Félicité Robert de (1782–1854), 323, 336
Lammert, Minna (b. 1852), 349
Lamond, Frederic Archibald (1868–1948), 470, 481, 533
   London recital (1886), 492–93
La Moutte (France), 47, 50, 53 and *n*.19, 81
Lamporecchio (Italy), 373
Lancy St. Georges (Switzerland), 189
Landberg, Dr. (Wagner's physician), 428
Landgraf, Dr. Karl, 510, 515
Láng, Adolf (1848–1913), 300
Lassen, Eduard (1830–1904), 17, 71, 80, 193, 196, 198, 256, 267, 269, 352, 414, 422, 463
   Incidental music to Goethe's "Faust," 368

Latour, Countess, 385
Laussot, Jessie (*née* Taylor) (1827–1905),
    15, 38 and *n*.15, 385
  Eugène (husband), 38
  Wagner and, 38*n*.15
Lebert, Sigmund (1822–1844), 41, 166 and
    n.38
Lebrun, General Barthelémi, 217
Lecomte, General, 222
Legány, Desző (b. 1916), 14, 292*n*.10
  Liszt and His Country, 14
Lehmann, Carl, 462
Lehmann, Lilli (1848–1929), 349
Lehmann, Liza (singer), 488, 489
Lehmann, Marie (1851–1931), 349
Leibniz, Gottfried Wilhelm (1646–1716),
    347 and *n*.15
Leipzig (Germany), 377, 391, 499
  Conservatory of Music, 200, 299
  Gewandhaus, 460
  St. Nicholas Church, 210
  St. Thomas's Church, 460
Leitert, Georg (1852–1901), 203*n*.23, 267
Lemberg (now Lvov, Ukraine), 171
Lenbach, Franz Seraph von (1836–1904),
    143, 210
Leo XIII, Pope (Pecci, Gioacchino
    Vincenzo) (1810–1903), 328,
    330–32, 384
Leopold II (1835–1909), King of the Bel-
    gians (1865–1909), 402
Lépessy, Ilona, 364
Le Play, Frédéric (1806–1882), 155
Lessmann, Otto (1844–1918), 12*n*.19, 509
Leuckart publishers (Leipzig), 188*n*.36
Levi, Hermann (1839–1900), 416, 418,
    430, 465
Levi, Primo (1854–1917), 330, 333
Lévy, Michel, 314
Lewald-Stahr, Fanny (1811–1889), 202
Lewes (England), 425*n*.18
Lewy, Carl, 271
Liber Ordinationum, 88*n*.12
Liberté, La (Paris), 101
Liber usualis, 263
Library of Congress, xix
Liebig, Baron Justus (1803–1873), 225
Liège (Belgium), 478
Ligorio, Pirro (c. 1500–1583), 165

Linz (Austria), 114
Lippi, Carlo (1845?–1906?), 60, 162
Liszt, Adam (father) (1776–1827), 337*n*.37
Liszt, Blandine-Rachel (daughter)
    (1835–1862). *See* Ollivier,
    Emile
Liszt, Cosima (daughter) (1837–1930). *See*
    Wagner, Richard
Liszt, Maria Anna (mother) (1788–1866),
    22*n*.5, 53*n*.19, 80, 86–87
  death of, 81, *95–97*
Liszt, Daniel Heinrich Franciscus Joseph
    (son) (1839–1859), 80
  Liszt visits his tomb, 80
Liszt, Eduard (uncle-cousin) (1817–1879),
    94, 207, 289, 319, 336, 364, 376,
    378, 529
  death of, 389
  Eduard (son) (1869–1961), 181*n*.24, 389
  Franz (son) (1851–1919), 400
  Hedwig (daughter) (1866–1941), 389
  Henriette (second wife) (1825–1920),
    204*n*.26, 366, 511
  Karolina (first wife) (1827–1854),
    204*n*.26
Liszt, Franz (1811–1886)
  accidents to
    (1876), 365
    (1881), 5, 403–05
  alcohol and, 5, 242, 411–12, 501
  America and, 9–10, 464
  Blandine and, 23, 44, 47, 529
  Bülow and, 145
  break with Wagner (1867), 125
  burial place of, 523–28
  church music and, 337
  conducting of, 91, 153 and *n*.14, 198,
    209, 240–41, 269
  Cosima and, 22–23, 81, 92, *134–36*,
    341–43, 462*n*.8, 465, 503
  Court Chamberlain, 193
  critics and, 14–15, 16
  cuts finger
    (1875), 279–80
    (1877), 367*n*.22
  decorations of (Appendix III)
  depressions of, 54, 369–70, 435, 437–38,
    510*n*.4
  dental problems of, 511*n*.8

Liszt, Franz (1811–1886) (*cont.*)
  descriptions of his piano playing
    (1864), 68
    (1869), 205
    (1873), 234–35
    (1875), 286
    (1880), 394–96
    (1882), 429
    (1883), 232–33
    (1884), 248
    (1886), 488, 496
  Dominicans and, 55
  failing eyesight of, 412, 465–66, 474,
      500–01, 505
  financial investments of, 378
  Franciscans and, 90–91
  funeral of, 519–20
  Grieg and, *168–70*
  holy orders and, 10–11, *85–89*
  illnesses of, 4, 245, 404–05, 466, 474, 500
  Jesuits and, 69–70
  Jewish question and, 336, *405–09*
  Jubilee celebrations (1873), 269–272
      and *n*.21
  Konzeptbücher, 357 and *n*.2
  last will and testament of, 319 and
      n.2, 530
  masterclasses, 202–03
  melancholia of, 369–70, 437–38
  Memento Journalier of, 23*n*.12, 33*n*.41, 46
  memorial museum (Budapest), xx,
      170*n*.49, 534, 535
  memorial museum (Weimar), 531
  Order of Franz Joseph, 150, 275
  Order of Leopold, 402
  physical descriptions of
    (1864), 68–69
    (1865), 86
    (1867), 161–62
    (1869), 205
    (1879), 388
    (1886), 486, 488
  as President of the Hungarian
      Academy of Music, 290
  priesthood and, *85–90*
  Princess Carolyne and, 22, 33–34, 94,
      299, 319–20, 466, 527
    correspondence with, 94, 152, 385
    quarrels with, 323*n*.12, 324, 336,
        343–44

Redeemer Medal (Vienna), 367
  as Royal Hungarian Councillor, 227
  Schumann (Clara) and, 298
  as secret agent, 223–25
  sight-reading of, 125, 169–70, 238, 389
  superstitious beliefs of, 435–36, 476
  "Technical Studies" of (1869–71), 164
      and *n*.32, 177–78, 231
  thwarted marriage to Carolyne, *22–30*
  tomb of, 528
  Wagner and, 125, 145, 278–80, 341–55,
      352–53, 409, 418*n*.7
    memorial concert in Weimar (1883),
        431–32
    rapprochement with (1872), *256–58,*
        341–42
    Wagner–Liszt letters, *434–35*
  Sword of Honour, 272, 534*n*.30
  as a teacher, *228–53, 295–99*
LISZT AT THE PIANO:
  fingering, 64, 232
  leaps, 246–47
  pedalling, 67, 127
  tremolos, 127, 247 and *n*.55
COMPOSING TECHNIQUES:
  atonality, 439–41
  chord building, 447–51
  "functional" harmony, 446–47
  gypsy scales, 451
  key characteristics, 43 and *n*.28, 52
      and *n*.17, 372, 441*n*.11
  ordre omnitonique, 440
  Sketches for a Harmony of the Future,
      440
WORKS:
Piano:
  Années de pèlerinage, 39, 532
  VOLUME I ("Suisse"):
    Au bord d'une source, 296, 372, 463,
        475, 534
    Vallée d'Obermann, 475
  VOLUME III, 338*n*.38, *370–72*
    Angelus! 376, *394–95,* 487*n*.20,
        488*n*.22
    Aux cyprès de la Villa d'Este
        (Threnodies I and II), 370–72
    Les jeux d'eaux à la Villa d'Este,
        247*n*.55, *372,* 376
    Marche funèbre, 158*n*.19
    Am Grabe Richard Wagners, 432, 433

Bagatelle without tonality, *444–46,* 471*n.27*

Ballade in B minor, 248

Beethoven's "kiss of consecration," 272

Beethoven symphony transcriptions, *62–68,* 89

Ceremonial March of the Holy Grail, from Parsifal (Wagner), *418*

Chants polonaises (Chopin), 484, 506

Charité, La (Rossini), 400

Christmas-tree Suite, 459

Concerto Pathétique, 368, 402

Concert Study in D-flat major ("Sospiro"), 484

"Confutatis" and "Lacrymosa" from Mozart's *Requiem, 44–46*

Consolations, 210

Csárdás macabre, 453–54

Don Giovanni Reminiscences (Mozart), 533

Elegy no. 1, 285

"Erlkönig" (Schubert), 10, 86

Ernani Paraphrase (Verdi), 236

Evocation à la Chapelle Sixtine (Mozart and Allegri), *42–44*

"Frühlingsglaube" (Schubert), 373

Harmonies poétiques et religieuses, 387
   Ave Maria, 68
   Bénédiction de Dieu dans la solitude, 166
   Cantique d'amour, 387, 484, 533
   Funérailles, 52*n.17*

Hungarian Historical Portraits, 225*n.37,* 439, 451–52

Hungarian March in C minor (Schubert), 362

Hungarian Rhapsodies, 375, 486, 496
   no. 2, in C-sharp minor, 237, 296, 422
   no. 9, in E-flat major (*Pesther Carnaval*), 423
   no. 12, in C-sharp minor, 92
   no. 15, in A minor (*Rákóczy* March), 225, 400
   no. 19, in D minor, 467–68

"Illustrations" from Meyerbeer's *L'Africaine,* 89

Isolde's "Liebestod" (Wagner), *126–28,* 247*n.55*

La campanella, 246

La lugubre gondola I & II, 426–28, 433

Liebestraum no. 1 ("Hohe Liebe"), 506

Mephisto Polka, 442

Mephisto Waltz no. 1, 71

Mephisto Waltz no. 2, 235, 458

Mephisto Waltz no. 3, 414, 450–51, 452

Nuages gris, 440–41

"Patineurs" Waltz from *Le Prophète* (Meyerbeer), 39

Polonaise Brillante (Weber), 269, 497

Polonaise no. 2, in E major, 398, 533

Polka oubliée, 438

Prelude and Fugue on the name "B.A.C.H.," 39, 284

Romance oubliée, 438

R.W.—Venezia, 431

Schlaflos! Frage und Antwort, 441–42 and *n.11*

"Serenade" (Schubert), 475

Soirées de Vienne (Schubert), 98, 163, 188*n.36,* 506

Sonata in B minor, 39 and *n.18,* 71, 367, 398, 472, 533

Sonnambula Fantasie (Bellini), 274

Spanish Rhapsody, 103

Studies
   Gnomenreigen, 42, 247, 398
   Waldesrauschen, 41–42, 398

"Szózat and Hymnus" paraphrase, 360

Tannhäuser Overture, 161

"Transcendental Studies" (1851)
   Feux-follets, 398
   Harmonies du soir, 247
   Mazeppa, 244, 296, 533
   Paysage, 398

Two Franciscan Legends, xviii, 92, 98
   St. Francis of Assisi preaching to the birds, 56–57, 72
   St. Francis of Paola walking on the waters, 58–59, 98

Unstern! Sinistre, Disastro, 443, 447

Valse oubliée, 438

Waltz from *Faust* (Gounod), 39, 102

Liszt, Franz (1811–1886): WORKS (*cont.*)
  "Weinen, Klagen" variations, 16, 51,
    264, 284, 362
ORGAN:
  Fantasy and Fugue on the name
    "B.A.C.H.," 421
SONGS:
  "Die drei Zigeuner," 61
  "Es muss ein Wunderbares sein," 71,
    202*n*.21
  "Go not, happy day," 442–43
  "Ich möchte hingehn," 371
  "König in Thule," 210
  "In liebeslust," 71
  "Die Lorelei," 371
  "Mignon's Lied," 71
ORCHESTRAL:
  Symphonic Poems
  Ce qu'on entend sur la montagne, 423
  Festklänge, 71, 242
  From the Cradle to the Grave, 439*n*.5
  Hamlet, 362 and *n*.14
  Heroïde funèbre, 52*n*.17
  Hunnenschlacht, 362, 402
  Les Préludes, 104
  Mazeppa, 402
  Orpheus, 497
  Prometheus, 362, 389
  Tasso, 104, 402, 463
  Dante Symphony, 38, 97, 104, 375,
    459, 472, 496
  Faust Symphony, 402, 406, 475
PIANO AND ORCHESTRA:
  Concerto no. 1, in E flat major, 460,
    488
  Concerto no. 2, in A major, 174, 459
  Concerto Pathétique, 402
  Hungarian Fantasy, 269, 379
  Ruins of Athens Fantasia
    (Beethoven), 274, 362
  Totentanz, 402, 533
  Wanderer Fantasy (Schubert), 103,
    273, 387
CHORAL:
  An den heiligen Franziskus von Paula,
    58–59, 360–61
  Ave Maris Stella, 393 and *n*.72
  The Bells of Strasbourg Cathedral, 168,
    240–41, 279–83, 432

Christus (Oratorio), xviii, 11, 16, 94,
    151, *258–67,* 271, 534
  "The Beatitudes," 256
  "Christmas Oratorio," 256
  composition of, 255–56
  Le Crucifix, 447
  "The March of the Three Holy
    Kings," 261, *488*
De Profundis, 448–49, 458
Die Legende von der heiligen Elisabeth
    (Oratorio), 79, 90–91, 151, 153,
    204, 284, 368, 463, 473, 477, 482,
    485–86, 494–96, 499, 523, 533
  "Miracle of the Roses," 153 and
    n.14, 165, 485, 486
"Gran" Mass, 97, *99–102,* 209–10,
    272, 362, 375, *478*
Hungarian Coronation Mass,
    149–50, 162, 205, 226, 463, 499
Legend of Saint Cecilia, 368
Missa Choralis, 89, 267, 286
Ossa arida, 449–50
Papsthymnus, 93
Prometheus Choruses, 94, 204, 362
Psalm 13, 71, 379
Psalm 125, 447–48
Psalm 129 (*De Profundis*) 447, 458,
    474
"Reapers' Chorus" from *Prometheus,*
    360*n*.8
Requiem for Male Voices, 285, 448,
    537
Rosario, 383
St. Cecilia Legend, 285
St. Stanislas (Oratorio), *464,*
    473–74
Septum sacramenta, 383
"Szekszárd" Mass, 92, 469
Ungarisches Königslied, 410, *411, 415*
Via Crucis, 381–84
  foreword to, 381
WRITINGS OF:
  Des Bohémiens et de leur musique en
    Hongrie, 373, 405–09, 410, 411
Liszt Memorial Museum and Research
    Centre (Budapest), xx, 170*n*.49
Liszt Museum (Weimar), 531
Liszt Prize (Allgemeiner Deutscher
    Musikverein), 453*n*.22

Liszt Scholarship (Budapest), 290n.9
Liszt Scholarship (RAM, England), 483–84
Liszt *Stiftung,* 530, 531, 532
Littleton, Alfred (1845–1914), 480, 520
Littleton, Henry (1823–1888), 480, 490, 492
Liverpool Music Festival, 9
Loën, Baron August von (1827–1887), 271, 519
Logier, Johann (1777–1846), 230
"Chiroplast," 230
London (England)
    Battersea, 481
    British Library and Museum, xix, 433
    Brompton Oratory, 496
    Buckingham Palace, 478, 486
    Chalk Farm, 481
    Chelsea, 481
    Colonial Exhibition of 1886, 424n.17
    Crystal Palace, 422n.14, 486, 488, 494
    Exeter Hall, 355
    Grosvenor Gallery, 487
    Guildhall School of Music, 481n.8
    Hampstead, 481
    London Academy of Music, 481n.8, 496n.34
    Lyceum Theatre, 490
    Marlborough House, 490
    Neumeyer Hall, 483
    Prince's Hall, 488, 489, 493, 496
    Queen's Concert Rooms, 483n.11
    Royal Academy of Music, 15, 477–78, 481n.8, 483–84 and n.13
    Royal Albert Hall, 355–56 and n.33
    Royal College of Music, 422n.14, 481n.8
    St. James's Church (Marylebone), 394
    St. James's Hall, 355, 422n.12, 485, 492
    St. James's Palace, 489
    Swiss Cottage, 481
    Trinity College of Music, 481n.8
    Victoria Station, 480 and n.5
    Westwood House, 496, 497
Longfellow, Henry Wadsworth (1807–82), 166–68, 281, 283–84
    Alice Mary (daughter) (1850–1928), 168
    Anne Pierce (sister) (1810–1901), 168
    Excelsior, 281 and n.49

The Golden Legend, 168, 281, 282
Loo Castle (Belgium), 284
Louis, Prince ("Child of France") (1856–1879), 215 and n.8
Louis-Philippe (1773–1850), "Citizen King" (1830–1848), 219n.17
Löwenberg (Germany), 22
Lucerne (Switzerland), 117, 121, 123n.23, 143
Ludwig II (1845–1886), King of Bavaria (1864–1886), 61 and n 18, 72
Luther, Martin (1843–1586), 153, 154, 342, 343n.5
Luxembourg Société de Musique, 505
Luxemburger Wort, 504, 505–06
Luxemburger Zeitung, 504n.19
Lynen, Victor Raymond (1834–1894), 498
Lyons (France), 23, 151

MacDowell, Edward (1861–1908), 419
    "Modern" Suite, 420
    Piano Concerto no. 1, in A minor, 419–20
Macfarren, Sir George Alexander (1813–1887), 15, 483, 484 and n.13
    John the Baptist, 483
Mackenzie, Sir Alexander Campbell (1847–1935), 480, 482–83, 494
    Violin Concerto, 483
MacMahon, Marshal Patrice (1808–1898), 216–17
Macmillan publishers, 278n.38
Magenta, Battle of (June 4, 1859), 328
Magdeburg (Germany), 368
Maggi, Monsignor Bernardino, 26, 27n.22, 28, 69
Magyarország és a Nagyvilág (Budapest), 375
Maier, Mathilde (1833–1910), 73–74
Mainz (Germany), 151, 303
Malibran, Maria Felicita (*née* Garcia) (1808–1836), 198
Manning, Cardinal Henry Edward (1808–1892), 93
Manns, Sir August (1825–1907), 480, 488–89, 494

Manon Lescaut, 70

Mansfeldt, Hugo Leonhardt (1844–1932), 464, 470
　first performance of "Bagatelle without tonality," *445–46*
　letter to Liszt, 470*n*.27

Marcello, Don, 86

Maria Pawlowna (1786–1859), Grand Duchess of Weimar (1828–1853), 531

Marini, Cardinal Pietro (1794–1863), 30*n*.32

Marmontel, Antoine François (1816–1898), 236

Marsches, Baron Eduard de, 499*n*.4

Marschner, Heinrich August (1795–1861)
　Hans Heiling, 124

Marseilles (France), 23, 24, 81, 117, 151

Martel, François, 50*n*.10

Martin, Henri (1810–1883), 314

Martindale, Louisa, 425*n*.18

Mason, William (1829–1908), 232

Mason and Risch (Toronto), 423 and *n*.16

Massenet, Jules (1842–1912), 102, 222, 387
　Le Cid, 478

Materna, Amalie (1844–1918), 355, 417, 520*n*.24

Mauro, Stephanie, 73*n*.42

Maximilian, Archduke (1832–1867), Emperor of Mexico (1864–1867), 157

Mayer, Friederike, 73*n*.42

Mazzini, Guiseppe (1805–72), 327

Mehlig-Falk, Anna (1843–1928), 203*n*.23

Meiningen (Germany), 144
　orchestra, 144 and *n*.25, 399

Melegari, Dora, 321–22

Meluzzi, Salvatore (Vatican Choir director) (1813–1897), 56

Mendelssohn, Felix (1809–1847), 39, 200, 237, 273, 395, 421
　A Midsummer Night's Dream, 42
　Prelude and Fugue, 298
　Rondo Capriccioso, 293

Ménestrel, Le (Paris), 103, 378, 499*n*.6

Menter, Sophie (1846–1918), 190, 205, 223, 225, 271, 364, 396, 473, 511, 533

Mérode, Monsignor Francesco Xaver Frédéric de (1820–1874), 55

Merseburg (Germany), 421

Messagero, Il (Rome), 332

Messiaen, Olivier (1908–1992), 57

Metternich, Princess Julie von, 98

Metternich, Princess Pauline von (1836–1921), 98, 103, 156, 426

Metternich, Prince Richard (1829–1895), 215*n*.6, 219

Metz (France), 215, 217

Meurin, Monsignor Luigi, Archbishop of Ascalon, 537

Meuse river, 218

Meyendorff, Baron Felix von (1834–1871), 37, 198

Meyendorff (*née* Princess Gortchakova), Baroness Olga von (1838–1926), 3, 185, 189, 198, 240, 271, 278, 336, 351, 369
　description of, 199
　first meetings with Liszt, 198–99

Meyer, Leopold de (1816–1883), 98

Meyerbeer, Giacomo (1791–1864), 23, 395, 408
　L'Africaine, 172*n*.3
　Le Prophète, 39

Meysenbug, Malwida von (1816–1903), 143, 536

Mézière, Alfred, 314

Michelangelo (1475–1564), 47

Mihalovich, Ödön (1842–1929), 178, 179, 225, 256, 274, 299, 376

Mikuli, Karol (1821–1897), 172

Milan (Italy), 122, 425

Milde, Hans Feodor von (1821–1899), 153, 196, 256
　Rosa (wife, *née* Aagthe) (1827–1906), 196, 274

Milesi Pironi Ferretti, Cardinal Giuseppe (1817–1873), 30*n*.32

Minghetti, Marco (1818–1886), 320, 335

Mirus, Adolf, 532*n*.26

Miscimarra, Giuseppe, 58*n*.13

Mohr, Father Joseph, 379

Moltke, Count Helmut von (1800–1891), 216, 220

Moniteur Universel (Paris), 271

Montalembert, Count Charles Forbes de
(1810–1870), 33*n*.41

Montebello steamship, 70

Montez, Lola (1818–1861) (Mrs. Eliza
Gilbert), 85, 109, 377*n*.42

Montreux (Switzerland), 17

Morel d'Arteux, Félix (lawyer), 315

Morelli, Father Francesco (b. 1799), 27

Morin-Chevillard String Quartet (Paris),
134

Moscheles, Ignaz (1794–1870), 200

Mosonyi, Mihály (pseud. for Michael
Brandt) (1815–1870), 91, 149

Moszkowski, Moritz (1854–1925), 237

Mottl, Felix (1856–1911), 388–89, 472, 473,
519

Mouchanoff-Kalergis, Marie von (*née*
Countess Nesselrode)
(1822–1874), 143, 228, 253*n*.58,
256, 271
  death of, 188, 285

Moulton, Lillie, 98–99

Mozart, Wolfgang Amadeus (1759–1791),
37, 39, 42, 102, 292
  Ave verum corpus, 43, 44
  Requiem, 44
  Rondo in A minor, 464

Mrazéck, Franz (1842–1898), 116
  Anna (wife), 76*n*.54

Müller, Eugénia (1866–after 1936), 293

Müller-Hartung, Carl (1834–1908), 152,
200 and *n*.17, 201, 209, 423, 431,
532

Muncker, Dr. Theodor von (1823–1900),
519

Munich (Germany), 61, 72, 93, 473
  Court orchestra, 144*n*.25
  Hotel Jôchum, 107, 109, 116
  Residenz Theatre, 112
  Royal Opera House, 107, 110, 122,
  210
  Royal Music School, 107, 110
  Royal Treasury, 110

Munkácsy, Mihály (1844–1900), 478, 499
and *n*.4
  Cécile (wife) (1845–1915), 478, 490,
  498, 504, 505

Musical Opinion, The (London), 481*n*.9

Musical Times, The (London), 480*n*.4, 490,
494

Music and Drama (New York), 253*n*.58,
417*n*.3, 461

Mussolini, Benito Amilcare Andrea
(1883–1945), 328

Nangis, Battle of (1814), 515*n*.46

Napoleon III (1808–1873), Emperor of
the French (1852–1870), 154,
212–13, 224, 311, 328
  death of, 222 and *n*.25
  Franco-Prussian War and, 212–20,
  222
  surrender at Sedan, 219 and *n*.16

Nardi, Monsignor Francesco (1808–1877),
37 and *n*.12, 60

Nazione, La (Rome), 29*n*.31

Nefftzer, Auguste (1820–1876), 309,
311

Neue Freie Presse (Vienna), 59*n*.15,
389*n*.63, 524

Neue Zeitschrift für Musik (Leipzig), 71*n*.37,
94

Neuer Bayerischer Kurier (Munich), 111

Neueste Nachrichten (Munich), 111, 119

Neu-Weimar-Verein, 79

Newcombe College (New Orleans),
232*n*.8

"New German School," 39*n*.20, 206

Newman, Ernest (1868–1959), 117*n*.18,
119*n*.19, 143*n*.22, 180,
399*n*.81

New York (America), 177, 471

New York Times, The, 346, 347*n*.13,
348*n*.16, 354*n*.27

Nicholas I (1796–1855), Tsar of Russia
(1825–1855), 272

Nicolai, Carl Otto Ehrenfried
(1810–1849), 124
  The Merry Wives of Windsor, 124

Niecks, Frederick (1845–1924), 484*n*.11

Nietzsche, Friedrich Wilhelm
(1844–1900), 134, 351

Nigra, Cavaliere Constantino
(1820–1907), 219

Nikisch, Arthur (1855–1922), 424

Nikolits, Sándor (1834–1895), 290
Nohl, Ludwig (1831–1885), 190, 207
Nonnenwerth (Germany), 310
Norddeutscher Allgemeine Zeitung, 214
Novello & Co. (London), 480
"Nun danket alle Gott," 219, 461
Nuremberg (Germany), 130, 277, 287, 424,
    425*n.*18

Obrist, Aloys (1867–1910), 532, 533
Obuda (Hungary), 358
Oedenburg (now Sopron, Hungary),
    400
Offenbach, Jacques (1819–1880), 156
    La Grand-Duchesse de Gérolstein, 156
Ollivier, Emile (1825–1913), 47–48, 50–51,
        88, 95, 96, 105, 224
    Adolphe (brother), 95, 96, 529–30
    Blandine-Rachel Liszt (first wife)
        (1835–62), 23, 97, 107*n.*3
    death of, xix, 44, *49–50,* 316, 529
    Daniel-Emile (son) (1862–1941),
        47–49, 53*n.*19, 316, 379, 465,
        478
    delivers Anna Liszt's eulogy, 96
    Démosthène (father) (1799–1884), 48
    Franco-Prussian War and, 221*n.*21, 215
        and *n.*7, 217
    Journal of, 50 *n.*10, 97, 305
    Marie-Thérèse Gravier (second wife)
        (1850–1934), 53*n.*19
Orczy, Baron Bódog (1835–1892), 496
Orloffsky, Princess, 28*n.*27
Ortigue, Joseph d' (1802–1866), 101, 102
L'Osservatore romano (Rome), 69*n.*27, 151,
        332
Ostend (Belgium), 77
Overbeck, Johann Friedrich (1789–1869),
        36, 527*n.*12

Pachmann, Vladimir de (1848–1943),
        462–63, 488
Paderewski, Ignace Jan (1860–1941),
        243*n.*37, 295
Padua (Italy), 37*n.*12
Paganini, Niccoló (1782–1840)

Palestrina, Giovanni Pierluigi (c.
        1525–1594), 36, 39, 68, 496
Palotásy, János (1831–1878), 375
Papp, Viktor (1881–1954), 525
Papperitz, George (painter), 418*n.*4
Paris (France), 357
    Arc de Triomphe, 220, 309
    Bastille, 220
    Bois de Boulogne, 156, 220
    Conservatoire of music, 35, 99, 289,
        499*n.*6
    Exhibition (1867), *154–57*
    Exhibition (1878), 378–79
    Hôtel de Ville, 156, 221
    Louvre, Le, 154, 219
    Montparnasse cemetery, 96
    Notre Dame, 154, 379
    Père-Lachaise cemetery, 221, 313
    Sainte-Clothilde, 102
    Saint-Eustache, 97, 99–100, 104, 478
    St. Thomas Aquinas, 96
    Siege of (1870), 220–21, 311
    Trocadéro, 103*n.*22, 499
    Tuileries Palace, 221, 224
Pascal, Blaise (1623–1662), 32*n.*40
Pasdeloup, Jules (1819–1887), 101
Pauer, Max (1866–1945), 422*n.*14
Pauler, Tivabar (1816–1886), 271
Pauline, Crown Princess of Weimar
        (b. 1852), 269
Pázmándy, Dénes (1848–1936), 398
Pecht, Friedrich (1814–1903), 109
Péchy, Támas (1829–1897), 359
Penge (England), 480
Perini, Gilda, 60, 162
Pesther Lloyd (Budapest), 280, 411, 528,
        535
Pesti Napló (*Budapest*), 91, 94
Petersen, Dori (1860–1944), 244 and *n.*42,
        245
    quarrel with Liszt, 412–14
Petersilia, Carlyle (1844–1903), 464
Pfistermeister, Franz Seraph von
        (1820–1912), 79*n.*64, 116
Pfordten, Baron Ludwig von der
        (1811–1880), 115, 116
Philharmonic Society of London, 531
Piccolomini, Cardinal, 159
Pickel, Augusta (maid), 77 and *n.*56,
        434

Piedmont (France), 328

Pinelli, Ettore (1843–1915), 60, 162, 459

Pinner, Max (1851–1887), 361

Pius VI, Pope (Braschi, Giannangelo) (1717–1799), 331

Pius IX, Pope (Mastai-Ferretti, Giovanni Maria) (1792–1878), xviii, 25, 30, 31, 36–37, 40, 55–56, 68–69 and *n*.29, 86, 90, 269, 326*n*.17, 327, 335
    First Vatican Council (1869–70), 323, 324*n*.15, 329, 335
    Quanta cura, 329
    Qui pluribus, 327
    Syllabus errorum, 329, 335

Planté, Francis (1839–1934), 104

Plotényi, Nándor (1844–1933), 225

Pocknell, Pauline, xx

Podmaniczky, Baron Frigyes (1824–1907), 410 and *n*.17

Pohl, Richard (1826–1896), 70, 114, 125

Pohlig, Karl (1858–1928), 271, 361, 384, 394, 500*n*.11

Poitiers (France), 382*n*.53

Poniatowska, Denise, 28

Popper, David (1843–1913), 271, 290

Porges, Heinrich (1837–1900), 430

Posse, Wilhelm (1852–1925), 419

Prague (Czech Republic), 73, 172, 399

Preller, Friedrich (1804–1878), 79, 195

Pressburg (now Bratislava, Slovakia), 399, 400, 468

Presse, La (Paris), 96*n*.4, *98, 309*

Preyer, Gottfried von (1807–1901), 149

Proudhon, Pierre-Joseph (1809–1865)

Prout, Ebenezer (1835–1909), 422*n*.14

Pückler-Muskau, Prince Hermann von (1785–1871), 343*n*.5

Pulszky, Ferenc (1814–1897), *272*

Punsch Magazine (Munich), 109, 110 and *n*.8

Pusinelli, Anton (1815–1878), 113, 117*n*.18

Pustet, Friedrich (1798–1882), 383

Quaglia, Monsignor Angele (1802–1872), 25*n*.19

Quirinal, The (steamship), 23, 26

Raab, Toni (Antonia) (1846–1902), 388, 442*n*.13

Raabe, Peter Carl Ludwig Hermann (1872–1945), 209*n*.36, 443, 532

Raff, Joseph Joachim (1822–1882), 114, 122, 207, 256, 380, 470
    Die Liebesfee, 461

Raiding (Austria; formerly Doborján, Hungary), 400–01, 523, 527

Rákóczy II, Prince Ferenc (1676–1735), 524*n*.4

Rákóczy Song, 410

Ralston, Susan, xx

Ramacciotti, Tullio (1819–1910), 36

Ramann, Lina (1833–1912), 12, 190, 207, 231, 287, 352, 409*n*.16
    Bibliothek (Weimar), 413*n*.25, 509*n*.2
    Franz Liszt's Oratorium "Christus" (1874), 275
    Lisztiana (1983), 277, 363, 509*n*.2
    as Liszt's biographer, 28*n*.26, *275–77,* 287, 363, 409 and *n*.16, 424, 440, 508*n*.2

Rampolla, Cardinal Mariano (1843–1913), 330

Randegger, Albert (1832–1911), 488

Rankau (Germany), 22

Ranouchewitsch, Katharina, 237, 420

Raphael Sanzio (1483–1520), 89

Ráth, Dr. Ferdinand, 480

Ráth, Károly (1821–1897), 373

Ratzenberger, Theodor (1840–1879), 207, 362

Ravasz, Ilona (1851–1922), 290*n*.9, 380

Ravel, Maurice-Joseph (1875–1937), 41, 372
    Jeux d'eau, 372
    "Ondine," 41

Redern, Count Friedrich Wilhelm (1802–1883), 72*n*.40

Redon, Odilon, 475

Regensburg (Germany), 205, 342, 383

Reichmann, Theodor (1849–1903), 417

Reisenauer, Alfred (1863–1907), 242, 361, 393, 419, 436, 458, 460, 519

Reményi, Ede (Eduard Hoffmann) (1830–1898), 61, 71, 92, 149–50 and *n*.7, 152, 196, 225–26

Remmert, Martha (1854–1941), 240, 267, 364, 419, 532

Reuss, Eduard (1851–1911), 519

Reutter, Isidore von, 120
Revue de Paris, 309
Revue et Gazette Musicale, La (Paris), 101
Revue Germanique (Paris), 311
Richter, Hans (1843–1916), 134, 143, 267,
    271, 279, 289, 312, 347, 353, 355,
    430
Riedel, Carl (1827–1888), 210, 256, 368,
    379–80, 460, 463
Riemann, Hugo (1849–1919), 502
Riesberg, Frederick W. (1863–1950), 446
Rietschel, Ernst (1804–1861), 225
Rietz, Julius (1812–1877), 35
Rimsky-Korsakoff, Nicolai (1844–1908),
    460
Risch, Vincent Michael (1833–1914),
    424n.17
Ritter, Alexander (1833–1896), 501
Ritter, Franziska (wife) (1829–1895),
    38n.15
Rohlfs, Gerhard (1831–1896), 199–200
    Leontine (wife), 199
Rohrer, Johann (1783–1868), 401
Rome (Italy)
    Academia Britannica, xviii
    Alibert Hotel, 457–58, 473, 474
    Baths of Diocletian, 68, 159, 396
    Colosseum, 35, 159, 162, 163, 182
    Dante Gallery, 36 and n.7, 97, 151, 384,
        256, 475
    Forum, 35, 163
    Madonna del Rosario, xvii, xviii, 10,
        54–56, 59–61, 80, 81
    Monte Mario, 55, 60
    Palazzo Barberini, 86, 100
    Palazzo Barca, 476
    Palazzo della Cancelleria, 327
    Pantheon, 35
    Piazza di Spagna, 23 and n.12, 33
    Piazza Trajane, 172
    Pretorian Camp, 68
    Quirinal Palace, 36, 326n.17, 327
    River Tiber, 59
    Romulus and Remus temple, 51
    St. Peter's, 55, 89, 165, 537
    San Carlo al Corso, 24, 27–28, 276, 321,
        457
    San Giacomo hospital, 5, 292n.11
    Sant' Andrea delle Fratte, 322

Santa Cecilia Academy, 38, 159n.23, 498
Santa Francesca Romana, 128, 159, 162,
    164, 168, 170, 182
Santa Maria degli Angeli, 36
Santa Maria Maggiore, 36, 159n.23, 330,
    333, 384
Santa Maria del Popolo, 33, 537 and
    n.39, 541
Sistine Chapel, 35, 42, 322
Via del Babuino, 172, 275, 287, 320, 321,
    407, 457, 537
Via Felice, 51, 52
Vicolo de' Greci, 159n.23, 205, 269
Villa Medici, 321, 458, 475
Ronchaud, Louis de (1816–1887), 104,
    306, 307, 308, 310. 313n.44
Rorate coeli desuper (plainchant), 260
Rosa, Carl (1842–1889), 480
Rosenthal, Moriz (1862–1946), 228, 234,
    235, 242, 380, 446, 533
Rosmini-Serbati, Father Antonio
    (1797–1855), 329, 336
    death of, 329–30
    diary of, 329–30
Rospigliosi, Prince, 373
Rossi, Pellegrino (1787–1848), 327
Rossini, Gioacchino (1792–1868), 102, 104,
    206, 207, 488, 524n.4, 527n.12
    Barber of Seville, 198n.12
    Stabat Mater, 68
    William Tell, 124
Roth, Bertrand (1855–1938), 380, 384
Rothschild's Bank (Paris), 319, 529
Rothschild, Baron Ferdinand
    (1839–1898), 319, 529, 530
Rózsavölgyi publishers, 292
Rubinstein, Anton (1829–1894), 23, 196,
    207, 239, 295, 380, 396, 424,
    462–63, 478
    conducts Liszt's "Christmas Oratorio,"
        256
    historical recitals, 481n.9
    Nero, 468
    "Staccato" Study, op. 25, 461
    "Yankee Doodle" Variations, 242, 471
Rugby School (England), 415n.30
Russell, Sir William Howard (1820–1907),
    217–18
Ryde, Isle of Wight, 220

Saarbrücken (Germany), 216
Sabinin, Martha Stepanova von
    (1831–1892), 360n.9
Sachsen-Weimar, Royal House of, 526
    burial vault, 526n.7
Sadler-Grün, Frederike (1836–1917), 355
Sadowska, Countess, 496–97
Saint-Cloud (France), 215
St. Francis of Assisi (1181–1226), 226, 343
St. Francis of Paola (c. 1416–1507), 59, 70,
    392, 408
St. John, Gospel According to, 372
Saint Laurent (steamship), 178
St. Mark, Gospel According to, 369
St. Matthew, Gospel According to, 262
St. Petersburg (Russia), 22, 25, 157, 271,
    473, 477
Saint-Saëns, Charles-Camille (1835–1921),
    98, 104, 207, 350, 379
    André (son), 379n.46
    Danse macabre, 363 and n.16, 534
    description of Liszt, 98
    Henry VIII, 464,
    Prometheus's Wedding Feast, 207n.32
    Samson et Dalila, 208n.32
    Variations on a theme of Beethoven
        (piano), 368
Saint-Tropez (France), 23, 50, 53n.19, 71,
    76, 107n.3, 526
Saissy, Amadé (1844–1901), 408n.14,
Salámon, Henrik, 511n.8
Salis-Schwabe, Julie, 112–13 and n.11
Salvagni, Fortunato (Liszt's manservant),
    34, 70, 86
Salzburg (Austria), 109n.5
San Francisco (America), 470
Santley, Sir Charles (1834–1922), 485
Sauer, Emil von (1862–1942), 7, 228, 234,
    242, 445, 464, 471, 533
Sauer, Captain Karl Theodor von, 121
Sayn-Wittgenstein, Princess Carolyne
        Jeanne Elisabeth von (*née*
        Iwanowska) (1819–1887), 3, 13,
        22, 51, 94, 435
    anti-Semitism of, 405–09
    correspondence with Liszt, 25n.19,
        152n.9, 385, 404–05
    death and burial of, 530, 536–38,
    death-notice of (Appendix I)

description of, 320–22
executrix of Liszt's will, 319 and n.2,
    319, 528–30
failing eyesight of, 321–22
Liszt and, 319–20, 521–22, 535–36
    quarrels with, *341–46*
marriage annulment of, *28–34*
placed on the Index, 323 and n.12
Pope Pius IX and, xviii, *55–56, 93,*
    321–22, 334
robbed of jewels, 321 and n.4
Schmalhausen and, 466, 500, 508,
    513–15
thwarted marriage to Liszt, *24–30*
WRITINGS OF:
    Buddhism and Christianity, 322
    catalogue of titles (Appendix IV),
        553–54
    Causes intérieures, 322–26, 334 and
        n.31, 407, 536, 537n.40
    *Practical Conversations for the Use of
        Society Ladies,* 322
    Simplicité des colombes, 347n.12
Sayn-Wittgenstein, Princess Marie von.
        See Hohenlohe-Schillingsfürst,
        Princess Marie von
Sayn-Wittgenstein, Prince Nicholas von
        (husband) (1812–1864), xix, 28
    death of, 32n.40
Sayn-Wittgenstein family. See family tree,
    vol. II, p. xviii
Scaria, Emil (1840–1886), 417
Scharwenka, Xaver (1850–1924), 237, 243,
    413 and n.27
Schauss, Dr. von, 113n.11
Scheffer, Ary (1795–1858), 77
    The Three Magi, 77
Schenker, Heinrich (1868–1935), 371
Schiaffino, Cardinal, 329
Schiller, Johann Christian Friedrich
        (1759–1805), 286, 526
    Stiftung, 79
    Wallenstein's Camp, 79
Schilling, Ernst, 420–21 and n.9, 458
Schlauch, Bishop Lőrinc (1824–1902),
    298
Schleinitz, Countess Marie von
        (1842–1912), 256
Schlosser, Karl Max (1835–1916), 355

Schlözer, Kurd von (1822–1894) (Prussian diplomat), 61, 86, 161
  Römische Briefe, 61
Schmalhausen, Lina (1864–1928), 412–13, 466, 500, 509–10
  accused of theft, 413–14
  amputation of leg, 414n.29
  diary of, 508–09 and n.2, 512–18, 522
  Liszt manuscripts and, 414n.29, 433
  piano playing of, 245, 414
Schmitt, Friedrich (1812–1884), 111
Schnappauf, Bernhard, 518–19
Schneider, Hortense, 156
Schnorr von Carolsfeld, Ludwig (1836–1865)
  death of, 114–15 and n.13, 120
  as Tristan, 112
Schnorr von Carolsfeld, Malvina (wife) (1832–1904), 120–21 and n.21, 122
  illness of, 120–21
  as Isolde, 112
Schoenberg, Arnold (1874–1951), 16, 371, 440, 452, 453, 454, 456
  First Chamber Symphony, 452
  Gurrelieder, 453
Scholz, Bernhard (1835–1916), 39 and n.20
Schopenhauer, Arthur (1788–1860), 347 and n.15, 450
  Parerga und Parolipomena, 456 and n.28, 466–67
Schorn, Adelheid von (1841–1916), 7, 26n.21, 153, 196, 197, 211, 244, 287, 336, 351, 403, 404 and n.2, 425, 458, 462, 510
  Henriette von (mother) (1807–1869), 196, 197 and n.11
  Ludwig von (father) (1793–1842), 197n.11
  Das Nachklassiche Weimar, 7
  Zwei Menschenalter, 7
Schröder, Carl (1848–1935), 501–02
Schubert, Franz Peter (1797–1828), 116, 292
  Divertissement hongroise, 487
  "Der Doppelgänger," 77
  "Erlkönig," 10, 86
  "Frühlingsglaube," 373
  Liszt's editions of, 166

String Quartet in E-flat major, 388
Wanderer Fantasy, 103, 273, 387
Schuberth, Julius (1804–1875), 177–78, 188, 256
Schultze, M., 114
Schumann, Robert (1810–1856), 235–36, 297, 442, 460
  Clara (wife) (1819–1896), 162, 200, 206–07, 298, 351, 362, 396, 488n.22
  Etudes Symphoniques, op. 13, 297
  Kinderscenen, op. 15, 442n.12
  Novellette in D major, op. 21, 235
  Piano Concerto in A minor, op. 54, 422n.14
  Sonata no. 1, in F-sharp minor, op. 11, 163
  Toccata in C major, op. 7, 237
  Two Grenadiers, The, 426
Schuszter, Bishop Konstantin, (1817–?), 298
Schütz, Miksa ("Saggitarius") (1852–1888)
  Franz Liszt über die Juden, 406
Schweitzer, Reverend Christian Wilhelm, 211
Schwendtner, Abbé Mihály (1820–1885), 90, 92, 93, 150, 294
  Resi (niece, Teréz Lavner), 90
Schwind, Moritz von (1804–1871), 153–54
Scitovszky, Cardinal János (1785–1866), 92
Searle, Humphrey (1915–1982), 437n.2, 450n.21
Secchi, Father Angelo (1818–1878), 69–70
Sedan, Battle of (September 1, 1870), 217–18, 219, 420
Seidl, Anton (1850–1898), 428
Seidl, Arthur (1863–1928), 460n.6
Seidl, Gabriel (architect), 528
Seifriz, Max (1827–1885), 71, 207
Semenenko, Father Pjotr (b. 1814), 29, 30 and n.33
Semper, Gottfried (1803–1879), 111, 348n.17, 309
Senfft von Pilsach, Baron Arnold (1834–1889), 188n.36
Senkrah, Arma (anagram for Mary Harkness) (1864–1900), 7, 471 and n.30, 472
Serov, Alexander (1820–1871), 71

Sertrich, Imre, 173

Servais, François-Mathieu (1846–1901), 207, 225, 472

Sgambati, Giovanni (1841–1914), 37, 38, 59, 97, 151, 162, 169, 256, 380, 459, 498
  Piano Quintet in F minor, 384

Shakespeare, William (conductor) (1849–1931), 483

Shaw, George Bernard (1856–1950), 356

Sheffield Town Hall (England), 103n.22

Sheridan, General Philip Henry (1831–1888), 217n.10

Sherwood, William Hall (1854–1911), 361

Sibelius, Jean (1865–1957), 200n.18
  Violin Concerto, 200n.18

Siemienski, Lucien, 473

Siloti, Alexander (1863–1845), 7, 228, 445, 501, 508, 509, 517n.20

Silvestri, Cardinal Pietro de (1803–1875), 30n.32

Simor, Cardinal János (1813–1891), 148, 280, 463

Singer, Edmund (1830–1912), 71, 152

Singer, Otto (1833–1894), 63

Sipka, Mihály ("Miska") (d. 1875), 5

Siposs, Antal (1839–1923), 226, 360n.8

Sitwell, Sir Sacheverell (1897–1988), 180

Sixtus V (1520–1590), Pope (1585–90) (Peretti, Felice), 331

Smetana, Bedrich (1824–1884), 470

Smith, Noble (surgeon), 230n.6

Solfanelli, Father Antonio (Liszt's theology tutor), 89, 163, 164

Solferino, Battle of (June 24, 1859), 328

Solomon, King, 75

Sondershausen (Germany), 209, 285, 362, 501, 503n.17

Sophie (1818–1877), Queen of the Netherlands (1849–1877), 103, 245

Sorabji, Kaikhosru (1892–1988), 16

Sourdeval, Zélie de, 48n.3

Spandau prison (Berlin), 219n.16

Spicheren (France), 217

Spontini, Mme Céleste, 96

Spontini, Gaspare Luigi Pacifico (1774–1851), 475
  Olympia, 475

Staegeman, Max (1843–1905), 460

Stahr, Adolf (1805–1876), 159–61, 202
  Anna (daughter) (1835–1909), 201–02, 510n.4, 514n.14
  Helene (daughter) (1838–1914), 201–02, 510n.4, 514n.14
  Weimar und Jena, 202

Stainer, Sir John (1840–1901), 480

Stanford, Sir Charles Villiers (1852–1924), 286

Stanislas, Saint (c. 1030–1079), 473

Starck-Bronsart, Ingeborg (1840–1913), 70, 71, 284, 354, 368, 443

Stark, Ludwig (1831–1884), 41

Starnberg Lake (Bavaria), 71, 72–74, 108
  Villa Pellet, 74

Stavenhagen, Bernhard (1862–1914), 7, 296, 466, 473, 480, 490, 492, 498, 504, 507, 517n.20
  London debut (1886), 489, 493–94

Stein, Octavie von, 210

Steinacker, Irma, 203n.23

Steinacker, Ödön (b.1839), 524n.4

Steinle, Edward Jakob (1810–1886), 58
  St. Francis of Paola, 58

Steinway & Sons (New York), 158, 352
  and n.24

Sterling, Antoinette (1850–1904), 492n.31

Stern, Professor Adolf (1835–1907), 209n.36, 531

Stiller, Dr. Mór (1842–1917), 529n.16

Stoker, Bram (1847–1912), 492
  Dracula, 492

Stomp, Guillaume (piano dealer), 505

Stör, Carl (1814–1889), 152

Stradal, August (1860–1930), 16, 176n.11, 299n.22, 456, 466, 468

Strasbourg (Germany), 70, 151, 282, 472

Strauss, Johann (1825–1899), 144n.25, 156, 468
  Blue Danube Waltz, 156

Strauss, Richard (1865–1949), 17, 144n.25, 200 and n.18, 262, 453, 534
  Don Juan, 17
  Franz (father) (1822–1905), 144n.25
  Macbeth, 17
  Suite for Winds, 144n.26

Stravinsky, Igor (1882–1971), 452

Street-Klindworth, Agnès (1825–1906), 71 and n.36, 224, 336n.37

Strelezki, Anton (pseud. for Theophilus
      Burnand) (1859–1907), 239
Stróbl, Alajos (1856–1926), 410
Stuttgart (Germany), 125
   Conservatory, 166*n*.38
Sudda Bey, Francesco della, 239, 247
Suffield, Lady, 490*n*.28
Sullivan, Sir Arthur Seymour
      (1842–1900), 422*n*.14, 480, 494
      and *n*.33
Suppé, Franz von (1819–1895), 350
Szabados, Béla (1867–1936), 293
Szabolcsi, Bence (1899–1973), 437*n*.2, 438
Széchenyi, Count Imre (1858–1905),
      180*n*.24, 289
Szeged (Hungary), 388
   flood of 1879, 385–87
Szekszárd (Hungary), 170, 174, 211, 225
   Hotel Szabó, 174
Szemere, Count Bertalan von
      (1812–1869), 175*n*.9
   Miriam (daughter), 179*n*.9
Szigeti, József (1892–1973), 374

Táborszky publishers (Budapest), 292
Táborszky, Nándor (1831–1888), 298,
      427*n*.23
Tageblatt (Budapest), 466
Tardieu, Malwida, 500
Taubert, Wilhelm (1811–1891), 35
Taubmann, Otto, 532
Tausig, Carl (1841–1871), 26*n*.21, 143, 194,
      207–09, 234, 238, 239, 271, 396,
      422
   death of, 208*n*.35
   Valse noble, 453
Tchaikovsky, Modest (1850–1916), 350
      and *n*.18
Tchaikovsky, Peter (1840–1893), 350*n*.18,
      458, 470
   Eugene Onegin, 350*n*.18
   meets Liszt, 350*n*.18
   Symphony no. 2, in C minor, 368
Teck, Duke of, 489*n*.26
Teck, Princess Mary of (1867–1953),
      489*n*.26
Temesvár (Hungary), 385

Temps, Le (Paris), 309
Ternant, André de, 475
Terry, Ellen (1847–1928), 492, 496
Teuscher, Dr. Gerhart (b. 1934), xx
Thaisz, Elek (1820–1892), 181*n*.24
Thaly, Kálmán (1839–1909), 524*n*.4
Theatre, The (London), 497
Theiner, Father Agostino (1804–1874),
      Prefect of the Vatican Secret
      Archive (1855–1870), 54 and
      n.4
Thern, Károly (1817–1886), 284
Thiers, Louis-Adolphe (1797–1877), 221
Thode, Dr. Henry (1857–1920), 503, 504,
      519
Thomán, István (1862–1940), 235, 458,
      473, 508
Thomas, Ambroise (1811–1896), 159, 285
Thomas, General Clément (1809–1871),
      222
Thomas, Theodore (1835–1905), 239
Thompson, Sir Henry, 222
Thurn und Taxis, Princess Marie von,
      333*n*.30
Tiefurt (Germany), 79
Timanova, Vera Victorovna (1855–1942),
      240, 362, 364, 533
Times, The (London), 156*n*.16, 218*n*.12,
      271, 356*n*.34, 482, 488
Tisza, Count Kálmán (1830–1902), Prime
      Minister of Hungary, 271, 359,
      410, 524*n*.4, 525
Tiszaeszlár (Hungary), 407
   "blood trial" of, 407–08
Tivoli (Italy), 88, 287, 333, 380, 393, 457, 526
Tisza River (Hungary), 385
Tonkünstler-Versammlung (1864), 70–72
Topp, Alide, 71
Toronto (Canada), 424
   Conservatory of Music, 424*n*.17
   Exhibition (1887), 424*n*.17,
Toulon (France), 81
Toulouse-Lautrec, Henri Marie de
      (1864–1901), 412*n*.23
Tovey, Sir Donald Francis (1875–1940), 63
Trefort, Ágoston (1817–1888), 271, 278,
      290, 292, 359, 365, 378
Tribert, Louis (1819–1899), 305, 306, 309,
      310, 315

Tribuna (Rome), 330
Triebschen (Switzerland), 117–18, 122,
      125, 145, 311–13
Tripoli (North Africa), 199
Trochu, General Louis (1815–1896), 220
Troisier de Diaz, Anne (b. 1917), 50n.10
Turgenev, Ivan Sergeyevich (1818–1883),
      198
Turin (Italy), 310

Ujpest (Hungary), 358
Ullathorne, Bishop William Bernard
      (1806–1889), 324n.15
Unger, Georg (1837–1887), 355
Univers Illustre L' (Paris), 101
Urspruch, Anton (1850–1907), 267

Vác (Hungary), 270
Vaszilievitz, Olga, 293
Vatican, The
   First Council (1869–70), 324n.15, 329
   Secret Archive, xviii, 28, 29n.31, 30n.32
Venantius Fortunatus (c. 540–c. 600),
      382n.53
Venice (Italy)
   Conservatory of Music, 428
   Grand Canal, 426, 429
   Palace of the Doges, 93
   Palazzo Vendramin, 424, 425, 426
   St. Mark's Cathedral, 93
   Teatro La Fenice, 428, 429
Verbunkos, 149
Verdi, Guiseppe (1813–1901), 263, 387, 478
   Trovatore, 124
Versailles (France), 132, 138n.16, 221
Vetzkó, Father Anton (1825–1869), 93
Veuillot, Louis (1813–1883), 40n.23
Vevey (Switzerland), 117
Vexilla Regis prodeunt (plainchant), 382
Vianesi, Auguste (1837–1908)
      (conductor), 499
Vianna da Motta, José (1869–1948), 470,
      532
Viardot-Garcia, Michelle Ferdinande
      Pauline (1821–1910), 71, 72

Le Dernier Sorcier, 198
Vicariato di Roma, 88n.12
Liber Ordinationum, 88n.12
Victor Emmanuel (1820–1878), King of
      Italy (1861–1878), 170, 211,
      327–28, 335
Victoria, Crown Princess (1840–1901),
      486n.18
Victoria (1819–1901), Queen of England
      (1837–1901), 150n.7, 155
   diary of, 486
   Liszt plays to, 486
Vidal, Paul (1863–1931), 475
Viel-Castel, Count Horace de
      (1798–1864), 314
Vienna (Austria), 24, 299, 357, 391
   Gesellschaft der Musikfreunde, 204,
      271, 389
   Imperial Chapel, 148
   Musikvereinsaal, 273
   St. Stephen's Cathedral, 149
   Schottenhof, 204, 364, 366, 389
Vieuxtemps, Henri (1820–1881), 362
Villa d'Este (Tivoli, Italy), xvii, 164, 287,
      321, 369, 370, 373
   historical background of, 165
Vogel, Mór, 460
Voigt, Hortense, 180n.24
Volckmann, Ida, 275
Volkmann, Richard von (1830–1889), 403,
      500, 509
Volkmann, Robert (1815–1883), 91, 289,
      290, 293
Volksblatt (Munich), 111
Volksbote (Munich), 118–19, 120
Voss, Richard (1851–1918), 322

Wachtel (tenor), 196
Wagner, Richard (1813–1883), 3, 72, 394,
      395
   banishment from Munich, 117–18
   Bayreuth festivals
      (1876), 346–55
      (1882), 416–18
   Briennerstrasse house, 108, 109
   "Brown Book," 74, 75n.47, 92, 131
   Bülow and, 131

Wagner, Richard (1813–1883) *(cont.)*
  caricatures of, 110 and *n*.8
  Christiane Wilhelmine ("Minna")
      (*née* Planer, first wife)
      (1809–1866)
    death of, 117 and *n*.18
  Cosima (*née* Liszt, second wife)
      (1837–1930), 22–23, 71, 336
    conversion to Protestantism,
        137*n*.14, 342–43 and *n*.5
    diaries of, 106, 133–34
    divorce from Bülow, 107, *136–43*
    marriage to Wagner, 143, 342
  Cosima and, 73–76, 116, 117–18, 430–31
      and *n*.31
  death of, 426, *429–30*
  debts of, 61, 73, 109*n*.5
  dog "Pohl," 116, 117*n*.18
  Eva (daughter) (1867–1942), 118, 123,
      132, 312, 514*n*.14, 515, 531
  "exile" from Munich, 116
  Isolde Ludowika Josepha (daughter)
      (1865–1919), 312, 515, 517
    illegitimate birth of, 76 *and n*.54, 91,
        112, 132
  Jessie Laussot and, 38*n*.15
  Liszt and, 278–80, 409
    ambivalence towards, 265–66
    Liszt-Wagner letters, 434–35
    rapprochement with (1872), *256–58,*
        341–42
    tributes to (1876), 354
        (1882), 353*n*.26
  London concerts of (1877), 355–56
  Ludwig II and, 61, 115–16, *118–22*
  Mein Leben, 73*n*.43, 367
  memorial concert in Weimar (1883),
      431–32
  Music School in Munich, 110
  nationalism of, 223 and *n*.27
  Siegfried (son) (1869–1930), 142,
      246*n*.50, 312, 425, 515, 528,
      533
    birth of, 132, 134
    Liszt and, 533
  Triebschen and, 117–18
  Wagner Society (London) 494
  Wahnfried, 351 and *n*.22, 352*n*.22, 362,
      363, 376, 508, 511

Works:
  Eine Kapitulation, 223*n*.27
  Der fliegende Holländer, 110, 114, 341,
      355, 435
  Huldigungsmarsch, 74*n*.46
  Kaiserlied, 312
  Kaisermarsch, 223*n*.27, 461
  Lohengrin, 110, 124, 129, 355, 435
  Die Meistersinger von Nürnberg, 118,
      75, 122, 123, 125, 355
    first performance of (1868),
        130–31
  Parsifal, 262, 283, 367, 368, 431, 465,
      503, 504, 509, 520
    first performance of (1882), 416–18
  Das Rheingold, 210
  Rienzi, 134, 355, 376, 377*n*.42
  Der Ring der Nibelungen, 111, 278,
      279, 363
    first performance of (1876),
        346–55, 416
  Symphony in C major, 428
  Tannhäuser, 99, 110, 114, 129, 337, 355,
      435
  Tristan und Isolde, 110, 122, 355, 371,
      503, 510, 511, 521
    first performance of (1865), *111–14*
  Die Walküre, 210
Walker, Bettina (d. 1893), 12–13, 236
Wallace, William (1860–1940), 86*n*.5
Walther, Frau Rosina, 152, 434*n*.37
"War of the Romantics," 203, 206, 351,
    488*n*.22
Warsaw (Poland), 176
Wartburg Castle (Germany), 151, 153, 198,
    204, 269, 285, 523
Wasielewski, Wilhelm Joseph von
    (1822–1896), 233*n*.12
Webbe, Septimus (1867–1943), 484
Weber, Carl Maria von (1786–1826), 232,
    524*n*.4
  Freischütz Overture, 506
  Invitation to the Dance, 86
  Liszt's editions of, 166
  Momento capriccioso, 274
  Oberon, 196
  Polonaise Brillante, 269, 497
Weber, Henri (conductor), 506
Wedell, Count Oskar von, 519

Weimar (Germany)
  Altenburg, the, 21, 76–79, 151–52, 195,
    360n.9, 366
  Armbrust's restaurant, 8 and n.10, 419
  Belvedere Castle, xvii
  Chemnicus restaurant, 464
  Erbprinz Hotel, 21, 239, 425
  Erholung, 201n.19
  Goethe Park, 7, 188, 195n.5, 502–03
  Herder Church, 79, 256, 275
  Hofgärtnerei, 4, 5, 194–95, 207, 229,
    403, 419, 424, 436, 445, 462, 464,
    470, 500, 503, 525, 531
  Liszt Hochschule für Musik, 201
  Liszt Museum, 531
  Orchesterschule, 200–01
  railway station, 21, 47, 76–77, 196, 240,
    500
  regimental garrison, 211
Weingartner, Felix (1863–1842), 234, 463,
    464 and n.13, 519, 520
  Sakuntala, 463–64
Weissbrod (sculptor), 518
Weissheimer, Wendelin (1838–1910), 131
  Theodor Körner, 131
Weisz, József (b. 1864), 293
Weitzmann, Carl Friedrich (1808–1880),
    23, 453 and n.23, 484n.11
Wellington, Duke of (Arthur Wellesley)
    (1769–1852), 484
Wenzel, Johanna, 230
Wesendonck, Mathilde (1828–1902),
    73n.42, 351
Wheelwright, Annie, 274
Widor, Charles-Marie (1844–1937), 103
Wieland, Christoph Martin (1733–1813),
    286
Wieniawski, Henryk (1835–1880), 285, 295
Wilhelm I (1797–1888) King of Prussia
    (1861–71) [Kaiser of a united
    Germany (1871–88)], 156, 213,
    216, 217, 351
Wilhelmj, August (1845–1908), 347, 353,
    355
Wilhelmsthal (Germany), xvii, 21, 22, 80,
    285, 362
Willem III (1817–1890), King of the
    Netherlands (1849–1890),
    284–85, 379

Willheim, Etelka, 241
Winding, August (1835–1899), 169
Windsor Castle (England), 150n.7, 486–87
Winkelmann, Hermann (1849–1912), 417
Winterberger, Alexander (1834–1914),
    164n.32, 178n.16
Witt, Franz Xaver (1834–1888), 290
Wohl, Janka (1846–1901), 8, 150
  describes Olga Janina's playing, 174–75,
    176
Wolff, Albert (critic), 100–01, 351
Wolfrum, Philip (1854–1919), 532, 533
Wolfsteiner, Dr. (Bavarian physician), 72
Wolkov-Mouromtzov, Alexeivich
    (1844–1928), 426
Wolzogen, Baron Ernst von (1855–1934)
  Der Kraft-Mayr, 9n.12
Wolzogen, Hans von (1848–1938), 519
Worms, Diet of (1521), 153
Woronince (Ukraine), 344
Wrana, Antoni, 172
Wylde, Dr. Henry (1822–1890), 485n.15,
    496n.34

Yale University Library, 494n.33

Zander, Dr., 119
Zarembski, Juliusz (1854–1885), 230, 361,
    458
  Galician Dances, 458
Zenelap (Budapest), 535n.31
Zenészeti Lapok (Budapest), 227
Zeyl, Henryk van, 237, 240, 458
Zichy, Count Géza (1849–1924), 365, 374,
    376, 387, 400, 527n.12
  arm injury, 365n.18
  Das Buch des Einarmigen (1915), 365n.18
Zielinska-Piasecka, Olga ("Olga Janina")
    (b. 1845), xix, 210, 225, 336
  addictions to drugs, 173
  concerts in Paris, 172 and n.3, 179–80
  disturbed personality of, 184–85, 210
  descriptions of
    (1870), 173n.4
    (1874), 184–85

Zielinska-Piasecka, Olga ("Olga Janina")
(b. 1845) (*cont.*)
first meeting with Liszt (1869), 172
Hélène (daughter), 172, 182
Karol Janina (first husband), 172, 181
Liszt's letter to, 176–77
Ludwik (father), 171, 174
Lopuszanska (mother, *née* Sabina), 171
Paul Guy Cézano (second husband),
189 and *n.*42
piano playing of, 174–75, 190
pseudonyms of, 180, 181*n.*25
suicide threats of, 175–76, 178–79

Wladislaw (brother), 171
WRITINGS OF:
*Les Amours d'une cosaque par un ami
de l'Abbé "X,"* 180
Le Roman du pianiste et de la cosaque,
180
Souvenirs d'une cosaque, 180, 181
Liszt's response to, 185–87
Souvenirs d'un pianiste, 180, 183,
185
"Zorelli, Sylvia," 180
Zürich (Switzerland), 119
Zschoscher, Johann (1821–1897), 210

A NOTE ON THE TYPE

The text of this book was set in Bembo, a facsimile of a typeface cut by Francesco Griffo for Aldus Manutius, the celebrated Venetian printer, in 1495. The face was named after Pietro Cardinal Bembo, the author of the small treatise entitled De Aetna *in which it first appeared. Through the research of Stanley Morison, it is now generally acknowledged that all old-style type designs up to the time of William Caslon can be traced to the Bembo cut.*

The present-day version of Bembo was introduced by the Monotype Corporation of London in 1929. Sturdy, well balanced, and finely proportioned, Bembo is a face of rare beauty and great legibility in all its sizes.

Composed by North Market Street Graphics,
Lancaster, Pennsylvania

Printed and bound by Quebecor Printing,
Martinsburg, West Virginia

Based on a design by
Dorothy Schmiderer Baker

LIBRARY
St. LOUIS COMMUNITY COLLEGE
AT FLORISSANT VALLEY.